HALFWAY THERE

A GRAPHIC MEMOIR OF SELF-DISCOVERY

LITTLE, BROWN AND COMPANY

NEW YORK   BOSTON

TO MY FAMILY IN JAPAN AND AMERICA,
WHO MAKE ME FEEL THEIR LOVE NO
MATTER WHERE I AM IN THE WORLD.

ABOUT THIS BOOK

THIS BOOK WAS EDITED BY ANDREA COLVIN AND DESIGNED BY ANN DWYER. THE PRODUCTION WAS SUPERVISED BY KIMBERLY STELLA, AND THE PRODUCTION EDITOR WAS LINDSAY WALTER-GREANEY. THE TEXT WAS SET IN MARI TEXT, AND THE DISPLAY TYPE IS GUESS SANS.

Copyright © 2024 by Christine Mari • Cover illustration copyright © 2024 by Christine Mari. Cover design by Ann Dwyer. • Cover copyright © 2024 by Hachette Book Group, Inc. • Hachette Book Group supports the right to free expression and the value of copyright. The purpose of copyright is to encourage writers and artists to produce the creative works that enrich our culture. • The scanning, uploading, and distribution of this book without permission is a theft of the author's intellectual property. If you would like permission to use material from the book (other than for review purposes), please contact permissions@hbgusa.com. Thank you for your support of the author's rights. • Little, Brown Ink • Hachette Book Group • 1290 Avenue of the Americas, New York, NY 10104 • Visit us at LBYR.com • First Edition: October 2024 • Little, Brown Ink is an imprint of Little, Brown and Company. The Little, Brown Ink name and logo are registered trademarks of Hachette Book Group, Inc. • The publisher is not responsible for websites (or their content) that are not owned by the publisher. • Little, Brown and Company books may be purchased in bulk for business, educational, or promotional use. For information, please contact your local bookseller or the Hachette Book Group Special Markets Department at special.markets@hbgusa.com.
• Library of Congress Cataloging-in-Publication Data • Names: Mari, Christine, author. • Title: Halfway there: a graphic memoir of self-discovery / Christine Mari. • Description: First edition. | New York : Little, Brown Ink, 2024. | Summary: "A Japanese American college student reconnects with her roots in Tokyo, Japan, while wrestling with feelings of loneliness, depression, and cultural identity confusion." — Provided by publisher. • Identifiers: LCCN 2023054824 | ISBN 9780316416658 (hardcover) | ISBN 9780316416726 (paperback) | ISBN 9780316416825 (ebook) • Subjects: LCSH: Mari, Christine—Comic books, strips, etc. | Cartoonists—United States—Biography—Comic books, strips, etc. | Japanese Americans—Biography—Comic books, strips, etc. | Women college students—Comic books, strips, etc. | Identity (Psychology)—Comic books, strips, etc. | LCGFT: Autobiographical comics. | Graphic novels. • Classification: LCC PN6727.M2423 Z46 2024 | DDC 741.5/973 [B]—dc23/eng/20231129 • LC record available at https://lccn.loc.gov/2023054824 • ISBNs: 978-0-316-41665-8 (hardcover), 978-0-316-41672-6 (paperback), 978-0-316-41682-5 (ebook) 978-0-316-57931-5 (ebook), 978-0-316-57932-2 (ebook) • PRINTED IN DONGGUAN, CHINA APS • Hardcover: 10 9 8 7 6 5 4 3 2 1 • Paperback: 10 9 8 7 6 5 4 3 2 1

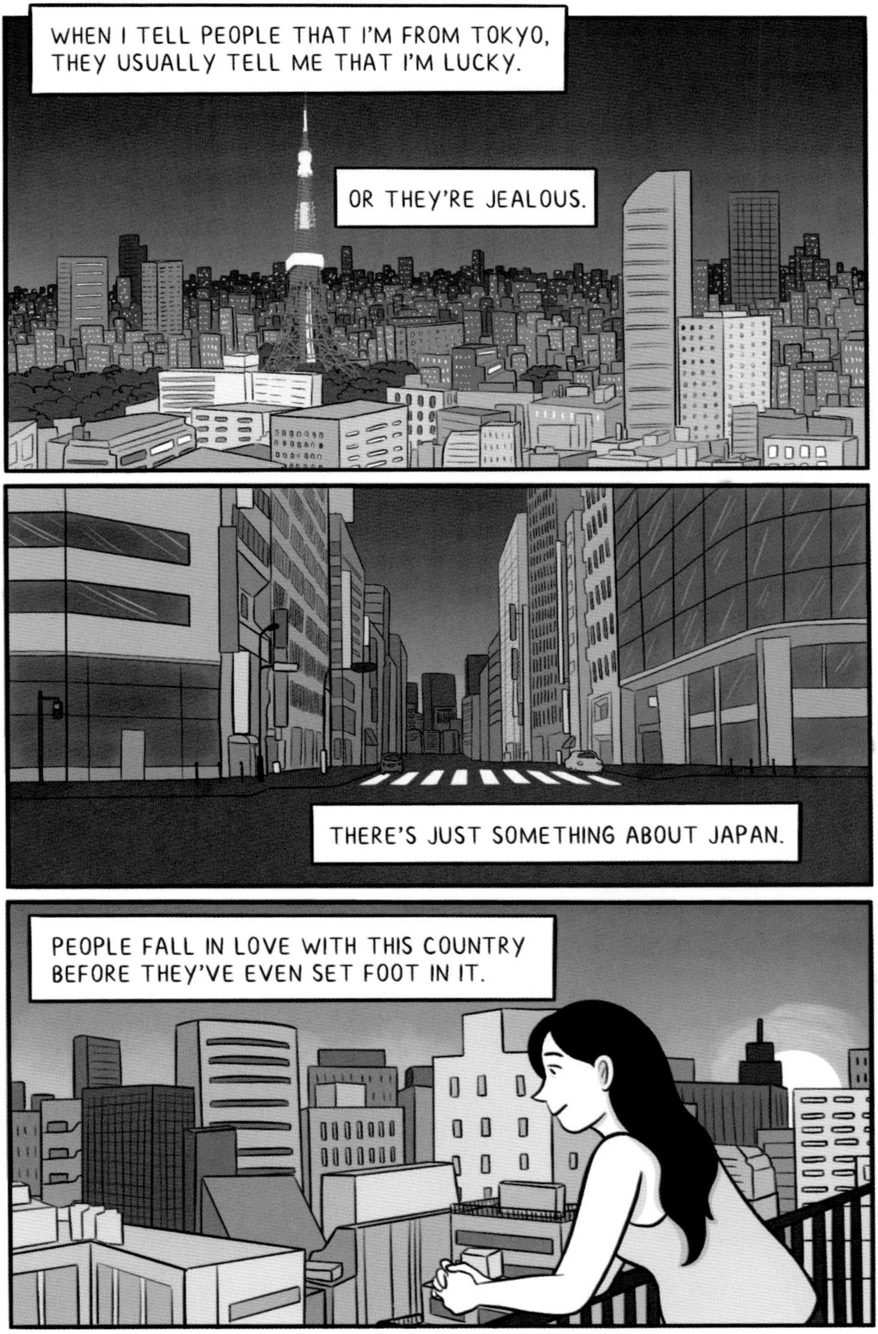
WHEN I TELL PEOPLE THAT I'M FROM TOKYO, THEY USUALLY TELL ME THAT I'M LUCKY.
OR THEY'RE JEALOUS.
THERE'S JUST SOMETHING ABOUT JAPAN.
PEOPLE FALL IN LOVE WITH THIS COUNTRY BEFORE THEY'VE EVEN SET FOOT IN IT.

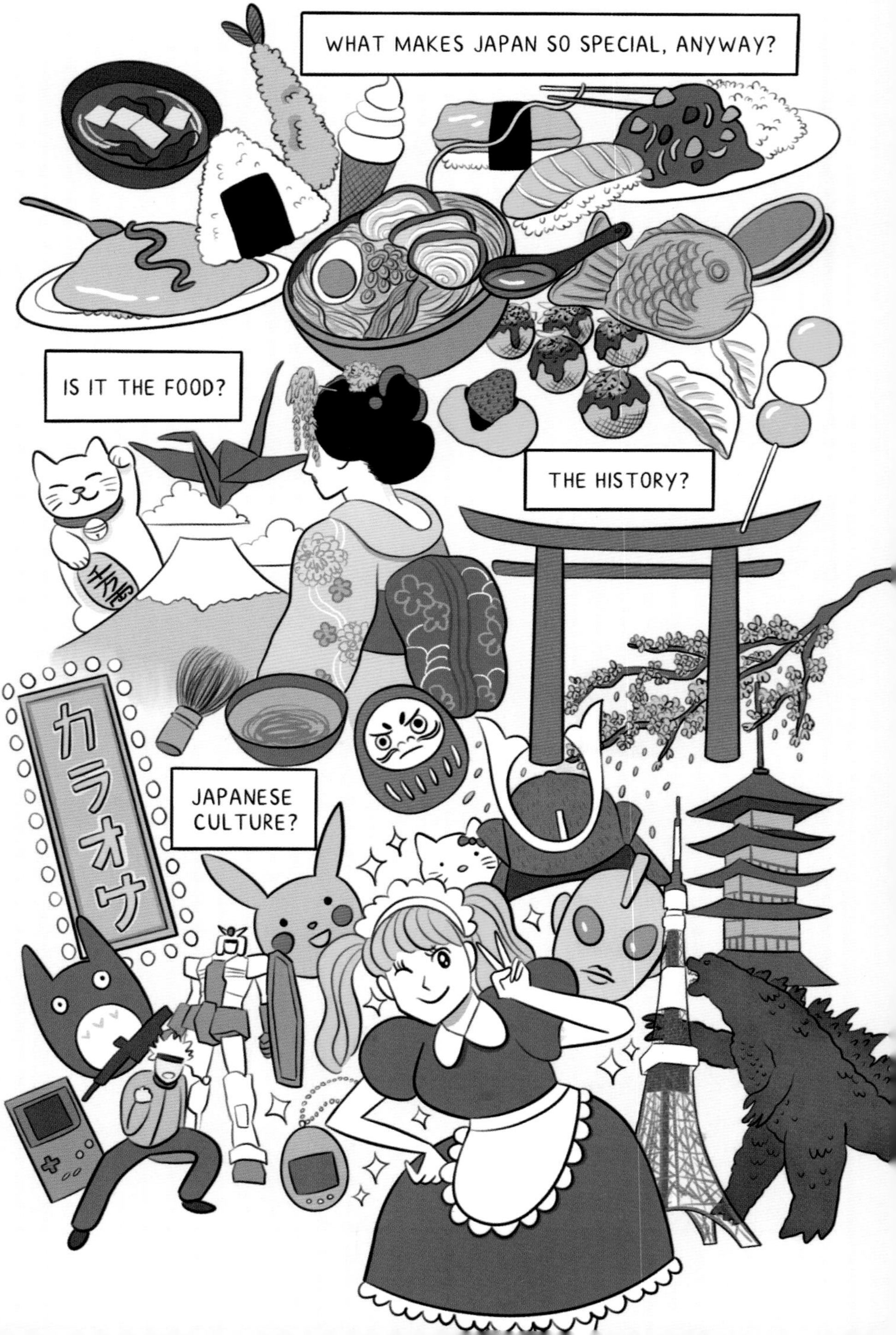
WHAT MAKES JAPAN SO SPECIAL, ANYWAY?
IS IT THE FOOD?
THE HISTORY?
カラオケ
JAPANESE CULTURE?

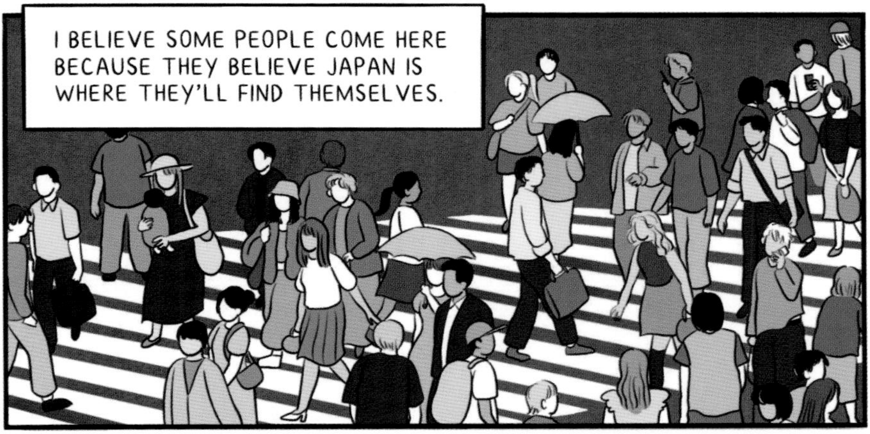
I BELIEVE SOME PEOPLE COME HERE BECAUSE THEY BELIEVE JAPAN IS WHERE THEY'LL FIND THEMSELVES.

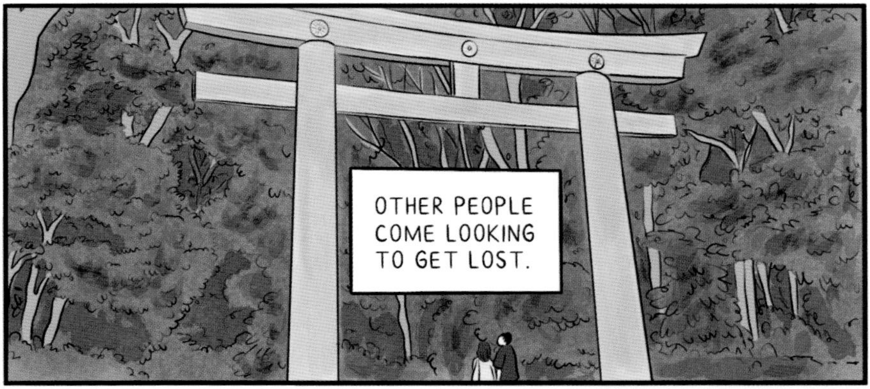
OTHER PEOPLE COME LOOKING TO GET LOST.

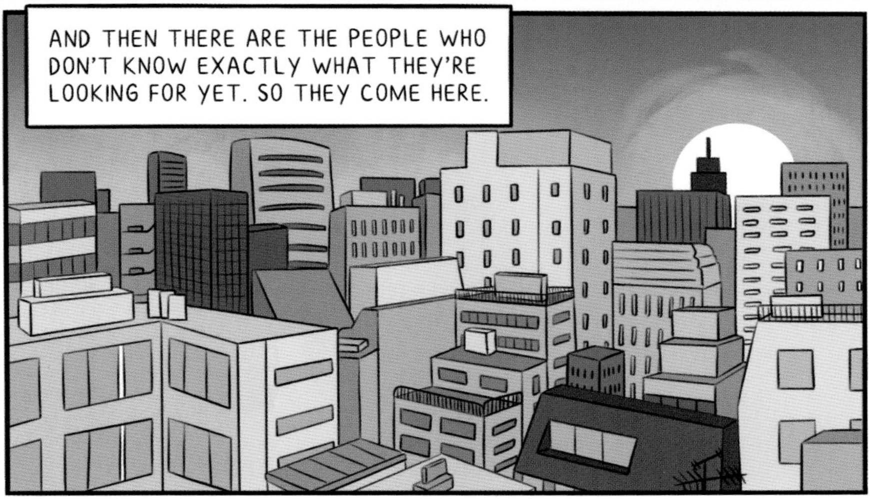
AND THEN THERE ARE THE PEOPLE WHO DON'T KNOW EXACTLY WHAT THEY'RE LOOKING FOR YET. SO THEY COME HERE.

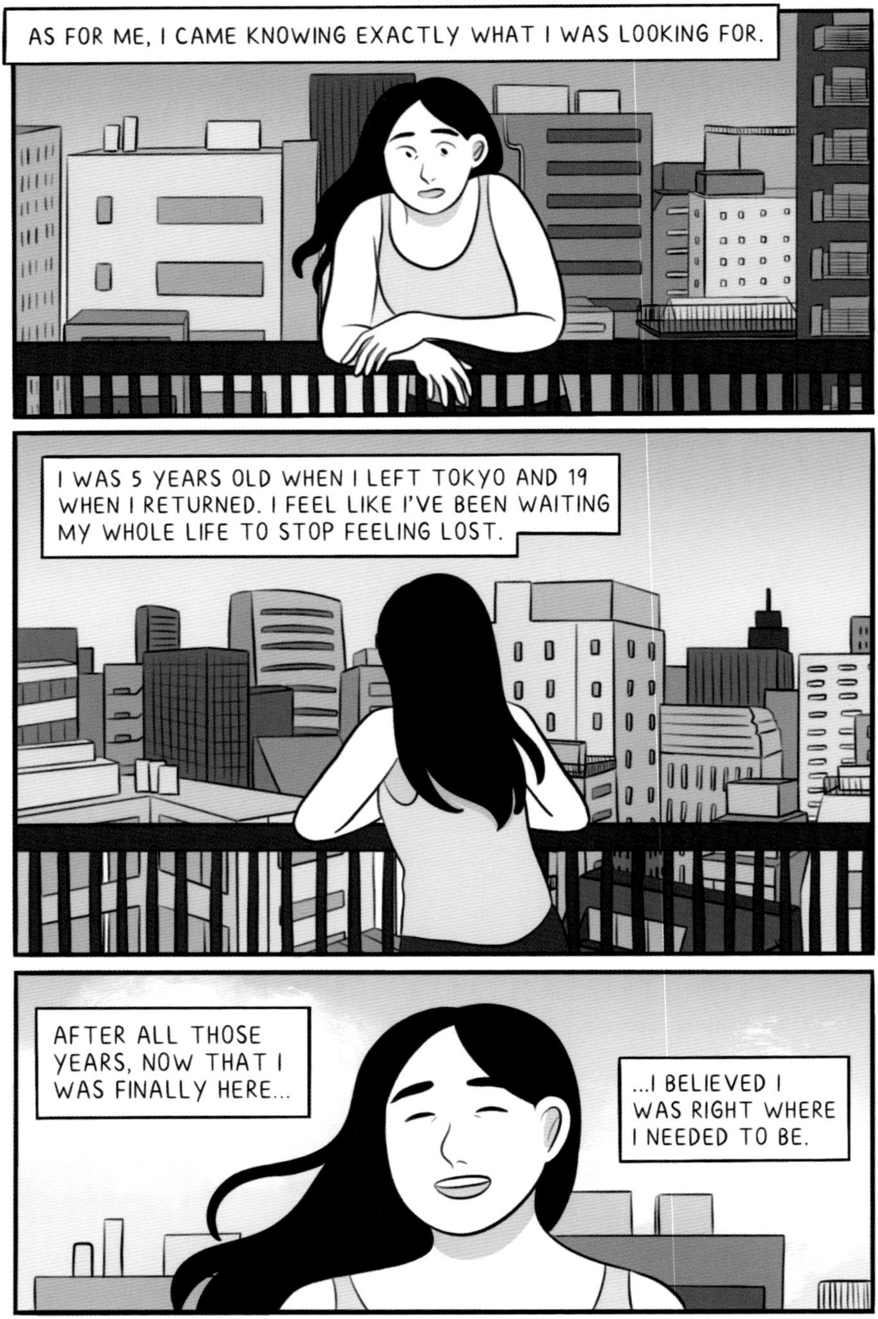
AS FOR ME, I CAME KNOWING EXACTLY WHAT I WAS LOOKING FOR.
I WAS 5 YEARS OLD WHEN I LEFT TOKYO AND 19 WHEN I RETURNED. I FEEL LIKE I'VE BEEN WAITING MY WHOLE LIFE TO STOP FEELING LOST.
AFTER ALL THOSE YEARS, NOW THAT I WAS FINALLY HERE...
...I BELIEVED I WAS RIGHT WHERE I NEEDED TO BE.

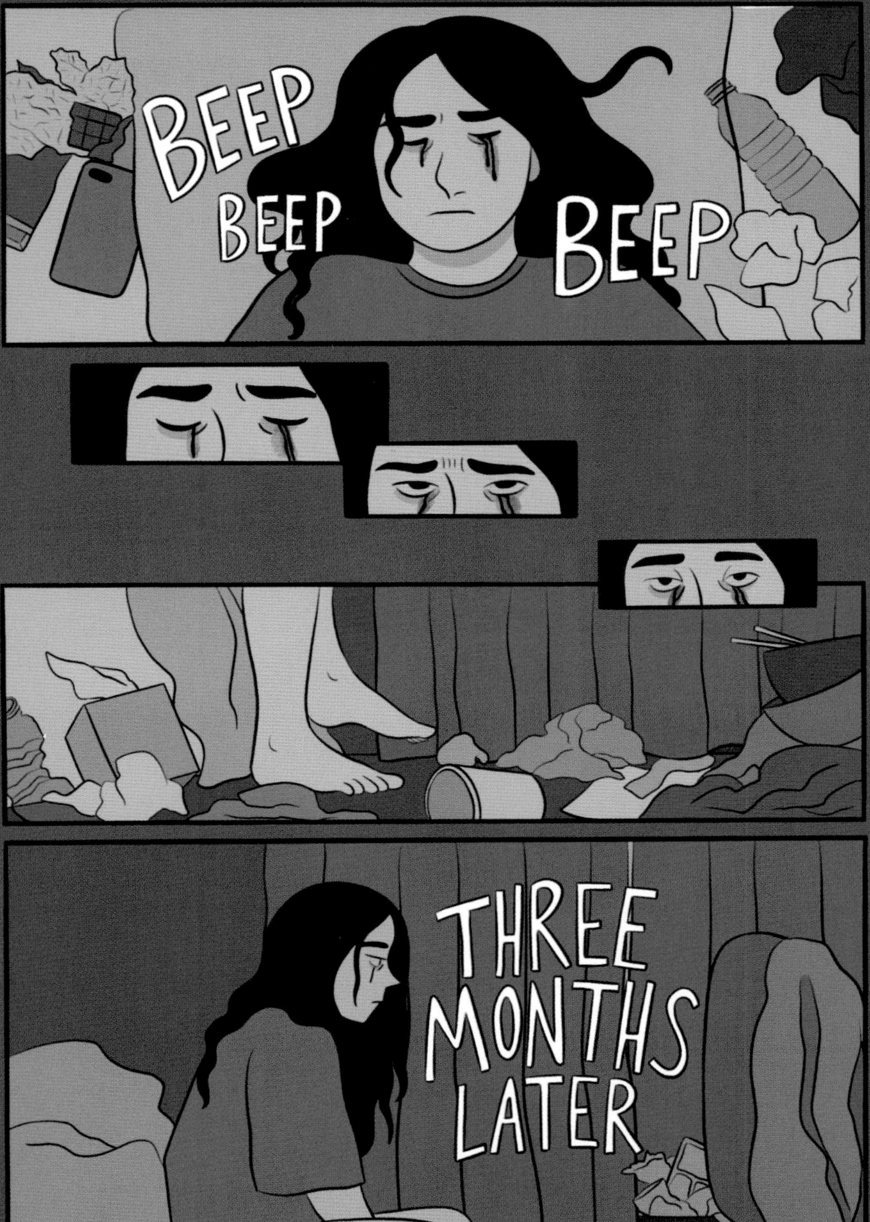
BEEP
BEEP
BEEP
THREE MONTHS LATER

I THINK I CONSUMED TOO MUCH FICTION AS A CHILD, BECAUSE I REALLY
BELIEVED THAT ONCE I GREW UP, LIFE WOULD MAKE MORE SENSE.

EVERYTHING I'VE BEEN TOLD ABOUT GROWING UP SEEMS WRONG NOW.

SO, WHERE DID IT GO WRONG?

WHERE DID I GO WRONG?

HOW FAR BACK DO I HAVE TO GO TO ANSWER THAT?

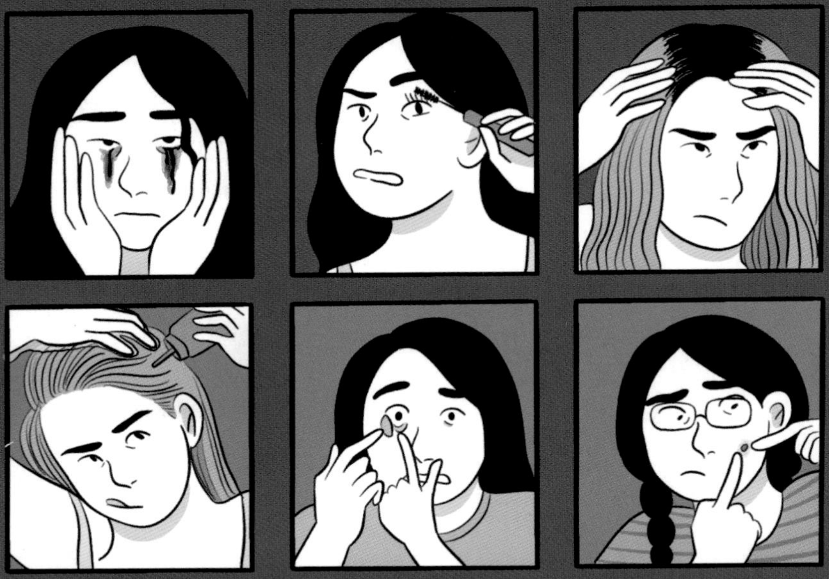

OR DO I HAVE TO START FROM THE BEGINNING?

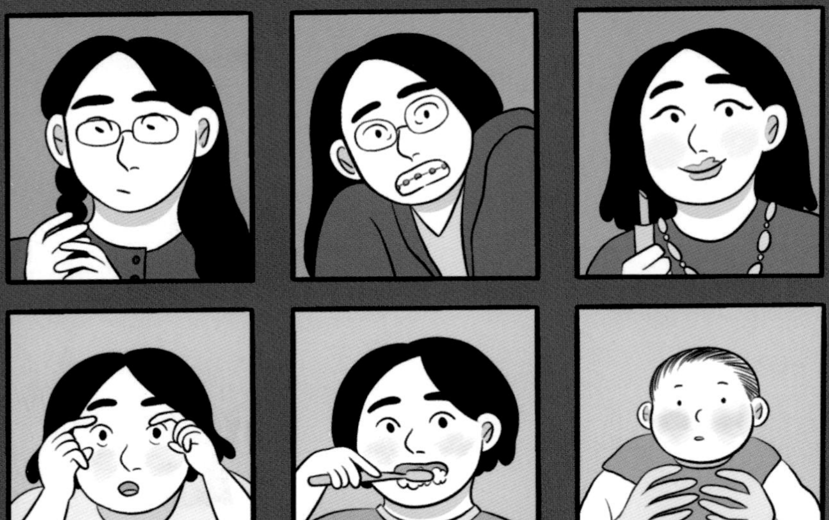

I WAS BORN IN TOKYO TO A JAPANESE
MOTHER AND AN AMERICAN FATHER.
APPARENTLY, THIS MAKES ME HALF.

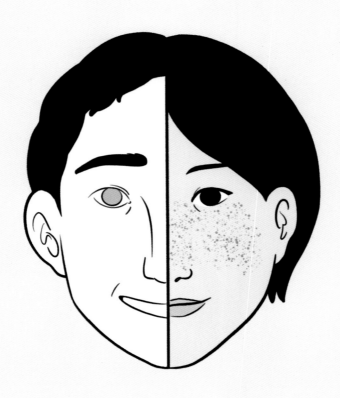

HALF-JAPANESE, HALF-AMERICAN.
HALF-ASIAN, HALF-WHITE.
HALF-MOM, HALF-DAD?

GROWING UP, PEOPLE CALLED ME ALL KINDS OF DIFFERENT THINGS, BUT THEY ALL SEEMED TO REVOLVE AROUND THE SAME IDEA.

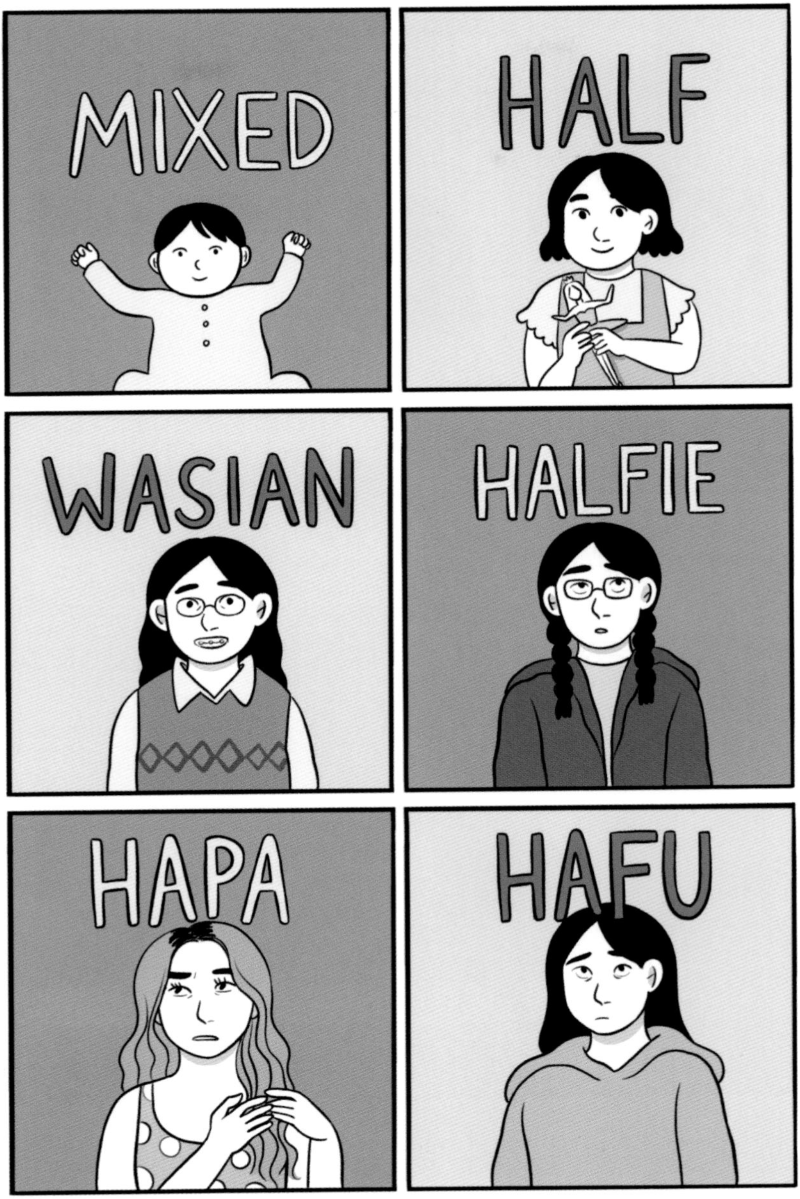
MIXED
HALF
WASIAN
HALFIE
HAPA
HAFU

IN ONE FORM OR ANOTHER, THE WORD *HALF* BECAME ENTANGLED WITH THE WAY I SAW MYSELF.

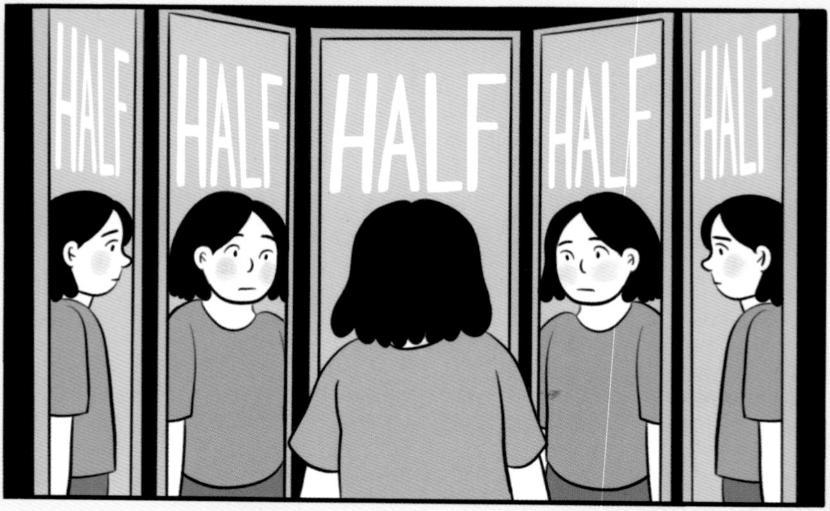
HALF
HALF
HALF
HALF
HALF

SO I KIND OF THINK, FROM THE VERY BEGINNING, I WAS DESTINED TO HAVE AN IDENTITY CRISIS.

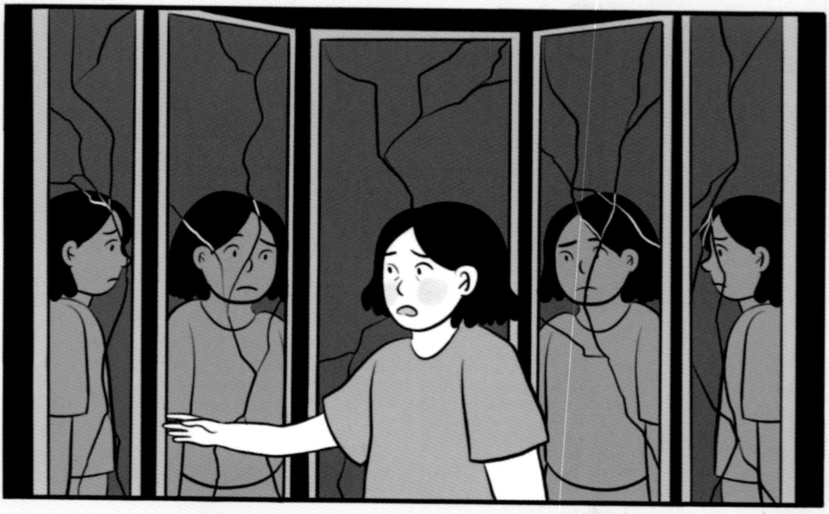

BECAUSE HOW CAN SOMEONE EVER FEEL WHOLE IF THEY'VE ALWAYS BEEN TOLD THEY'RE ONLY HALF OF SOMETHING?

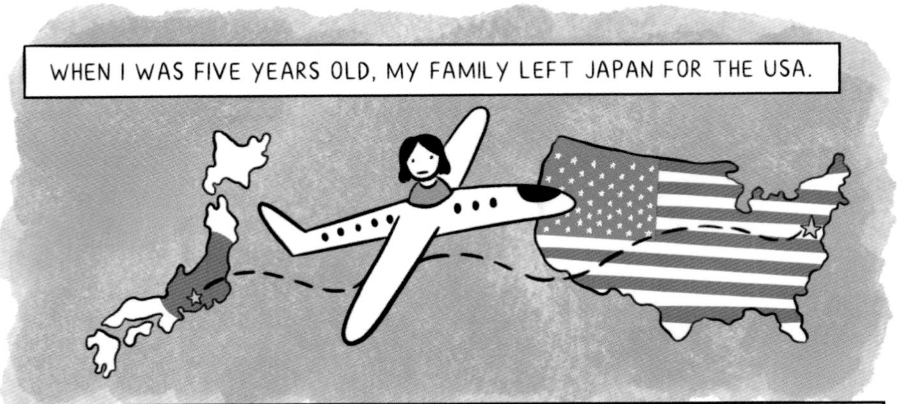
WHEN I WAS FIVE YEARS OLD, MY FAMILY LEFT JAPAN FOR THE USA.

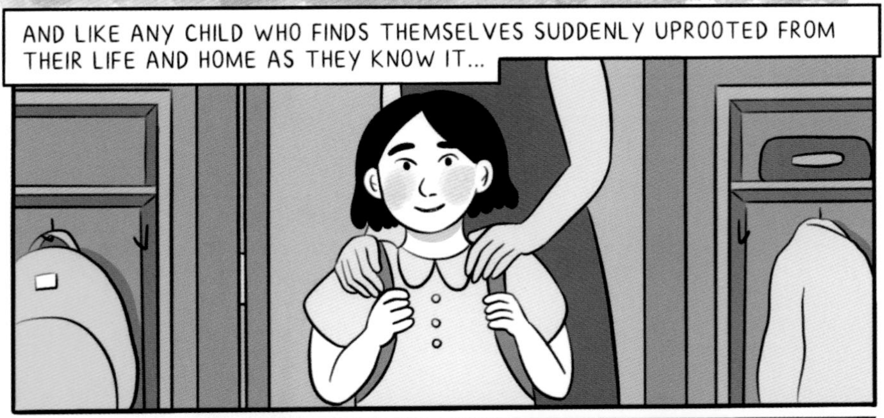
AND LIKE ANY CHILD WHO FINDS THEMSELVES SUDDENLY UPROOTED FROM THEIR LIFE AND HOME AS THEY KNOW IT...

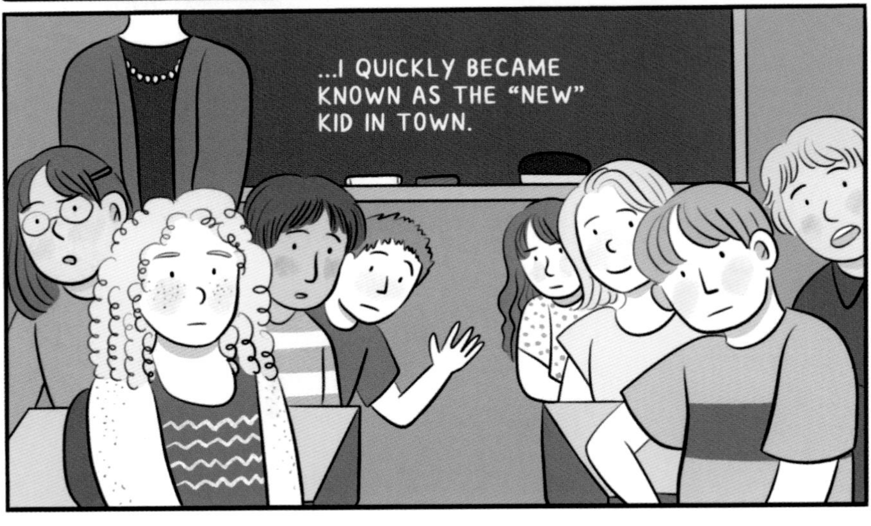
...I QUICKLY BECAME KNOWN AS THE "NEW" KID IN TOWN.

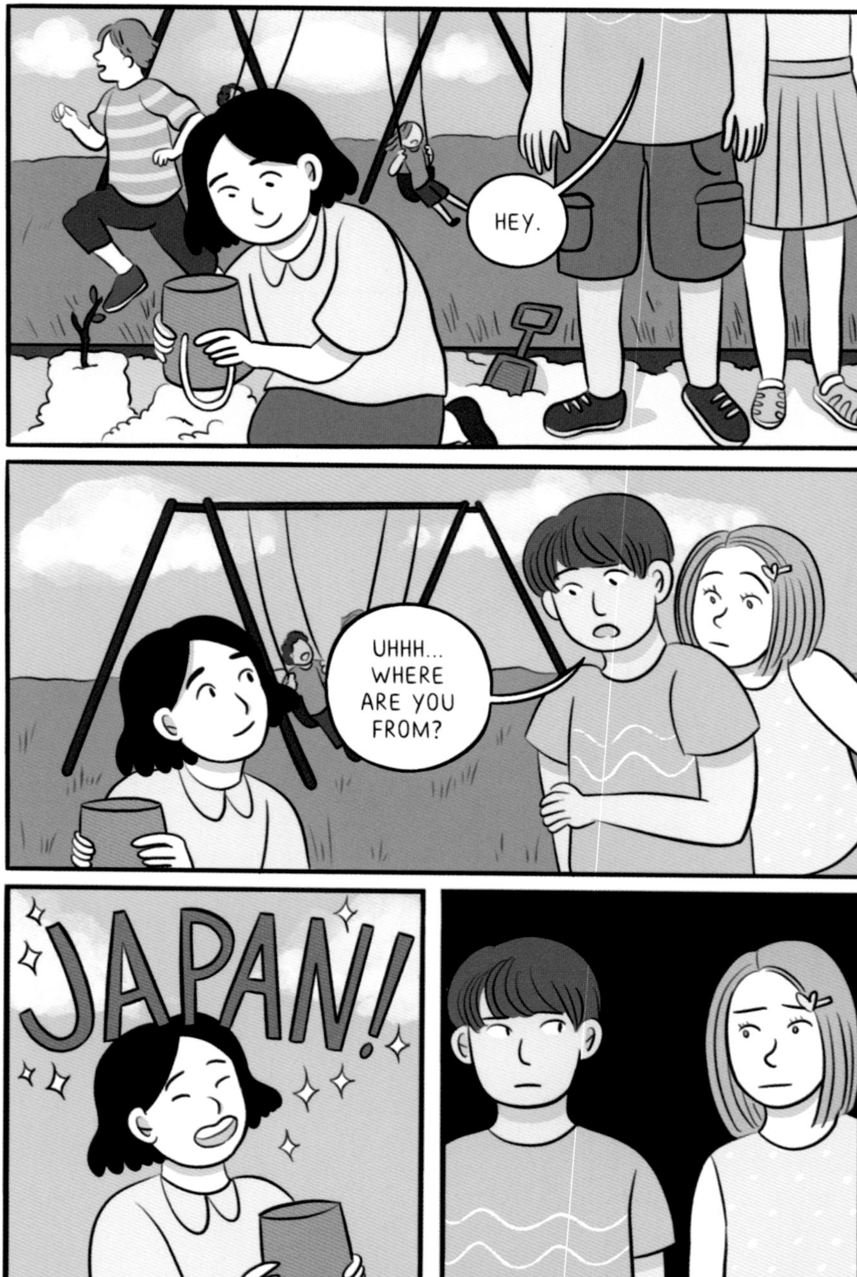
HEY.
UHHH... WHERE ARE YOU FROM?
JAPAN!

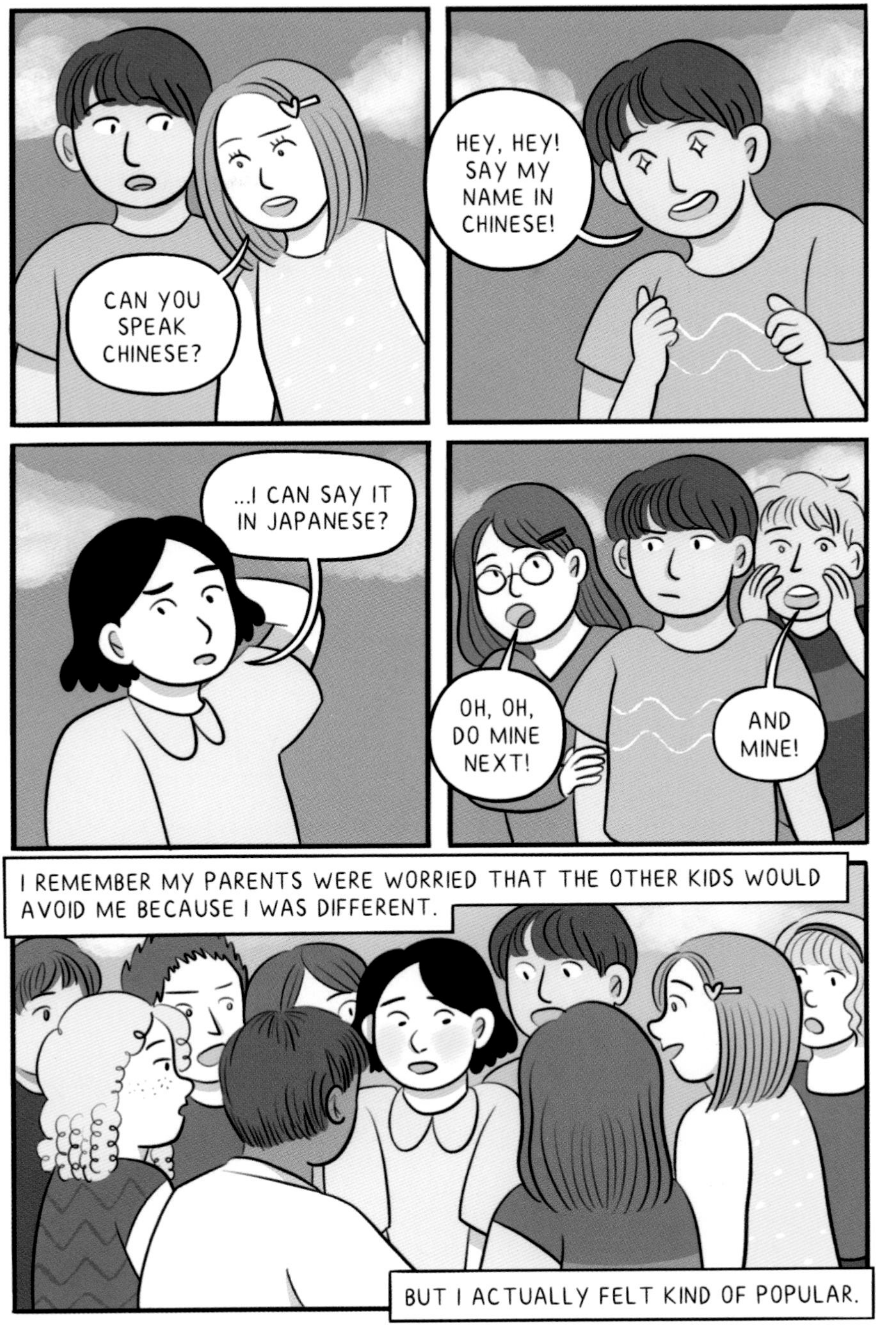
CAN YOU SPEAK CHINESE?
HEY, HEY! SAY MY NAME IN CHINESE!
...I CAN SAY IT IN JAPANESE?
OH, OH, DO MINE NEXT!
AND MINE!
I REMEMBER MY PARENTS WERE WORRIED THAT THE OTHER KIDS WOULD AVOID ME BECAUSE I WAS DIFFERENT.
BUT I ACTUALLY FELT KIND OF POPULAR.

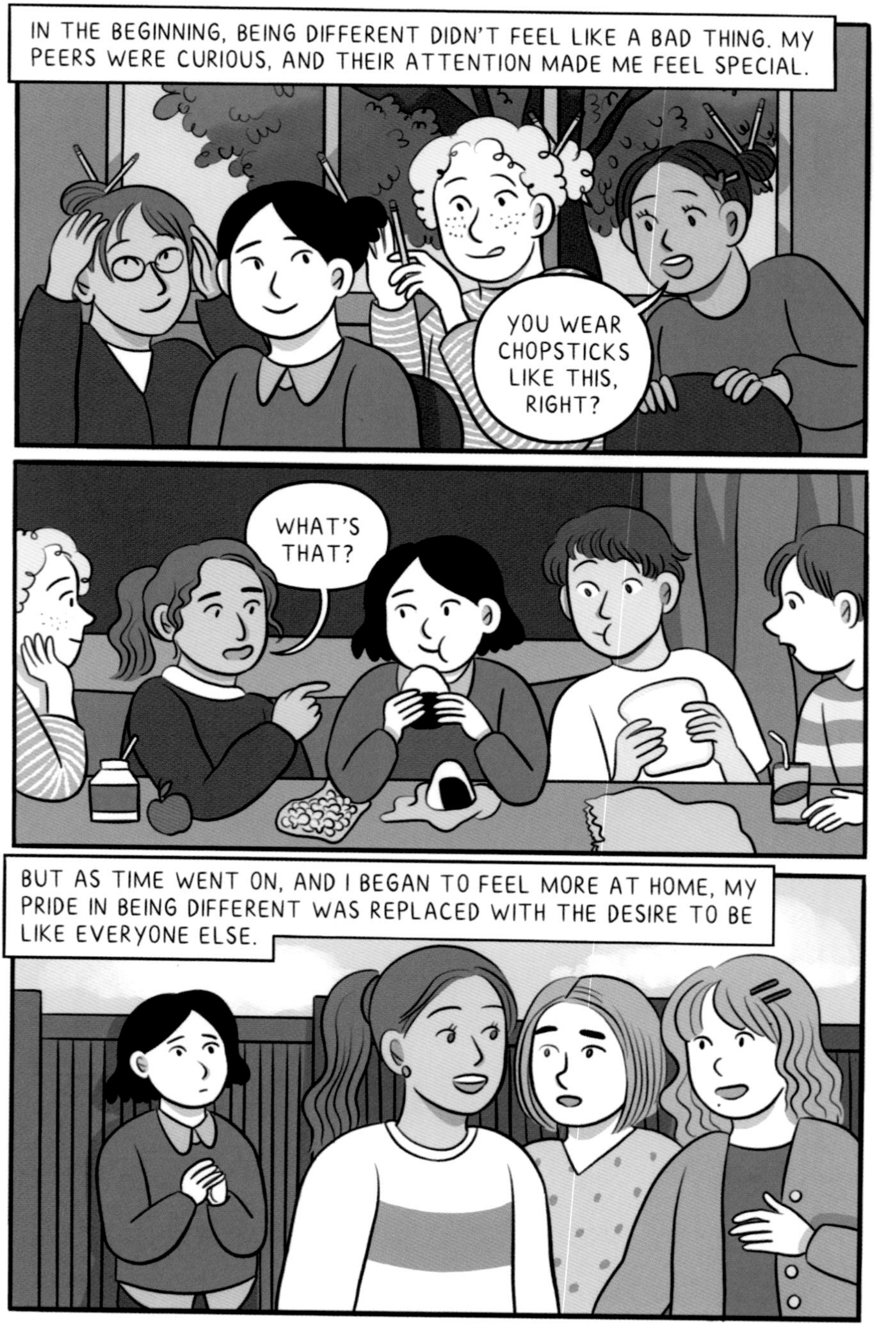
IN THE BEGINNING, BEING DIFFERENT DIDN'T FEEL LIKE A BAD THING. MY PEERS WERE CURIOUS, AND THEIR ATTENTION MADE ME FEEL SPECIAL.
YOU WEAR CHOPSTICKS LIKE THIS, RIGHT?
WHAT'S THAT?
BUT AS TIME WENT ON, AND I BEGAN TO FEEL MORE AT HOME, MY PRIDE IN BEING DIFFERENT WAS REPLACED WITH THE DESIRE TO BE LIKE EVERYONE ELSE.

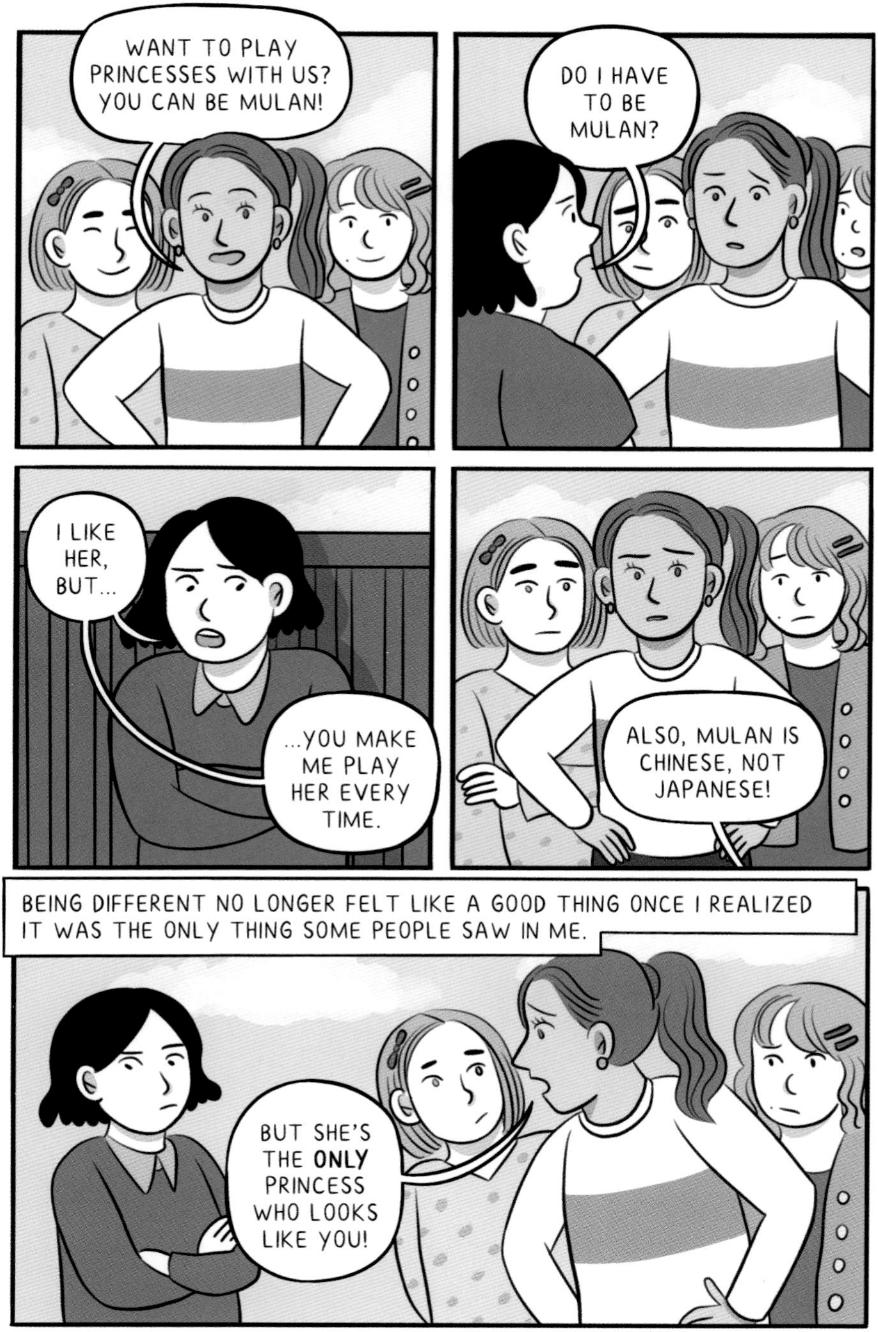
WANT TO PLAY PRINCESSES WITH US? YOU CAN BE MULAN!
DO I HAVE TO BE MULAN?
I LIKE HER, BUT...
...YOU MAKE ME PLAY HER EVERY TIME.
ALSO, MULAN IS CHINESE, NOT JAPANESE!
BEING DIFFERENT NO LONGER FELT LIKE A GOOD THING ONCE I REALIZED IT WAS THE ONLY THING SOME PEOPLE SAW IN ME.
BUT SHE'S THE **ONLY** PRINCESS WHO LOOKS LIKE YOU!

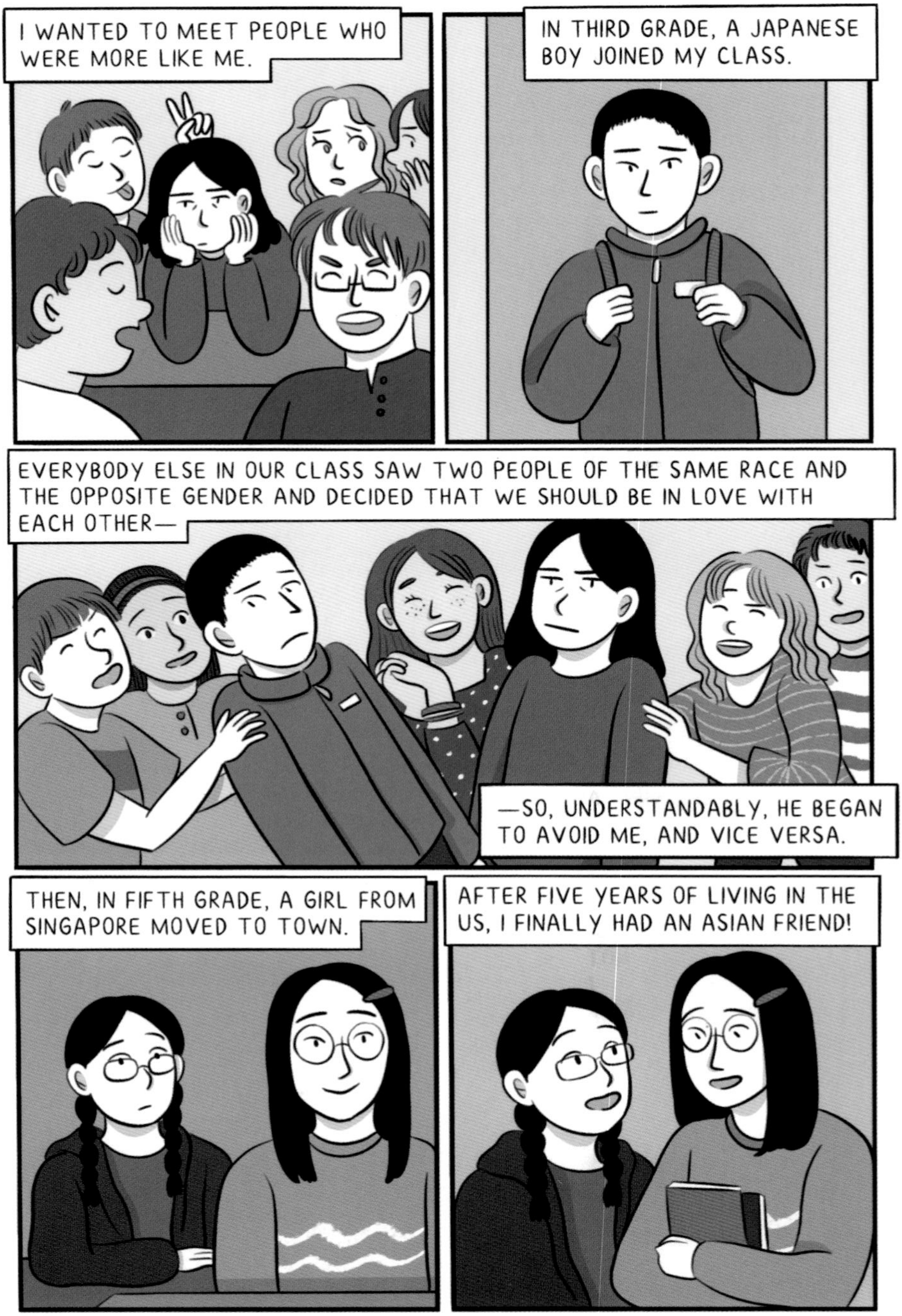
I WANTED TO MEET PEOPLE WHO WERE MORE LIKE ME.
IN THIRD GRADE, A JAPANESE BOY JOINED MY CLASS.
EVERYBODY ELSE IN OUR CLASS SAW TWO PEOPLE OF THE SAME RACE AND THE OPPOSITE GENDER AND DECIDED THAT WE SHOULD BE IN LOVE WITH EACH OTHER—
—SO, UNDERSTANDABLY, HE BEGAN TO AVOID ME, AND VICE VERSA.
THEN, IN FIFTH GRADE, A GIRL FROM SINGAPORE MOVED TO TOWN.
AFTER FIVE YEARS OF LIVING IN THE US, I FINALLY HAD AN ASIAN FRIEND!

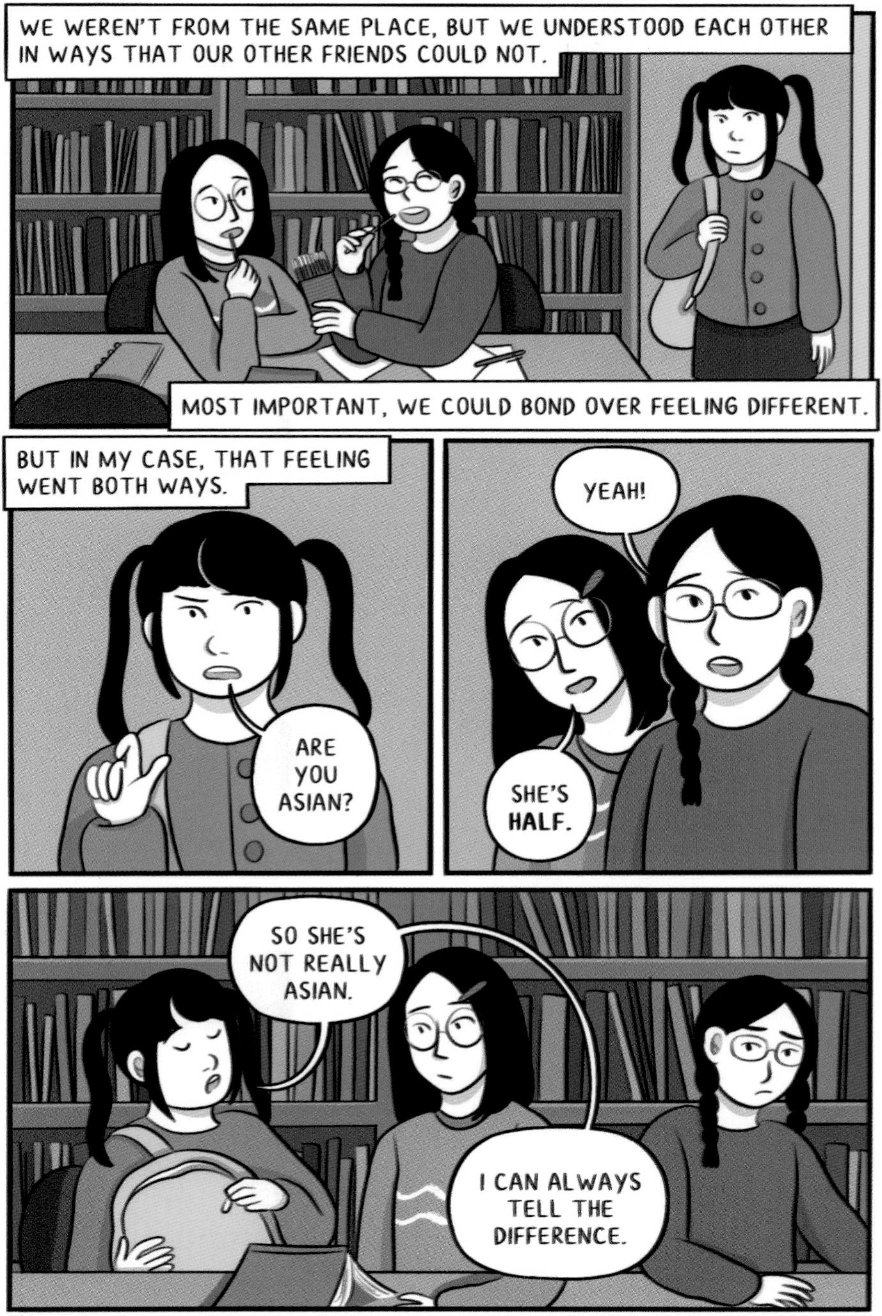
WE WEREN'T FROM THE SAME PLACE, BUT WE UNDERSTOOD EACH OTHER IN WAYS THAT OUR OTHER FRIENDS COULD NOT.
MOST IMPORTANT, WE COULD BOND OVER FEELING DIFFERENT.
BUT IN MY CASE, THAT FEELING WENT BOTH WAYS.
ARE YOU ASIAN?
YEAH!
SHE'S **HALF.**
SO SHE'S NOT REALLY ASIAN.
I CAN ALWAYS TELL THE DIFFERENCE.

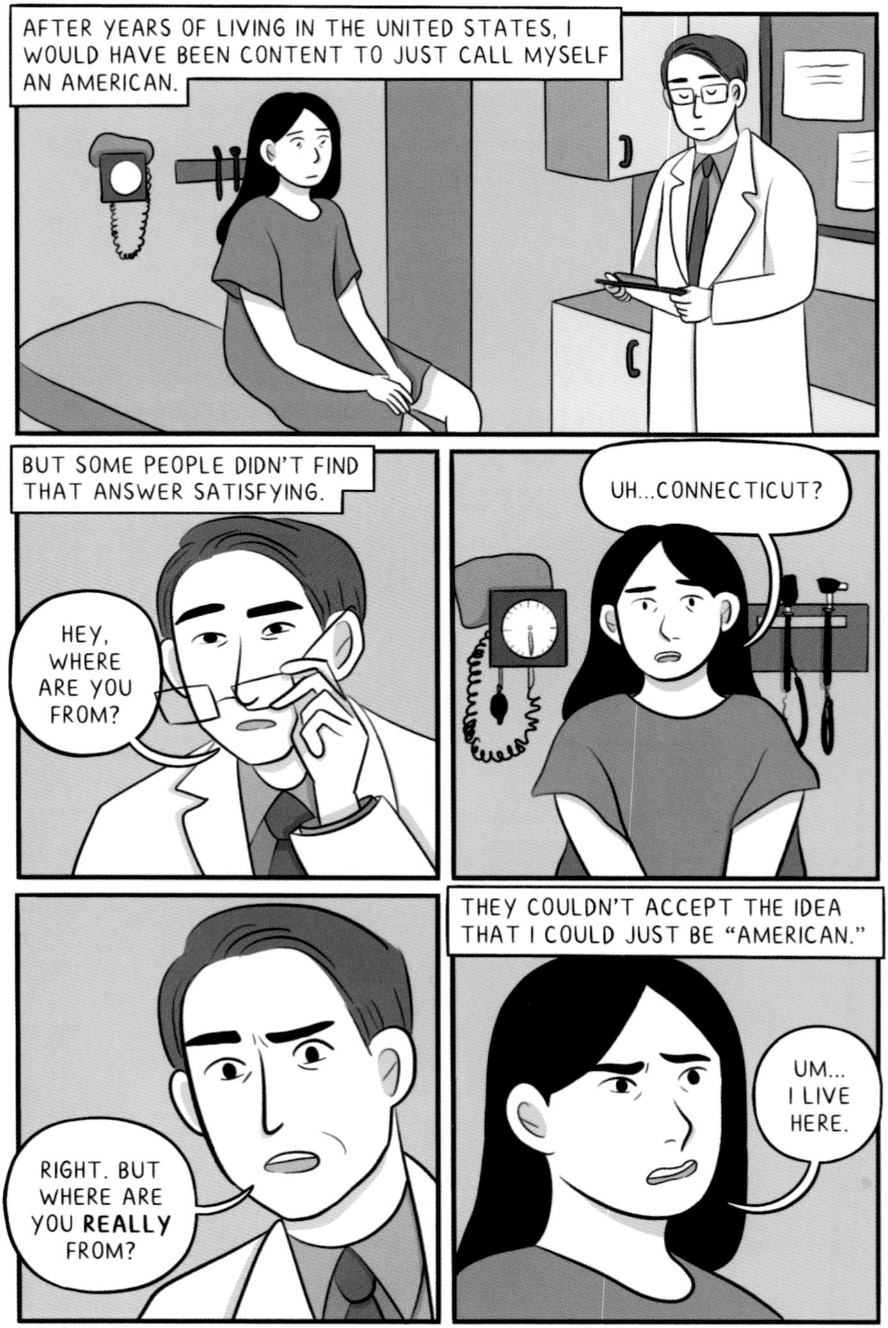
AFTER YEARS OF LIVING IN THE UNITED STATES, I WOULD HAVE BEEN CONTENT TO JUST CALL MYSELF AN AMERICAN.
BUT SOME PEOPLE DIDN'T FIND THAT ANSWER SATISFYING.
HEY, WHERE ARE YOU FROM?
UH...CONNECTICUT?
RIGHT. BUT WHERE ARE YOU **REALLY** FROM?
THEY COULDN'T ACCEPT THE IDEA THAT I COULD JUST BE "AMERICAN."
UM... I LIVE HERE.

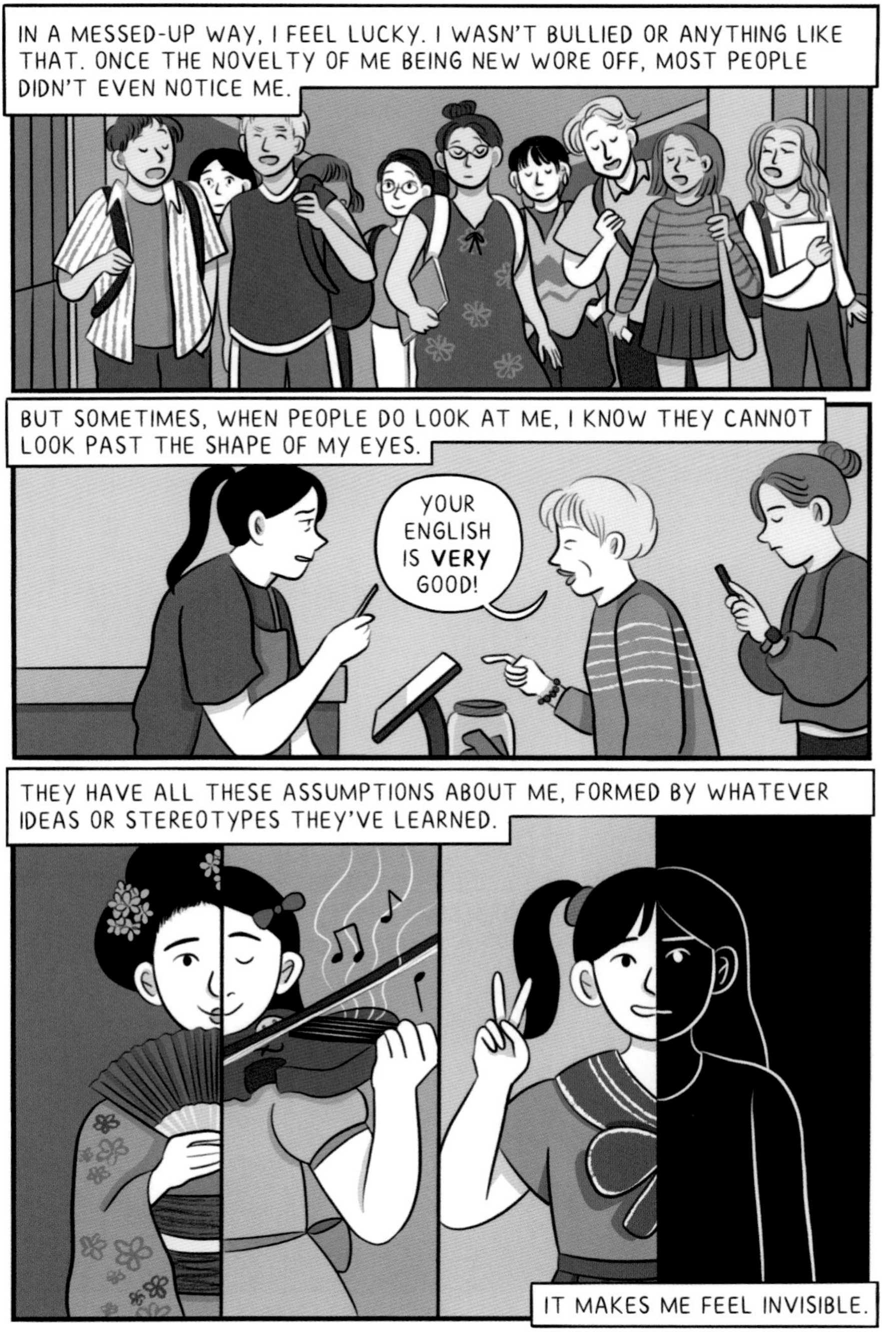
IN A MESSED-UP WAY, I FEEL LUCKY. I WASN'T BULLIED OR ANYTHING LIKE THAT. ONCE THE NOVELTY OF ME BEING NEW WORE OFF, MOST PEOPLE DIDN'T EVEN NOTICE ME.
BUT SOMETIMES, WHEN PEOPLE DO LOOK AT ME, I KNOW THEY CANNOT LOOK PAST THE SHAPE OF MY EYES.
YOUR ENGLISH IS **VERY** GOOD!
THEY HAVE ALL THESE ASSUMPTIONS ABOUT ME, FORMED BY WHATEVER IDEAS OR STEREOTYPES THEY'VE LEARNED.
IT MAKES ME FEEL INVISIBLE.

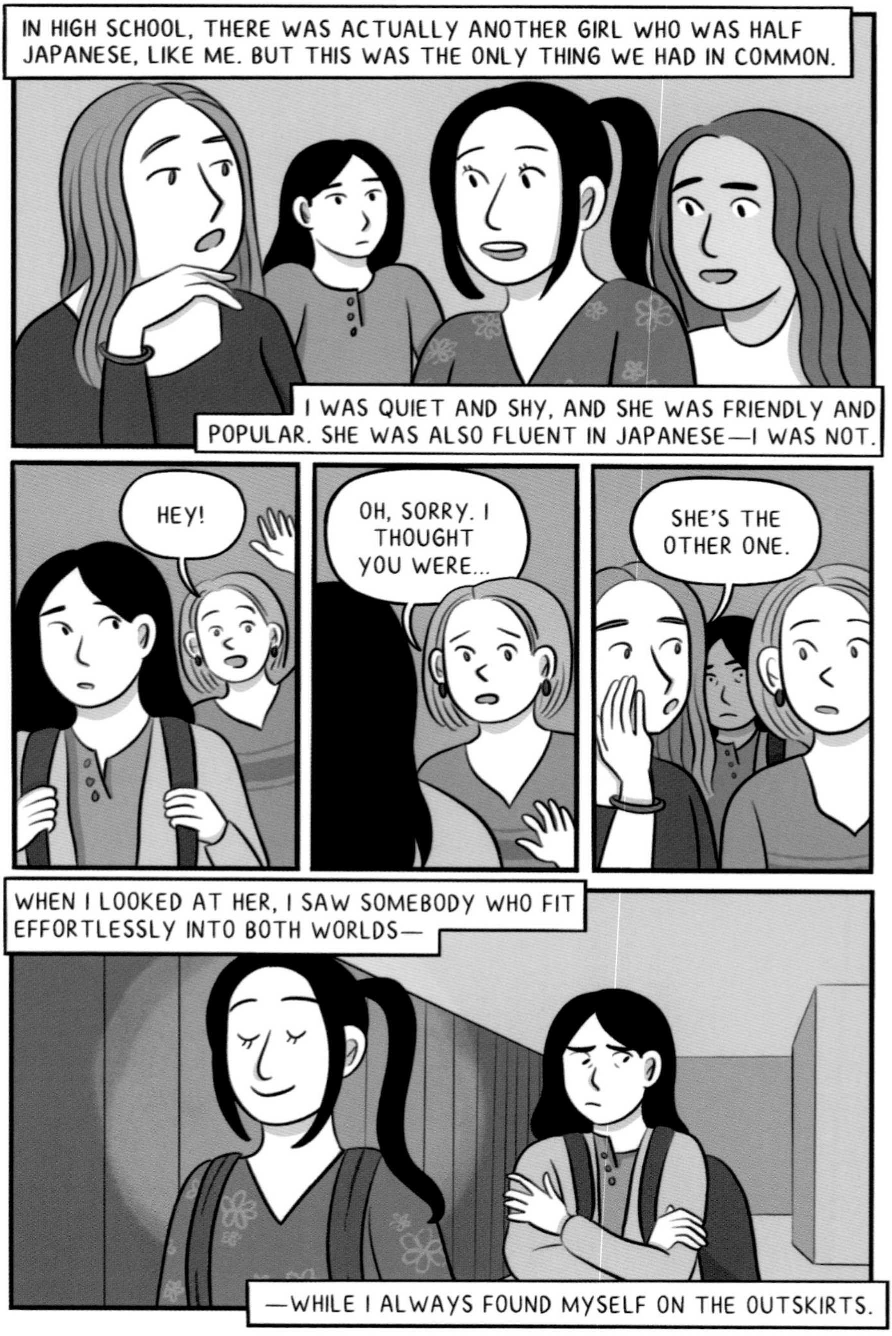
IN HIGH SCHOOL, THERE WAS ACTUALLY ANOTHER GIRL WHO WAS HALF JAPANESE, LIKE ME. BUT THIS WAS THE ONLY THING WE HAD IN COMMON.
I WAS QUIET AND SHY, AND SHE WAS FRIENDLY AND POPULAR. SHE WAS ALSO FLUENT IN JAPANESE—I WAS NOT.
HEY!
OH, SORRY. I THOUGHT YOU WERE...
SHE'S THE OTHER ONE.
WHEN I LOOKED AT HER, I SAW SOMEBODY WHO FIT EFFORTLESSLY INTO BOTH WORLDS—
—WHILE I ALWAYS FOUND MYSELF ON THE OUTSKIRTS.

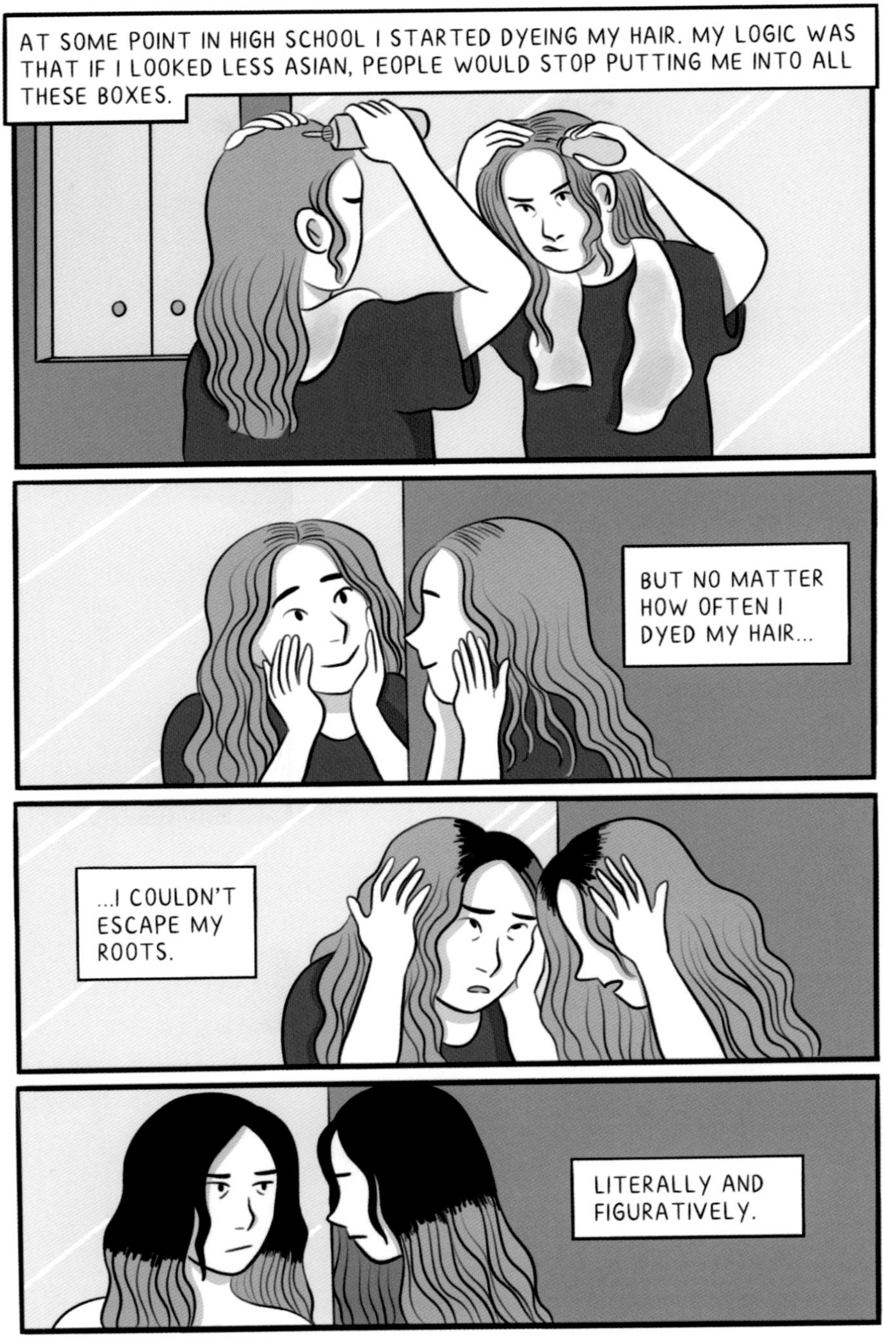
AT SOME POINT IN HIGH SCHOOL I STARTED DYEING MY HAIR. MY LOGIC WAS THAT IF I LOOKED LESS ASIAN, PEOPLE WOULD STOP PUTTING ME INTO ALL THESE BOXES.
BUT NO MATTER HOW OFTEN I DYED MY HAIR...
...I COULDN'T ESCAPE MY ROOTS.
LITERALLY AND FIGURATIVELY.

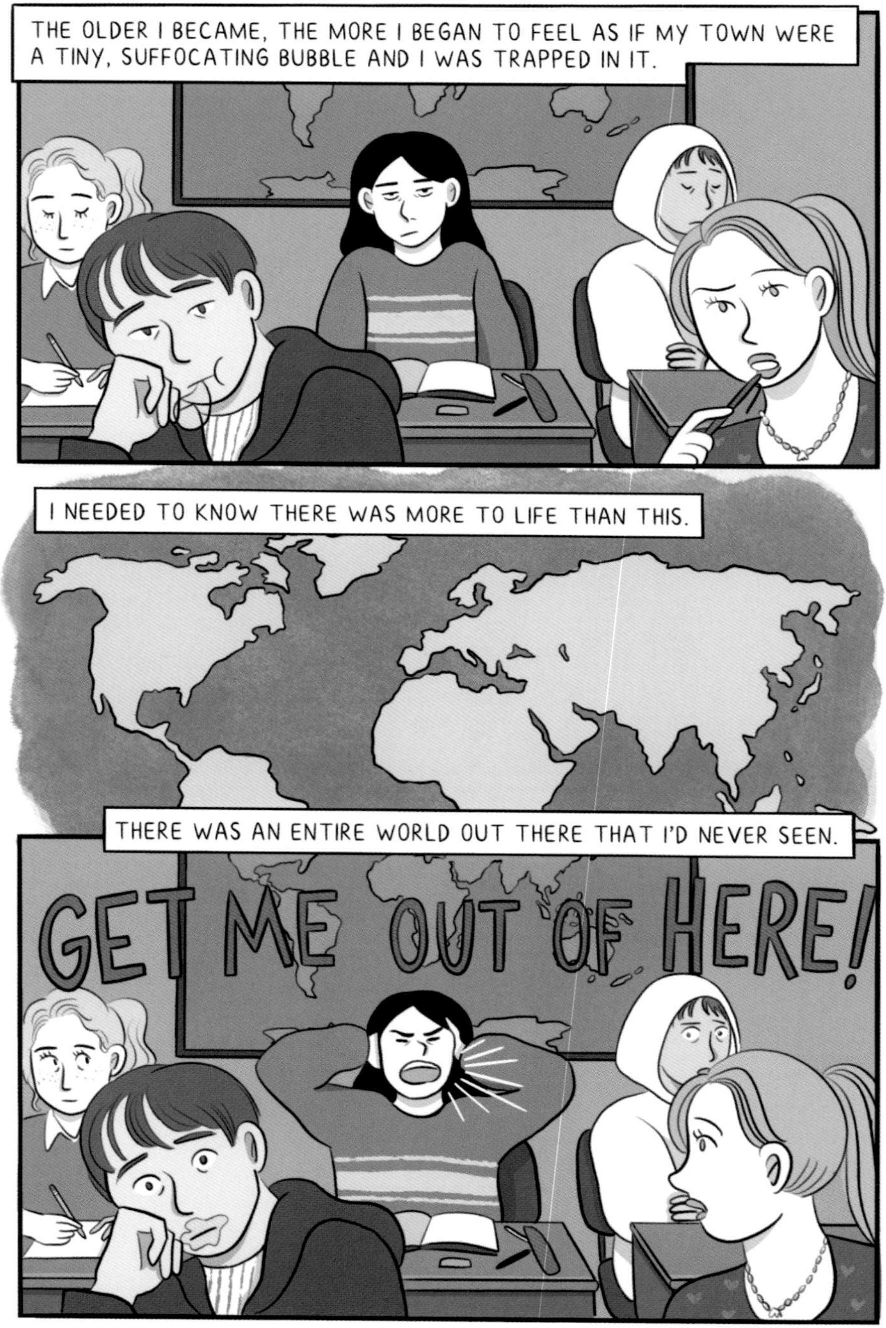
THE OLDER I BECAME, THE MORE I BEGAN TO FEEL AS IF MY TOWN WERE A TINY, SUFFOCATING BUBBLE AND I WAS TRAPPED IN IT.
I NEEDED TO KNOW THERE WAS MORE TO LIFE THAN THIS.
THERE WAS AN ENTIRE WORLD OUT THERE THAT I'D NEVER SEEN.
GET ME OUT OF HERE!

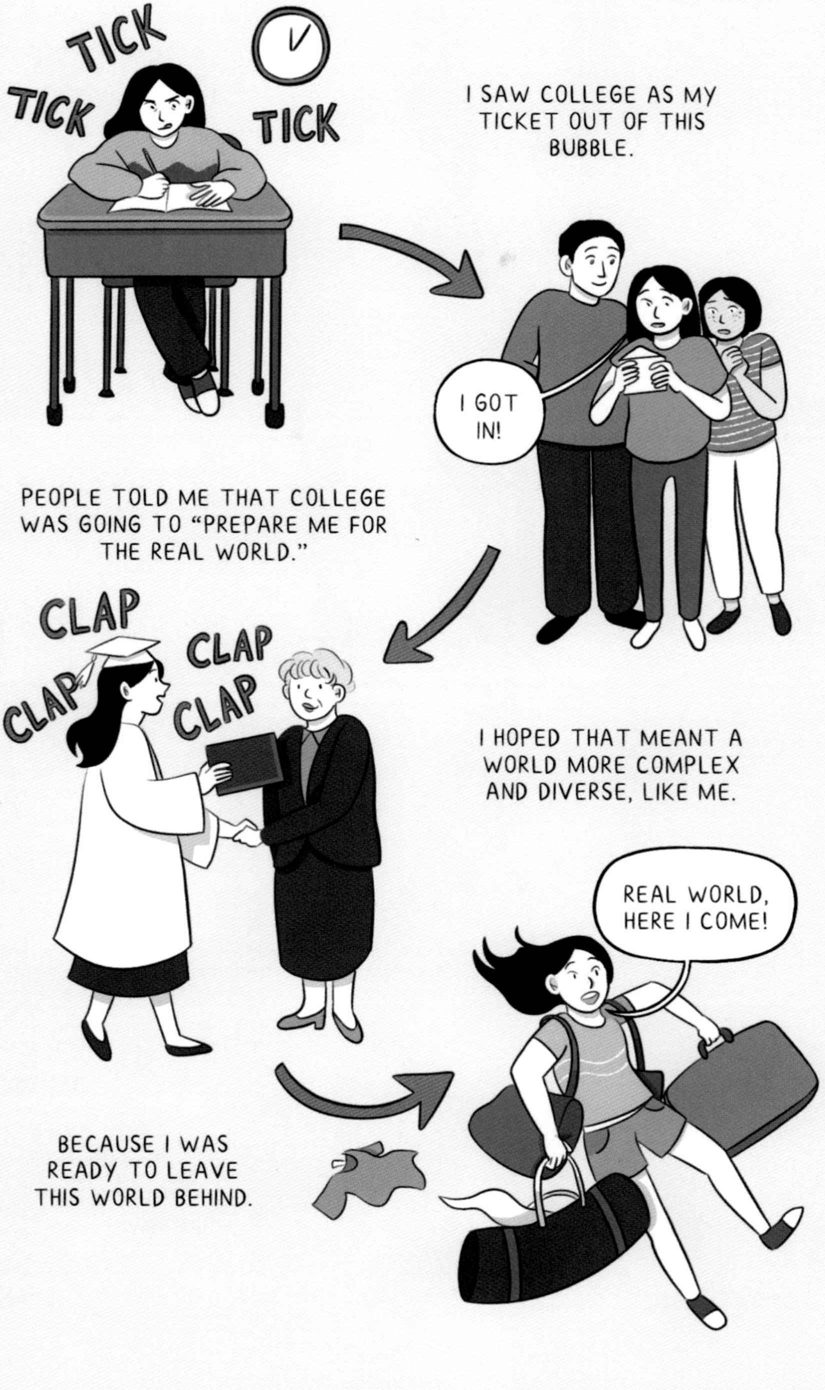
TICK
TICK
TICK
I SAW COLLEGE AS MY TICKET OUT OF THIS BUBBLE.
I GOT IN!
PEOPLE TOLD ME THAT COLLEGE WAS GOING TO "PREPARE ME FOR THE REAL WORLD."
CLAP
CLAP
CLAP
CLAP
I HOPED THAT MEANT A WORLD MORE COMPLEX AND DIVERSE, LIKE ME.
BECAUSE I WAS READY TO LEAVE THIS WORLD BEHIND.
REAL WORLD, HERE I COME!

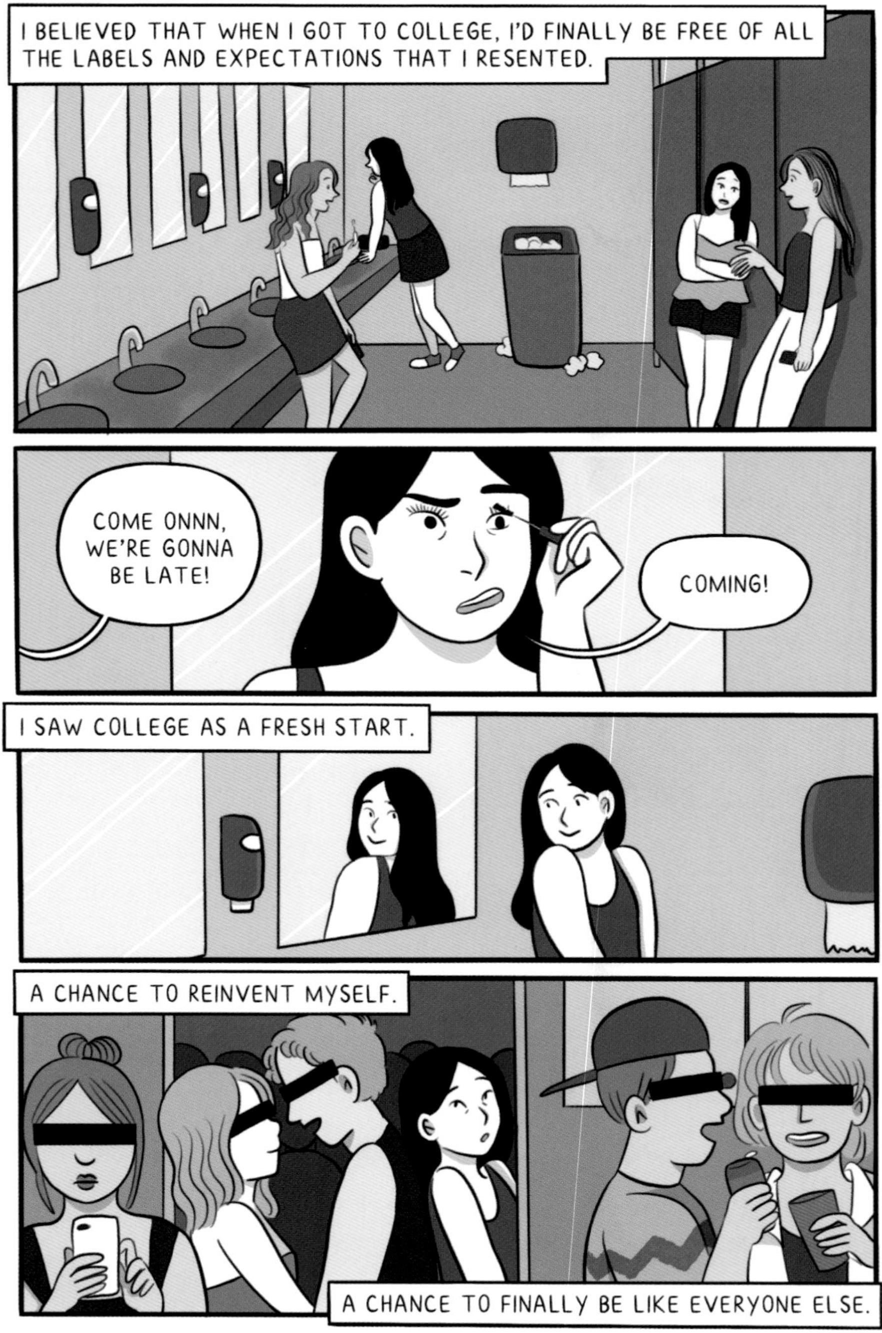
I BELIEVED THAT WHEN I GOT TO COLLEGE, I'D FINALLY BE FREE OF ALL THE LABELS AND EXPECTATIONS THAT I RESENTED.
COME ONNN, WE'RE GONNA BE LATE!
COMING!
I SAW COLLEGE AS A FRESH START.
A CHANCE TO REINVENT MYSELF.
A CHANCE TO FINALLY BE LIKE EVERYONE ELSE.

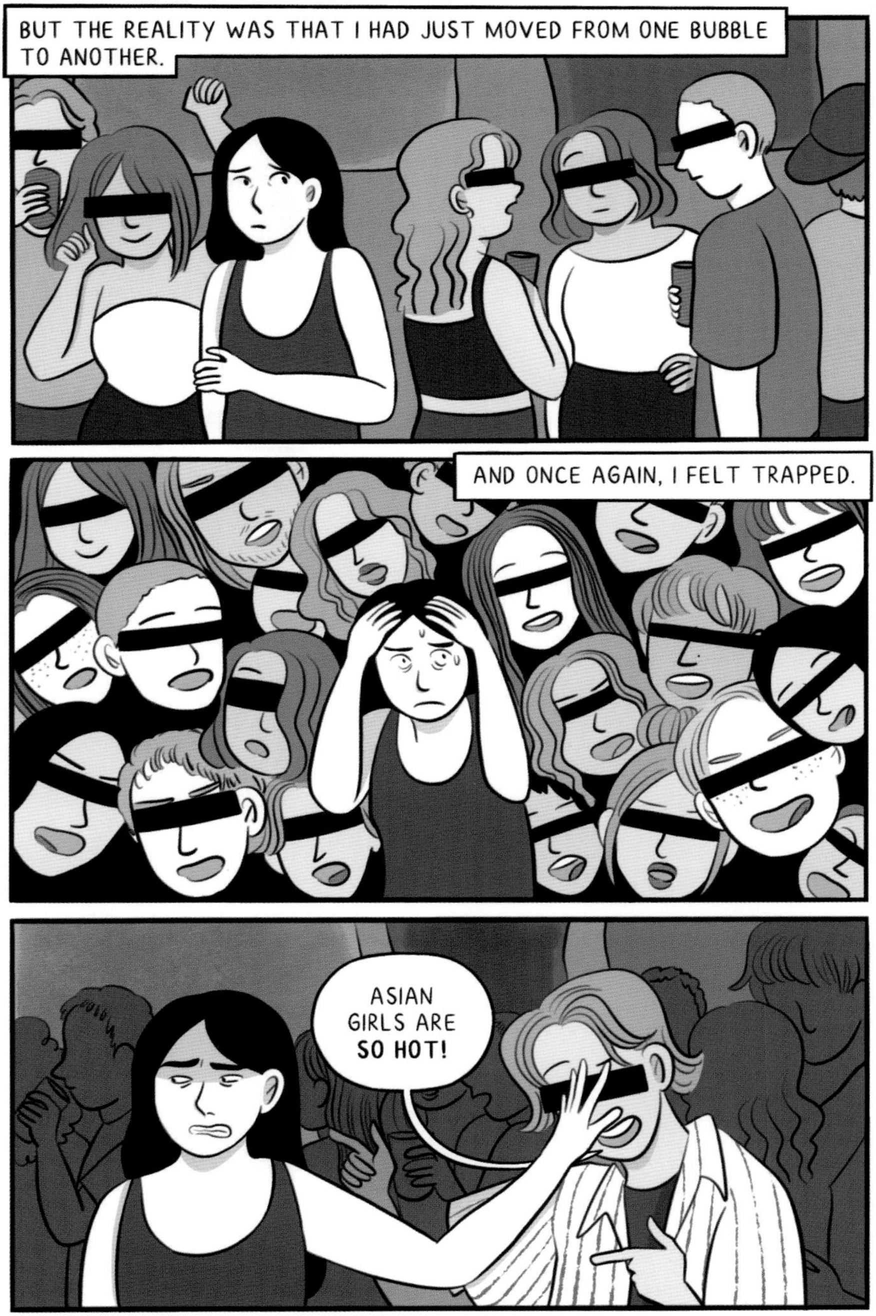
BUT THE REALITY WAS THAT I HAD JUST MOVED FROM ONE BUBBLE TO ANOTHER.
AND ONCE AGAIN, I FELT TRAPPED.
ASIAN GIRLS ARE **SO HOT!**

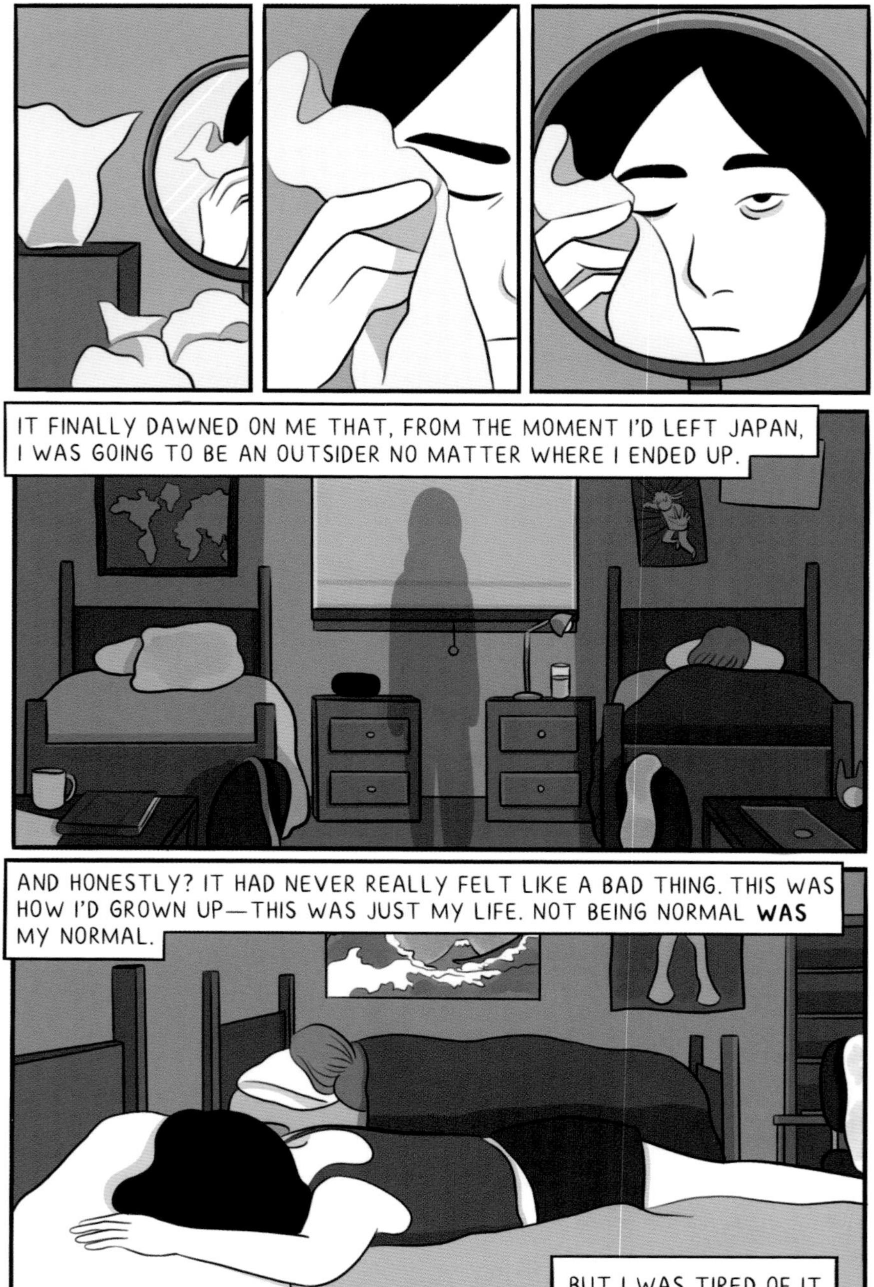
IT FINALLY DAWNED ON ME THAT, FROM THE MOMENT I'D LEFT JAPAN, I WAS GOING TO BE AN OUTSIDER NO MATTER WHERE I ENDED UP.
AND HONESTLY? IT HAD NEVER REALLY FELT LIKE A BAD THING. THIS WAS HOW I'D GROWN UP—THIS WAS JUST MY LIFE. NOT BEING NORMAL **WAS** MY NORMAL.
BUT I WAS TIRED OF IT.

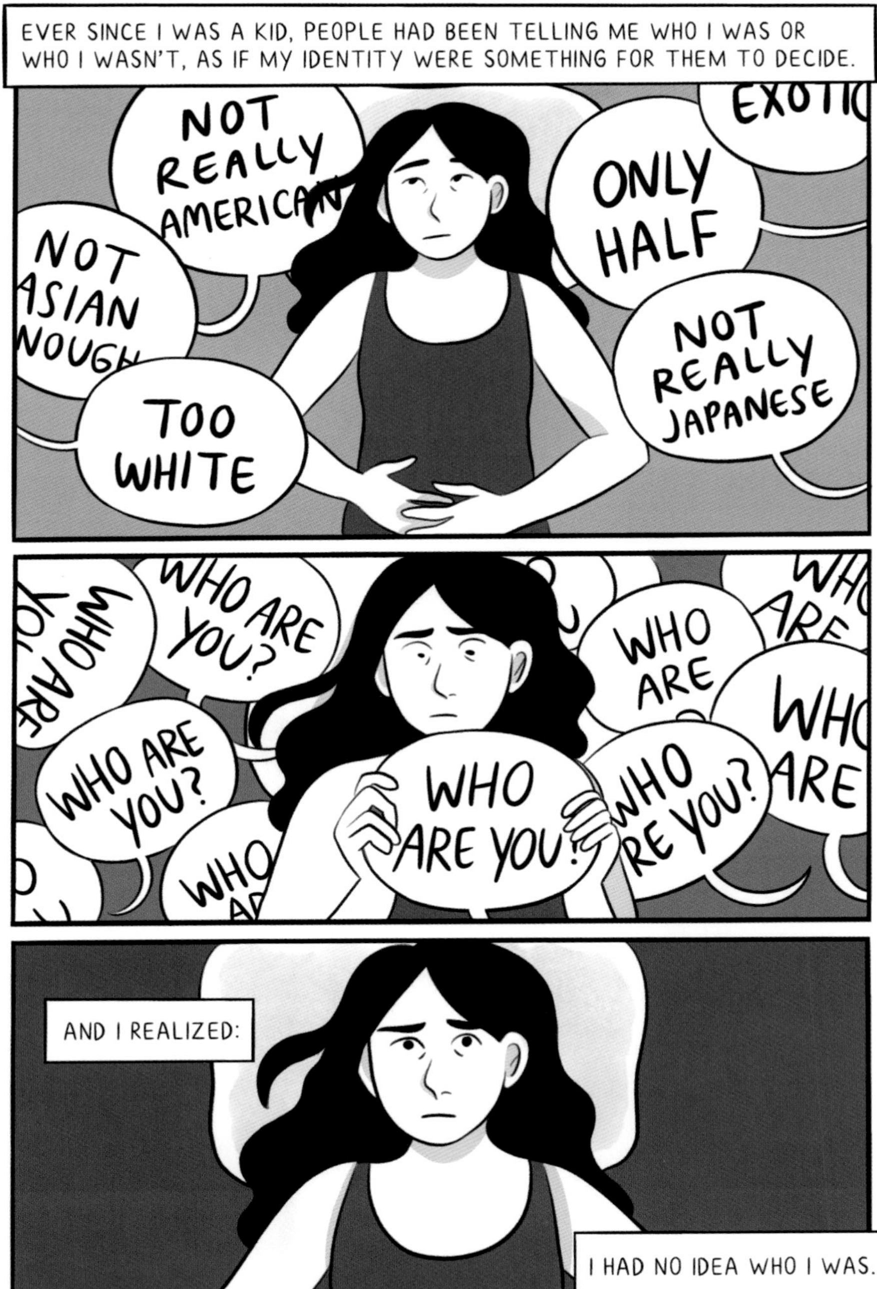
EVER SINCE I WAS A KID, PEOPLE HAD BEEN TELLING ME WHO I WAS OR WHO I WASN'T, AS IF MY IDENTITY WERE SOMETHING FOR THEM TO DECIDE.
NOT REALLY AMERICAN
ONLY HALF
TOO WHITE
NOT REALLY JAPANESE
WHO ARE YOU?
WHO ARE YOU?
WHO ARE YOU?
WHO ARE YOU?
AND I REALIZED:
I HAD NO IDEA WHO I WAS.

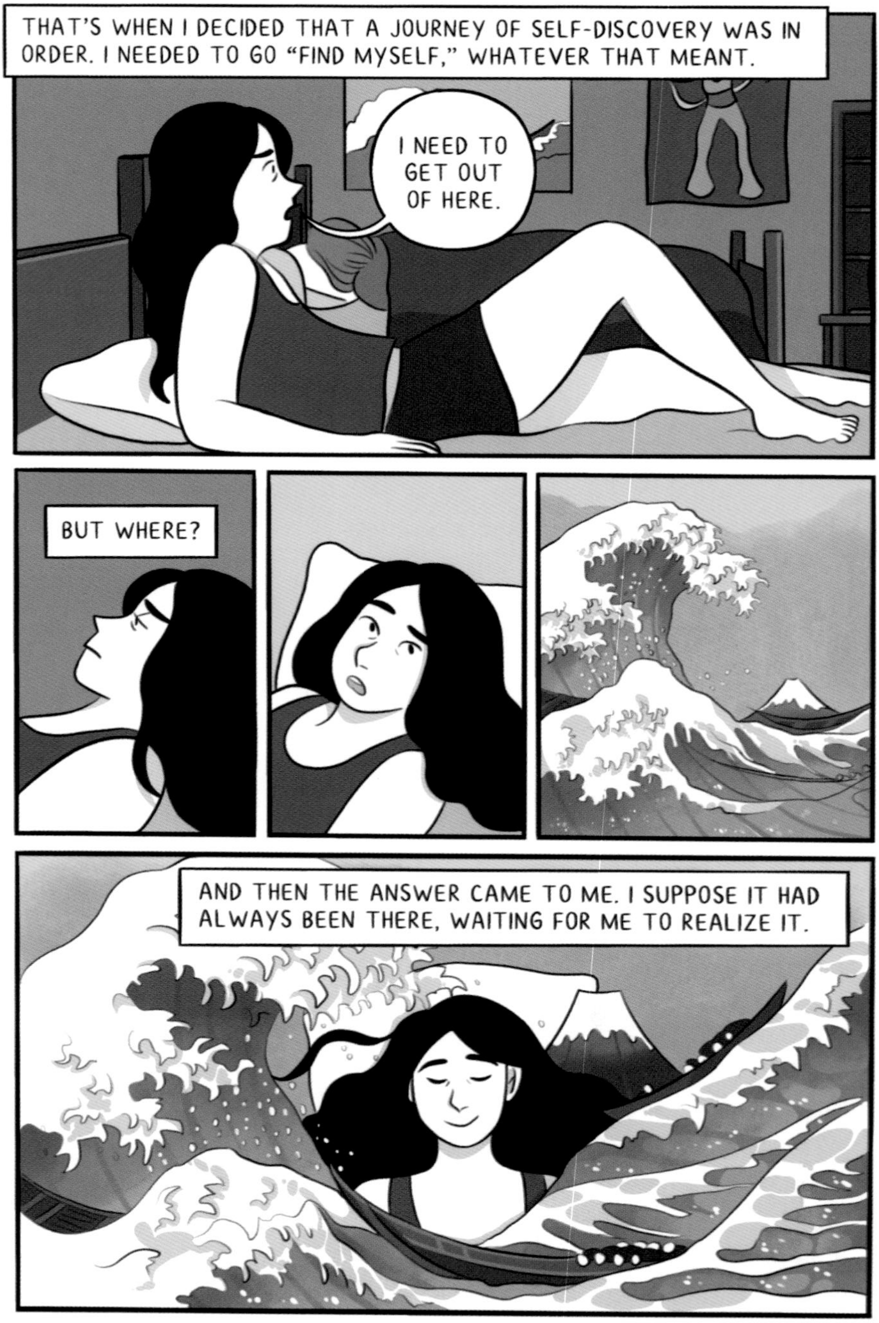
THAT'S WHEN I DECIDED THAT A JOURNEY OF SELF-DISCOVERY WAS IN ORDER. I NEEDED TO GO "FIND MYSELF," WHATEVER THAT MEANT.
I NEED TO GET OUT OF HERE.
BUT WHERE?
AND THEN THE ANSWER CAME TO ME. I SUPPOSE IT HAD ALWAYS BEEN THERE, WAITING FOR ME TO REALIZE IT.

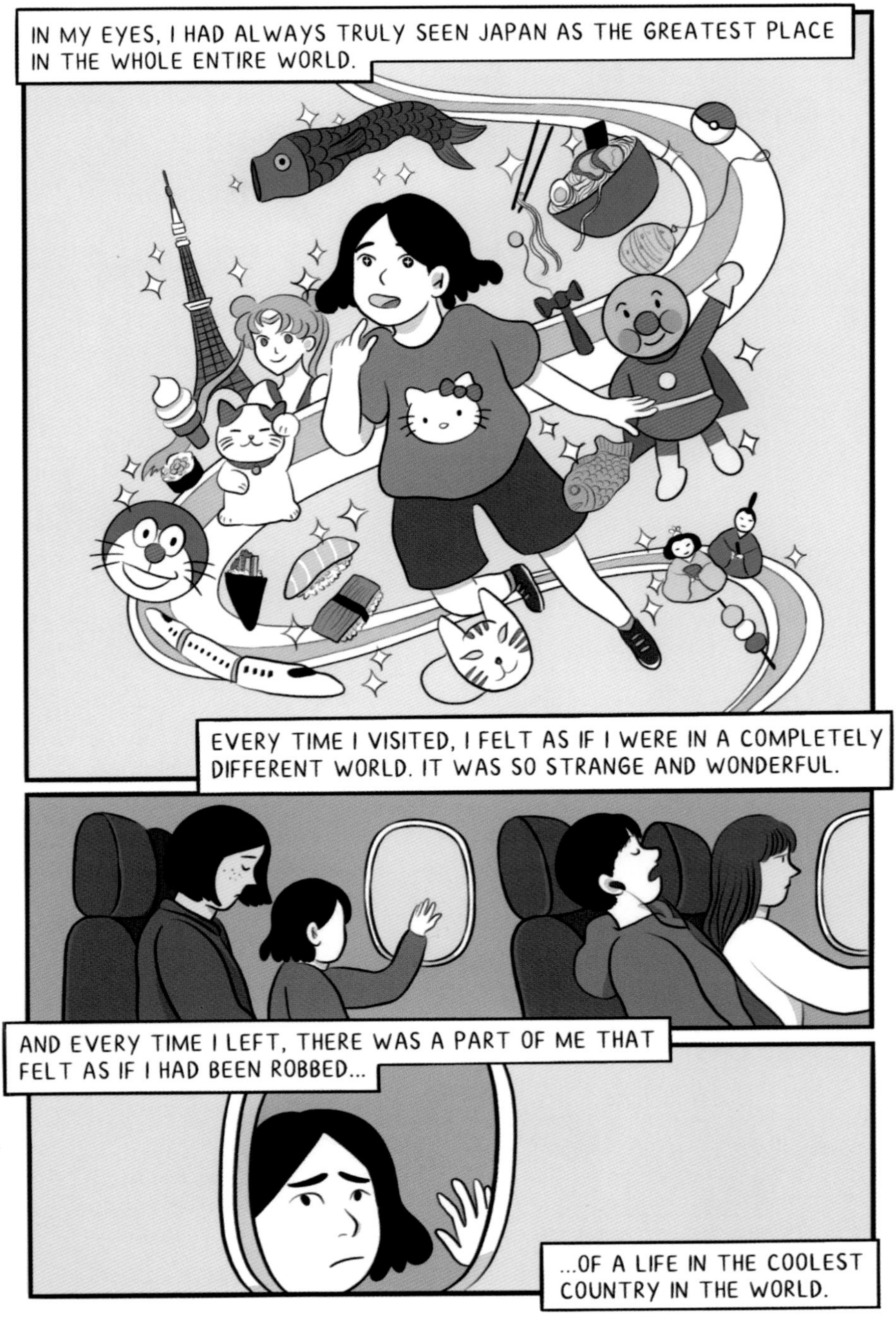
IN MY EYES, I HAD ALWAYS TRULY SEEN JAPAN AS THE GREATEST PLACE IN THE WHOLE ENTIRE WORLD.
EVERY TIME I VISITED, I FELT AS IF I WERE IN A COMPLETELY DIFFERENT WORLD. IT WAS SO STRANGE AND WONDERFUL.
AND EVERY TIME I LEFT, THERE WAS A PART OF ME THAT FELT AS IF I HAD BEEN ROBBED...
...OF A LIFE IN THE COOLEST COUNTRY IN THE WORLD.

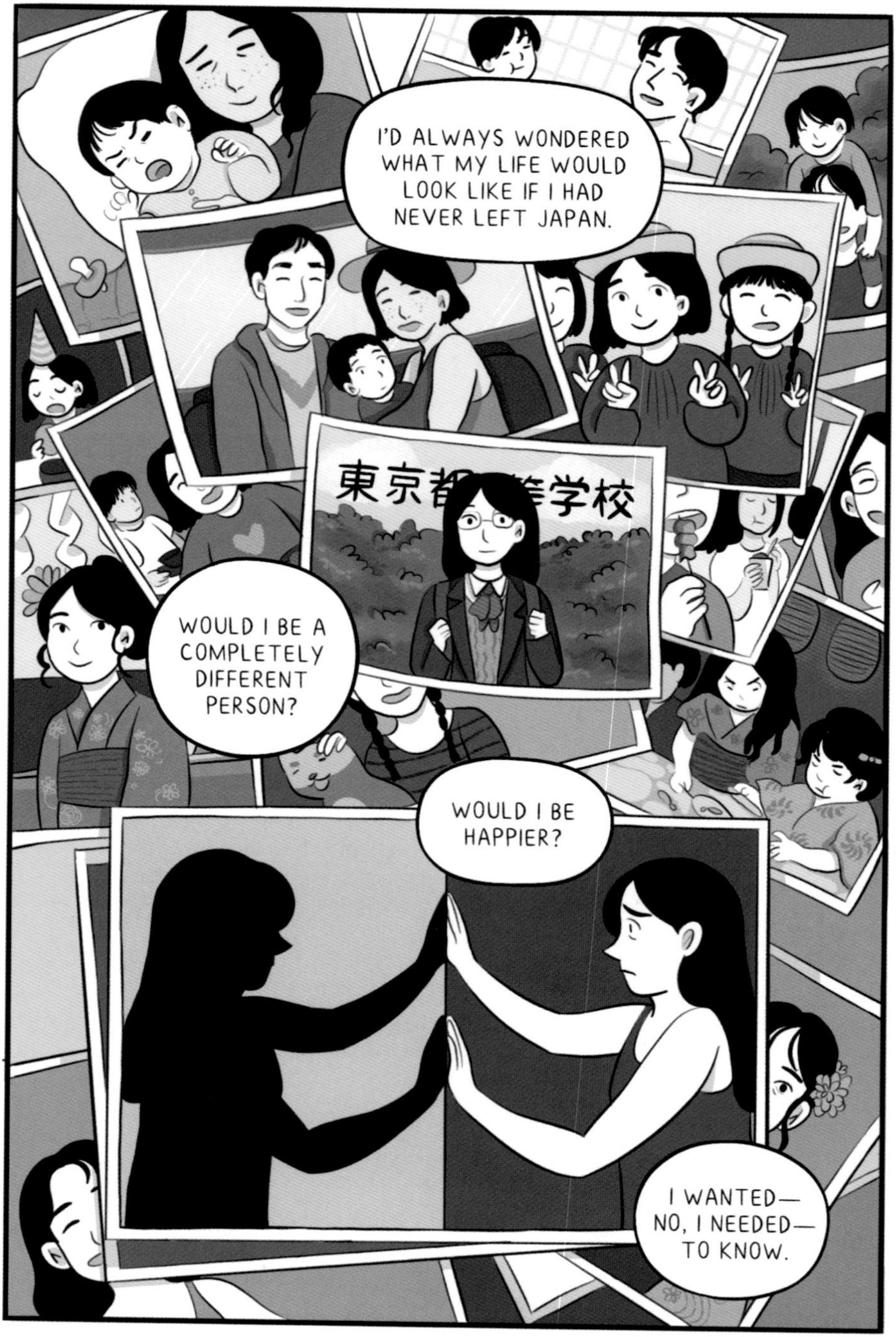
I'D ALWAYS WONDERED WHAT MY LIFE WOULD LOOK LIKE IF I HAD NEVER LEFT JAPAN.
東京都 学校
WOULD I BE A COMPLETELY DIFFERENT PERSON?
WOULD I BE HAPPIER?
I WANTED—NO, I NEEDED—TO KNOW.

SO, AS SOON AS I SAW THE FIRST CHANCE TO LEAVE, I TOOK IT.

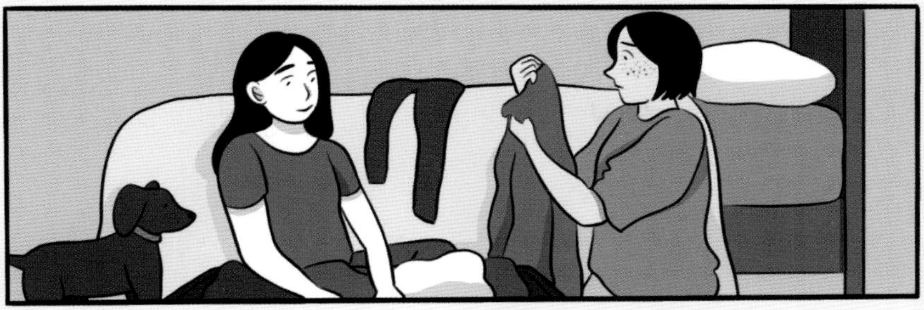

I SIGNED UP TO STUDY JAPANESE AT A BIG UNIVERSITY IN TOKYO.

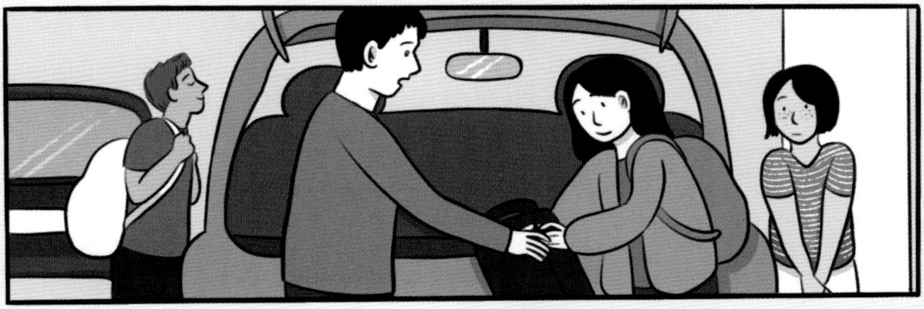

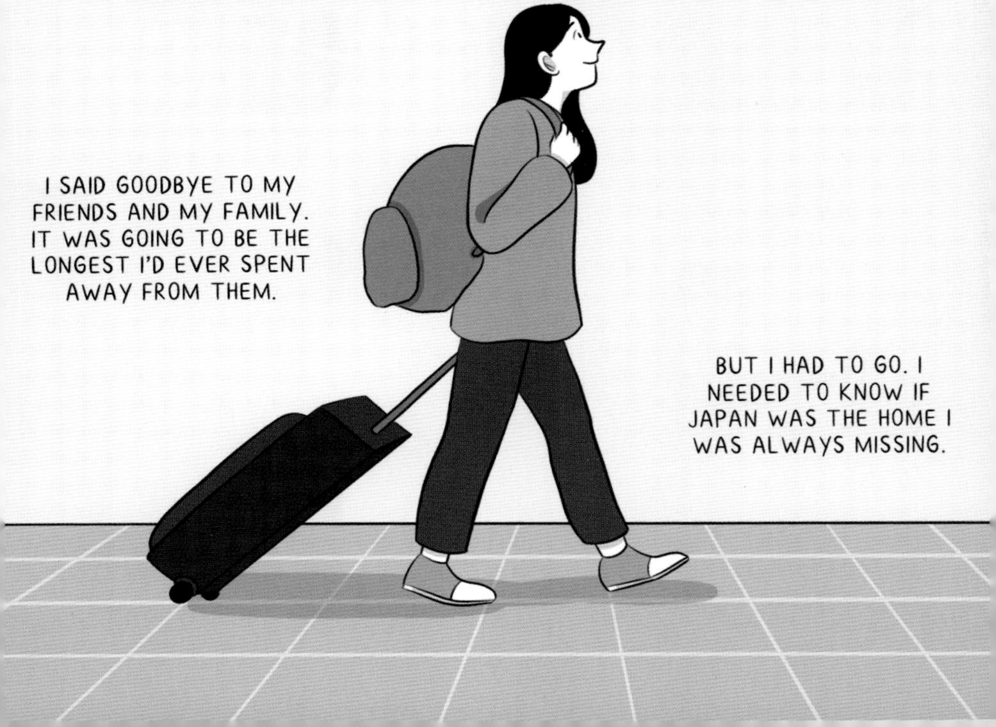
I SAID GOODBYE TO MY FRIENDS AND MY FAMILY. IT WAS GOING TO BE THE LONGEST I'D EVER SPENT AWAY FROM THEM.
BUT I HAD TO GO. I NEEDED TO KNOW IF JAPAN WAS THE HOME I WAS ALWAYS MISSING.

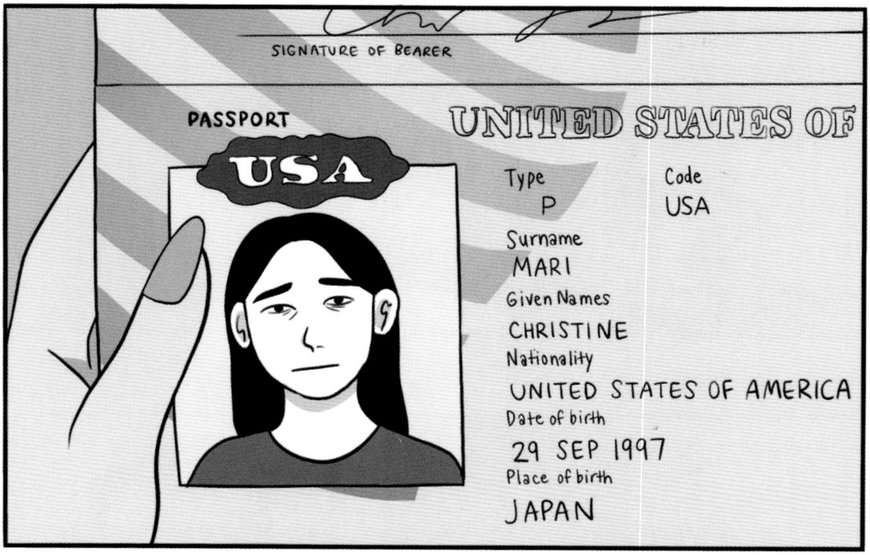
SIGNATURE OF BEARER
PASSPORT
UNITED STATES OF
USA
Type
P
Code
USA
Surname
MARI
Given Names
CHRISTINE
Nationality
UNITED STATES OF AMERICA
Date of birth
29 SEP 1997
Place of birth
JAPAN

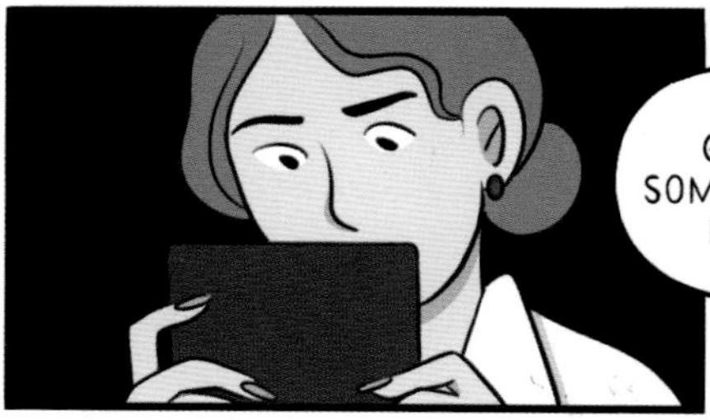

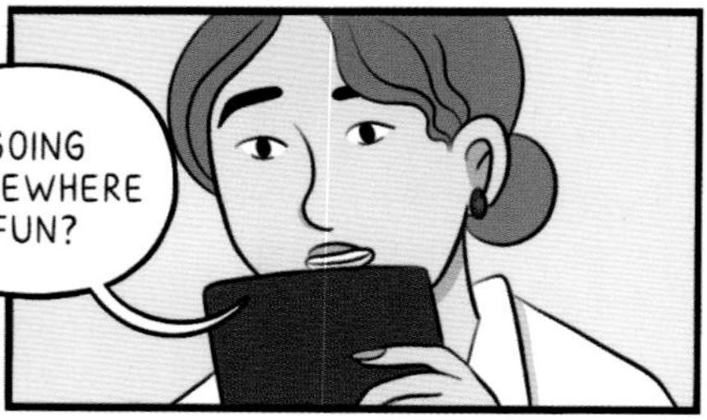
GOING SOMEWHERE FUN?

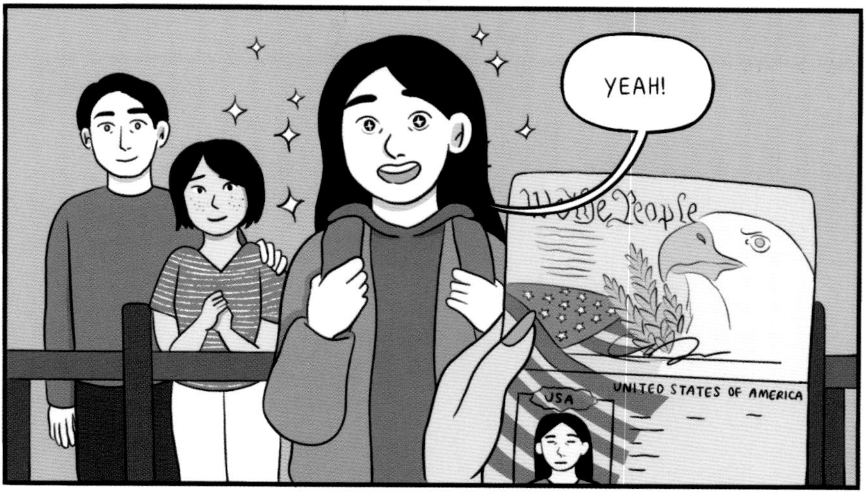
YEAH!
We the People
USA
UNITED STATES OF AMERICA

夏

SUMMER

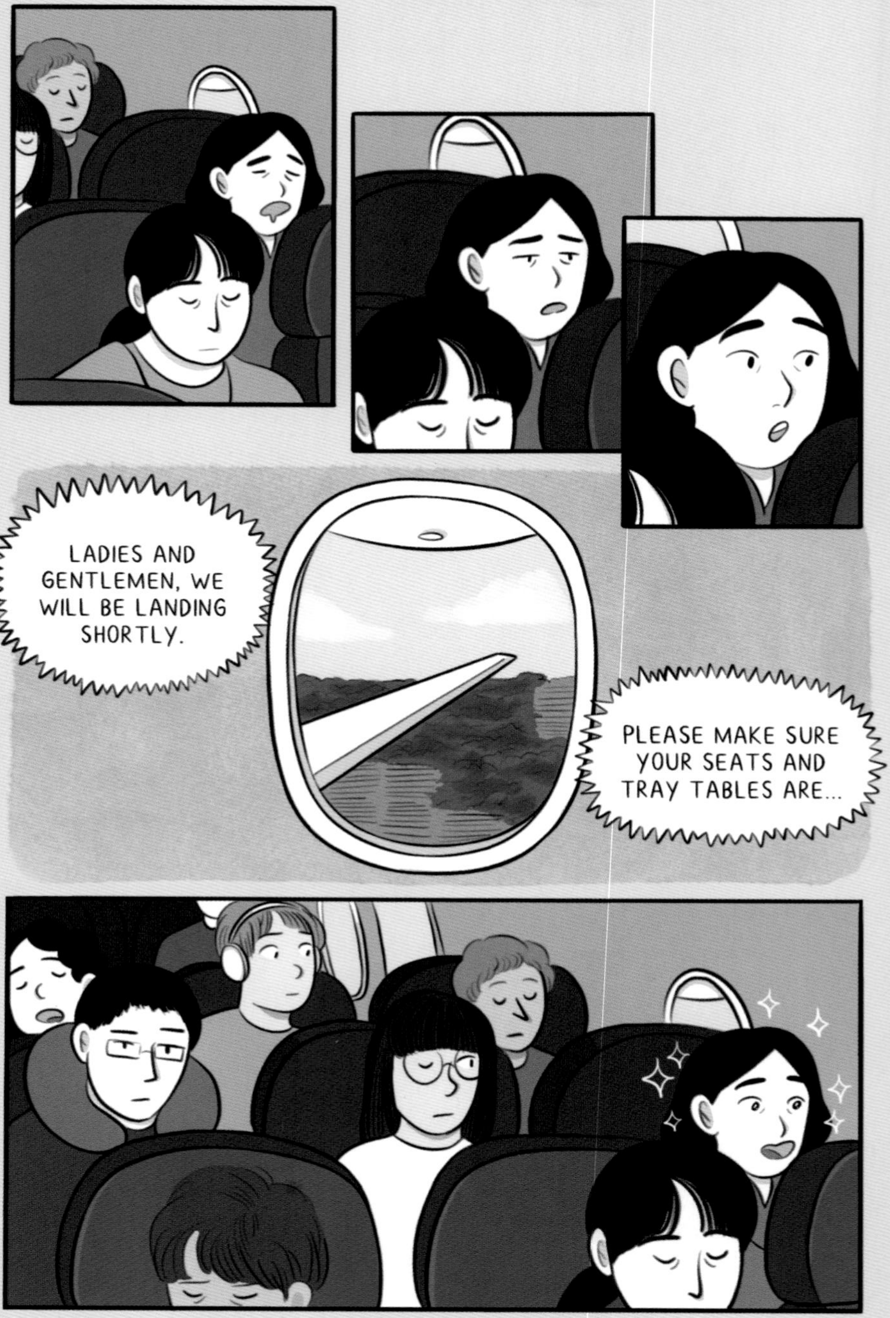
LADIES AND GENTLEMEN, WE WILL BE LANDING SHORTLY.
PLEASE MAKE SURE YOUR SEATS AND TRAY TABLES ARE...

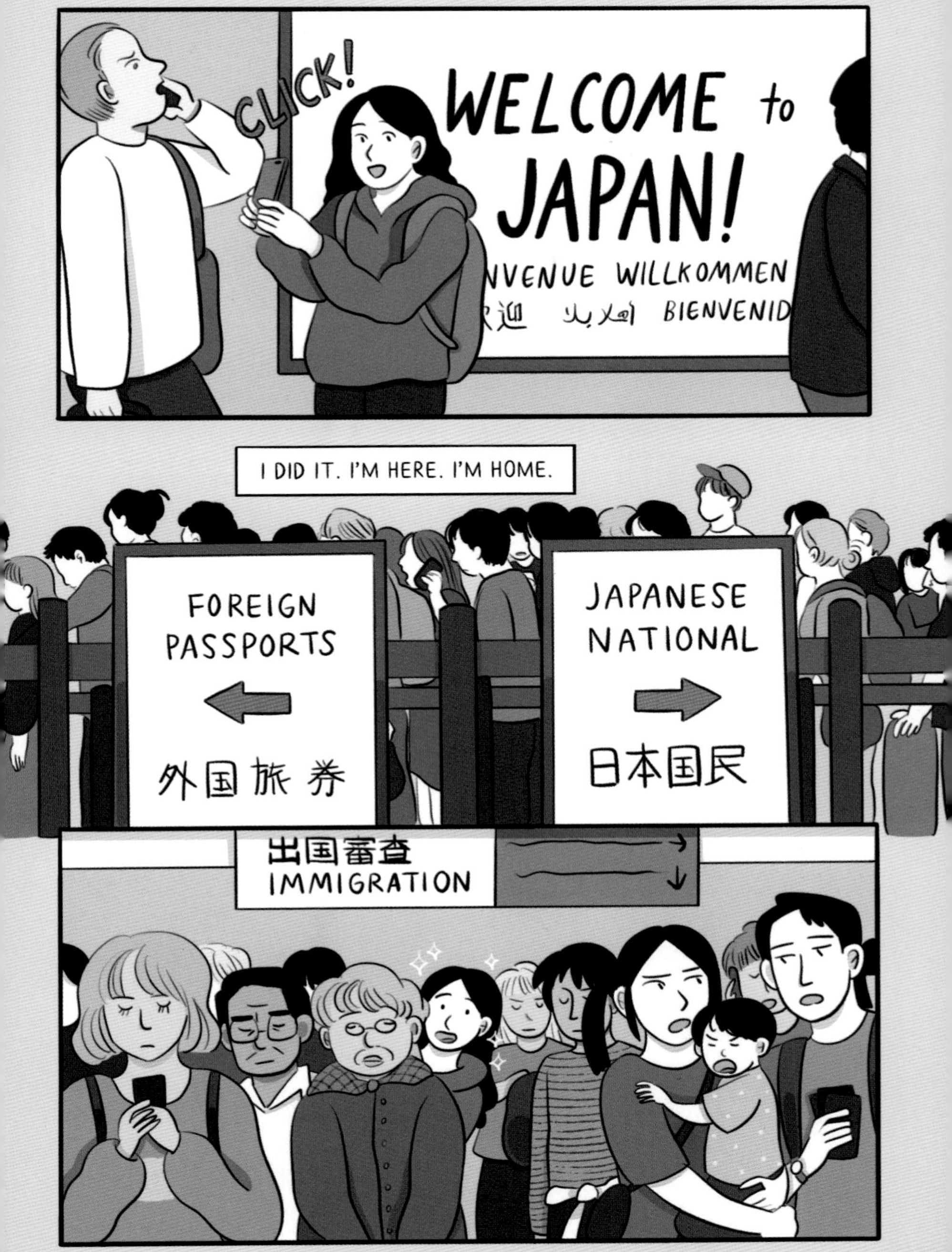
CLICK!
WELCOME to JAPAN!
NVENUE WILLKOMMEN
迎
BIENVENID
I DID IT. I'M HERE. I'M HOME.
FOREIGN PASSPORTS
外国旅券
JAPANESE NATIONAL
日本国民
出国審査
IMMIGRATION

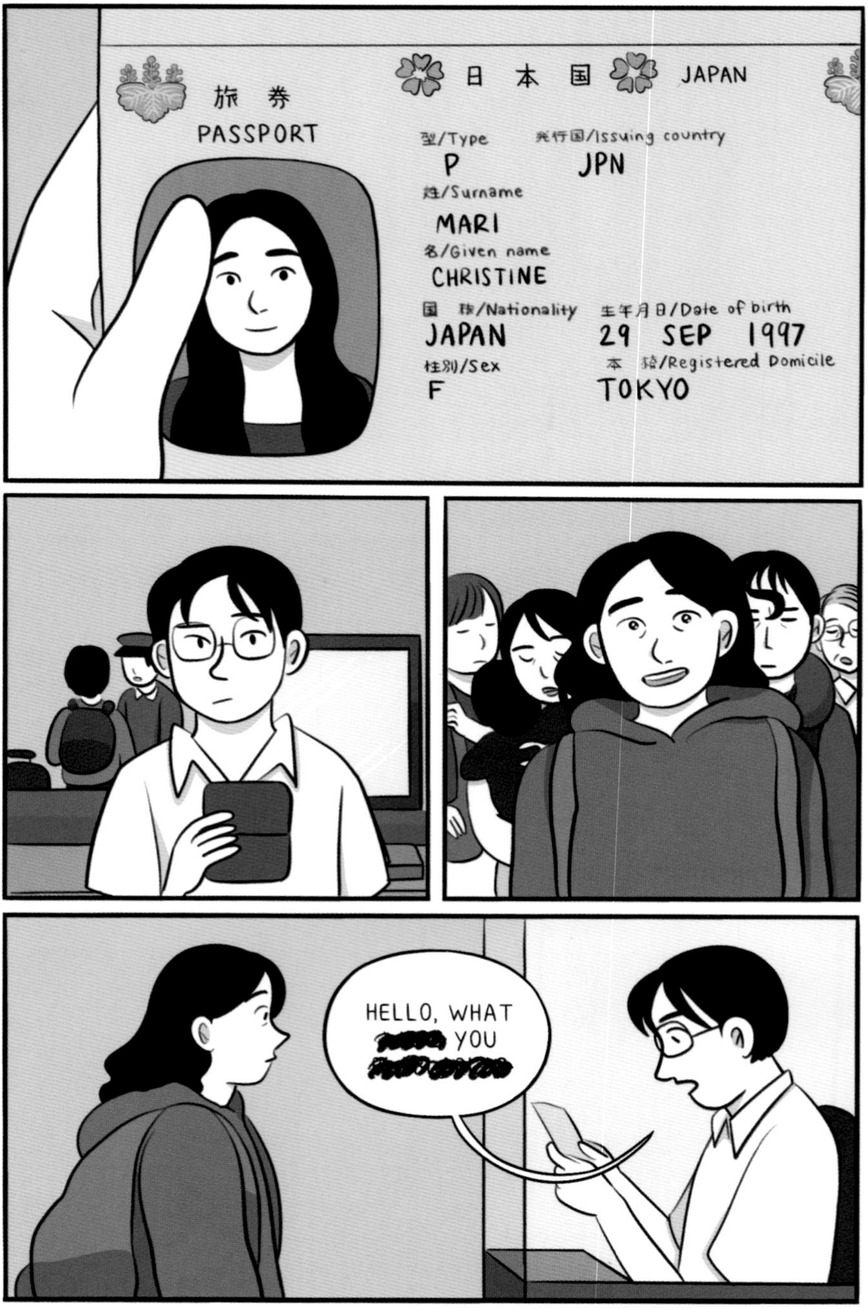
日本国 JAPAN
旅券
PASSPORT
型/Type
P
発行国/Issuing country
JPN
姓/Surname
MARI
名/Given name
CHRISTINE
国籍/Nationality
JAPAN
生年月日/Date of birth
29 SEP 1997
性別/Sex
F
本籍/Registered Domicile
TOKYO
HELLO, WHAT [redacted] YOU [redacted]

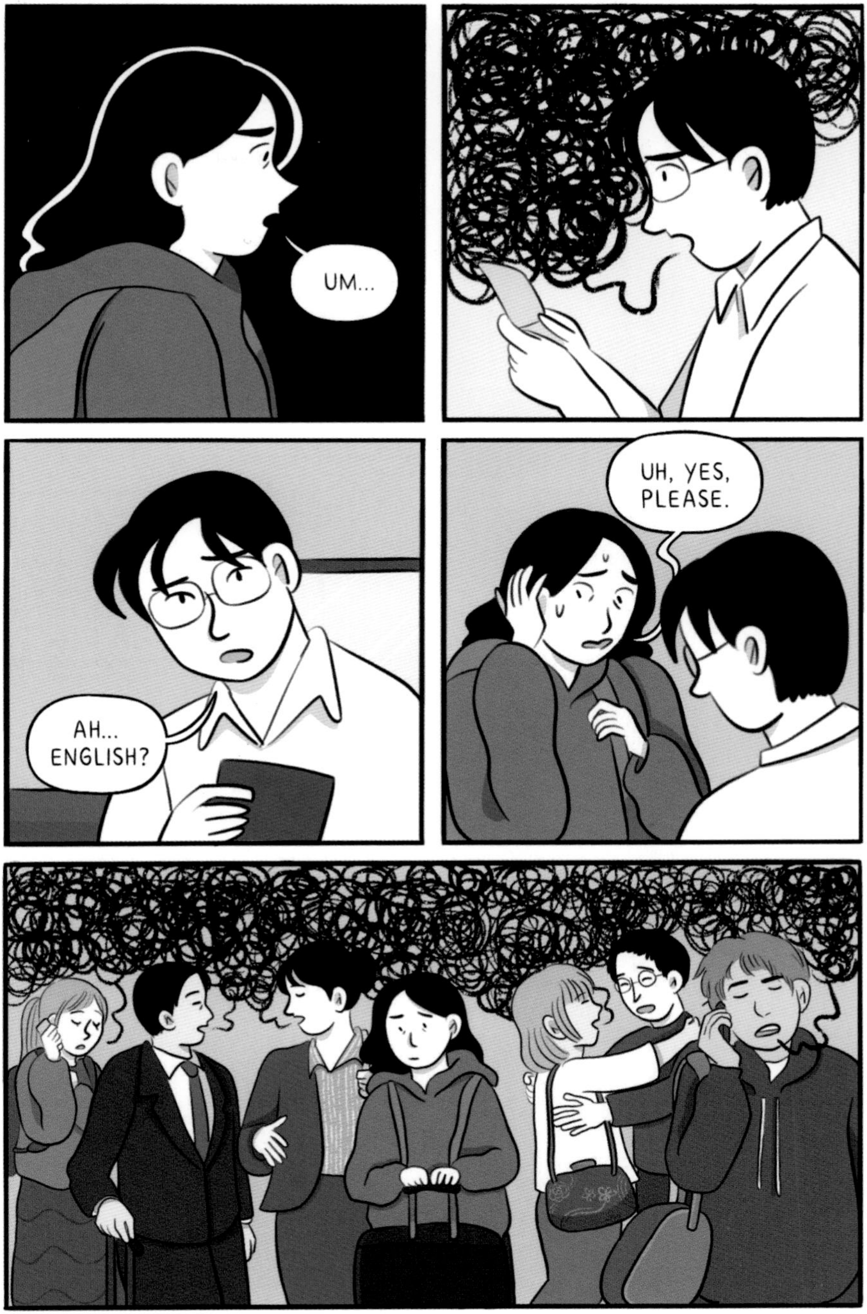
UM...
AH... ENGLISH?
UH, YES, PLEASE.

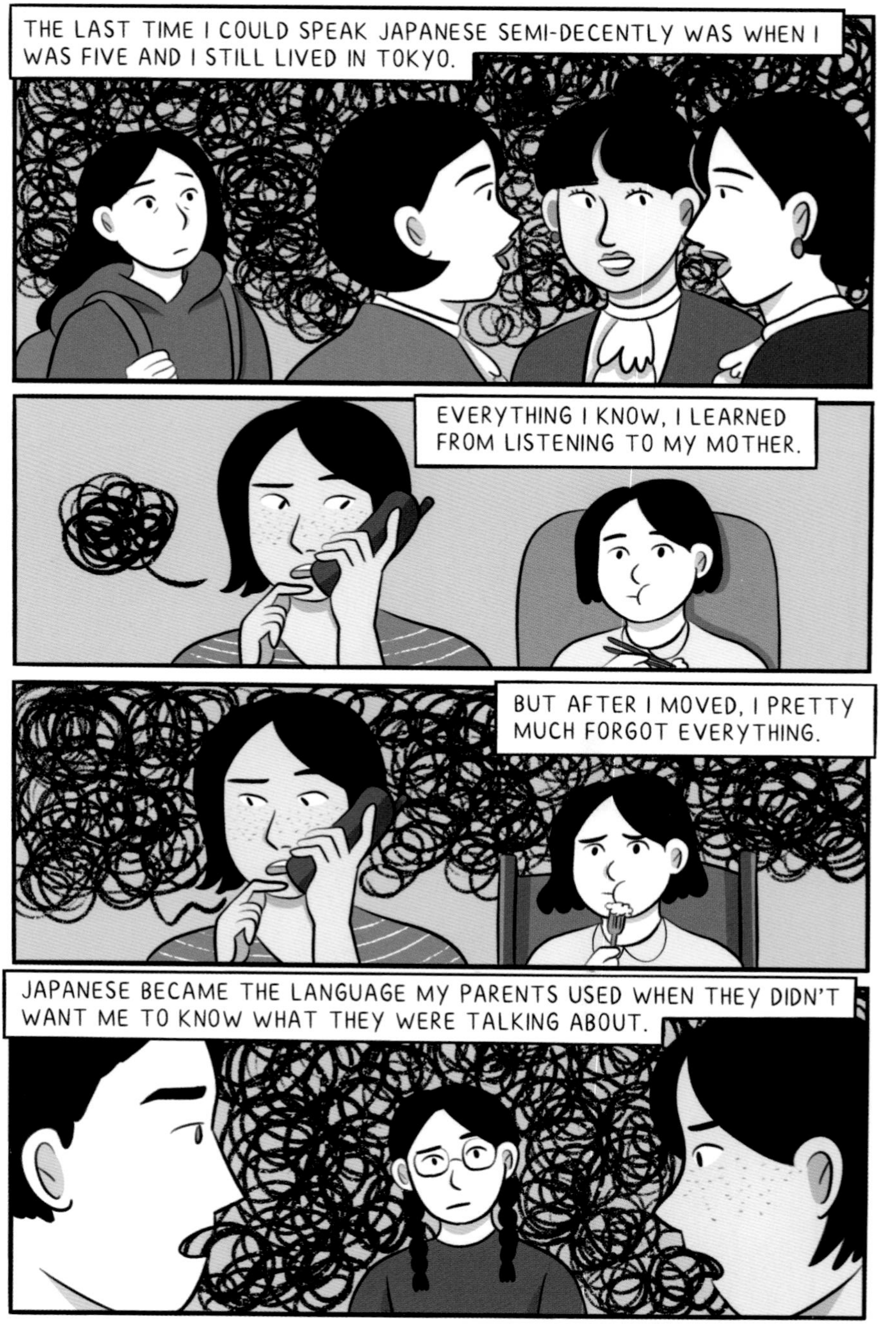
THE LAST TIME I COULD SPEAK JAPANESE SEMI-DECENTLY WAS WHEN I WAS FIVE AND I STILL LIVED IN TOKYO.
EVERYTHING I KNOW, I LEARNED FROM LISTENING TO MY MOTHER.
BUT AFTER I MOVED, I PRETTY MUCH FORGOT EVERYTHING.
JAPANESE BECAME THE LANGUAGE MY PARENTS USED WHEN THEY DIDN'T WANT ME TO KNOW WHAT THEY WERE TALKING ABOUT.

BUT THE WORST PART ABOUT NOT KNOWING JAPANESE WAS WHEN I REALIZED I WAS NO LONGER CAPABLE OF TALKING TO MY OWN GRANDPARENTS.

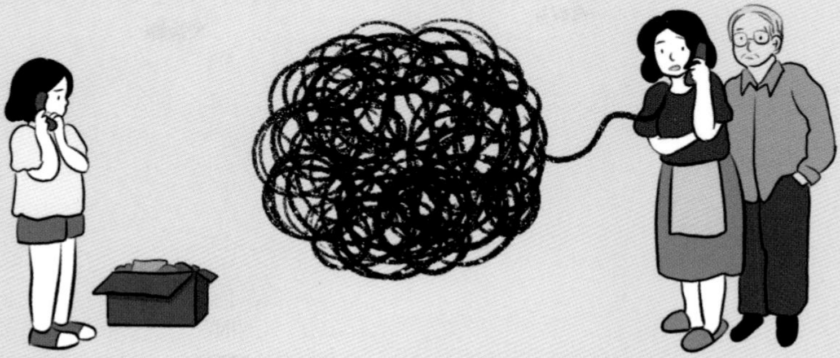

I DIDN'T WANT THEM TO KNOW HOW BAD MY JAPANESE HAD GOTTEN.

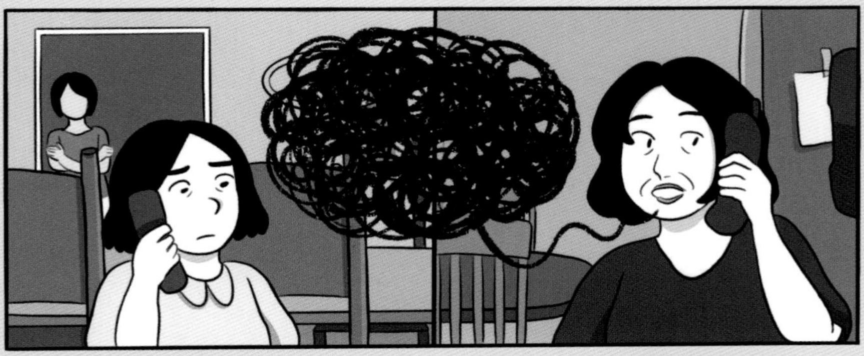

WHENEVER THEY CALLED ME, I WAS SO ANXIOUS, I COULDN'T SPEAK.

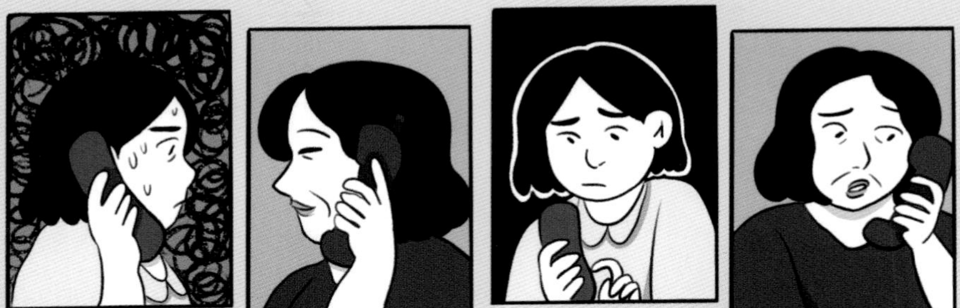

AND I'D ALWAYS TRY TO END THE CALL AS QUICKLY AS POSSIBLE.

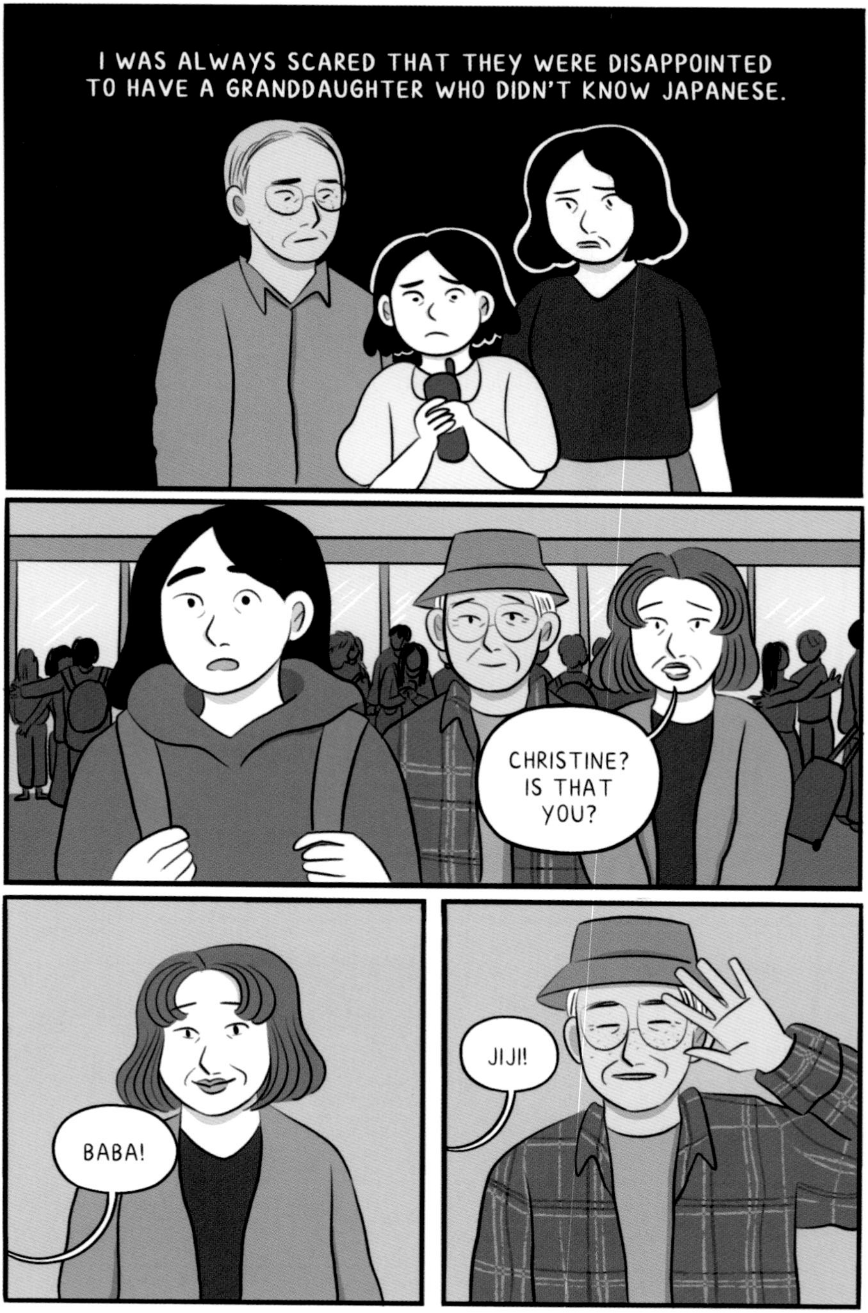
I WAS ALWAYS SCARED THAT THEY WERE DISAPPOINTED TO HAVE A GRANDDAUGHTER WHO DIDN'T KNOW JAPANESE.
CHRISTINE? IS THAT YOU?
BABA!
JIJI!

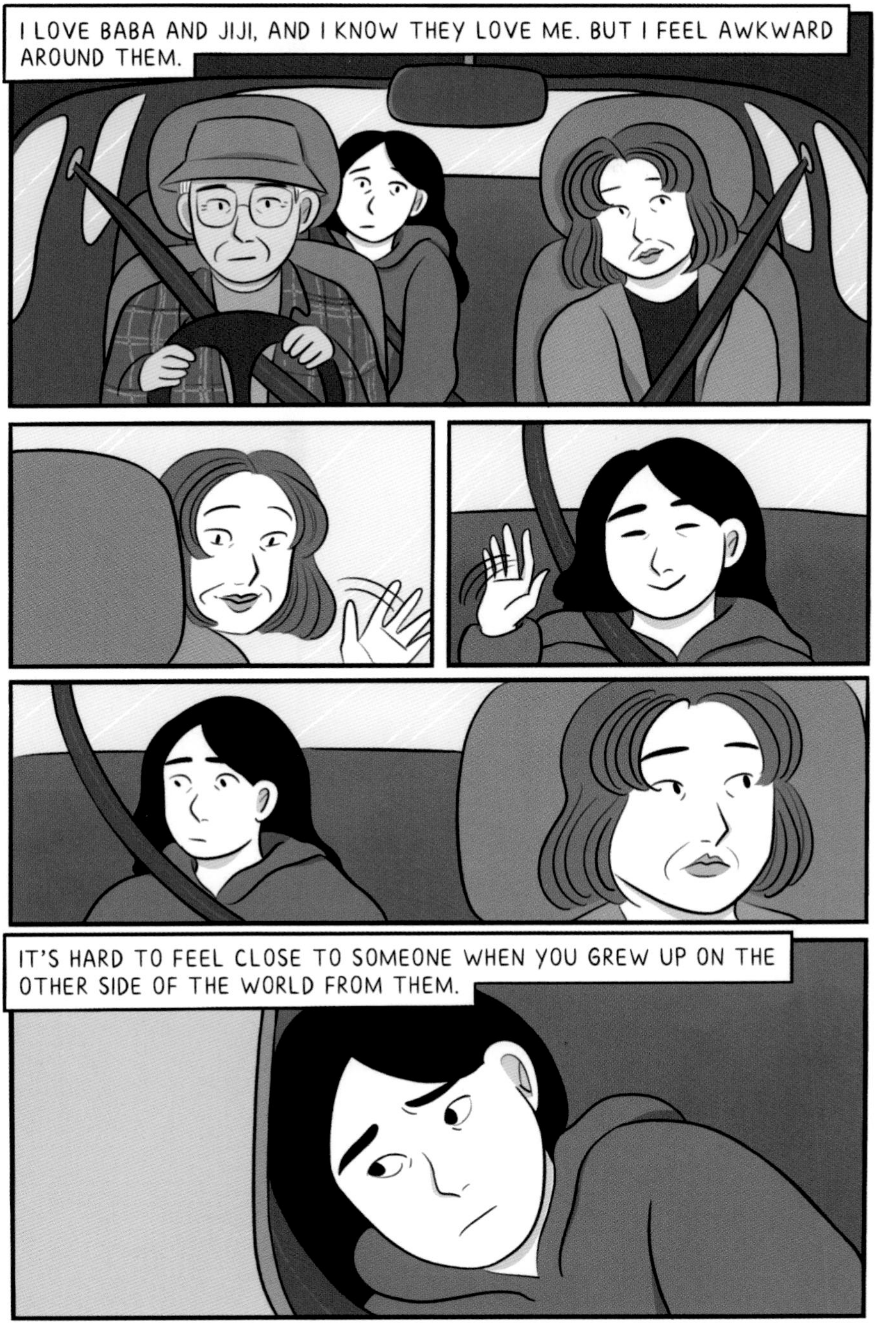
I LOVE BABA AND JIJI, AND I KNOW THEY LOVE ME. BUT I FEEL AWKWARD AROUND THEM.
IT'S HARD TO FEEL CLOSE TO SOMEONE WHEN YOU GREW UP ON THE OTHER SIDE OF THE WORLD FROM THEM.

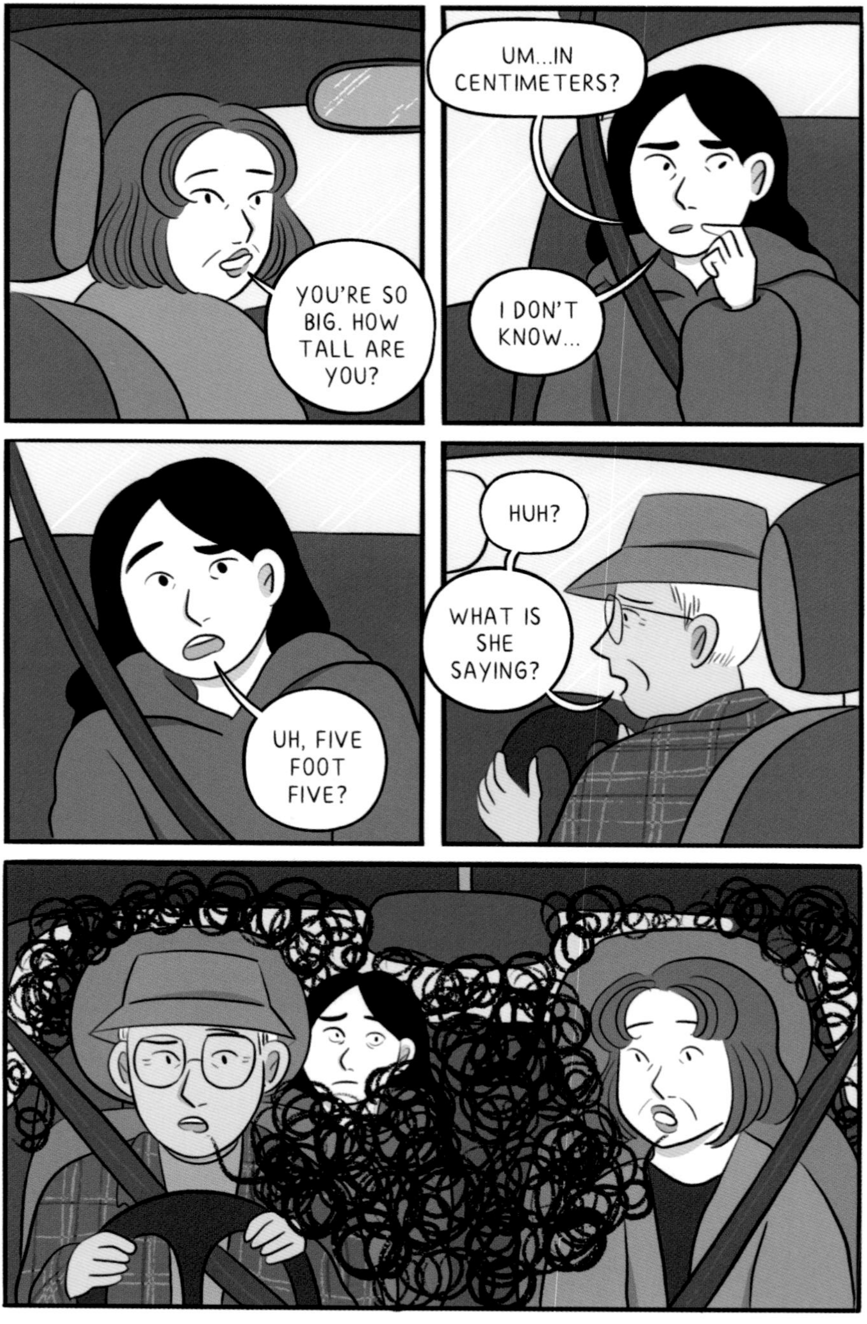
YOU'RE SO BIG. HOW TALL ARE YOU?
UM...IN CENTIMETERS?
I DON'T KNOW...
UH, FIVE FOOT FIVE?
HUH?
WHAT IS SHE SAYING?

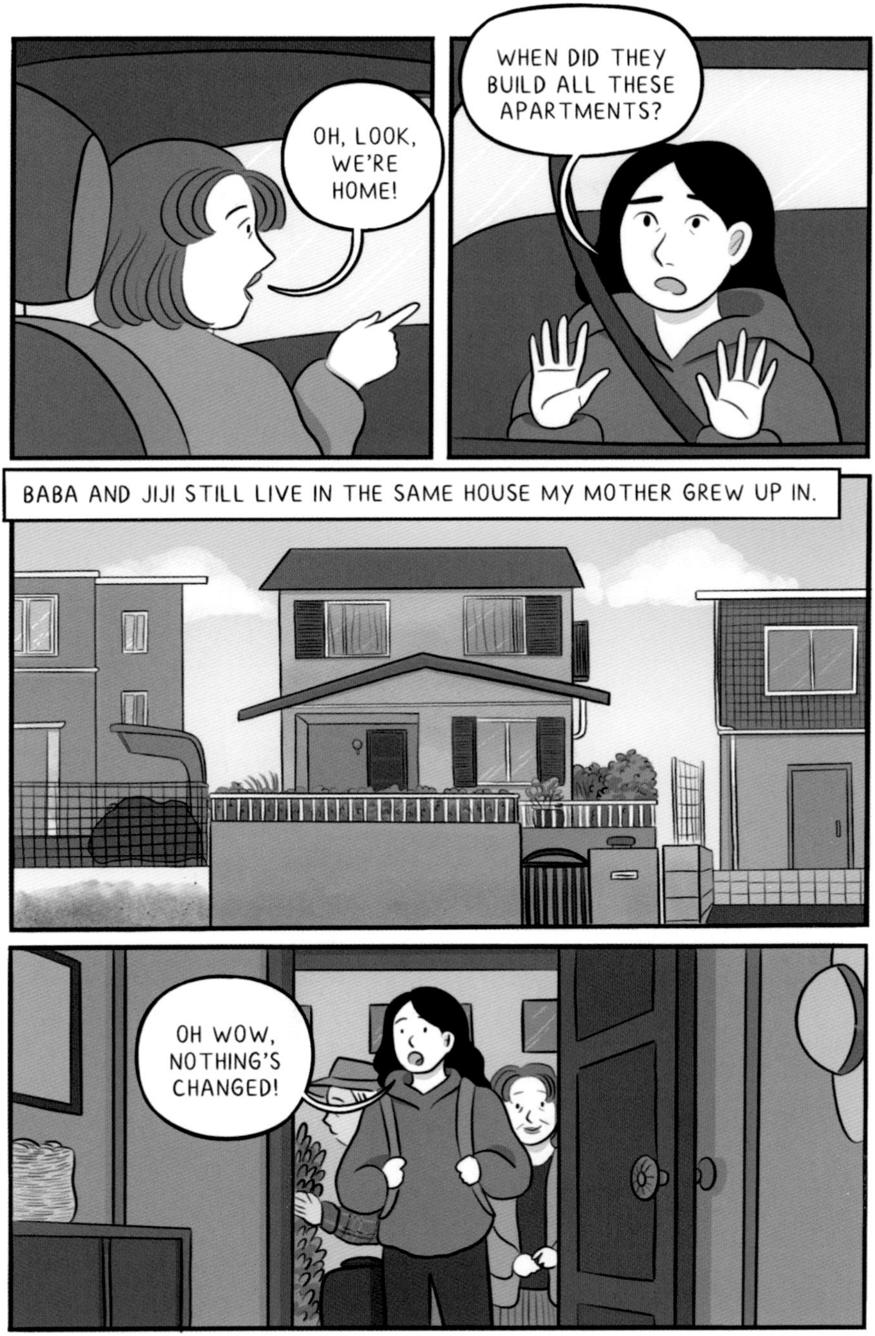
OH, LOOK, WE'RE HOME!
WHEN DID THEY BUILD ALL THESE APARTMENTS?
BABA AND JIJI STILL LIVE IN THE SAME HOUSE MY MOTHER GREW UP IN.
OH WOW, NOTHING'S CHANGED!

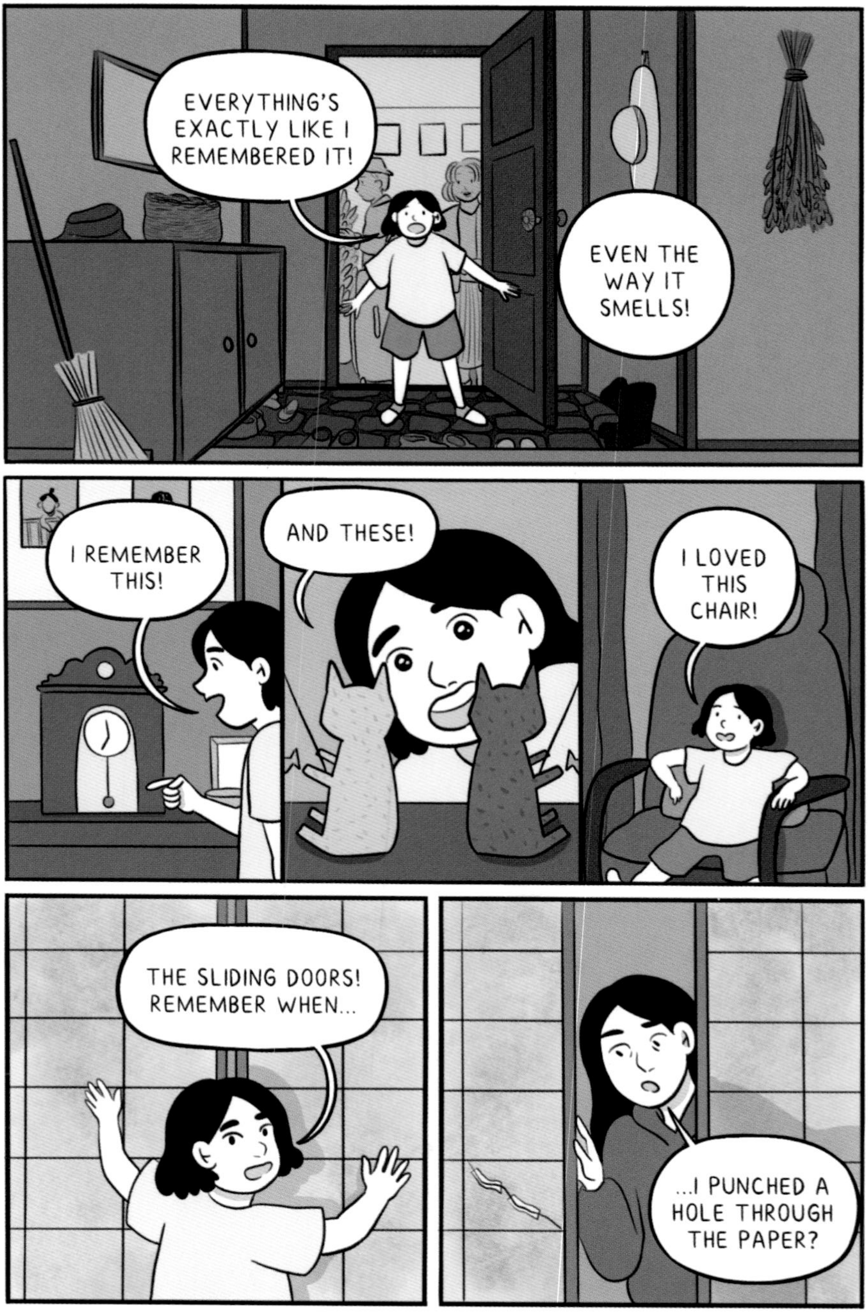
EVERYTHING'S EXACTLY LIKE I REMEMBERED IT!
EVEN THE WAY IT SMELLS!
I REMEMBER THIS!
AND THESE!
I LOVED THIS CHAIR!
THE SLIDING DOORS! REMEMBER WHEN...
...I PUNCHED A HOLE THROUGH THE PAPER?

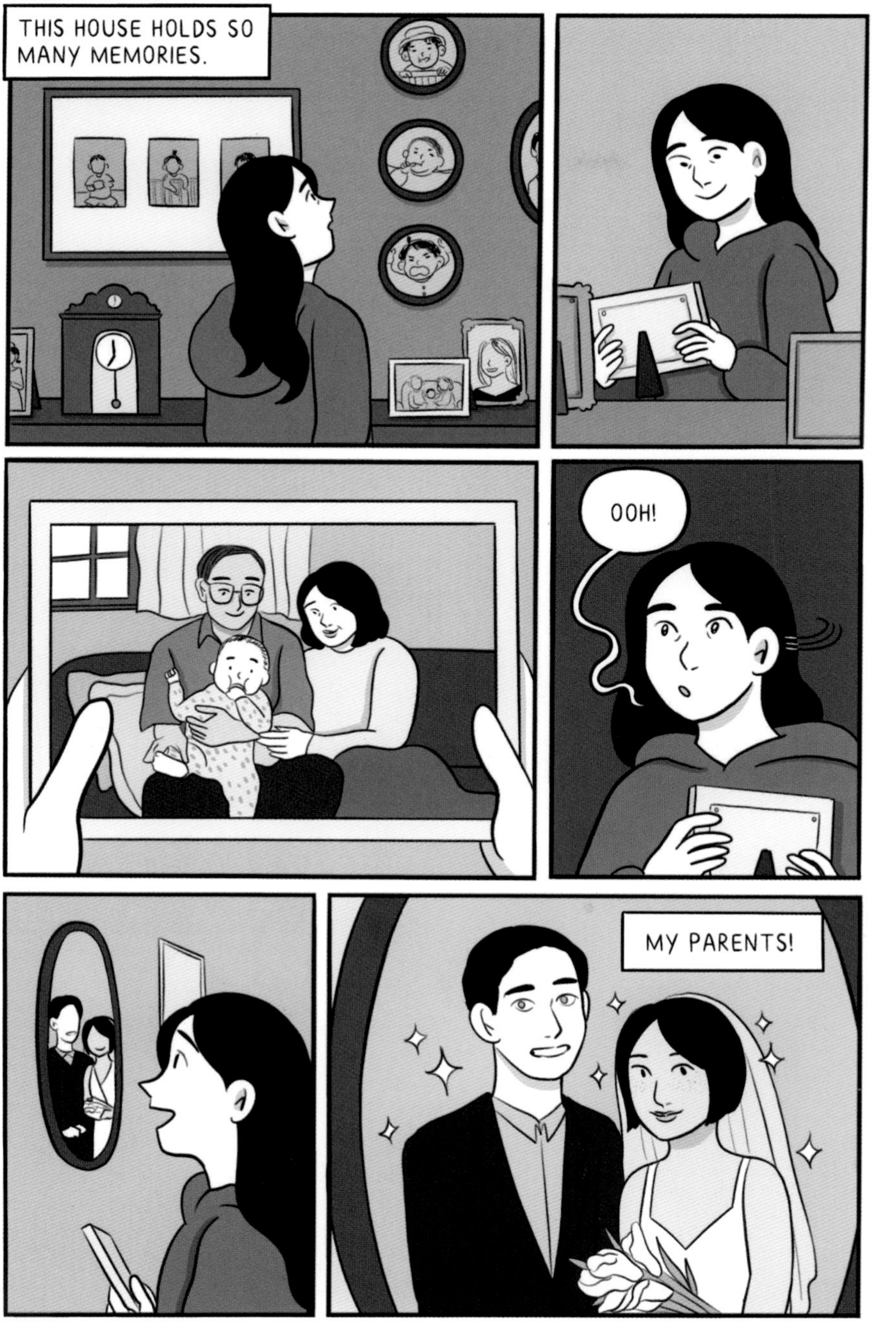
THIS HOUSE HOLDS SO MANY MEMORIES.
OOH!
MY PARENTS!

SOMETIMES I THINK ABOUT HOW, IN A DIFFERENT UNIVERSE, MY PARENTS' PATHS PROBABLY WOULD HAVE NEVER CROSSED.

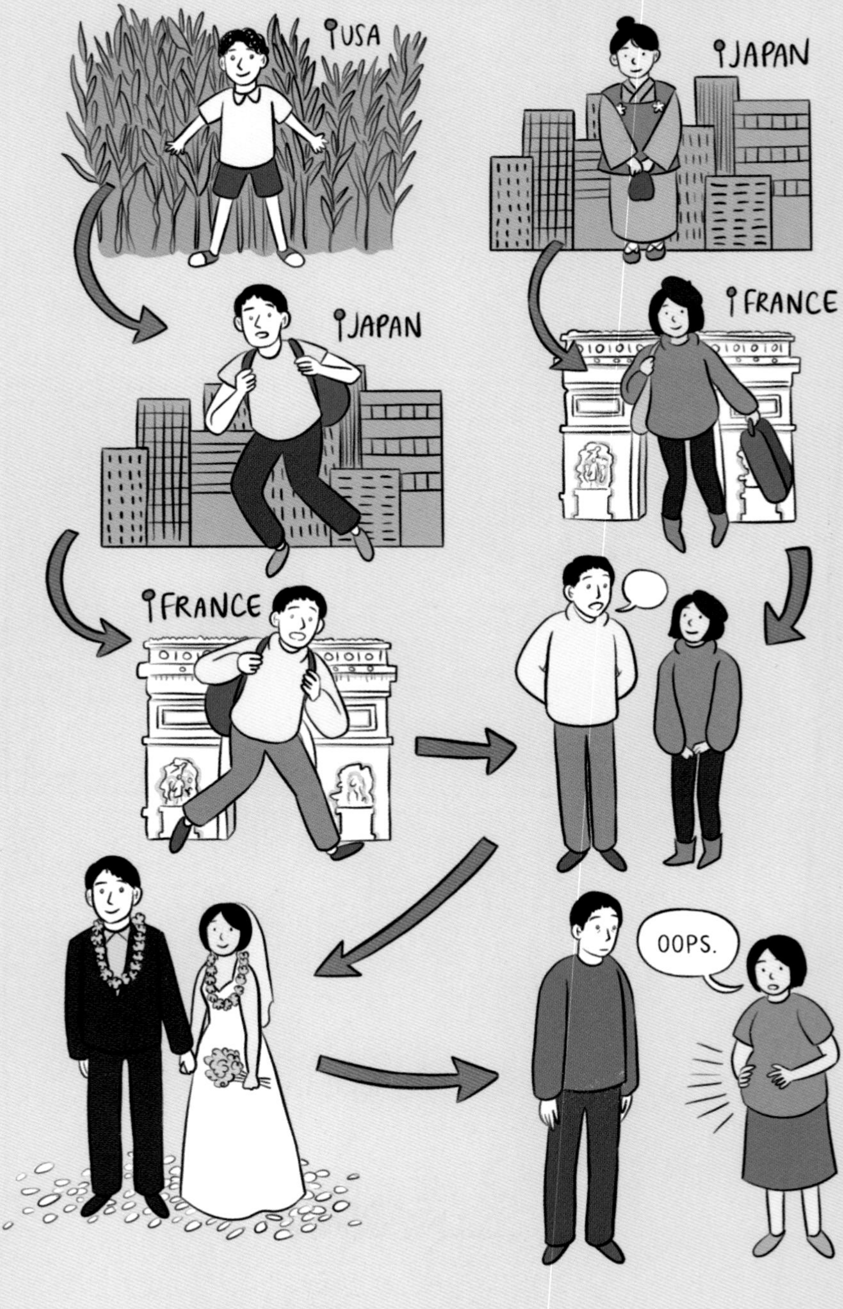
USA
JAPAN
JAPAN
FRANCE
FRANCE
OOPS.

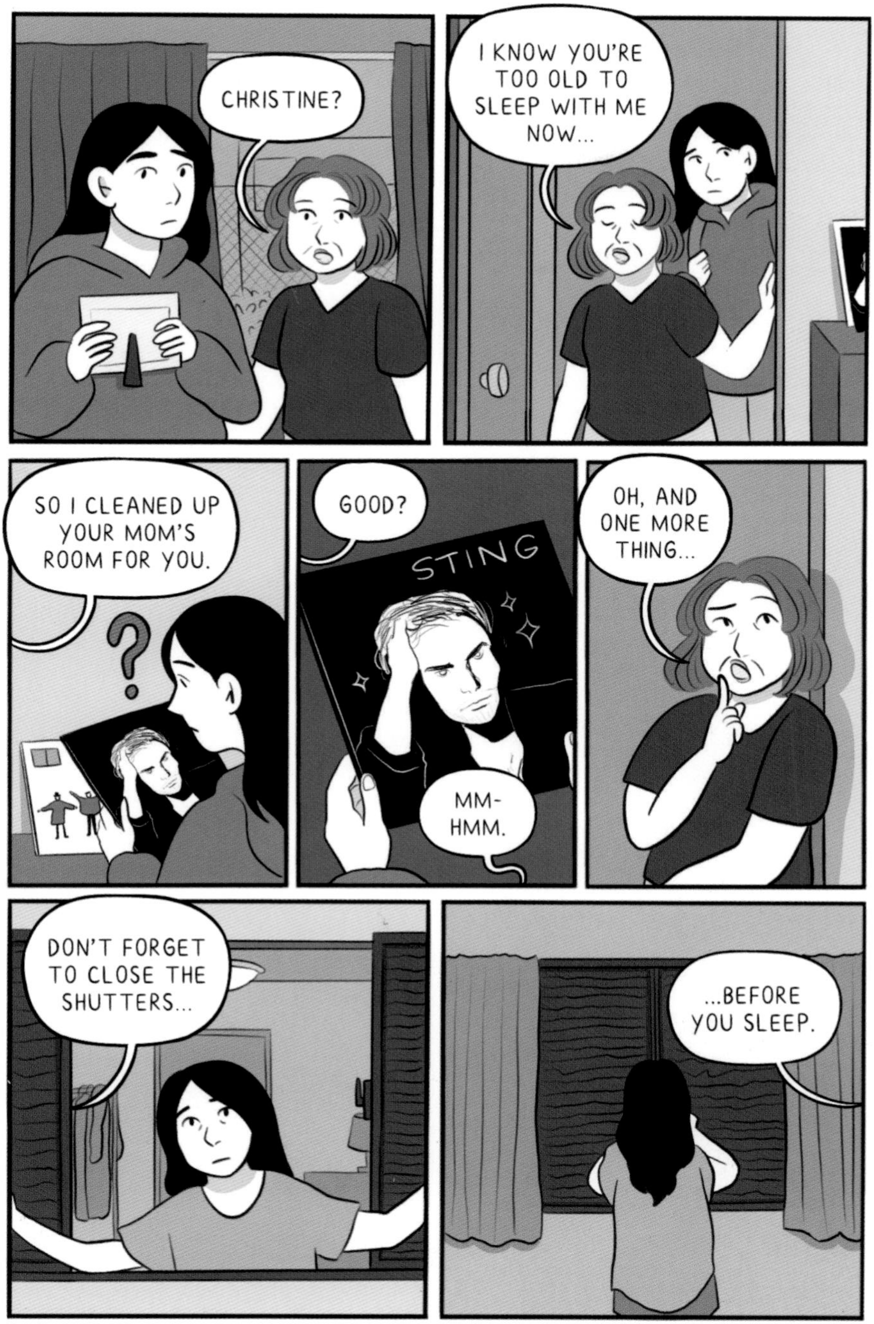
CHRISTINE?
I KNOW YOU'RE TOO OLD TO SLEEP WITH ME NOW...
SO I CLEANED UP YOUR MOM'S ROOM FOR YOU.
?
GOOD?
STING
MM-HMM.
OH, AND ONE MORE THING...
DON'T FORGET TO CLOSE THE SHUTTERS...
...BEFORE YOU SLEEP.

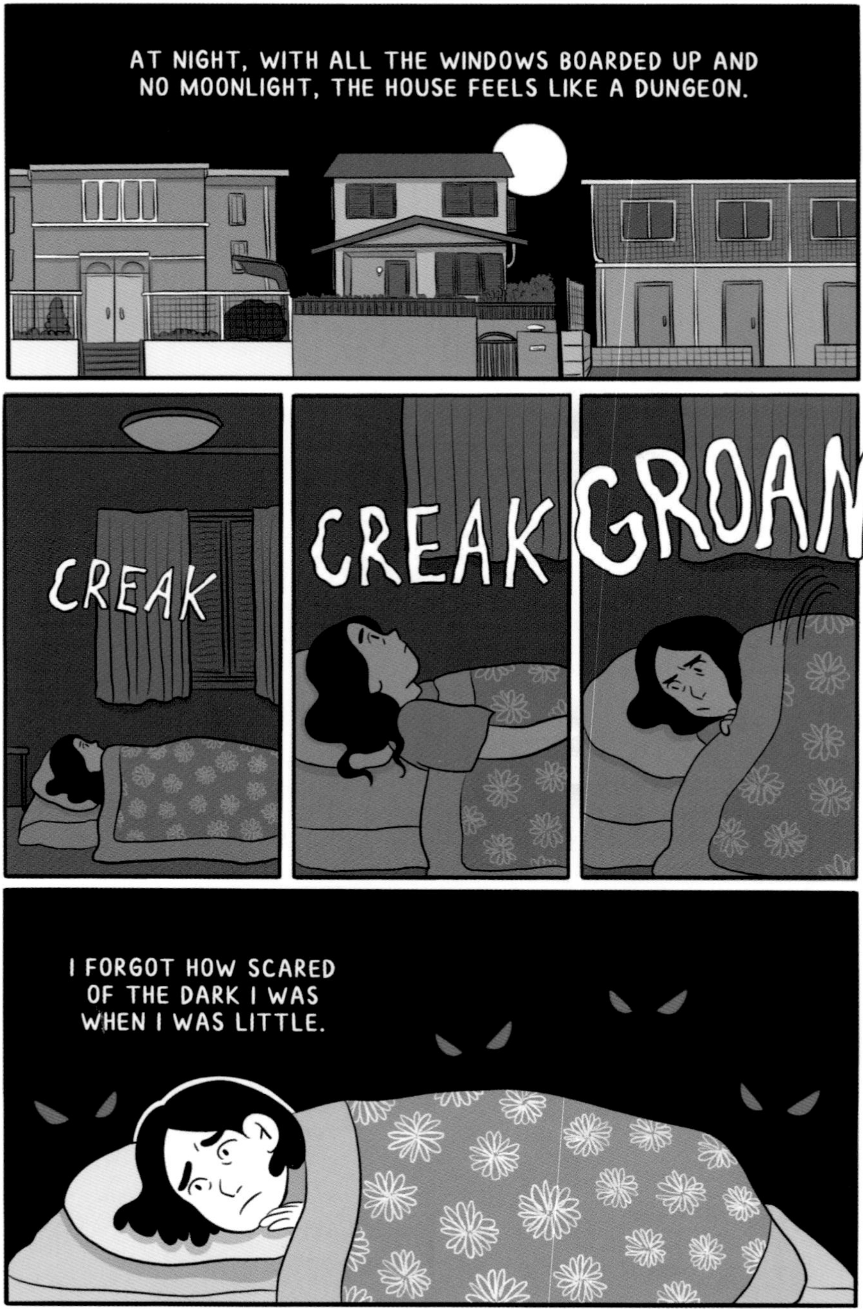
AT NIGHT, WITH ALL THE WINDOWS BOARDED UP AND NO MOONLIGHT, THE HOUSE FEELS LIKE A DUNGEON.
CREAK
CREAK
GROAN
I FORGOT HOW SCARED OF THE DARK I WAS WHEN I WAS LITTLE.

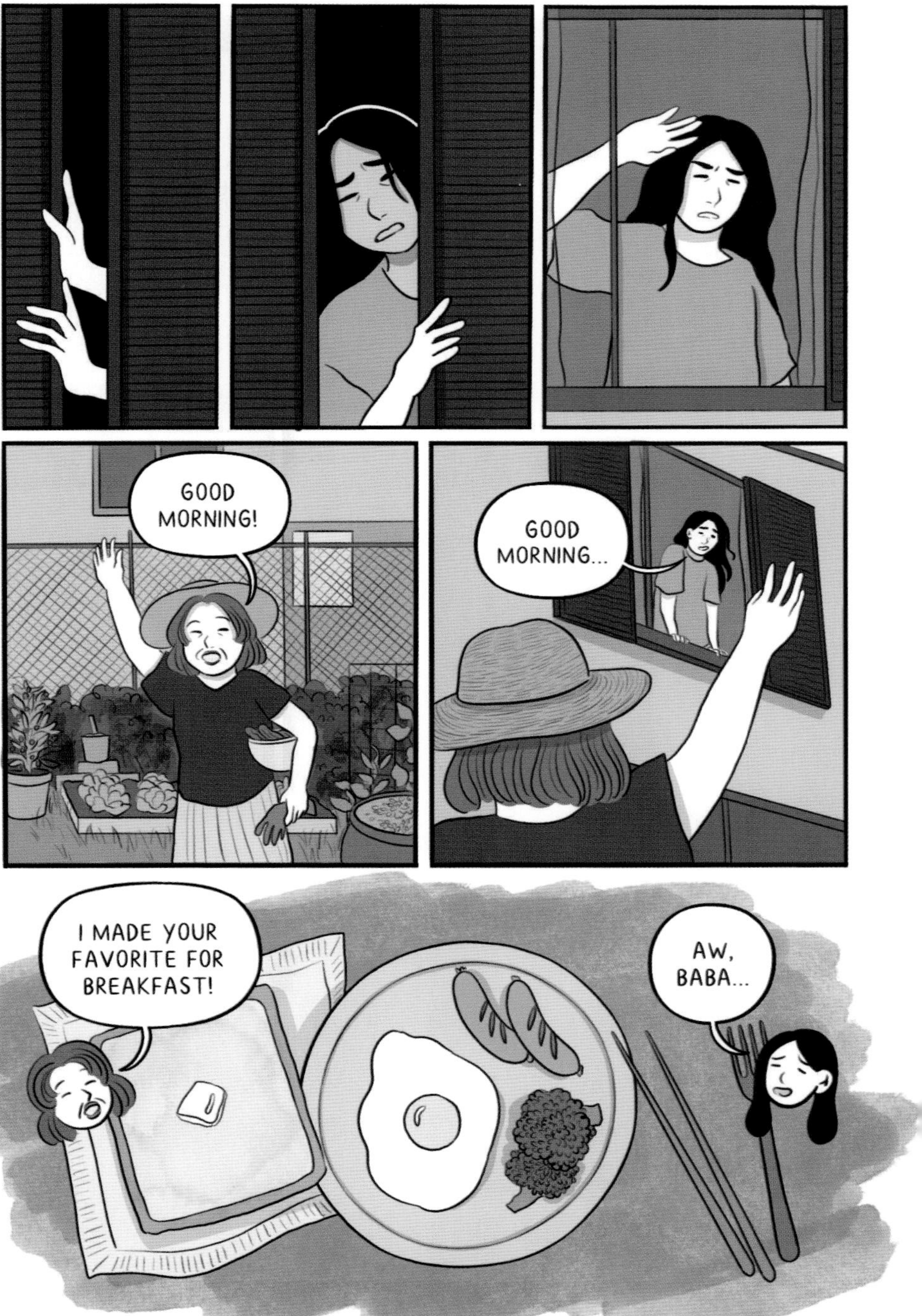
GOOD MORNING!
GOOD MORNING...
I MADE YOUR FAVORITE FOR BREAKFAST!
AW, BABA...

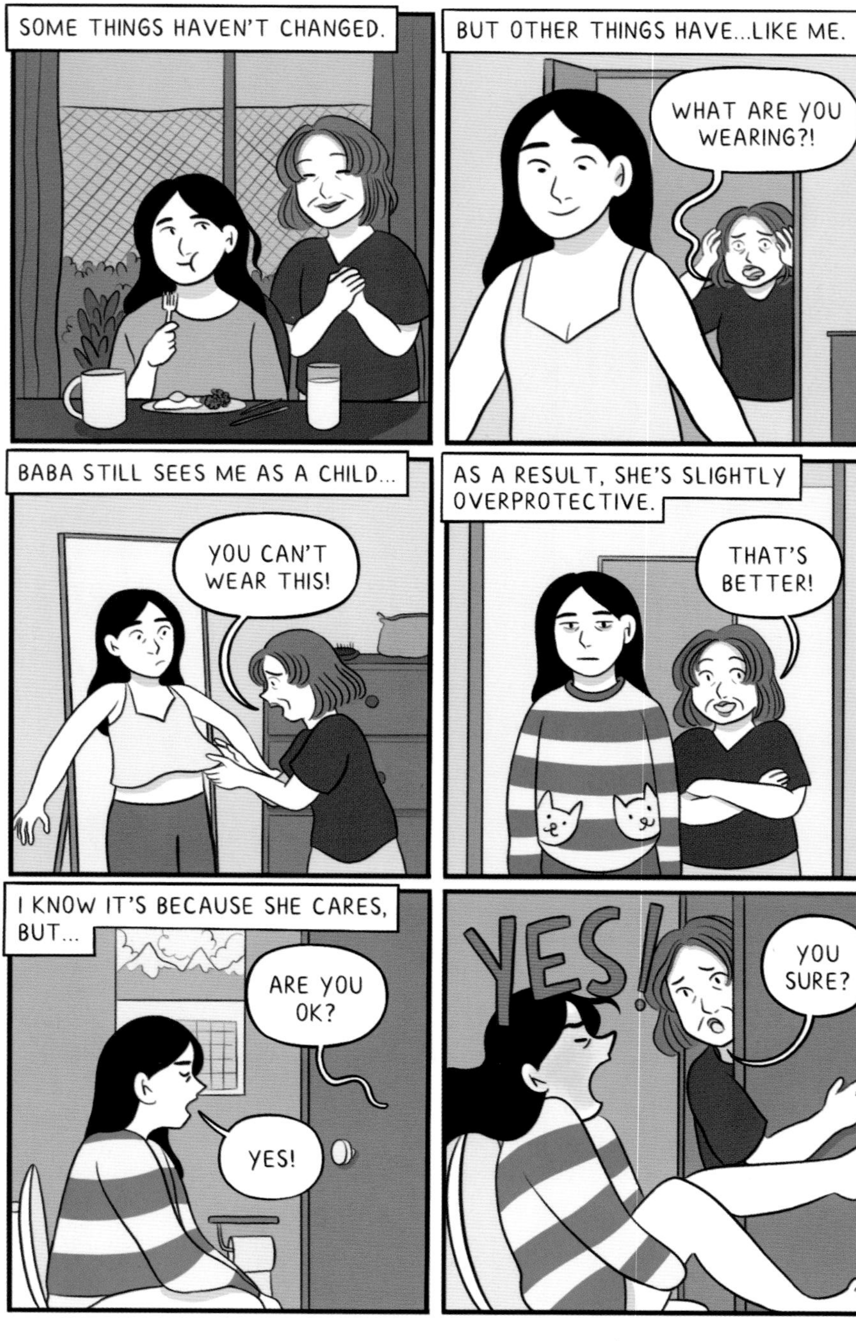
SOME THINGS HAVEN'T CHANGED.
BUT OTHER THINGS HAVE...LIKE ME.
WHAT ARE YOU WEARING?!
BABA STILL SEES ME AS A CHILD...
YOU CAN'T WEAR THIS!
AS A RESULT, SHE'S SLIGHTLY OVERPROTECTIVE.
THAT'S BETTER!
I KNOW IT'S BECAUSE SHE CARES, BUT...
ARE YOU OK?
YES!
YES!
YOU SURE?

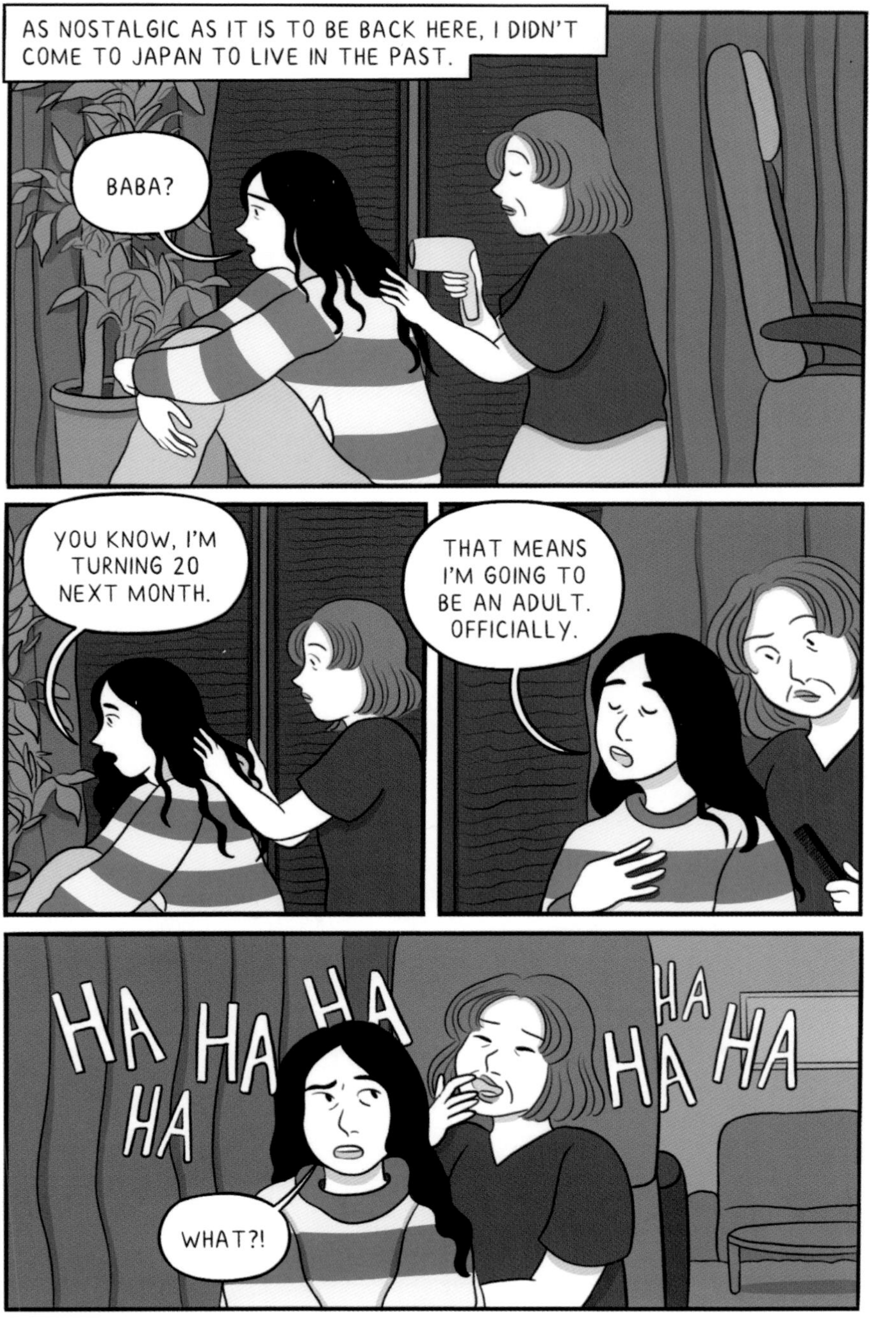
AS NOSTALGIC AS IT IS TO BE BACK HERE, I DIDN'T COME TO JAPAN TO LIVE IN THE PAST.
BABA?
YOU KNOW, I'M TURNING 20 NEXT MONTH.
THAT MEANS I'M GOING TO BE AN ADULT. OFFICIALLY.
HA HA HA HA
HA
HA HA HA HA
WHAT?!

IN JAPAN, TURNING 20 IS A BIG DEAL. IT MEANS THAT YOU'RE OFFICIALLY AN ADULT.* THERE'S EVEN A SPECIAL HOLIDAY FOR ALL THE NEW ADULTS TO CELEBRATE.

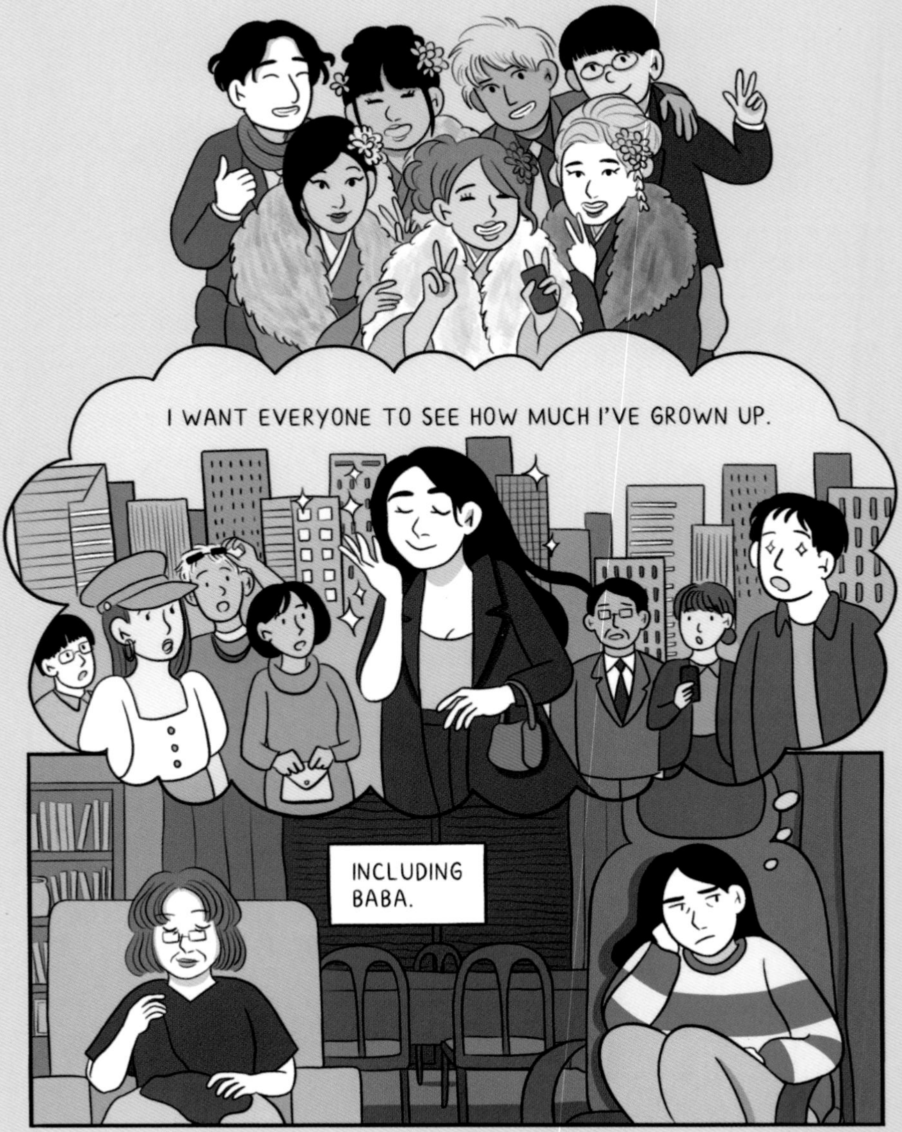
I WANT EVERYONE TO SEE HOW MUCH I'VE GROWN UP.
INCLUDING BABA.

*SINCE I DREW THIS, THEY LOWERED THE AGE TO 18.

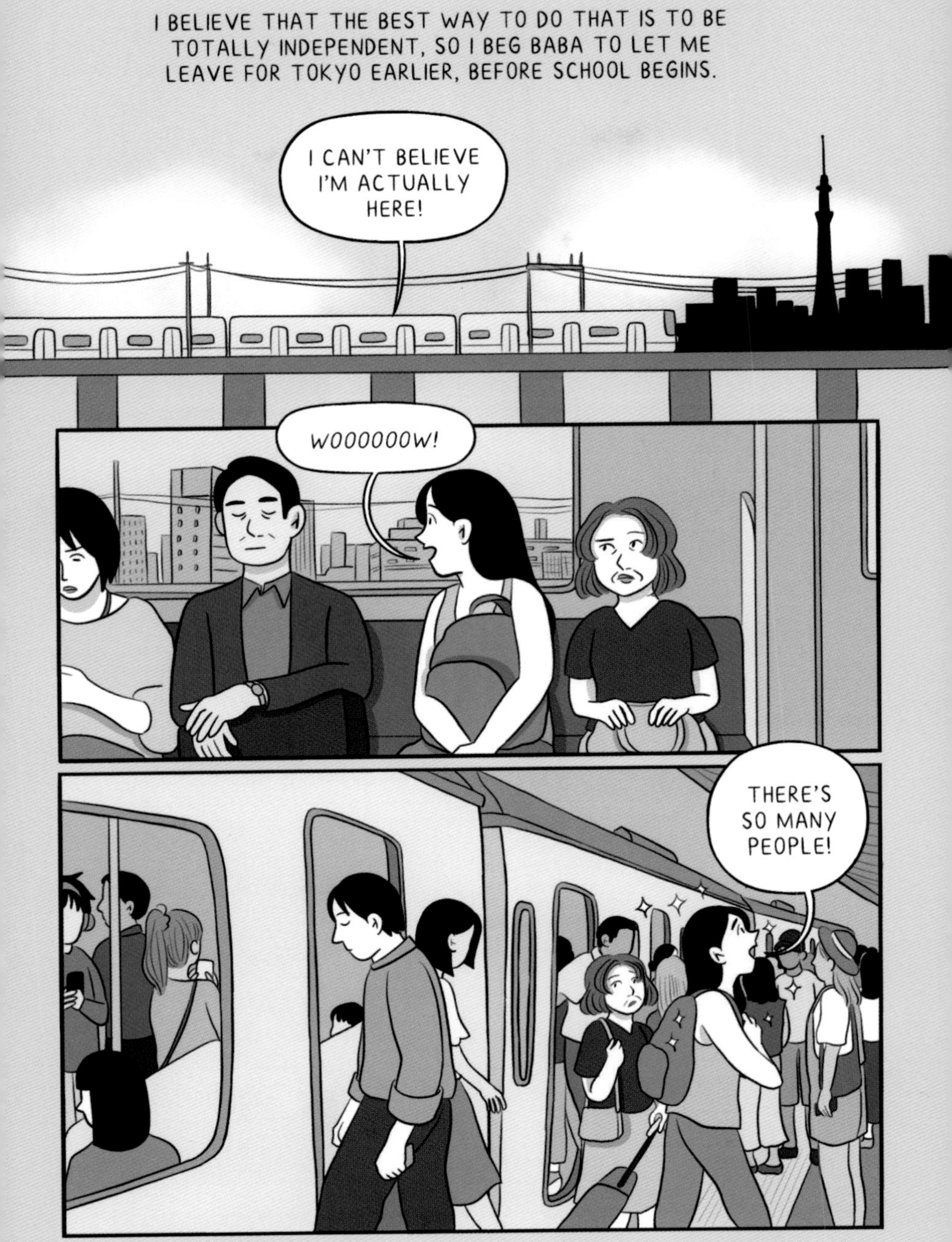
I BELIEVE THAT THE BEST WAY TO DO THAT IS TO BE TOTALLY INDEPENDENT, SO I BEG BABA TO LET ME LEAVE FOR TOKYO EARLIER, BEFORE SCHOOL BEGINS.
I CAN'T BELIEVE I'M ACTUALLY HERE!
WOOOOOOW!
THERE'S SO MANY PEOPLE!

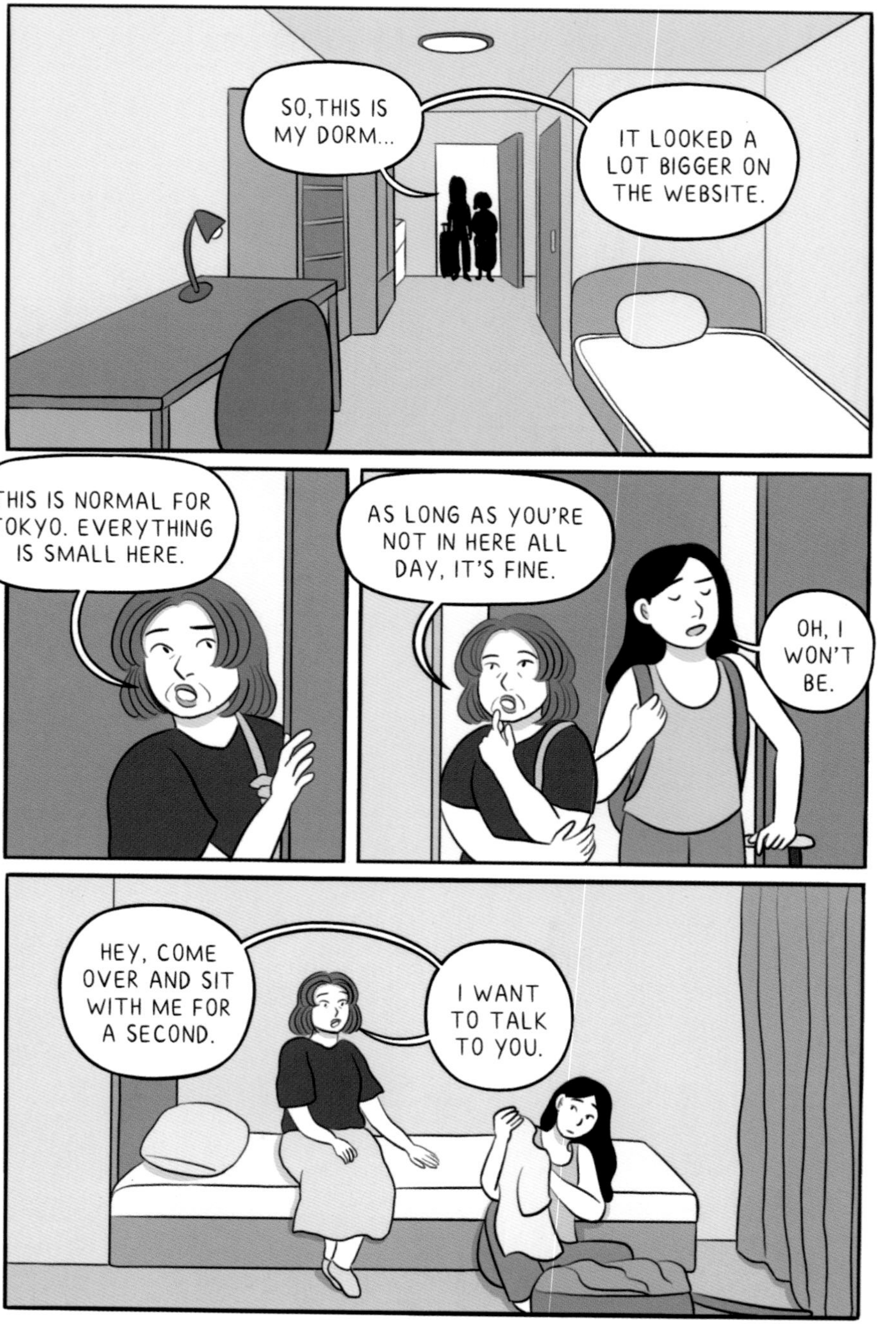
SO, THIS IS MY DORM...
IT LOOKED A LOT BIGGER ON THE WEBSITE.
THIS IS NORMAL FOR TOKYO. EVERYTHING IS SMALL HERE.
AS LONG AS YOU'RE NOT IN HERE ALL DAY, IT'S FINE.
OH, I WON'T BE.
HEY, COME OVER AND SIT WITH ME FOR A SECOND.
I WANT TO TALK TO YOU.

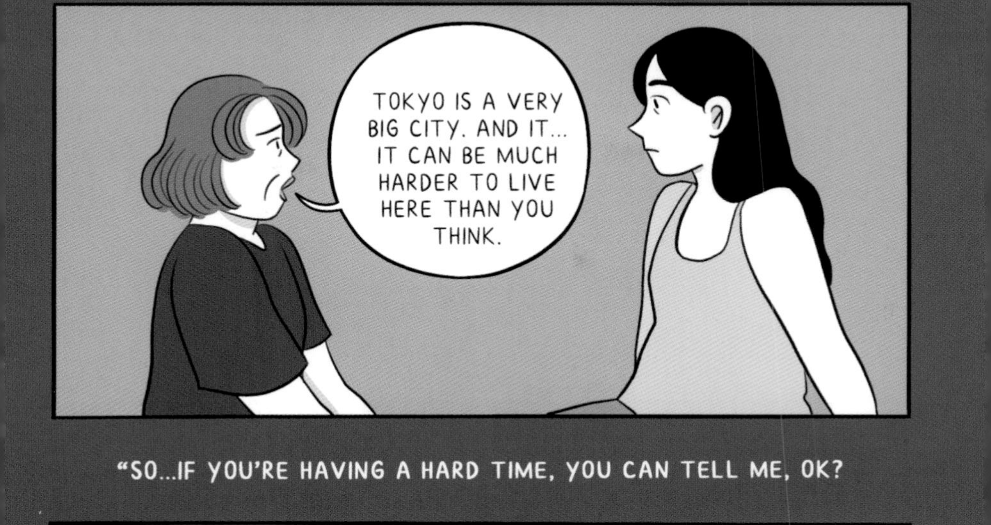
TOKYO IS A VERY BIG CITY. AND IT... IT CAN BE MUCH HARDER TO LIVE HERE THAN YOU THINK.

"SO...IF YOU'RE HAVING A HARD TIME, YOU CAN TELL ME, OK?

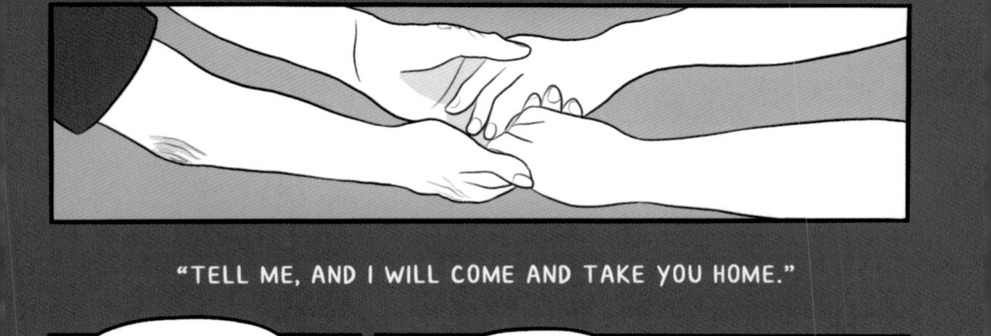

"TELL ME, AND I WILL COME AND TAKE YOU HOME."

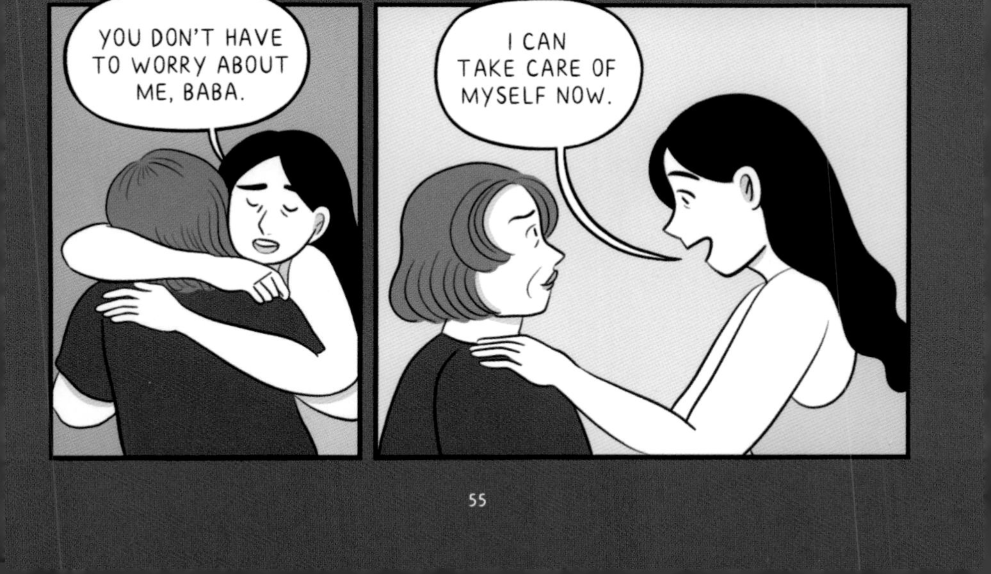
YOU DON'T HAVE TO WORRY ABOUT ME, BABA.
I CAN TAKE CARE OF MYSELF NOW.

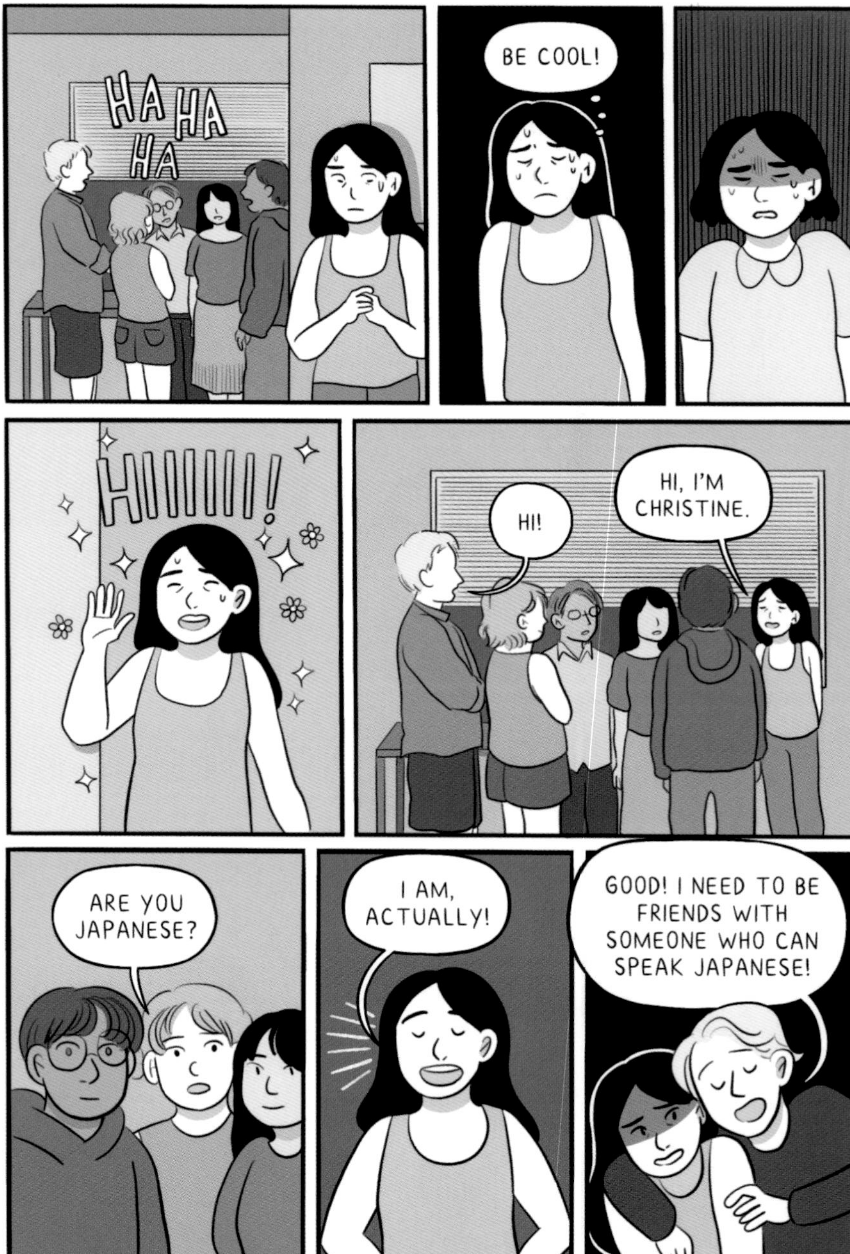
HA HA HA HA
BE COOL!
HIIIIIII!
HI!
HI, I'M CHRISTINE.
ARE YOU JAPANESE?
I AM, ACTUALLY!
GOOD! I NEED TO BE FRIENDS WITH SOMEONE WHO CAN SPEAK JAPANESE!

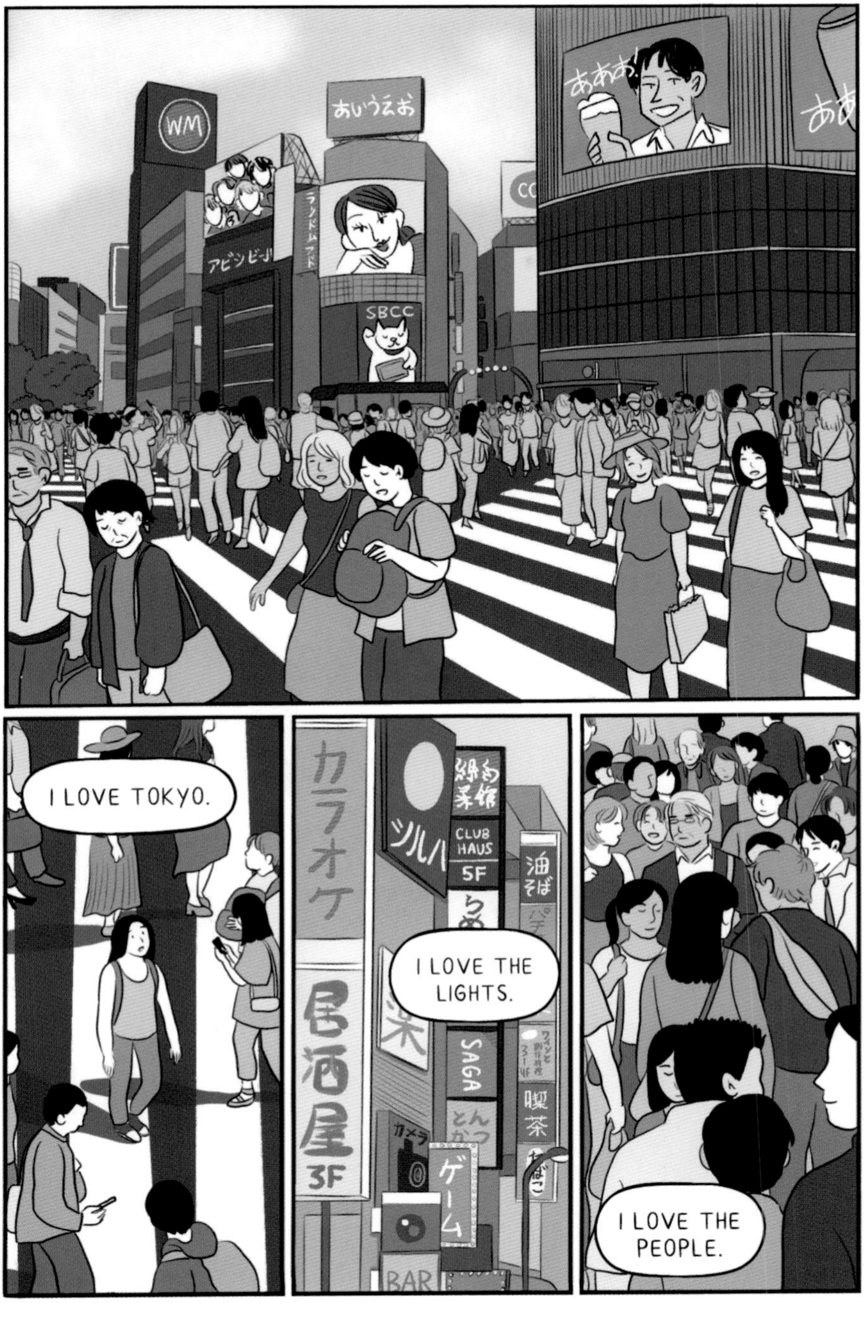
WM
あいうえお
SBCC
I LOVE TOKYO.
カラオケ
ツルハ
CLUB HAUS 5F
油そば
I LOVE THE LIGHTS.
居酒屋 3F
SAGA
とんかつ
喫茶
カメラ
ゲーム
BAR
I LOVE THE PEOPLE.

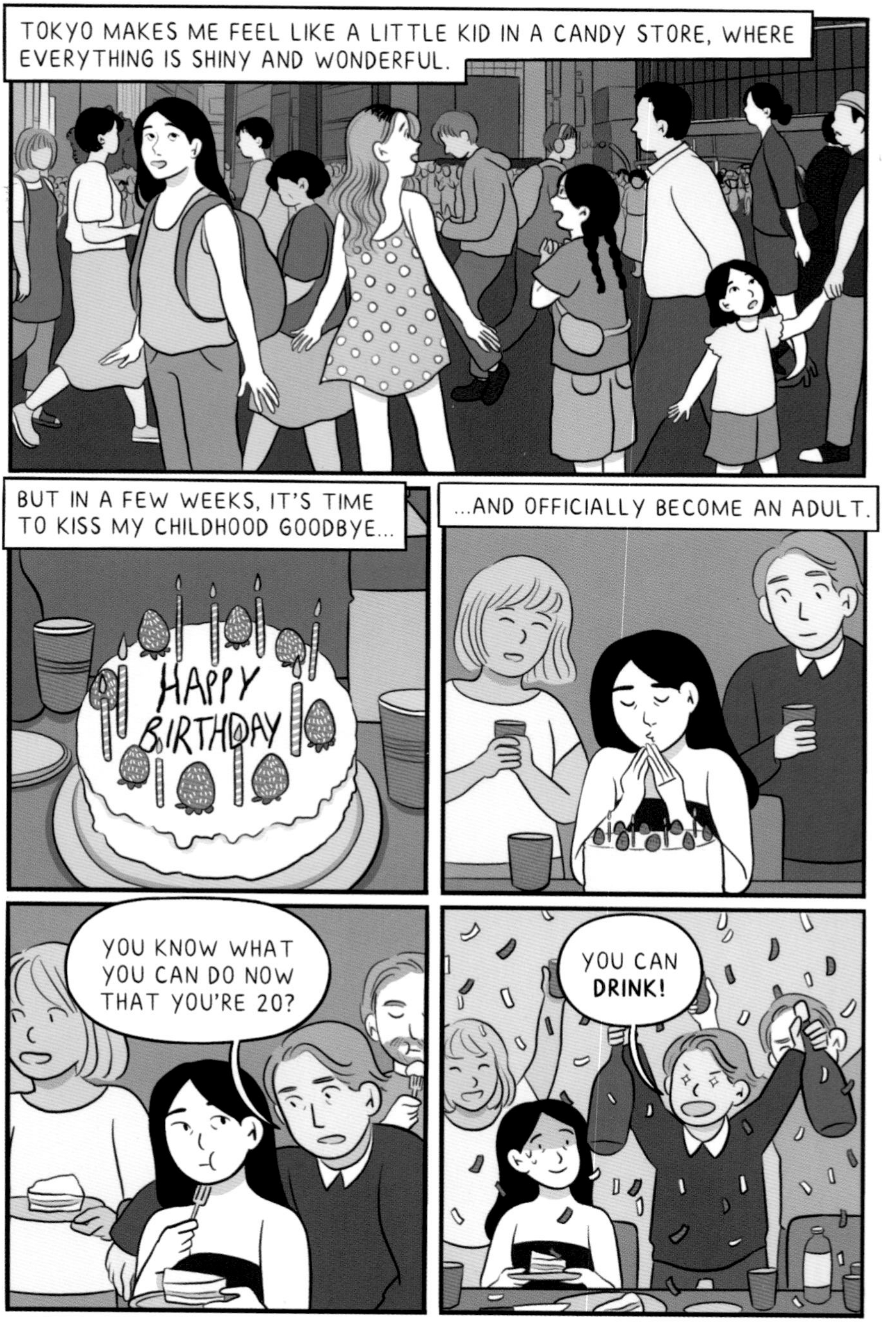
TOKYO MAKES ME FEEL LIKE A LITTLE KID IN A CANDY STORE, WHERE EVERYTHING IS SHINY AND WONDERFUL.
BUT IN A FEW WEEKS, IT'S TIME TO KISS MY CHILDHOOD GOODBYE...
HAPPY BIRTHDAY
...AND OFFICIALLY BECOME AN ADULT.
YOU KNOW WHAT YOU CAN DO NOW THAT YOU'RE 20?
YOU CAN **DRINK!**

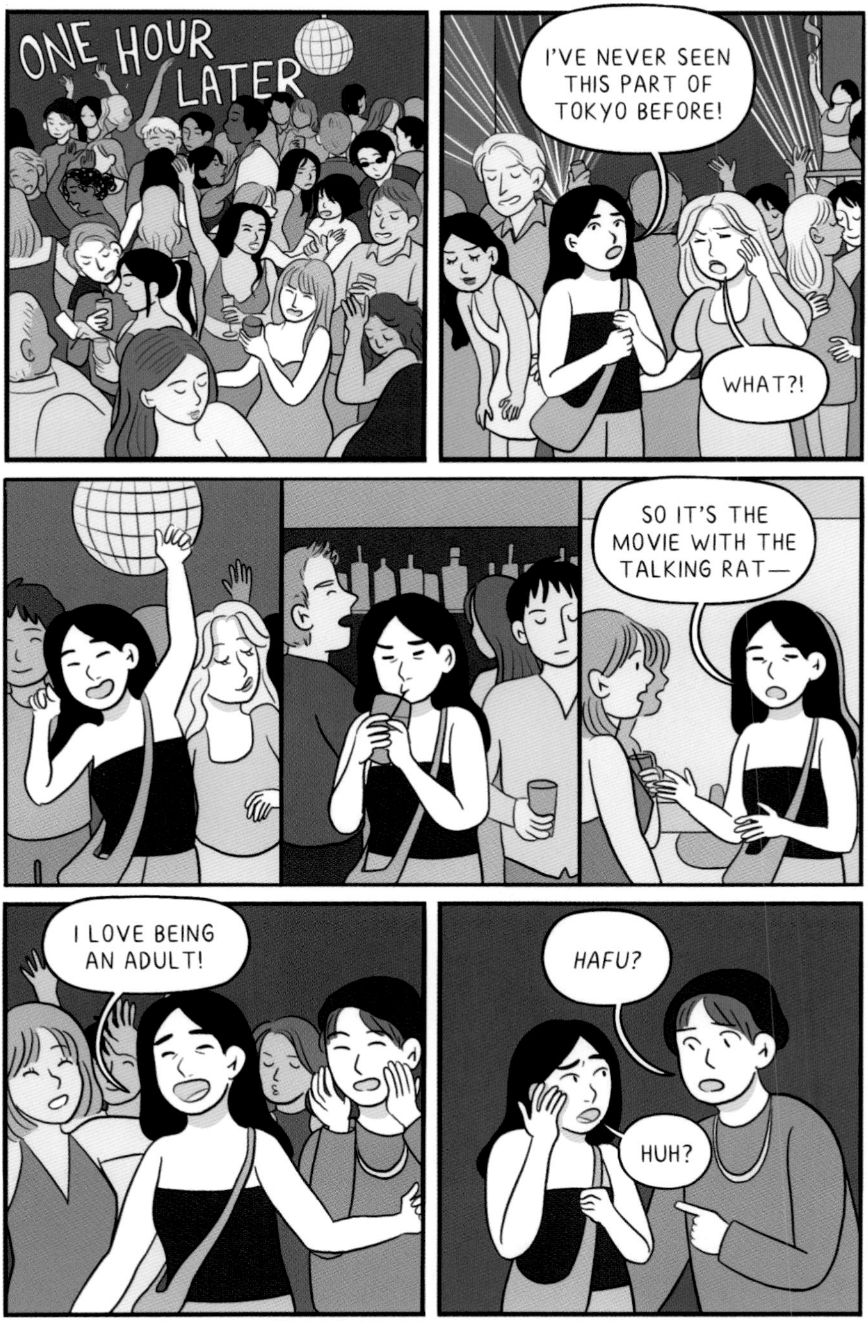
ONE HOUR LATER
I'VE NEVER SEEN THIS PART OF TOKYO BEFORE!
WHAT?!
SO IT'S THE MOVIE WITH THE TALKING RAT—
I LOVE BEING AN ADULT!
HAFU?
HUH?

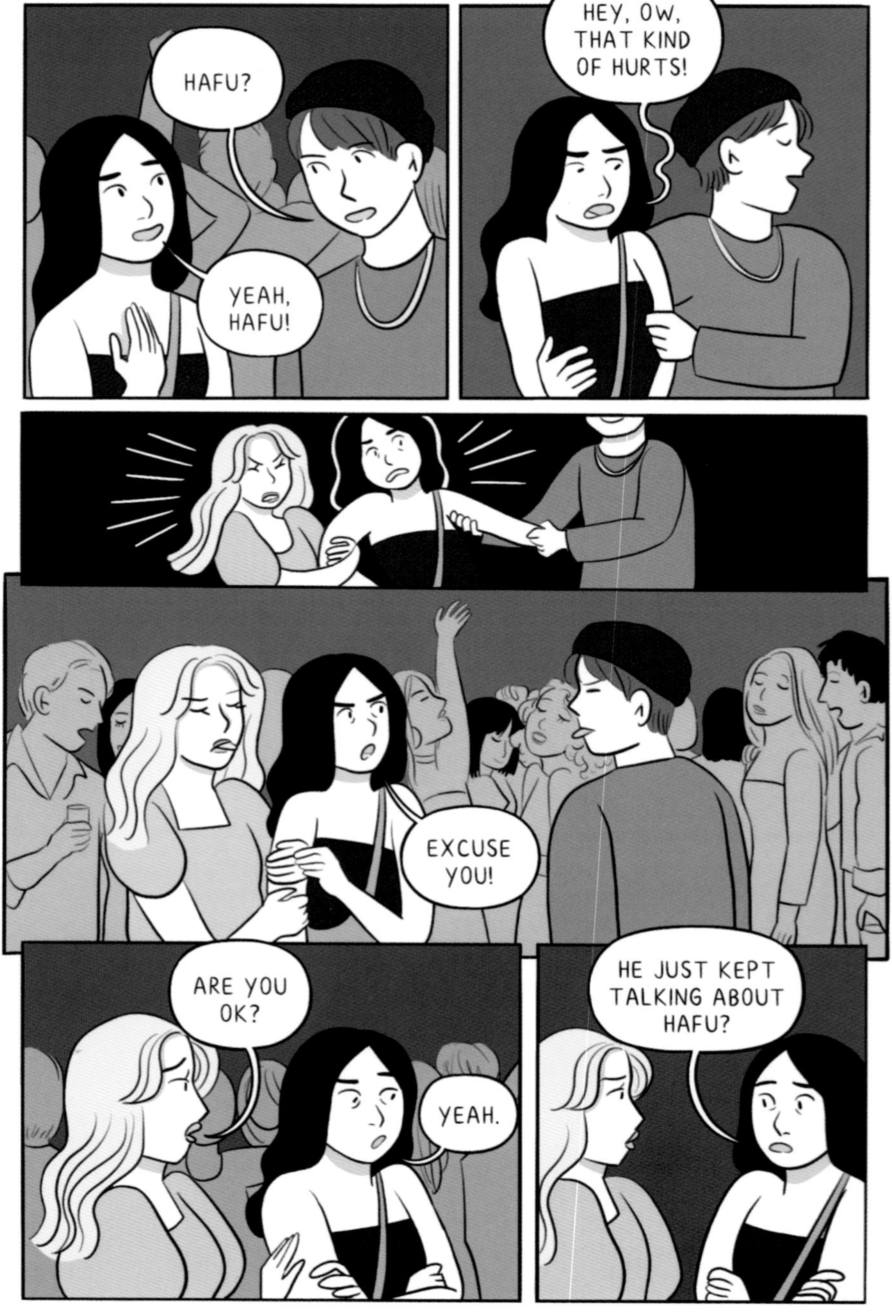
HAFU?
YEAH, HAFU!
HEY, OW, THAT KIND OF HURTS!
EXCUSE YOU!
ARE YOU OK?
YEAH.
HE JUST KEPT TALKING ABOUT HAFU?

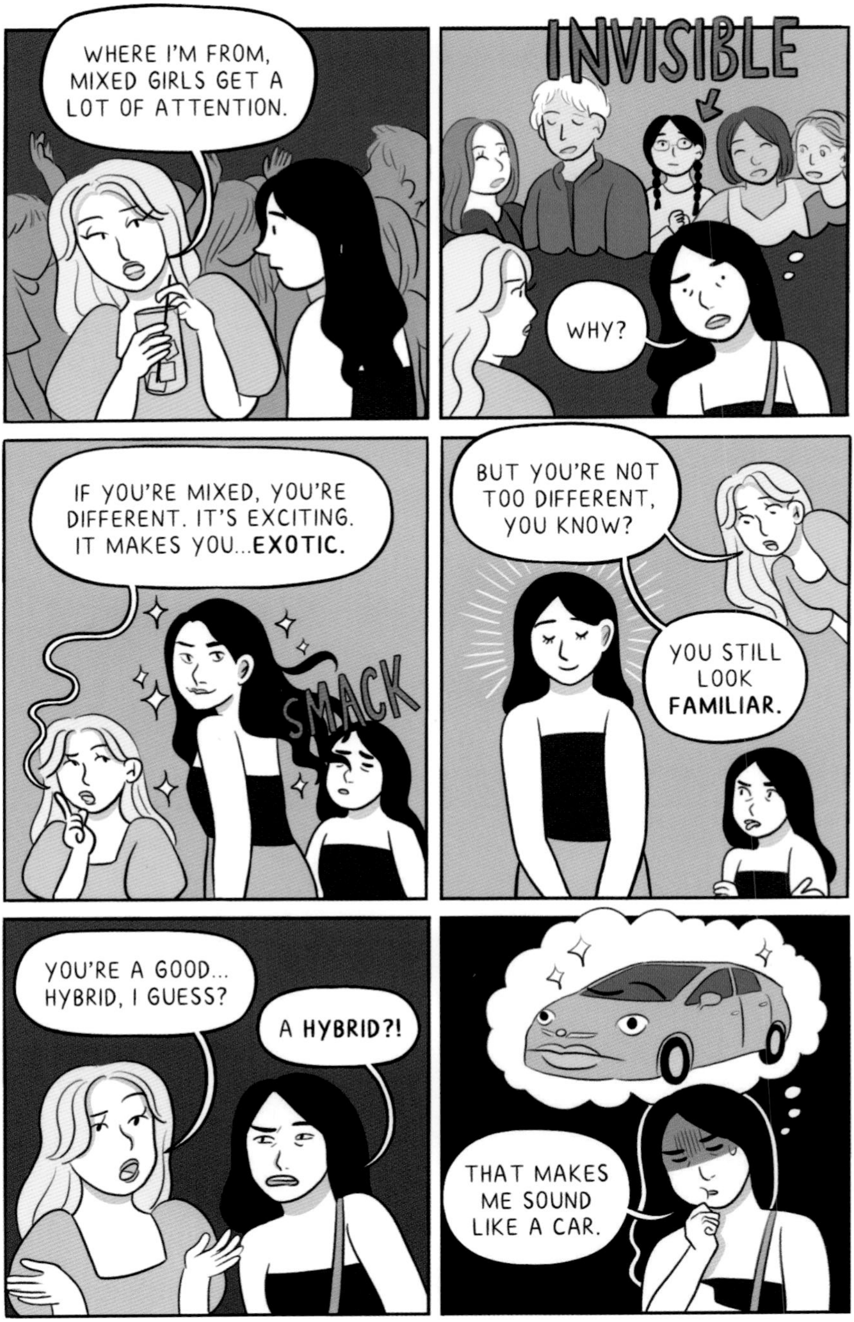
WHERE I'M FROM, MIXED GIRLS GET A LOT OF ATTENTION.
INVISIBLE
WHY?
IF YOU'RE MIXED, YOU'RE DIFFERENT. IT'S EXCITING. IT MAKES YOU...**EXOTIC.**
SMACK
BUT YOU'RE NOT TOO DIFFERENT, YOU KNOW?
YOU STILL LOOK **FAMILIAR.**
YOU'RE A GOOD... HYBRID, I GUESS?
A **HYBRID?!**
THAT MAKES ME SOUND LIKE A CAR.

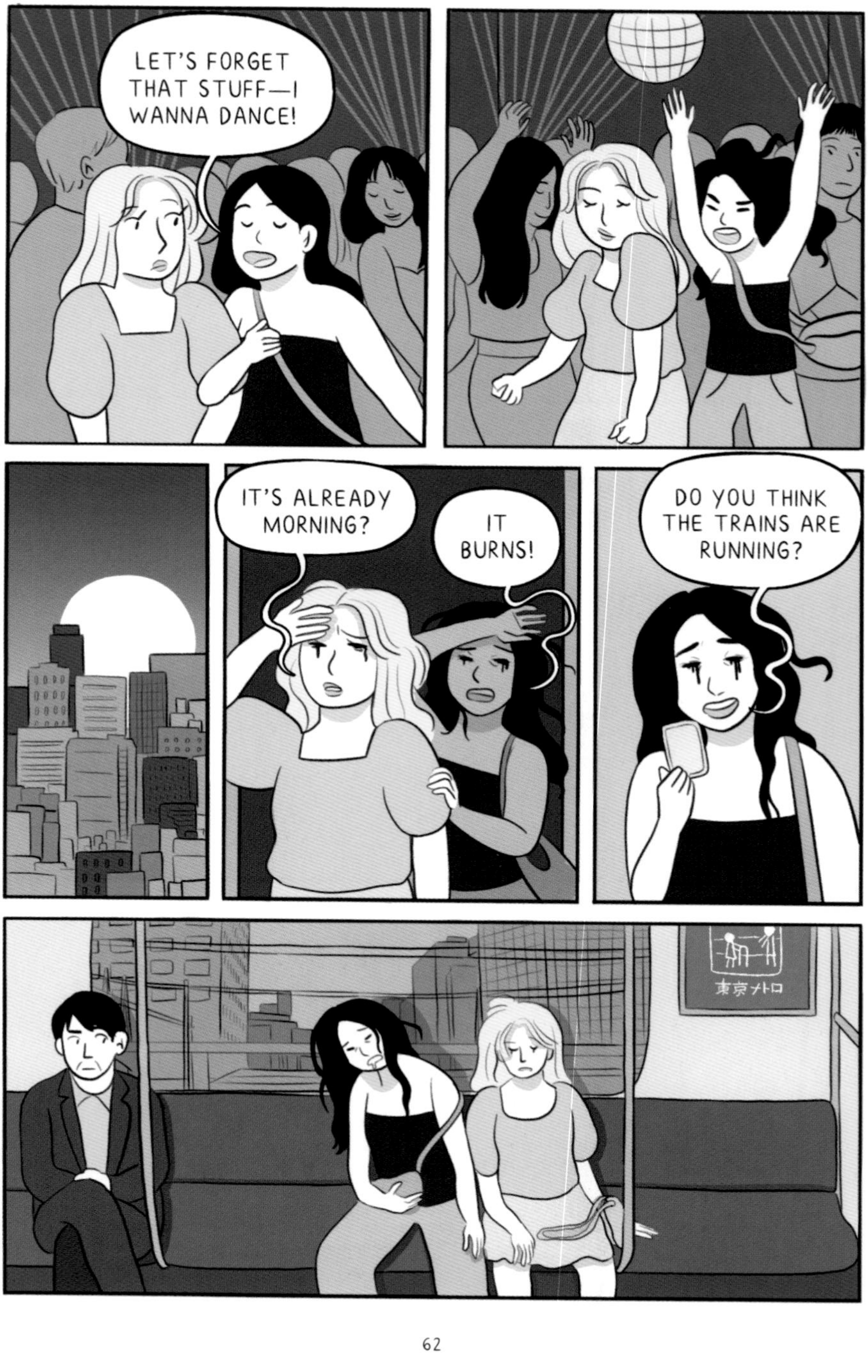
LET'S FORGET THAT STUFF—I WANNA DANCE!
IT'S ALREADY MORNING?
IT BURNS!
DO YOU THINK THE TRAINS ARE RUNNING?
東京メトロ

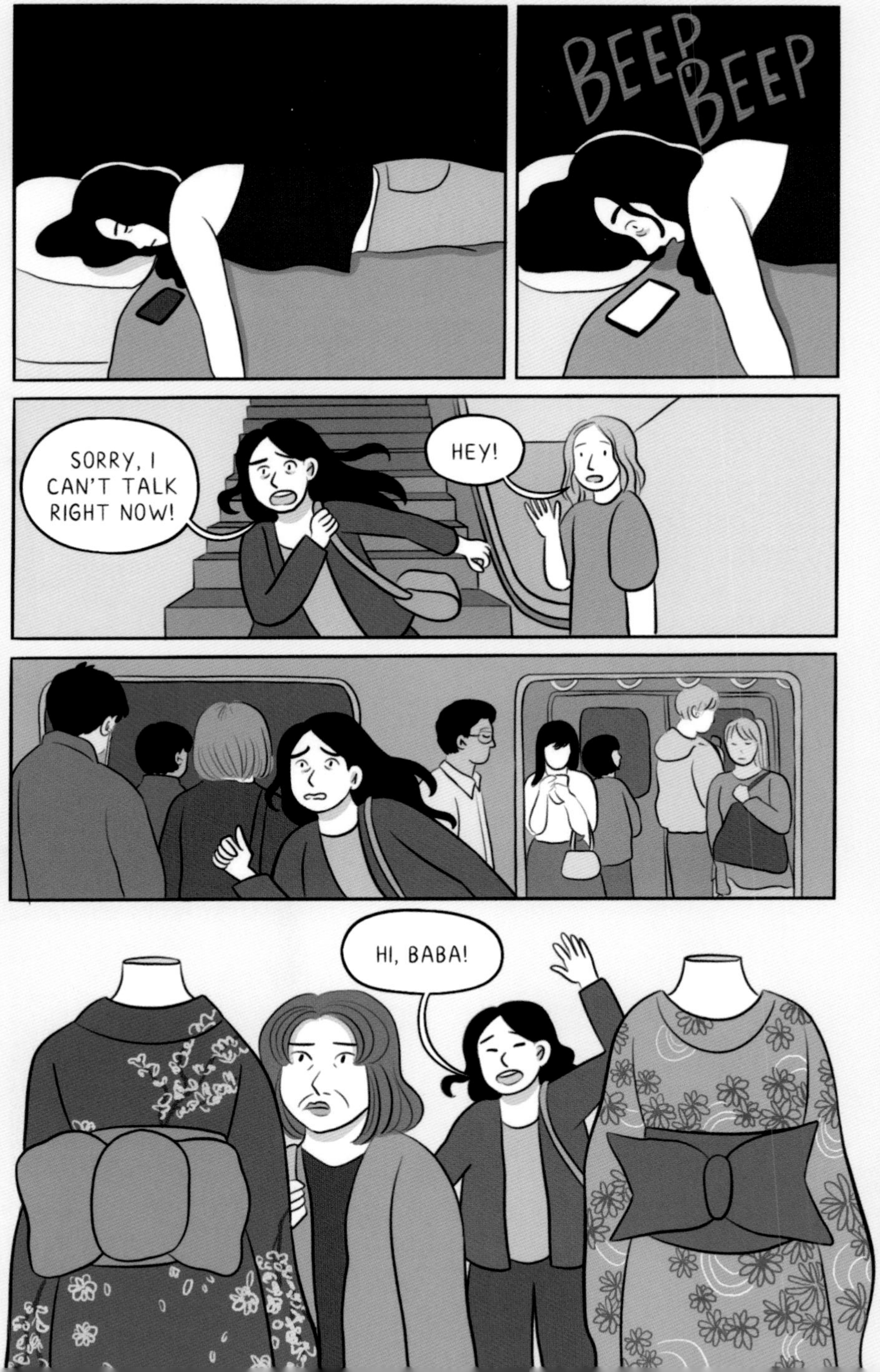
BEEP BEEP
SORRY, I CAN'T TALK RIGHT NOW!
HEY!
HI, BABA!

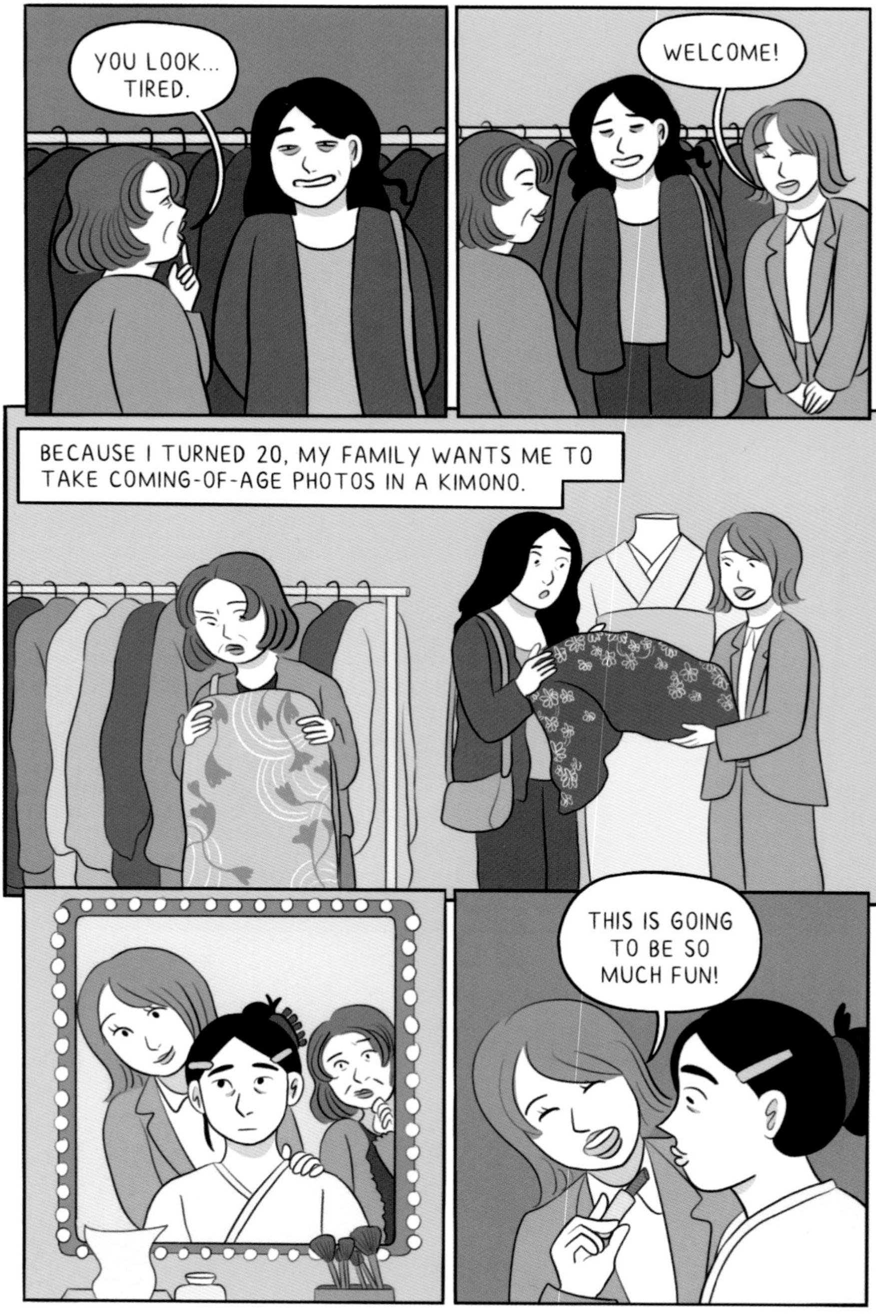
YOU LOOK... TIRED.
WELCOME!
BECAUSE I TURNED 20, MY FAMILY WANTS ME TO TAKE COMING-OF-AGE PHOTOS IN A KIMONO.
THIS IS GOING TO BE SO MUCH FUN!

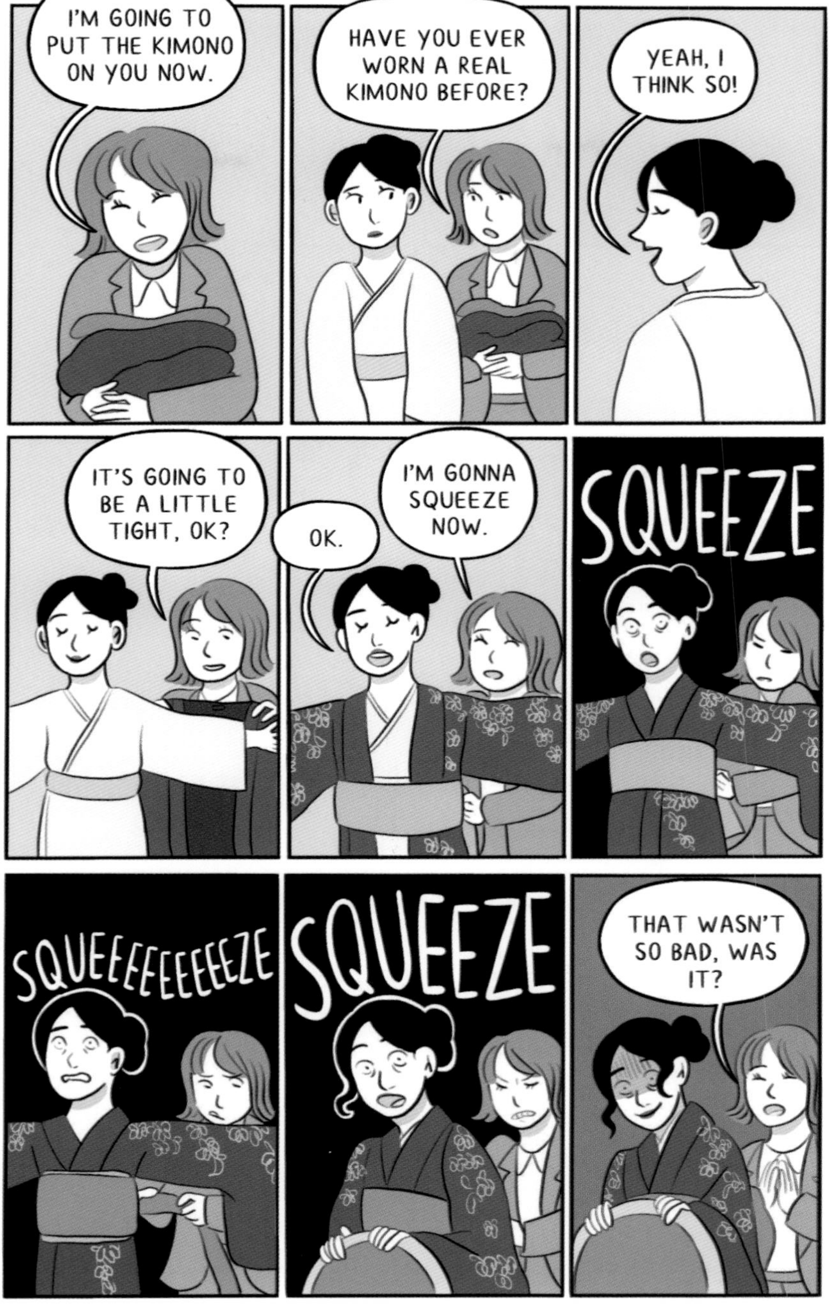
I'M GOING TO PUT THE KIMONO ON YOU NOW.
HAVE YOU EVER WORN A REAL KIMONO BEFORE?
YEAH, I THINK SO!
IT'S GOING TO BE A LITTLE TIGHT, OK?
OK.
I'M GONNA SQUEEZE NOW.
SQUEEZE
SQUEEEEEEEEEEZE
SQUEEZE
THAT WASN'T SO BAD, WAS IT?

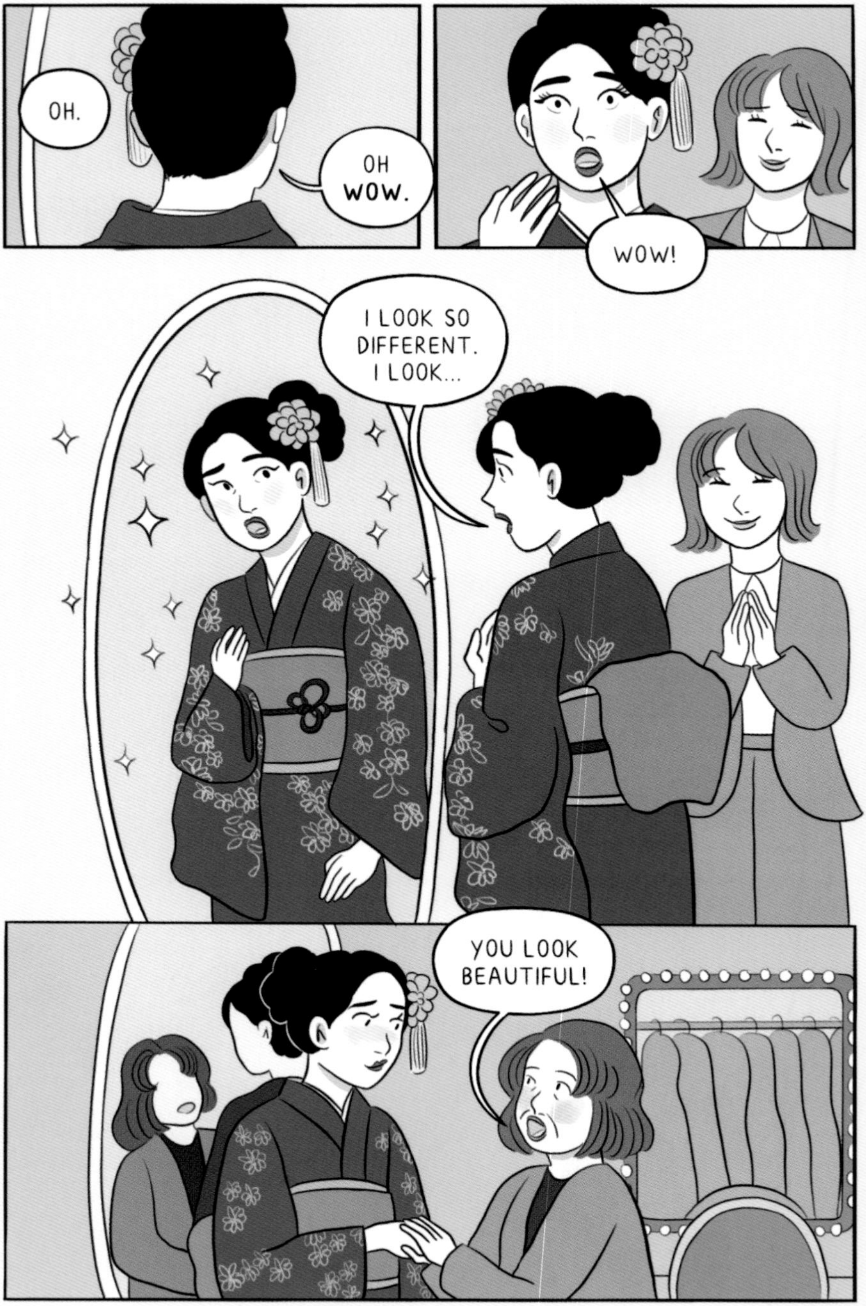
OH.
OH WOW.
WOW!
I LOOK SO DIFFERENT. I LOOK...
YOU LOOK BEAUTIFUL!

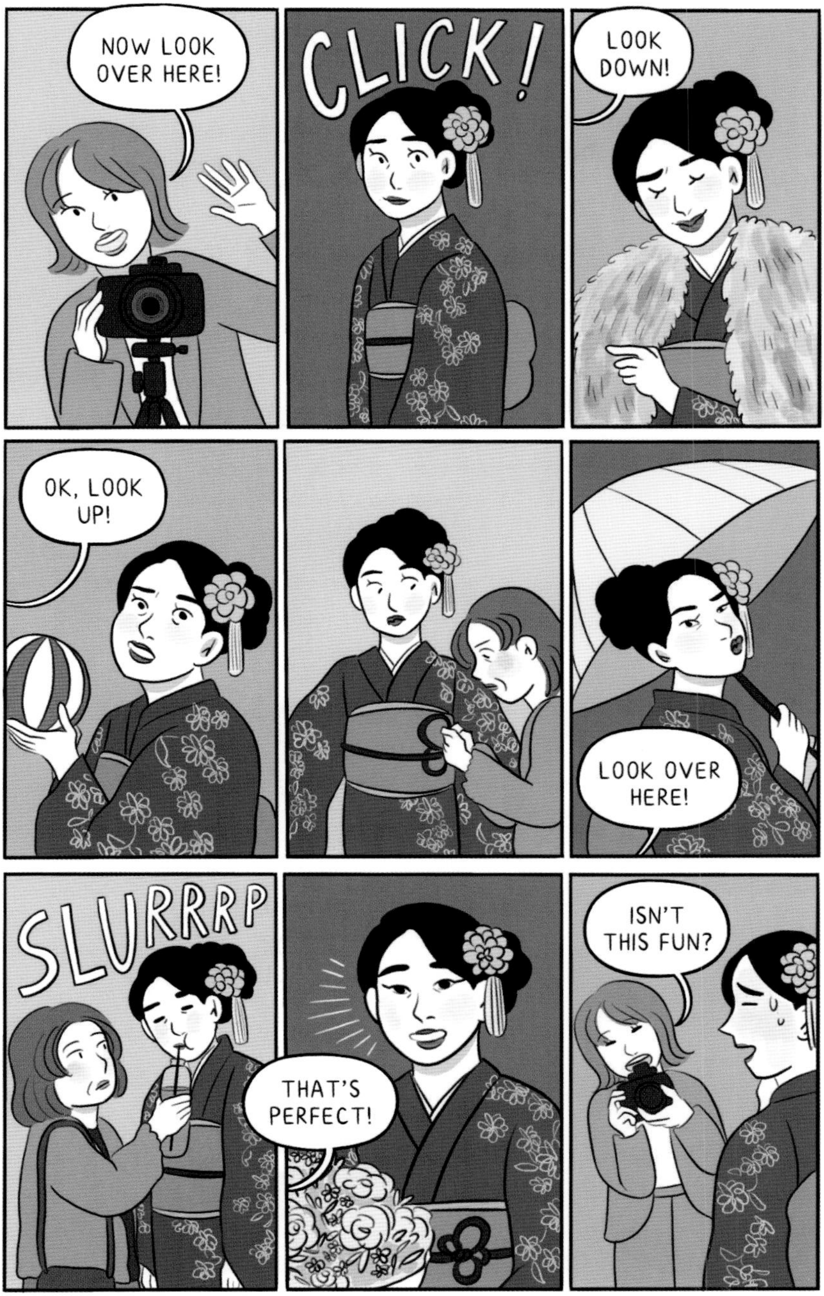

NOW LOOK OVER HERE!
CLICK!
LOOK DOWN!
OK, LOOK UP!
LOOK OVER HERE!
SLURRRP
THAT'S PERFECT!
ISN'T THIS FUN?

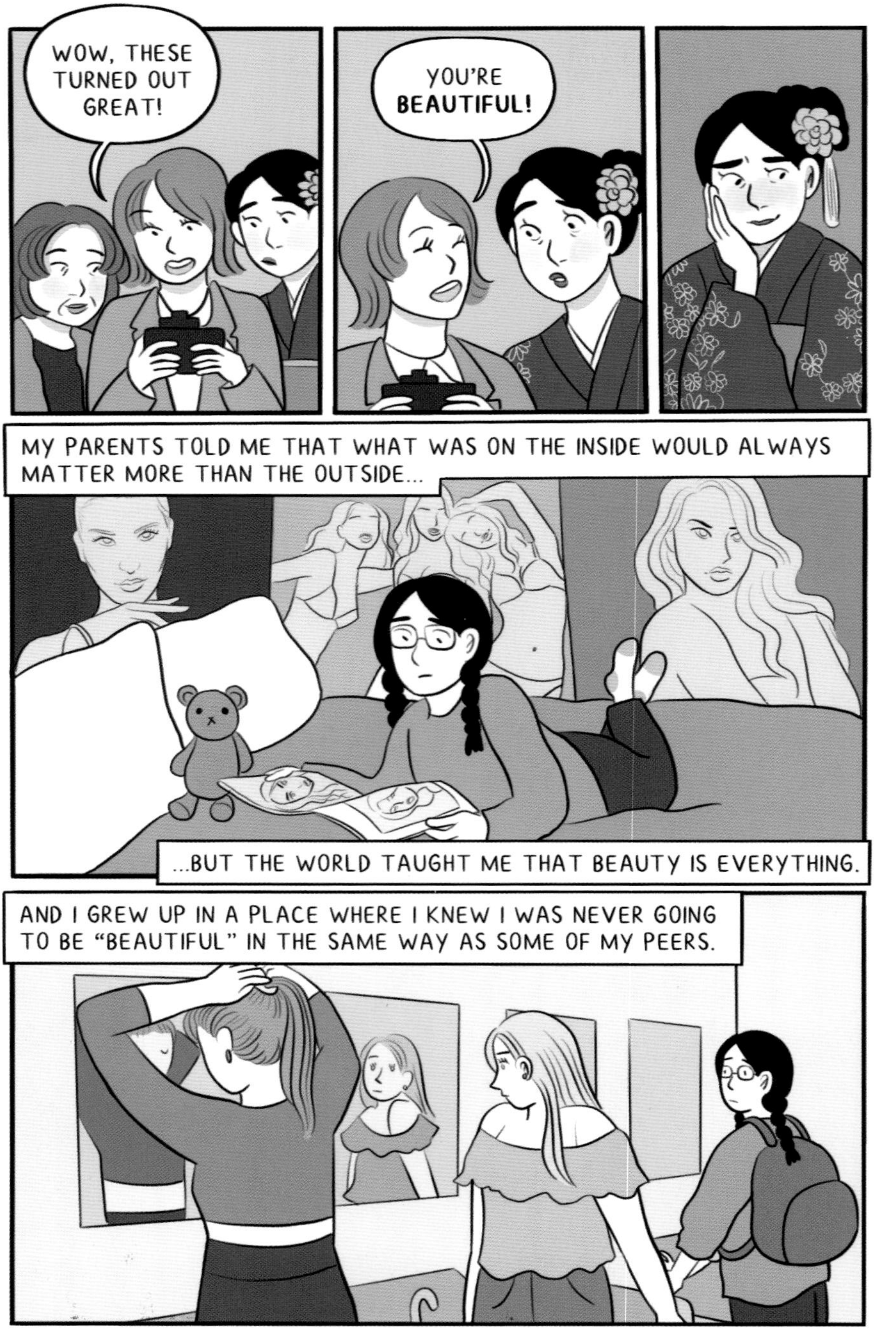
WOW, THESE TURNED OUT GREAT!
YOU'RE **BEAUTIFUL!**
MY PARENTS TOLD ME THAT WHAT WAS ON THE INSIDE WOULD ALWAYS MATTER MORE THAN THE OUTSIDE...
...BUT THE WORLD TAUGHT ME THAT BEAUTY IS EVERYTHING.
AND I GREW UP IN A PLACE WHERE I KNEW I WAS NEVER GOING TO BE "BEAUTIFUL" IN THE SAME WAY AS SOME OF MY PEERS.

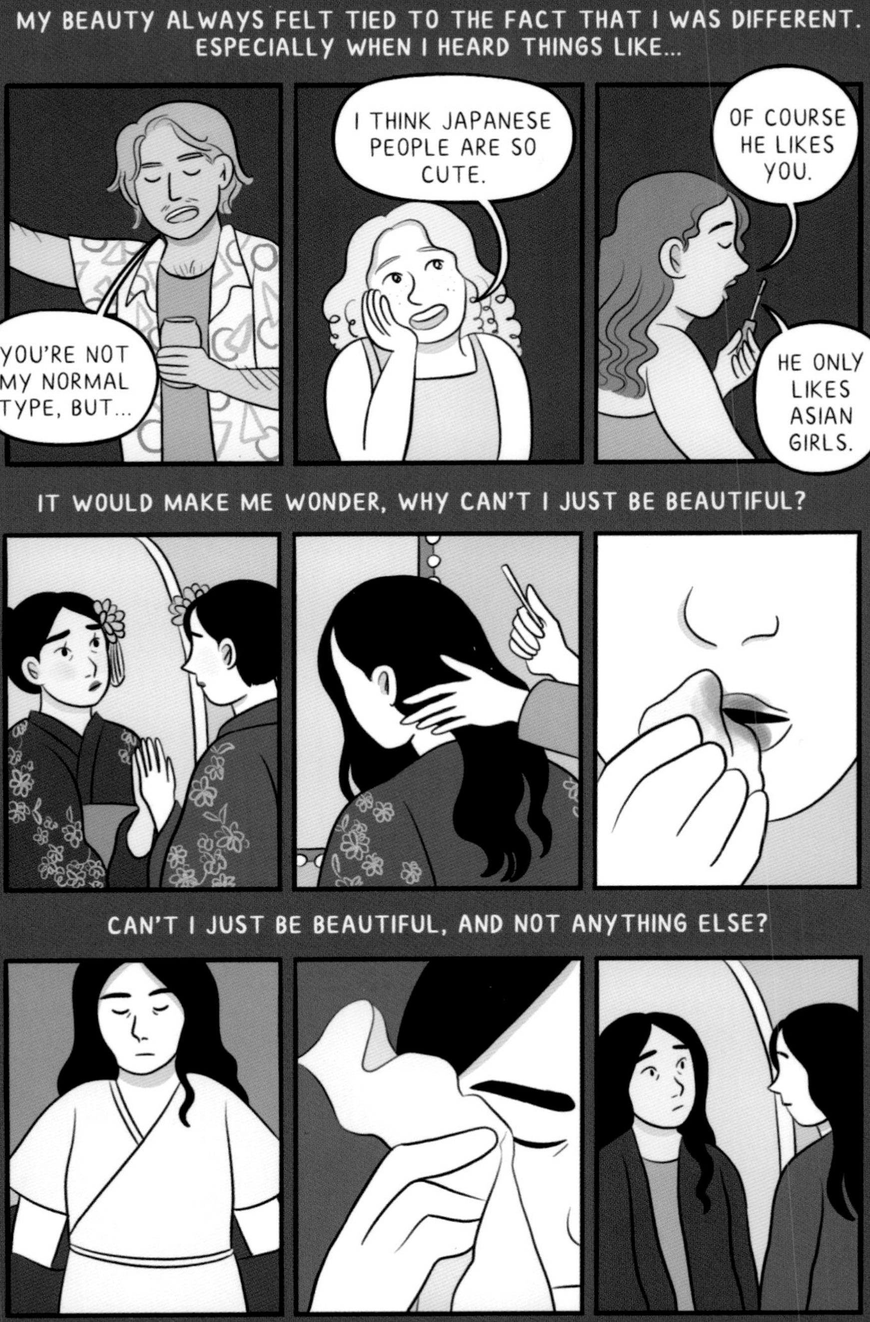
MY BEAUTY ALWAYS FELT TIED TO THE FACT THAT I WAS DIFFERENT. ESPECIALLY WHEN I HEARD THINGS LIKE...
YOU'RE NOT MY NORMAL TYPE, BUT...
I THINK JAPANESE PEOPLE ARE SO CUTE.
OF COURSE HE LIKES YOU.
HE ONLY LIKES ASIAN GIRLS.
IT WOULD MAKE ME WONDER, WHY CAN'T I JUST BE BEAUTIFUL?
CAN'T I JUST BE BEAUTIFUL, AND NOT ANYTHING ELSE?

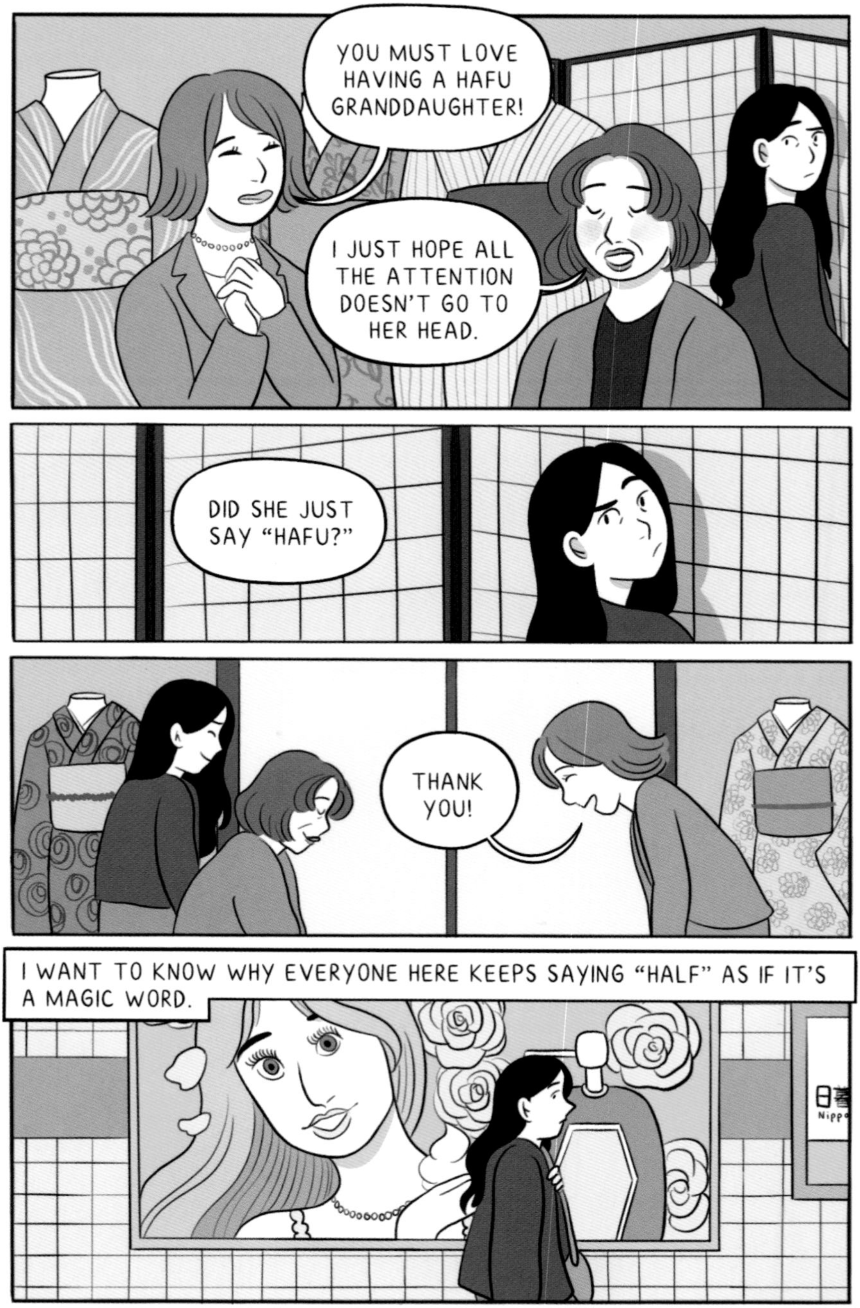
YOU MUST LOVE HAVING A HAFU GRANDDAUGHTER!
I JUST HOPE ALL THE ATTENTION DOESN'T GO TO HER HEAD.
DID SHE JUST SAY "HAFU?"
THANK YOU!
I WANT TO KNOW WHY EVERYONE HERE KEEPS SAYING "HALF" AS IF IT'S A MAGIC WORD.

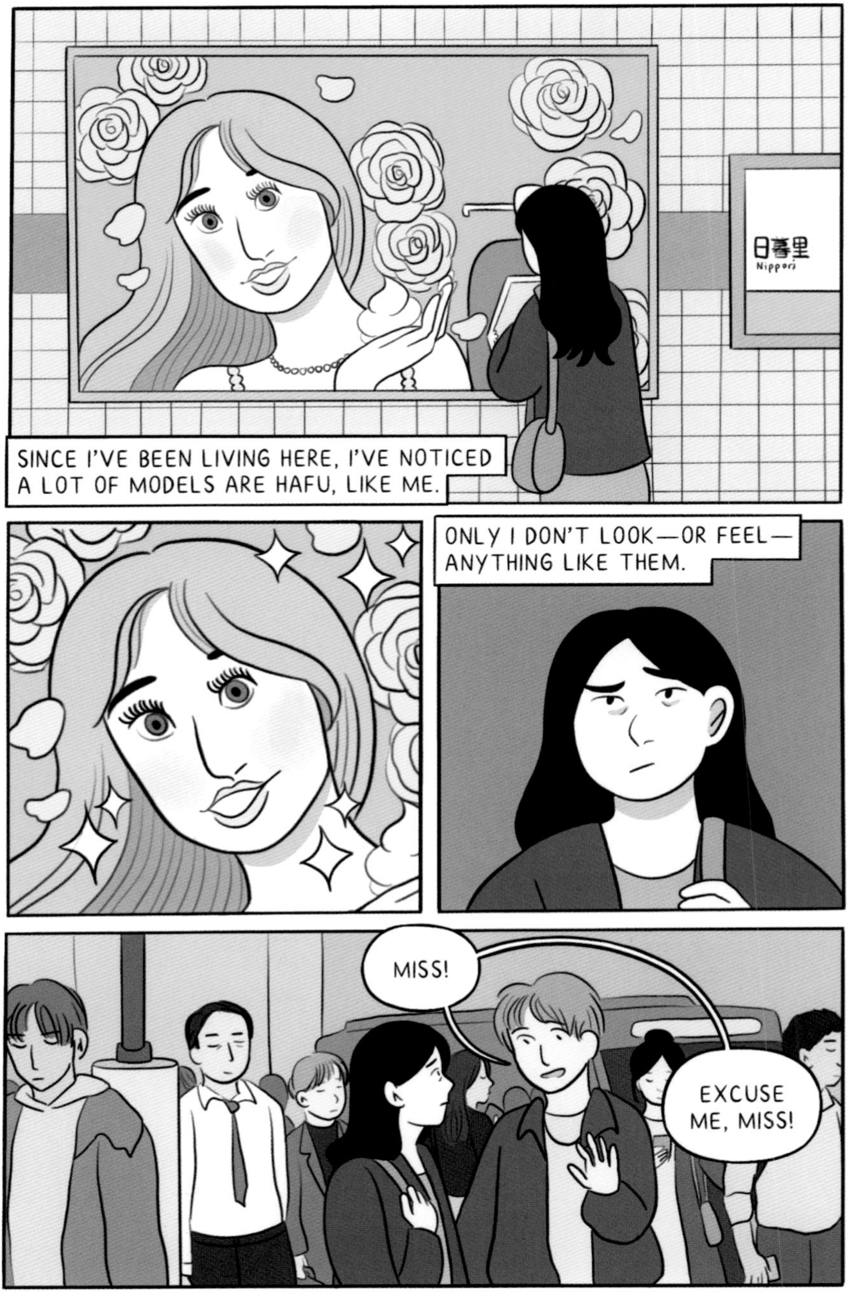
日暮里
Nippori
SINCE I'VE BEEN LIVING HERE, I'VE NOTICED A LOT OF MODELS ARE HAFU, LIKE ME.
ONLY I DON'T LOOK—OR FEEL—ANYTHING LIKE THEM.
MISS!
EXCUSE ME, MISS!

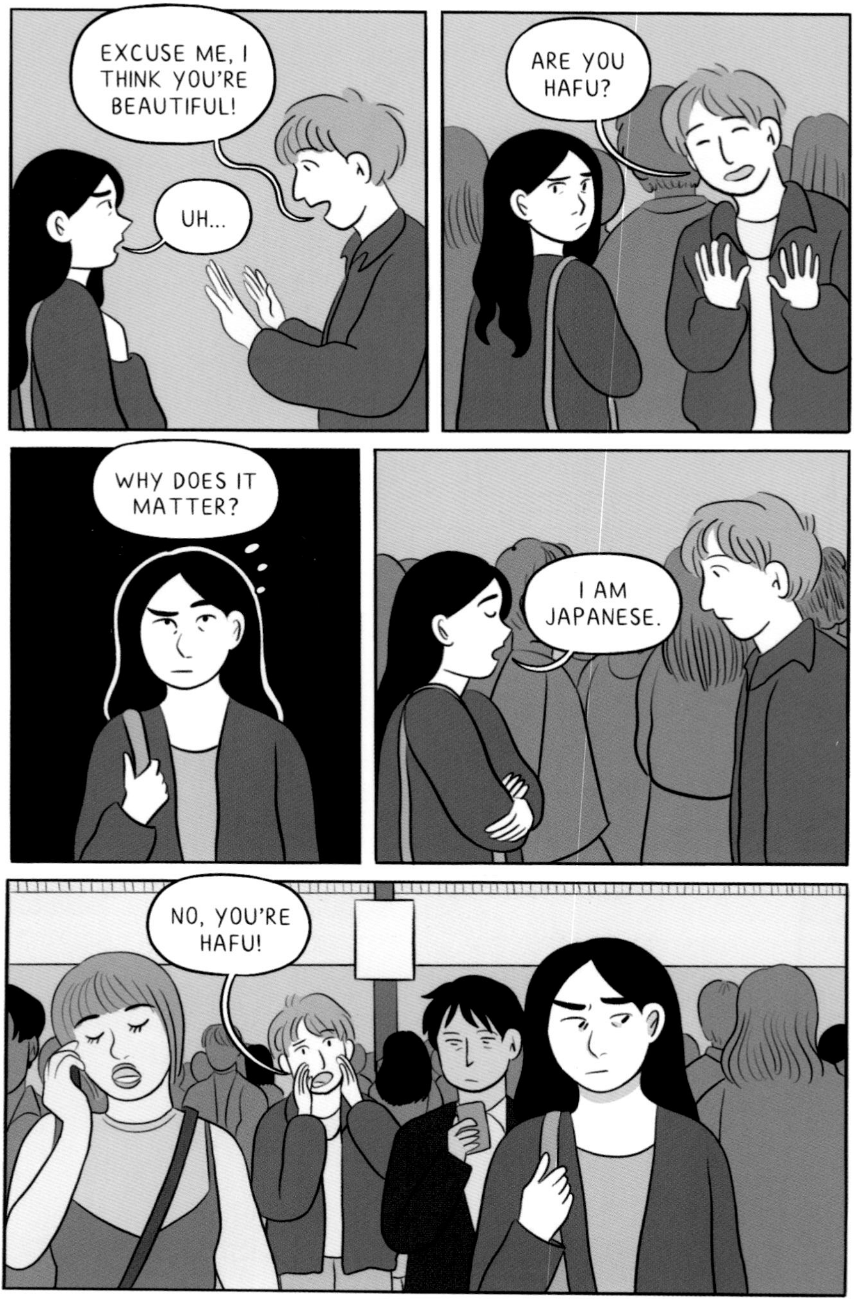
EXCUSE ME, I THINK YOU'RE BEAUTIFUL!
UH...
ARE YOU HAFU?
WHY DOES IT MATTER?
I AM JAPANESE.
NO, YOU'RE HAFU!

I THINK THE BEAUTY OF BEING HAFU IS THAT IT LOOKS DIFFERENT FOR EVERY SINGLE PERSON.

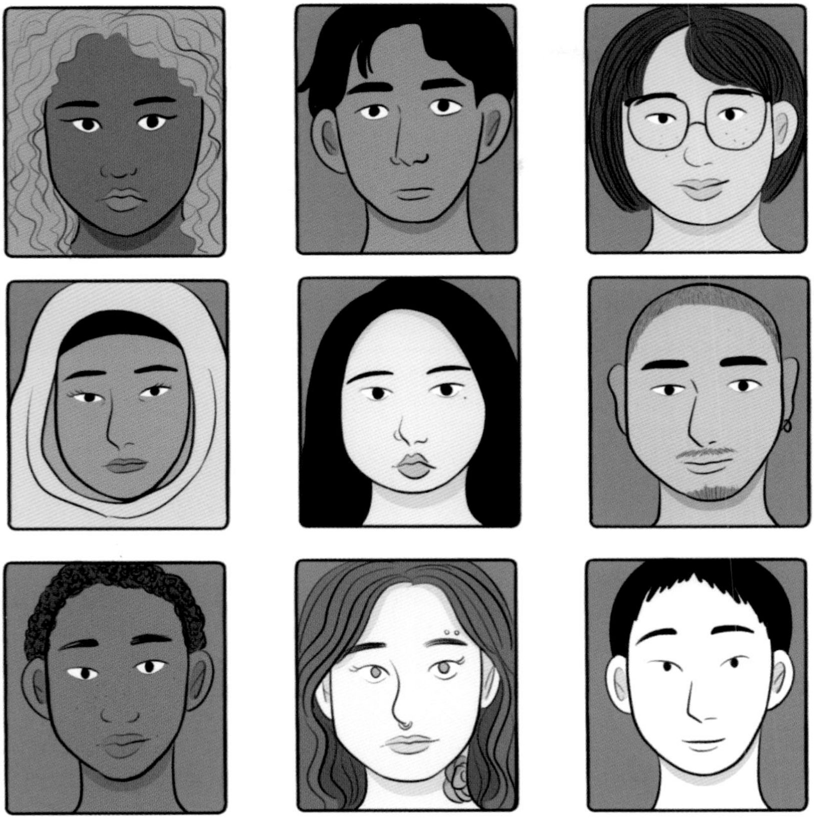

BUT WHEN PEOPLE IN JAPAN THINK OF HAFU, IT SEEMS THEY ONLY THINK OF A CERTAIN TYPE OF PERSON, WHO LOOKS A CERTAIN WAY.

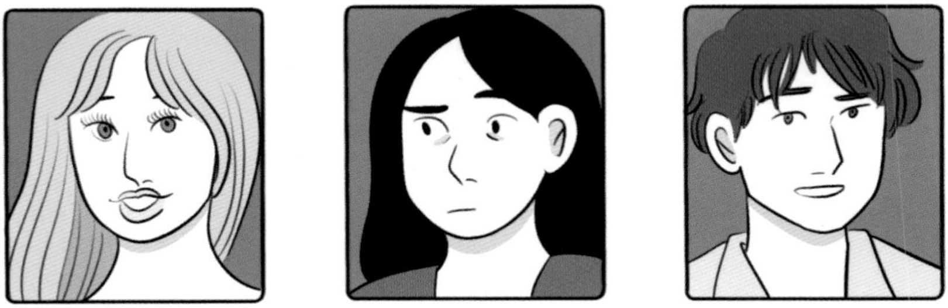

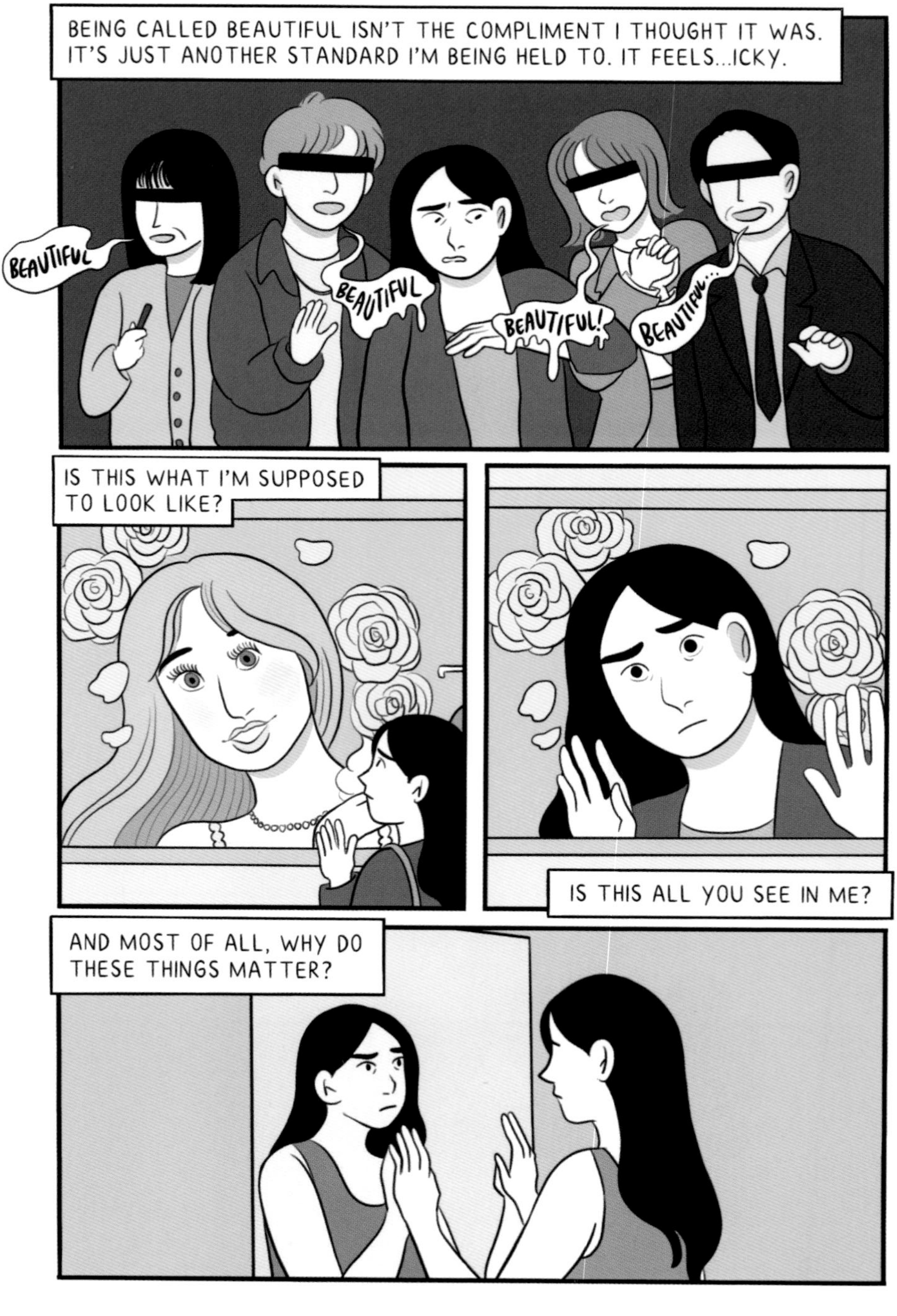
BEING CALLED BEAUTIFUL ISN'T THE COMPLIMENT I THOUGHT IT WAS. IT'S JUST ANOTHER STANDARD I'M BEING HELD TO. IT FEELS...ICKY.
BEAUTIFUL
BEAUTIFUL
BEAUTIFUL!
BEAUTIFUL...
IS THIS WHAT I'M SUPPOSED TO LOOK LIKE?
IS THIS ALL YOU SEE IN ME?
AND MOST OF ALL, WHY DO THESE THINGS MATTER?

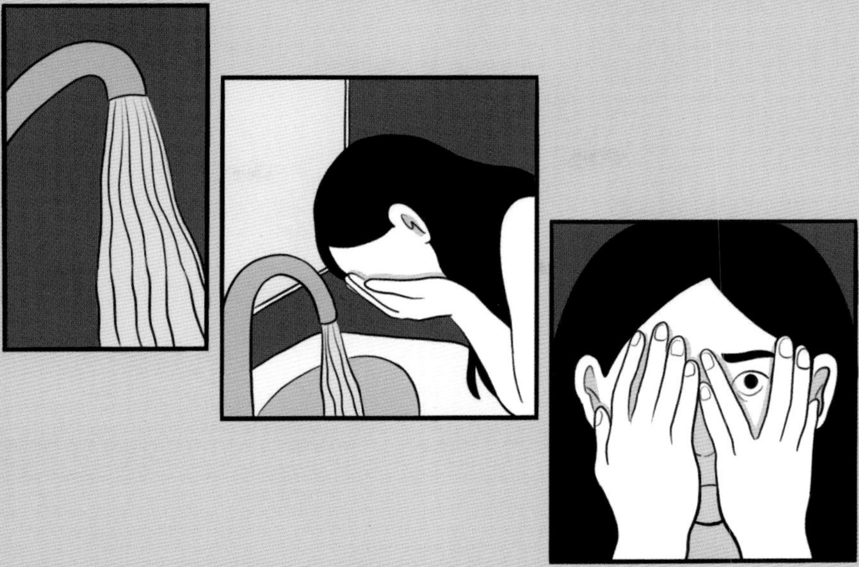

IT'S NOT REALLY ME WHO'S BEAUTIFUL. IT'S **HAFU.**

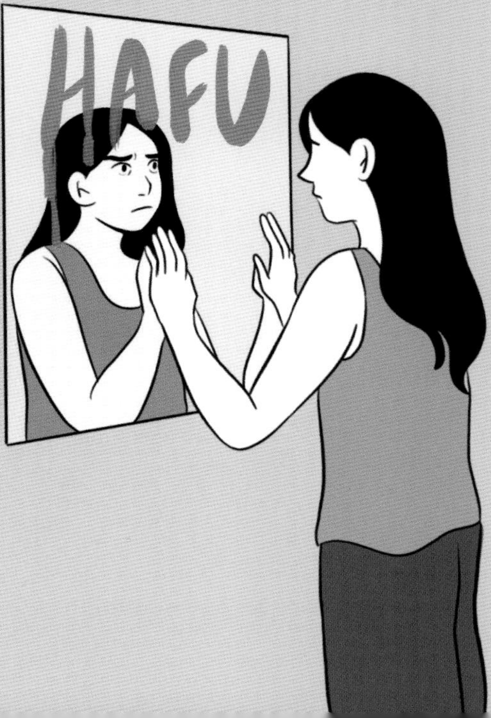
HAFU

秋
FALL

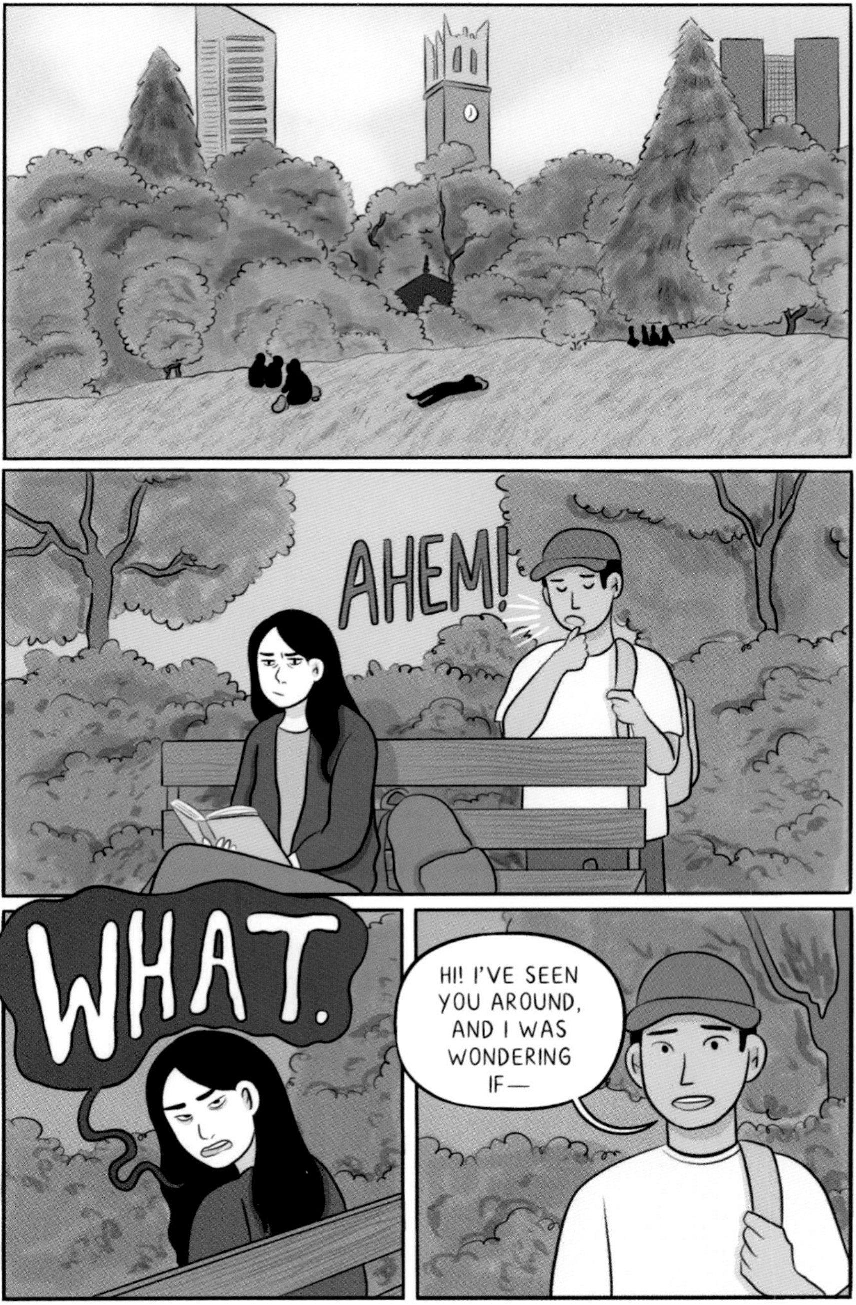
AHEM!
WHAT.
HI! I'VE SEEN YOU AROUND, AND I WAS WONDERING IF—

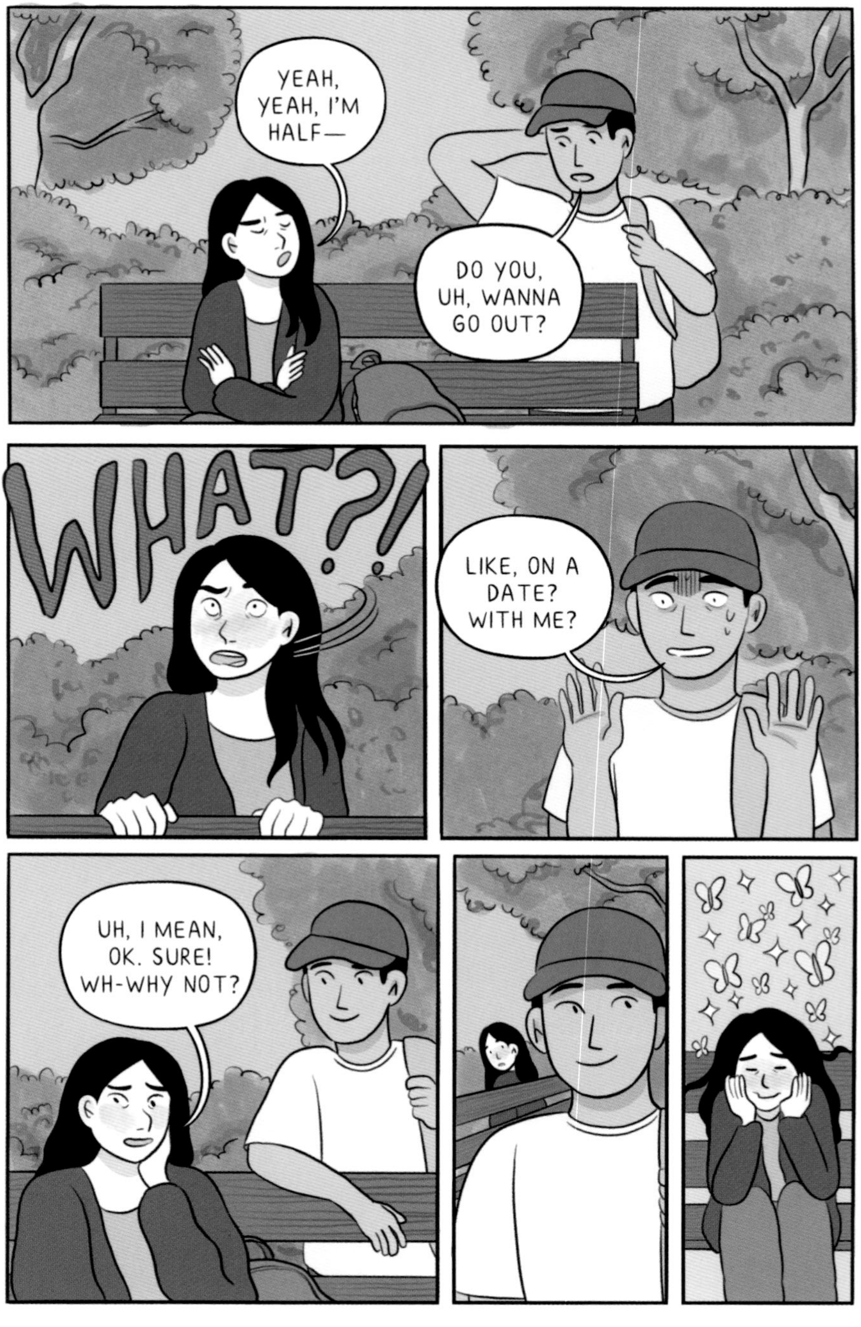
YEAH, YEAH, I'M HALF—
DO YOU, UH, WANNA GO OUT?
WHAT?!
LIKE, ON A DATE? WITH ME?
UH, I MEAN, OK. SURE! WH-WHY NOT?

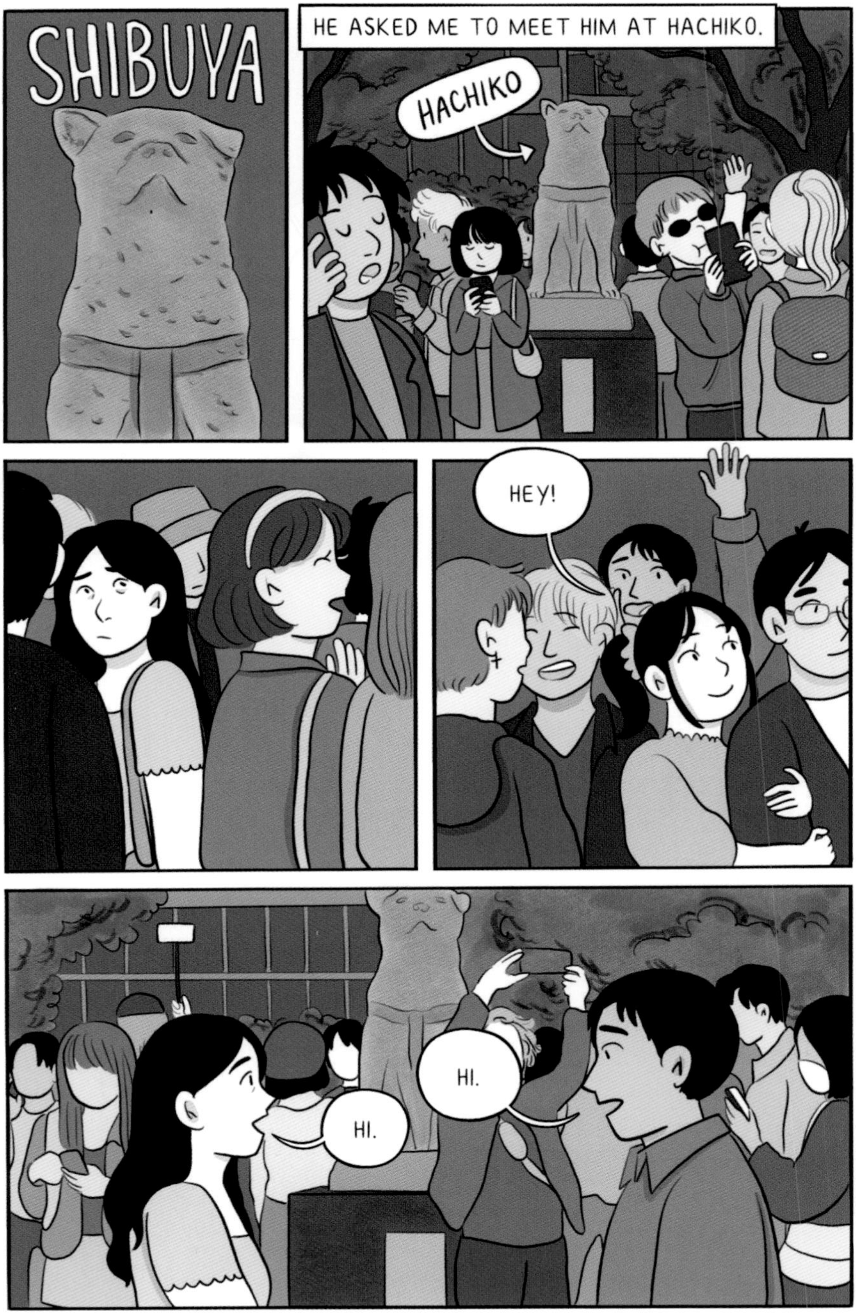
SHIBUYA
HE ASKED ME TO MEET HIM AT HACHIKO.
HACHIKO
HEY!
HI.
HI.

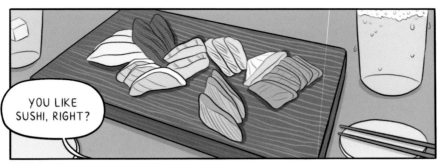

YOU LIKE SUSHI, RIGHT?

UH, I'M JAPANESE, TOO. OF COURSE I LIKE IT!

DID I DO SOMETHING WEIRD? WHY ARE YOU STARING LIKE THAT?

OH, IT'S NOTHING, REALLY! I JUST NOTICED THAT...

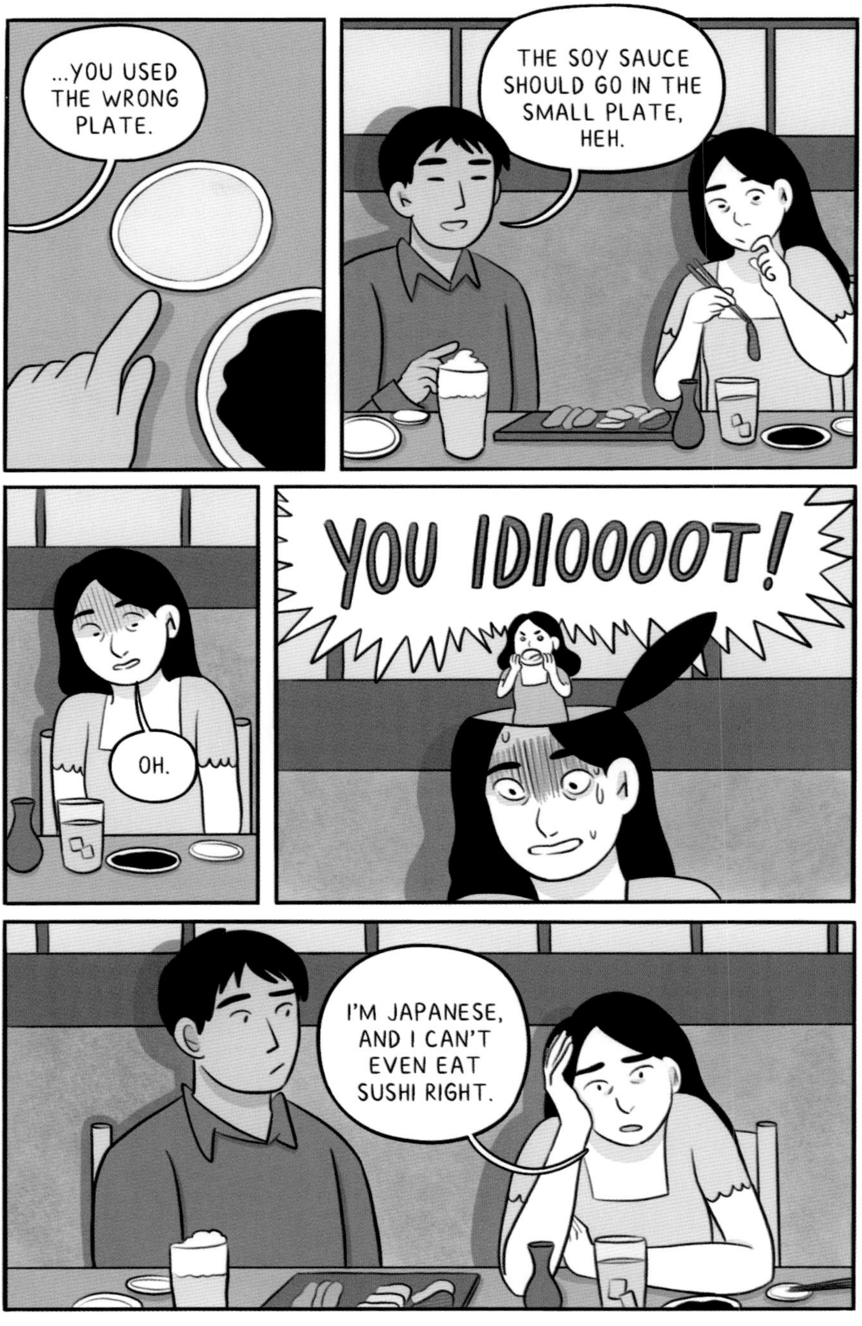
...YOU USED THE WRONG PLATE.
THE SOY SAUCE SHOULD GO IN THE SMALL PLATE, HEH.
OH.
YOU IDIOOOOT!
I'M JAPANESE, AND I CAN'T EVEN EAT SUSHI RIGHT.

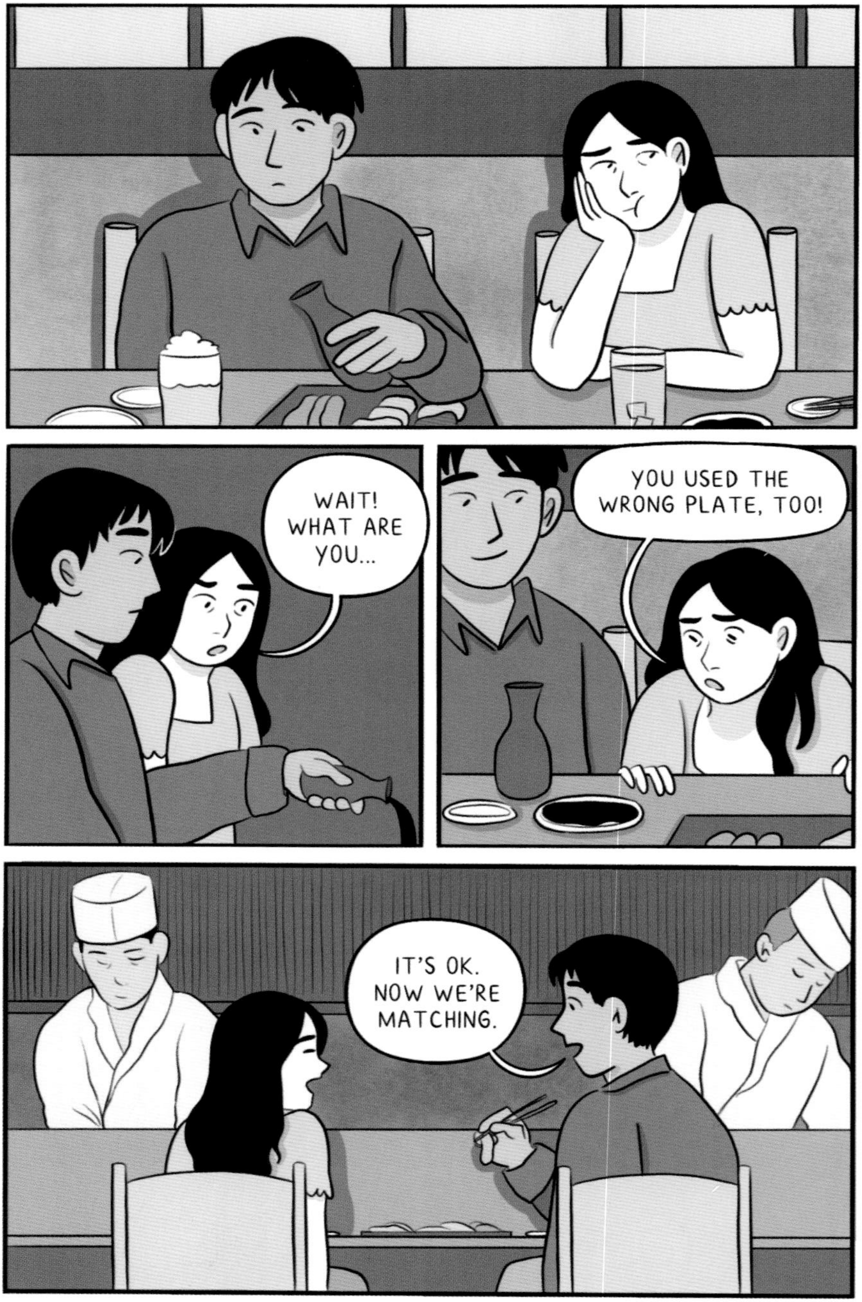
WAIT! WHAT ARE YOU...
YOU USED THE WRONG PLATE, TOO!
IT'S OK. NOW WE'RE MATCHING.

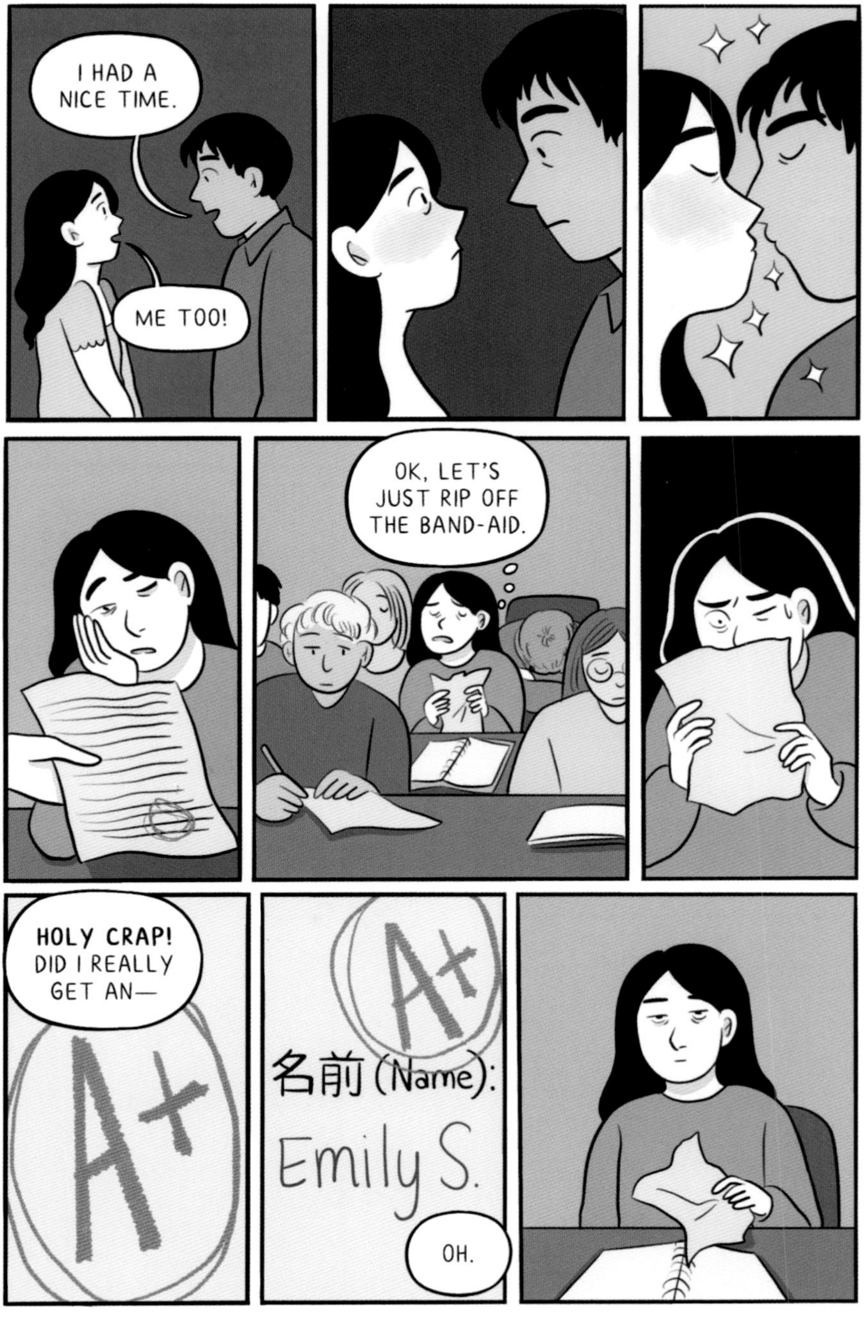
I HAD A NICE TIME.
ME TOO!
OK, LET'S JUST RIP OFF THE BAND-AID.
HOLY CRAP! DID I REALLY GET AN—
A+
A+
名前(Name):
Emily S.
OH.

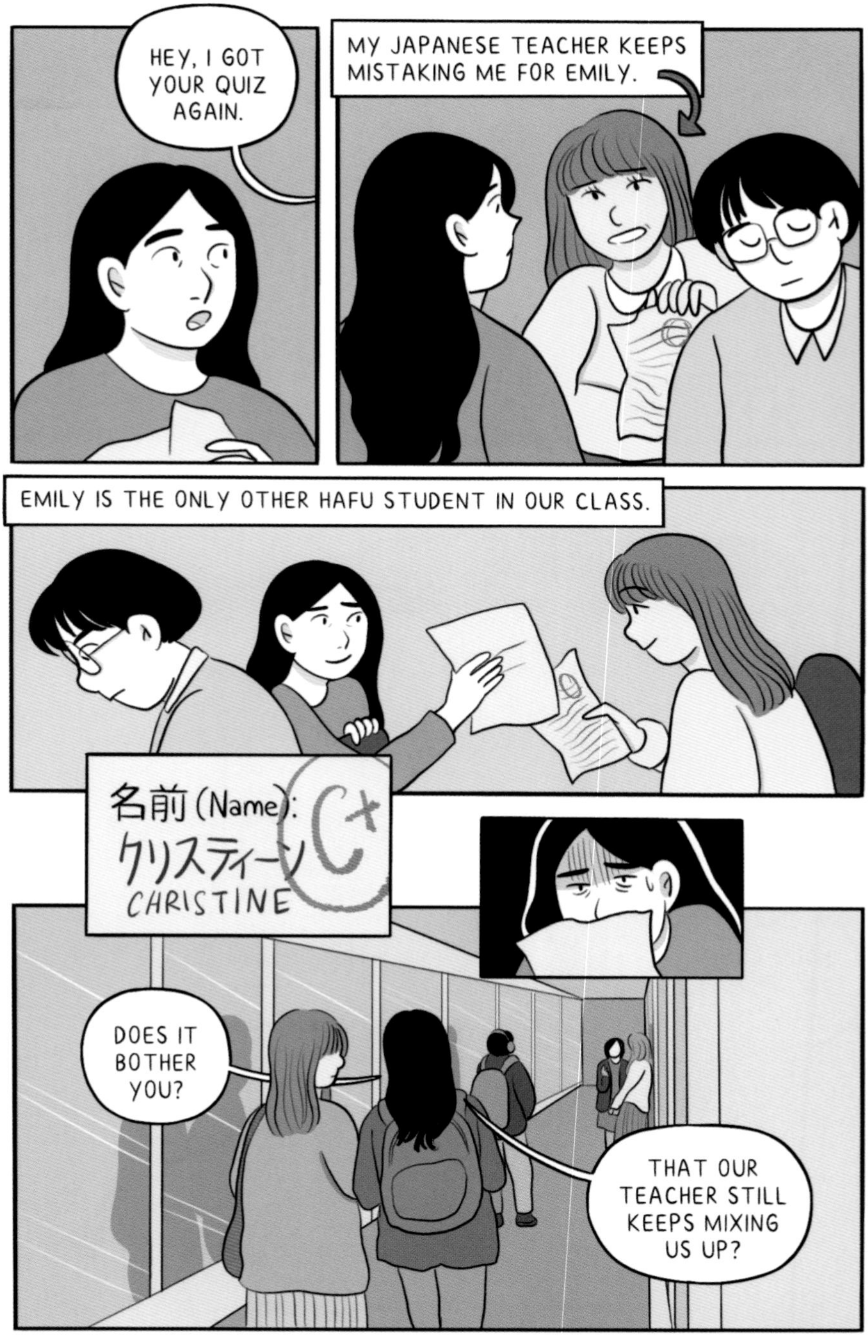
HEY, I GOT YOUR QUIZ AGAIN.
MY JAPANESE TEACHER KEEPS MISTAKING ME FOR EMILY.
EMILY IS THE ONLY OTHER HAFU STUDENT IN OUR CLASS.
名前 (Name): クリスティーン CHRISTINE
C+
DOES IT BOTHER YOU?
THAT OUR TEACHER STILL KEEPS MIXING US UP?

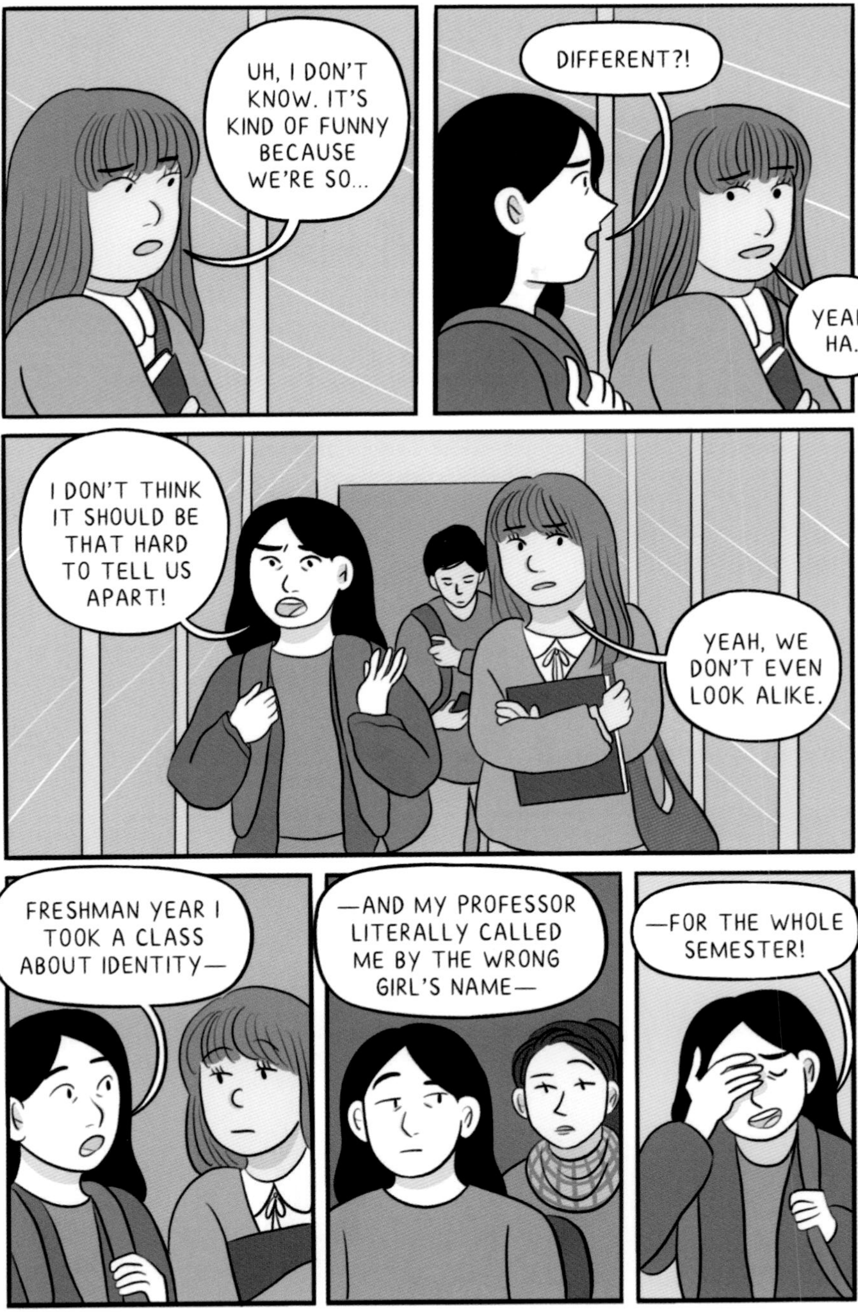
UH, I DON'T KNOW. IT'S KIND OF FUNNY BECAUSE WE'RE SO...
DIFFERENT?!
YEAH, HA.
I DON'T THINK IT SHOULD BE THAT HARD TO TELL US APART!
YEAH, WE DON'T EVEN LOOK ALIKE.
FRESHMAN YEAR I TOOK A CLASS ABOUT IDENTITY—
—AND MY PROFESSOR LITERALLY CALLED ME BY THE WRONG GIRL'S NAME—
—FOR THE WHOLE SEMESTER!

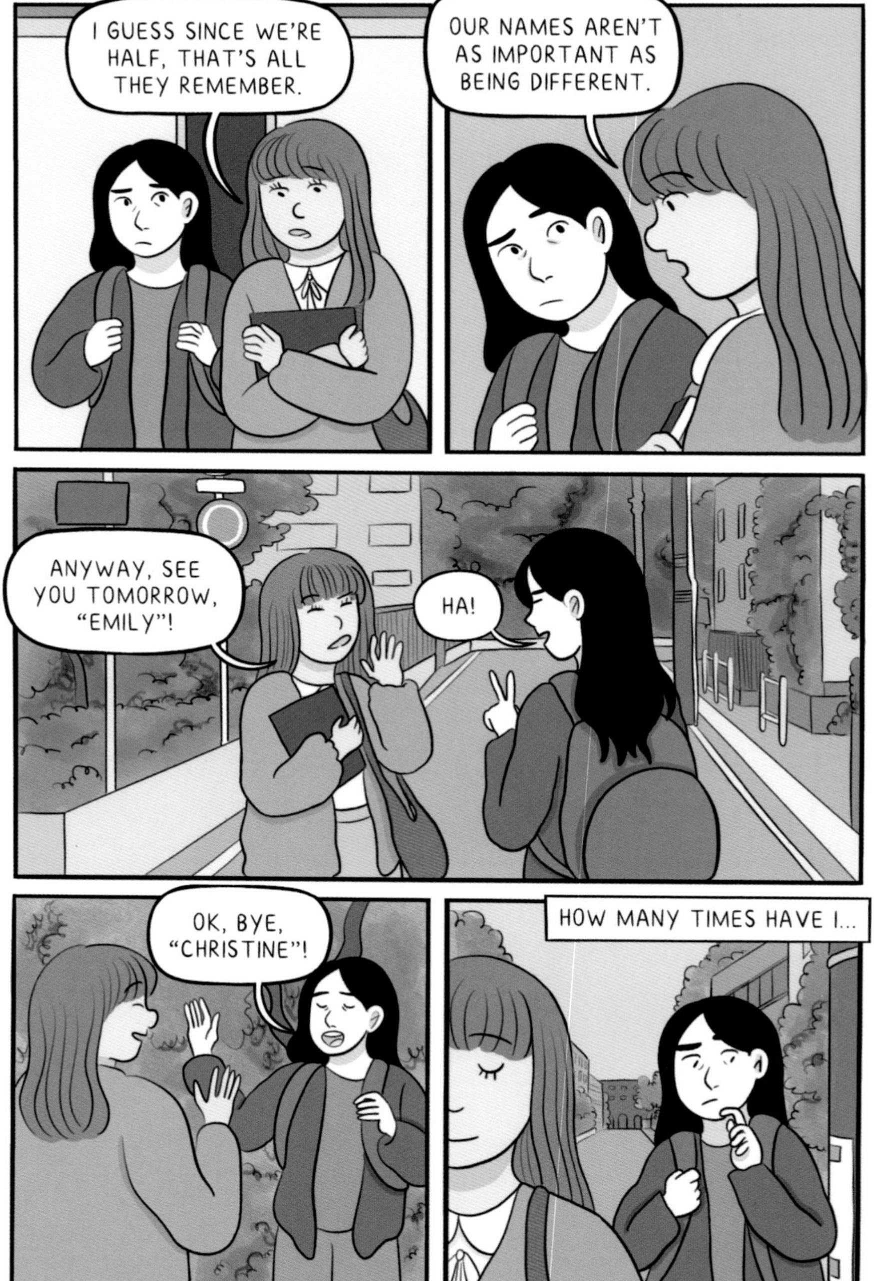

I GUESS SINCE WE'RE HALF, THAT'S ALL THEY REMEMBER.
OUR NAMES AREN'T AS IMPORTANT AS BEING DIFFERENT.
ANYWAY, SEE YOU TOMORROW, "EMILY"!
HA!
OK, BYE, "CHRISTINE"!
HOW MANY TIMES HAVE I...

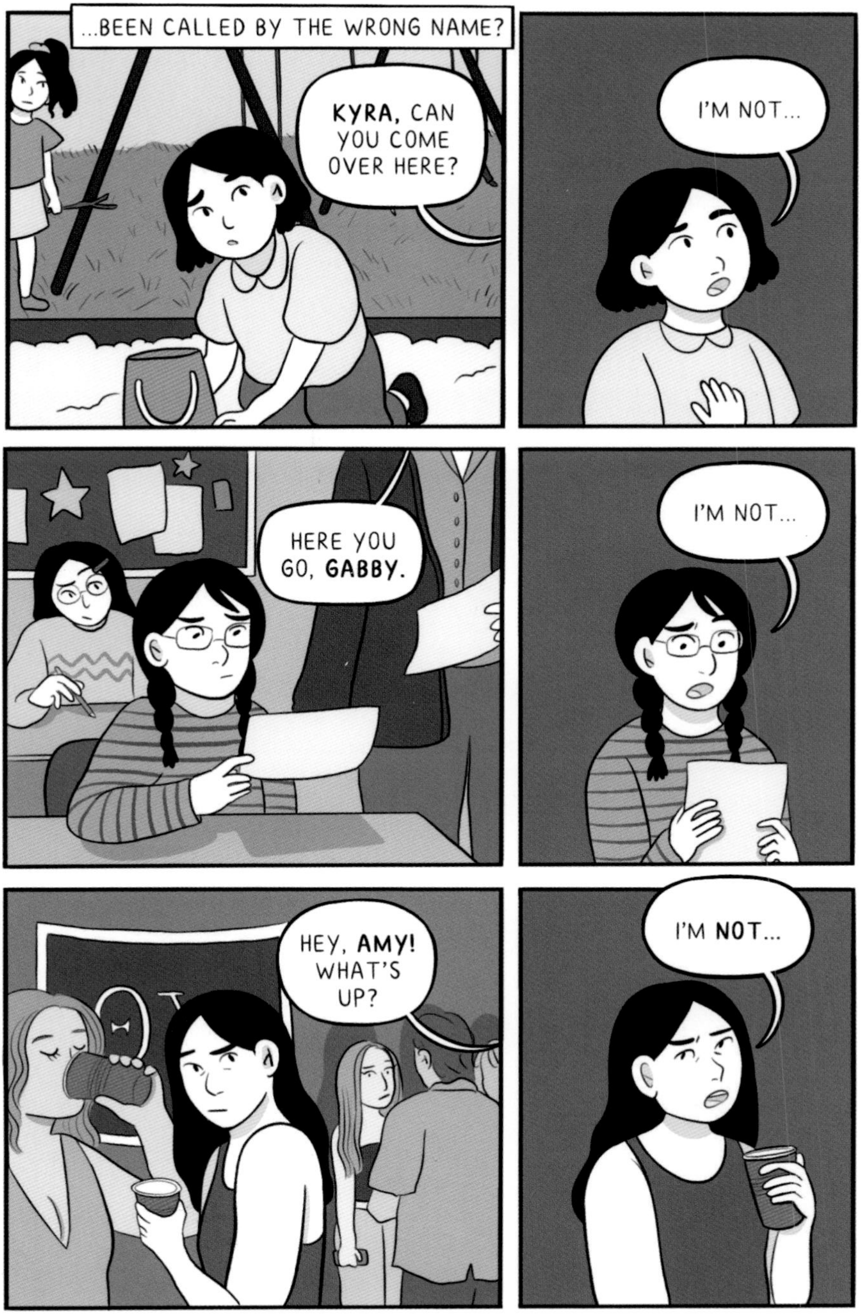
...BEEN CALLED BY THE WRONG NAME?
KYRA, CAN YOU COME OVER HERE?
I'M NOT...
HERE YOU GO, **GABBY.**
I'M NOT...
HEY, **AMY!** WHAT'S UP?
I'M **NOT**...

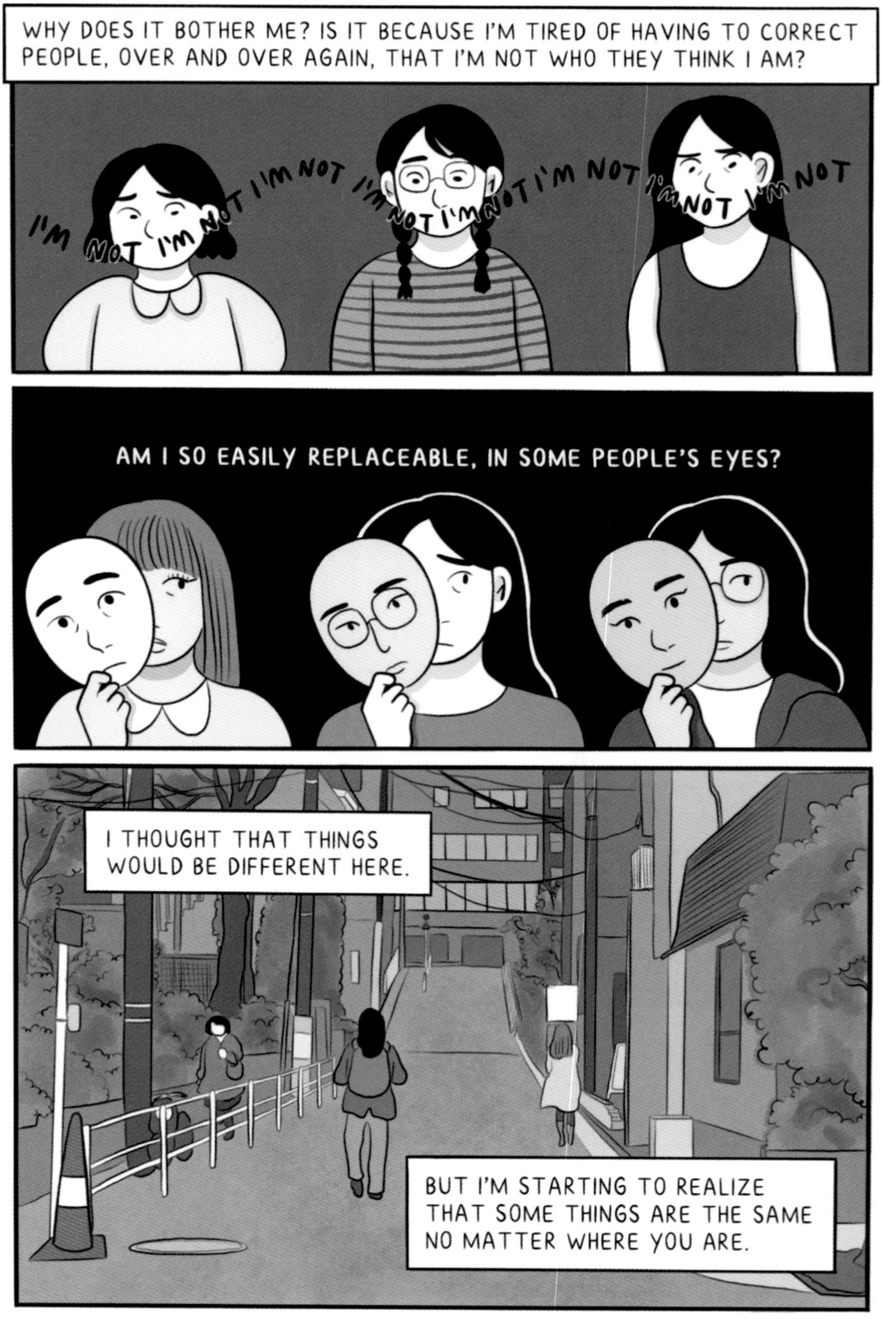
WHY DOES IT BOTHER ME? IS IT BECAUSE I'M TIRED OF HAVING TO CORRECT PEOPLE, OVER AND OVER AGAIN, THAT I'M NOT WHO THEY THINK I AM?
I'M NOT I'M NOT I'M NOT
I'M NOT I'M NOT I'M NOT
I'M NOT I'M NOT I'M NOT
AM I SO EASILY REPLACEABLE, IN SOME PEOPLE'S EYES?
I THOUGHT THAT THINGS WOULD BE DIFFERENT HERE.
BUT I'M STARTING TO REALIZE THAT SOME THINGS ARE THE SAME NO MATTER WHERE YOU ARE.

Exercise 2

A 鈴木さん、いまどこに（いる／います）

B いま喫茶店に_____。

A 言吾さんは沖縄にいる（の／んですか）

B 三者さんは沖縄には_____

A 東京は虫が多い（の／んですか）？

B 東京には虫があまり_____

A 学校に日本語の辞書は（ある／ありま

B （うん／はい）、学校の図書館に___

A 家にトイレが何個（ある／ありますか

GOOD NIGHT, YOU GUYS!

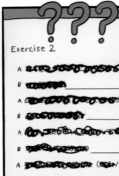

Exercise 2

UUUGHH

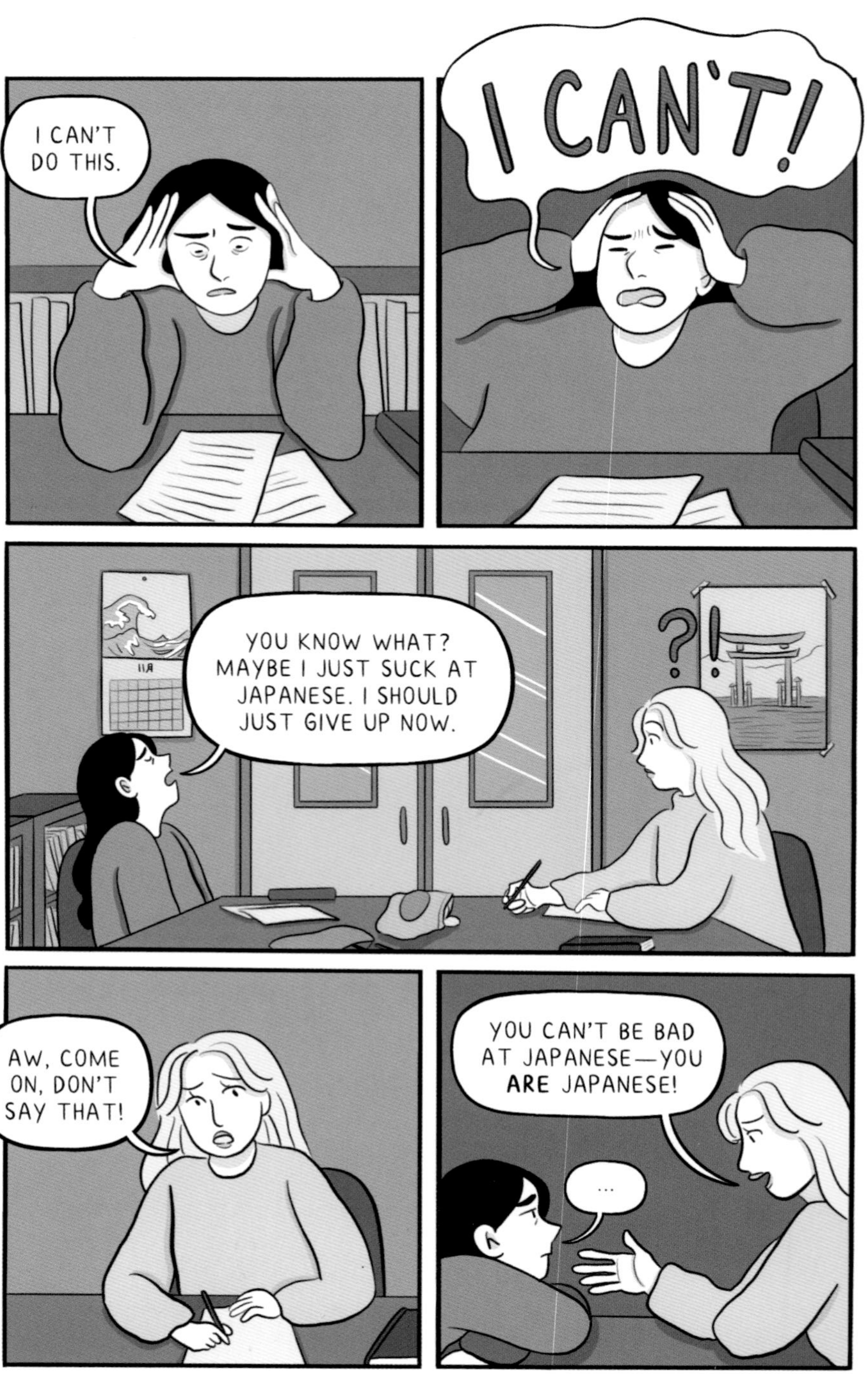
I CAN'T DO THIS.
I CAN'T!
YOU KNOW WHAT? MAYBE I JUST SUCK AT JAPANESE. I SHOULD JUST GIVE UP NOW.
?!
AW, COME ON, DON'T SAY THAT!
YOU CAN'T BE BAD AT JAPANESE—YOU **ARE** JAPANESE!
...

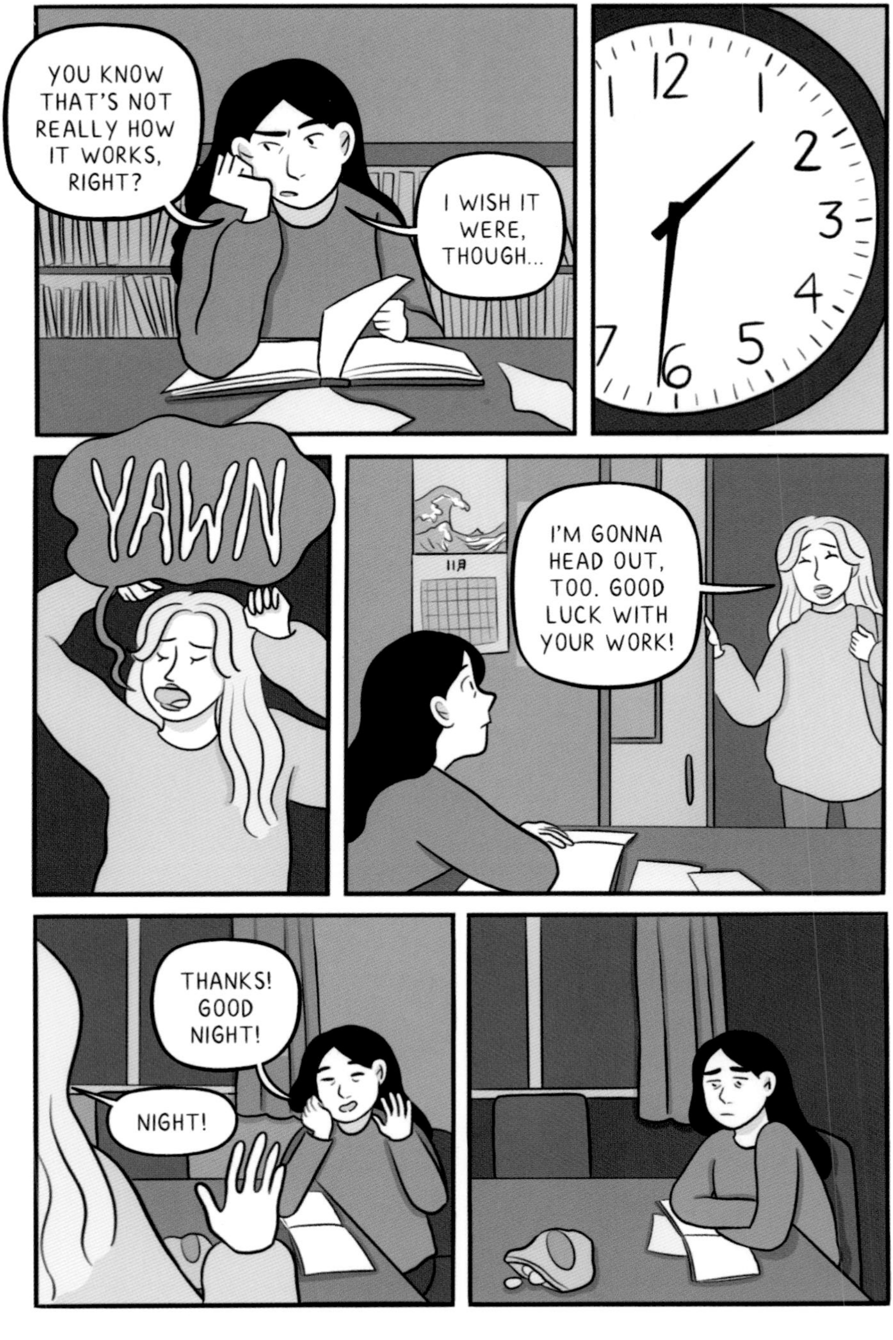
YOU KNOW THAT'S NOT REALLY HOW IT WORKS, RIGHT?
I WISH IT WERE, THOUGH...
YAWN
I'M GONNA HEAD OUT, TOO. GOOD LUCK WITH YOUR WORK!
THANKS! GOOD NIGHT!
NIGHT!

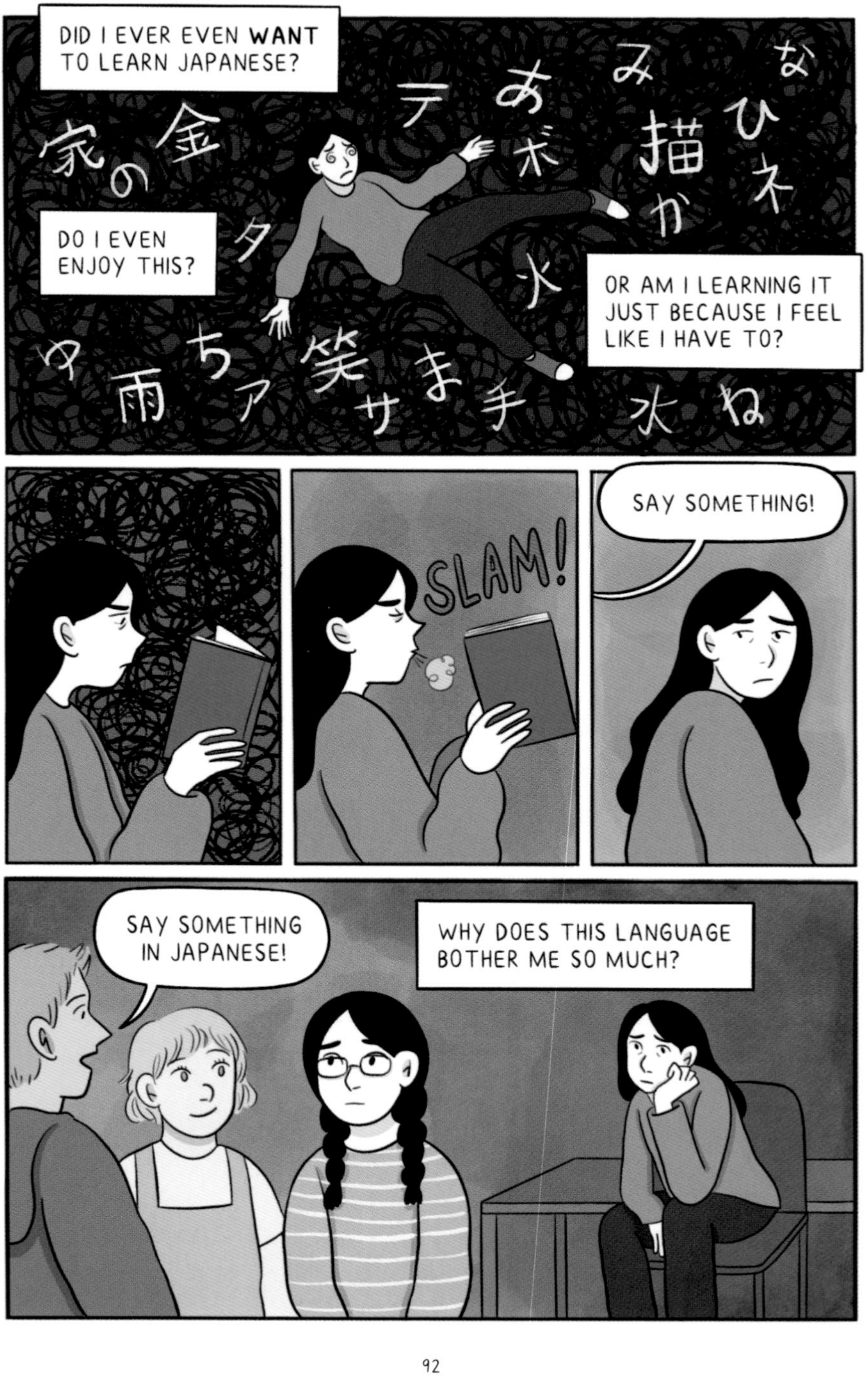
DID I EVER EVEN **WANT** TO LEARN JAPANESE?
家の金テあみな描ひネボタかゆ雨ちア笑サまて火水ね
DO I EVEN ENJOY THIS?
OR AM I LEARNING IT JUST BECAUSE I FEEL LIKE I HAVE TO?
SLAM!
SAY SOMETHING!
SAY SOMETHING IN JAPANESE!
WHY DOES THIS LANGUAGE BOTHER ME SO MUCH?

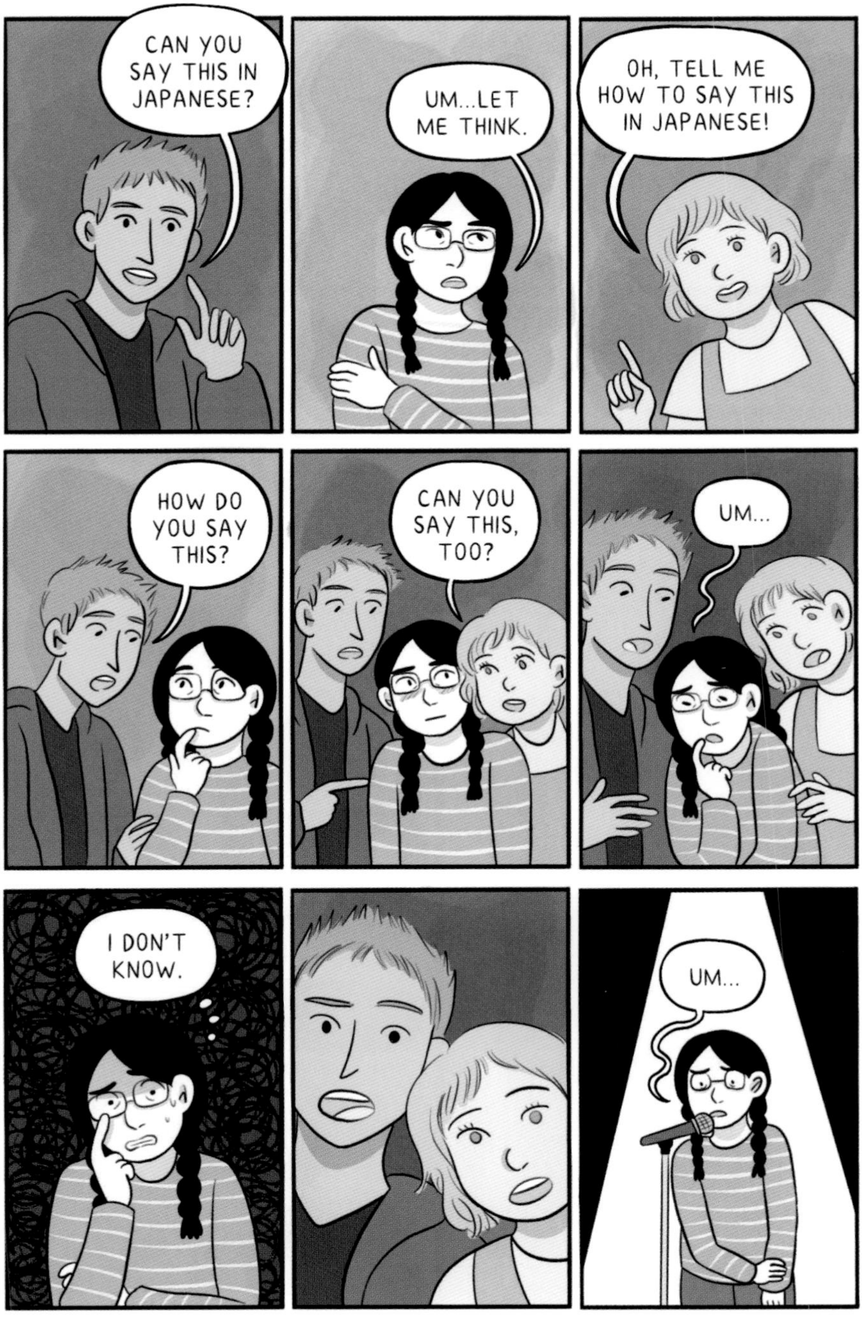
CAN YOU SAY THIS IN JAPANESE?
UM...LET ME THINK.
OH, TELL ME HOW TO SAY THIS IN JAPANESE!
HOW DO YOU SAY THIS?
CAN YOU SAY THIS, TOO?
UM...
I DON'T KNOW.
UM...

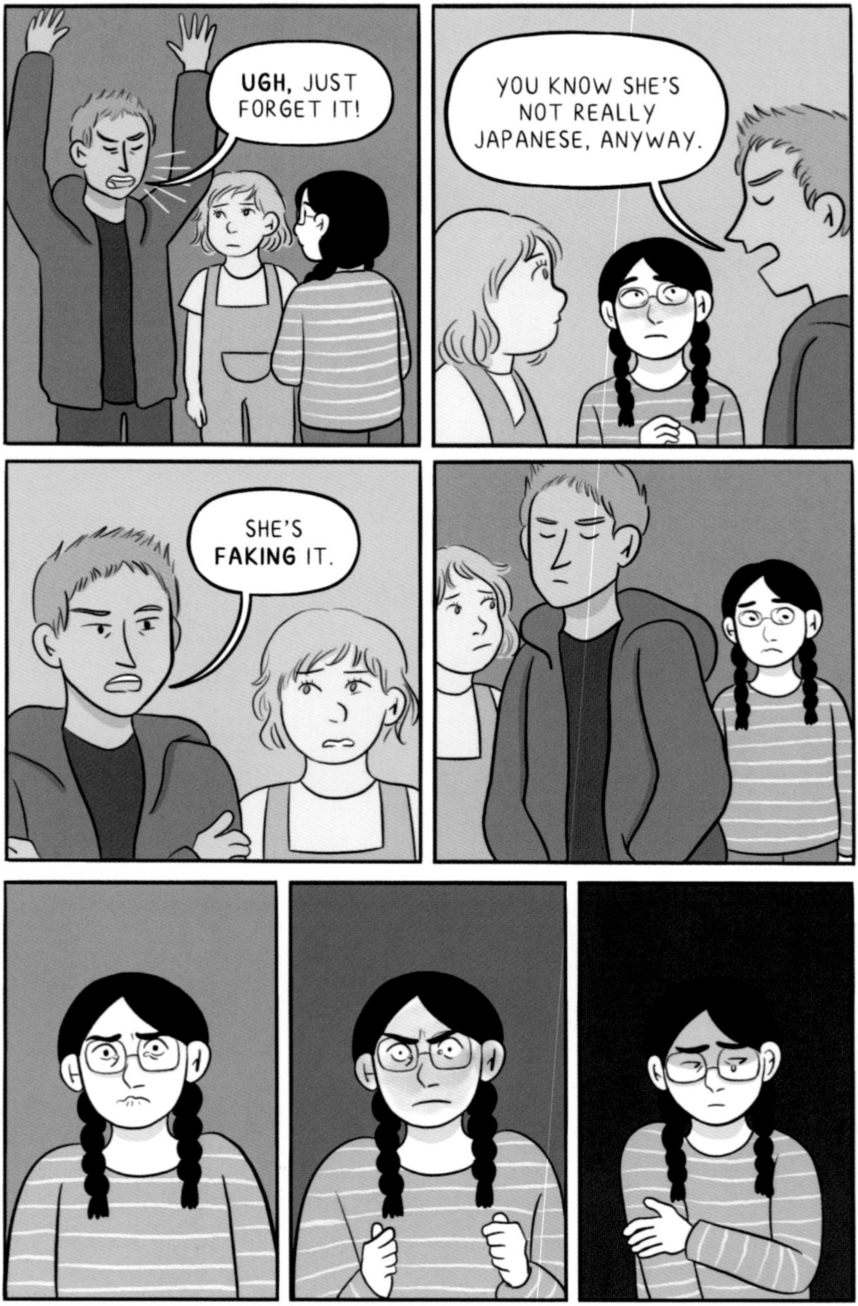
UGH, JUST FORGET IT!
YOU KNOW SHE'S NOT REALLY JAPANESE, ANYWAY.
SHE'S FAKING IT.

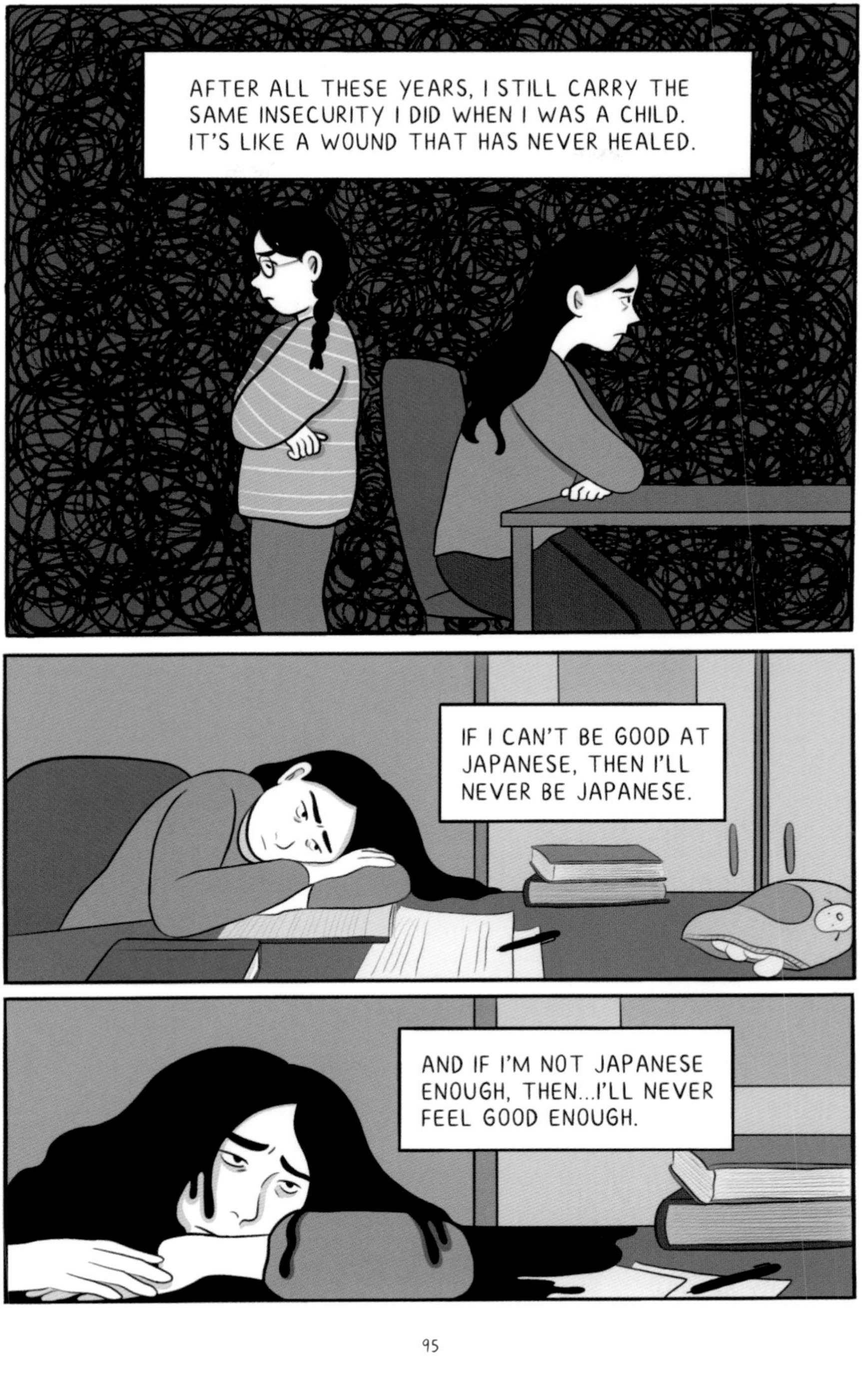
AFTER ALL THESE YEARS, I STILL CARRY THE SAME INSECURITY I DID WHEN I WAS A CHILD. IT'S LIKE A WOUND THAT HAS NEVER HEALED.
IF I CAN'T BE GOOD AT JAPANESE, THEN I'LL NEVER BE JAPANESE.
AND IF I'M NOT JAPANESE ENOUGH, THEN...I'LL NEVER FEEL GOOD ENOUGH.

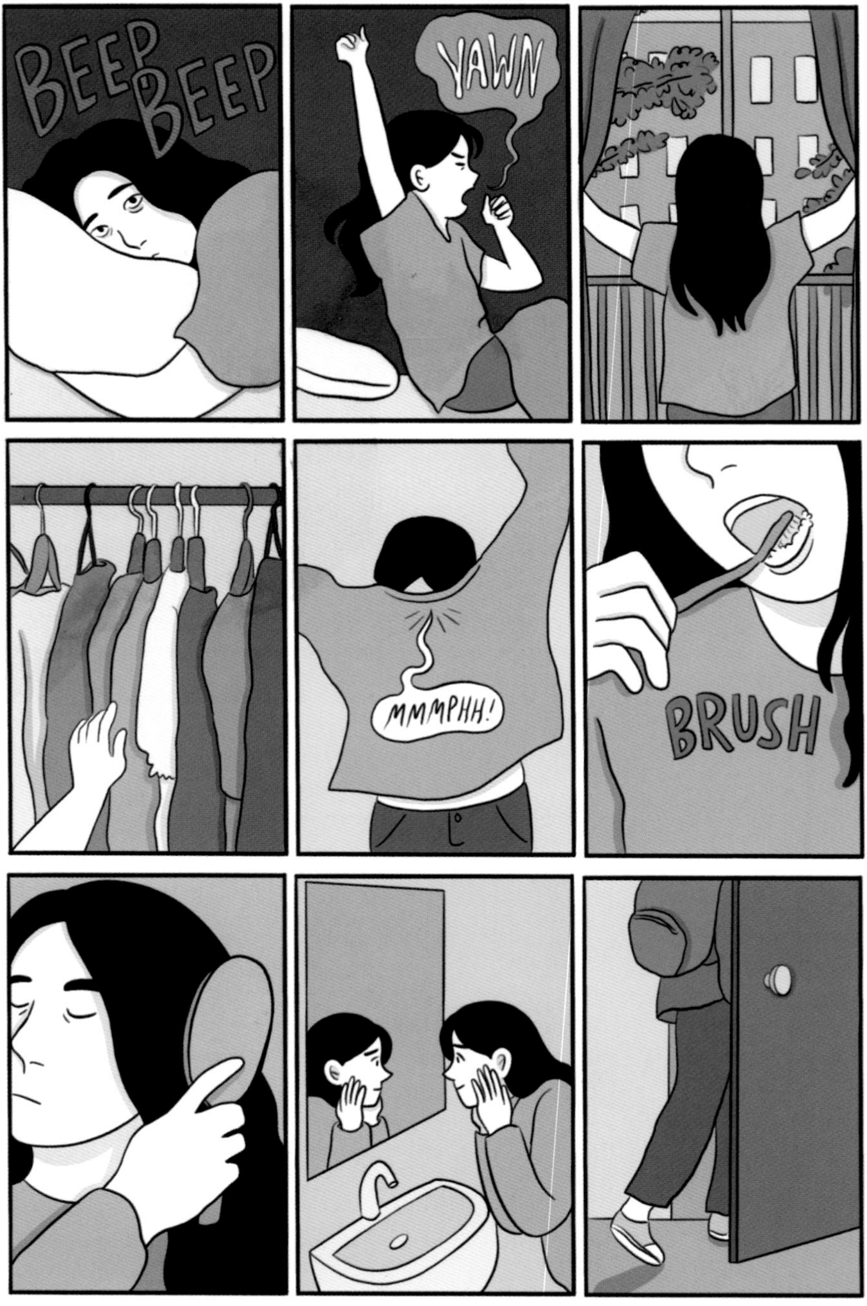
BEEP BEEP
YAWN
MMMPHH!
BRUSH

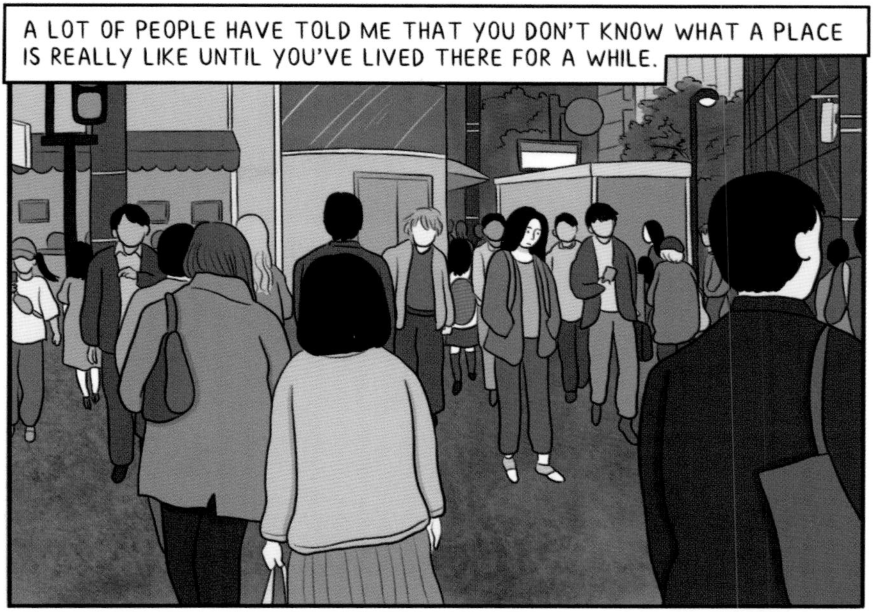
A LOT OF PEOPLE HAVE TOLD ME THAT YOU DON'T KNOW WHAT A PLACE IS REALLY LIKE UNTIL YOU'VE LIVED THERE FOR A WHILE.

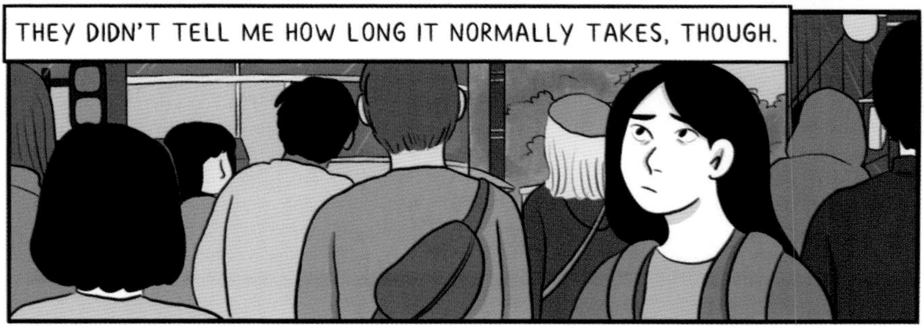
THEY DIDN'T TELL ME HOW LONG IT NORMALLY TAKES, THOUGH.

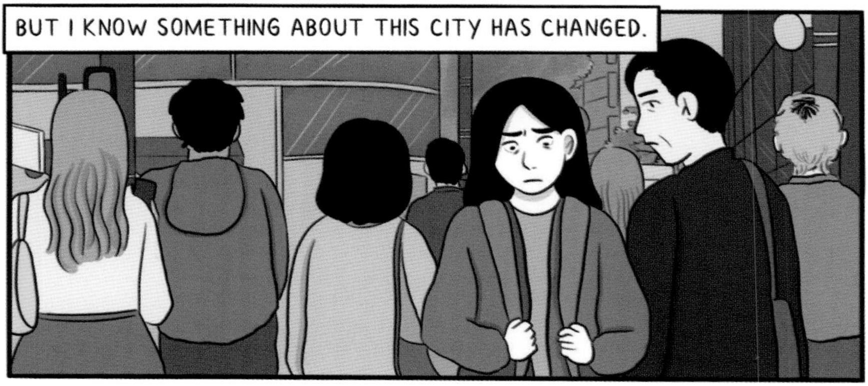
BUT I KNOW SOMETHING ABOUT THIS CITY HAS CHANGED.

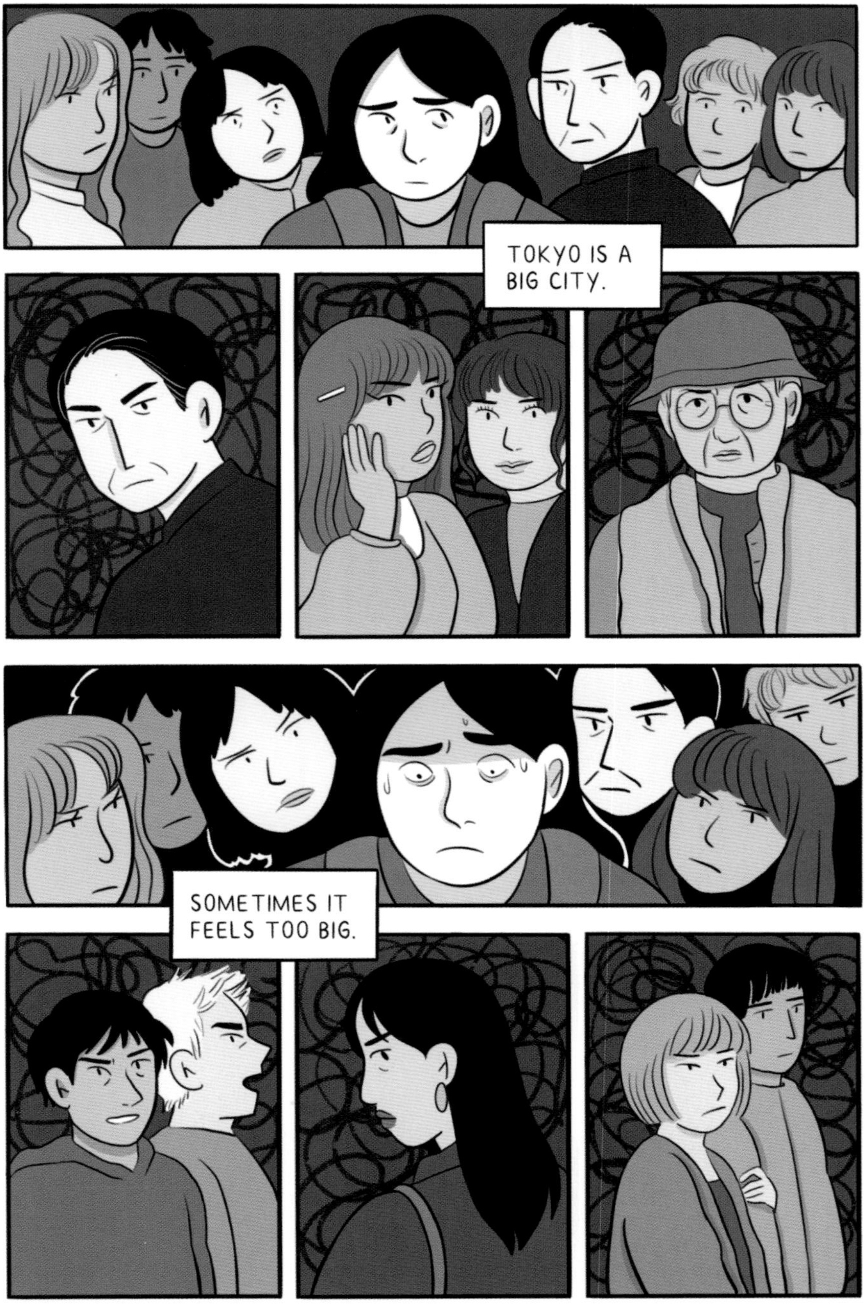
TOKYO IS A BIG CITY.
SOMETIMES IT FEELS TOO BIG.

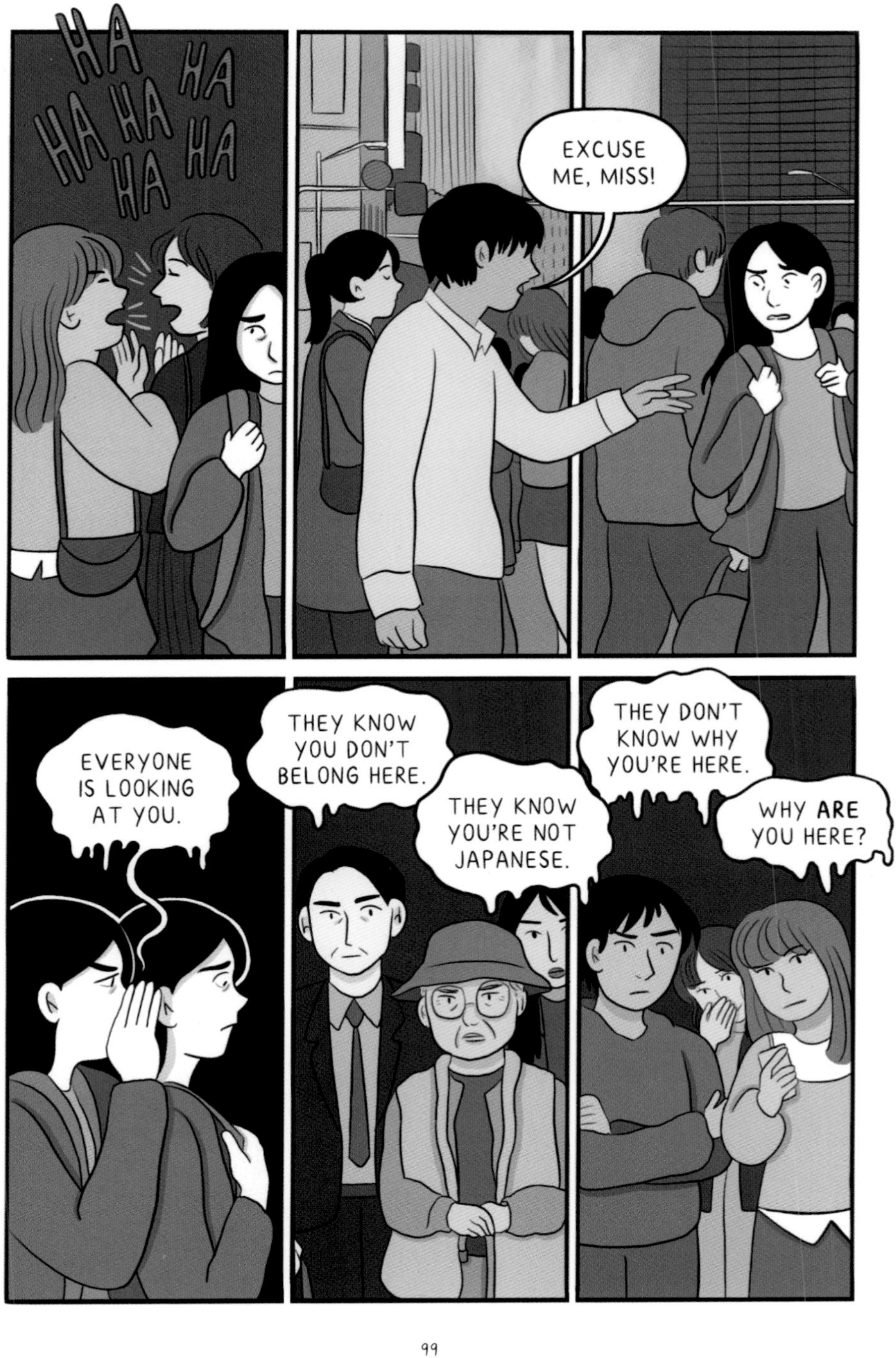
HA HA HA HA HA HA HA
EXCUSE ME, MISS!
EVERYONE IS LOOKING AT YOU.
THEY KNOW YOU DON'T BELONG HERE.
THEY KNOW YOU'RE NOT JAPANESE.
THEY DON'T KNOW WHY YOU'RE HERE.
WHY **ARE** YOU HERE?

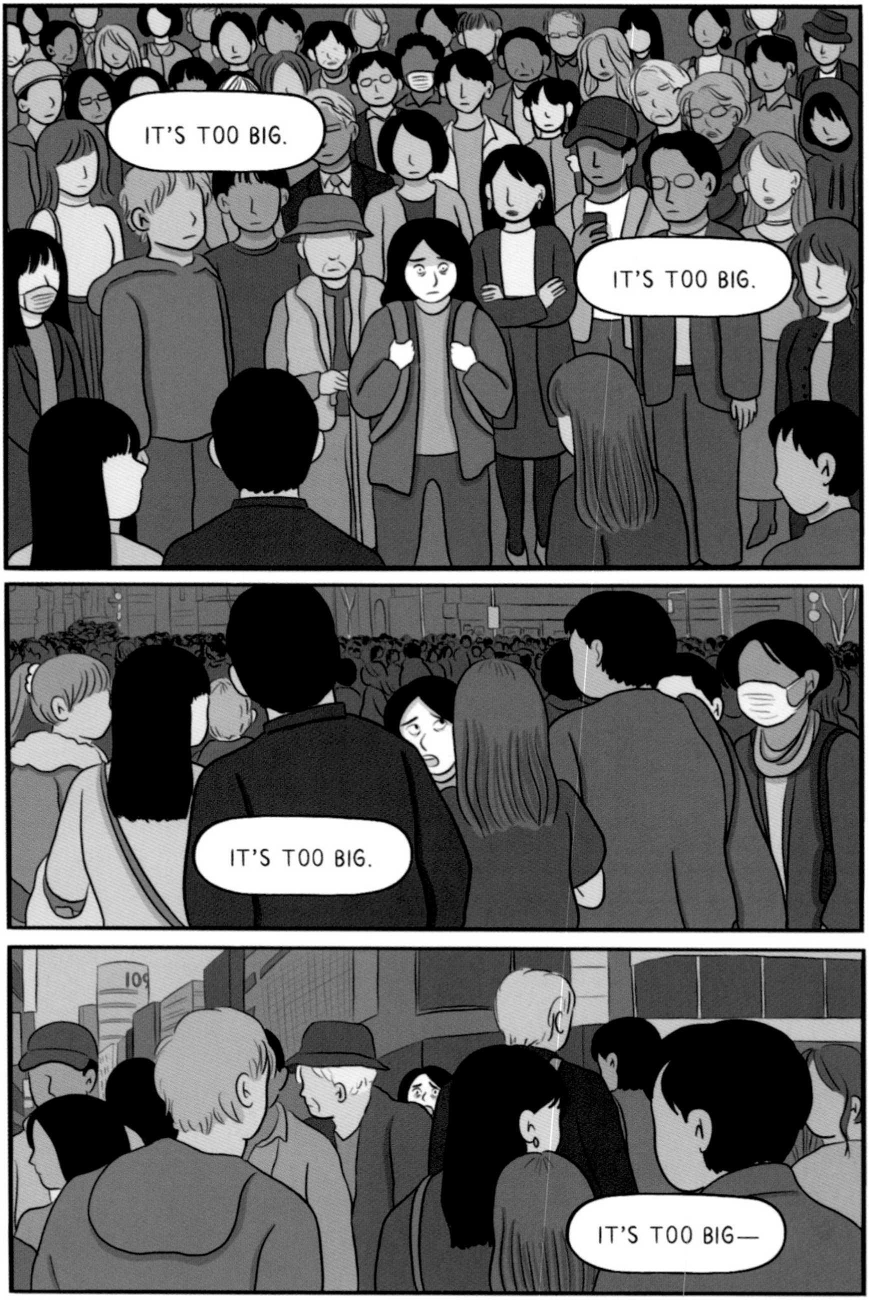
IT'S TOO BIG.
IT'S TOO BIG.
IT'S TOO BIG.
IT'S TOO BIG—

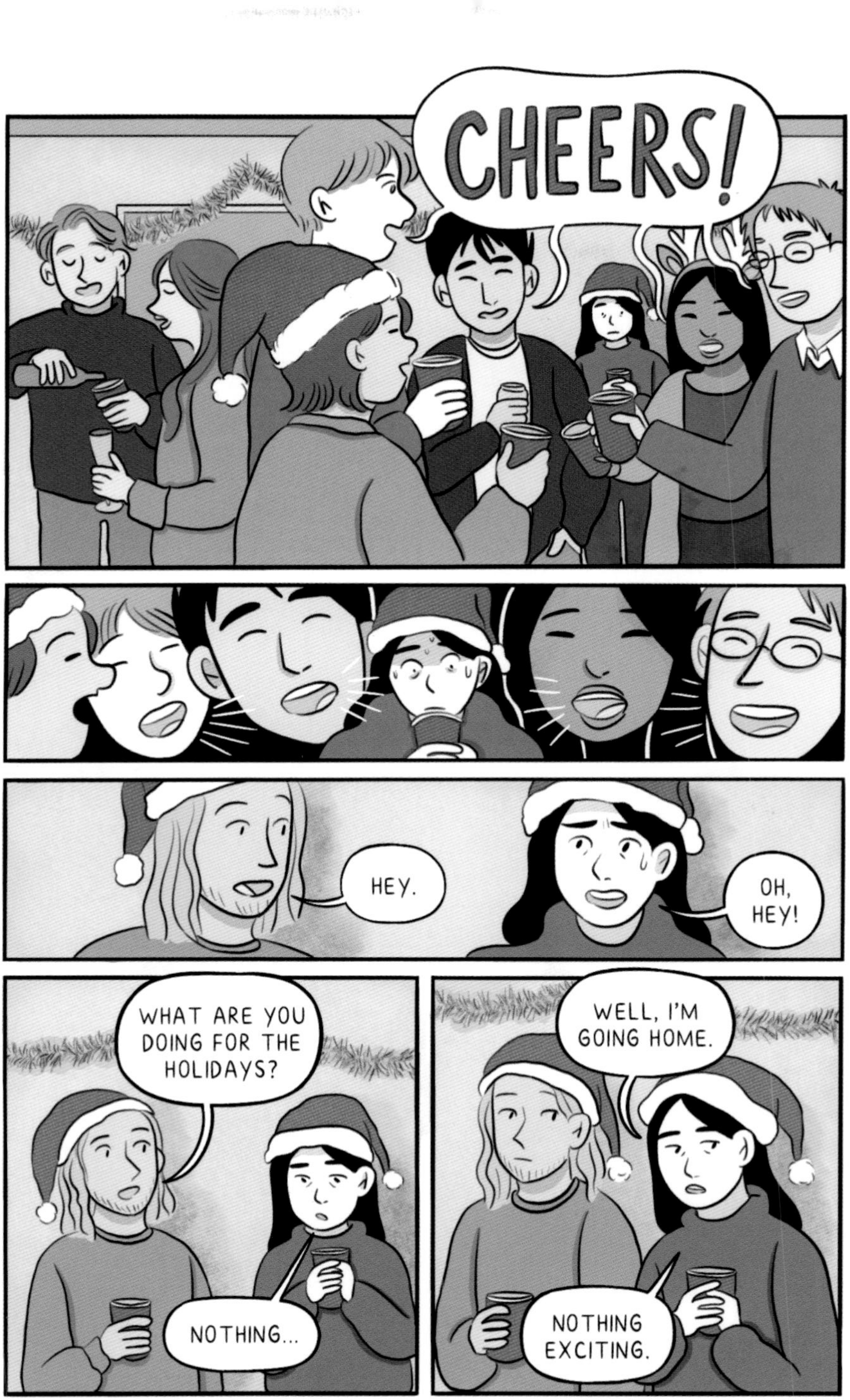
CHEERS!
HEY.
OH, HEY!
WHAT ARE YOU DOING FOR THE HOLIDAYS?
NOTHING...
WELL, I'M GOING HOME.
NOTHING EXCITING.

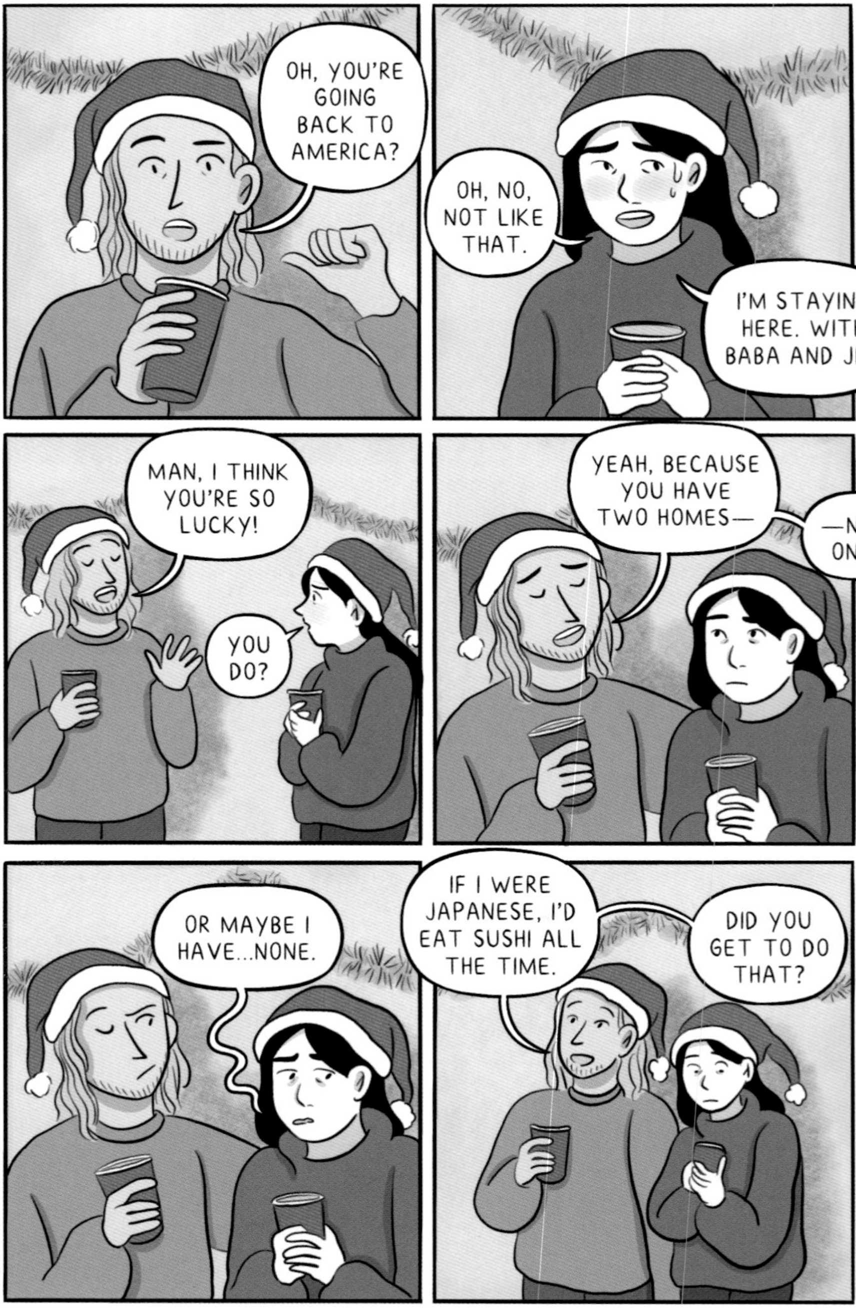
OH, YOU'RE GOING BACK TO AMERICA?
OH, NO, NOT LIKE THAT.
I'M STAYING HERE. WITH BABA AND JIJI.
MAN, I THINK YOU'RE SO LUCKY!
YOU DO?
YEAH, BECAUSE YOU HAVE TWO HOMES—
—NOT ONE!
OR MAYBE I HAVE...NONE.
IF I WERE JAPANESE, I'D EAT SUSHI ALL THE TIME.
DID YOU GET TO DO THAT?

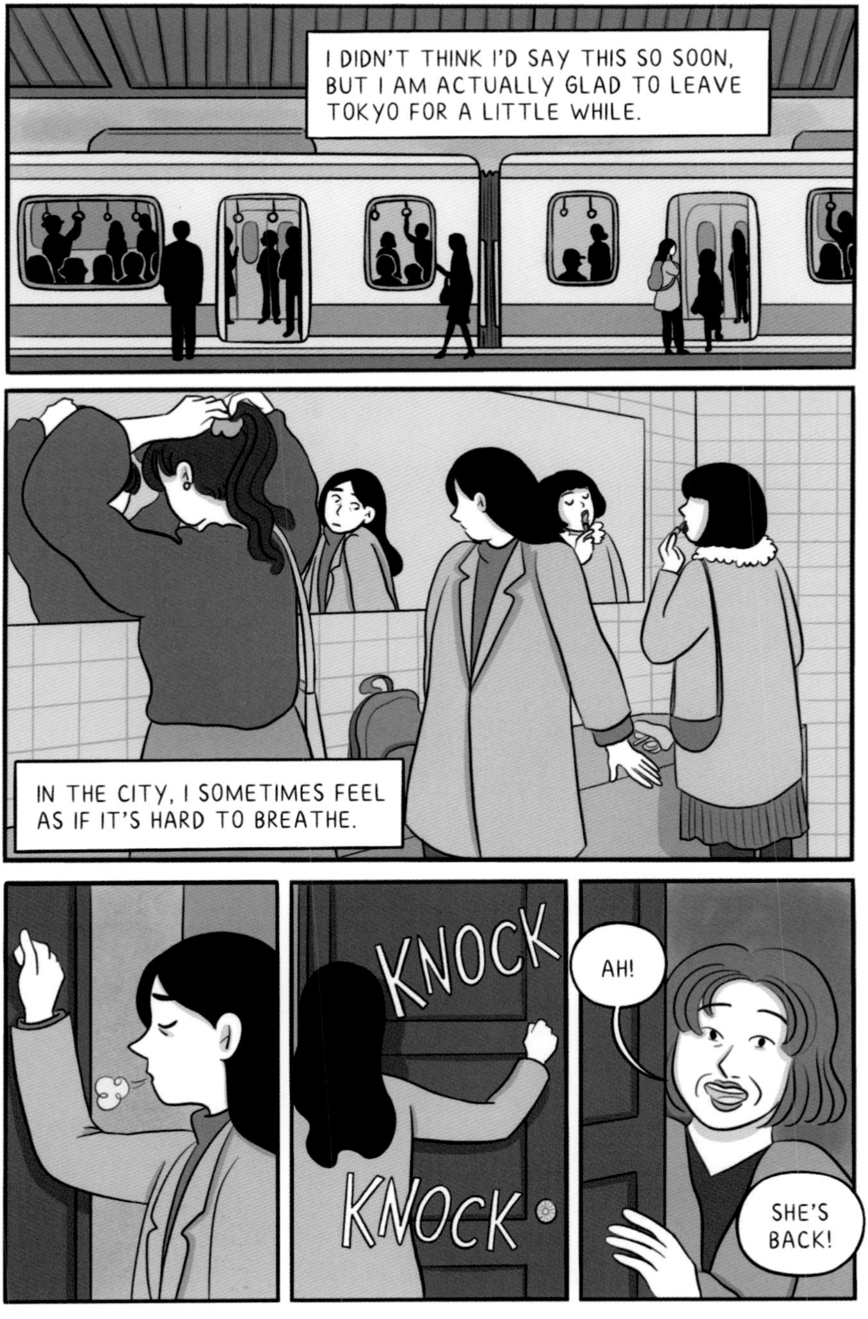
I DIDN'T THINK I'D SAY THIS SO SOON, BUT I AM ACTUALLY GLAD TO LEAVE TOKYO FOR A LITTLE WHILE.
IN THE CITY, I SOMETIMES FEEL AS IF IT'S HARD TO BREATHE.
KNOCK
KNOCK
AH!
SHE'S BACK!

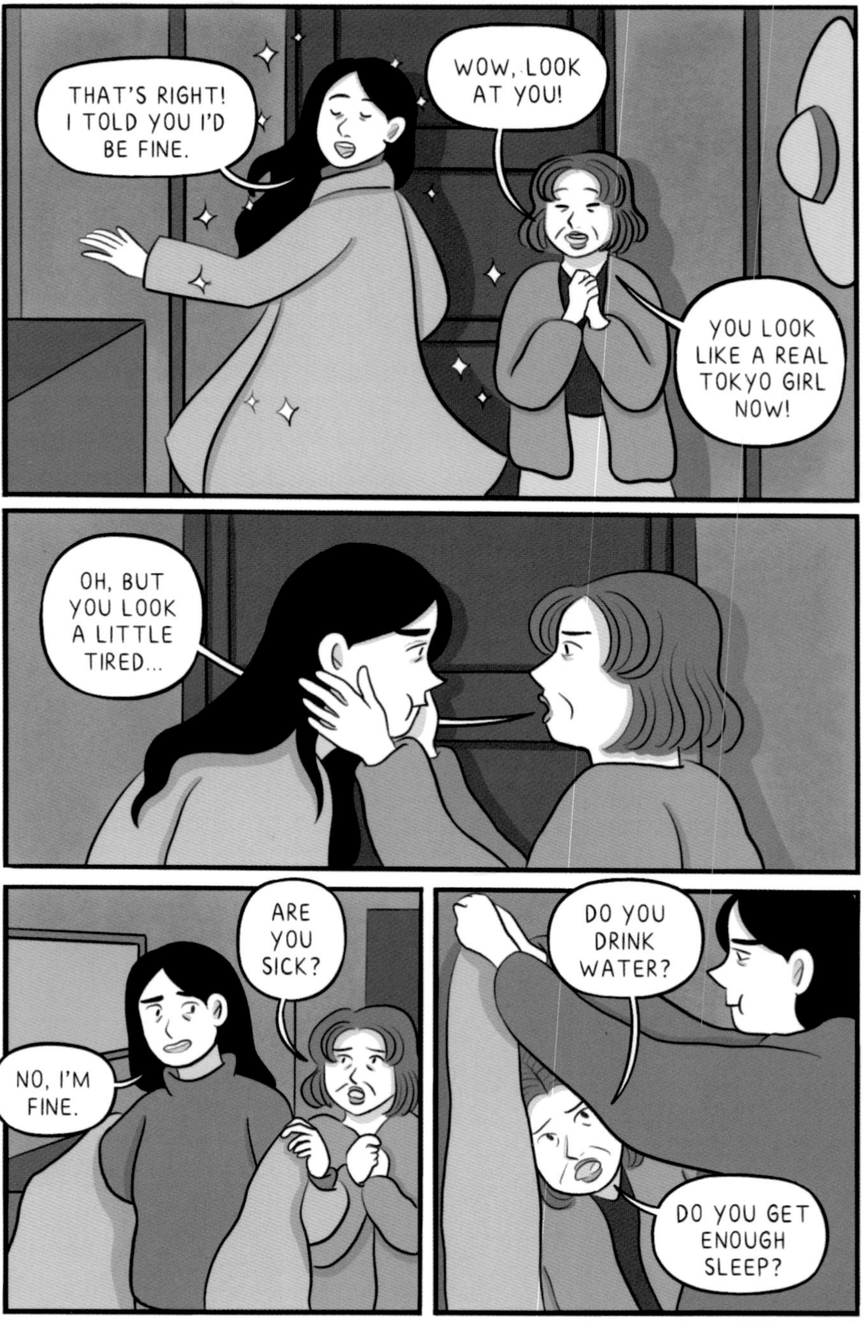
THAT'S RIGHT! I TOLD YOU I'D BE FINE.
WOW, LOOK AT YOU!
YOU LOOK LIKE A REAL TOKYO GIRL NOW!
OH, BUT YOU LOOK A LITTLE TIRED...
ARE YOU SICK?
NO, I'M FINE.
DO YOU DRINK WATER?
DO YOU GET ENOUGH SLEEP?

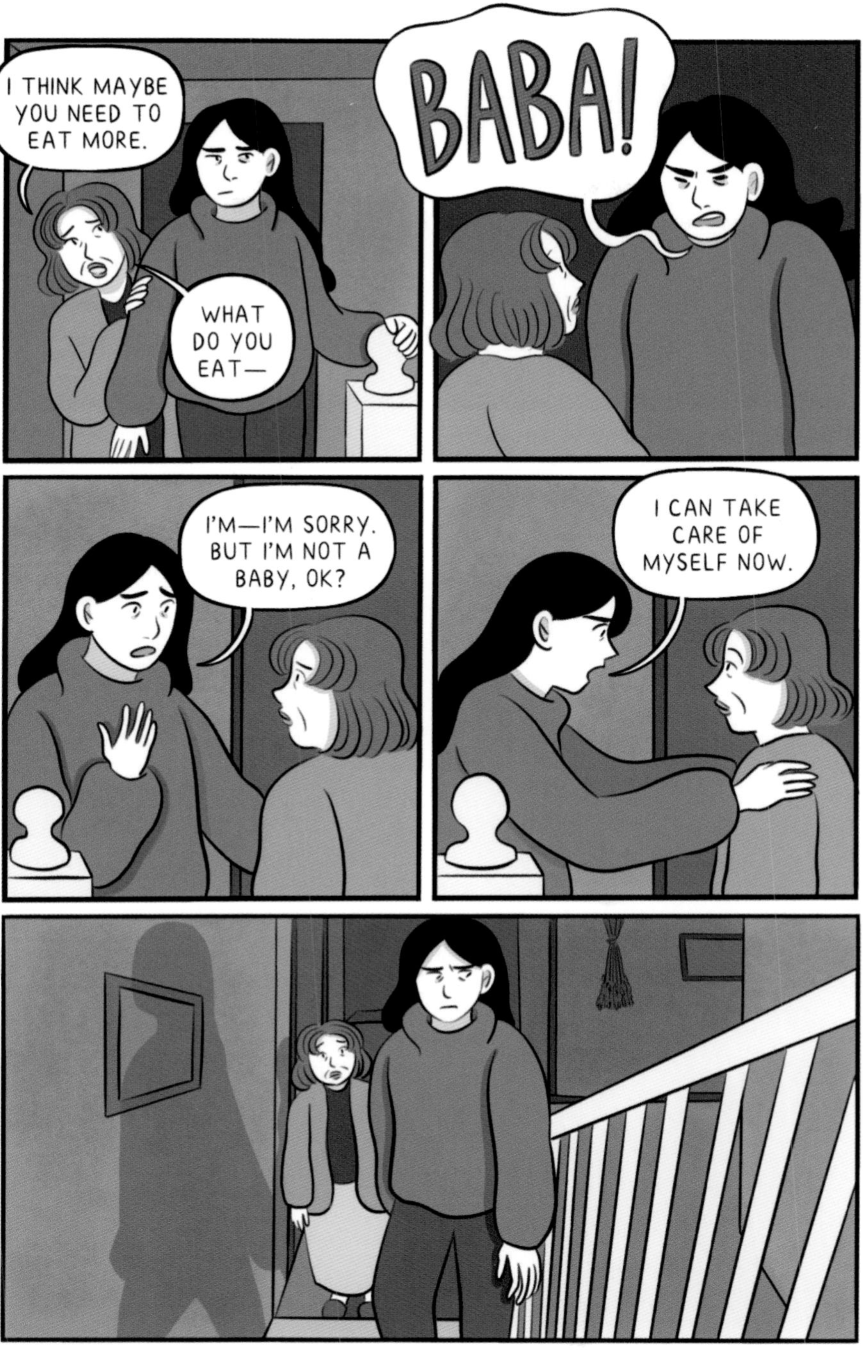
I THINK MAYBE YOU NEED TO EAT MORE.
WHAT DO YOU EAT—
BABA!
I'M—I'M SORRY. BUT I'M NOT A BABY, OK?
I CAN TAKE CARE OF MYSELF NOW.

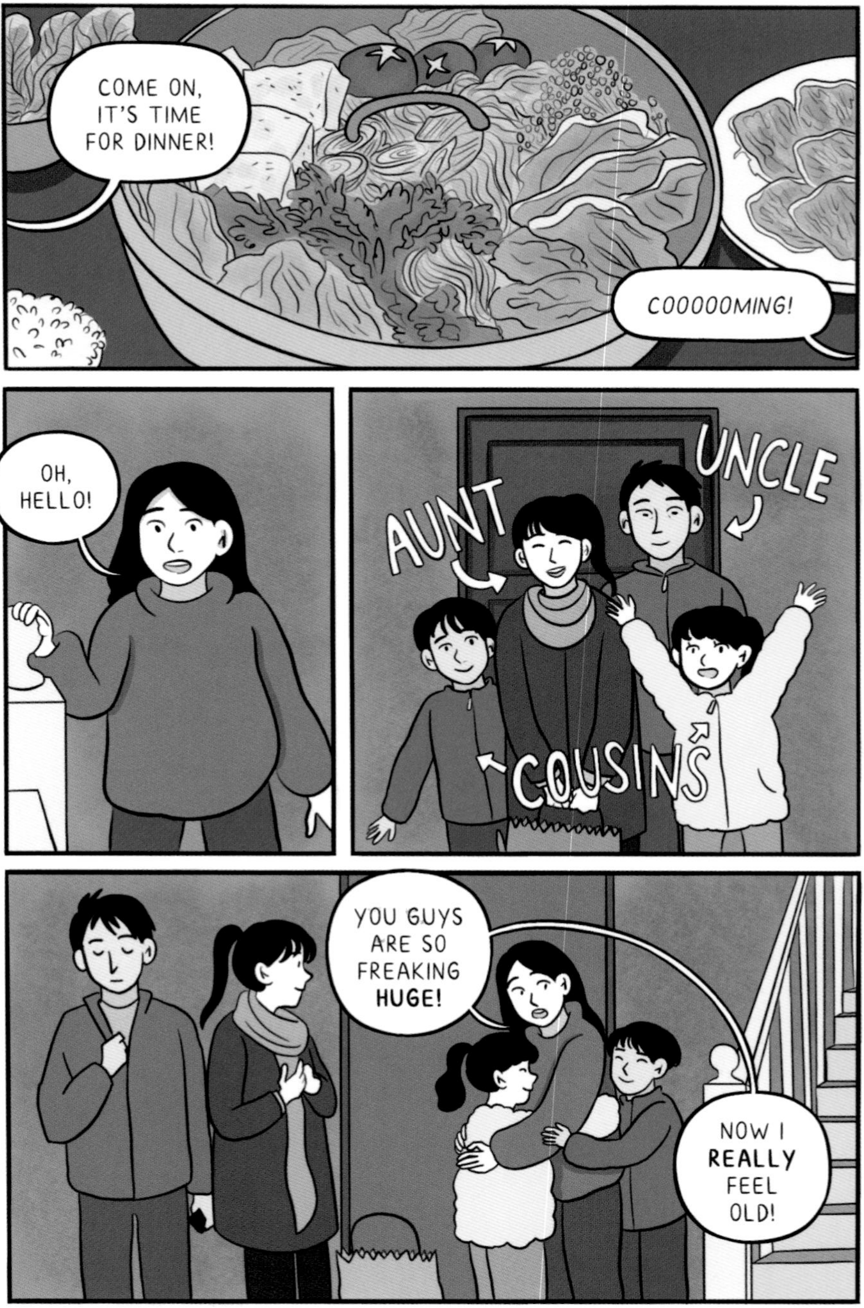
COME ON, IT'S TIME FOR DINNER!
COOOOOMING!
OH, HELLO!
AUNT
UNCLE
COUSINS
YOU GUYS ARE SO FREAKING **HUGE!**
NOW I **REALLY** FEEL OLD!

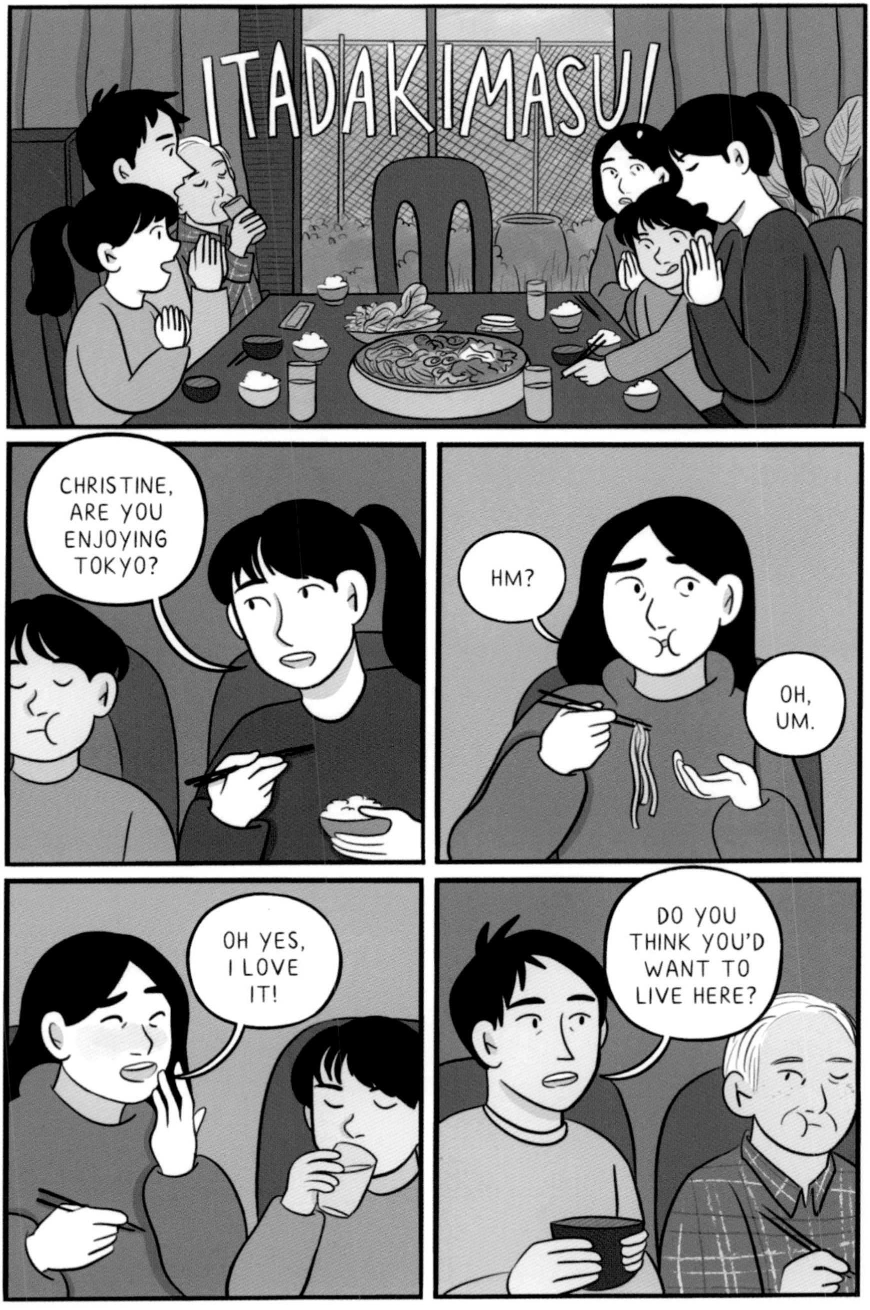
ITADAKIMASU!
CHRISTINE, ARE YOU ENJOYING TOKYO?
HM?
OH, UM.
OH YES, I LOVE IT!
DO YOU THINK YOU'D WANT TO LIVE HERE?

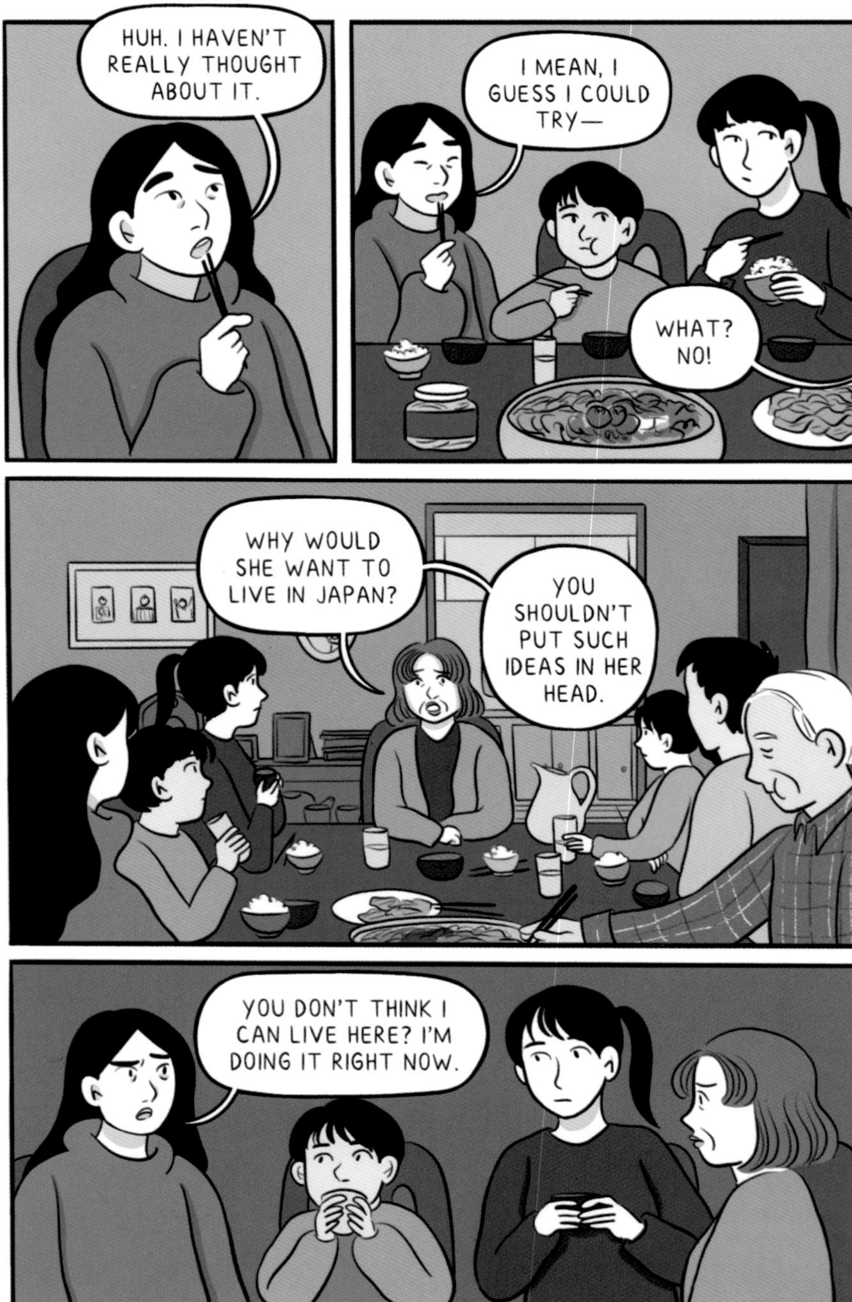
HUH. I HAVEN'T REALLY THOUGHT ABOUT IT.
I MEAN, I GUESS I COULD TRY—
WHAT? NO!
WHY WOULD SHE WANT TO LIVE IN JAPAN?
YOU SHOULDN'T PUT SUCH IDEAS IN HER HEAD.
YOU DON'T THINK I CAN LIVE HERE? I'M DOING IT RIGHT NOW.

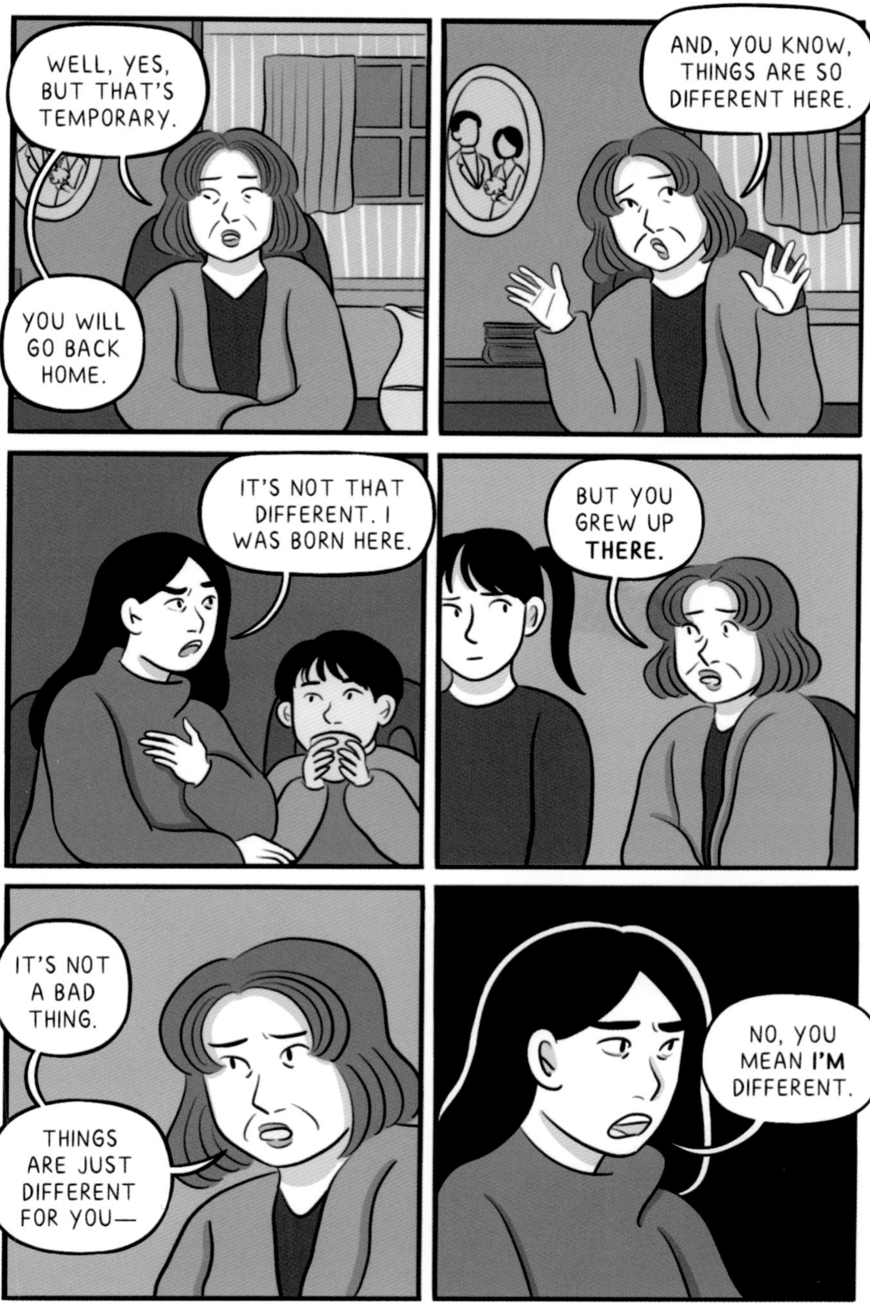
WELL, YES, BUT THAT'S TEMPORARY.
YOU WILL GO BACK HOME.
AND, YOU KNOW, THINGS ARE SO DIFFERENT HERE.
IT'S NOT THAT DIFFERENT. I WAS BORN HERE.
BUT YOU GREW UP **THERE.**
IT'S NOT A BAD THING.
THINGS ARE JUST DIFFERENT FOR YOU—
NO, YOU MEAN **I'M** DIFFERENT.

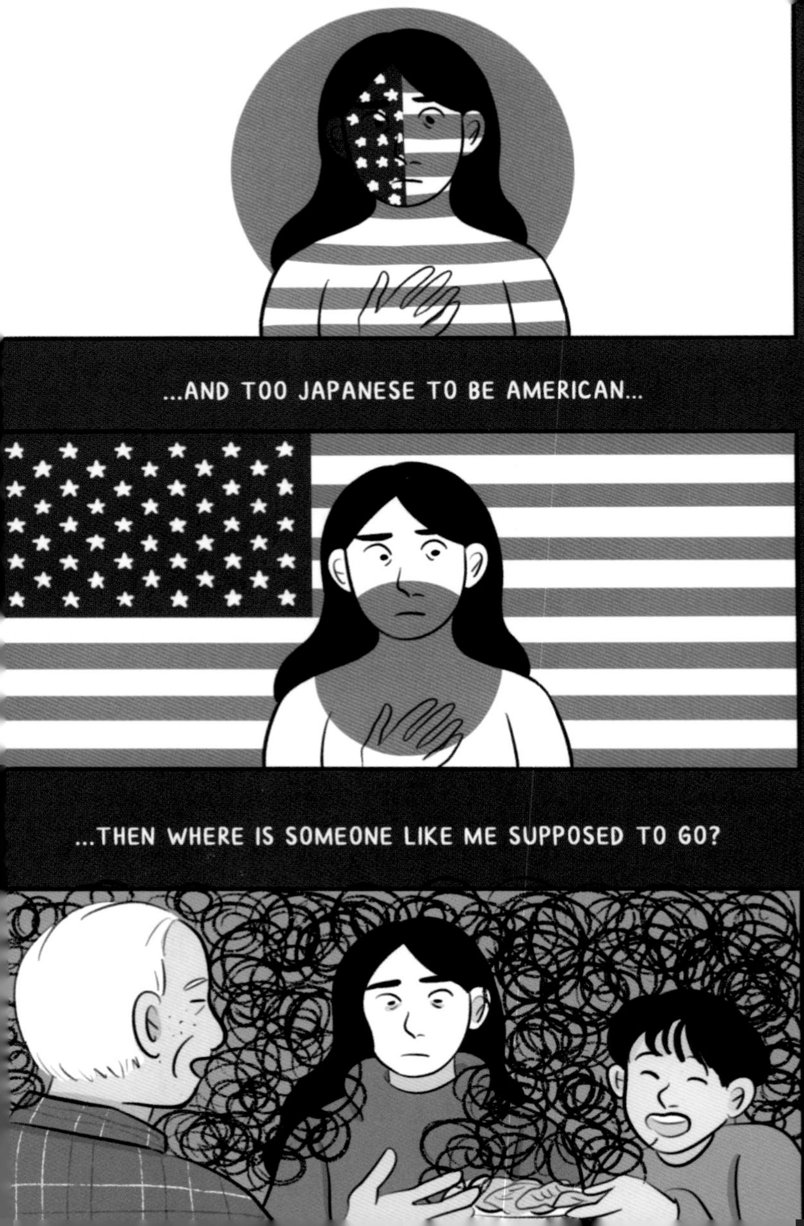
...AND TOO JAPANESE TO BE AMERICAN...
...THEN WHERE IS SOMEONE LIKE ME SUPPOSED TO GO?

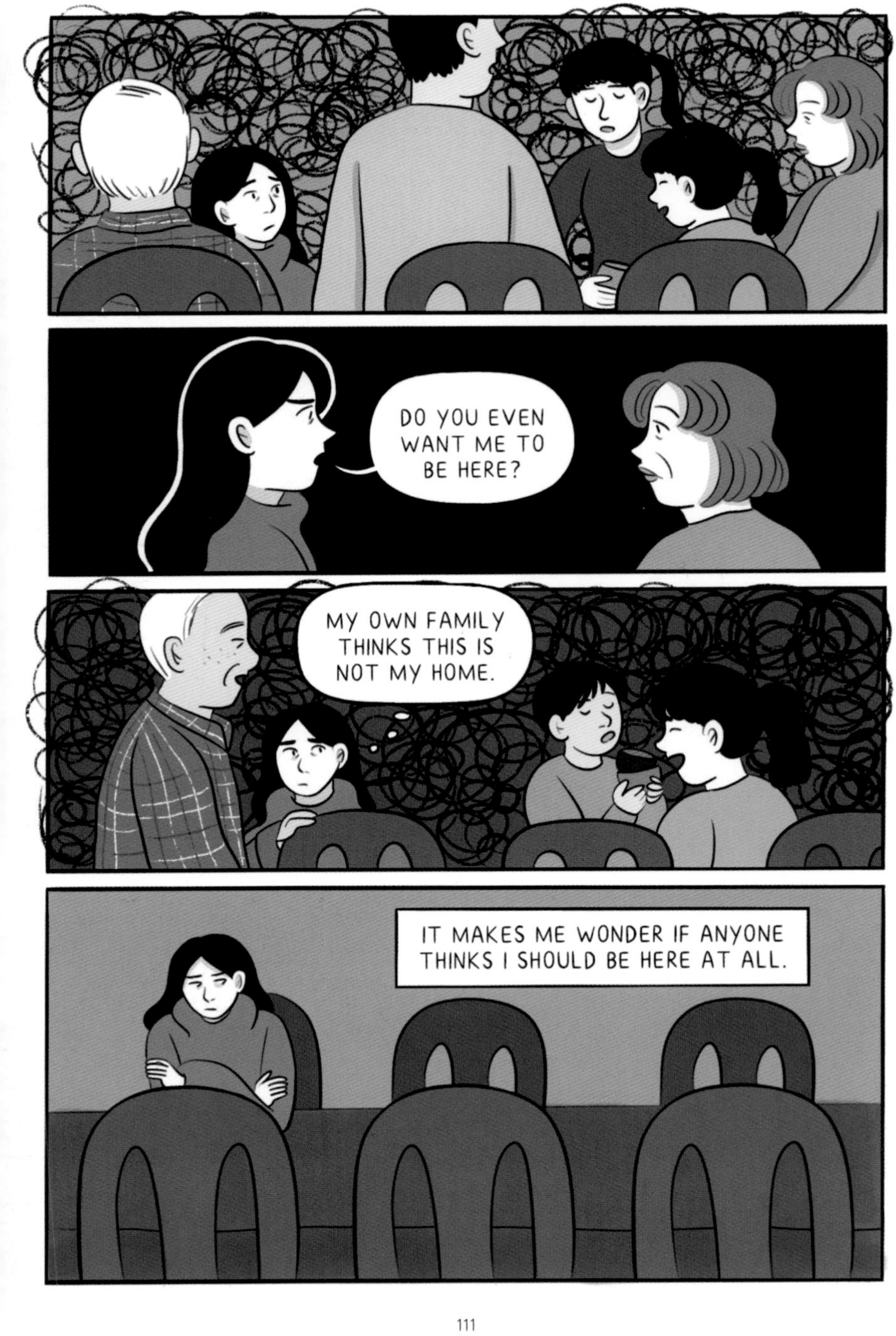
DO YOU EVEN WANT ME TO BE HERE?
MY OWN FAMILY THINKS THIS IS NOT MY HOME.
IT MAKES ME WONDER IF ANYONE THINKS I SHOULD BE HERE AT ALL.

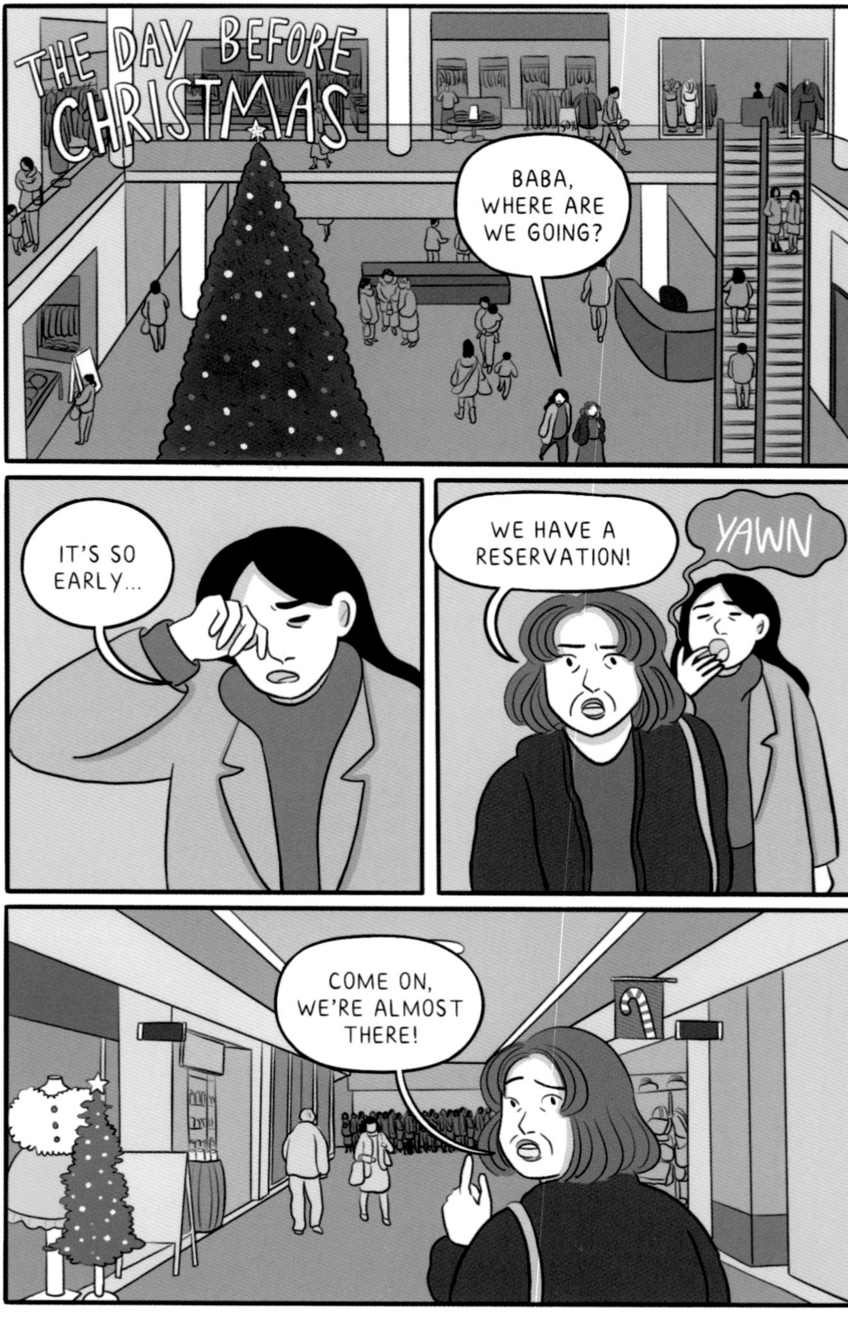
THE DAY BEFORE CHRISTMAS
BABA, WHERE ARE WE GOING?
IT'S SO EARLY...
WE HAVE A RESERVATION!
YAWN
COME ON, WE'RE ALMOST THERE!

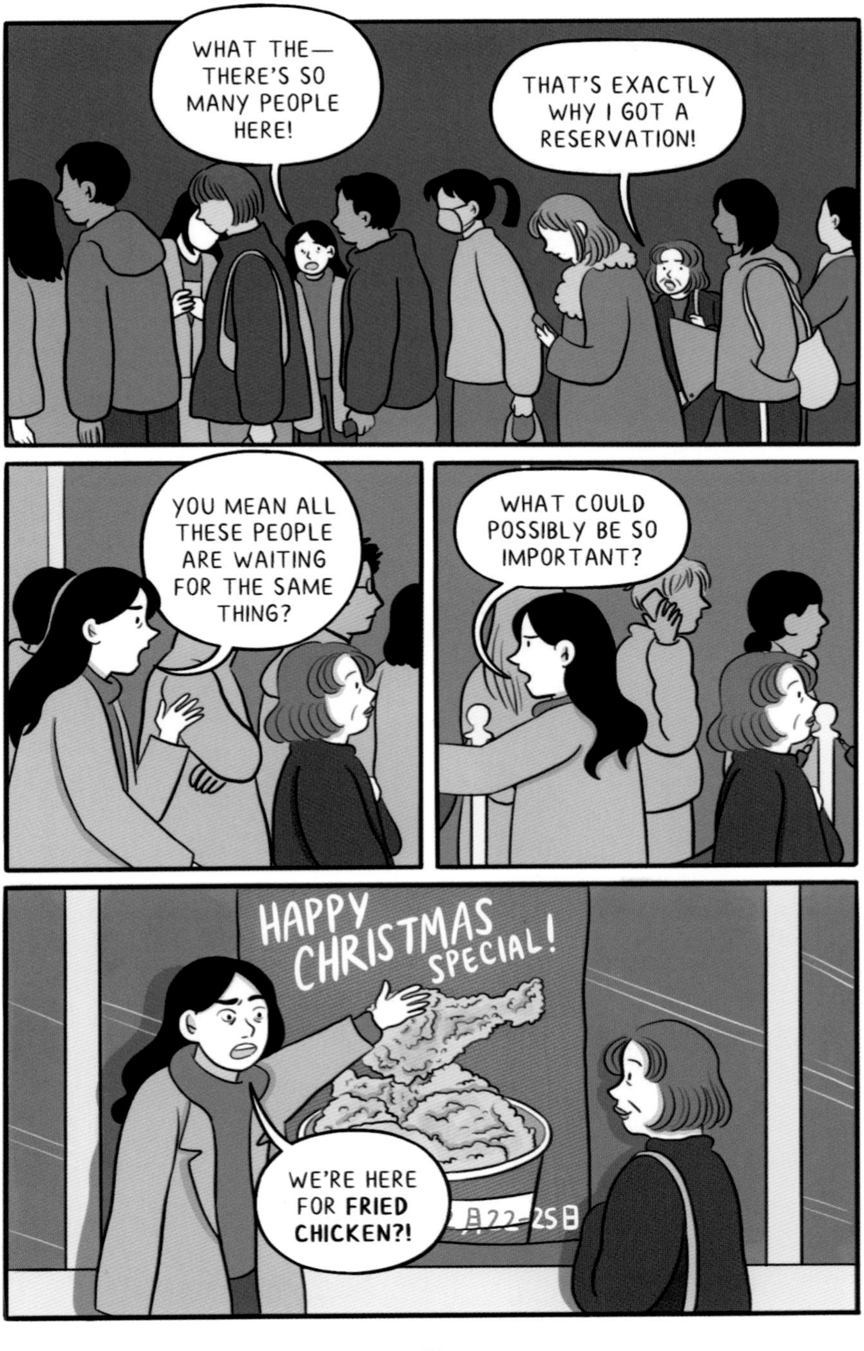
WHAT THE— THERE'S SO MANY PEOPLE HERE!
THAT'S EXACTLY WHY I GOT A RESERVATION!
YOU MEAN ALL THESE PEOPLE ARE WAITING FOR THE SAME THING?
WHAT COULD POSSIBLY BE SO IMPORTANT?
HAPPY CHRISTMAS SPECIAL!
WE'RE HERE FOR **FRIED CHICKEN?!**

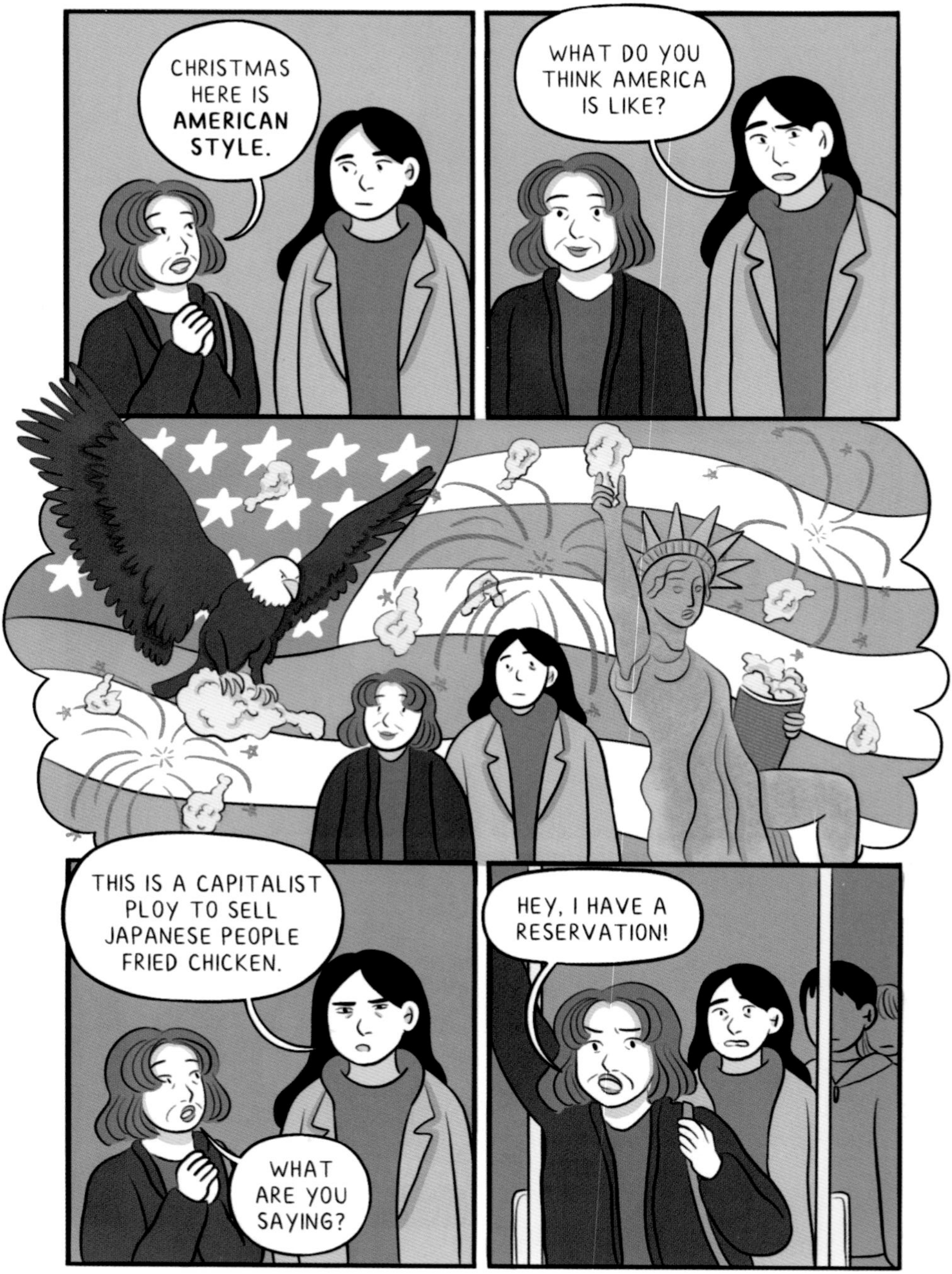
CHRISTMAS HERE IS **AMERICAN STYLE.**
WHAT DO YOU THINK AMERICA IS LIKE?
THIS IS A CAPITALIST PLOY TO SELL JAPANESE PEOPLE FRIED CHICKEN.
WHAT ARE YOU SAYING?
HEY, I HAVE A RESERVATION!

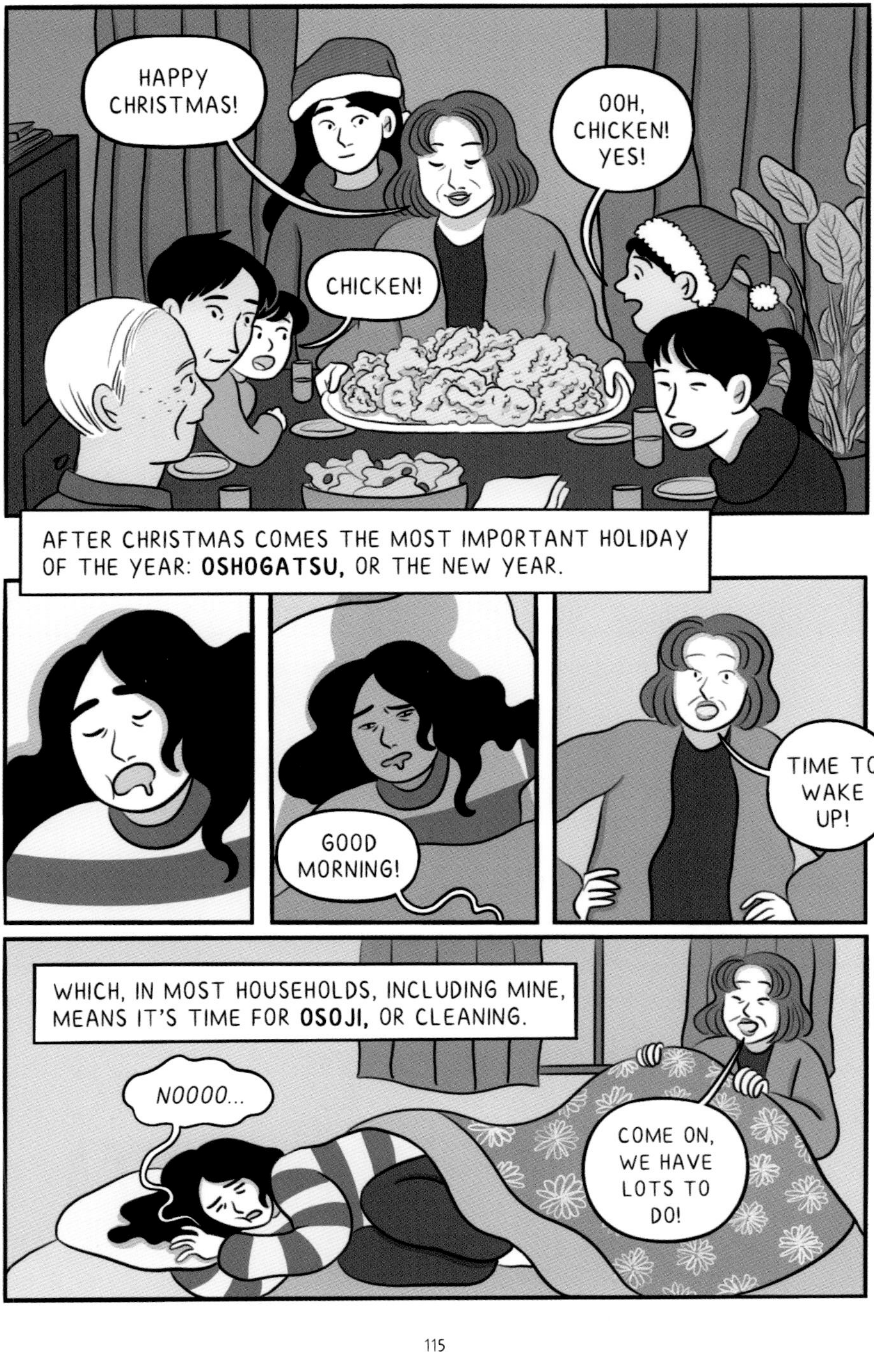
HAPPY CHRISTMAS!
OOH, CHICKEN! YES!
CHICKEN!
AFTER CHRISTMAS COMES THE MOST IMPORTANT HOLIDAY OF THE YEAR: **OSHOGATSU,** OR THE NEW YEAR.
GOOD MORNING!
TIME TO WAKE UP!
WHICH, IN MOST HOUSEHOLDS, INCLUDING MINE, MEANS IT'S TIME FOR **OSOJI,** OR CLEANING.
NOOOO...
COME ON, WE HAVE LOTS TO DO!

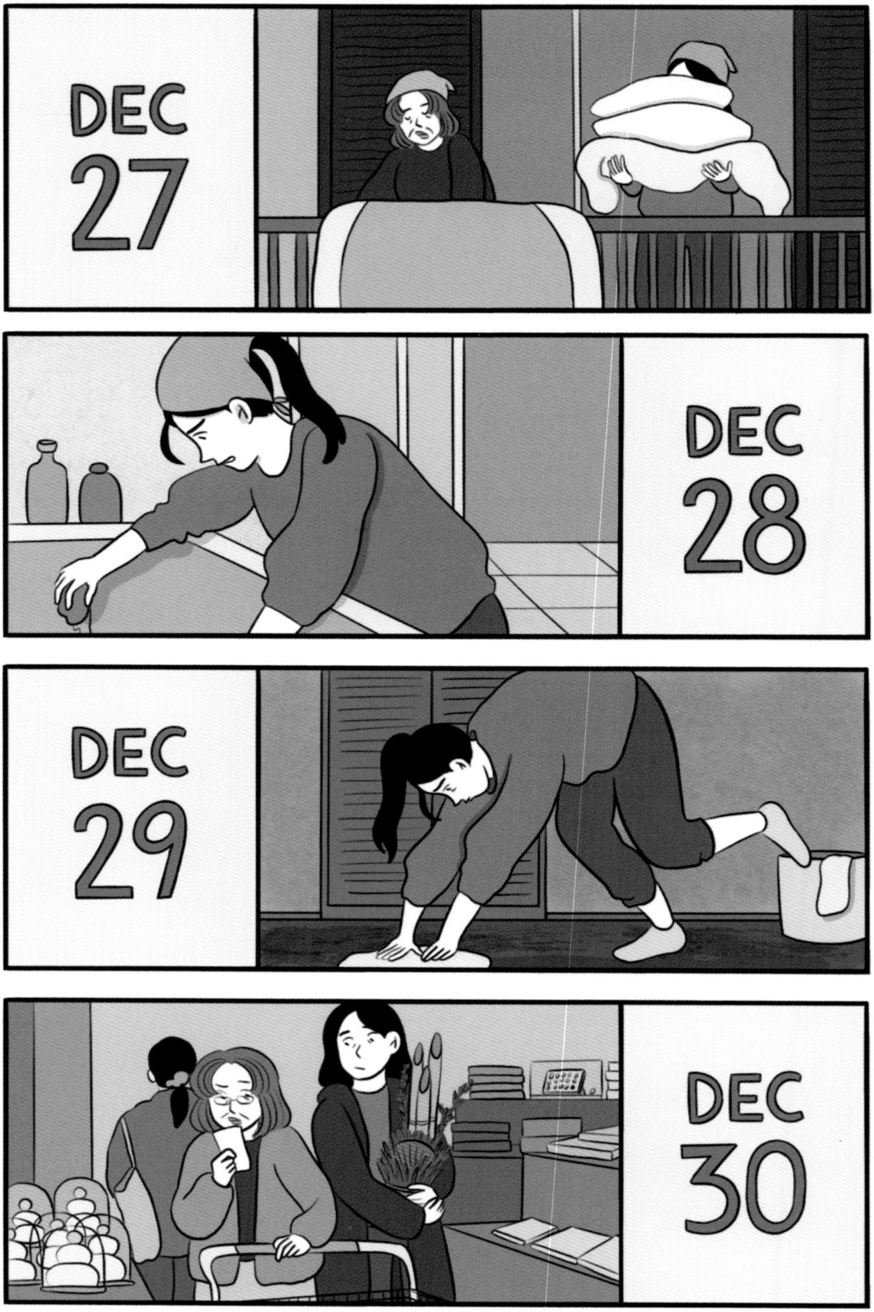
DEC 27
DEC 28
DEC 29
DEC 30

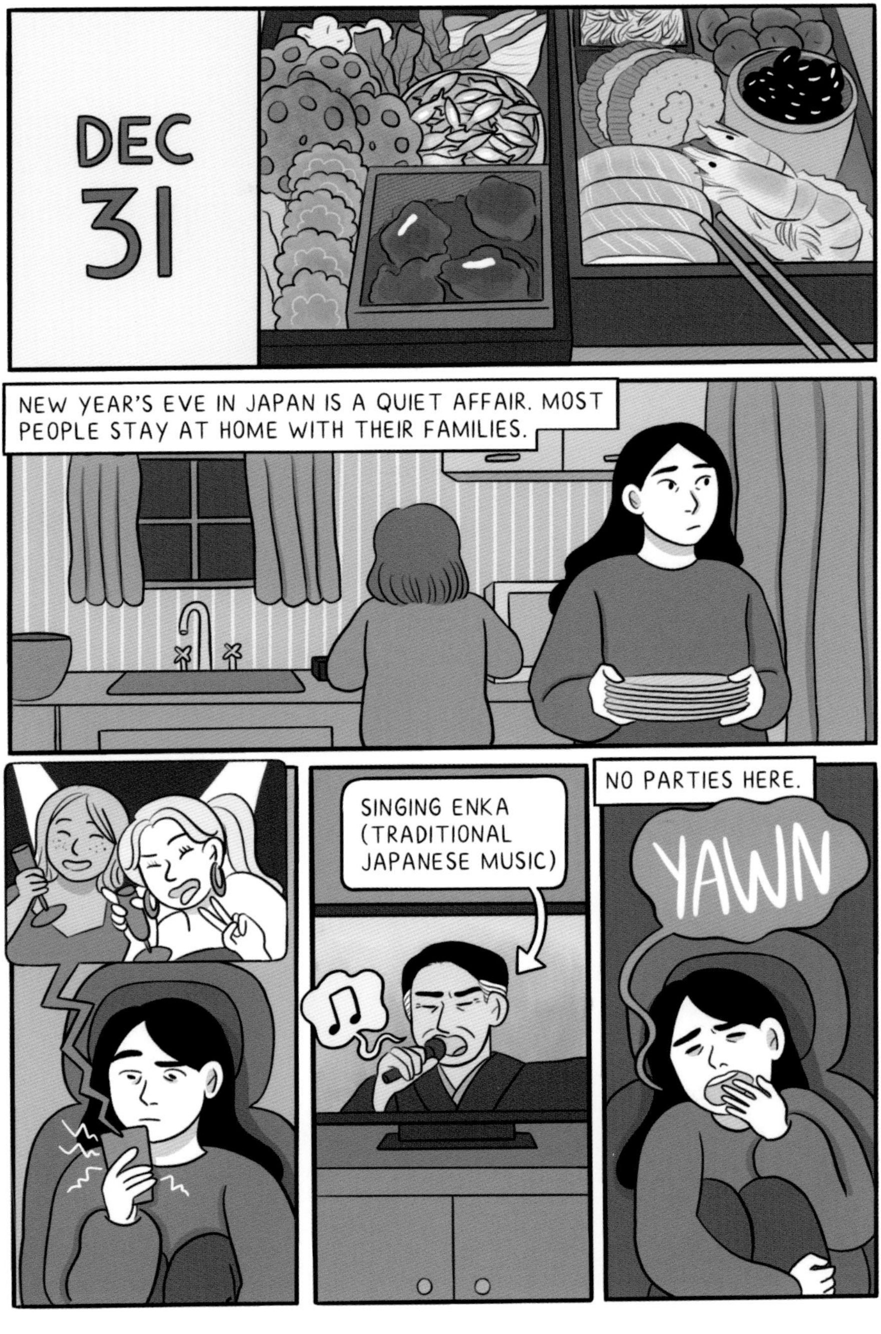
DEC 31
NEW YEAR'S EVE IN JAPAN IS A QUIET AFFAIR. MOST PEOPLE STAY AT HOME WITH THEIR FAMILIES.
SINGING ENKA (TRADITIONAL JAPANESE MUSIC)
NO PARTIES HERE.
YAWN

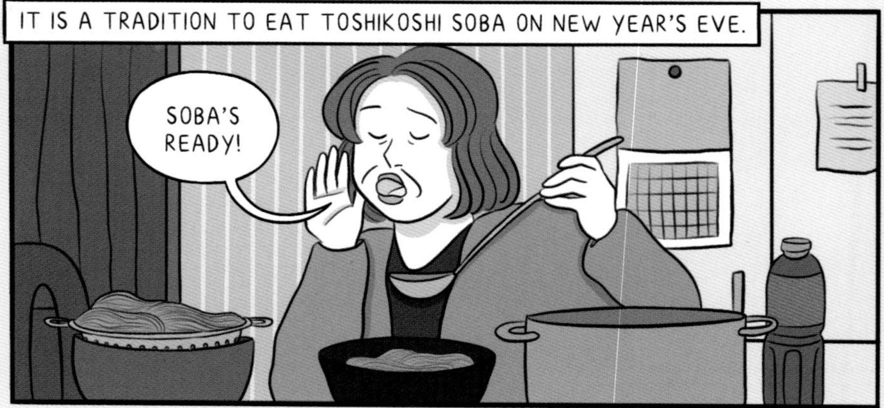
IT IS A TRADITION TO EAT TOSHIKOSHI SOBA ON NEW YEAR'S EVE.
SOBA'S LONG READY!

THE LONG NOODLES ARE SUPPOSED TO REPRESENT A LONG AND HEALTHY LIFE.

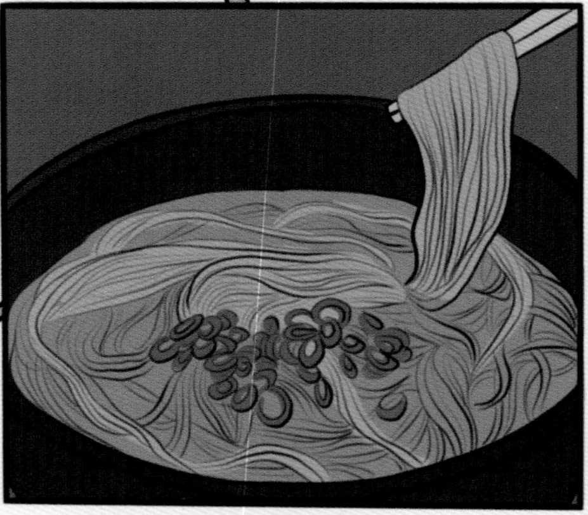

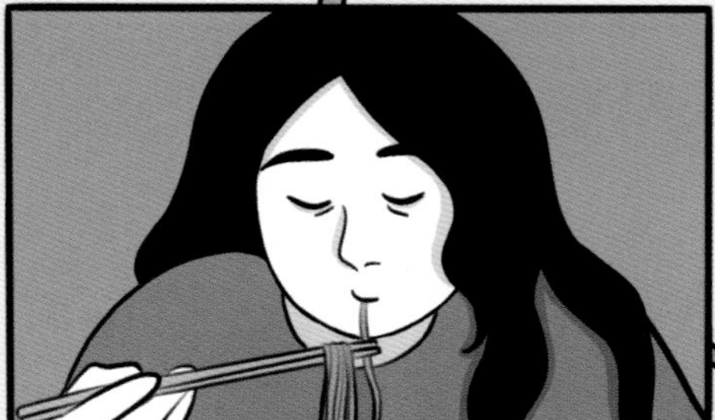

AND BECAUSE SOBA IS EASY TO EAT, IT'S MEANT TO SIGNIFY AN END TO THE HARDSHIPS OF THE YEAR.

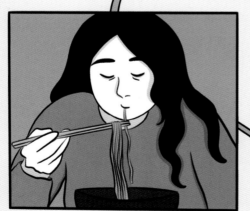

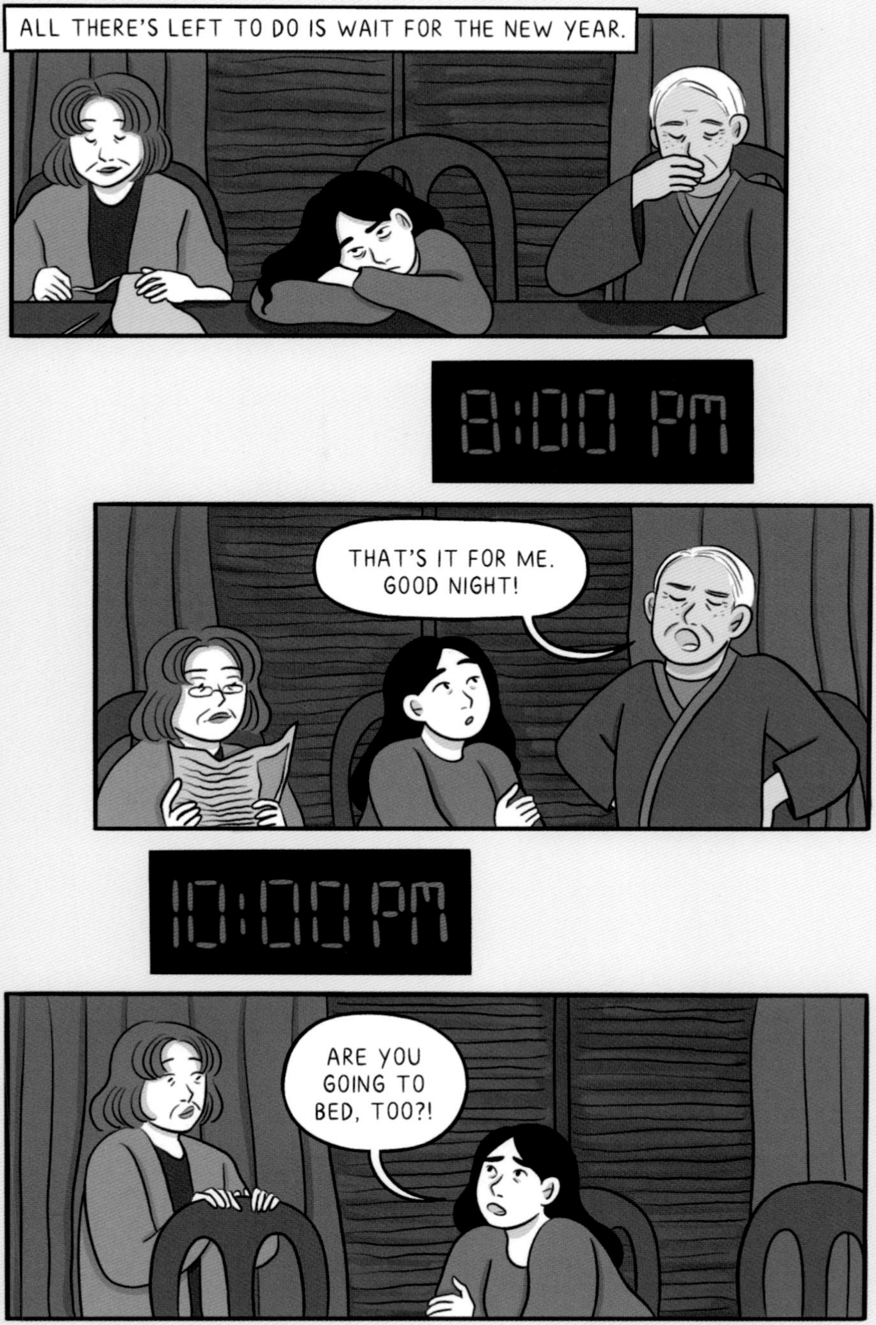
ALL THERE'S LEFT TO DO IS WAIT FOR THE NEW YEAR.
8:00 PM
THAT'S IT FOR ME. GOOD NIGHT!
10:00 PM
ARE YOU GOING TO BED, TOO?!

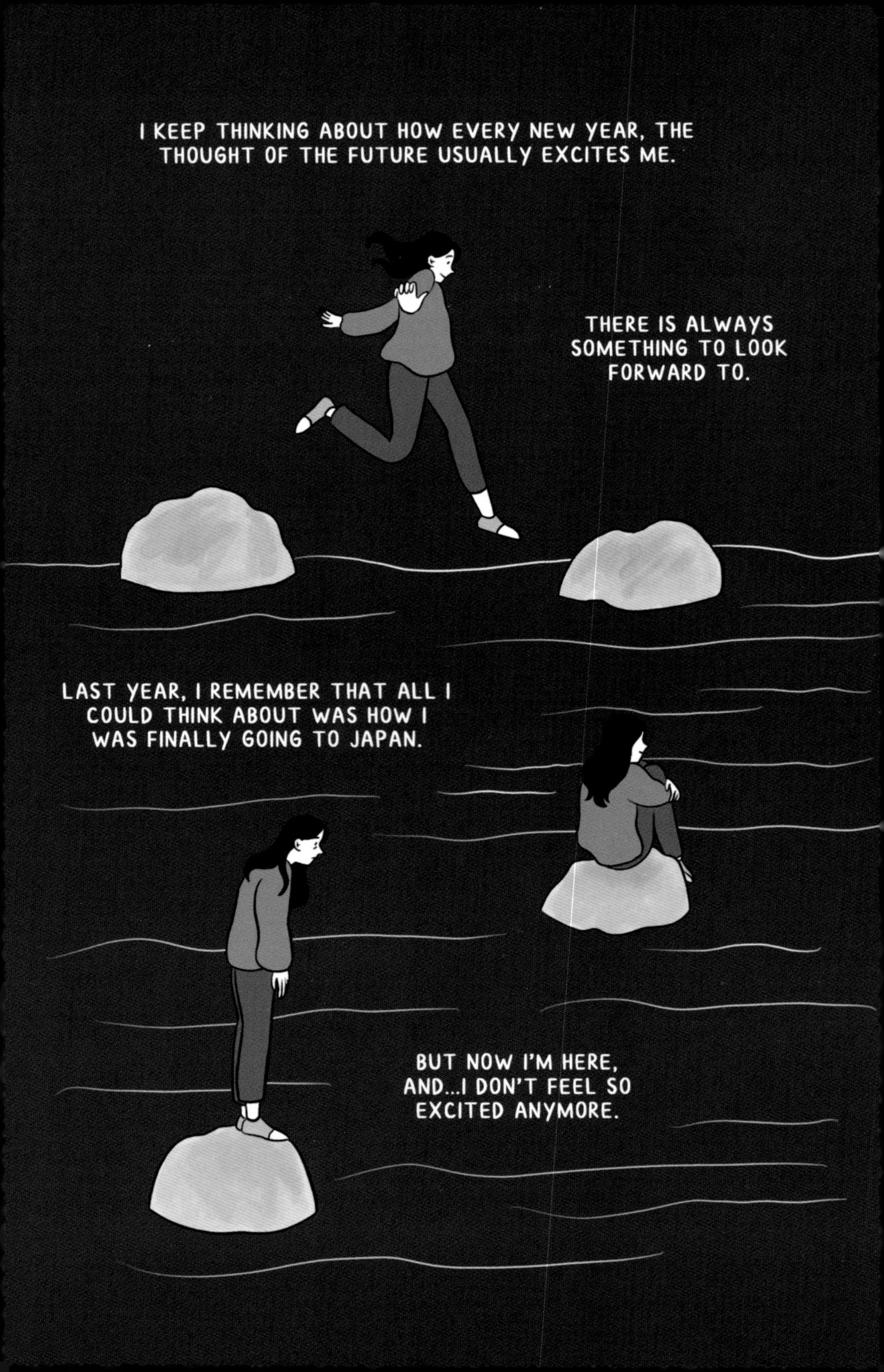
I KEEP THINKING ABOUT HOW EVERY NEW YEAR, THE THOUGHT OF THE FUTURE USUALLY EXCITES ME.
THERE IS ALWAYS SOMETHING TO LOOK FORWARD TO.
LAST YEAR, I REMEMBER THAT ALL I COULD THINK ABOUT WAS HOW I WAS FINALLY GOING TO JAPAN.
BUT NOW I'M HERE, AND...I DON'T FEEL SO EXCITED ANYMORE.

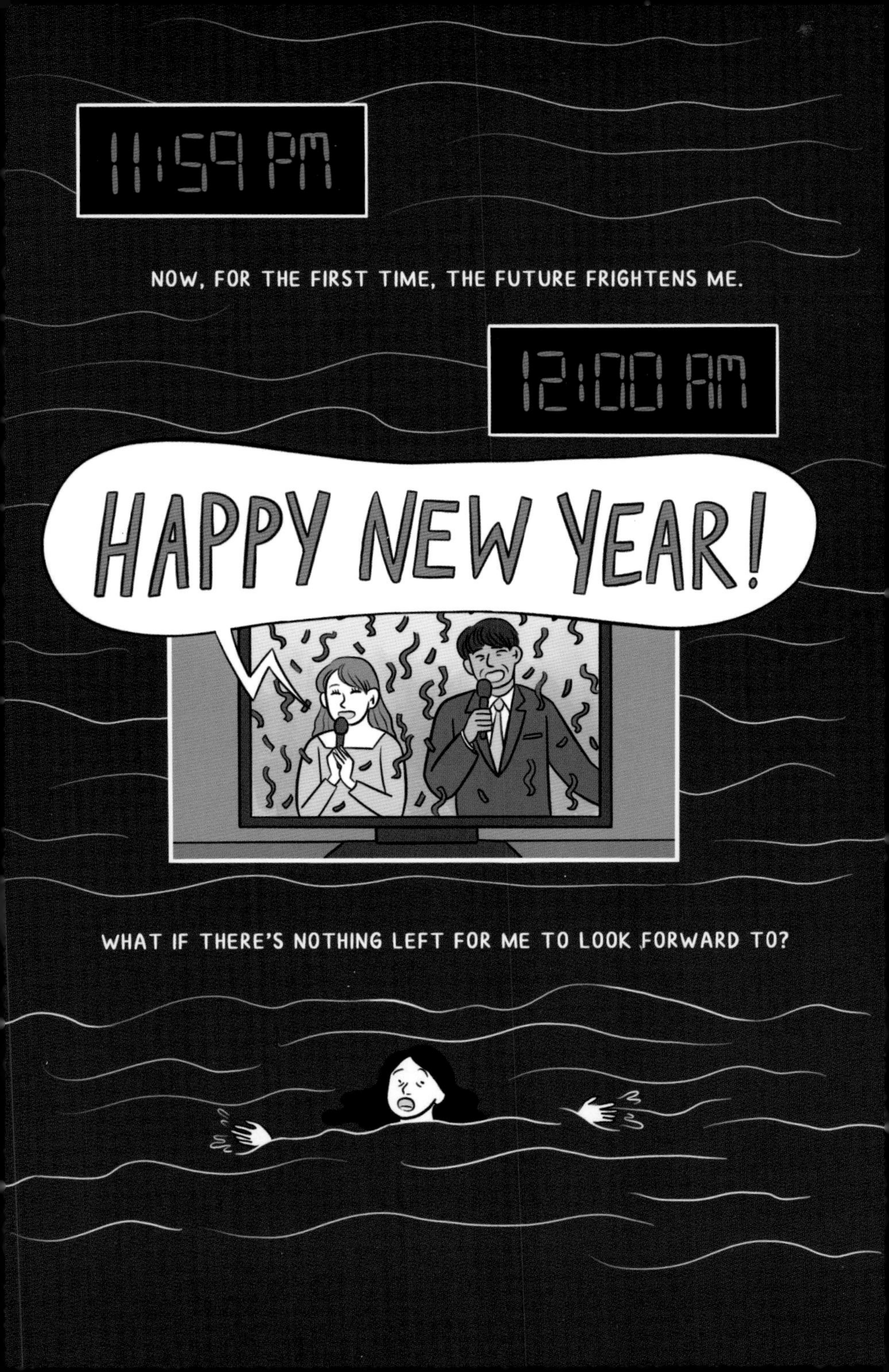
11:59 PM
NOW, FOR THE FIRST TIME, THE FUTURE FRIGHTENS ME.
12:00 AM
HAPPY NEW YEAR!
WHAT IF THERE'S NOTHING LEFT FOR ME TO LOOK FORWARD TO?

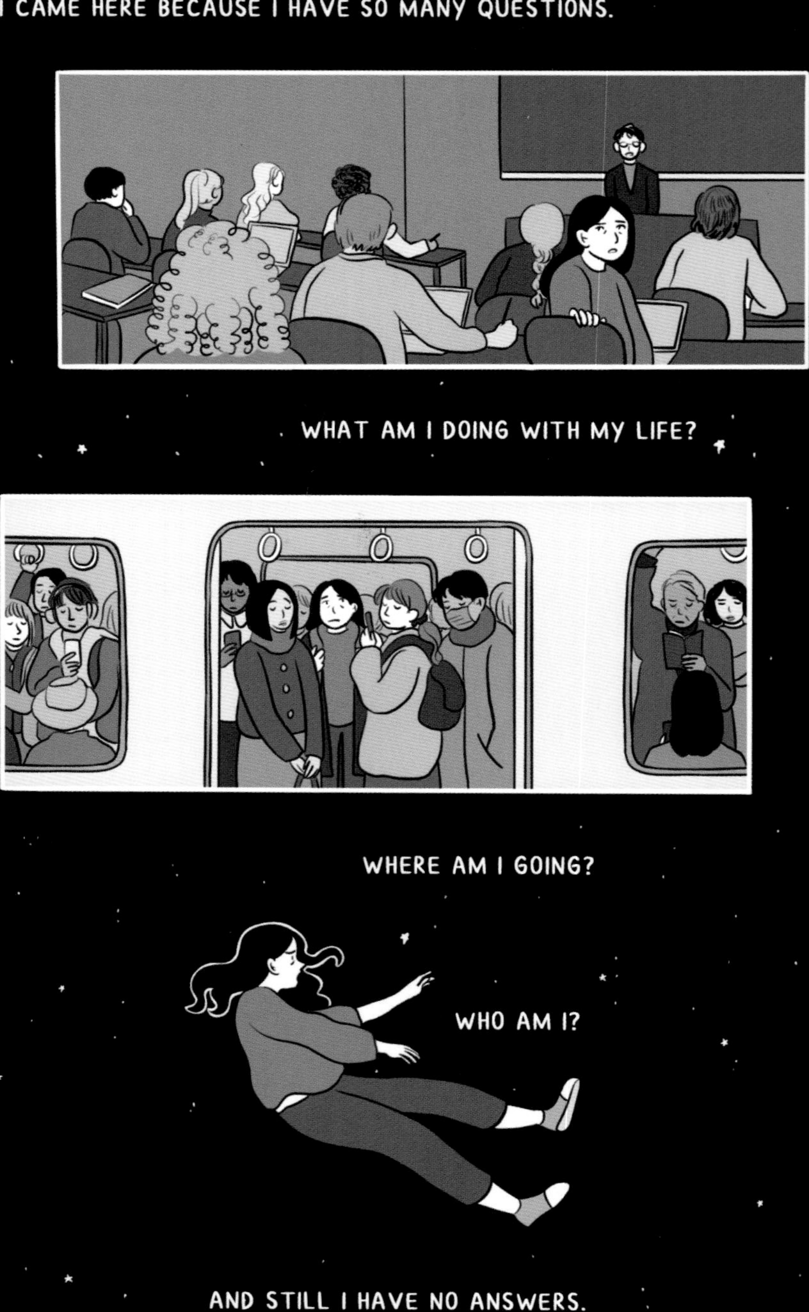
I CAME HERE BECAUSE I HAVE SO MANY QUESTIONS.
WHAT AM I DOING WITH MY LIFE?
WHERE AM I GOING?
WHO AM I?
AND STILL I HAVE NO ANSWERS.

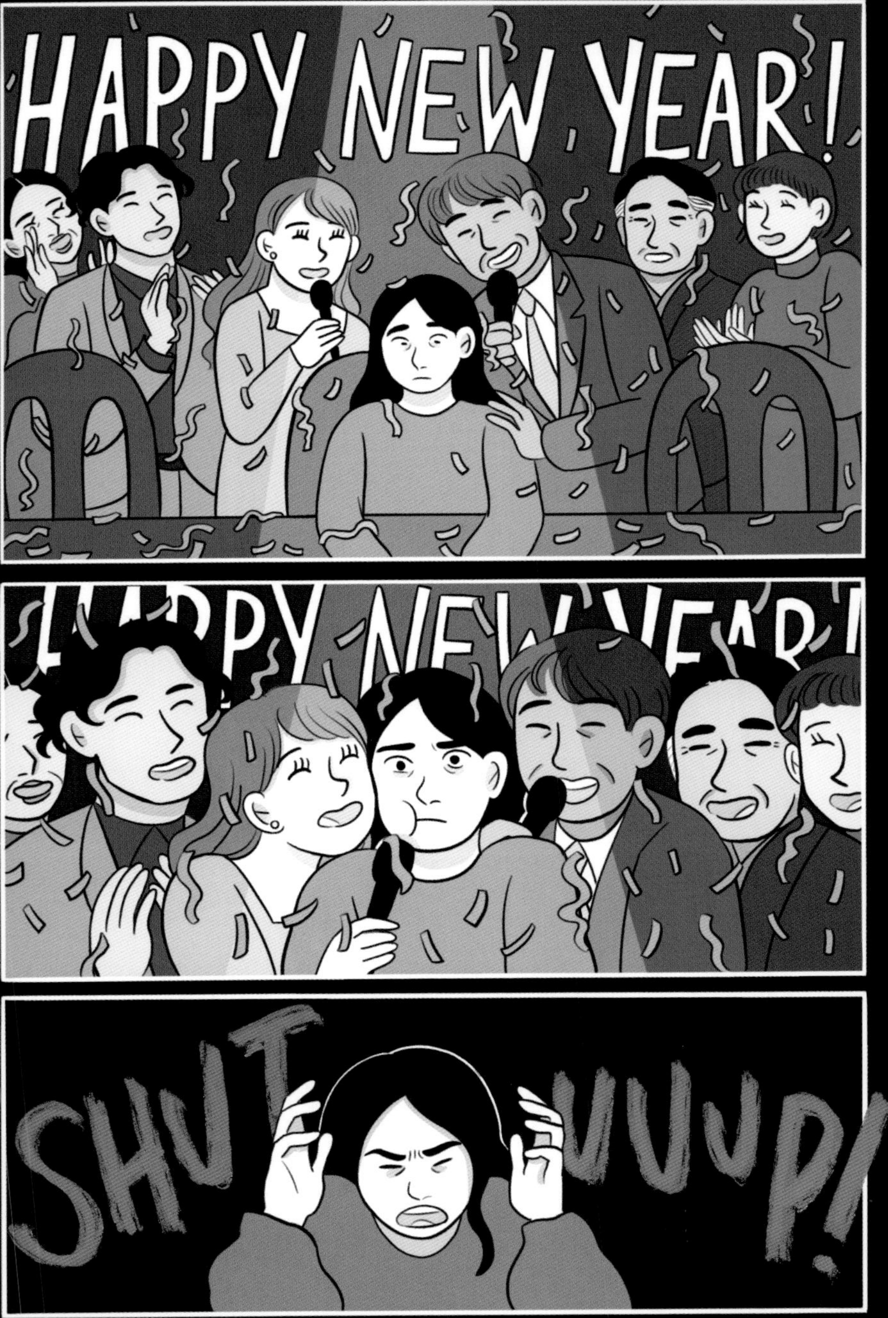
HAPPY NEW YEAR!
SHUT UUUP!

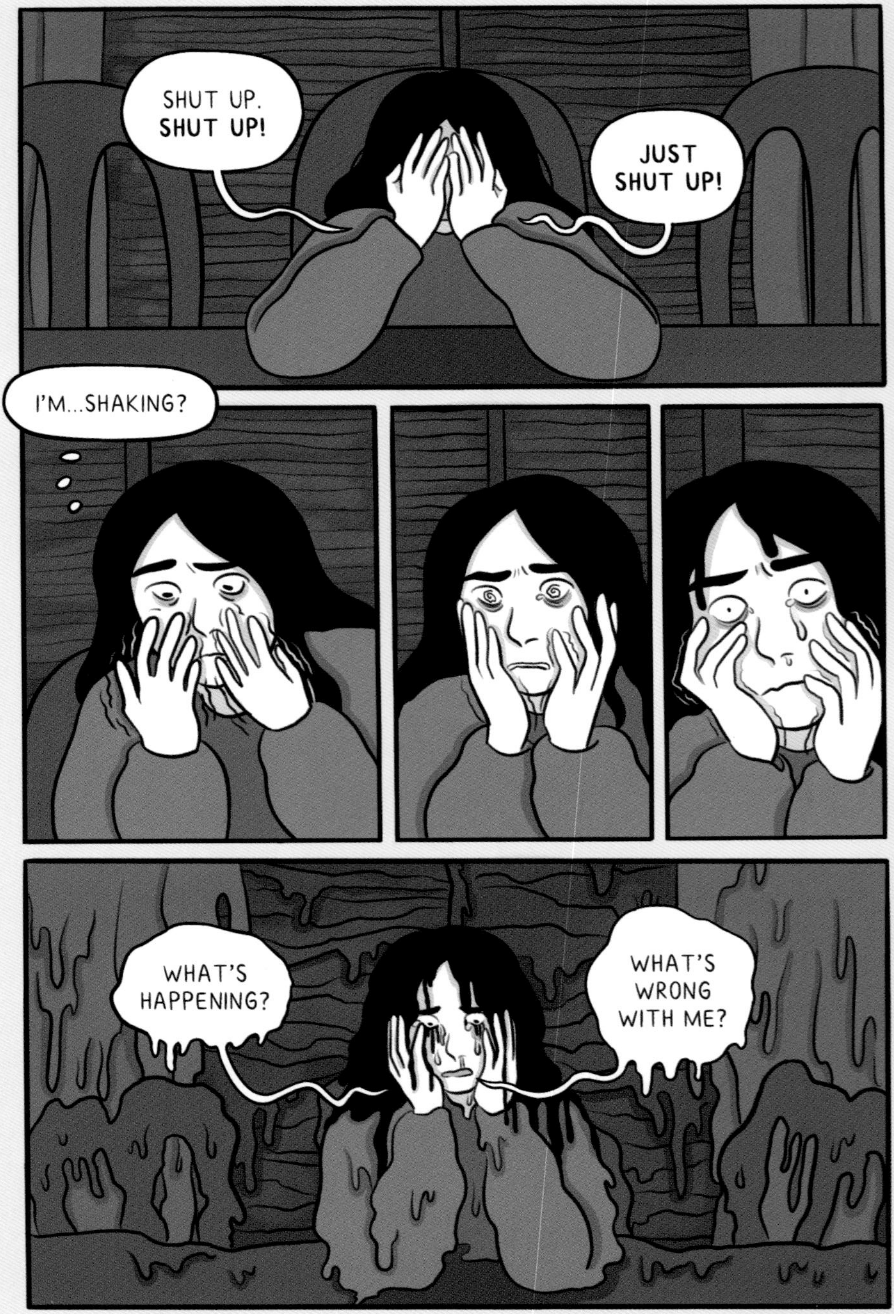
SHUT UP. SHUT UP!
JUST SHUT UP!
I'M...SHAKING?
WHAT'S HAPPENING?
WHAT'S WRONG WITH ME?

THE NEW YEAR IS SUPPOSED TO BE A CLEAN START.

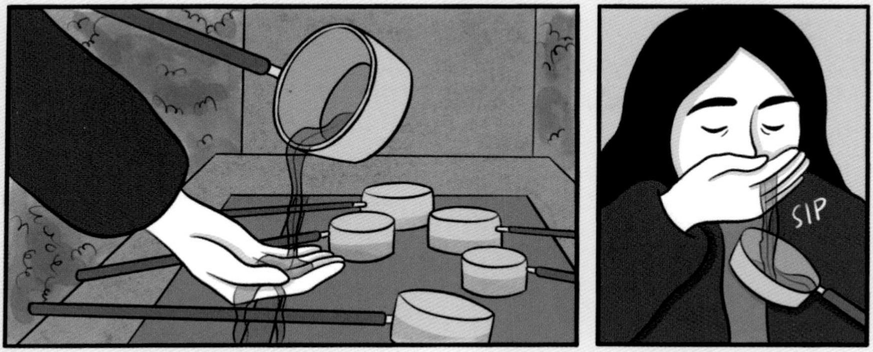
SIP

A CHANCE TO MAKE THINGS BETTER THAN THEY WERE BEFORE.

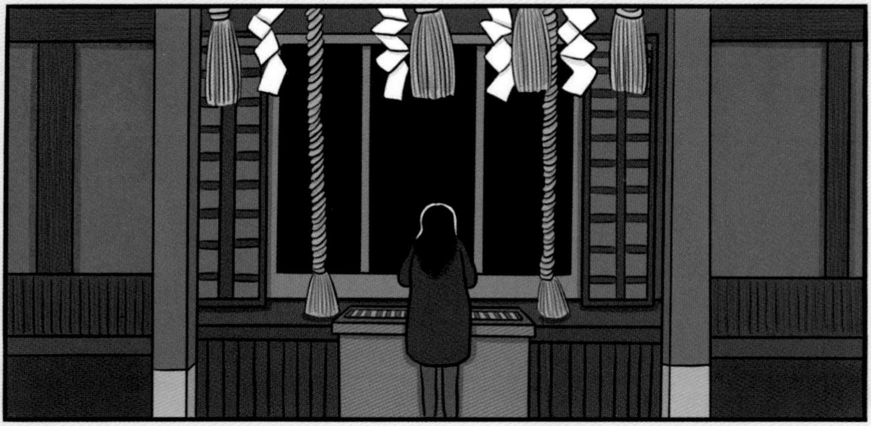

BUT WHAT IF IT DOESN'T GET BETTER? WHAT IF I CAN'T BE BETTER?

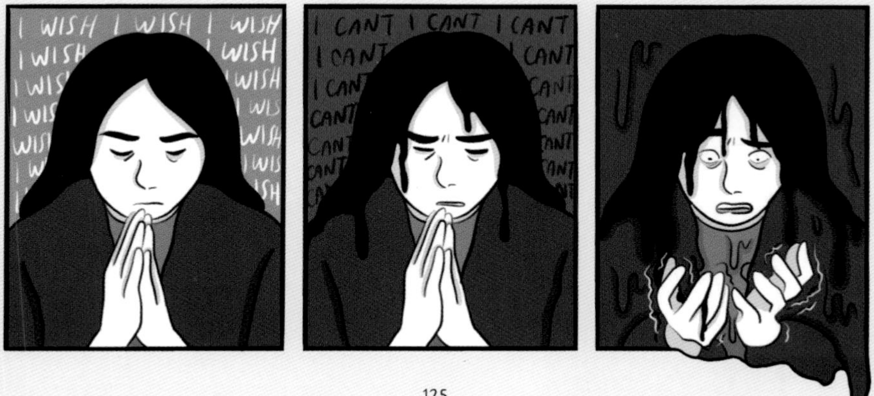
I WISH I WISH I WISH
I CANT I CANT I CANT

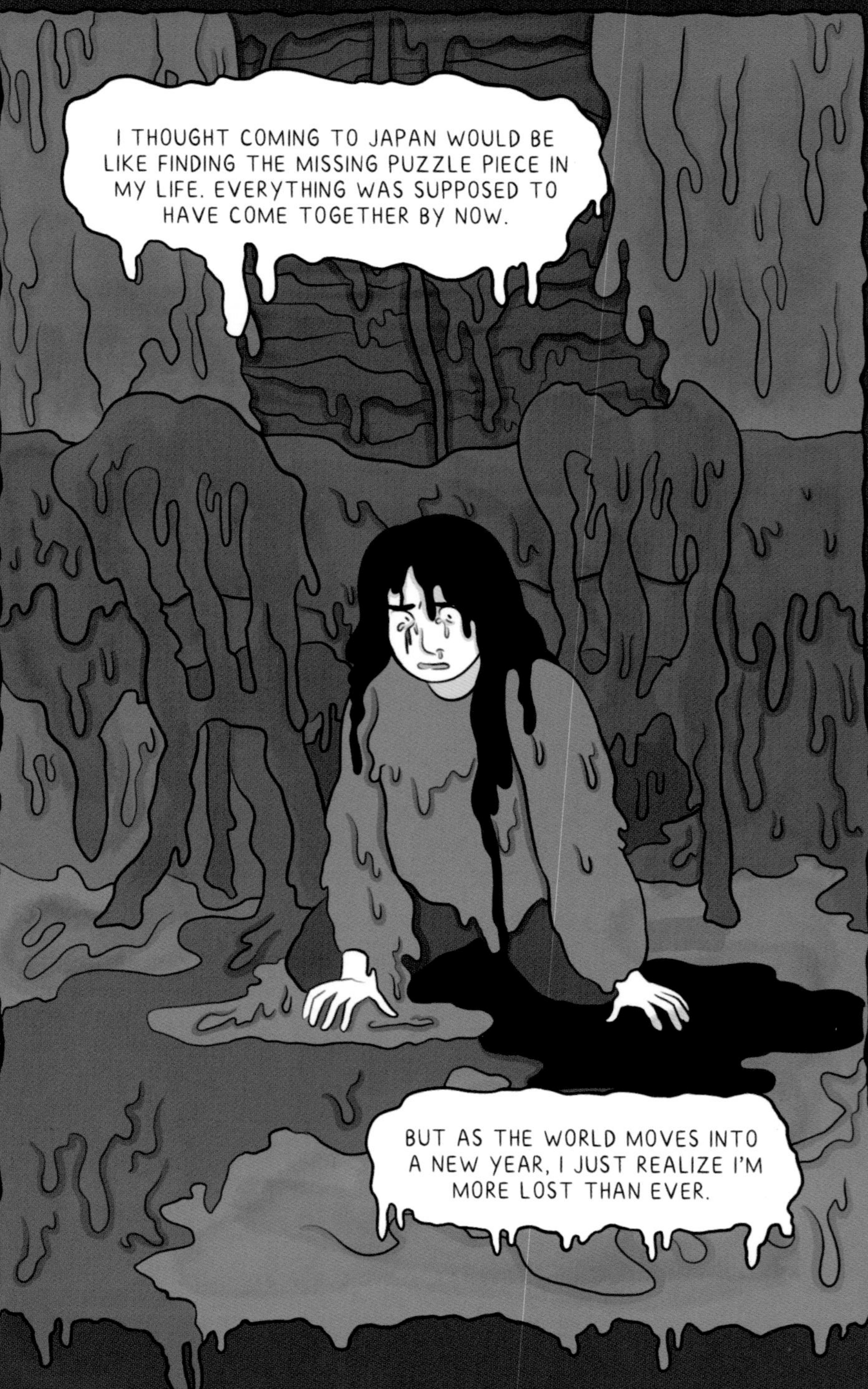
I THOUGHT COMING TO JAPAN WOULD BE LIKE FINDING THE MISSING PUZZLE PIECE IN MY LIFE. EVERYTHING WAS SUPPOSED TO HAVE COME TOGETHER BY NOW.
BUT AS THE WORLD MOVES INTO A NEW YEAR, I JUST REALIZE I'M MORE LOST THAN EVER.

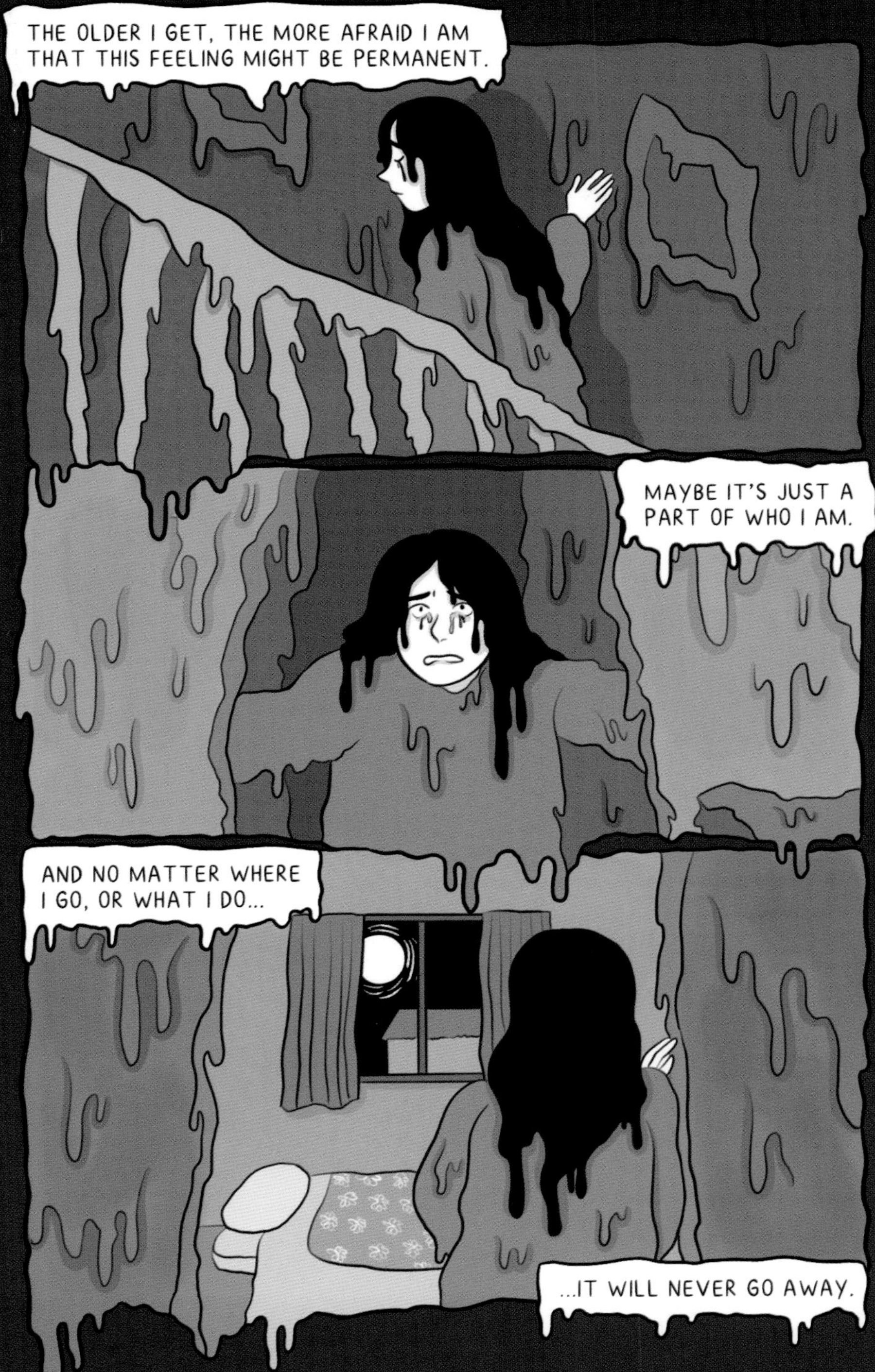
THE OLDER I GET, THE MORE AFRAID I AM THAT THIS FEELING MIGHT BE PERMANENT.
MAYBE IT'S JUST A PART OF WHO I AM.
AND NO MATTER WHERE I GO, OR WHAT I DO...
...IT WILL NEVER GO AWAY.

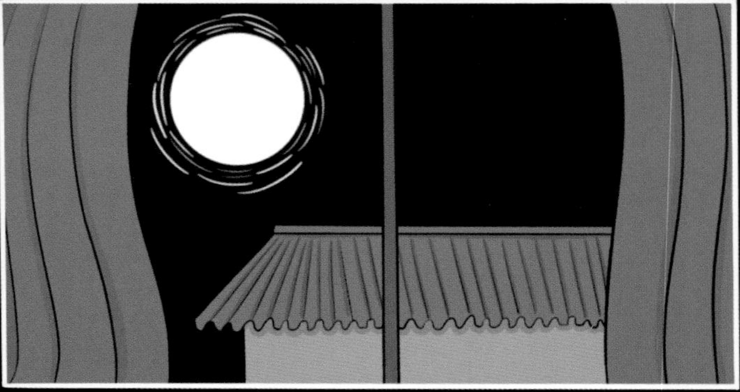

WHAT A LONELY WAY TO FEEL.

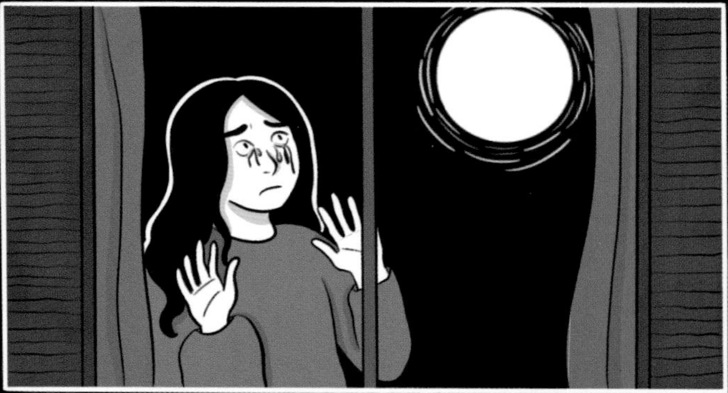

I DON'T THINK I'VE EVER FELT SO LONELY BEFORE.

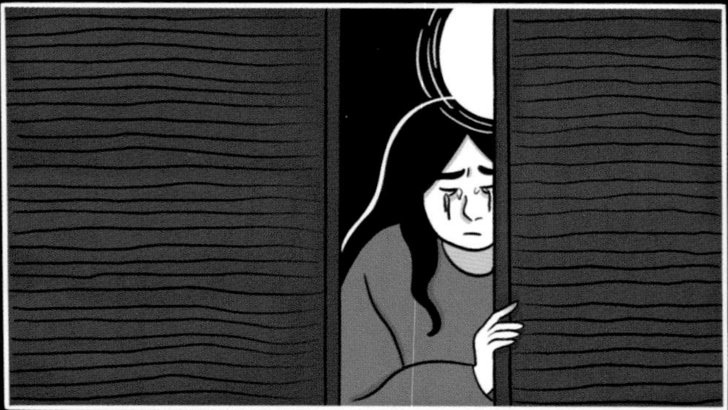

冬

WINTER

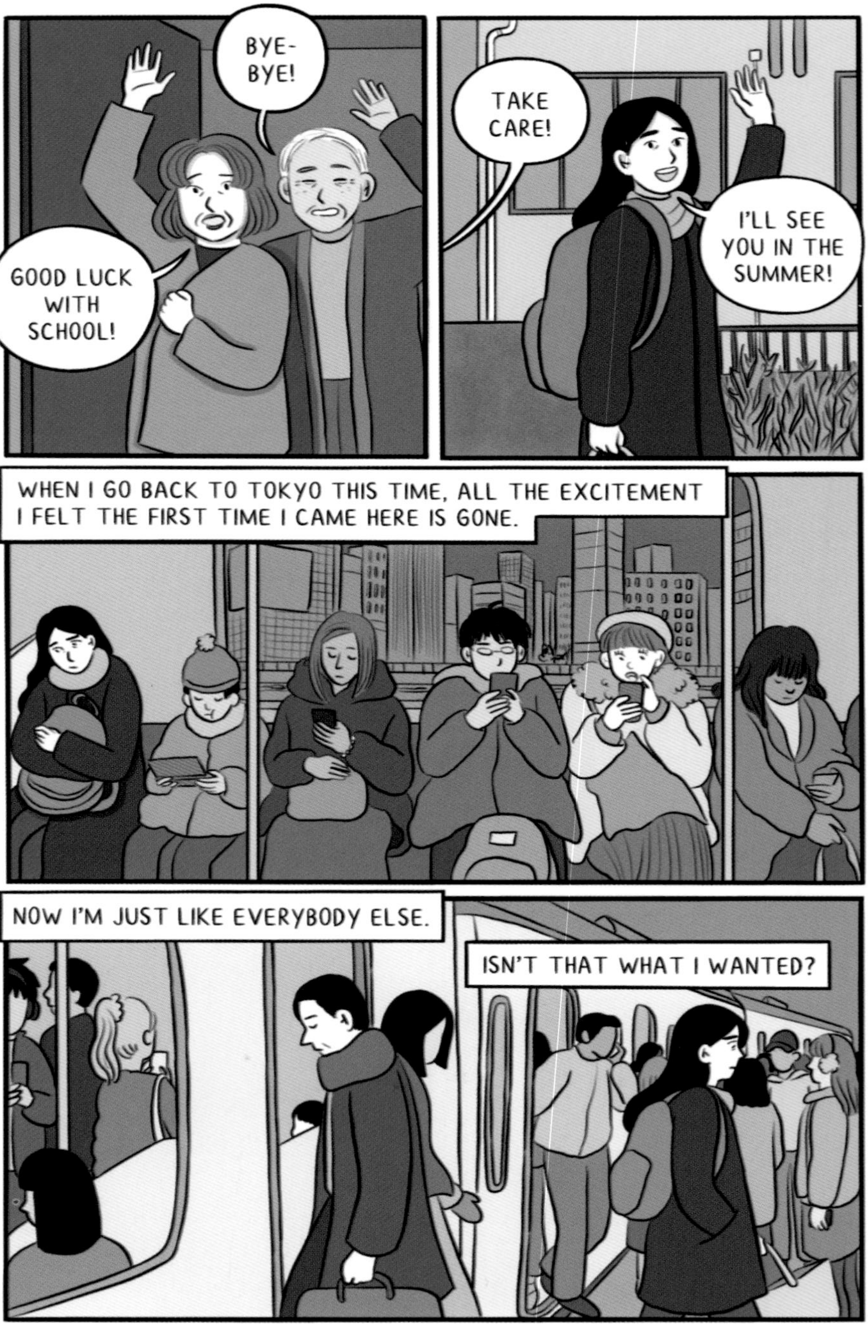
BYE-BYE!
GOOD LUCK WITH SCHOOL!
TAKE CARE!
I'LL SEE YOU IN THE SUMMER!
WHEN I GO BACK TO TOKYO THIS TIME, ALL THE EXCITEMENT I FELT THE FIRST TIME I CAME HERE IS GONE.
NOW I'M JUST LIKE EVERYBODY ELSE.
ISN'T THAT WHAT I WANTED?

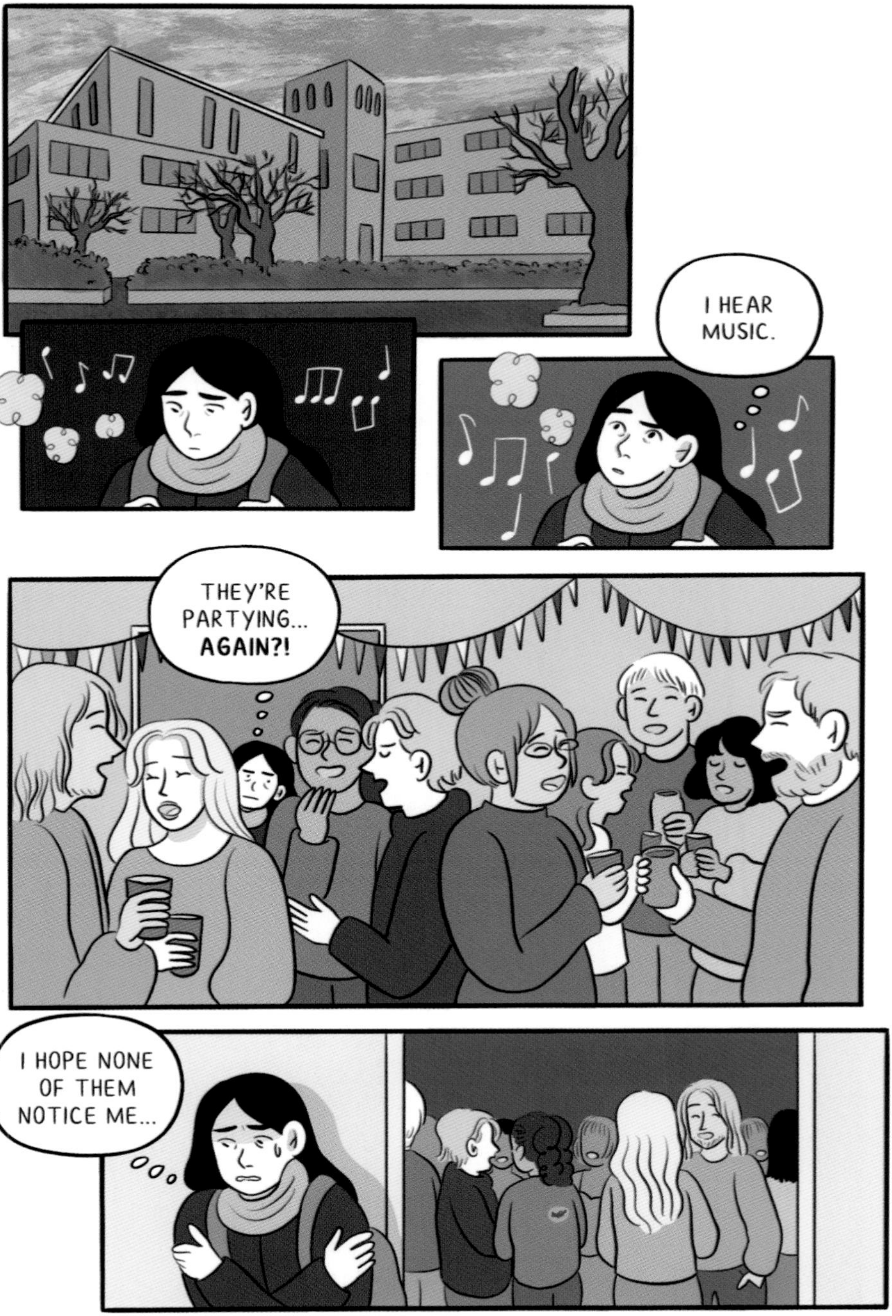
I HEAR MUSIC.
THEY'RE PARTYING... **AGAIN?!**
I HOPE NONE OF THEM NOTICE ME...

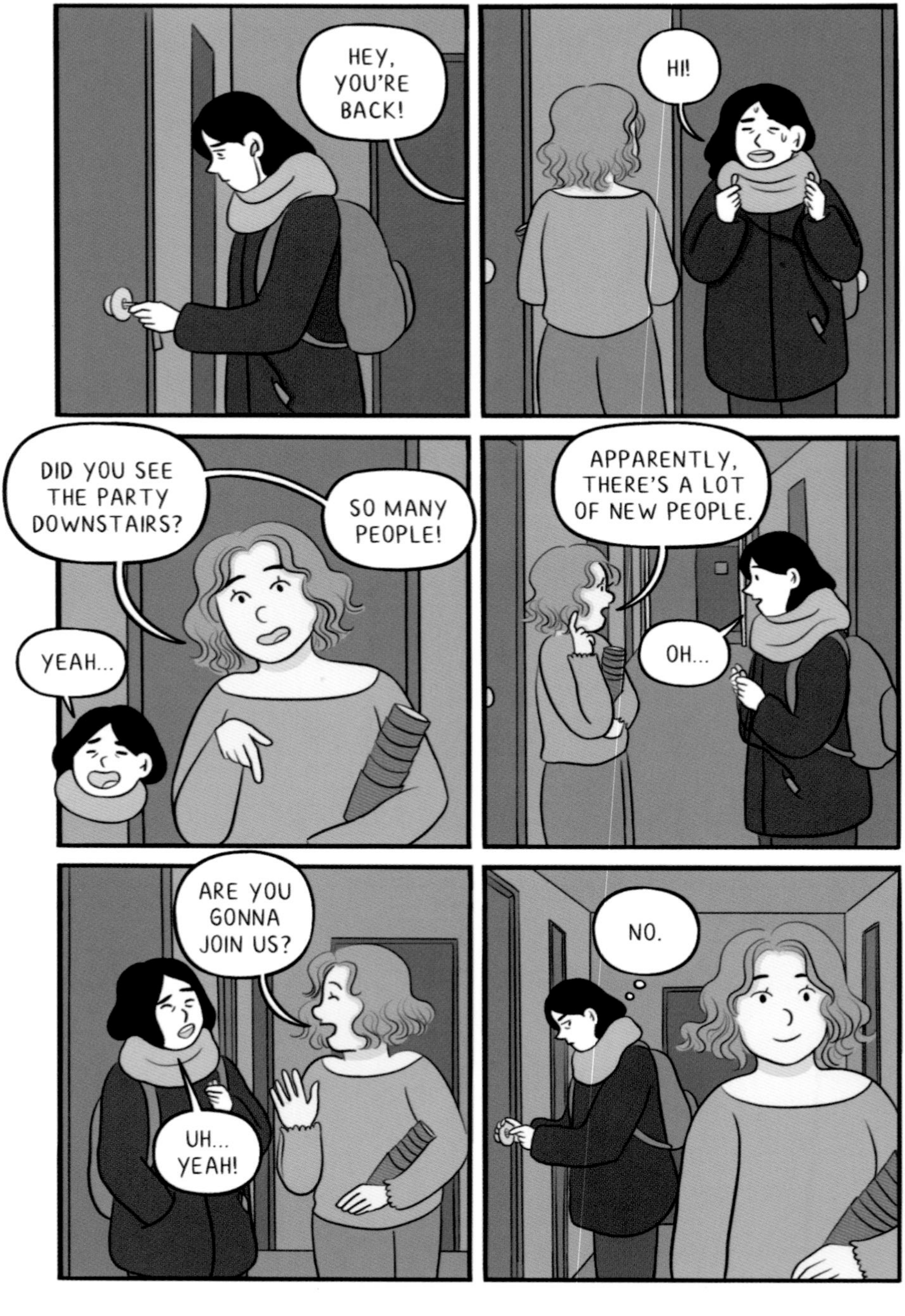
HEY, YOU'RE BACK!
HI!
DID YOU SEE THE PARTY DOWNSTAIRS?
SO MANY PEOPLE!
YEAH...
APPARENTLY, THERE'S A LOT OF NEW PEOPLE.
OH...
ARE YOU GONNA JOIN US?
UH... YEAH!
NO.

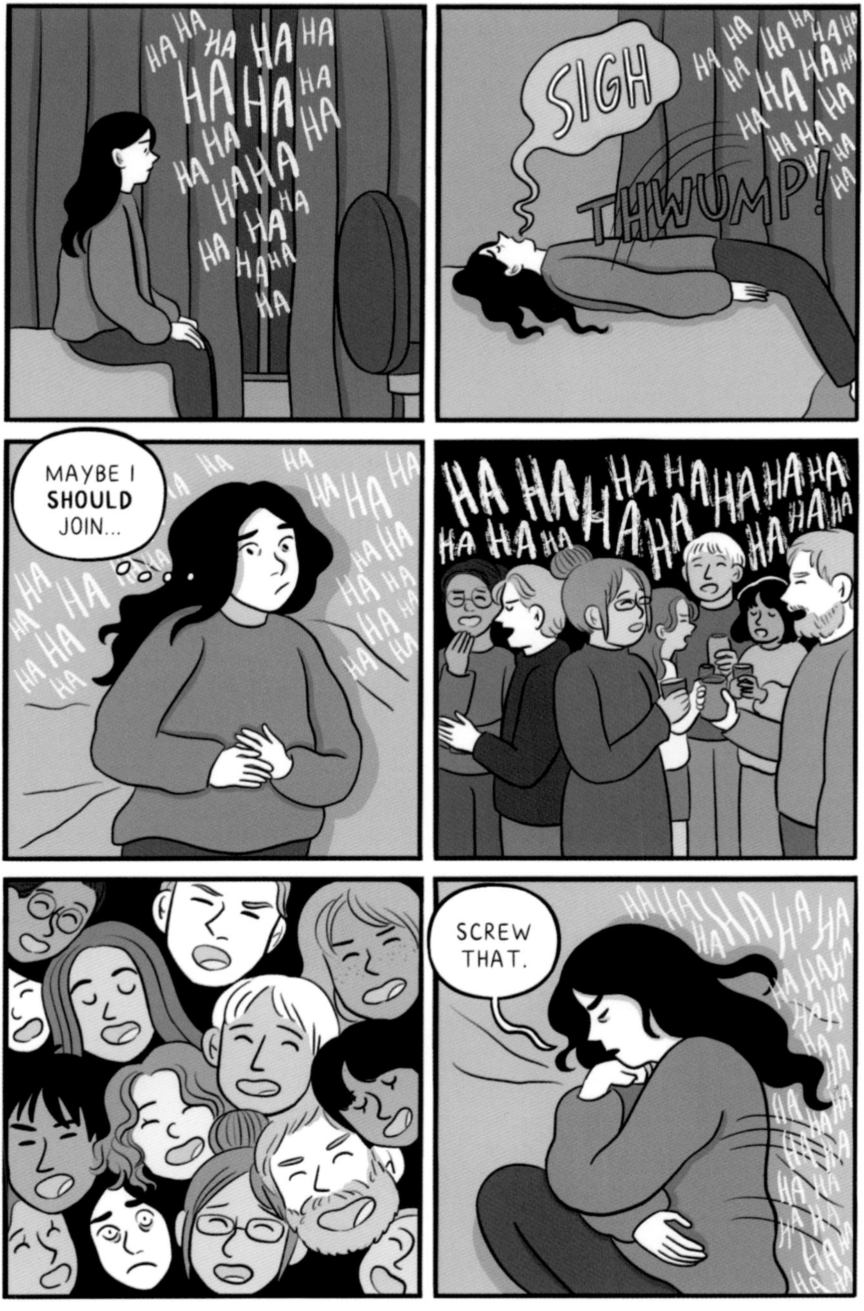
HA HA HA HA HA HA HA HA HA HA HA HA HA HA HA HA HA HA
SIGH
HA HA HA HA HA HA HA HA HA HA HA HA HA HA
THWUMP!
MAYBE I **SHOULD** JOIN...
HA HA HA HA HA HA HA HA HA HA HA HA HA
HA HA HA HA HA HA HA HA HA HA HA HA HA HA HA HA
SCREW THAT.
HA HA HA HA HA HA HA HA HA HA HA HA HA HA HA HA HA

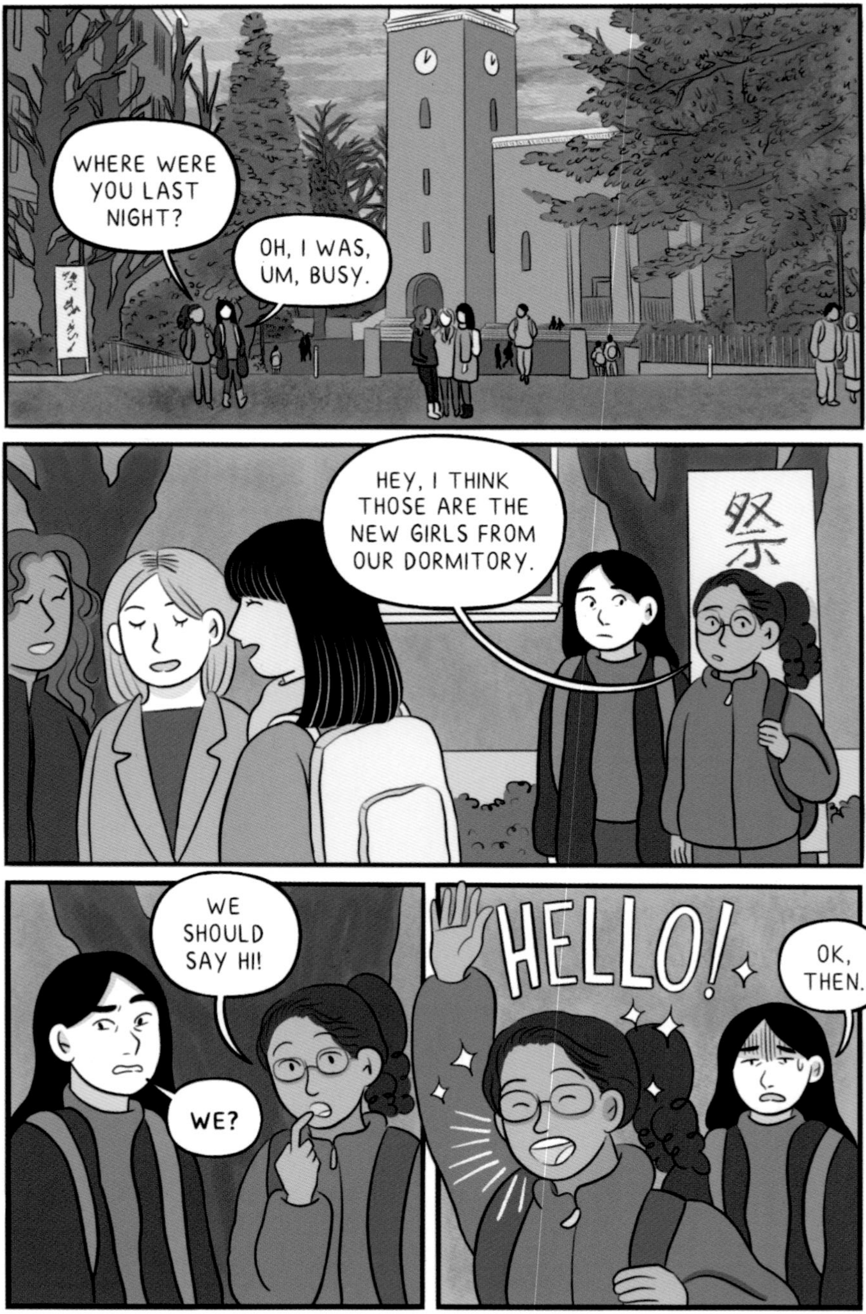
WHERE WERE YOU LAST NIGHT?
OH, I WAS, UM, BUSY.
HEY, I THINK THOSE ARE THE NEW GIRLS FROM OUR DORMITORY.
祭
WE SHOULD SAY HI!
WE?
HELLO!
OK, THEN.

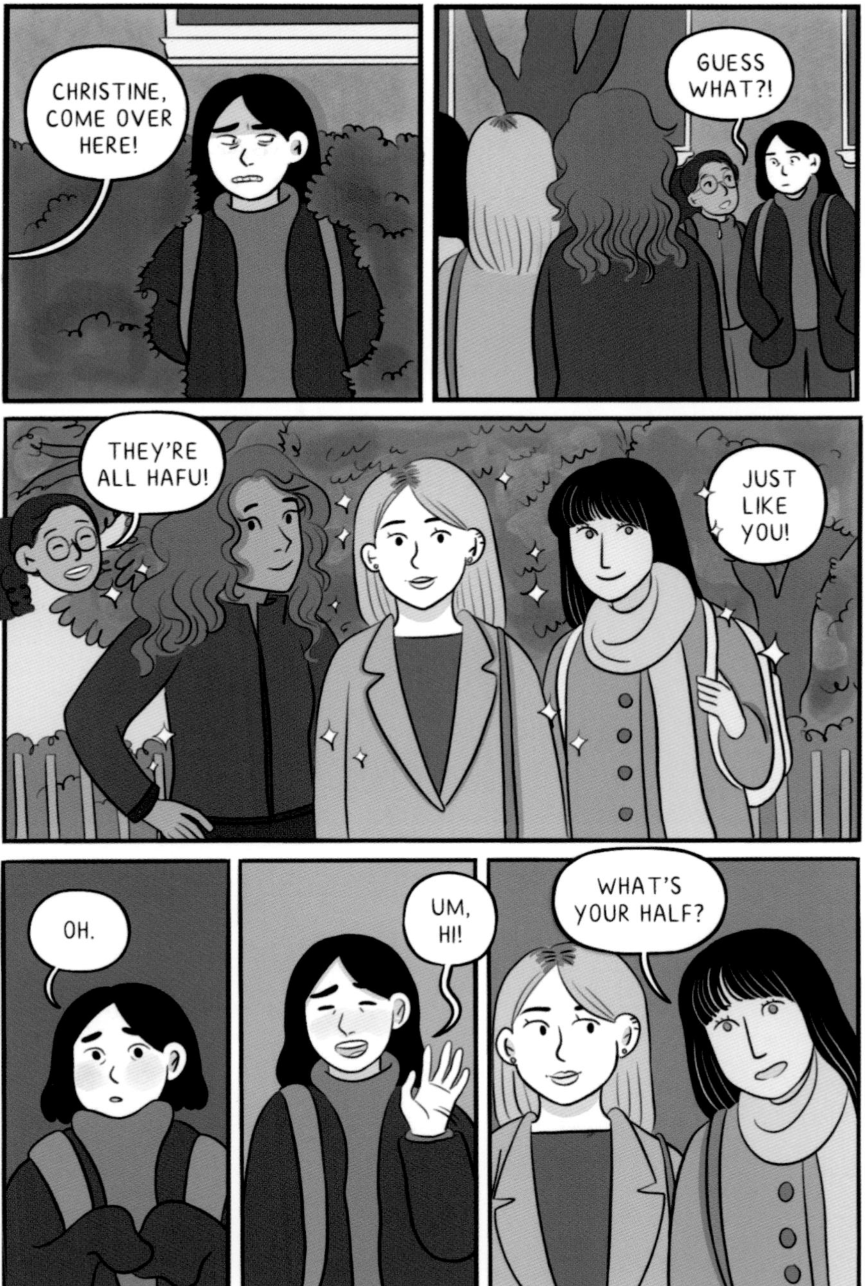

CHRISTINE, COME OVER HERE!
GUESS WHAT?!
THEY'RE ALL HAFU!
JUST LIKE YOU!
OH.
UM, HI!
WHAT'S YOUR HALF?

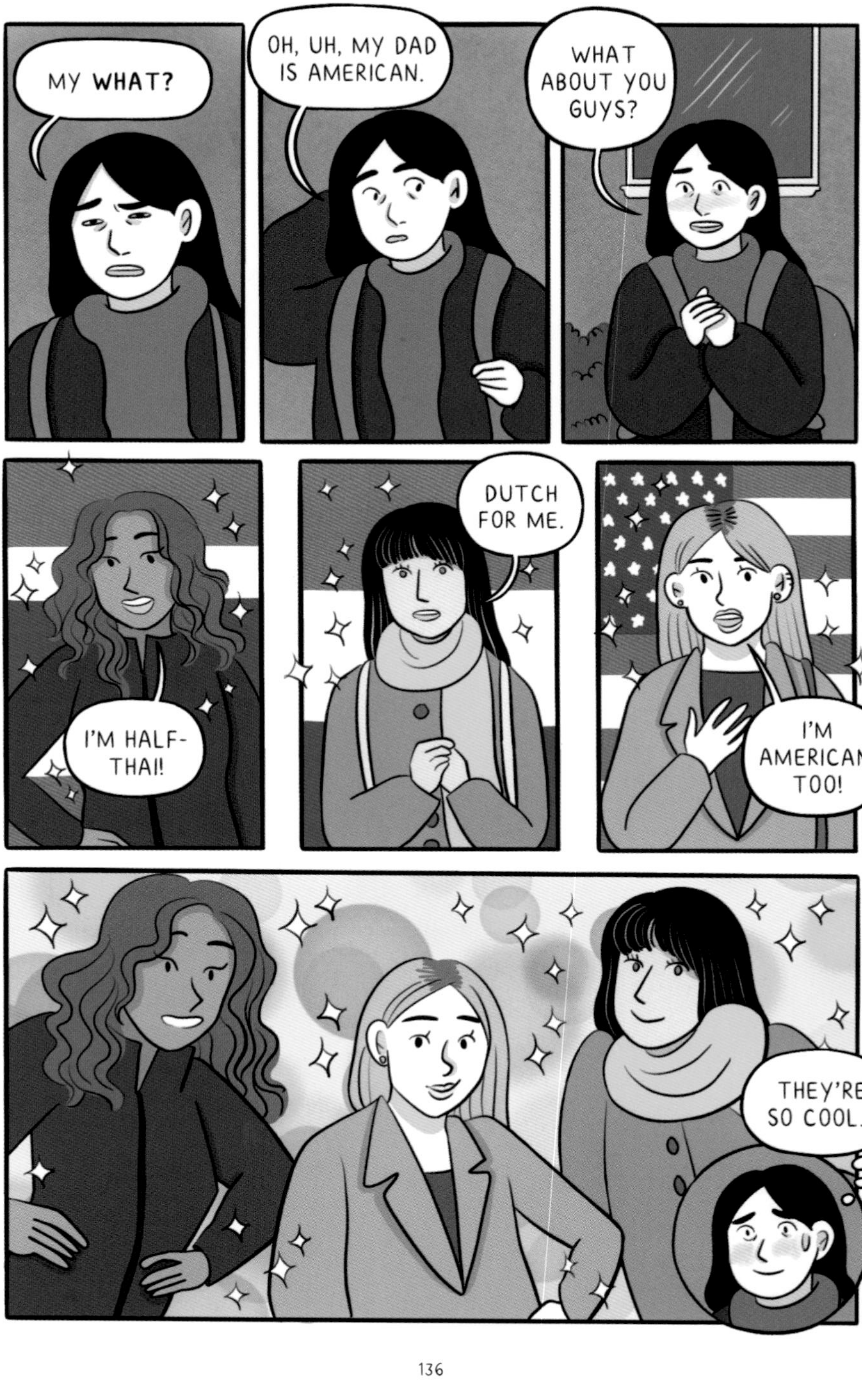

MY **WHAT?**
OH, UH, MY DAD IS AMERICAN.
WHAT ABOUT YOU GUYS?
I'M HALF-THAI!
DUTCH FOR ME.
I'M AMERICAN, TOO!
THEY'RE SO COOL...

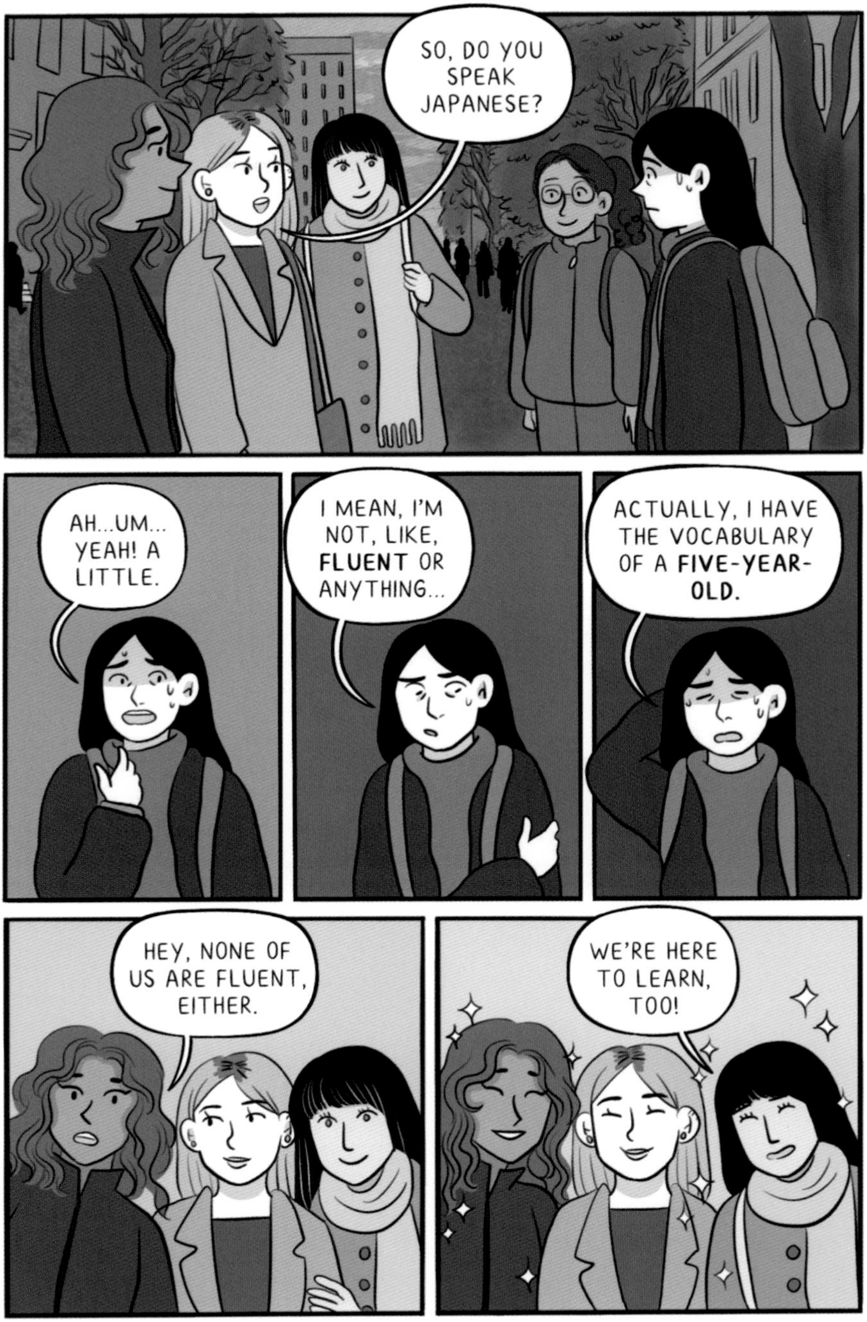
SO, DO YOU SPEAK JAPANESE?
AH...UM... YEAH! A LITTLE.
I MEAN, I'M NOT, LIKE, **FLUENT** OR ANYTHING...
ACTUALLY, I HAVE THE VOCABULARY OF A **FIVE-YEAR-OLD.**
HEY, NONE OF US ARE FLUENT, EITHER.
WE'RE HERE TO LEARN, TOO!

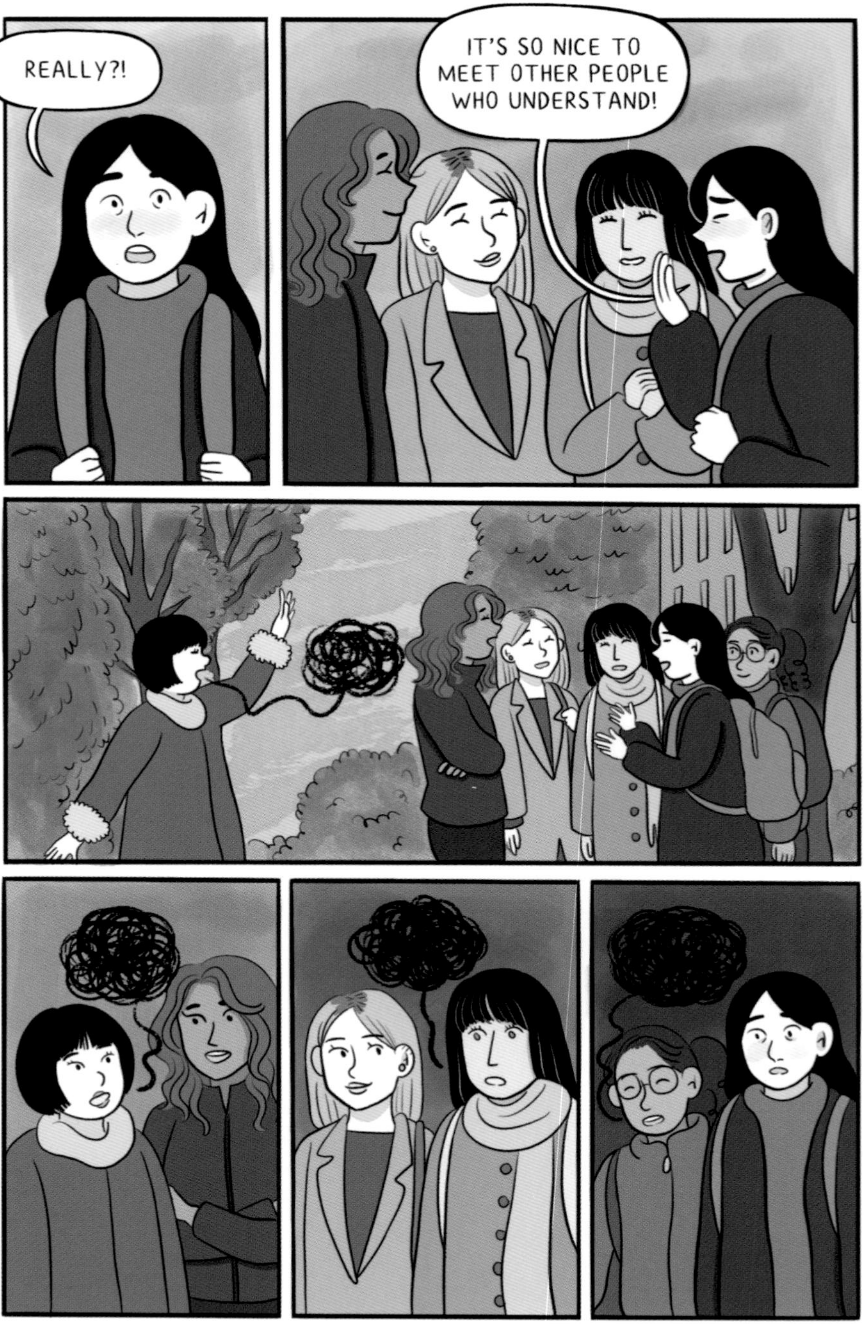
REALLY?!
IT'S SO NICE TO MEET OTHER PEOPLE WHO UNDERSTAND!

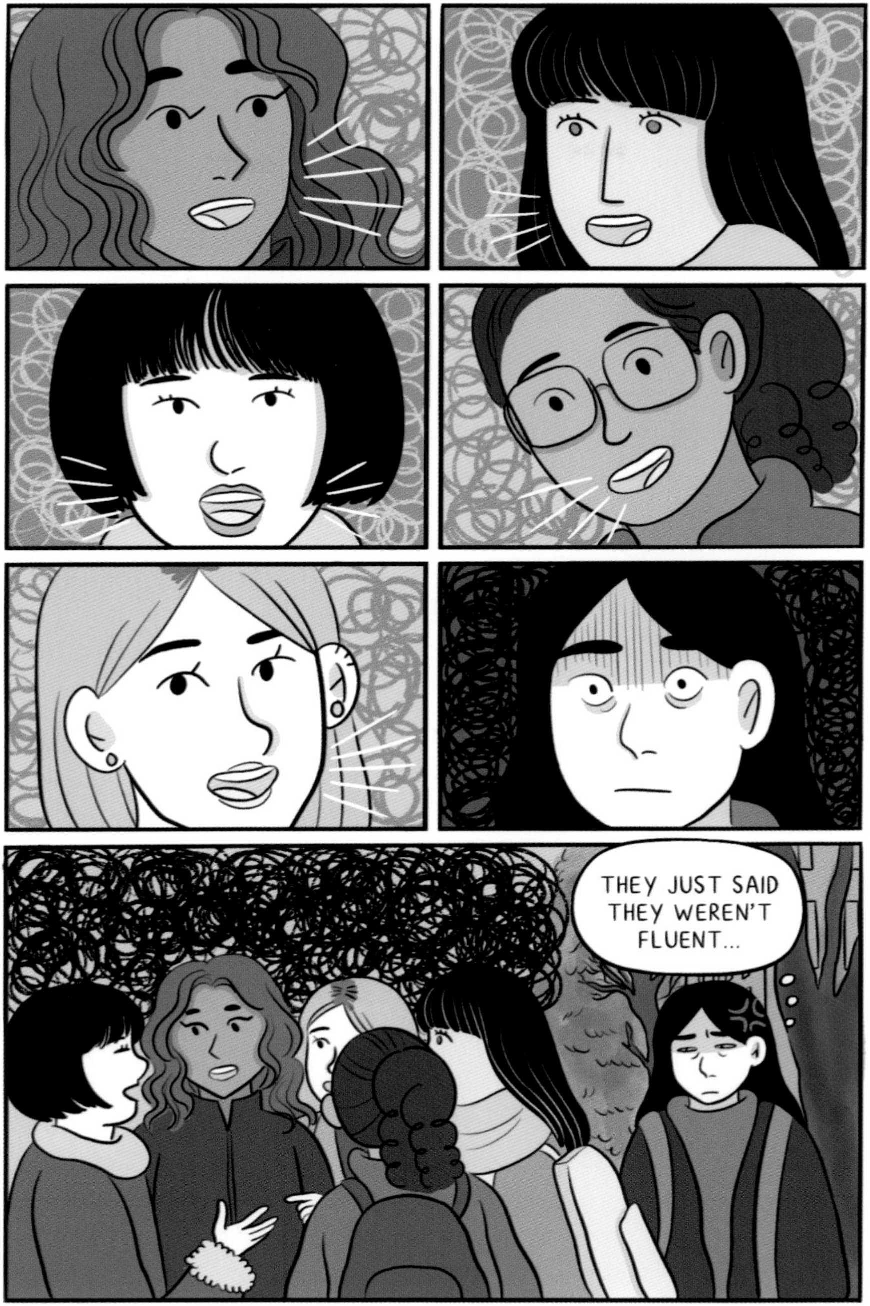
THEY JUST SAID THEY WEREN'T FLUENT...

WE MIGHT ALL BE HAFU, BUT THAT'S ALL I HAVE IN COMMON WITH THEM.

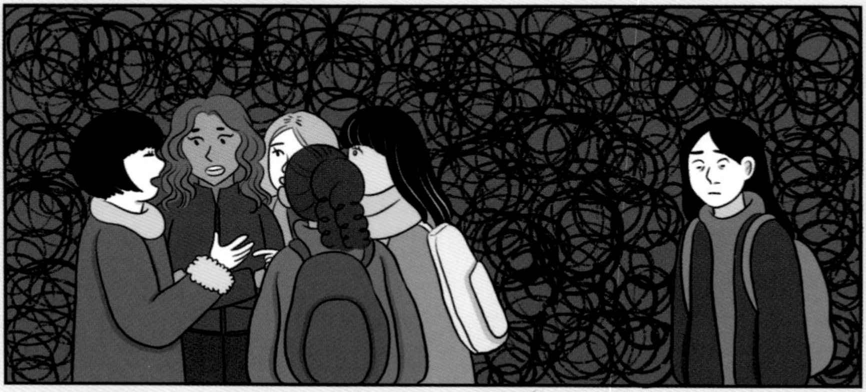

I'M ALWAYS THE ONE STANDING ON THE OUTSIDE, LOOKING IN.

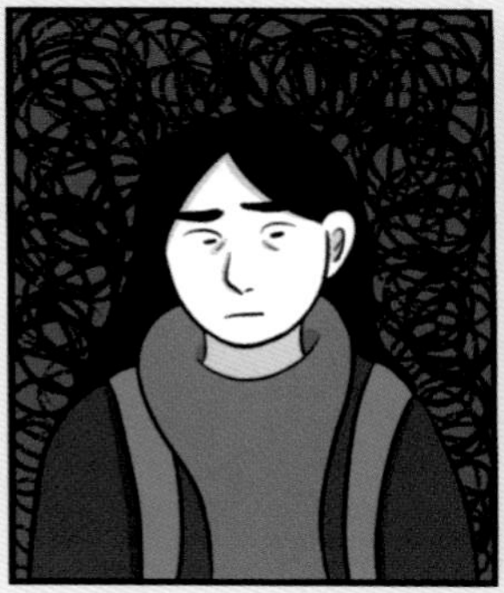

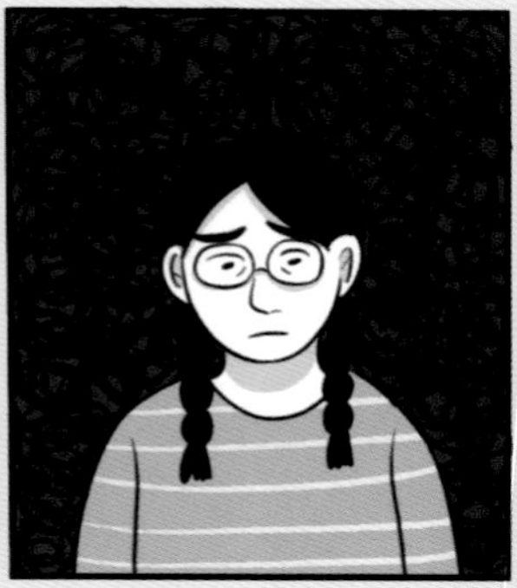

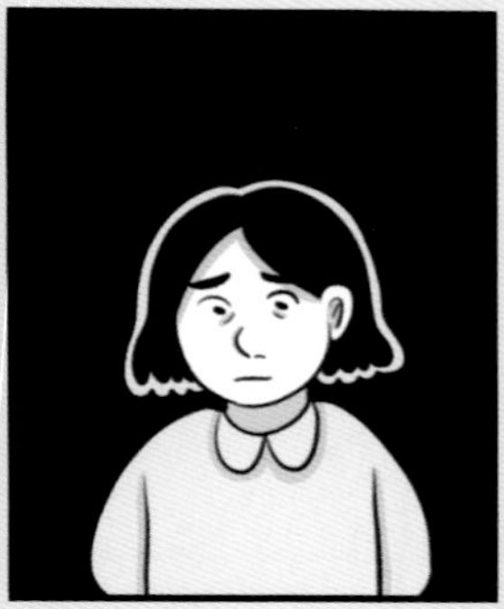

NOW I JUST FEEL LIKE I'M NOT EVEN GOOD AT BEING HALF.

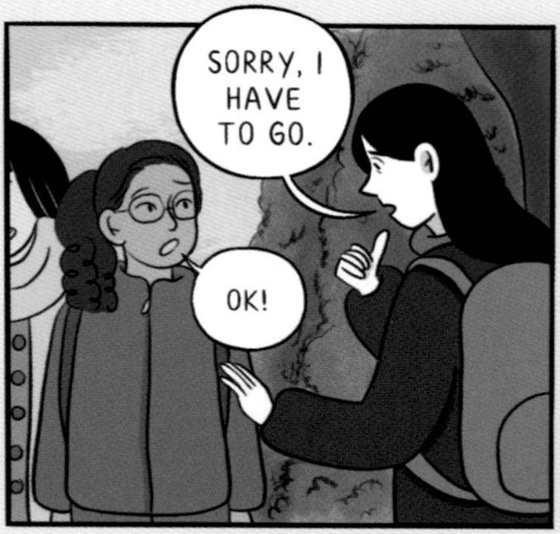
SORRY, I HAVE TO GO.
OK!

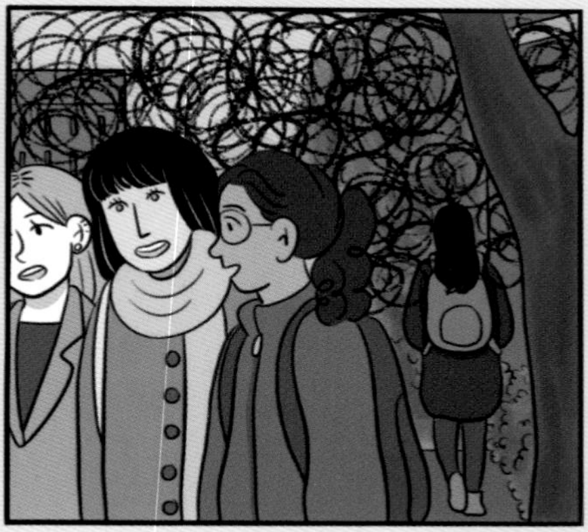

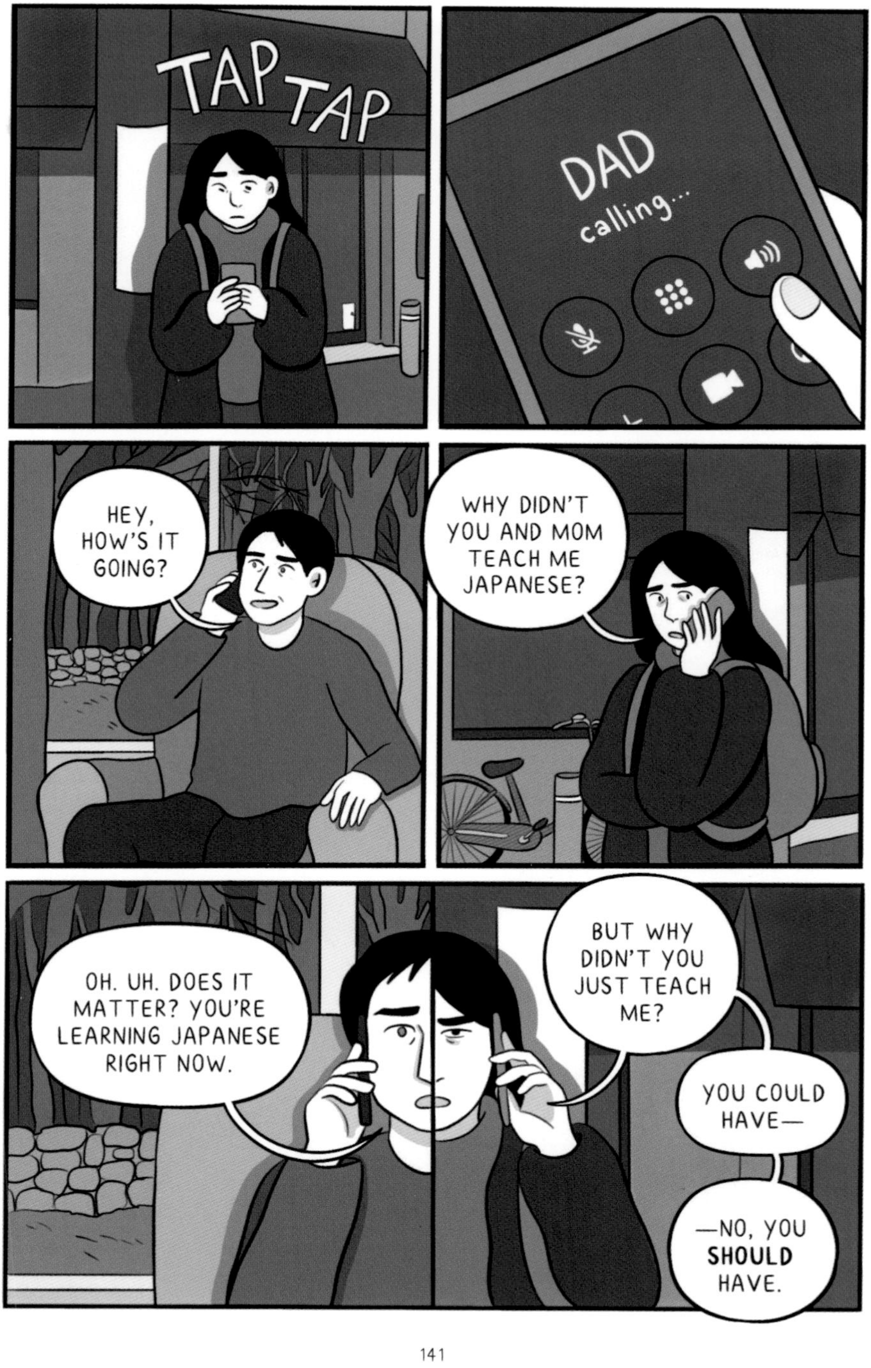
TAP TAP
DAD
calling...
HEY, HOW'S IT GOING?
WHY DIDN'T YOU AND MOM TEACH ME JAPANESE?
OH. UH. DOES IT MATTER? YOU'RE LEARNING JAPANESE RIGHT NOW.
BUT WHY DIDN'T YOU JUST TEACH ME?
YOU COULD HAVE—
—NO, YOU **SHOULD** HAVE.

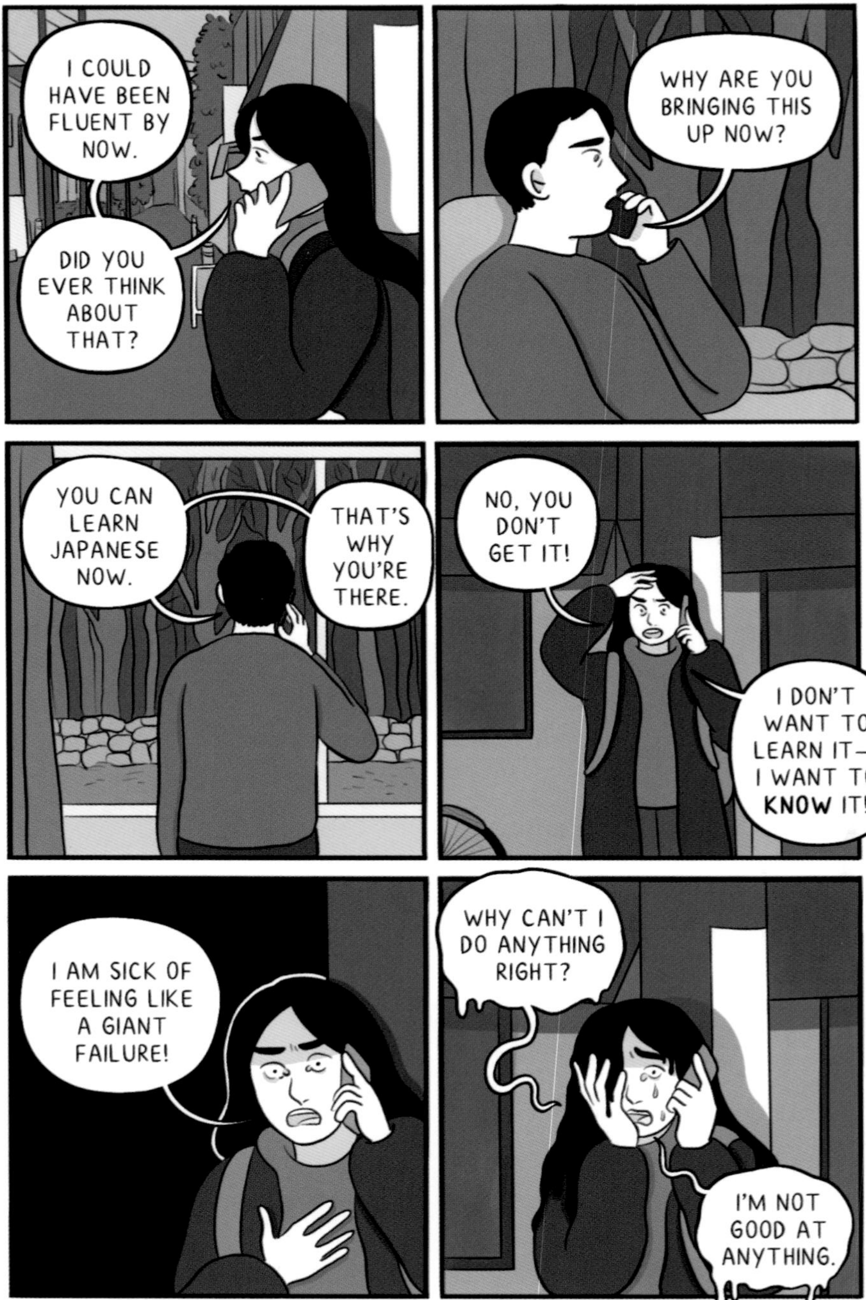
I COULD HAVE BEEN FLUENT BY NOW.
DID YOU EVER THINK ABOUT THAT?
WHY ARE YOU BRINGING THIS UP NOW?
YOU CAN LEARN JAPANESE NOW.
THAT'S WHY YOU'RE THERE.
NO, YOU DON'T GET IT!
I DON'T WANT TO LEARN IT— I WANT TO **KNOW** IT!
I AM SICK OF FEELING LIKE A GIANT FAILURE!
WHY CAN'T I DO ANYTHING RIGHT?
I'M NOT GOOD AT ANYTHING.

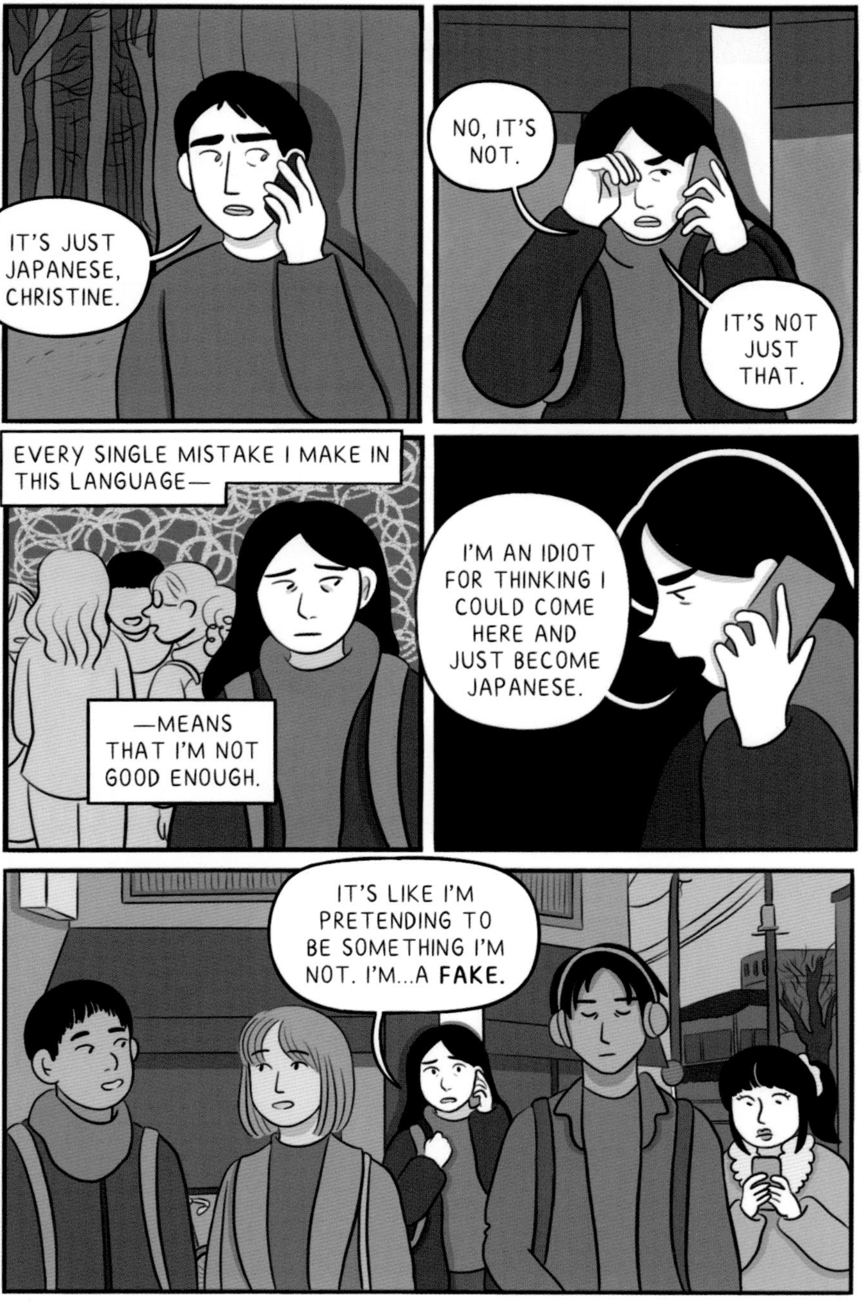
IT'S JUST JAPANESE, CHRISTINE.
NO, IT'S NOT.
IT'S NOT JUST THAT.
EVERY SINGLE MISTAKE I MAKE IN THIS LANGUAGE—
—MEANS THAT I'M NOT GOOD ENOUGH.
I'M AN IDIOT FOR THINKING I COULD COME HERE AND JUST BECOME JAPANESE.
IT'S LIKE I'M PRETENDING TO BE SOMETHING I'M NOT. I'M...A **FAKE.**

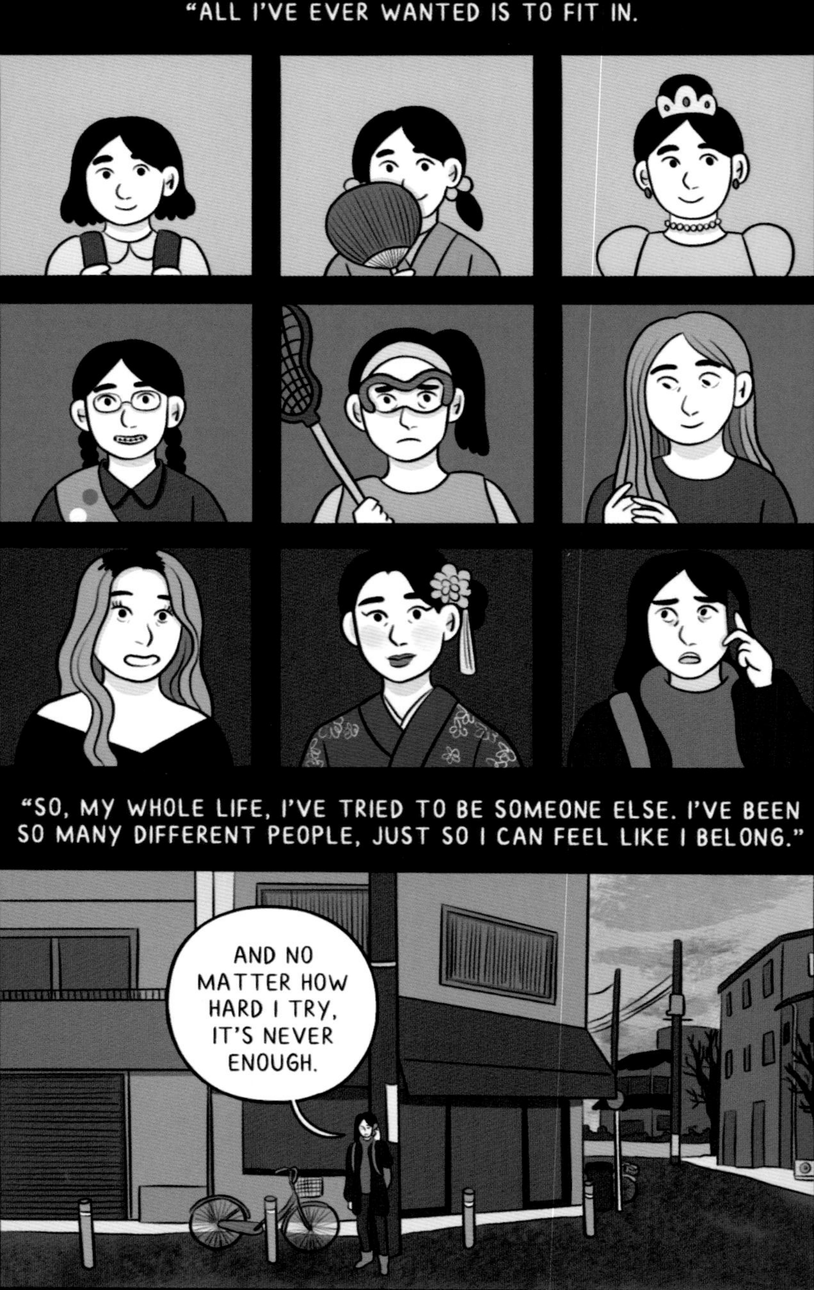
"ALL I'VE EVER WANTED IS TO FIT IN.
"SO, MY WHOLE LIFE, I'VE TRIED TO BE SOMEONE ELSE. I'VE BEEN SO MANY DIFFERENT PEOPLE, JUST SO I CAN FEEL LIKE I BELONG."
AND NO MATTER HOW HARD I TRY, IT'S NEVER ENOUGH.

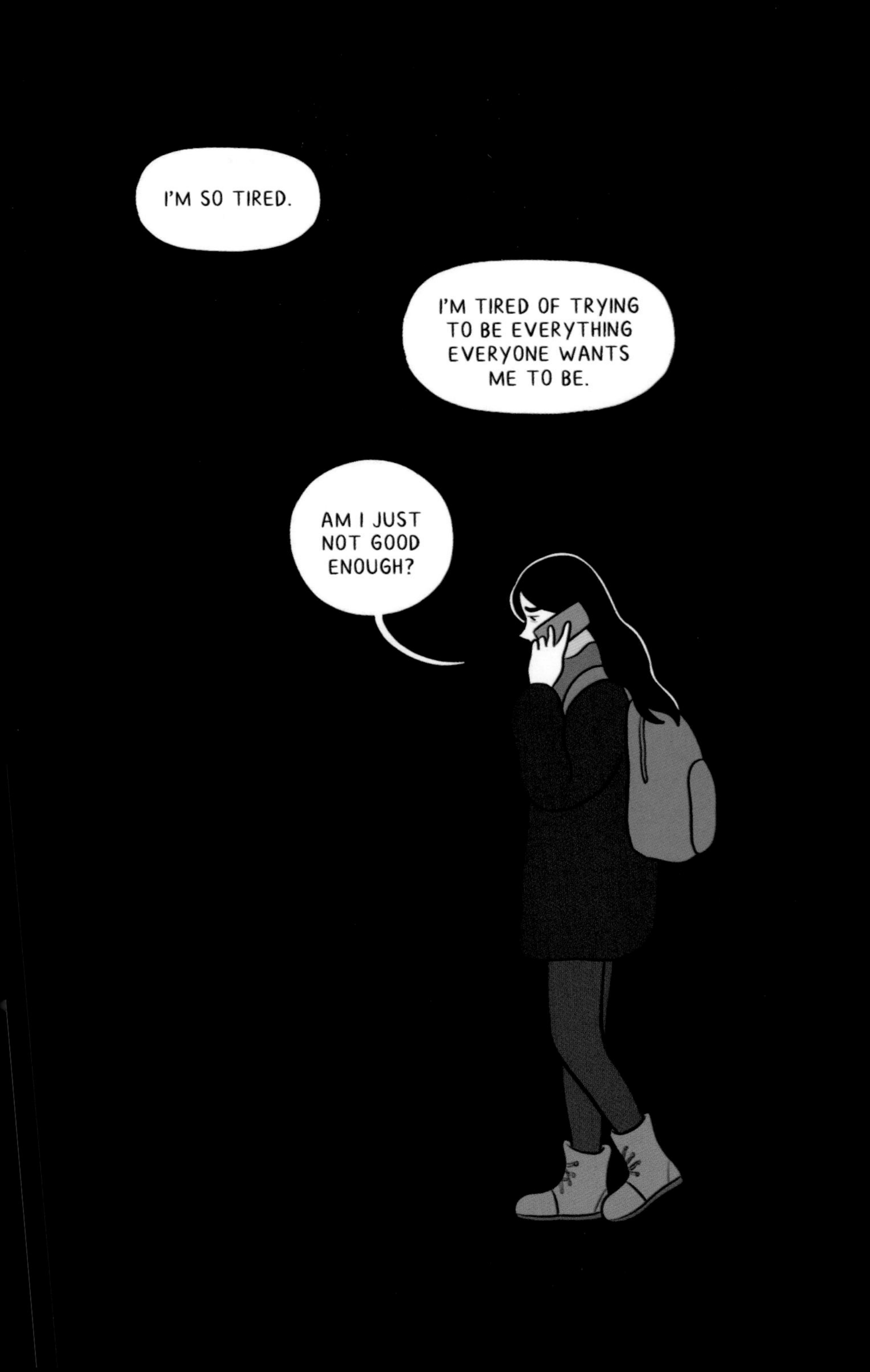
I'M SO TIRED.
I'M TIRED OF TRYING TO BE EVERYTHING EVERYONE WANTS ME TO BE.
AM I JUST NOT GOOD ENOUGH?

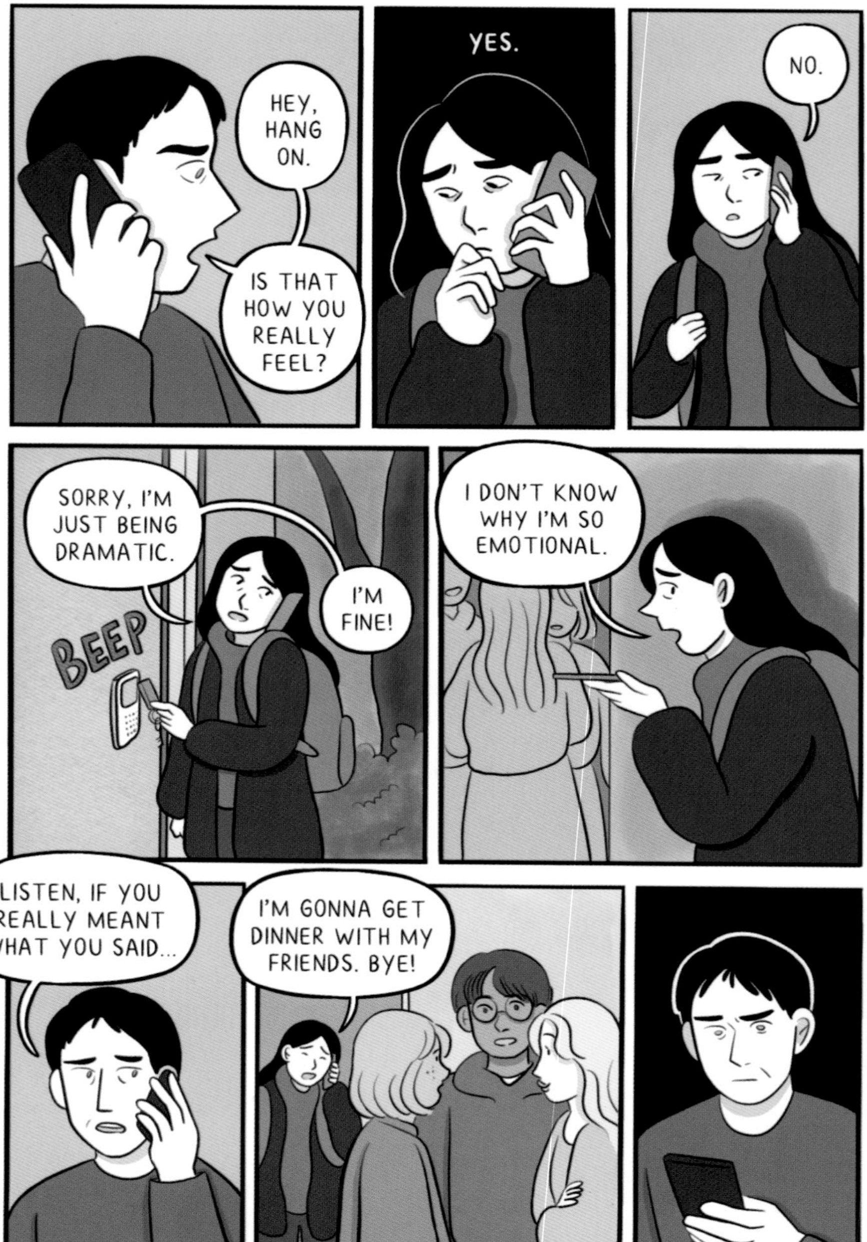
HEY, HANG ON.
IS THAT HOW YOU REALLY FEEL?
YES.
NO.
SORRY, I'M JUST BEING DRAMATIC.
I'M FINE!
BEEP
I DON'T KNOW WHY I'M SO EMOTIONAL.
LISTEN, IF YOU REALLY MEANT WHAT YOU SAID...
I'M GONNA GET DINNER WITH MY FRIENDS. BYE!

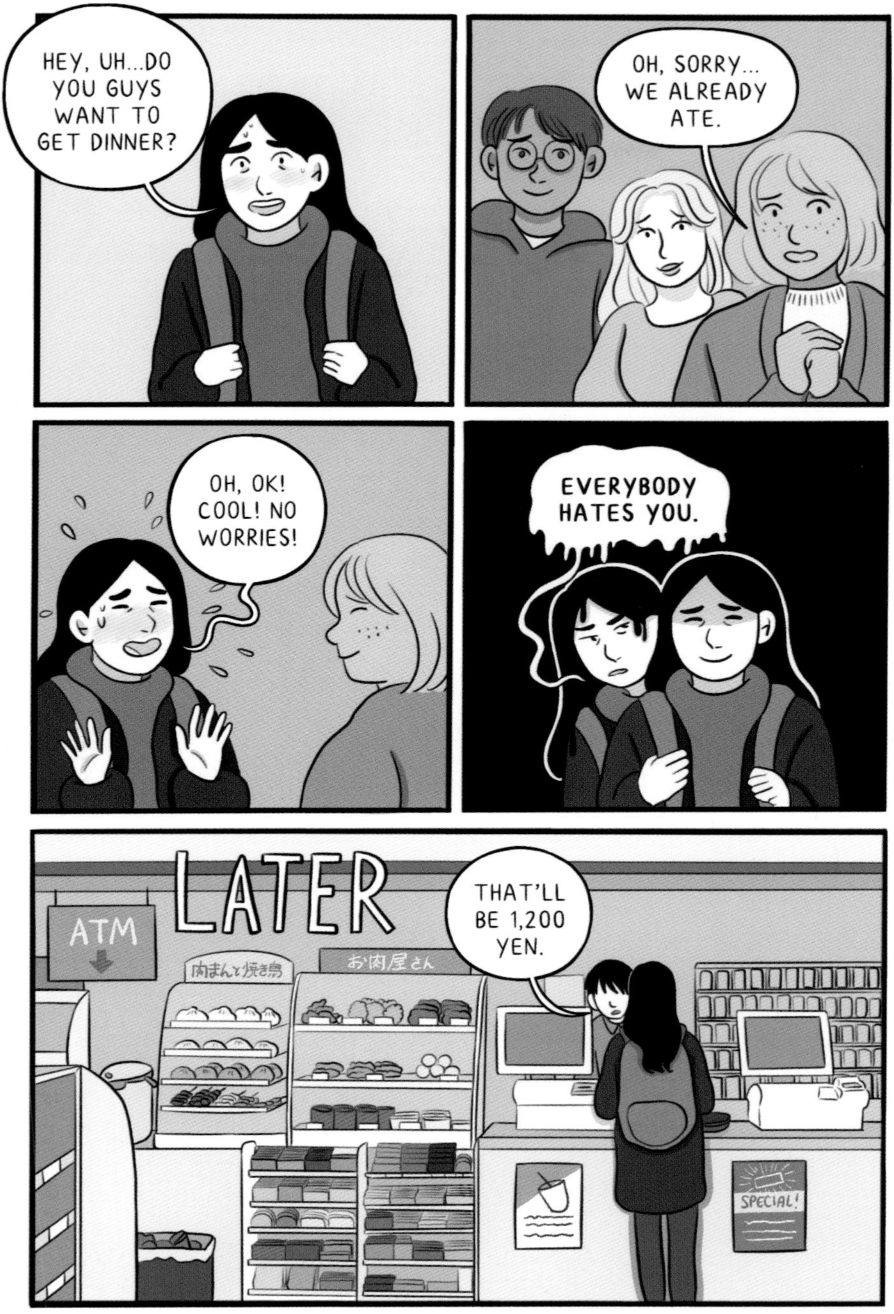
HEY, UH...DO YOU GUYS WANT TO GET DINNER?
OH, SORRY... WE ALREADY ATE.
OH, OK! COOL! NO WORRIES!
EVERYBODY HATES YOU.
LATER
ATM
肉まんと焼き鳥
お肉屋さん
THAT'LL BE 1,200 YEN.
SPECIAL!

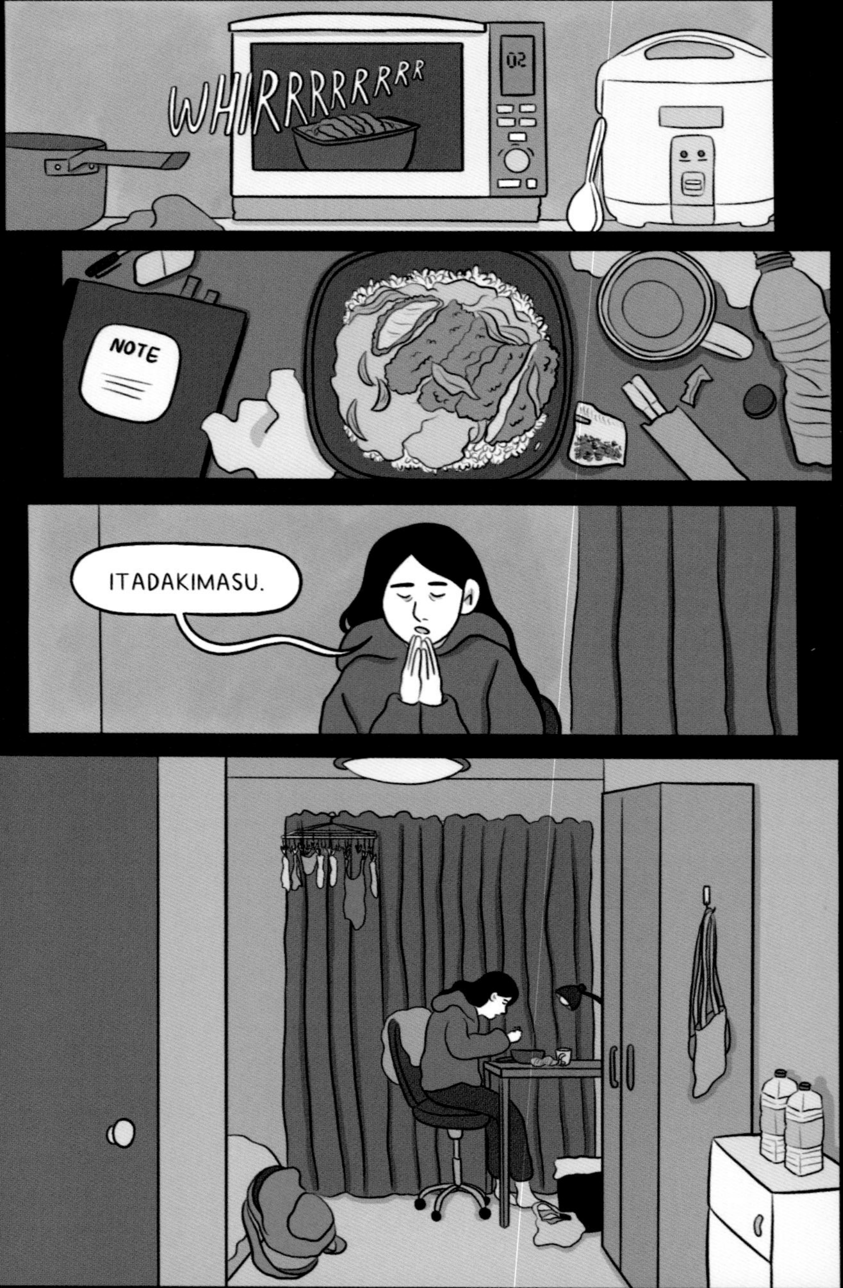
WHIRRRRRRRR
02
NOTE
ITADAKIMASU.

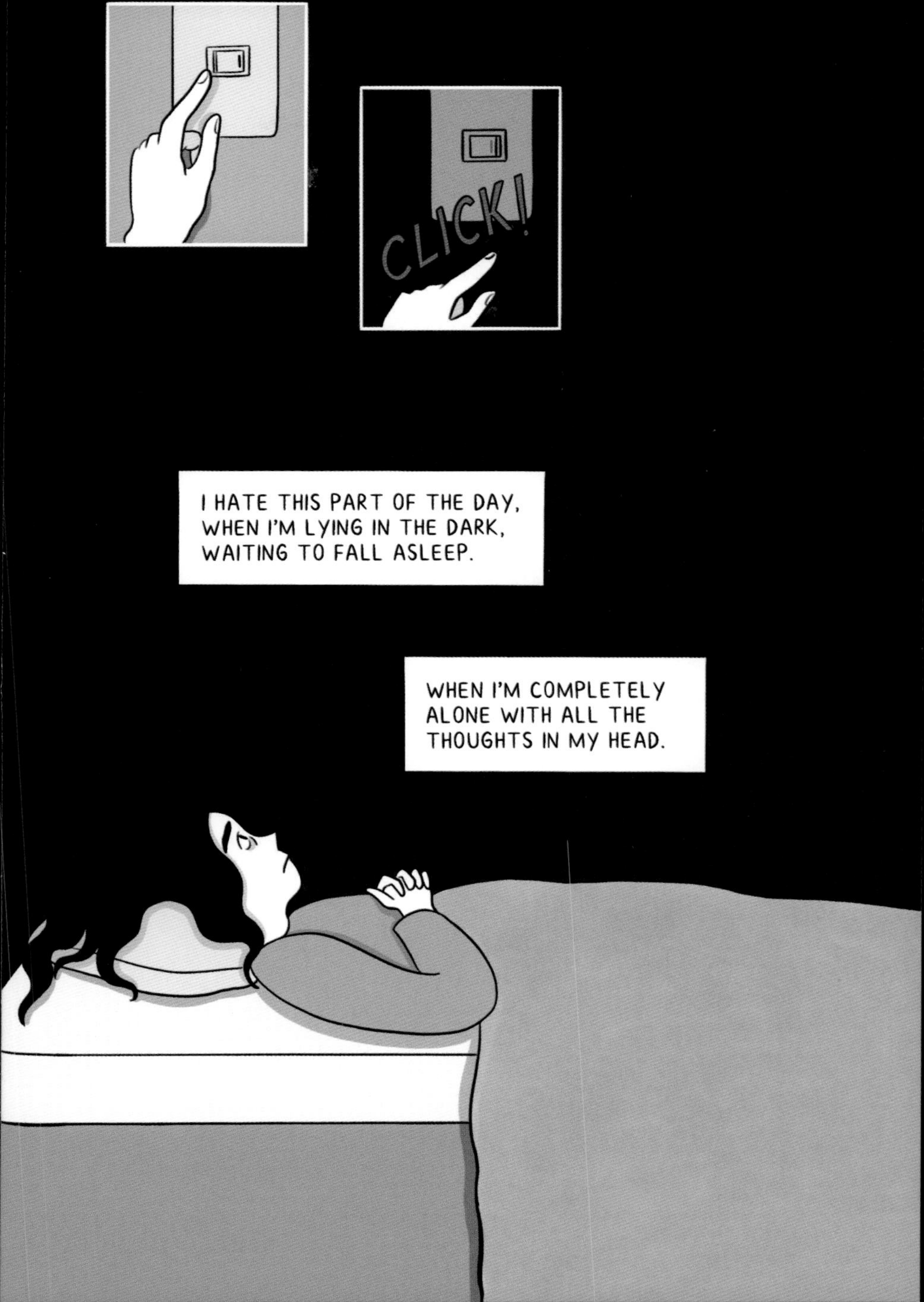
CLICK!
I HATE THIS PART OF THE DAY, WHEN I'M LYING IN THE DARK, WAITING TO FALL ASLEEP.
WHEN I'M COMPLETELY ALONE WITH ALL THE THOUGHTS IN MY HEAD.

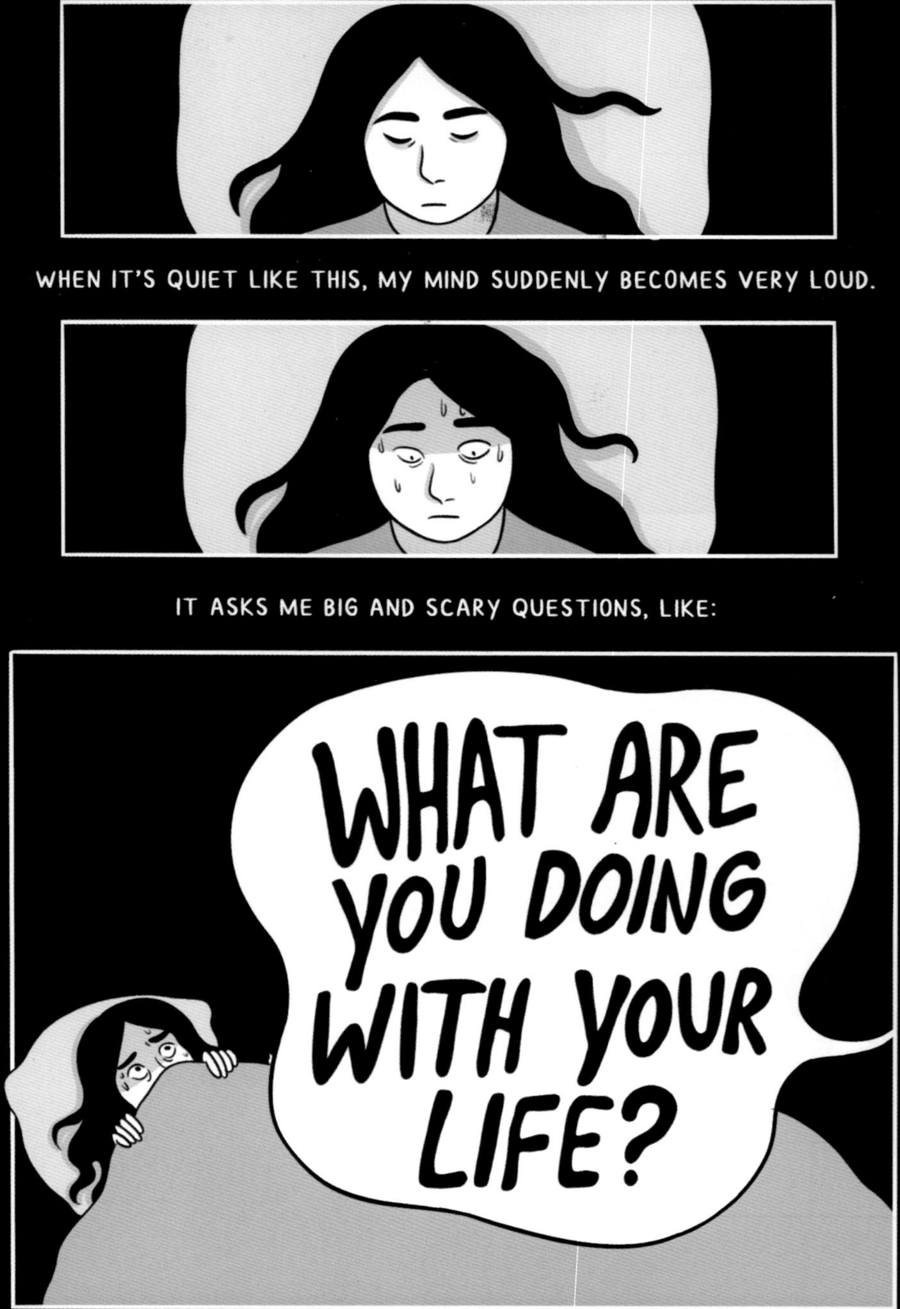
WHEN IT'S QUIET LIKE THIS, MY MIND SUDDENLY BECOMES VERY LOUD.
IT ASKS ME BIG AND SCARY QUESTIONS, LIKE:
WHAT ARE YOU DOING WITH YOUR LIFE?

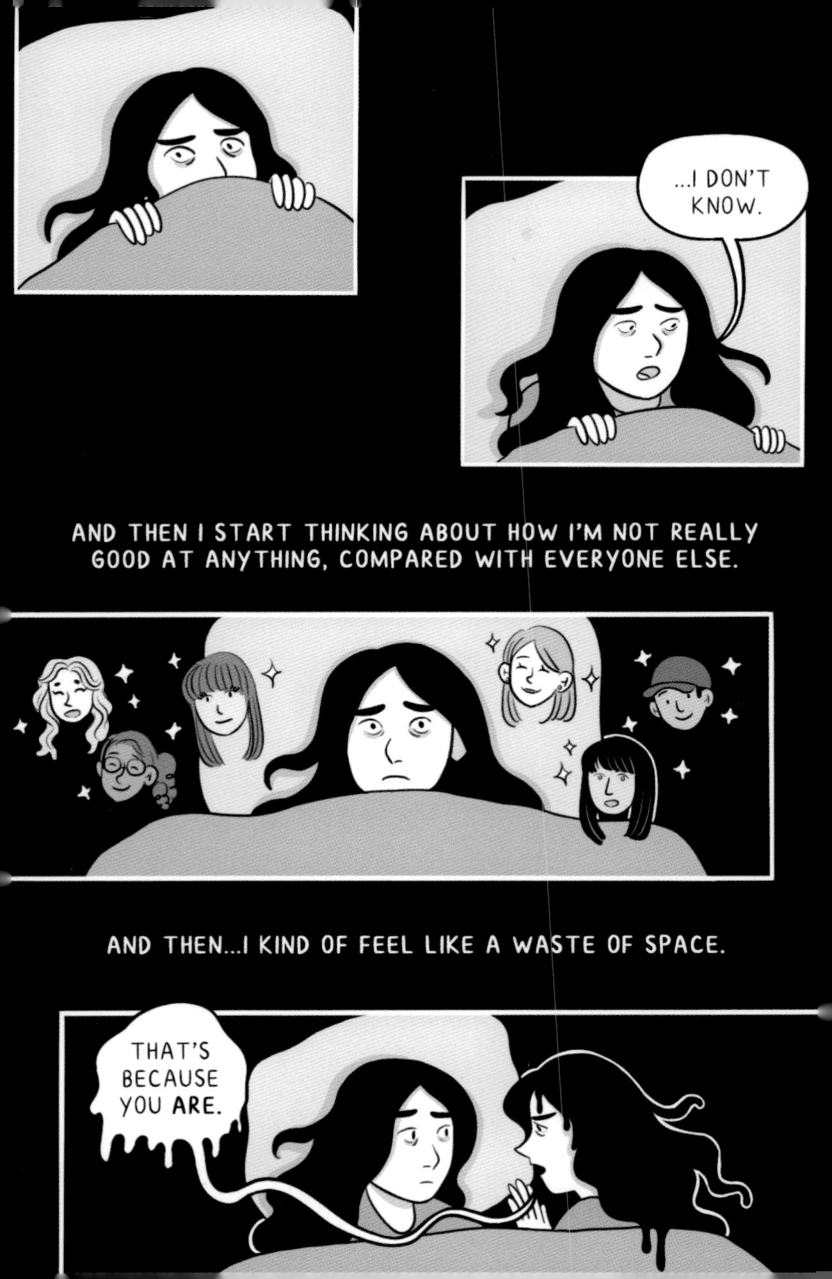
...I DON'T KNOW.
AND THEN I START THINKING ABOUT HOW I'M NOT REALLY GOOD AT ANYTHING, COMPARED WITH EVERYONE ELSE.
AND THEN...I KIND OF FEEL LIKE A WASTE OF SPACE.
THAT'S BECAUSE YOU **ARE**.

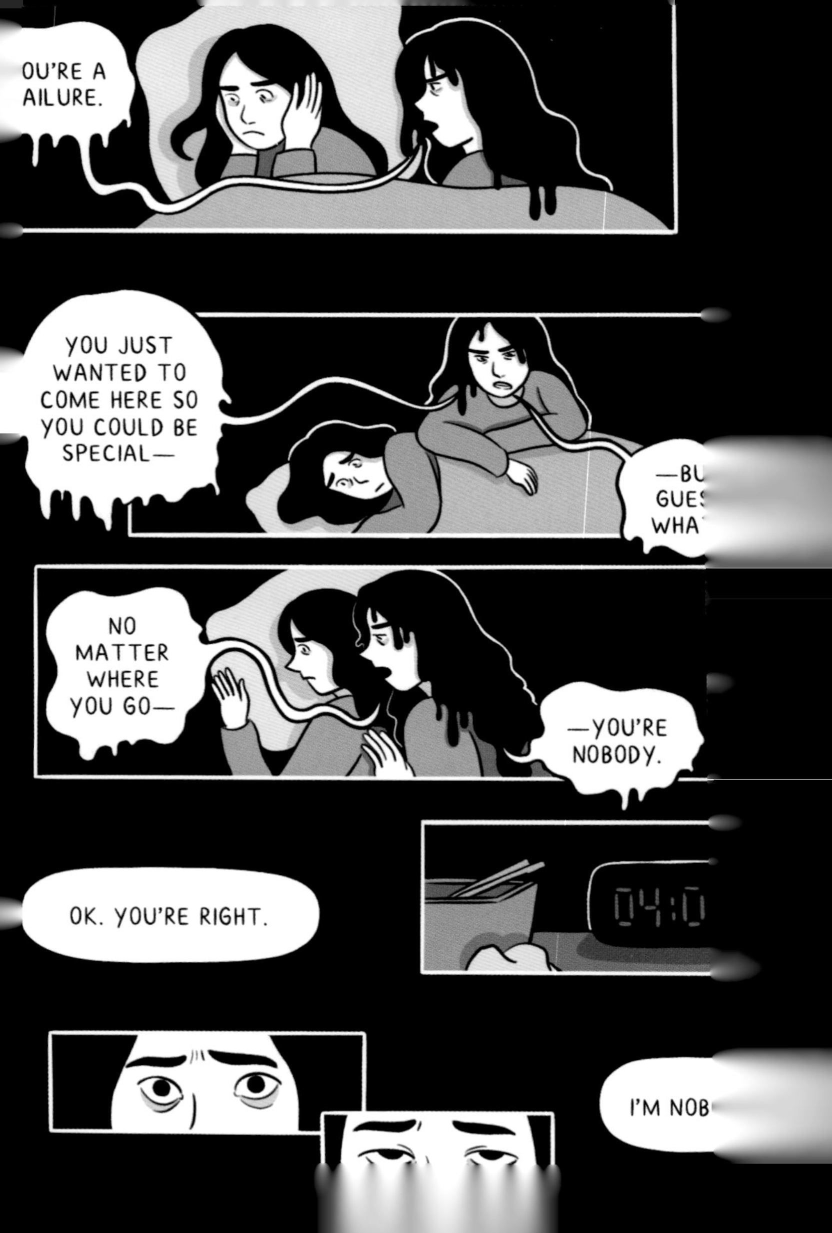
OU'RE A AILURE.
YOU JUST WANTED TO COME HERE SO YOU COULD BE SPECIAL—
—BU GUES WHA
NO MATTER WHERE YOU GO—
—YOU'RE NOBODY.
OK. YOU'RE RIGHT.
04:0
I'M NOB

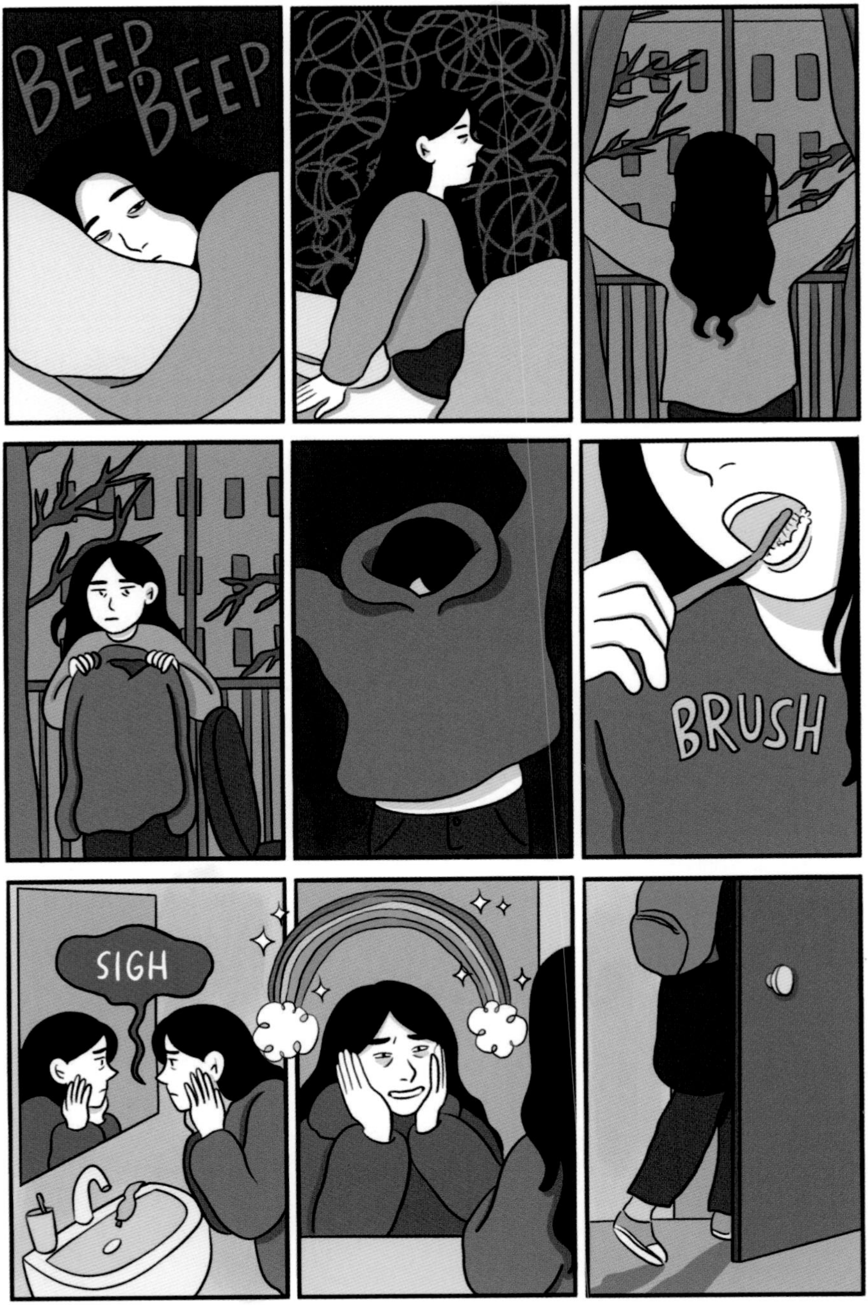
BEEP BEEP
BRUSH
SIGH

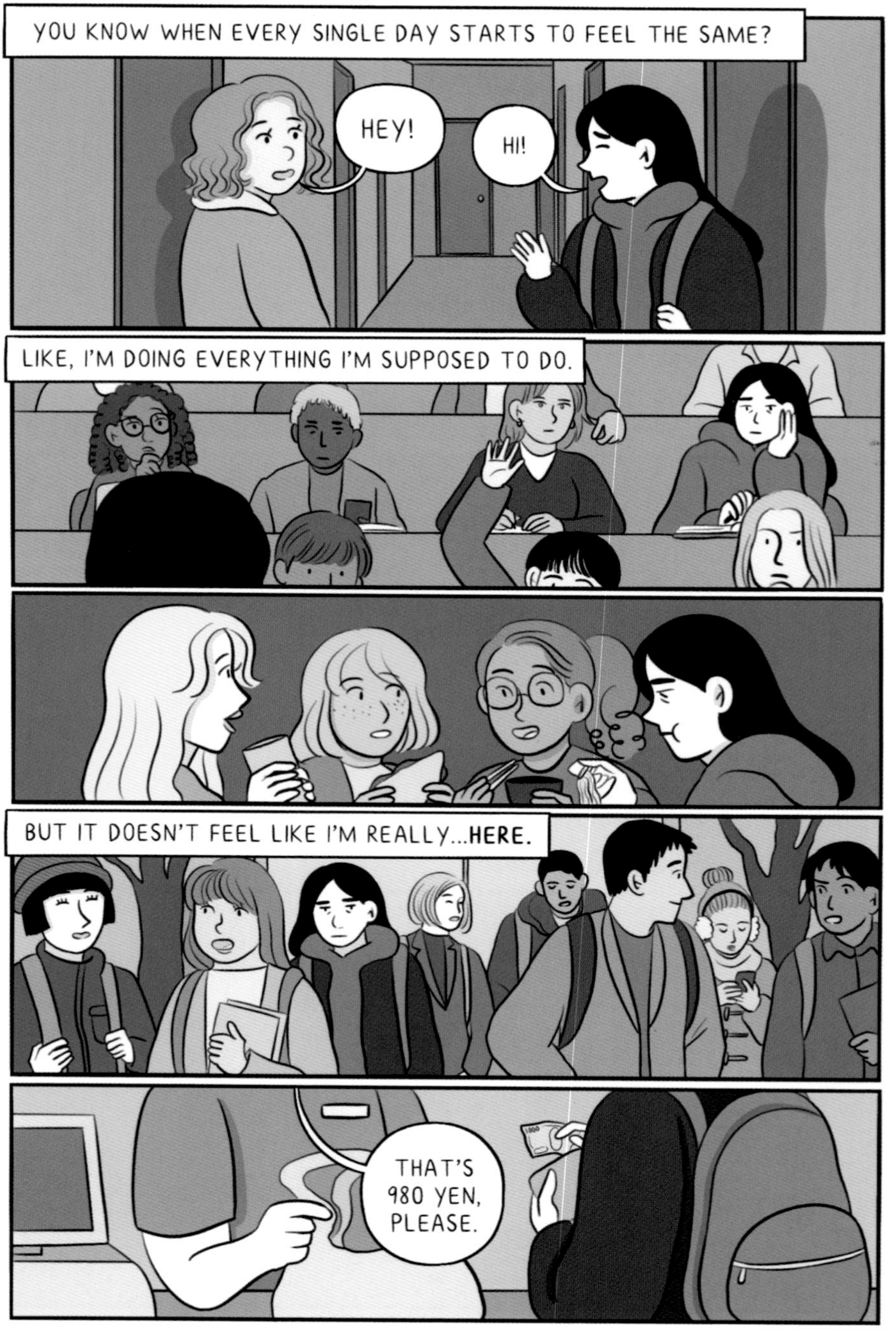
YOU KNOW WHEN EVERY SINGLE DAY STARTS TO FEEL THE SAME?
HEY!
HI!
LIKE, I'M DOING EVERYTHING I'M SUPPOSED TO DO.
BUT IT DOESN'T FEEL LIKE I'M REALLY...**HERE.**
THAT'S 980 YEN, PLEASE.

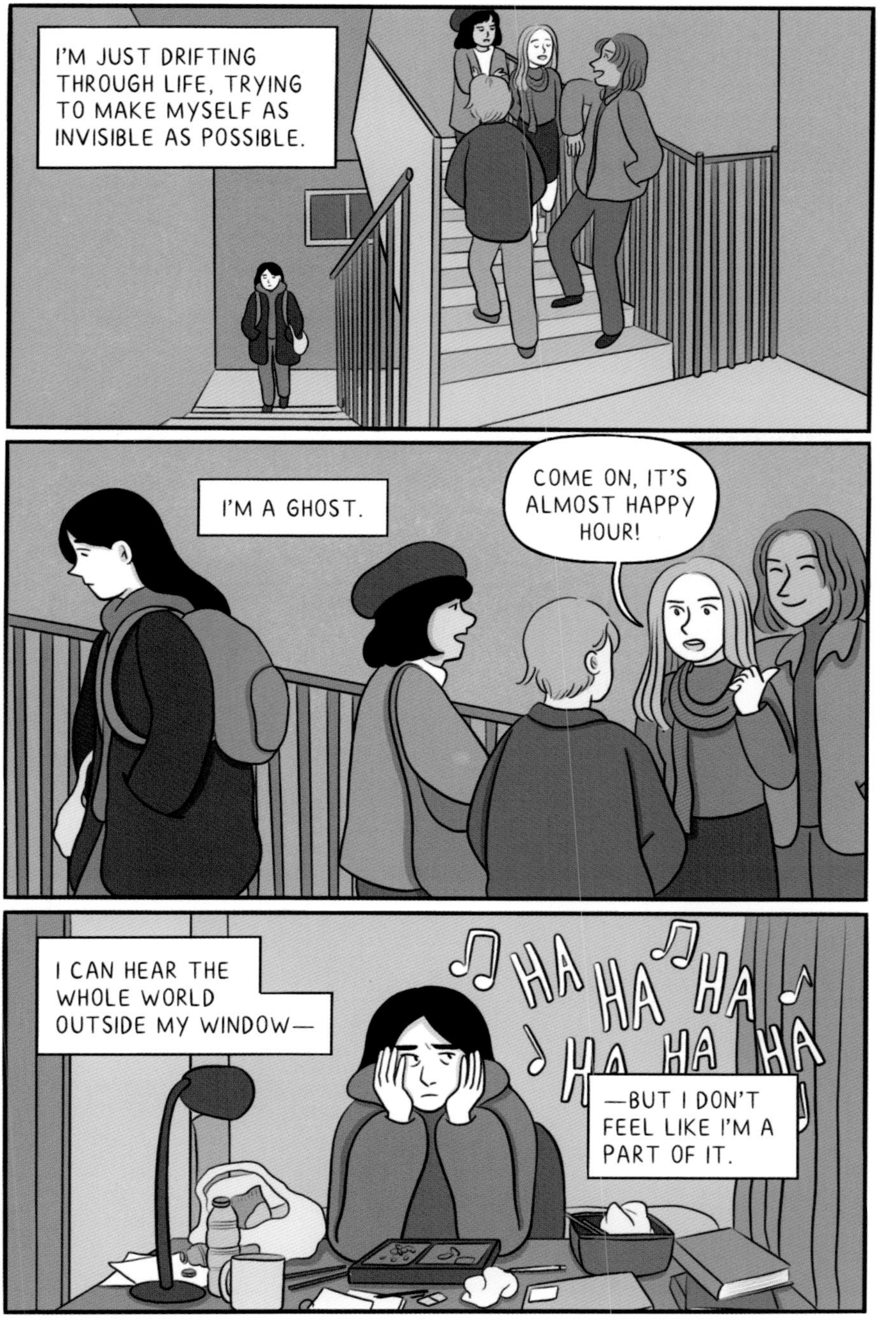
I'M JUST DRIFTING THROUGH LIFE, TRYING TO MAKE MYSELF AS INVISIBLE AS POSSIBLE.
I'M A GHOST.
COME ON, IT'S ALMOST HAPPY HOUR!
I CAN HEAR THE WHOLE WORLD OUTSIDE MY WINDOW—
HA HA HA
HA HA HA
—BUT I DON'T FEEL LIKE I'M A PART OF IT.

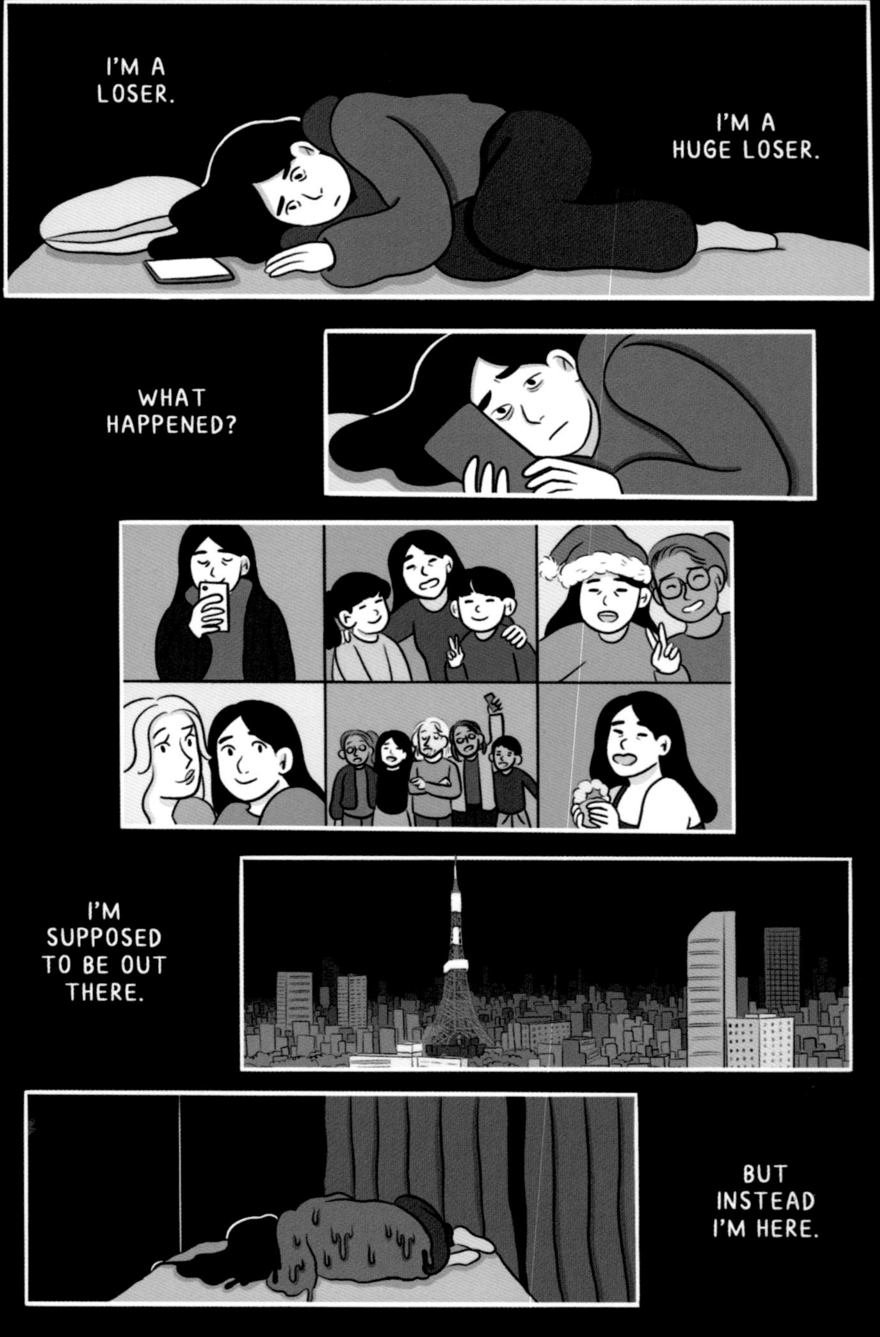
I'M A LOSER.
I'M A HUGE LOSER.
WHAT HAPPENED?
I'M SUPPOSED TO BE OUT THERE.
BUT INSTEAD I'M HERE.

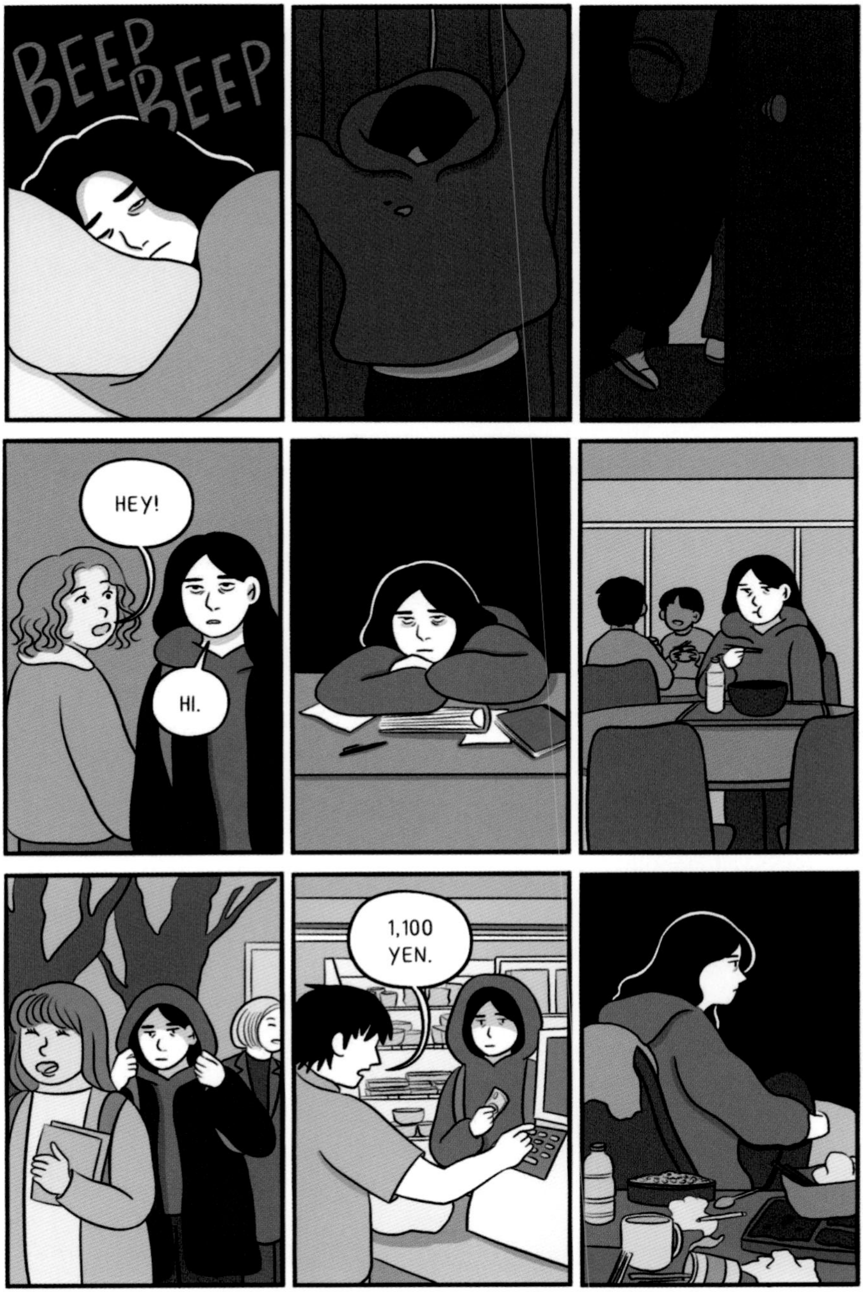
BEEP BEEP
HEY!
HI.
1,100 YEN.

I'VE BEEN EATING CONVENIENCE STORE FOOD EVERY DAY, TO THE POINT WHERE I'M TOO EMBARRASSED TO EVEN GO INSIDE BECAUSE THE GUY WHO WORKS THERE WILL RECOGNIZE ME.

BUT I STILL HAVE TO EAT.

GROWL

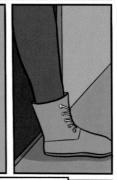

LUCKILY, THIS IS TOKYO—GOOD FOOD IS NEVER VERY HARD TO FIND.

ESPECIALLY IF IT'S RAMEN.

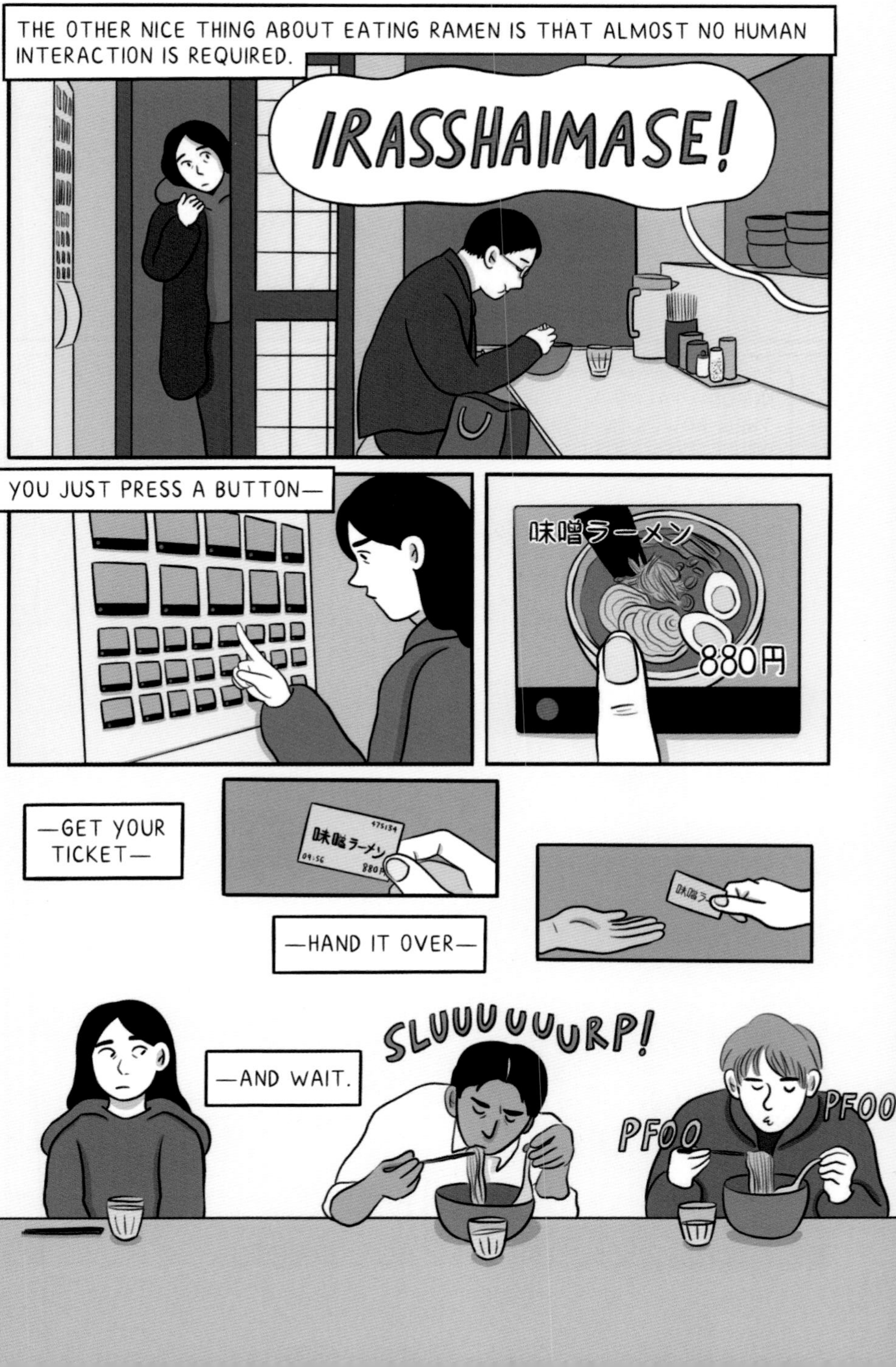
THE OTHER NICE THING ABOUT EATING RAMEN IS THAT ALMOST NO HUMAN INTERACTION IS REQUIRED.
IRASSHAIMASE!
YOU JUST PRESS A BUTTON—
味噌ラーメン
880円
—GET YOUR TICKET—
味噌ラーメン
—HAND IT OVER—
—AND WAIT.
SLUUUUUURP!
PFOO
PFOO

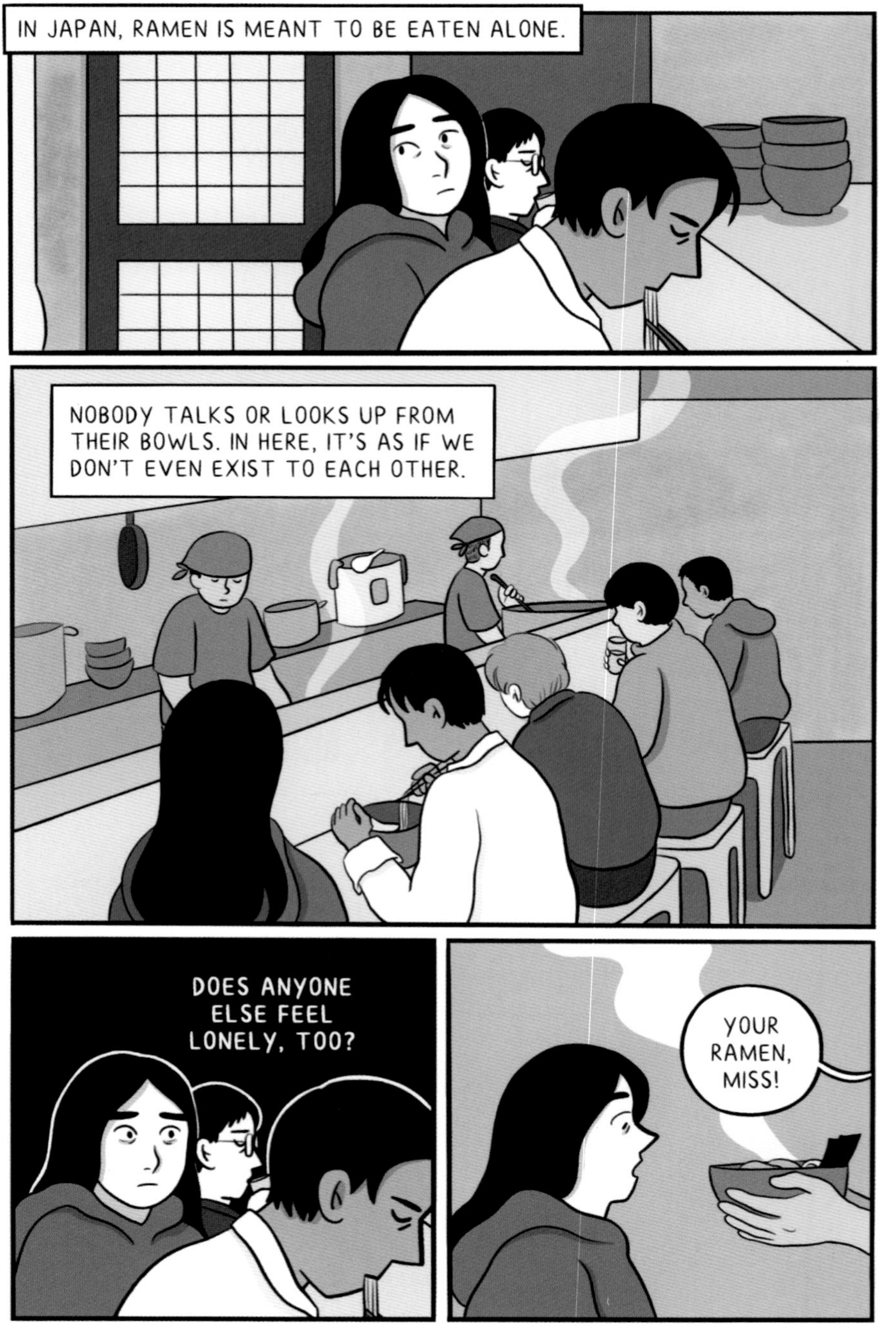
IN JAPAN, RAMEN IS MEANT TO BE EATEN ALONE.
NOBODY TALKS OR LOOKS UP FROM THEIR BOWLS. IN HERE, IT'S AS IF WE DON'T EVEN EXIST TO EACH OTHER.
DOES ANYONE ELSE FEEL LONELY, TOO?
YOUR RAMEN, MISS!

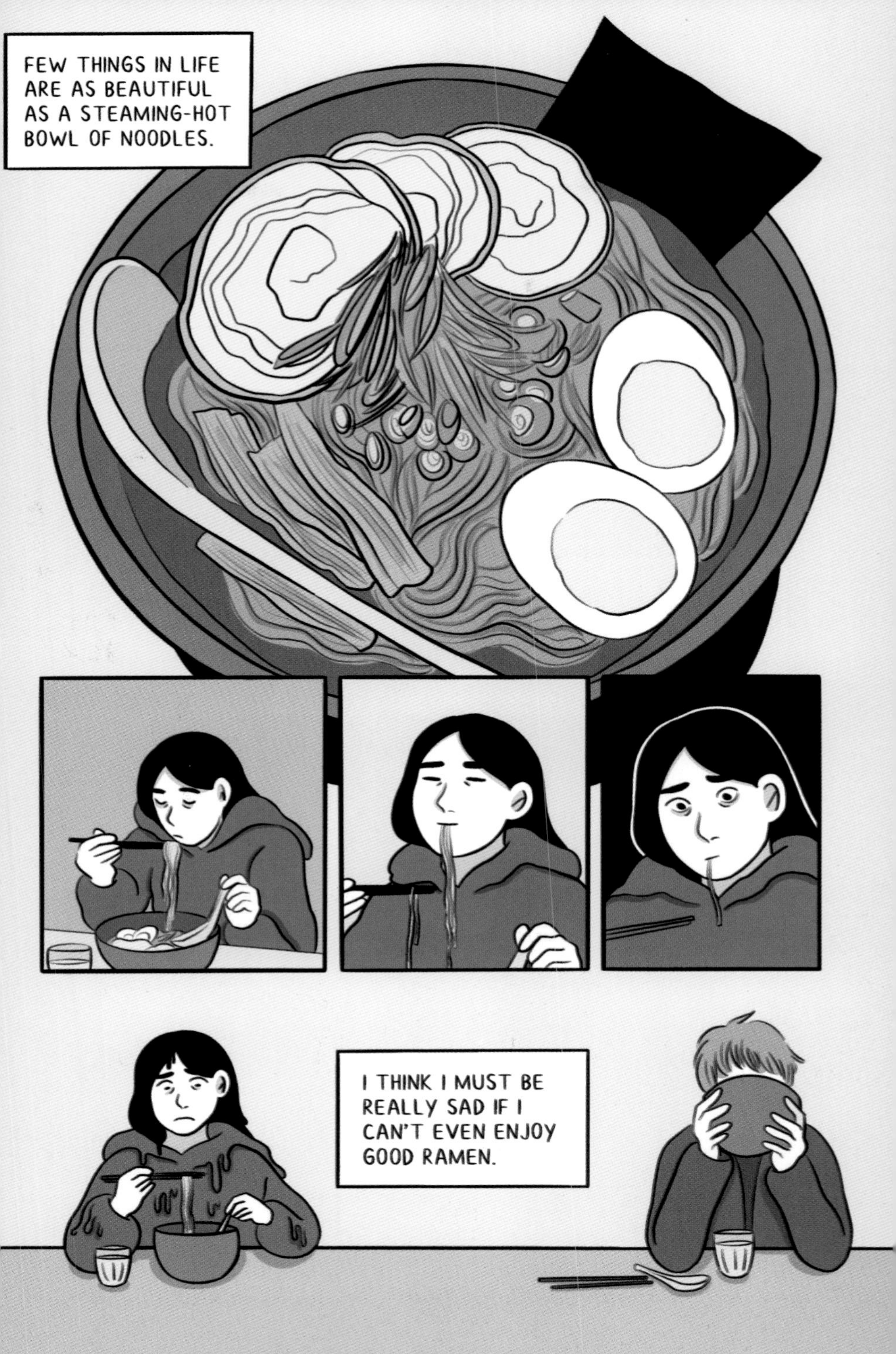
FEW THINGS IN LIFE ARE AS BEAUTIFUL AS A STEAMING-HOT BOWL OF NOODLES.
I THINK I MUST BE REALLY SAD IF I CAN'T EVEN ENJOY GOOD RAMEN.

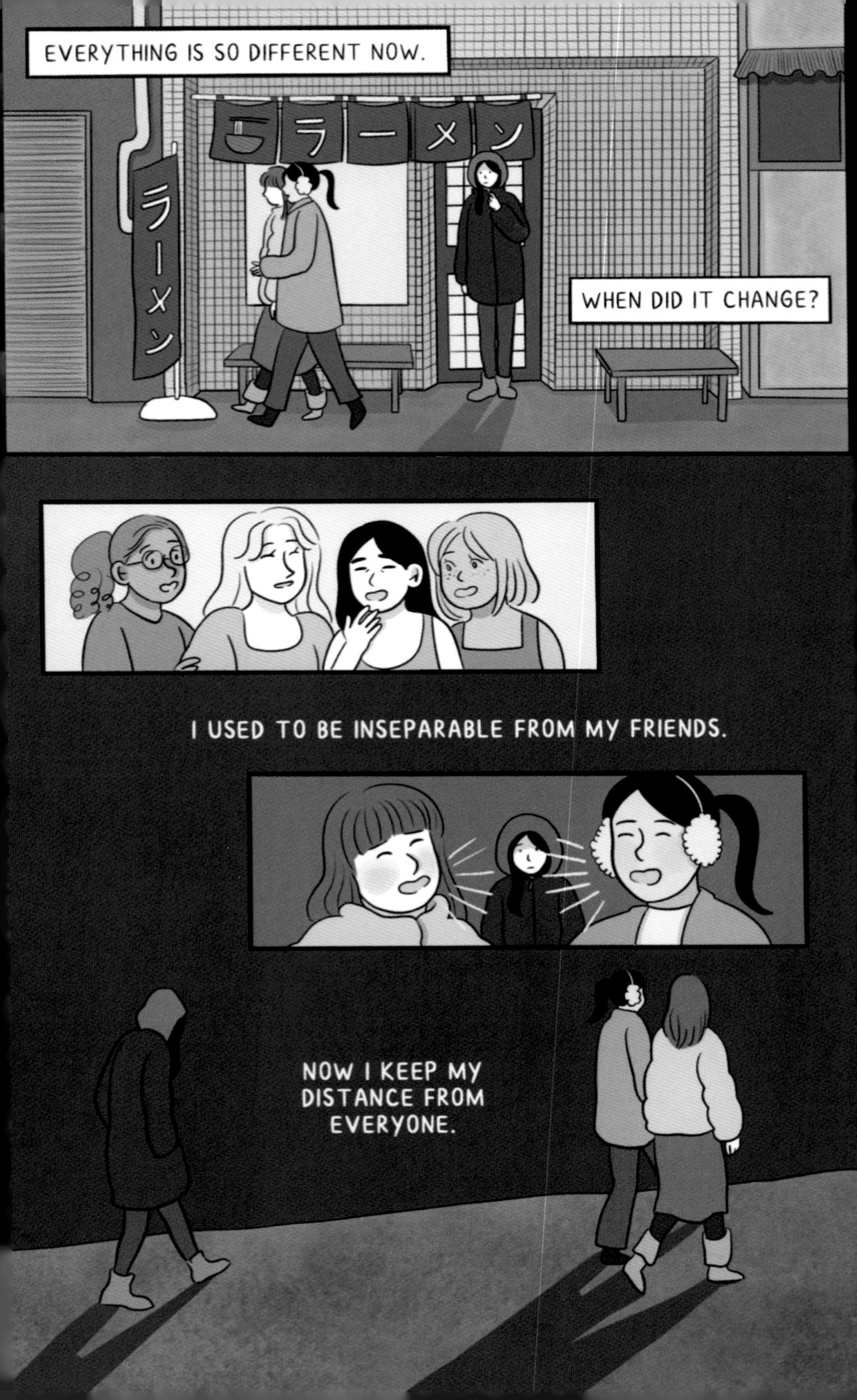
EVERYTHING IS SO DIFFERENT NOW.
ラーメン
ラーメン
WHEN DID IT CHANGE?
I USED TO BE INSEPARABLE FROM MY FRIENDS.
NOW I KEEP MY DISTANCE FROM EVERYONE.

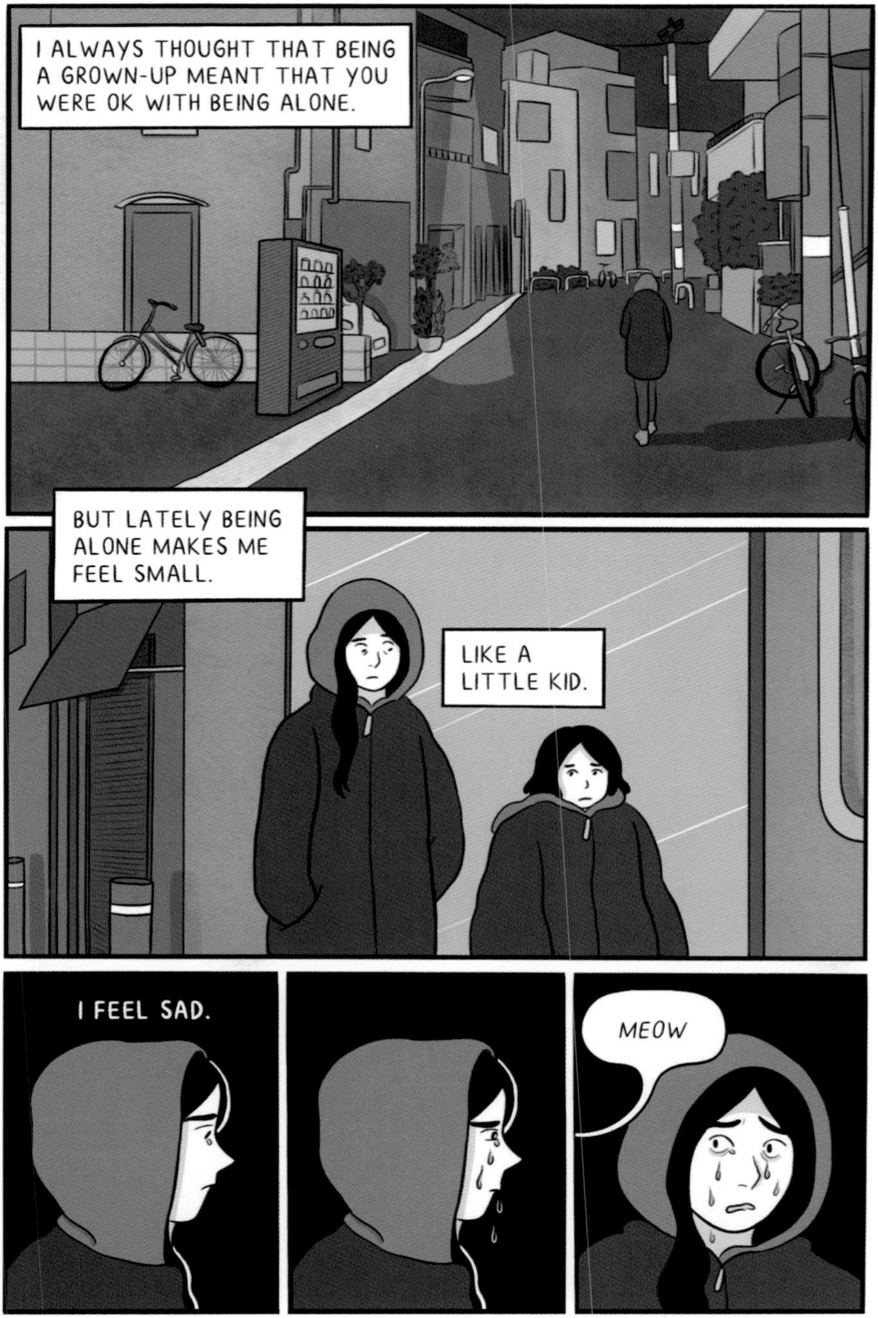
I ALWAYS THOUGHT THAT BEING A GROWN-UP MEANT THAT YOU WERE OK WITH BEING ALONE.
BUT LATELY BEING ALONE MAKES ME FEEL SMALL.
LIKE A LITTLE KID.
I FEEL SAD.
MEOW

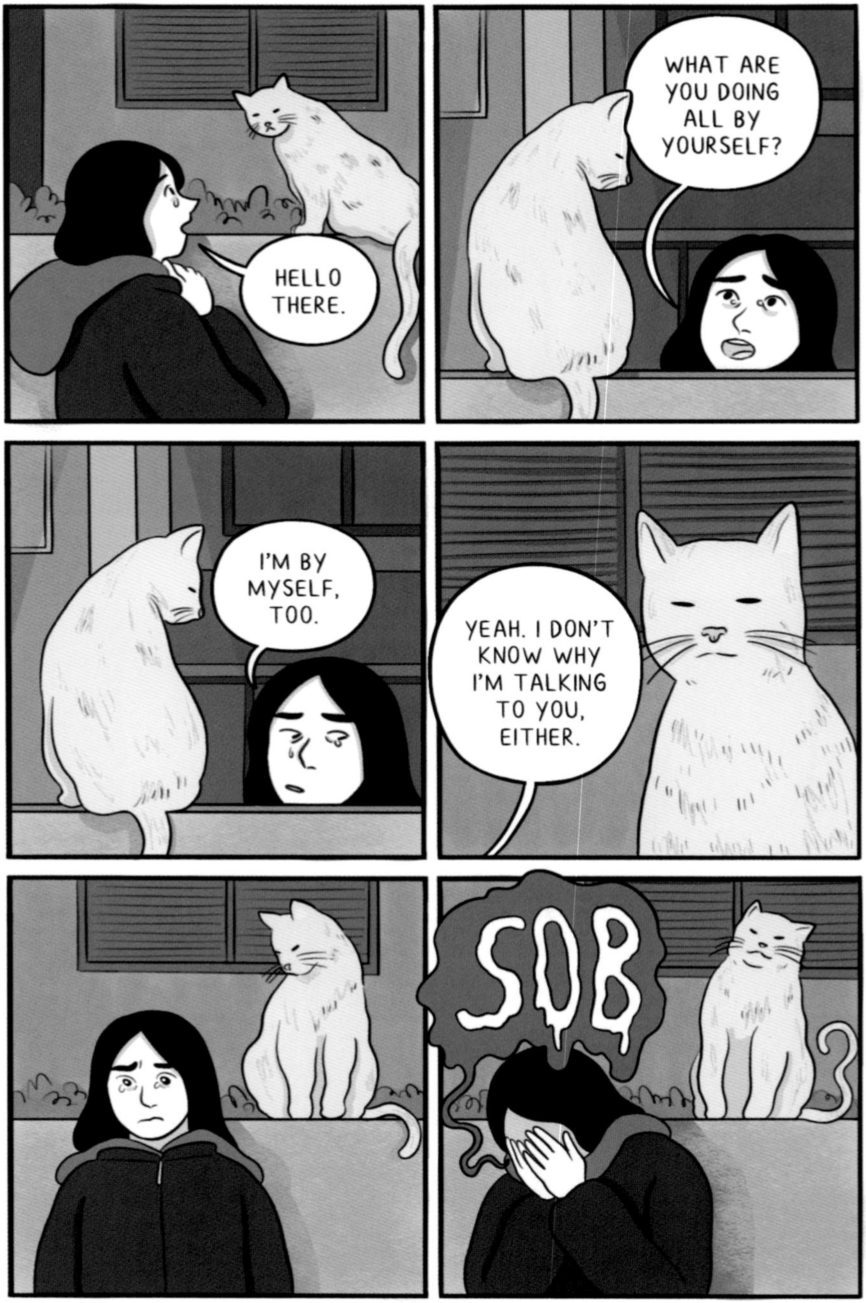
HELLO THERE.
WHAT ARE YOU DOING ALL BY YOURSELF?
I'M BY MYSELF, TOO.
YEAH. I DON'T KNOW WHY I'M TALKING TO YOU, EITHER.
SOB

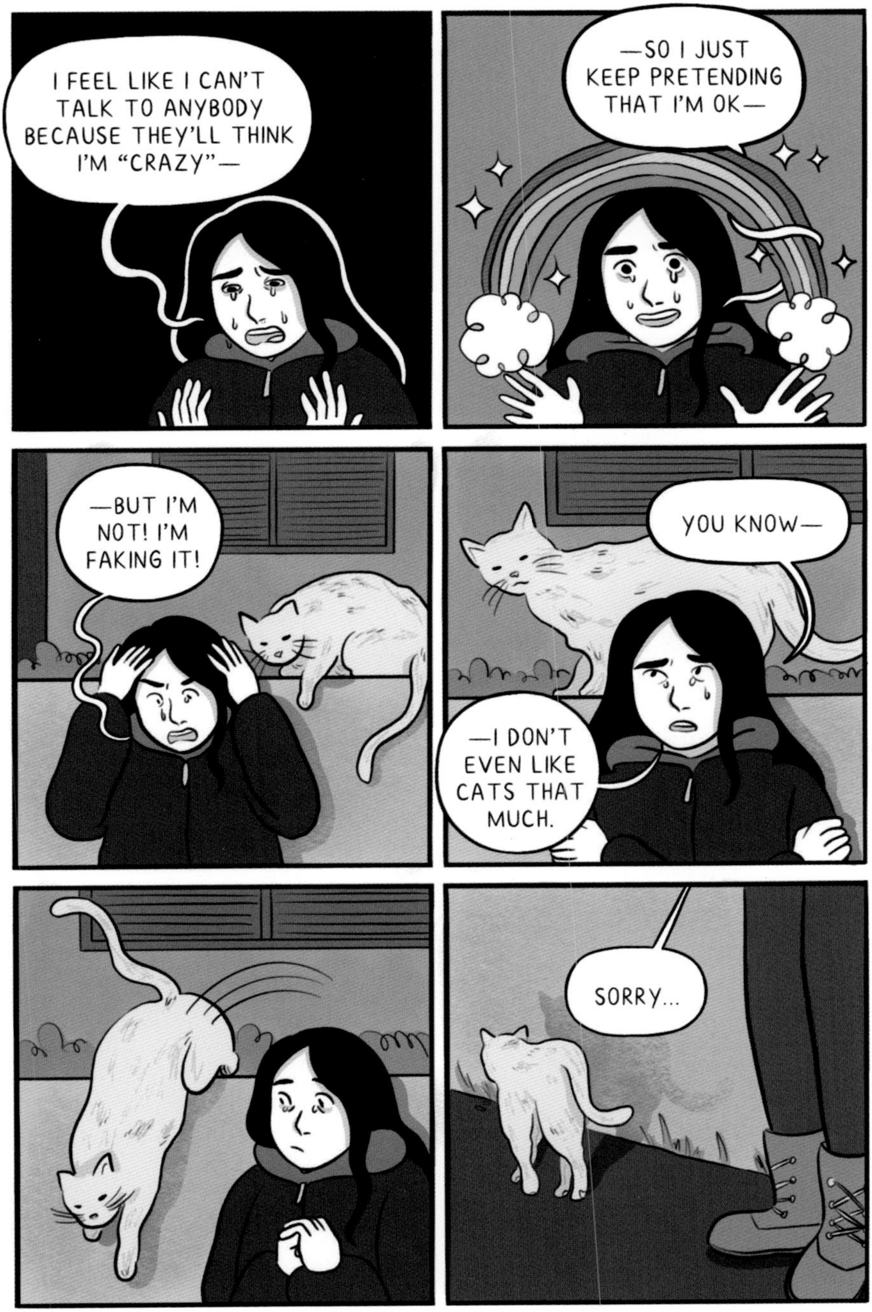
I FEEL LIKE I CAN'T TALK TO ANYBODY BECAUSE THEY'LL THINK I'M "CRAZY"—
—SO I JUST KEEP PRETENDING THAT I'M OK—
—BUT I'M NOT! I'M FAKING IT!
YOU KNOW—
—I DON'T EVEN LIKE CATS THAT MUCH.
SORRY...

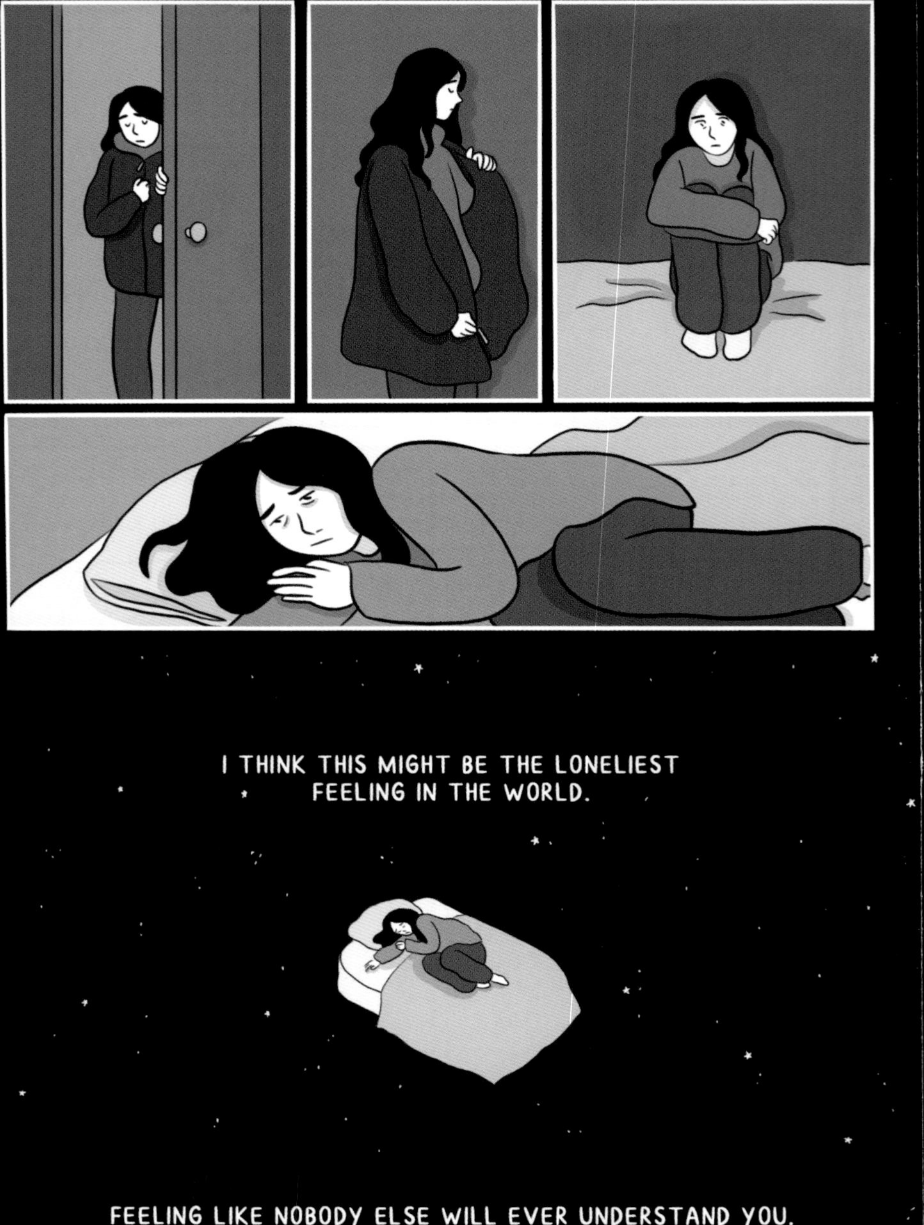
I THINK THIS MIGHT BE THE LONELIEST FEELING IN THE WORLD.
FEELING LIKE NOBODY ELSE WILL EVER UNDERSTAND YOU.

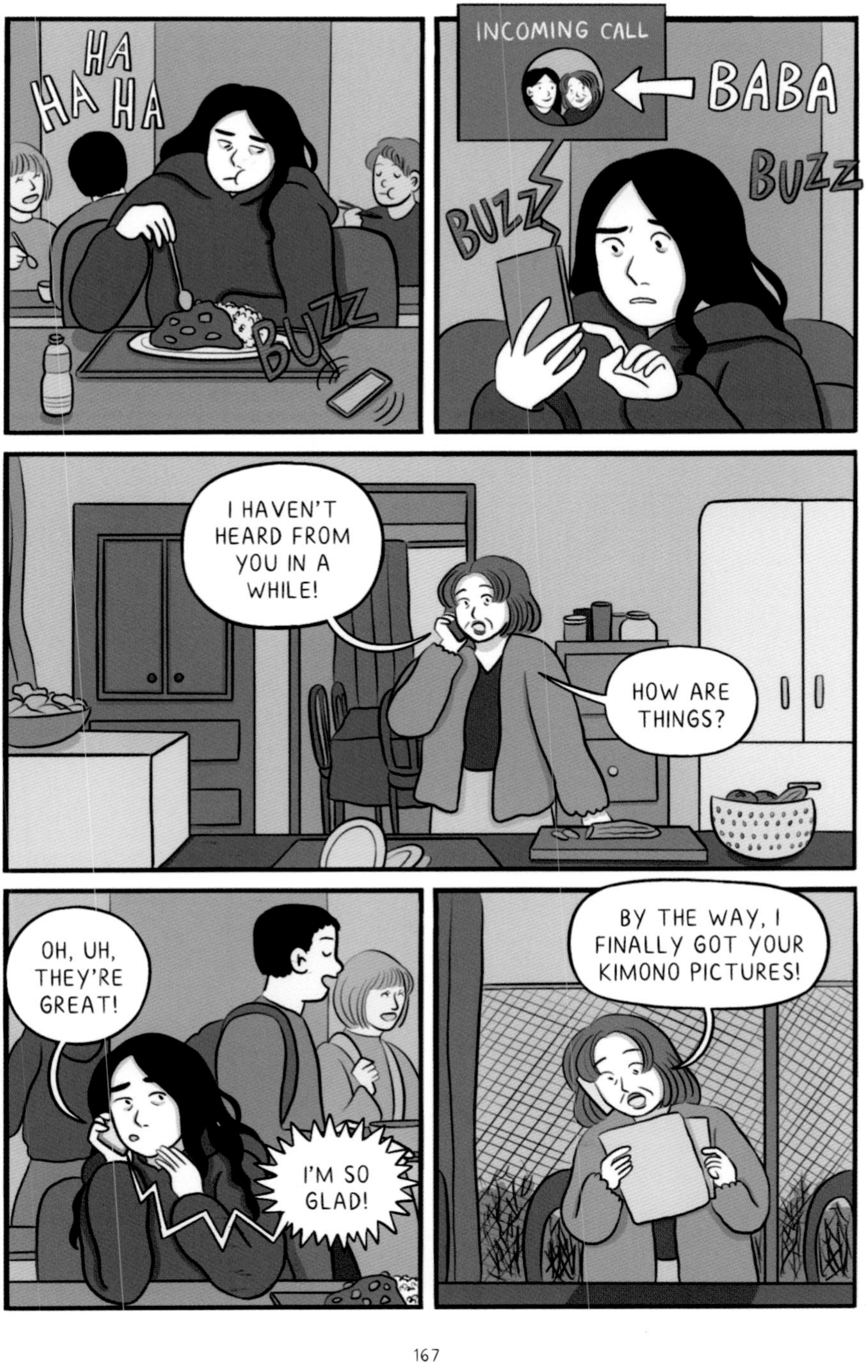
HA
HA HA
HA
BUZZ
INCOMING CALL
BABA
BUZZ
BUZZ
I HAVEN'T HEARD FROM YOU IN A WHILE!
HOW ARE THINGS?
OH, UH, THEY'RE GREAT!
I'M SO GLAD!
BY THE WAY, I FINALLY GOT YOUR KIMONO PICTURES!

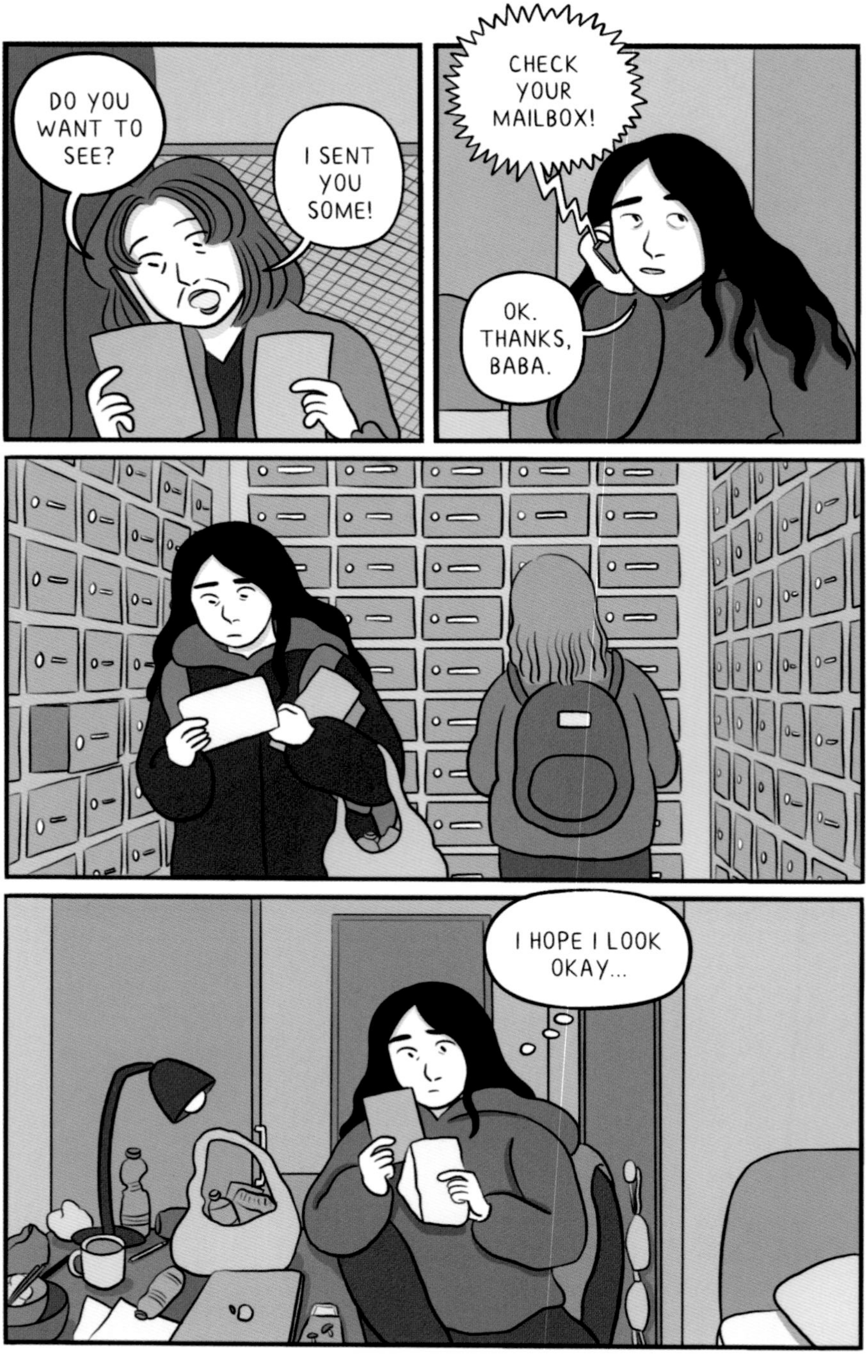
DO YOU WANT TO SEE?
I SENT YOU SOME!
CHECK YOUR MAILBOX!
OK. THANKS, BABA.
I HOPE I LOOK OKAY...

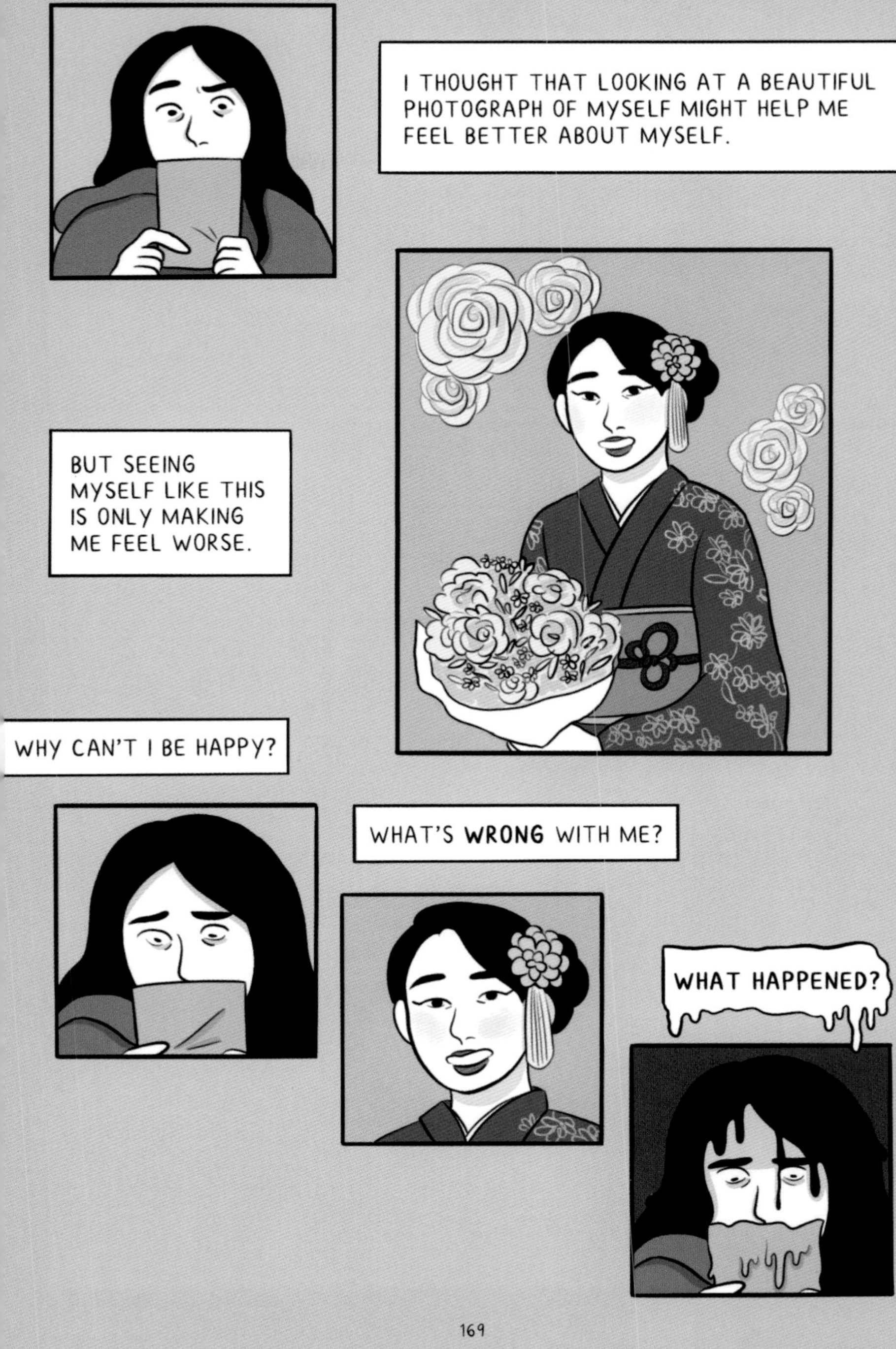
I THOUGHT THAT LOOKING AT A BEAUTIFUL PHOTOGRAPH OF MYSELF MIGHT HELP ME FEEL BETTER ABOUT MYSELF.
BUT SEEING MYSELF LIKE THIS IS ONLY MAKING ME FEEL WORSE.
WHY CAN'T I BE HAPPY?
WHAT'S **WRONG** WITH ME?
WHAT HAPPENED?

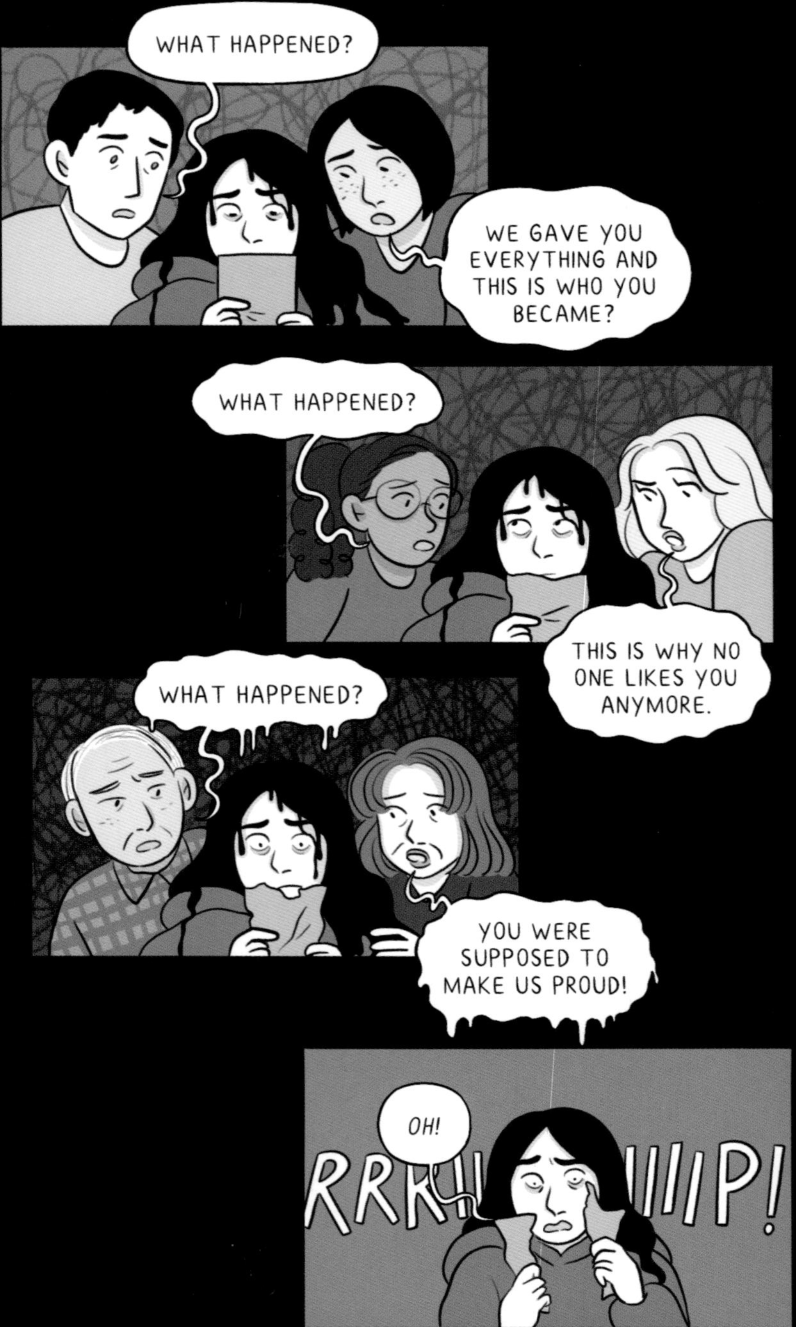
WHAT HAPPENED?
WE GAVE YOU EVERYTHING AND THIS IS WHO YOU BECAME?
WHAT HAPPENED?
THIS IS WHY NO ONE LIKES YOU ANYMORE.
WHAT HAPPENED?
YOU WERE SUPPOSED TO MAKE US PROUD!
OH!
RRR

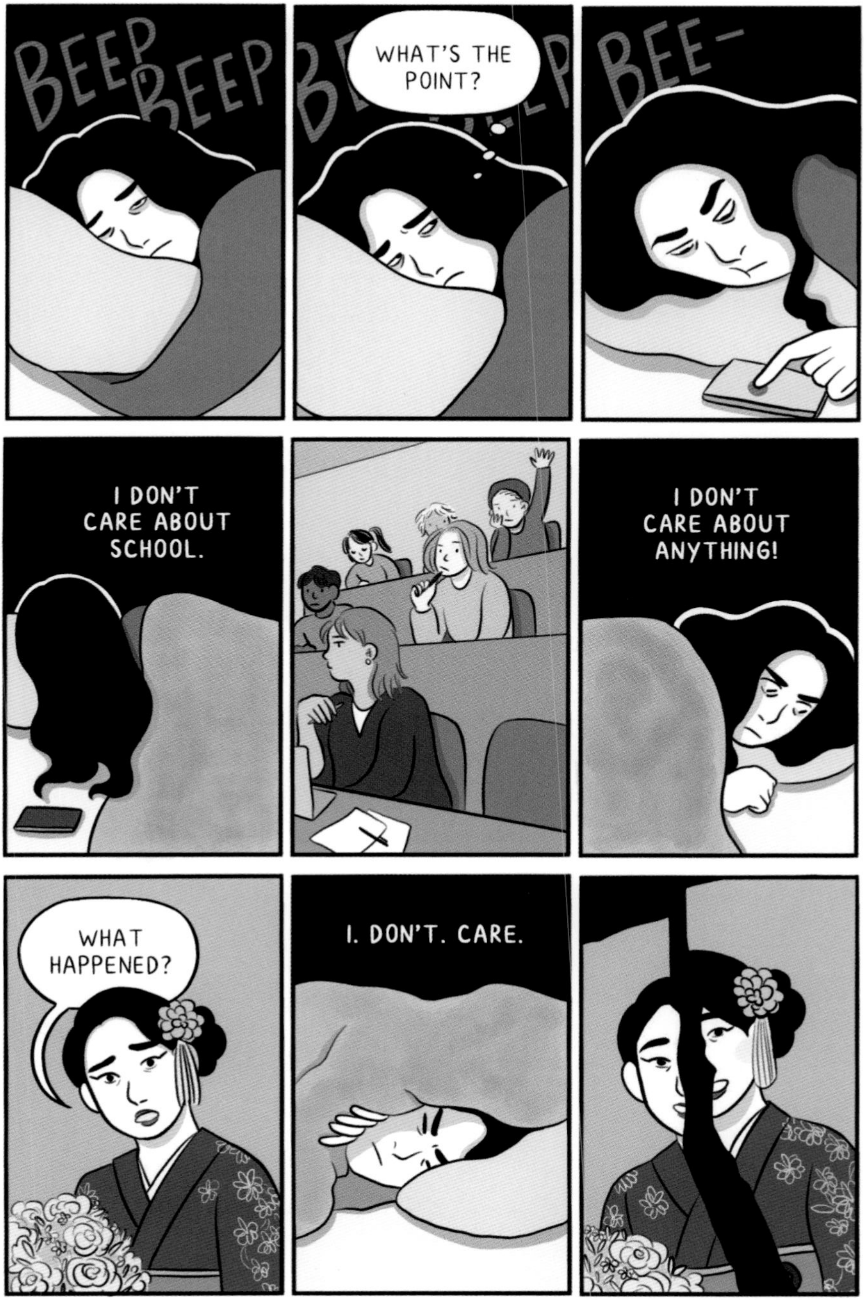
BEEP BEEP
WHAT'S THE POINT?
BEE-
I DON'T CARE ABOUT SCHOOL.
I DON'T CARE ABOUT ANYTHING!
WHAT HAPPENED?
I. DON'T. CARE.

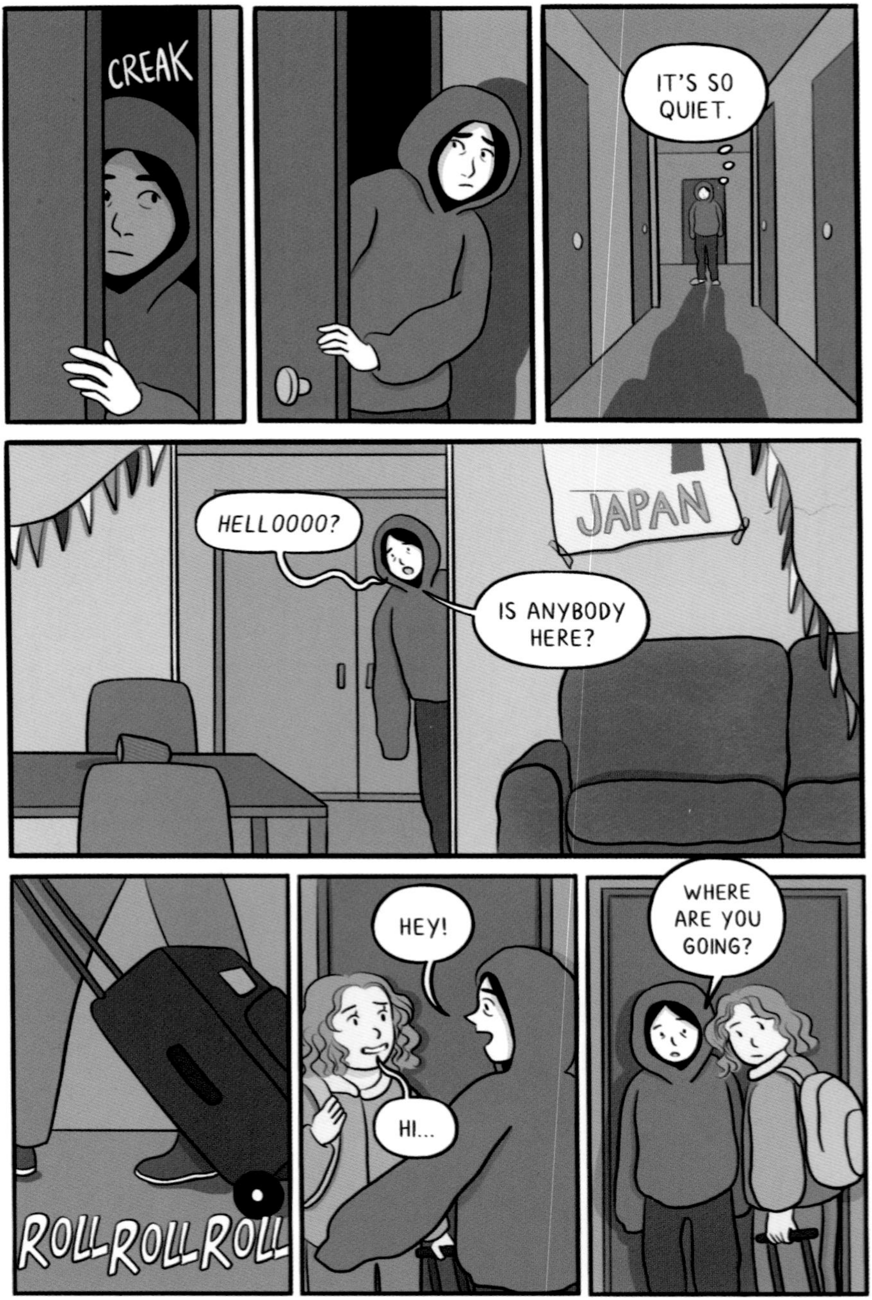
CREAK
IT'S SO QUIET.
HELLOOOO?
IS ANYBODY HERE?
ROLL ROLL ROLL
HEY!
HI...
WHERE ARE YOU GOING?

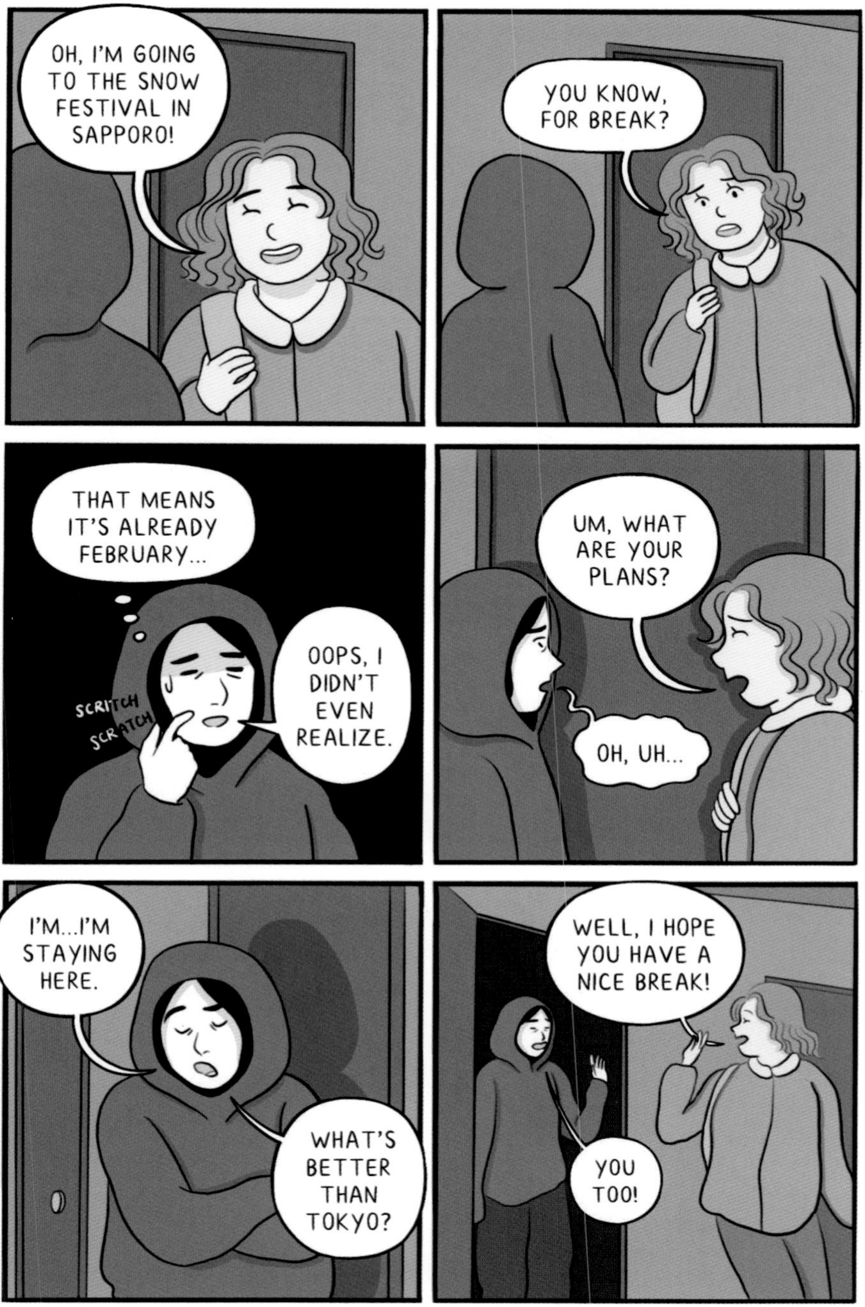
OH, I'M GOING TO THE SNOW FESTIVAL IN SAPPORO!
YOU KNOW, FOR BREAK?
THAT MEANS IT'S ALREADY FEBRUARY...
SCRITCH SCRATCH
OOPS, I DIDN'T EVEN REALIZE.
UM, WHAT ARE YOUR PLANS?
OH, UH...
I'M...I'M STAYING HERE.
WHAT'S BETTER THAN TOKYO?
WELL, I HOPE YOU HAVE A NICE BREAK!
YOU TOO!

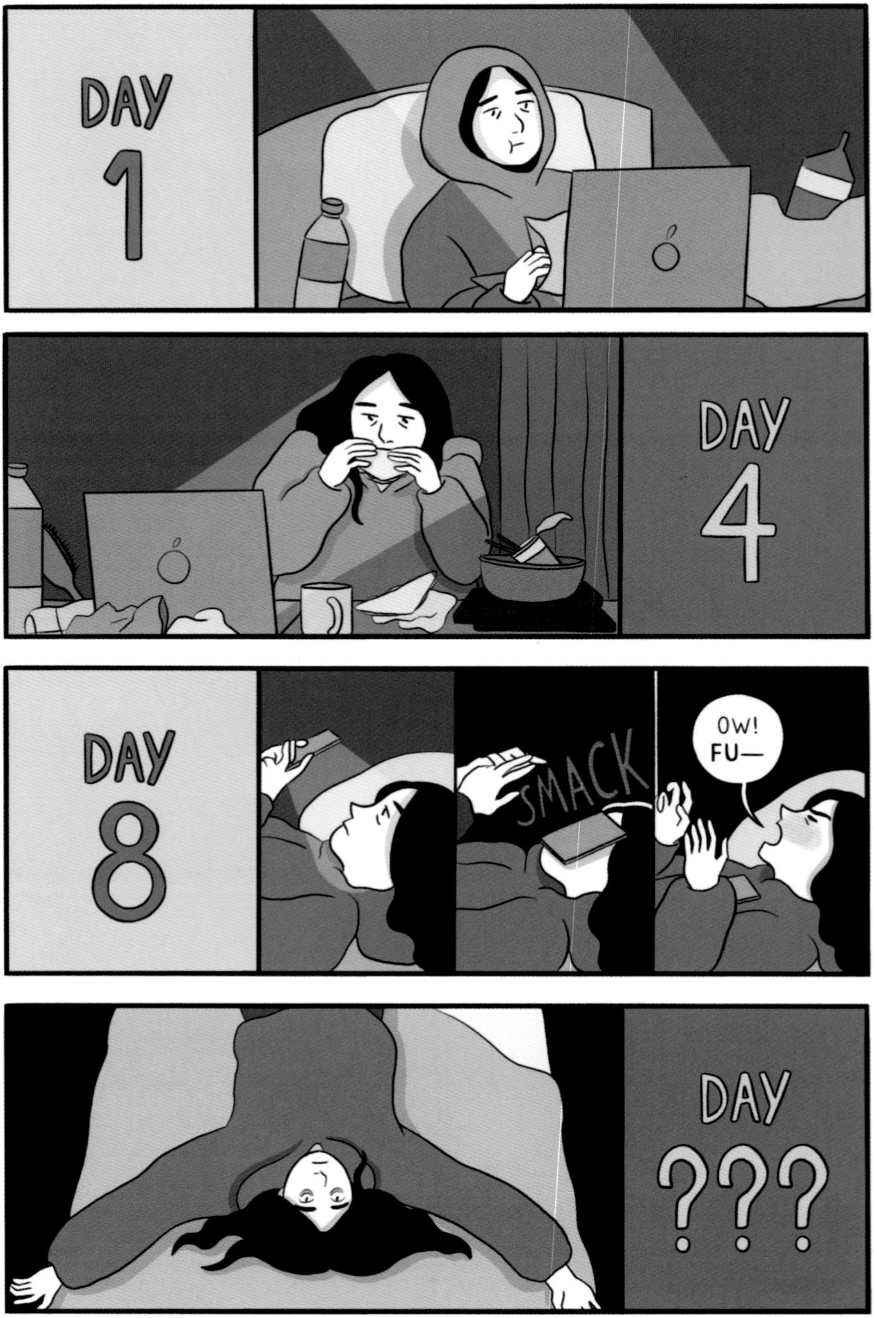
DAY
1
DAY
4
DAY
8
SMACK
OW!
FU—
DAY
???

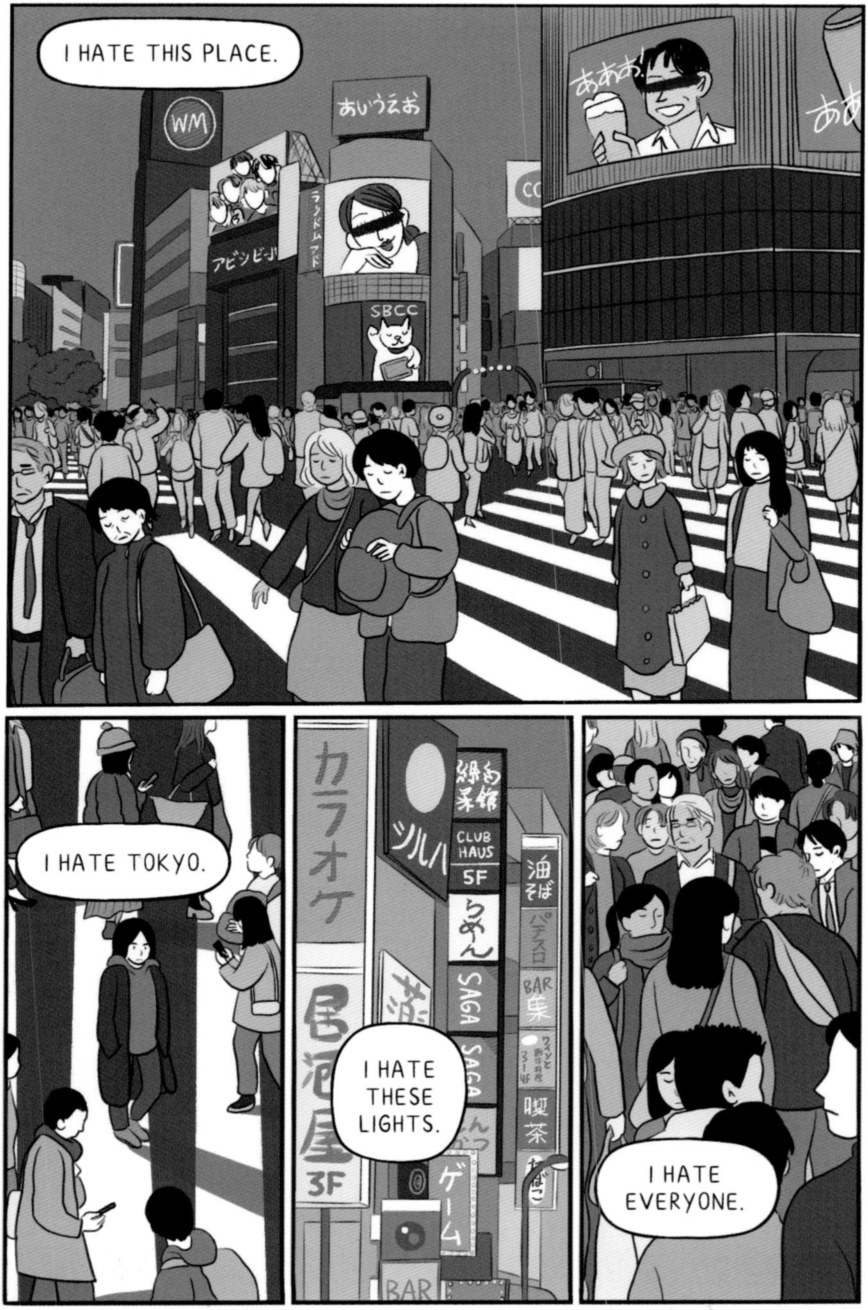
I HATE THIS PLACE.
I HATE TOKYO.
I HATE THESE LIGHTS.
I HATE EVERYONE.

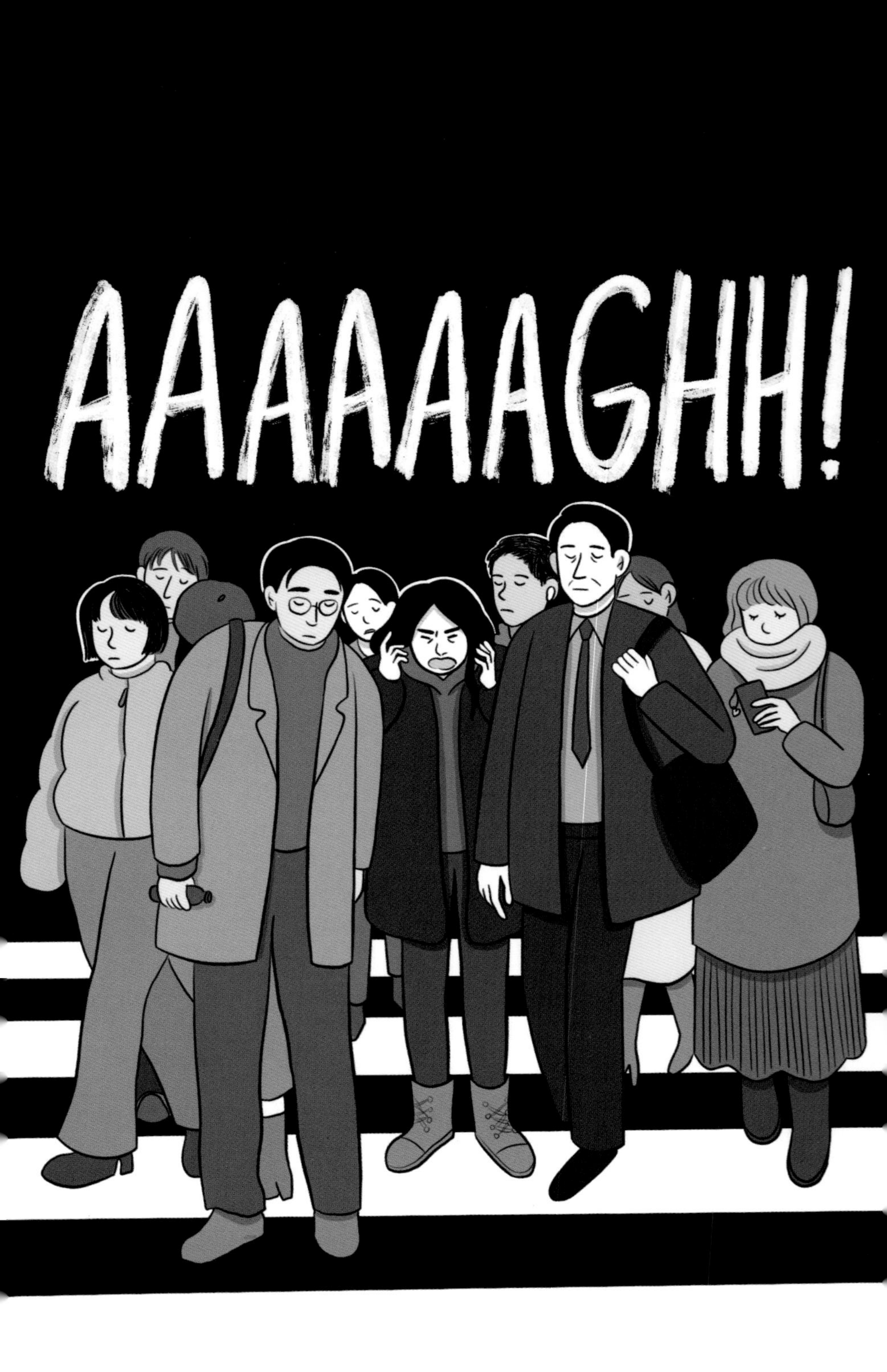
AAAAAAGHH!

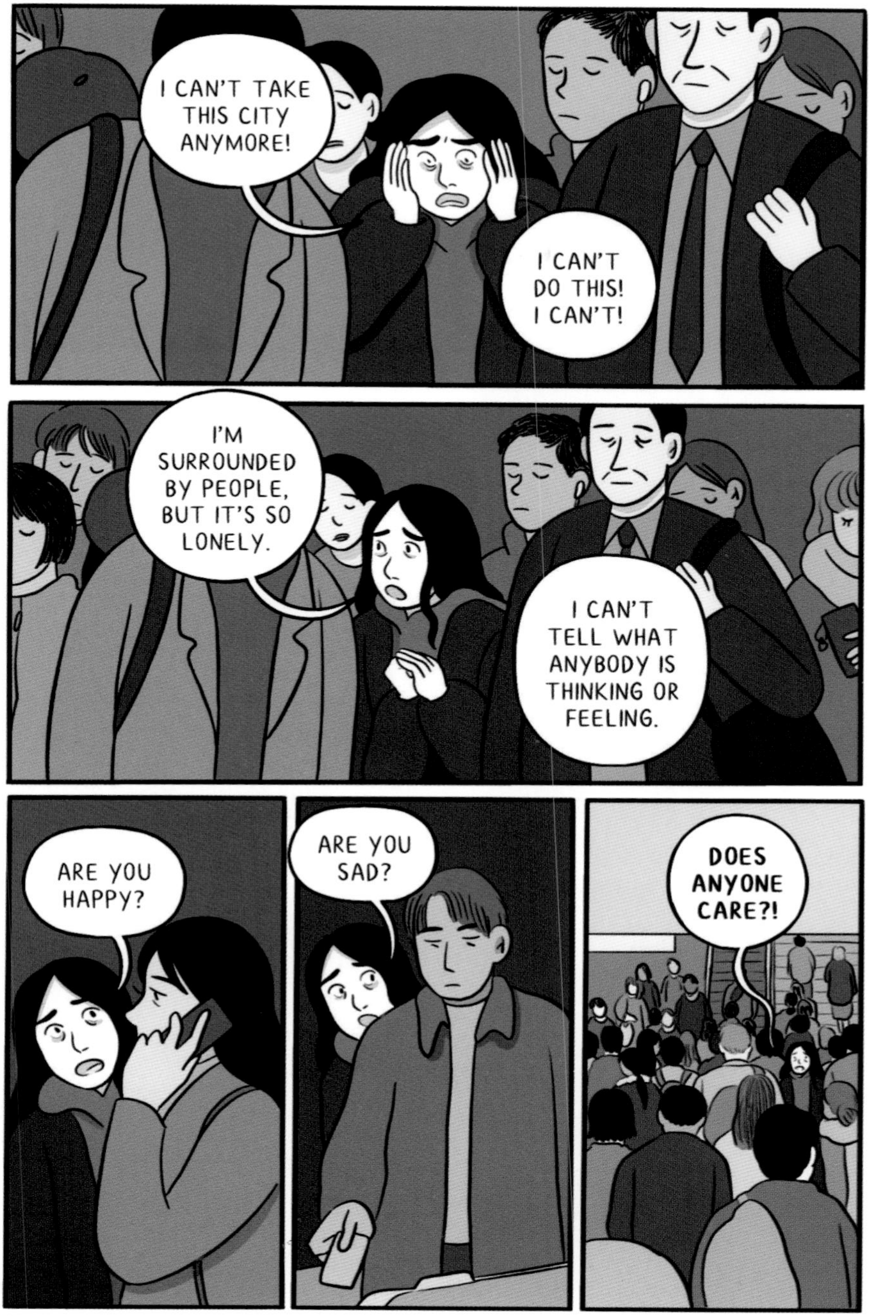
I CAN'T TAKE THIS CITY ANYMORE!
I CAN'T DO THIS! I CAN'T!
I'M SURROUNDED BY PEOPLE, BUT IT'S SO LONELY.
I CAN'T TELL WHAT ANYBODY IS THINKING OR FEELING.
ARE YOU HAPPY?
ARE YOU SAD?
DOES ANYONE CARE?!

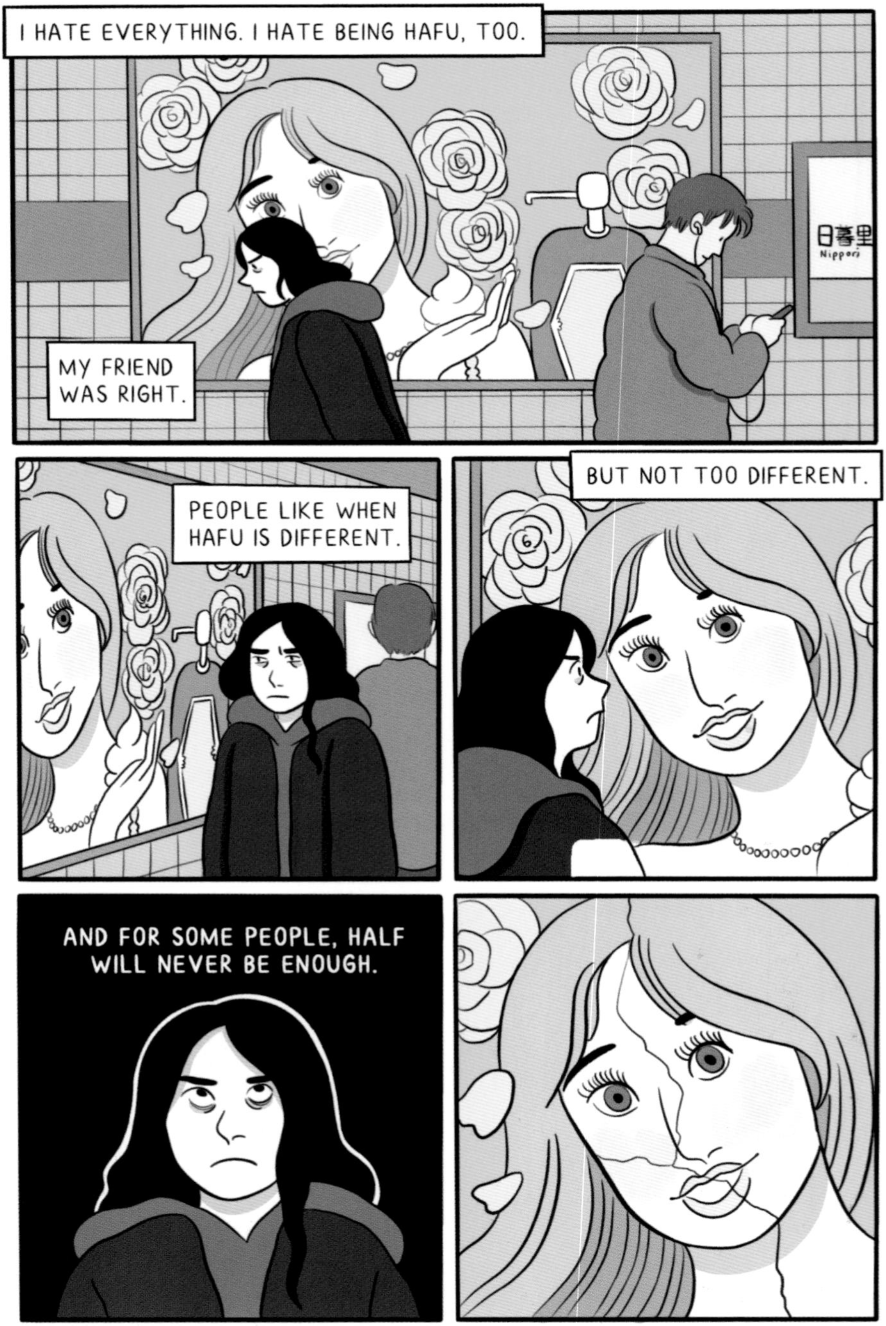
I HATE EVERYTHING. I HATE BEING HAFU, TOO.
日暮里
Nippori
MY FRIEND WAS RIGHT.
PEOPLE LIKE WHEN HAFU IS DIFFERENT.
BUT NOT TOO DIFFERENT.
AND FOR SOME PEOPLE, HALF WILL NEVER BE ENOUGH.

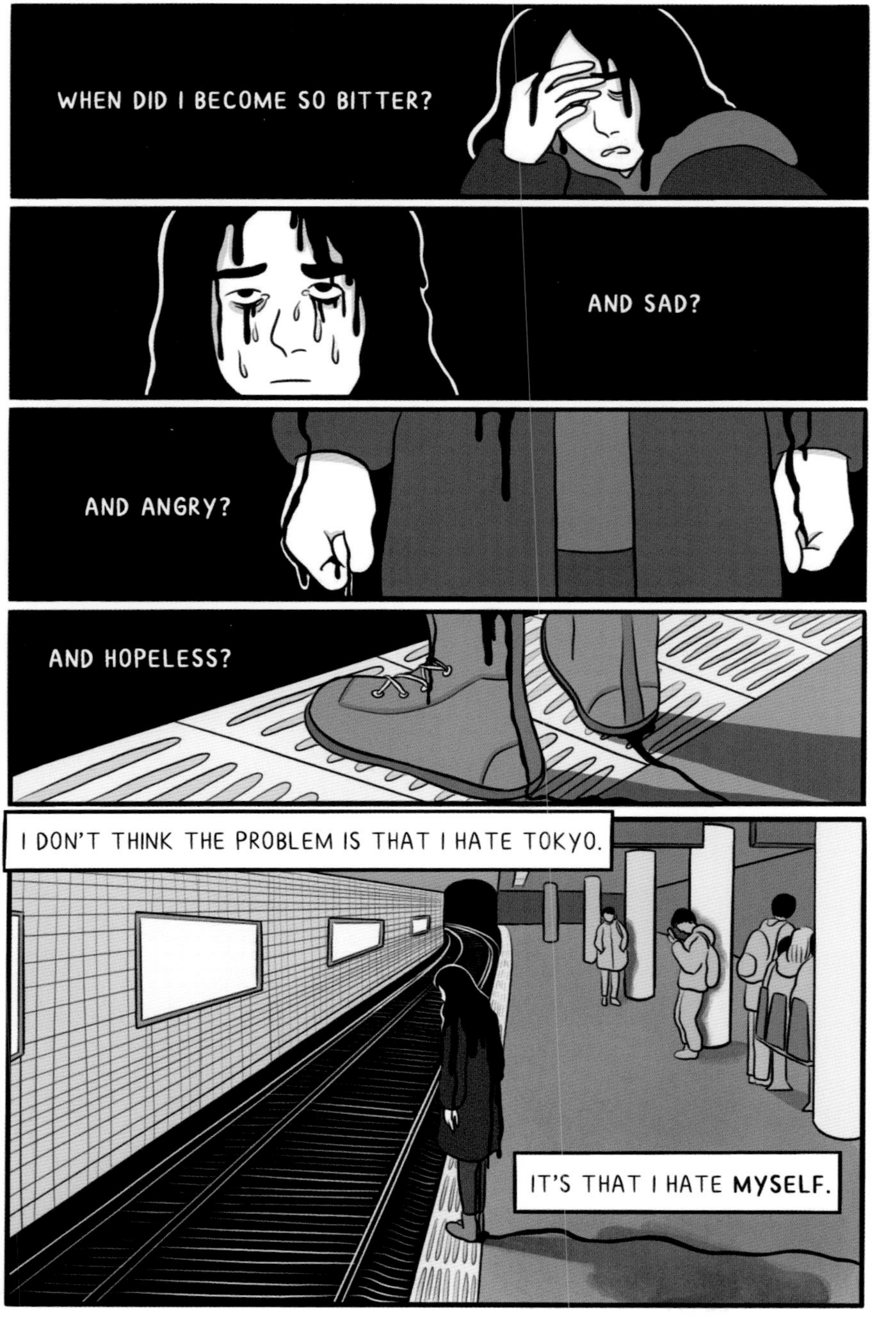
WHEN DID I BECOME SO BITTER?
AND SAD?
AND ANGRY?
AND HOPELESS?
I DON'T THINK THE PROBLEM IS THAT I HATE TOKYO.
IT'S THAT I HATE **MYSELF**.

YES, THAT'S IT. I HATE MYSELF.

I HATE MYSELF.

I. HATE. MYSELF.

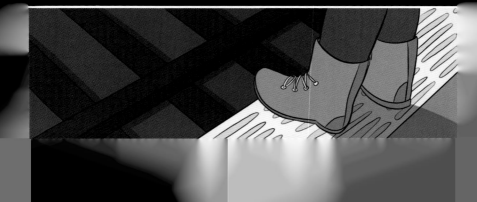

WHOOO OOOSHH

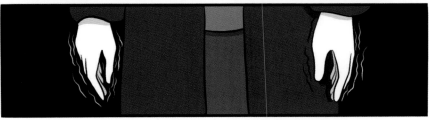

WHAT HAPPENED?

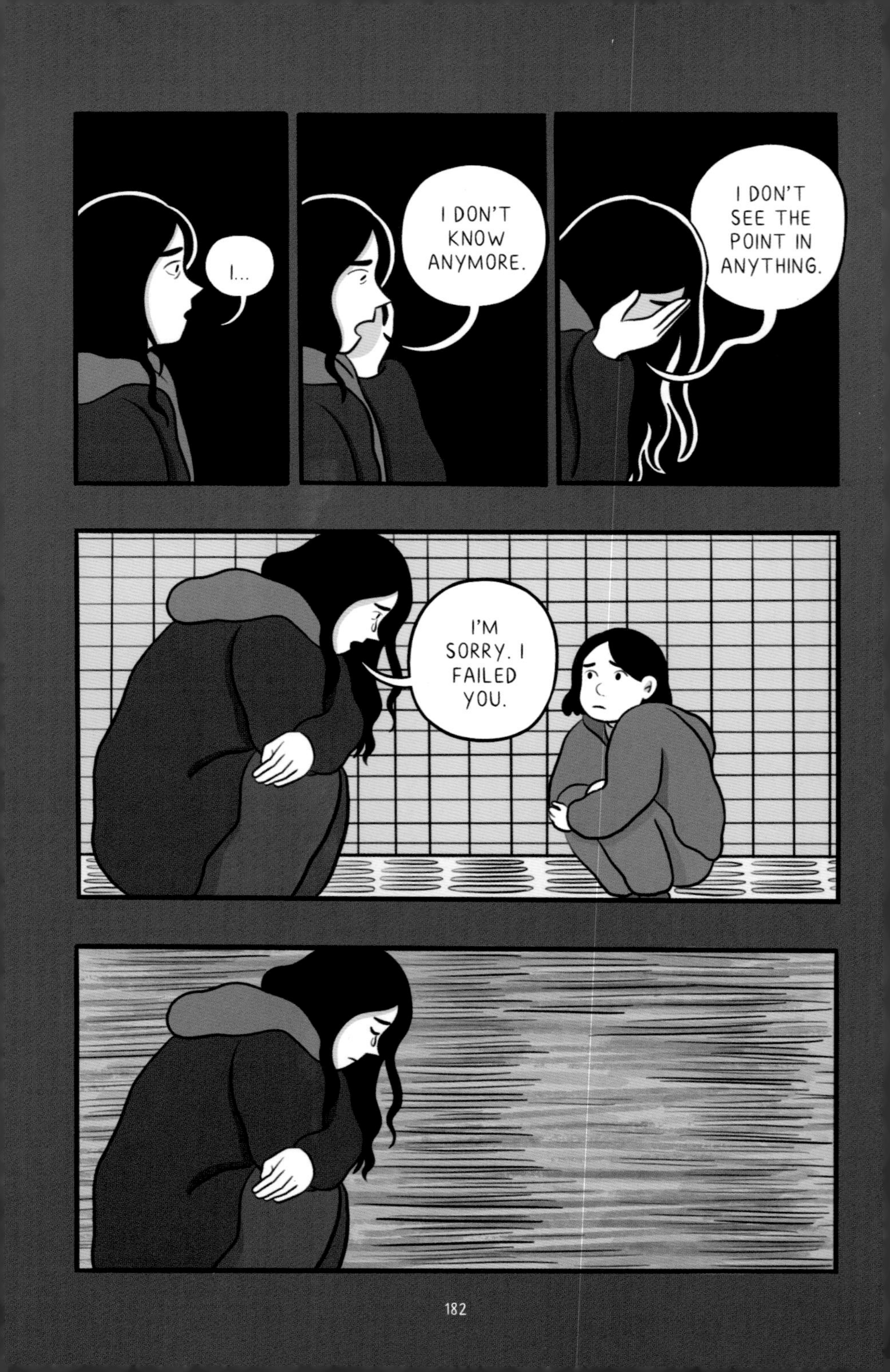

I...
I DON'T KNOW ANYMORE.
I DON'T SEE THE POINT IN ANYTHING.
I'M SORRY. I FAILED YOU.

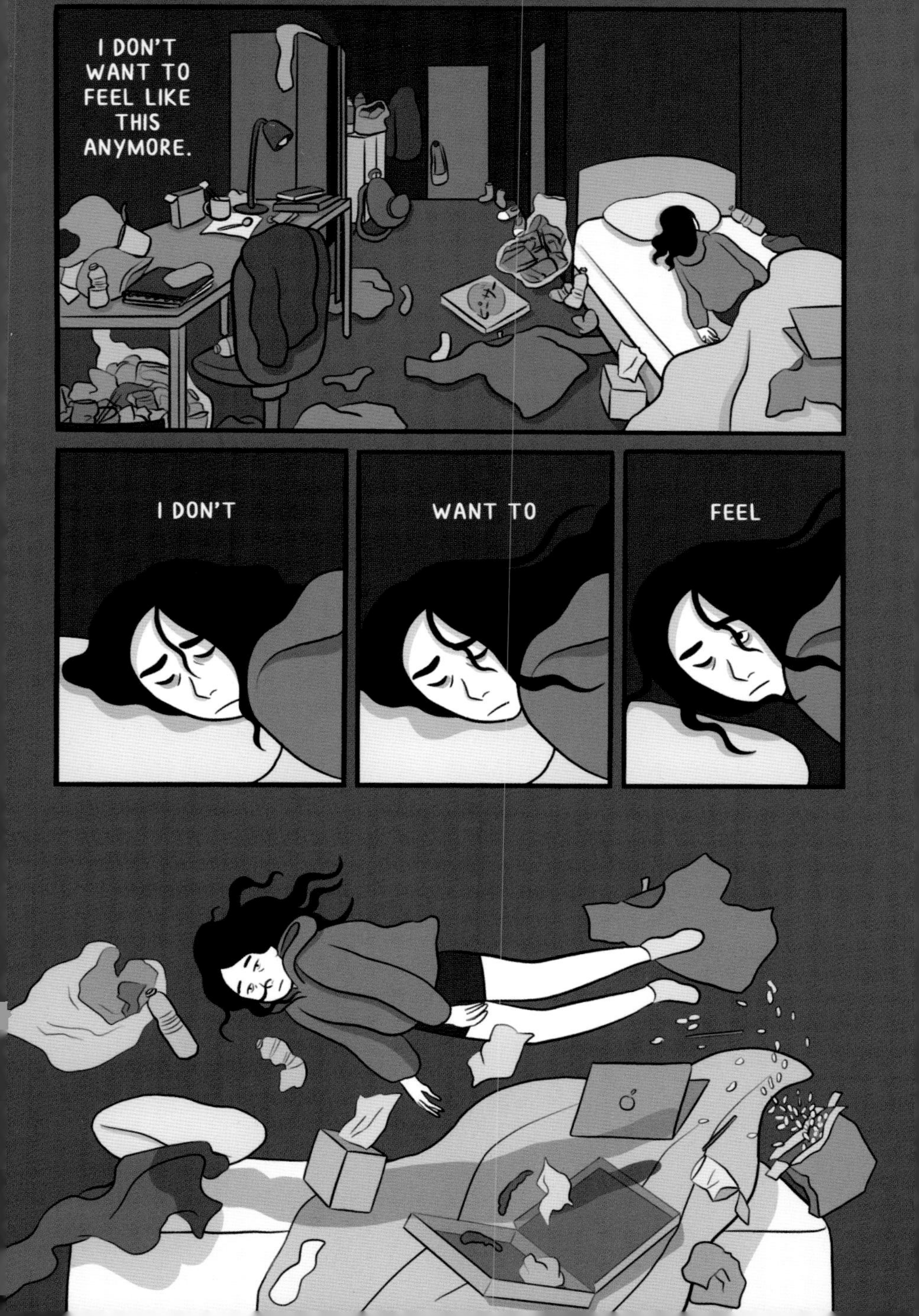
I DON'T WANT TO FEEL LIKE THIS ANYMORE.
I DON'T
WANT TO
FEEL

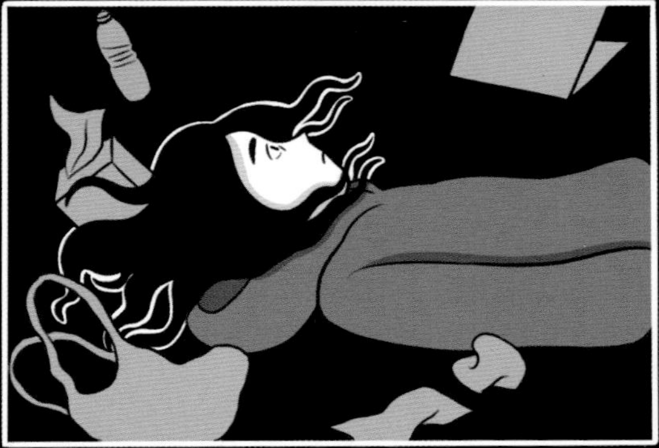

I FEEL NOTHING.

I DON'T FEEL SAD.

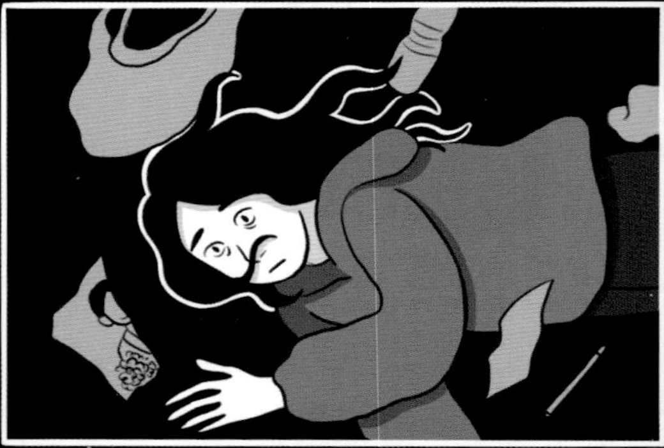

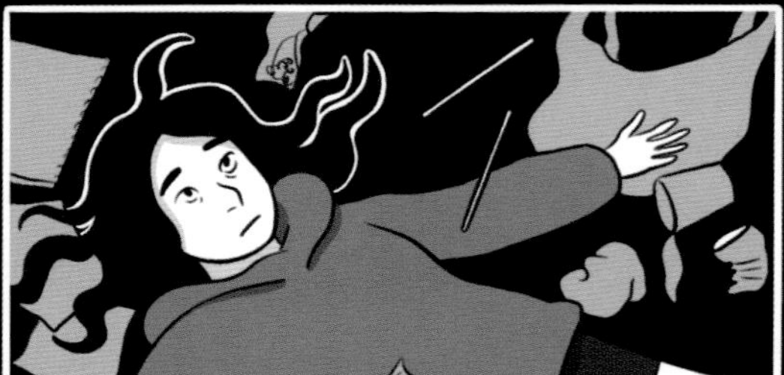

I DON'T FEEL ANGRY.

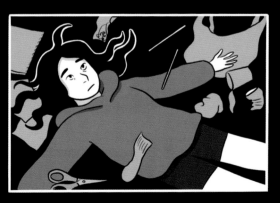

I DON'T EVEN THINK I CAN FEEL PAIN.

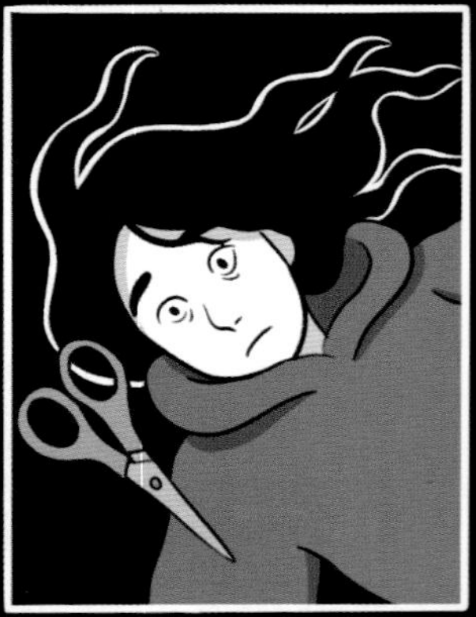

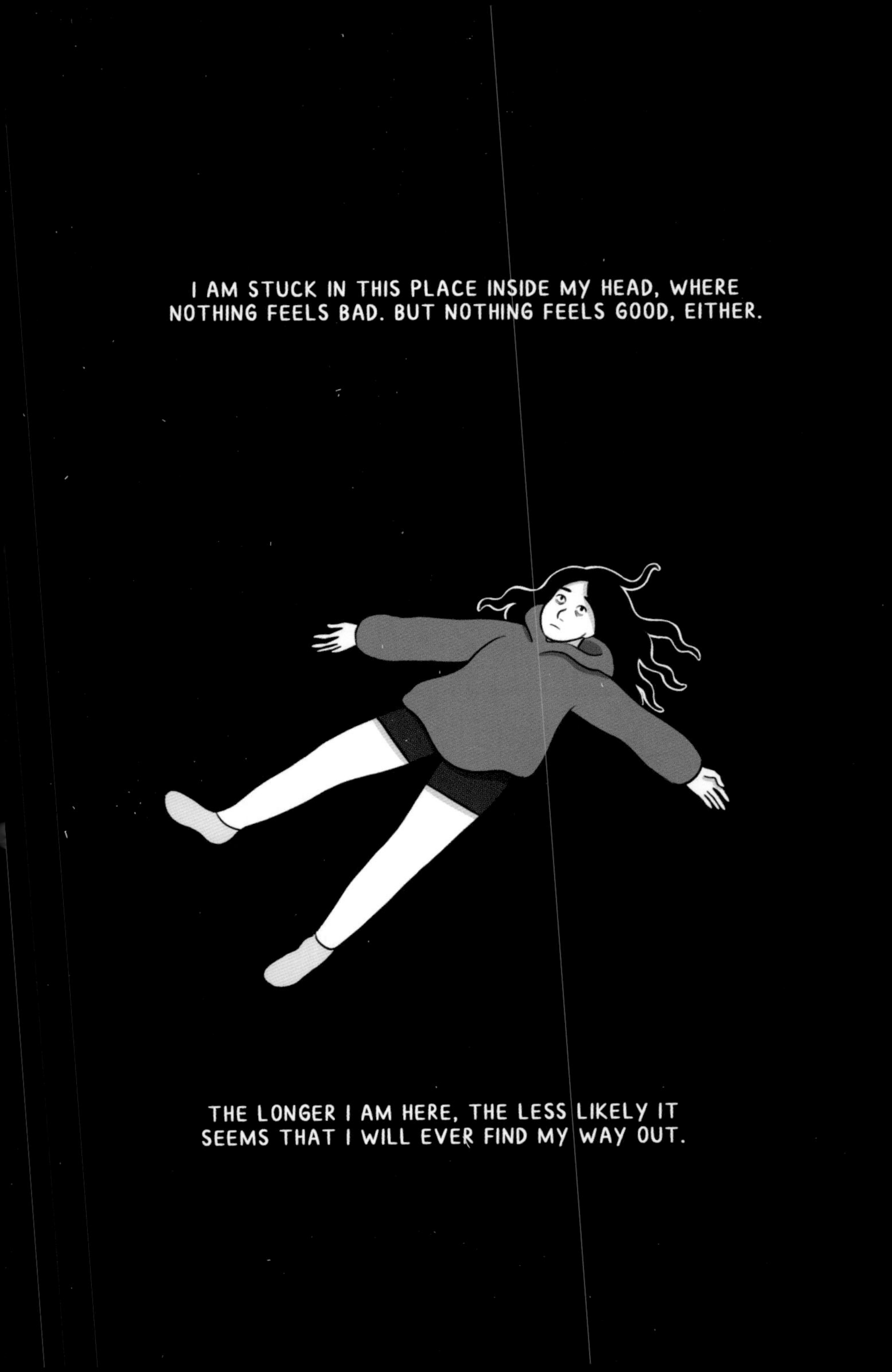
I AM STUCK IN THIS PLACE INSIDE MY HEAD, WHERE NOTHING FEELS BAD. BUT NOTHING FEELS GOOD, EITHER.
THE LONGER I AM HERE, THE LESS LIKELY IT SEEMS THAT I WILL EVER FIND MY WAY OUT.

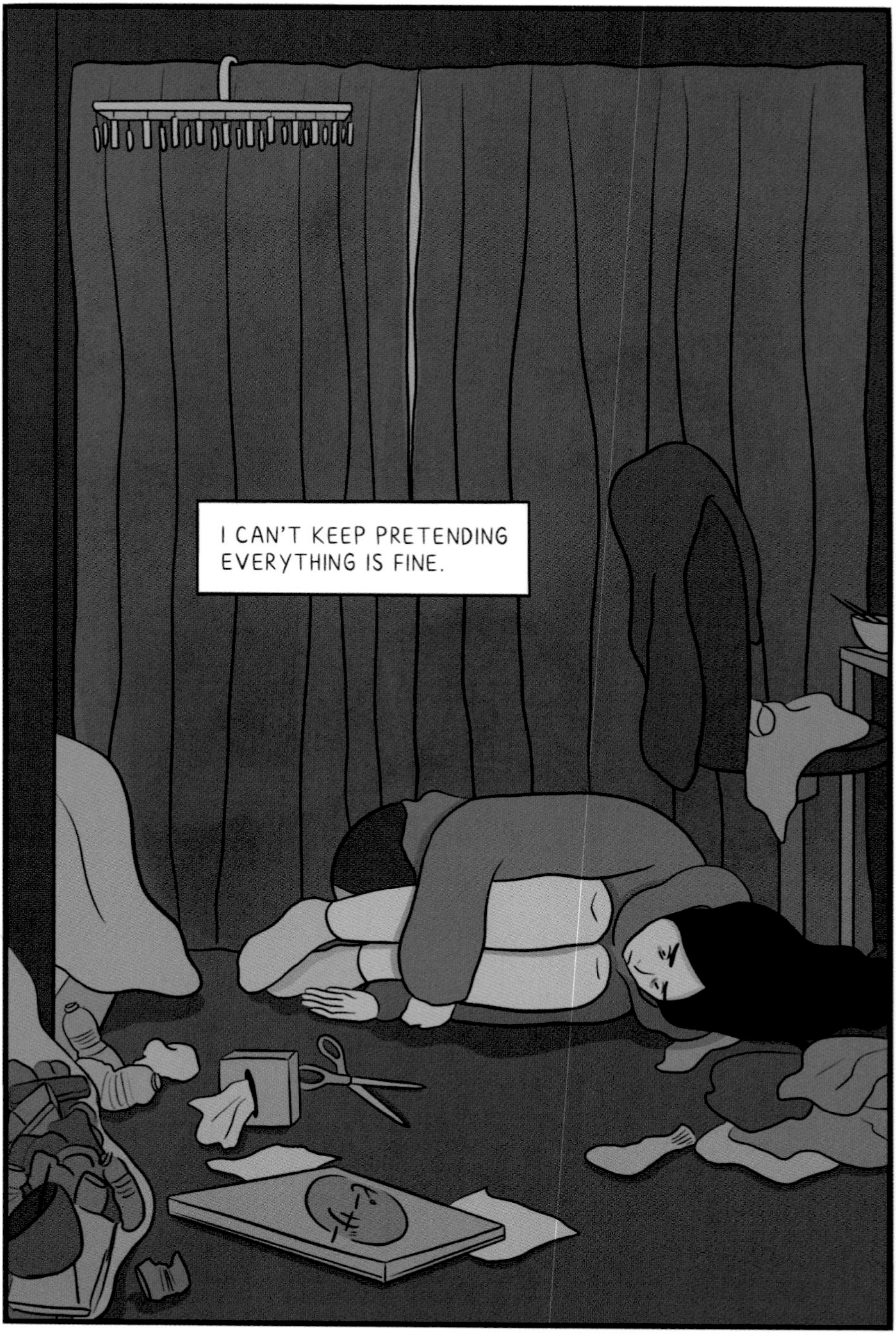
I CAN'T KEEP PRETENDING EVERYTHING IS FINE.

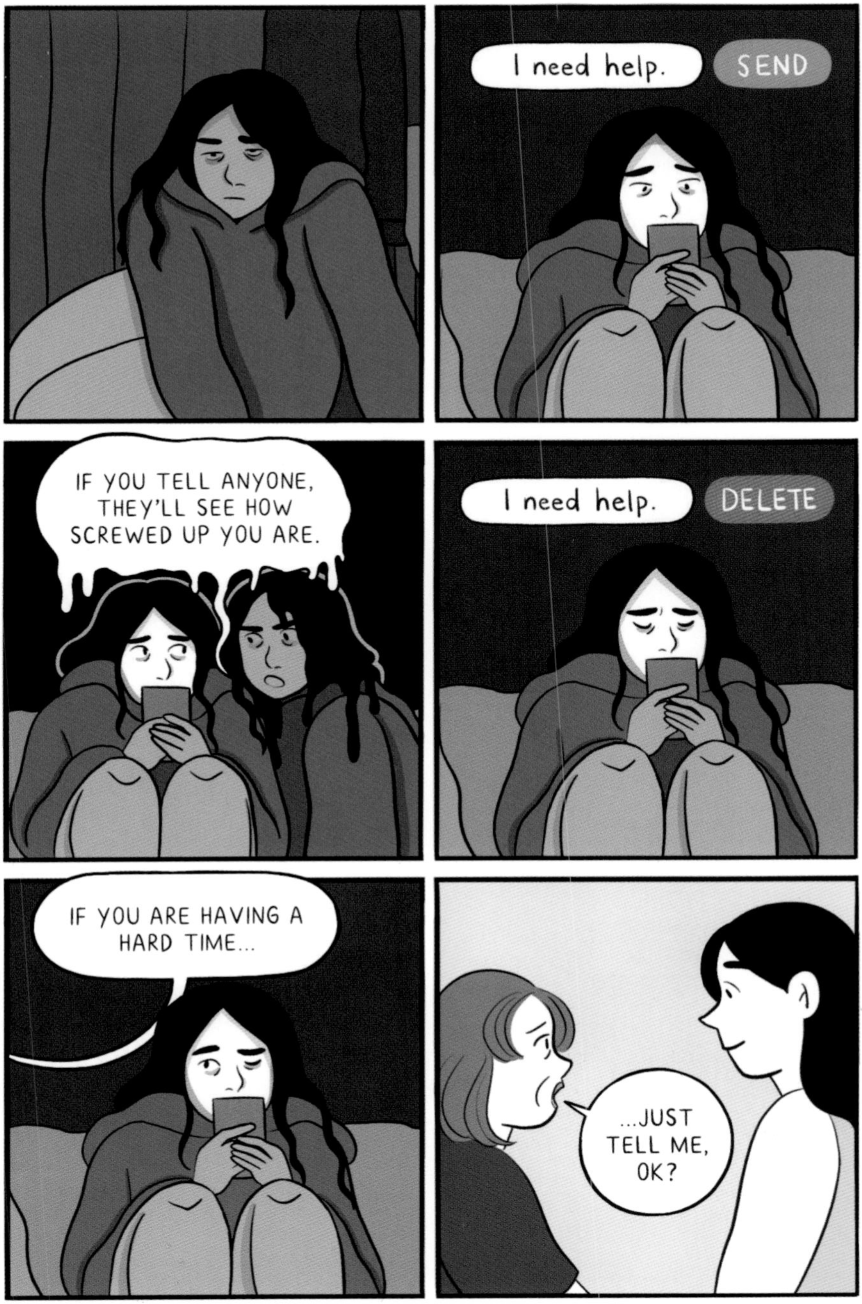
I need help.
SEND
IF YOU TELL ANYONE, THEY'LL SEE HOW SCREWED UP YOU ARE.
I need help.
DELETE
IF YOU ARE HAVING A HARD TIME...
...JUST TELL ME, OK?

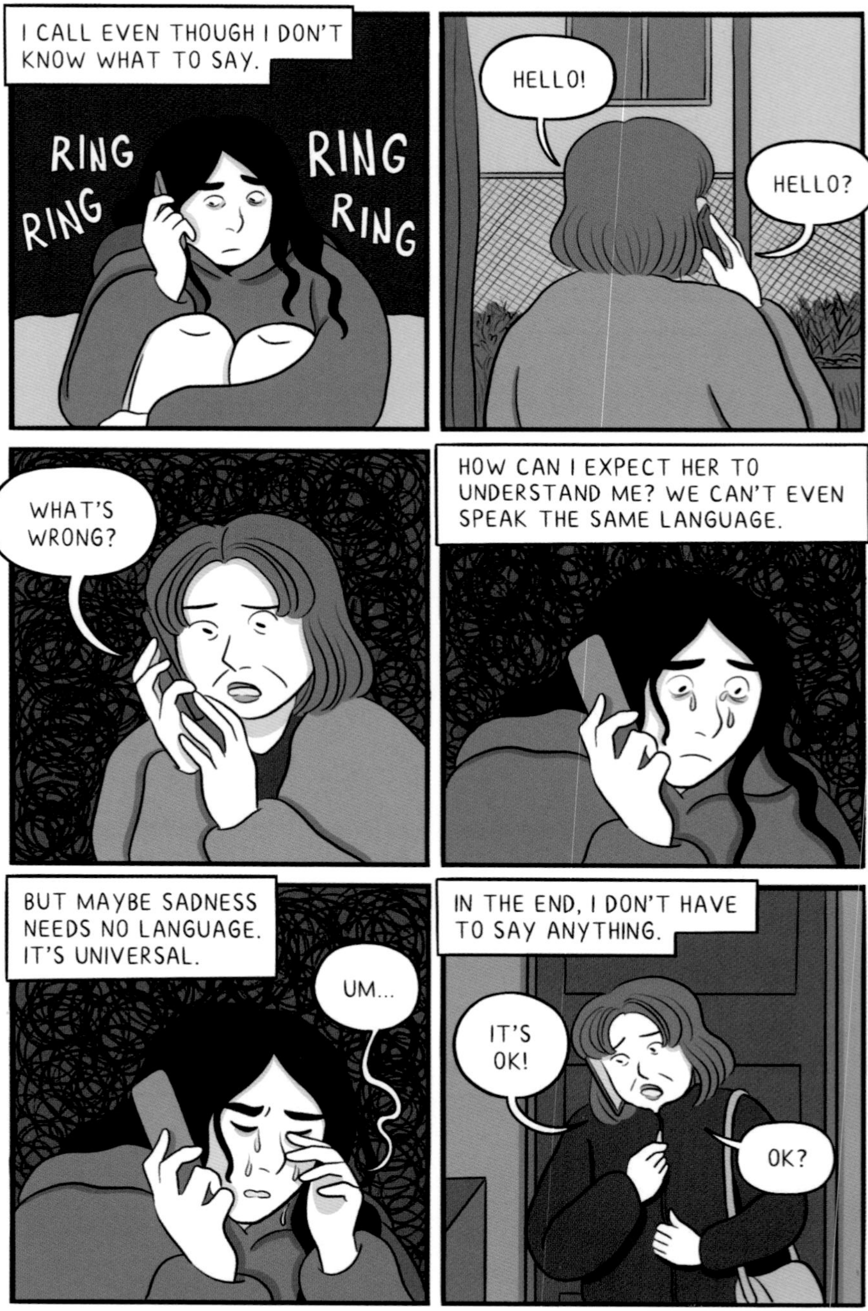
I CALL EVEN THOUGH I DON'T KNOW WHAT TO SAY.
RING RING
RING RING
HELLO!
HELLO?
WHAT'S WRONG?
HOW CAN I EXPECT HER TO UNDERSTAND ME? WE CAN'T EVEN SPEAK THE SAME LANGUAGE.
BUT MAYBE SADNESS NEEDS NO LANGUAGE. IT'S UNIVERSAL.
UM...
IN THE END, I DON'T HAVE TO SAY ANYTHING.
IT'S OK!
OK?

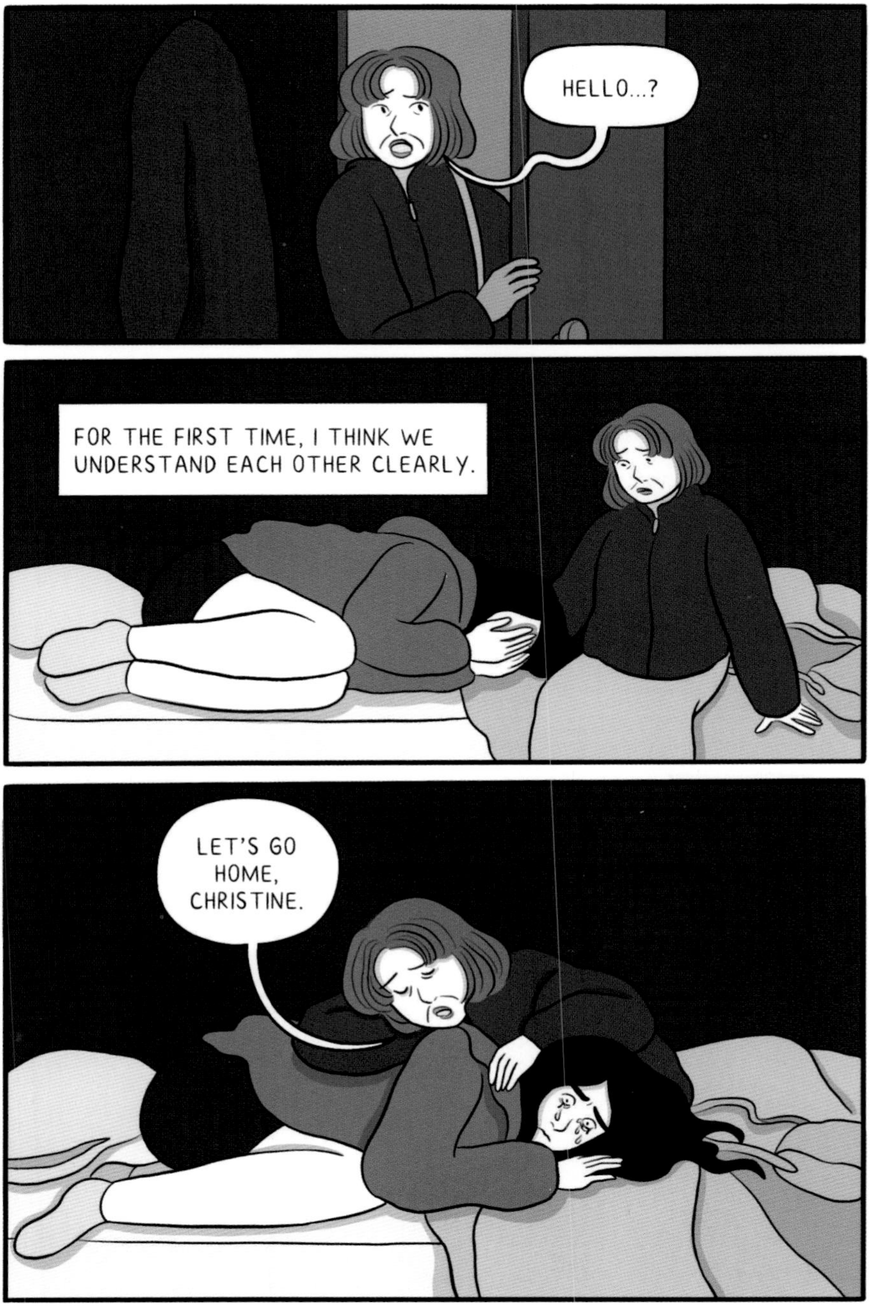
HELLO...?
FOR THE FIRST TIME, I THINK WE UNDERSTAND EACH OTHER CLEARLY.
LET'S GO HOME, CHRISTINE.

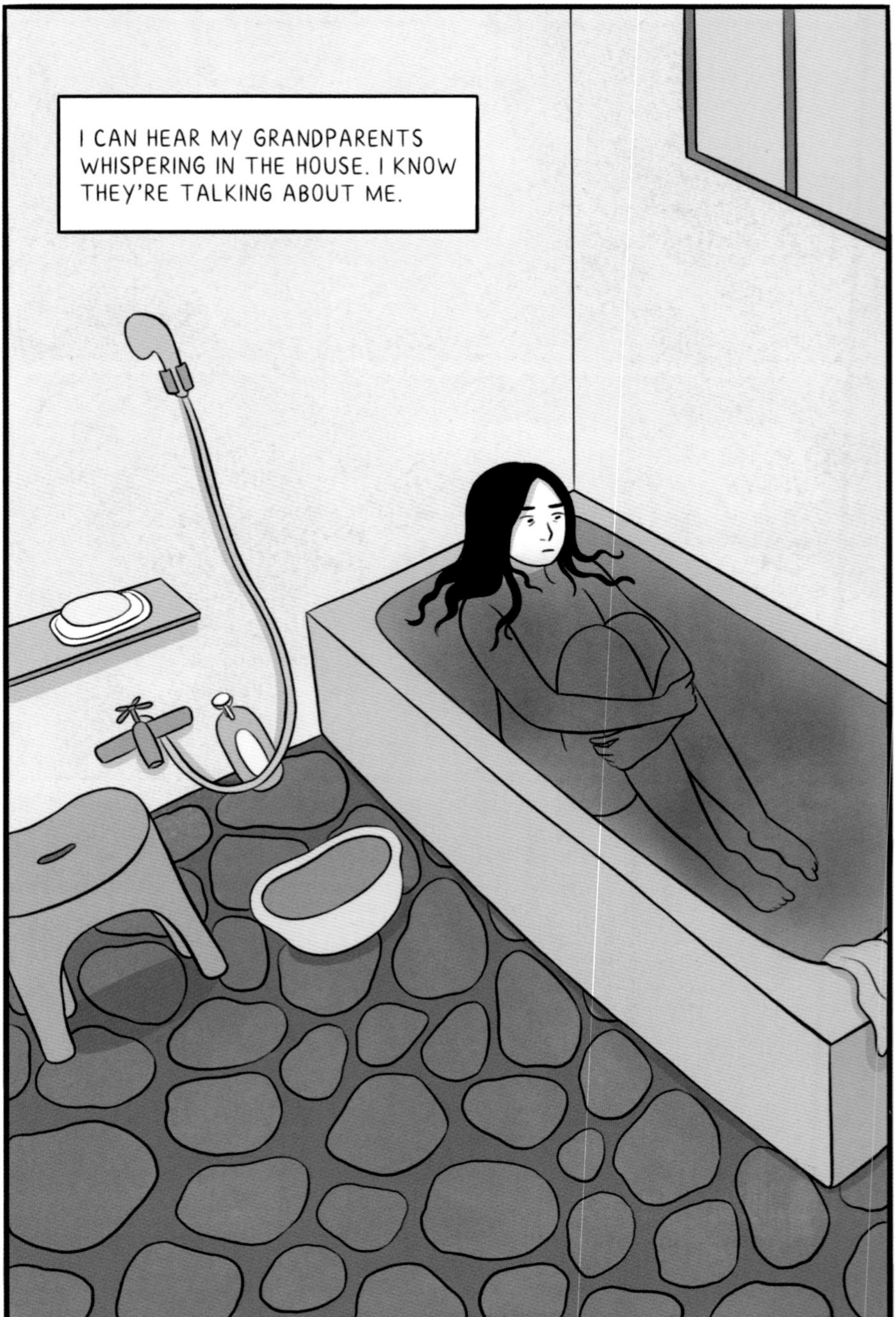
I CAN HEAR MY GRANDPARENTS WHISPERING IN THE HOUSE. I KNOW THEY'RE TALKING ABOUT ME.

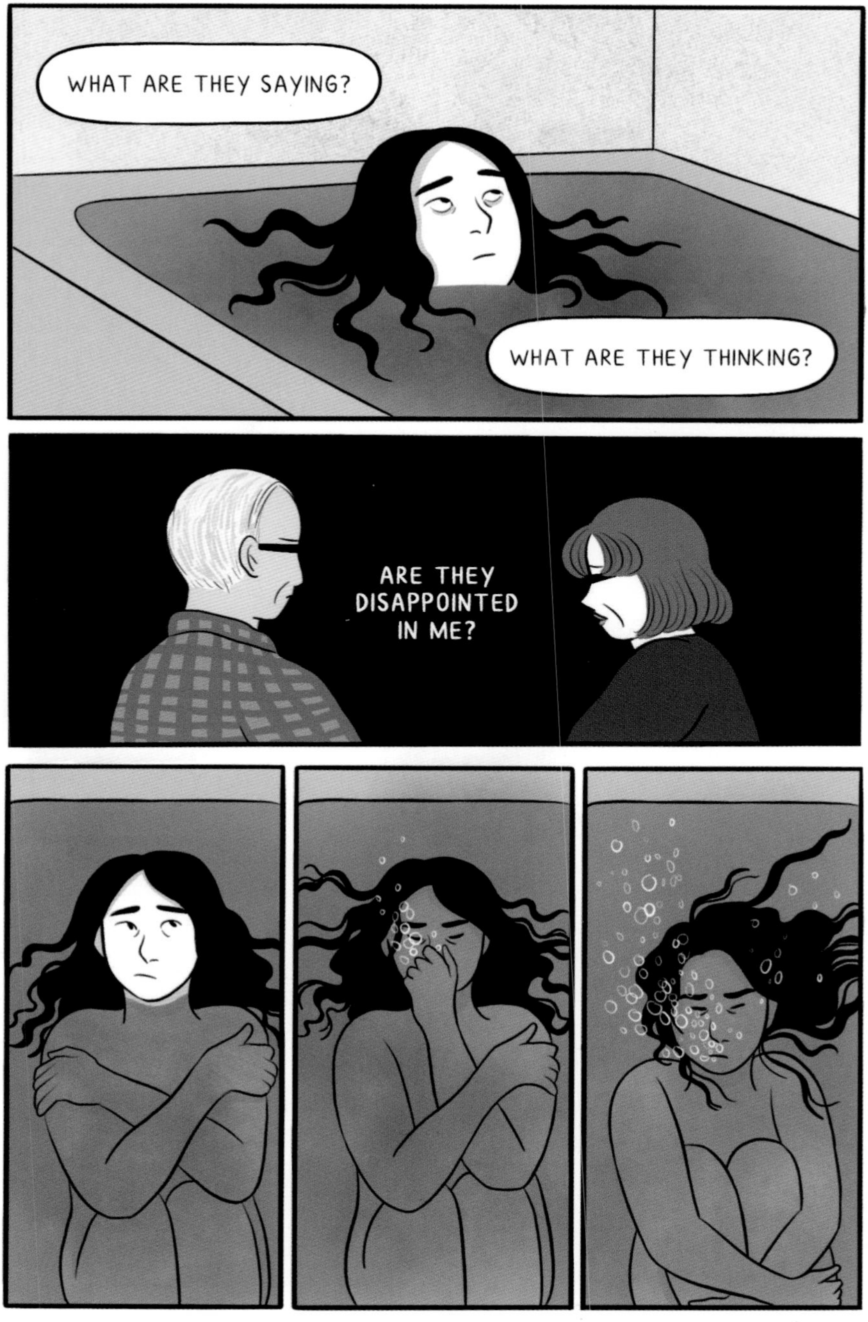
WHAT ARE THEY SAYING?
WHAT ARE THEY THINKING?
ARE THEY DISAPPOINTED IN ME?

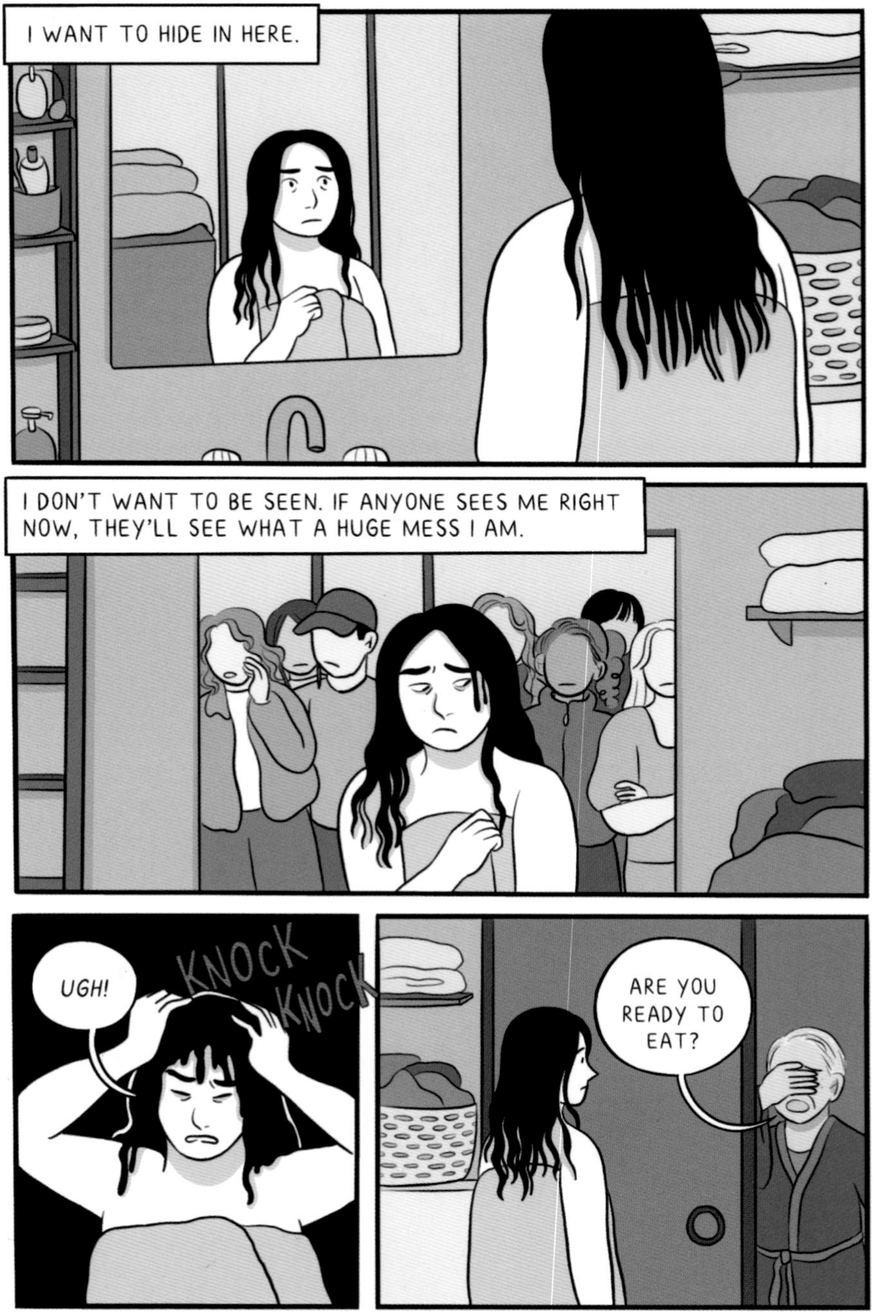
I WANT TO HIDE IN HERE.
I DON'T WANT TO BE SEEN. IF ANYONE SEES ME RIGHT NOW, THEY'LL SEE WHAT A HUGE MESS I AM.
UGH!
KNOCK KNOCK
ARE YOU READY TO EAT?

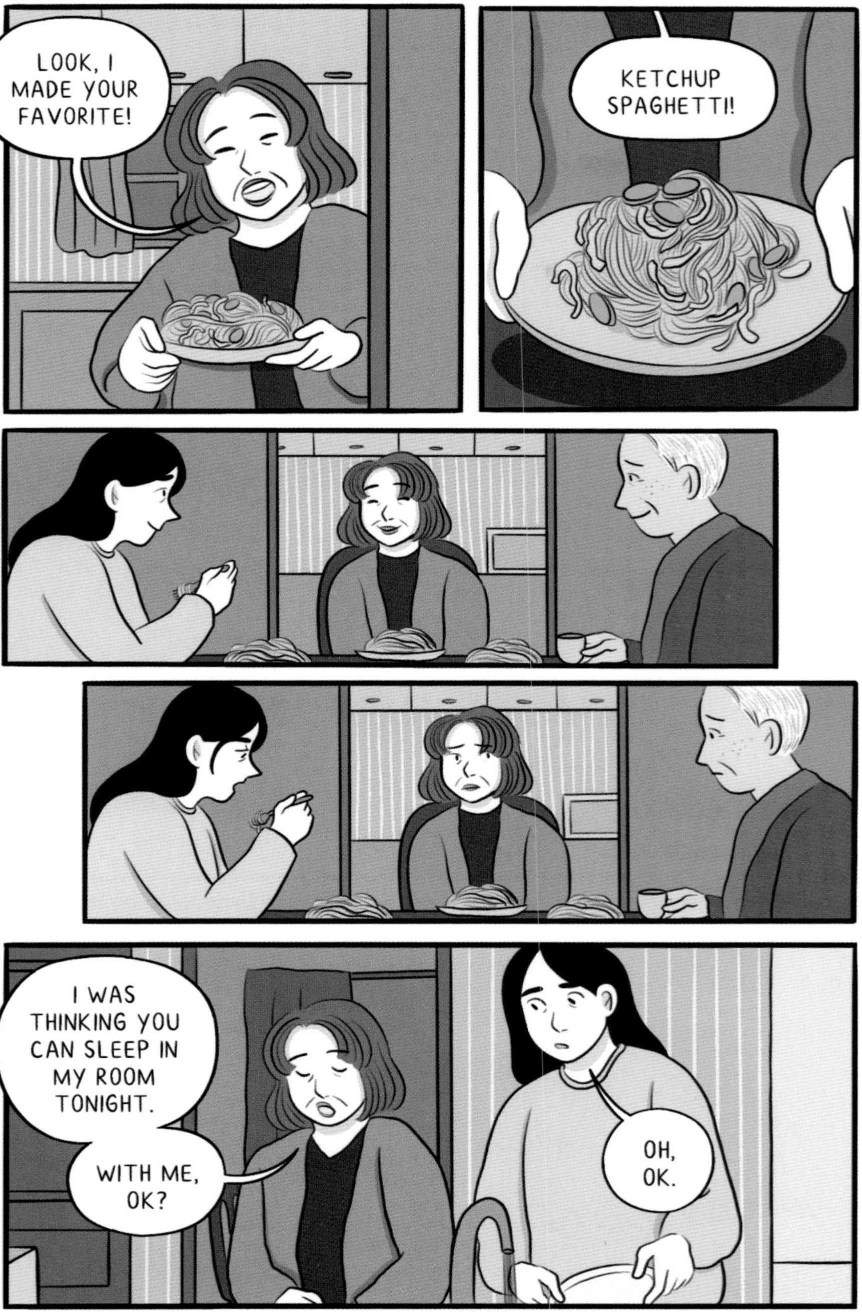

LOOK, I MADE YOUR FAVORITE!
KETCHUP SPAGHETTI!
I WAS THINKING YOU CAN SLEEP IN MY ROOM TONIGHT.
WITH ME, OK?
OH, OK.

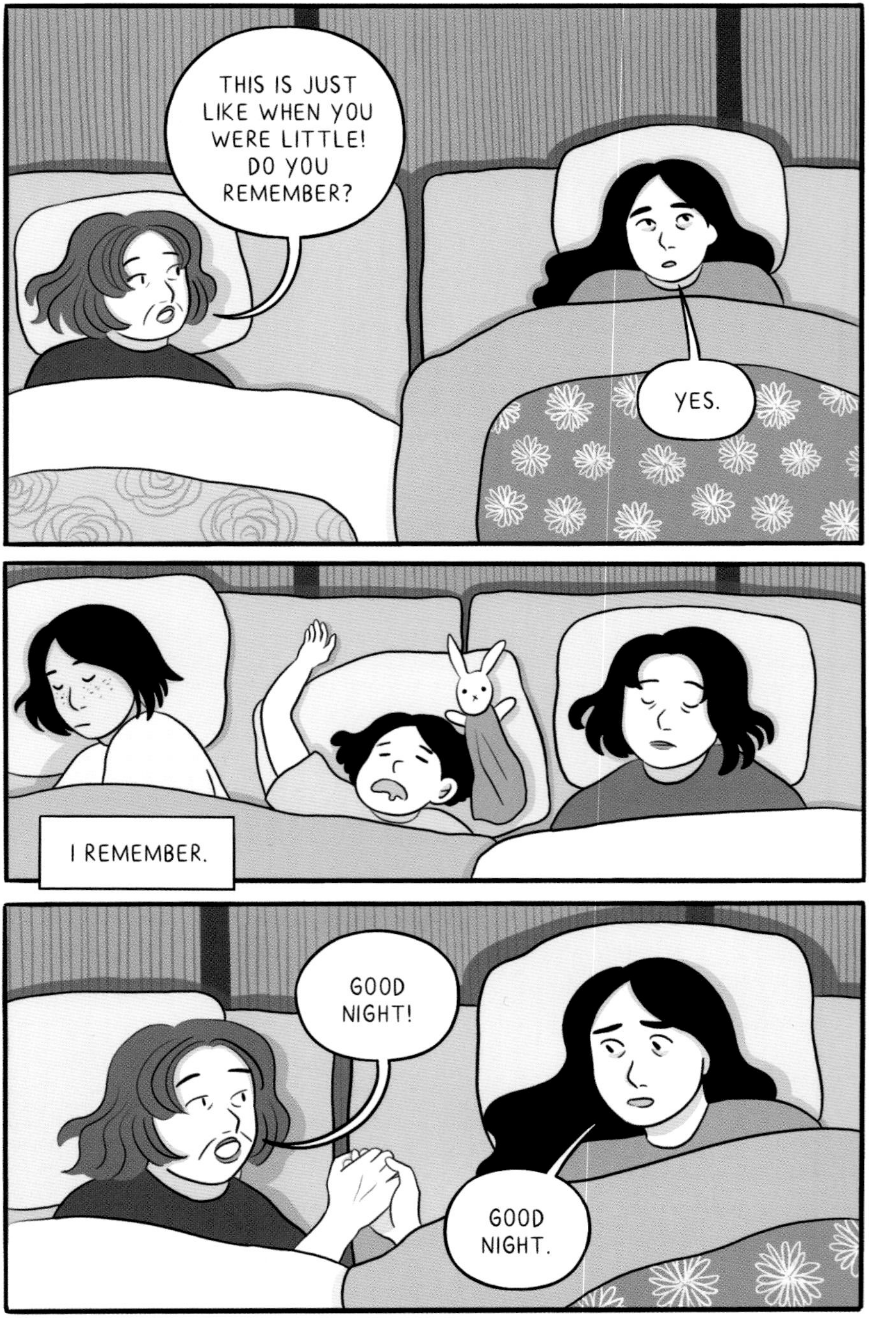
THIS IS JUST LIKE WHEN YOU WERE LITTLE! DO YOU REMEMBER?
YES.
I REMEMBER.
GOOD NIGHT!
GOOD NIGHT.

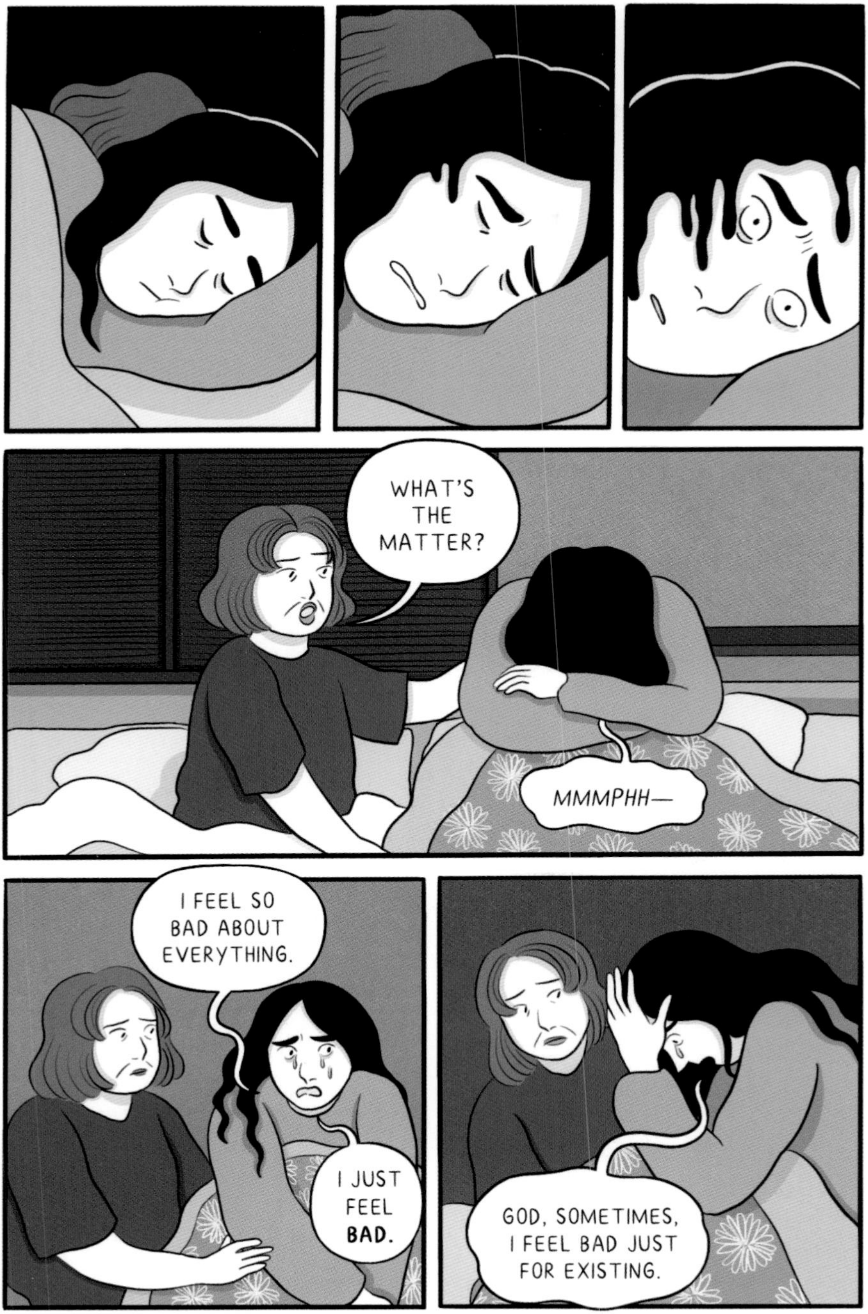
WHAT'S THE MATTER?
MMMPHH—
I FEEL SO BAD ABOUT EVERYTHING.
I JUST FEEL **BAD.**
GOD, SOMETIMES, I FEEL BAD JUST FOR EXISTING.

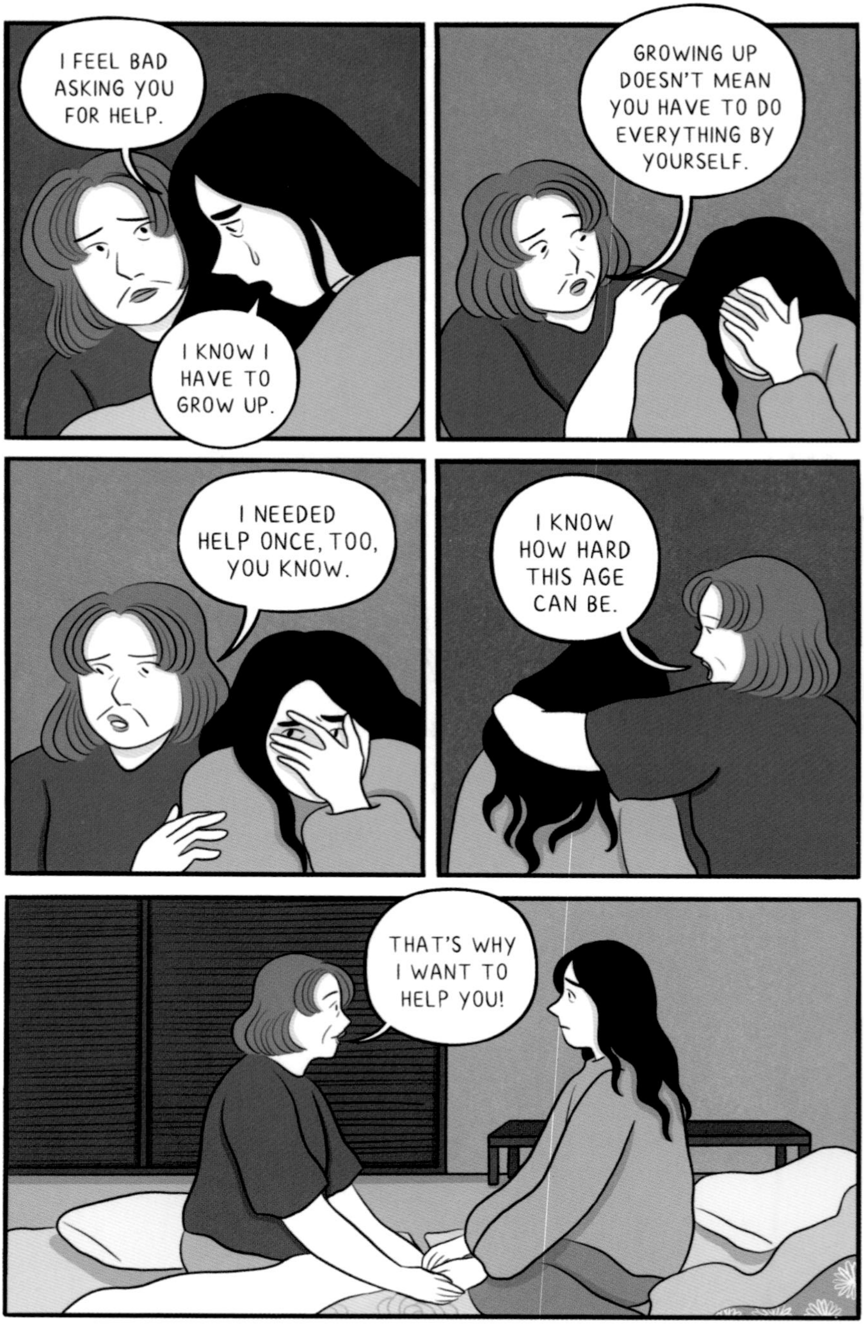
I FEEL BAD ASKING YOU FOR HELP.
I KNOW I HAVE TO GROW UP.
GROWING UP DOESN'T MEAN YOU HAVE TO DO EVERYTHING BY YOURSELF.
I NEEDED HELP ONCE, TOO, YOU KNOW.
I KNOW HOW HARD THIS AGE CAN BE.
THAT'S WHY I WANT TO HELP YOU!

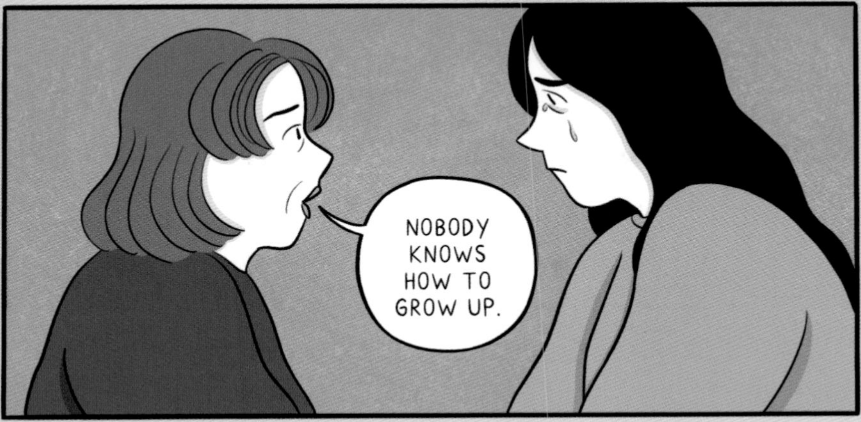
NOBODY KNOWS HOW TO GROW UP.

"YOU'LL EXPERIENCE ALL KINDS OF THINGS. SOME GOOD, SOME BAD. THAT'S HOW YOU LEARN. HOW YOU BECOME STRONGER.

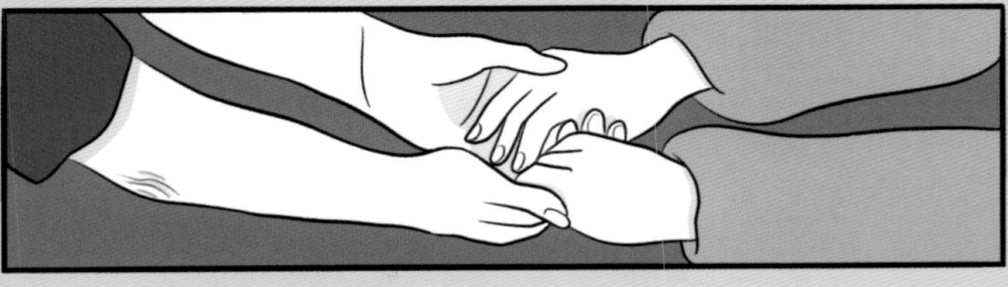

"AND ONE DAY YOU'LL BE OLDER, LIKE ME. AND THEN IT WILL BE YOUR TURN TO HELP SOMEBODY ELSE WHO'S LOST."

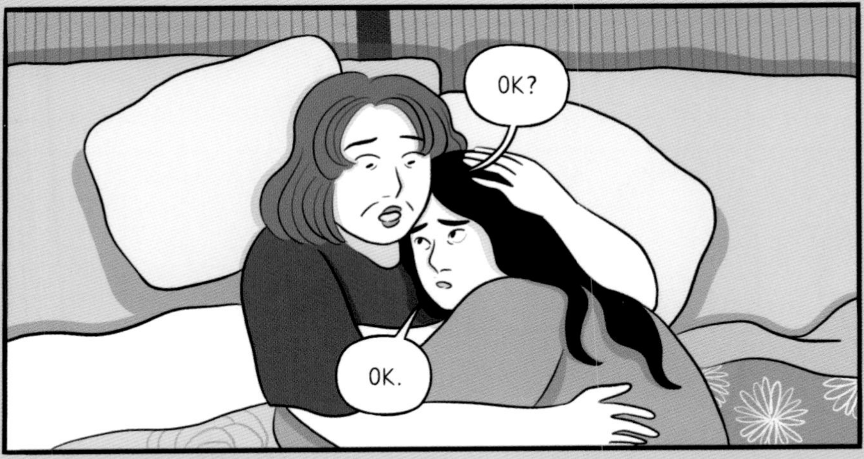
OK?
OK.

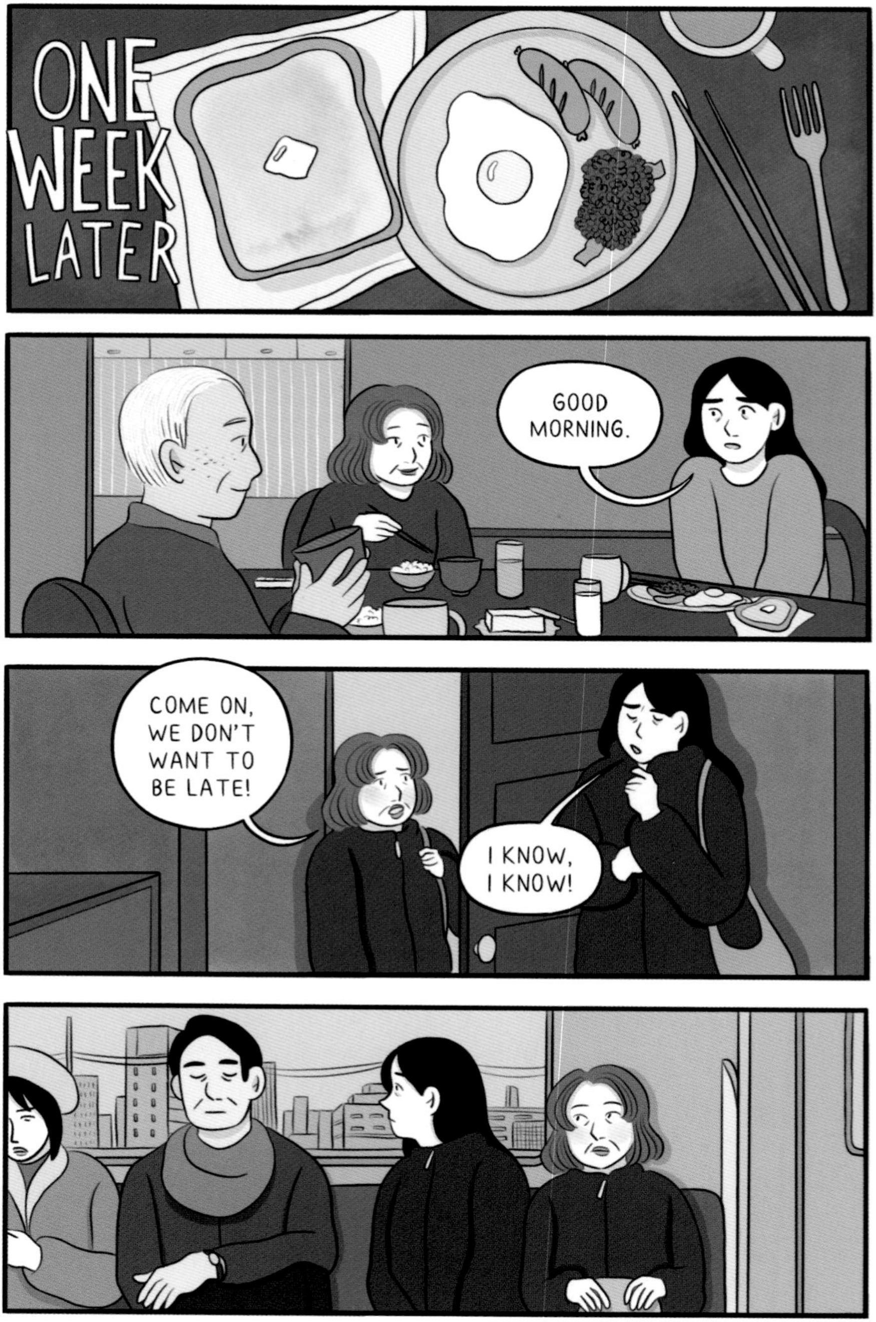

ONE WEEK LATER
GOOD MORNING.
COME ON, WE DON'T WANT TO BE LATE!
I KNOW, I KNOW!

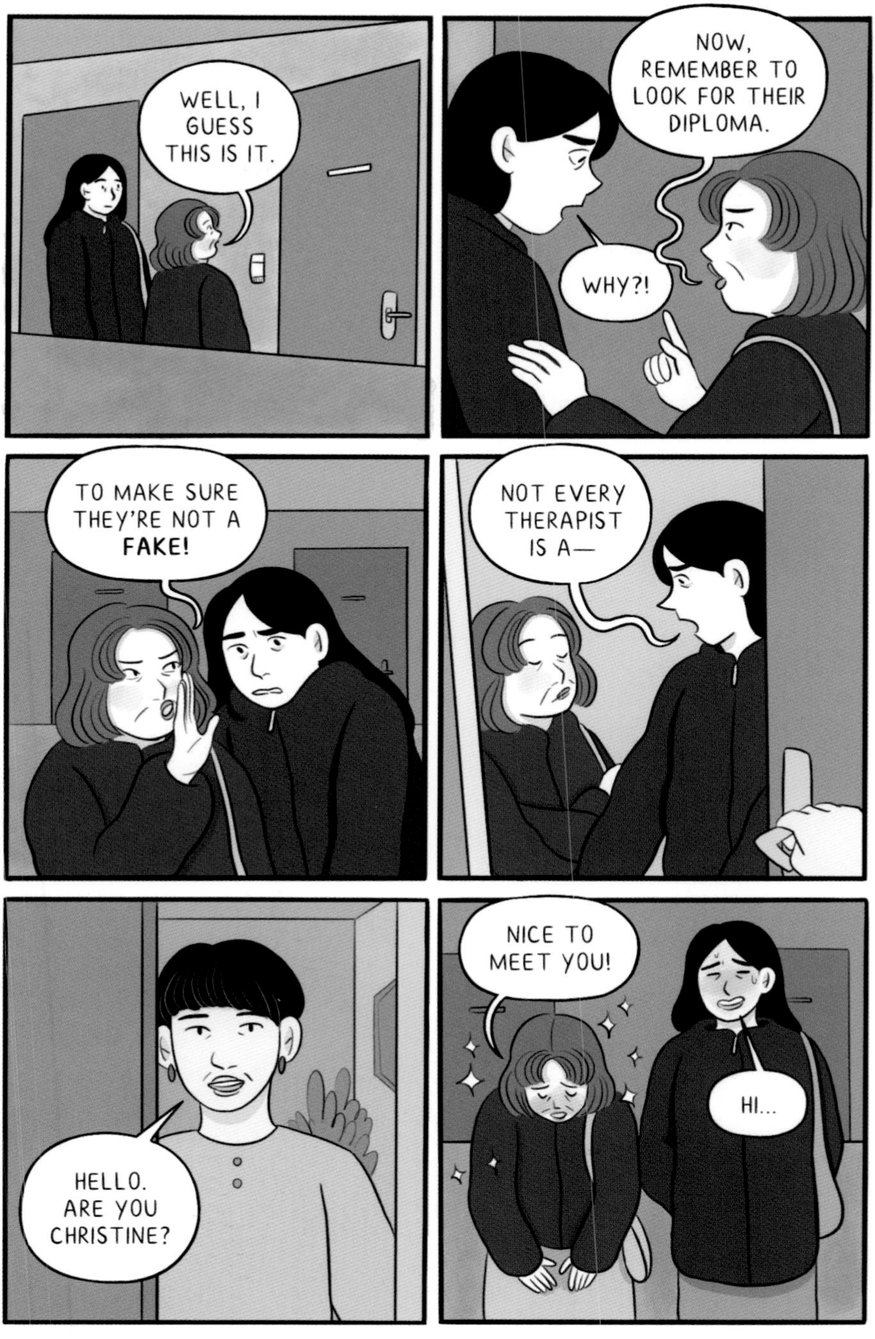
WELL, I GUESS THIS IS IT.
NOW, REMEMBER TO LOOK FOR THEIR DIPLOMA.
WHY?!
TO MAKE SURE THEY'RE NOT A **FAKE!**
NOT EVERY THERAPIST IS A—
HELLO. ARE YOU CHRISTINE?
NICE TO MEET YOU!
HI...

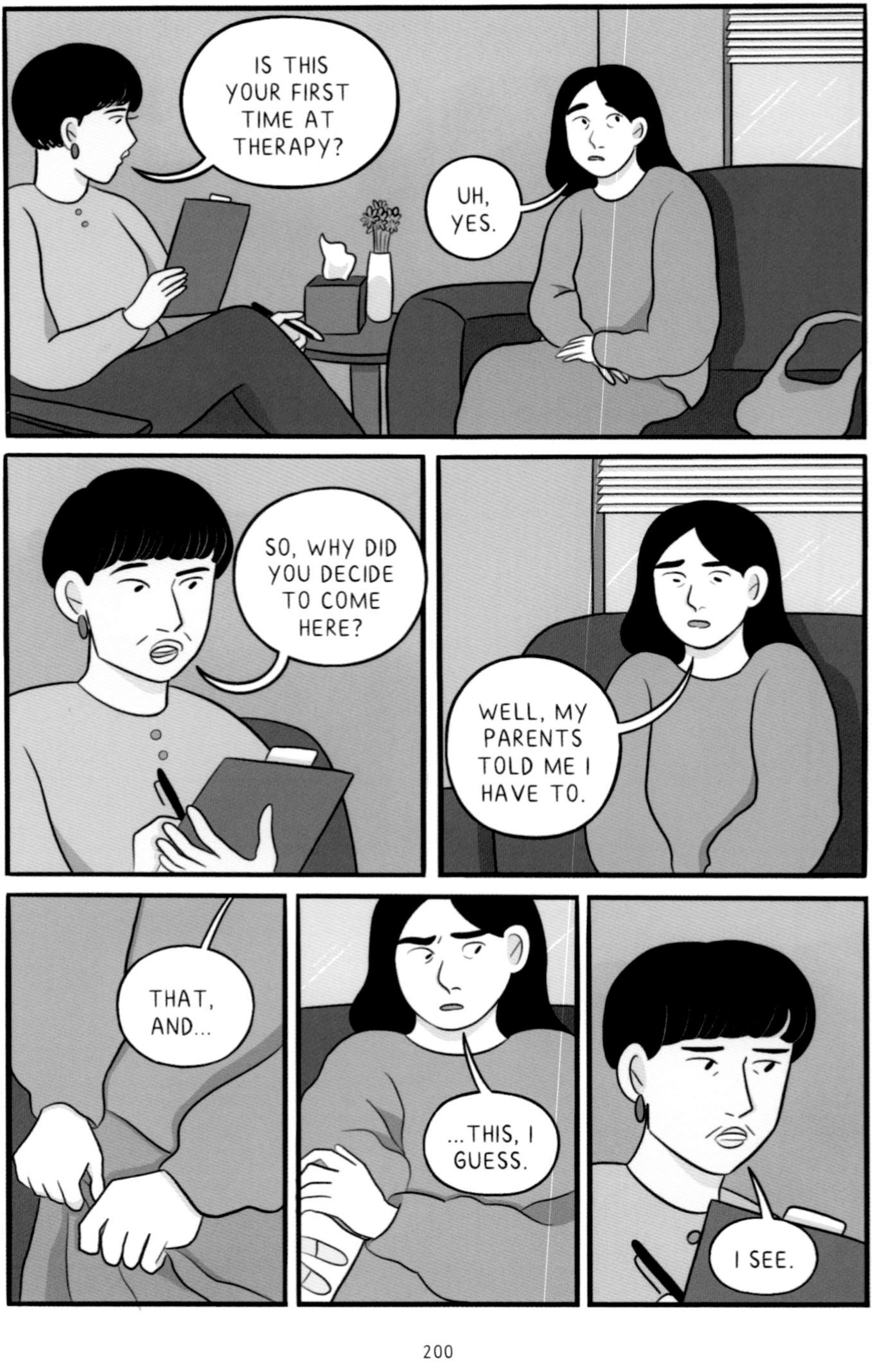
IS THIS YOUR FIRST TIME AT THERAPY?
UH, YES.
SO, WHY DID YOU DECIDE TO COME HERE?
WELL, MY PARENTS TOLD ME I HAVE TO.
THAT, AND...
...THIS, I GUESS.
I SEE.

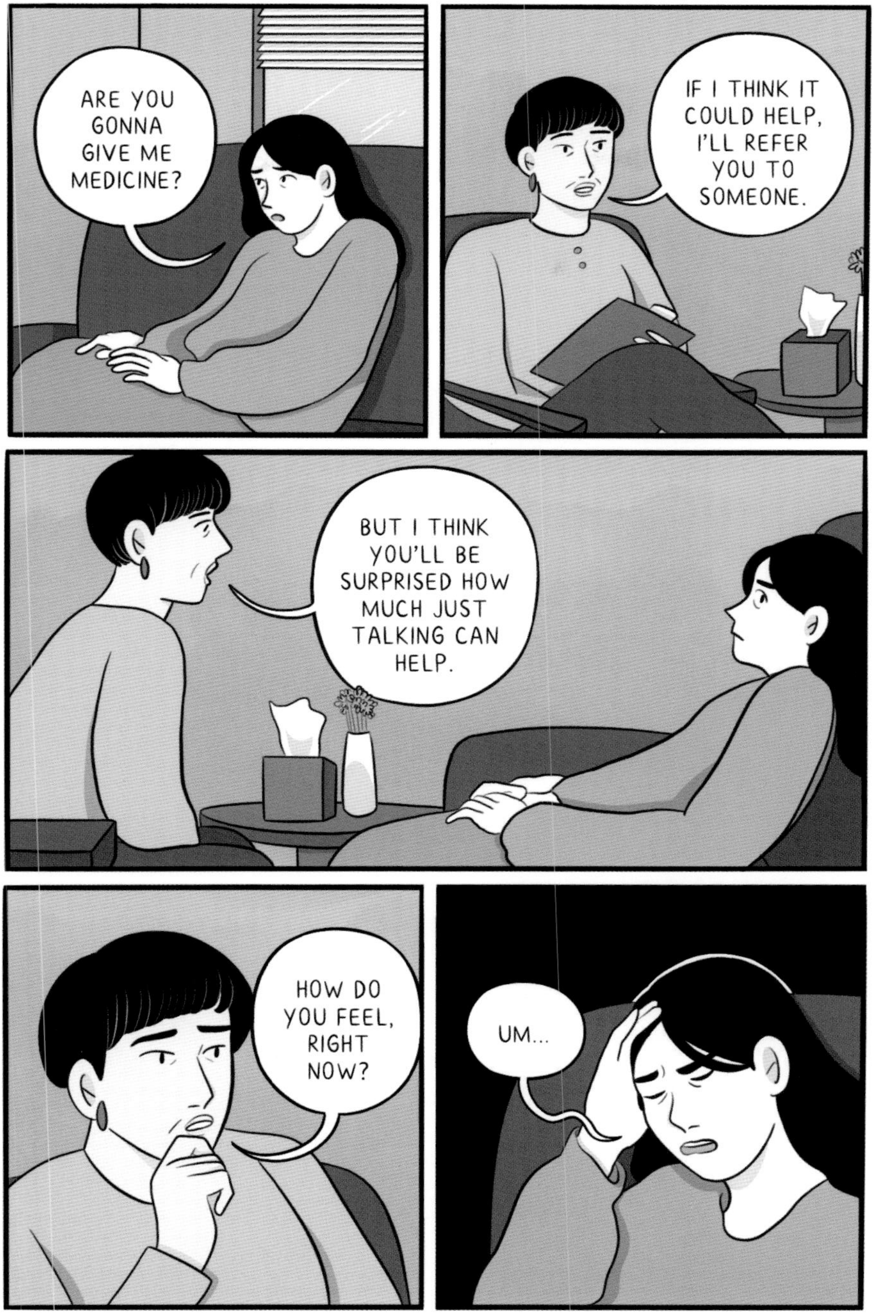
ARE YOU GONNA GIVE ME MEDICINE?
IF I THINK IT COULD HELP, I'LL REFER YOU TO SOMEONE.
BUT I THINK YOU'LL BE SURPRISED HOW MUCH JUST TALKING CAN HELP.
HOW DO YOU FEEL, RIGHT NOW?
UM...

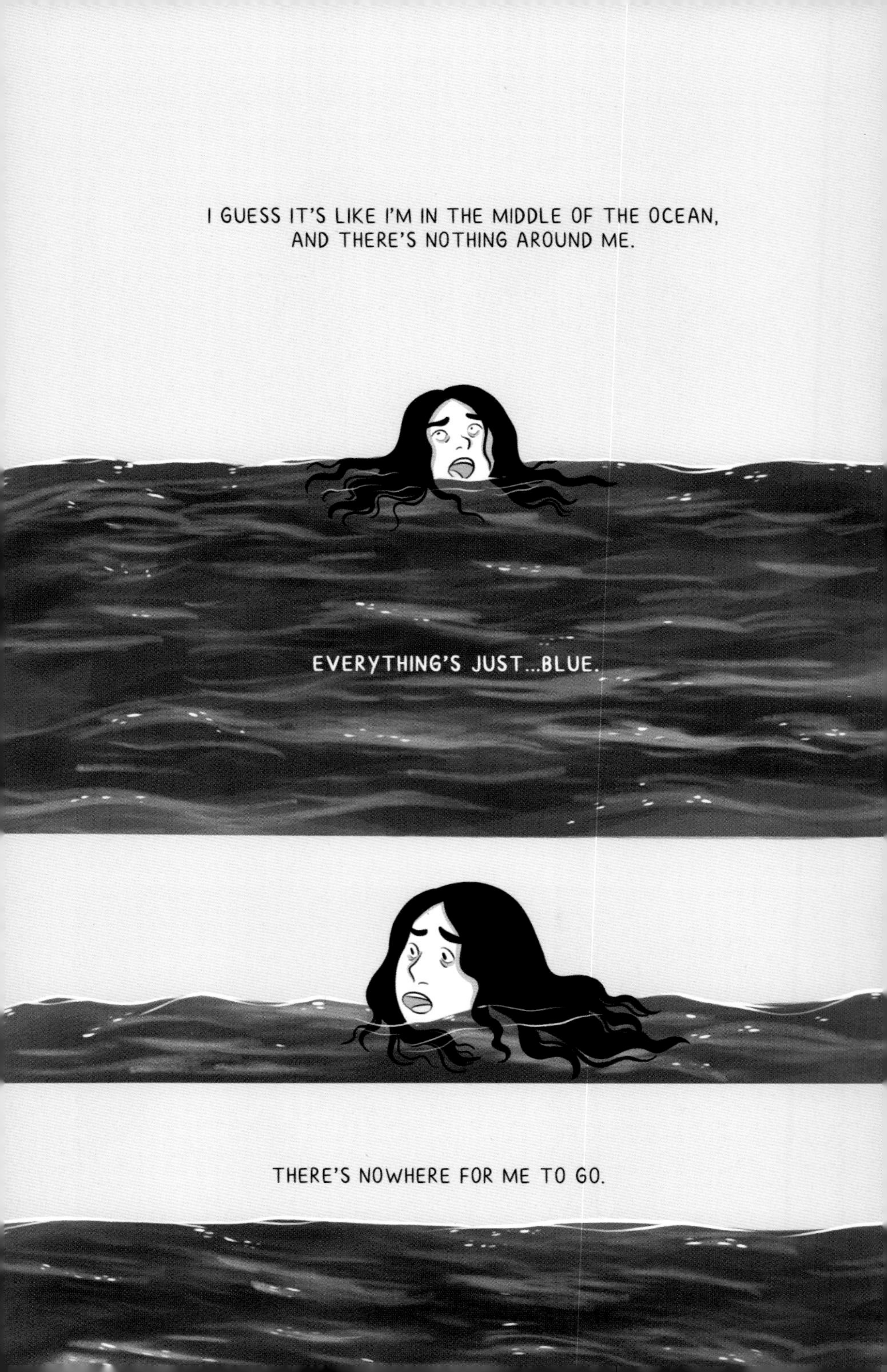
I GUESS IT'S LIKE I'M IN THE MIDDLE OF THE OCEAN, AND THERE'S NOTHING AROUND ME.
EVERYTHING'S JUST...BLUE.
THERE'S NOWHERE FOR ME TO GO.

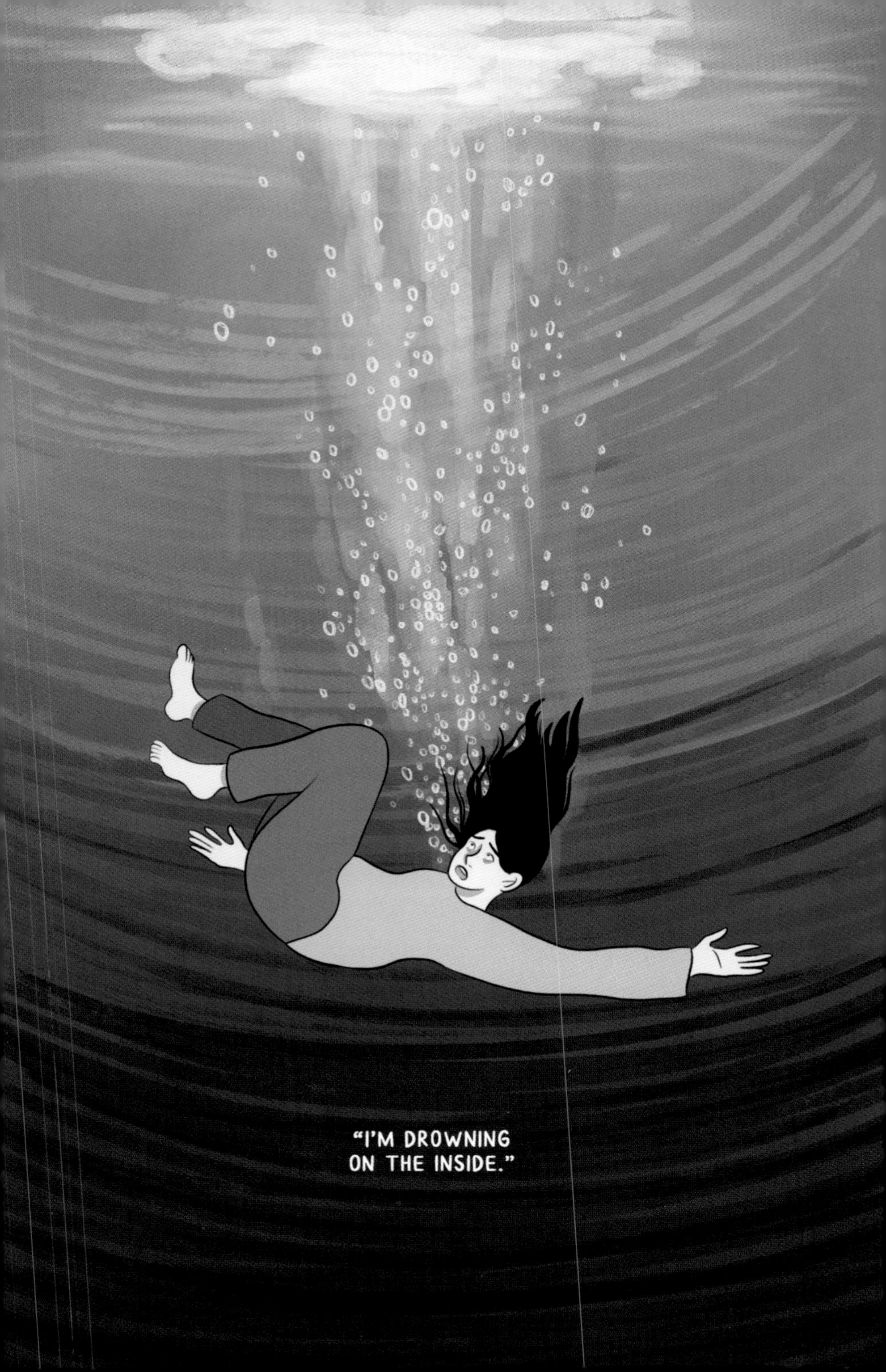
"I'M DROWNING
ON THE INSIDE."

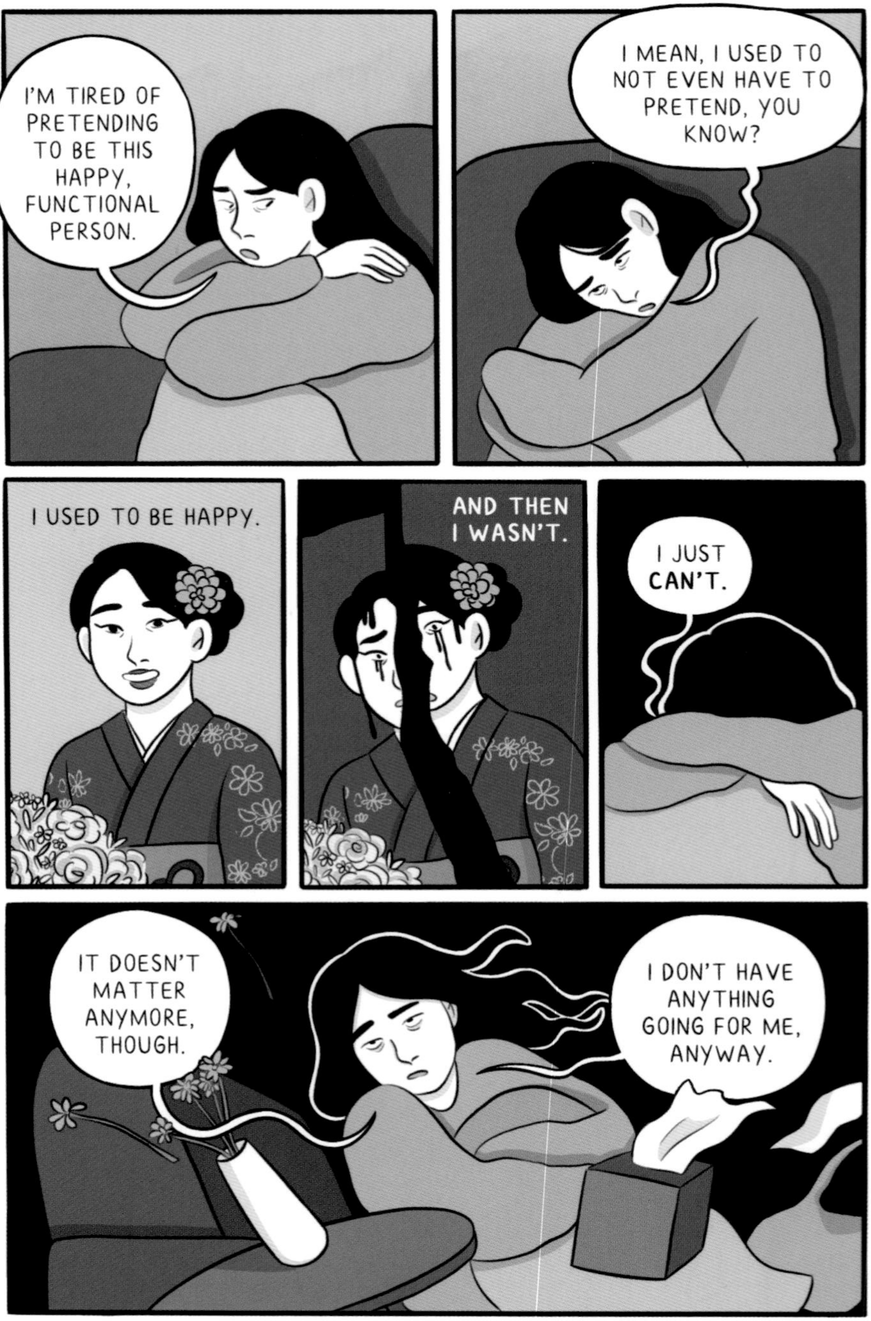
I'M TIRED OF PRETENDING TO BE THIS HAPPY, FUNCTIONAL PERSON.
I MEAN, I USED TO NOT EVEN HAVE TO PRETEND, YOU KNOW?
I USED TO BE HAPPY.
AND THEN I WASN'T.
I JUST **CAN'T.**
IT DOESN'T MATTER ANYMORE, THOUGH.
I DON'T HAVE ANYTHING GOING FOR ME, ANYWAY.

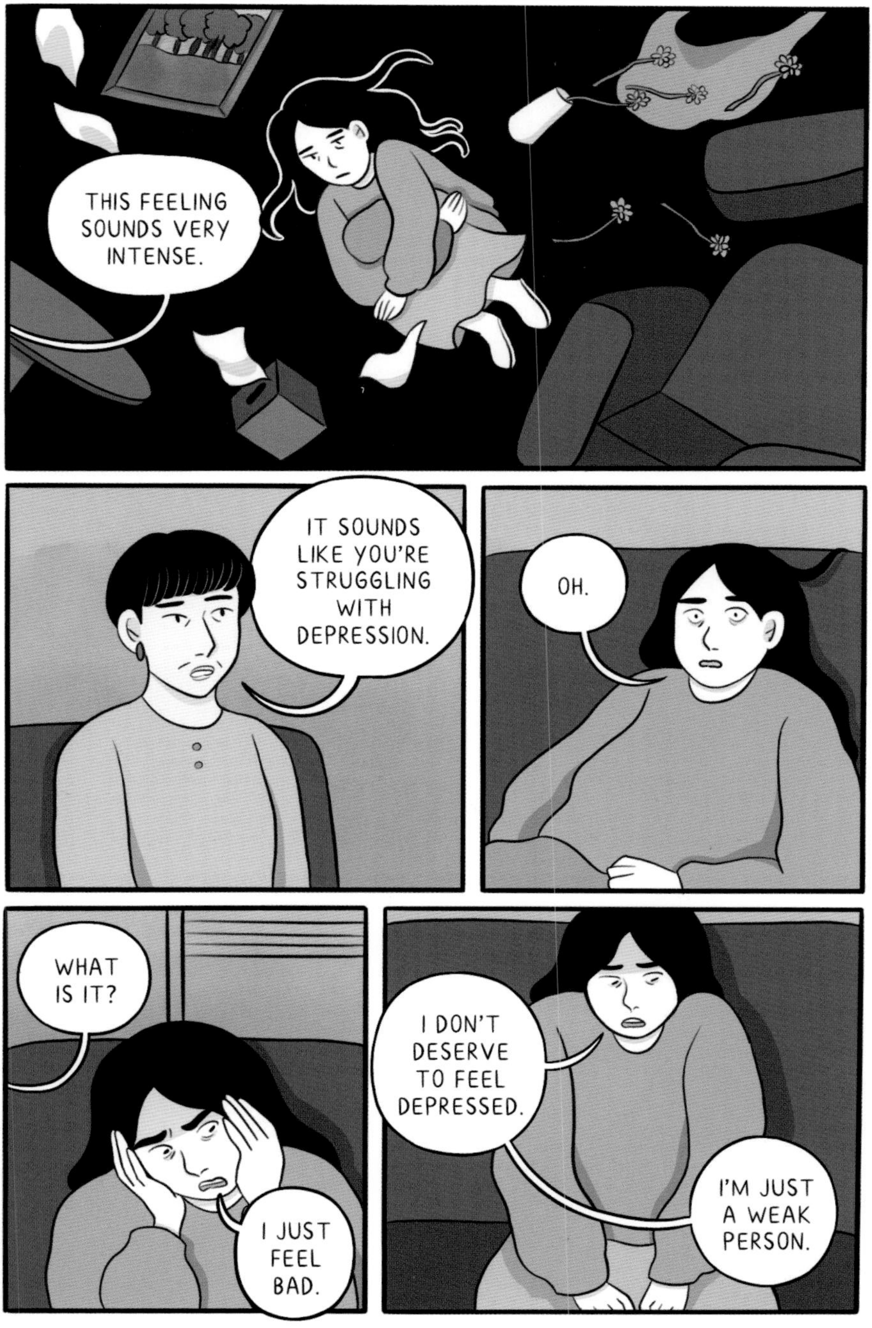
THIS FEELING SOUNDS VERY INTENSE.
IT SOUNDS LIKE YOU'RE STRUGGLING WITH DEPRESSION.
OH.
WHAT IS IT?
I JUST FEEL BAD.
I DON'T DESERVE TO FEEL DEPRESSED.
I'M JUST A WEAK PERSON.

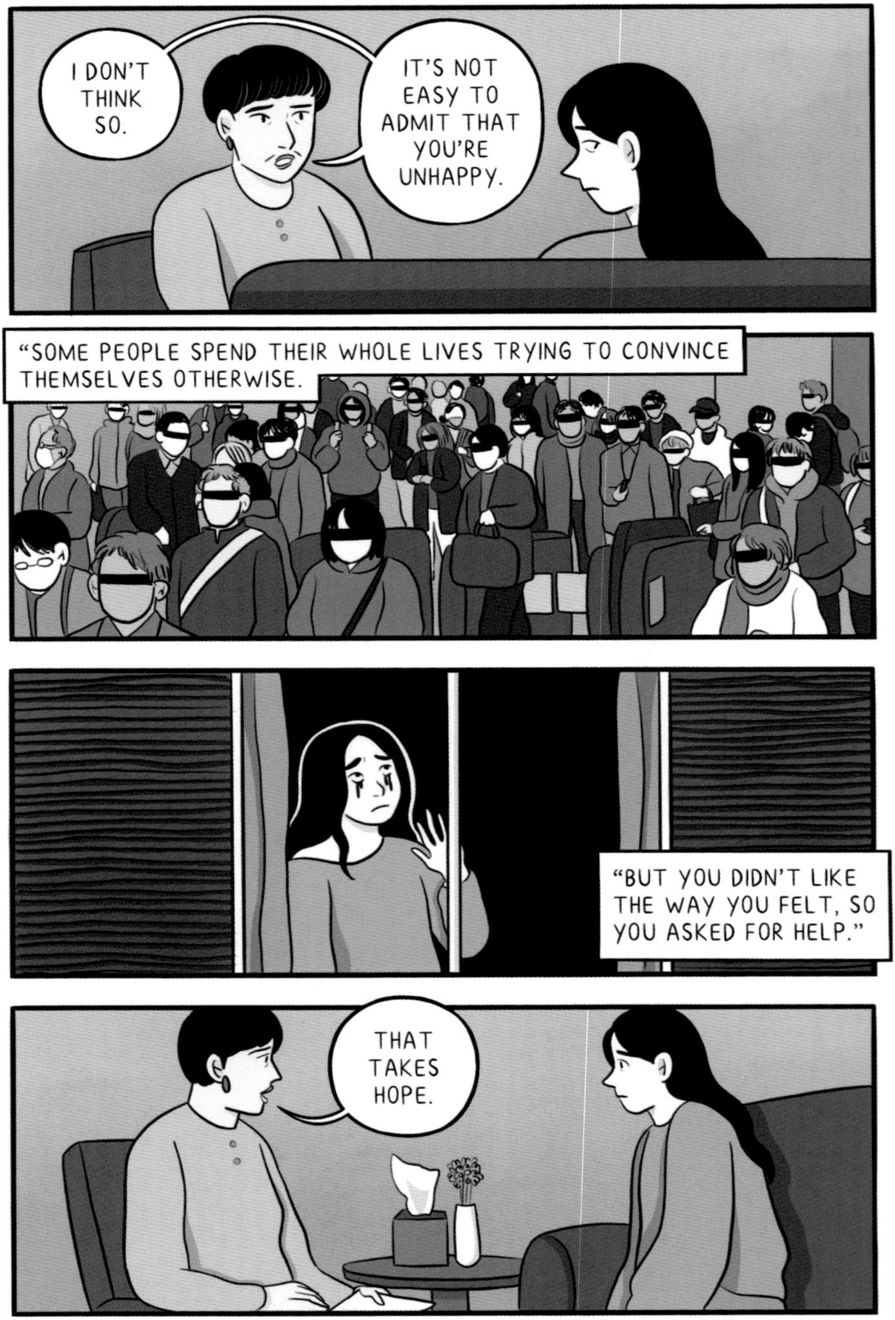
I DON'T THINK SO.
IT'S NOT EASY TO ADMIT THAT YOU'RE UNHAPPY.
"SOME PEOPLE SPEND THEIR WHOLE LIVES TRYING TO CONVINCE THEMSELVES OTHERWISE.
"BUT YOU DIDN'T LIKE THE WAY YOU FELT, SO YOU ASKED FOR HELP."
THAT TAKES HOPE.

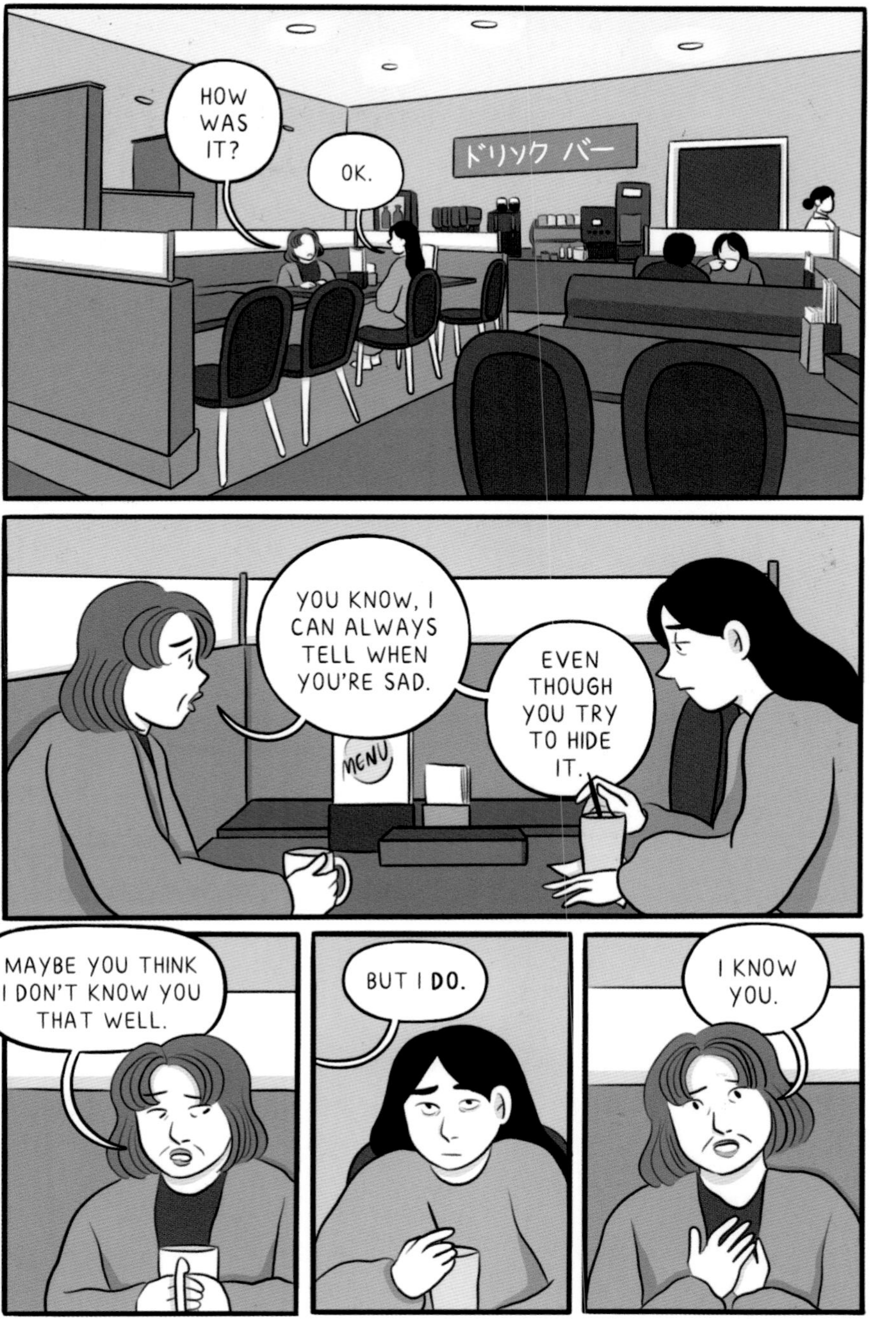
HOW WAS IT?
OK.
ドリンク バー
YOU KNOW, I CAN ALWAYS TELL WHEN YOU'RE SAD.
EVEN THOUGH YOU TRY TO HIDE IT.
MENU
MAYBE YOU THINK I DON'T KNOW YOU THAT WELL.
BUT I **DO.**
I KNOW YOU.

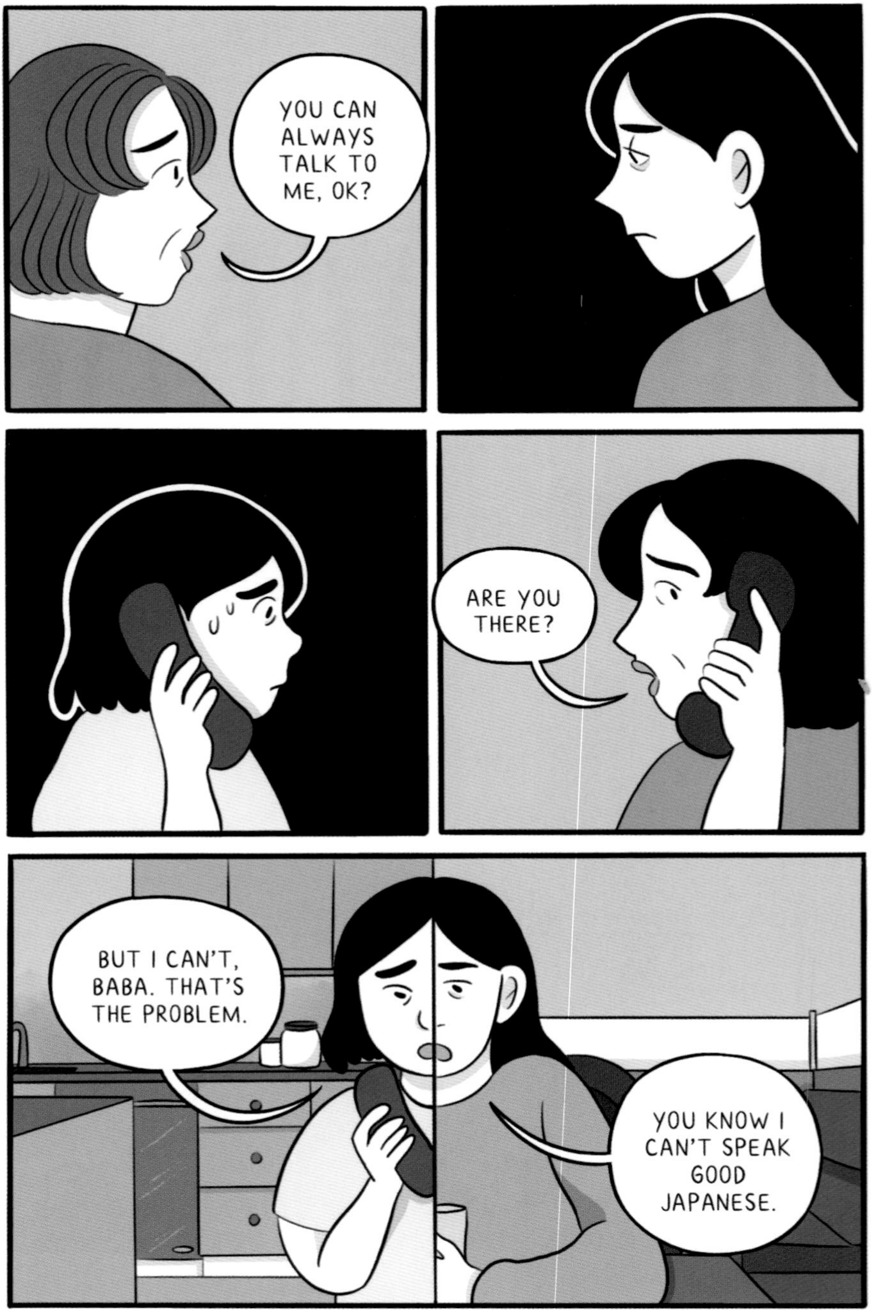
YOU CAN ALWAYS TALK TO ME, OK?
ARE YOU THERE?
BUT I CAN'T, BABA. THAT'S THE PROBLEM.
YOU KNOW I CAN'T SPEAK GOOD JAPANESE.

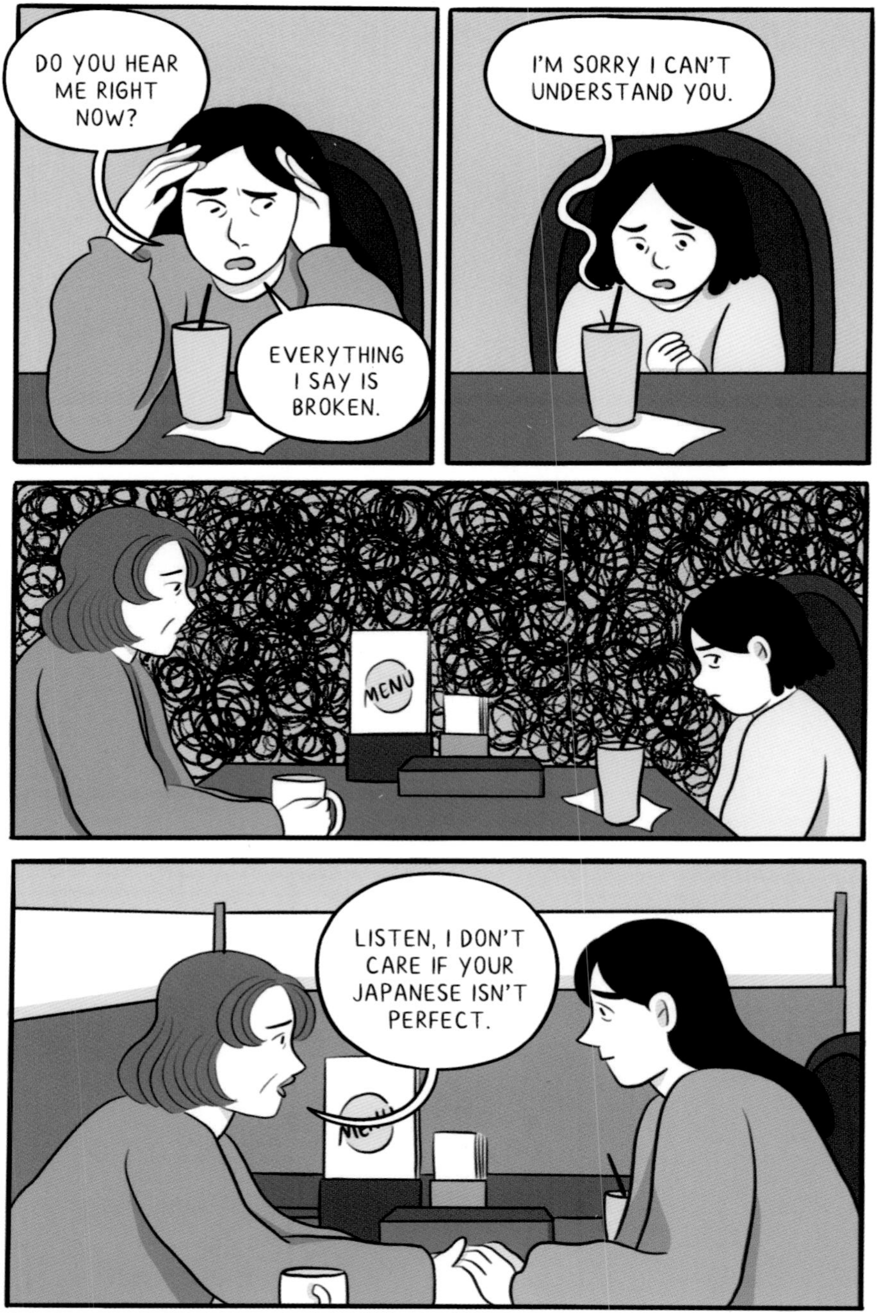
DO YOU HEAR ME RIGHT NOW?
EVERYTHING I SAY IS BROKEN.
I'M SORRY I CAN'T UNDERSTAND YOU.
MENU
LISTEN, I DON'T CARE IF YOUR JAPANESE ISN'T PERFECT.

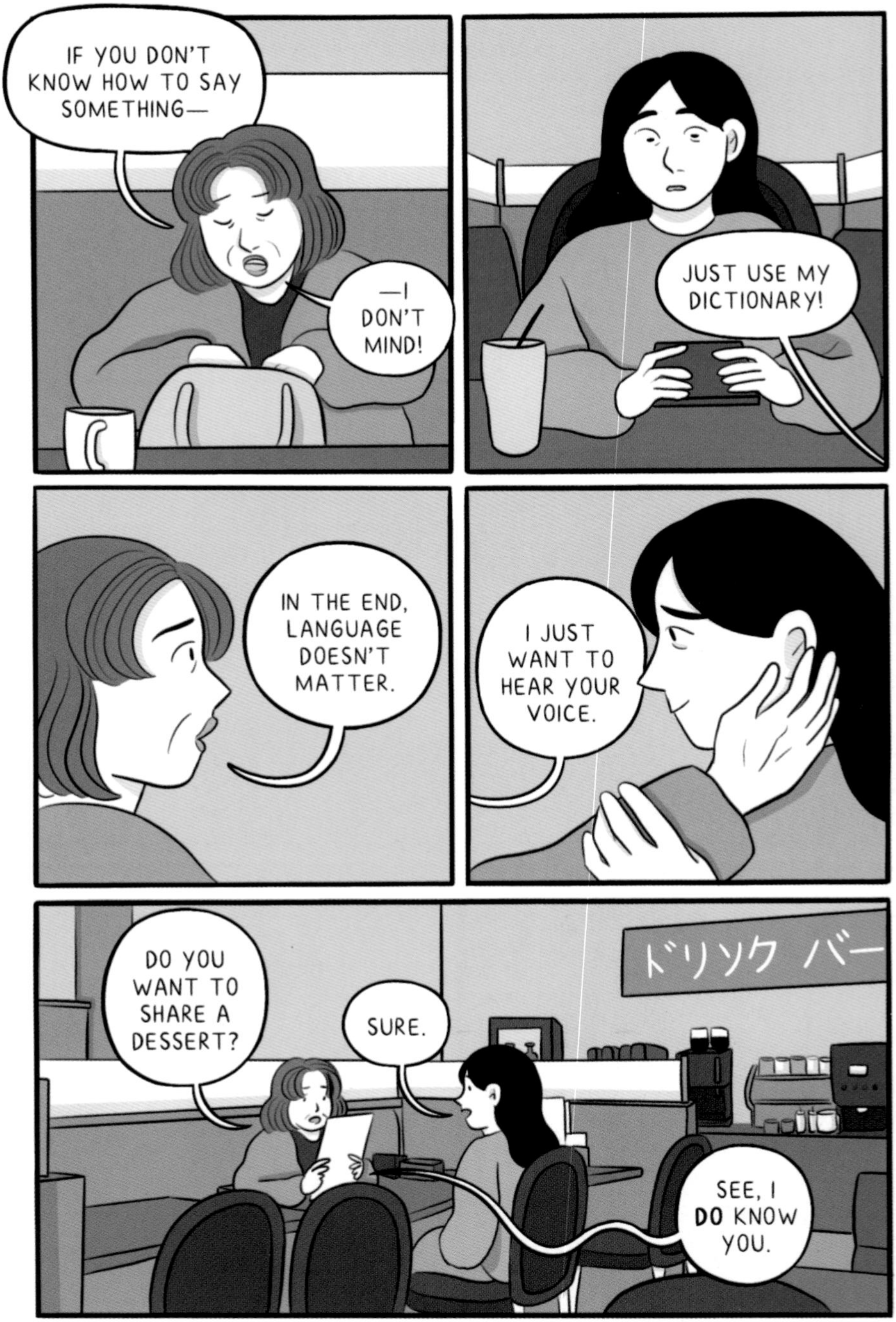
IF YOU DON'T KNOW HOW TO SAY SOMETHING—
—I DON'T MIND!
JUST USE MY DICTIONARY!
IN THE END, LANGUAGE DOESN'T MATTER.
I JUST WANT TO HEAR YOUR VOICE.
DO YOU WANT TO SHARE A DESSERT?
SURE.
ドリンク バー
SEE, I **DO** KNOW YOU.

春
SPRING

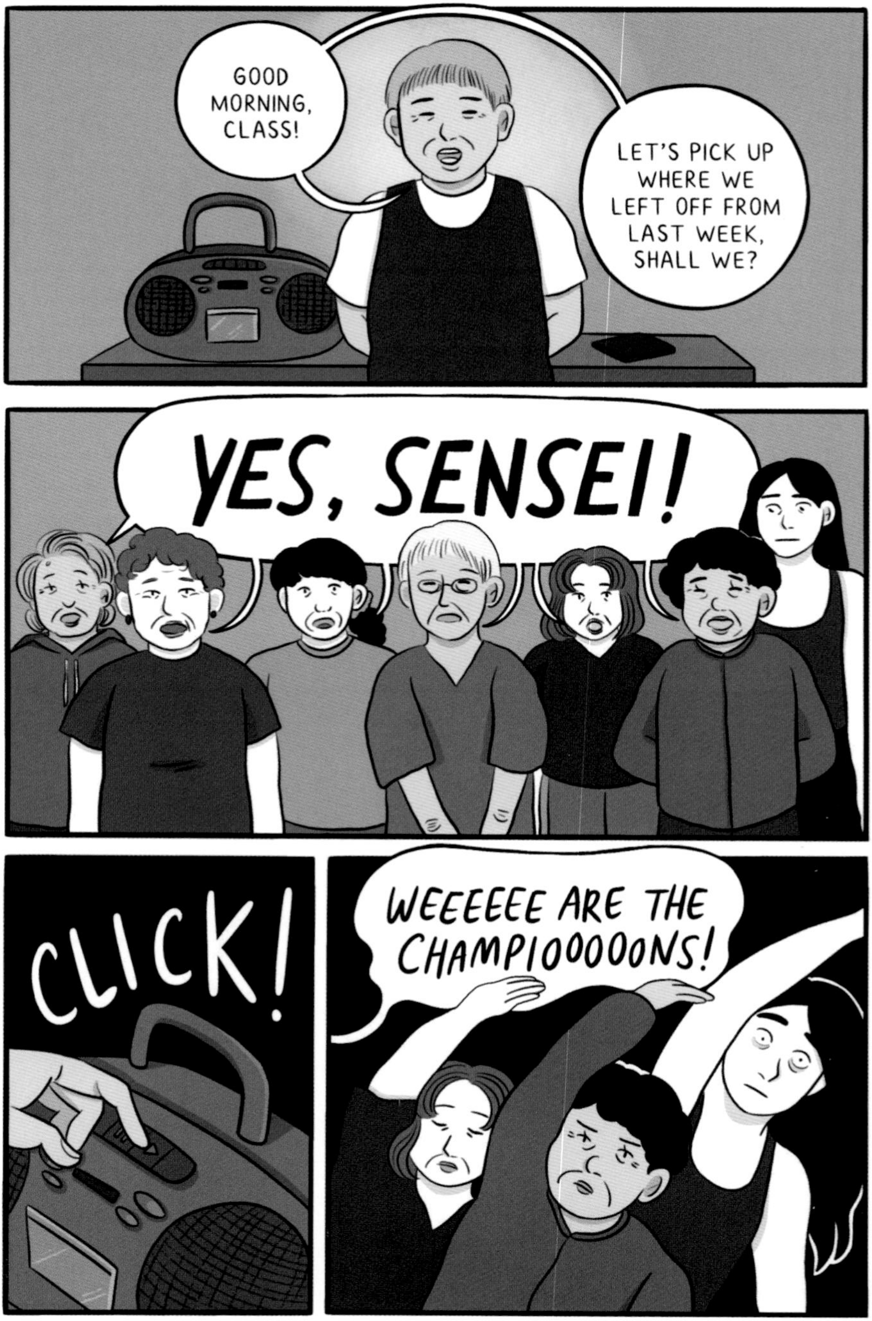
GOOD MORNING, CLASS!
LET'S PICK UP WHERE WE LEFT OFF FROM LAST WEEK, SHALL WE?
YES, SENSEI!
CLICK!
WEEEEEE ARE THE CHAMPIOOOOONS!

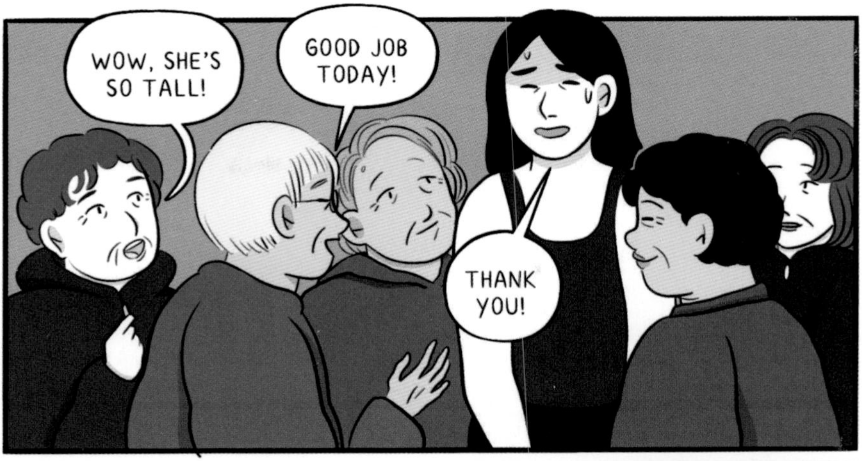
WOW, SHE'S SO TALL!
GOOD JOB TODAY!
THANK YOU!

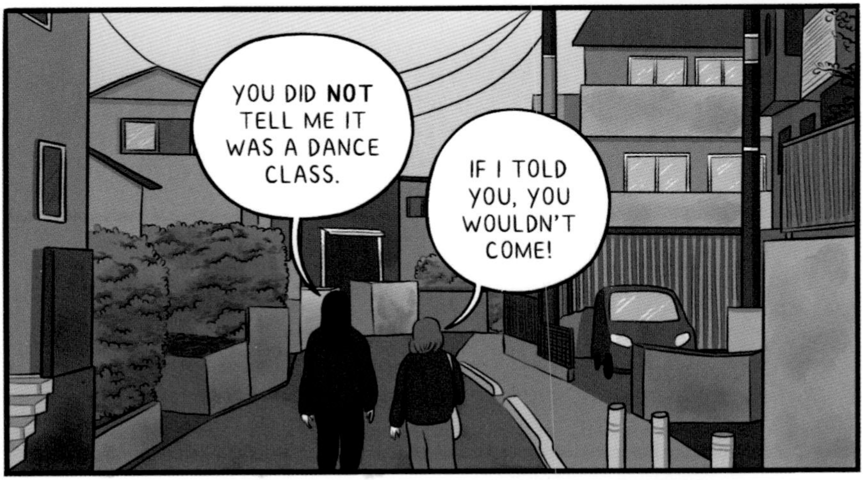
YOU DID **NOT** TELL ME IT WAS A DANCE CLASS.
IF I TOLD YOU, YOU WOULDN'T COME!

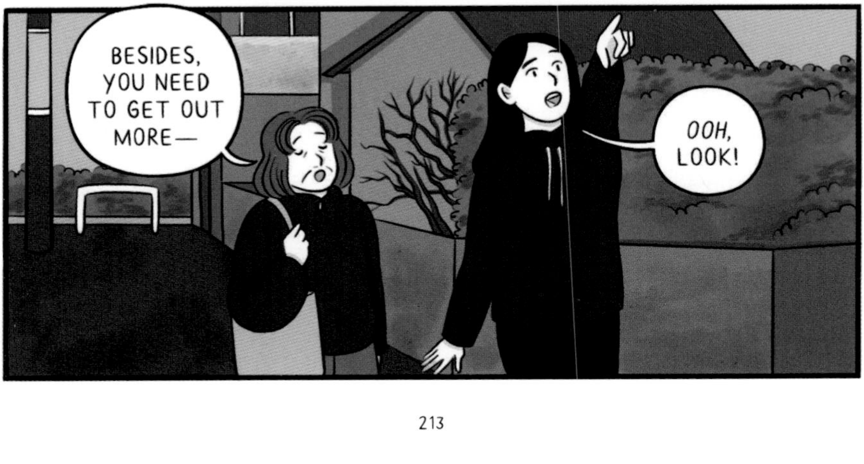
BESIDES, YOU NEED TO GET OUT MORE—
OOH, LOOK!

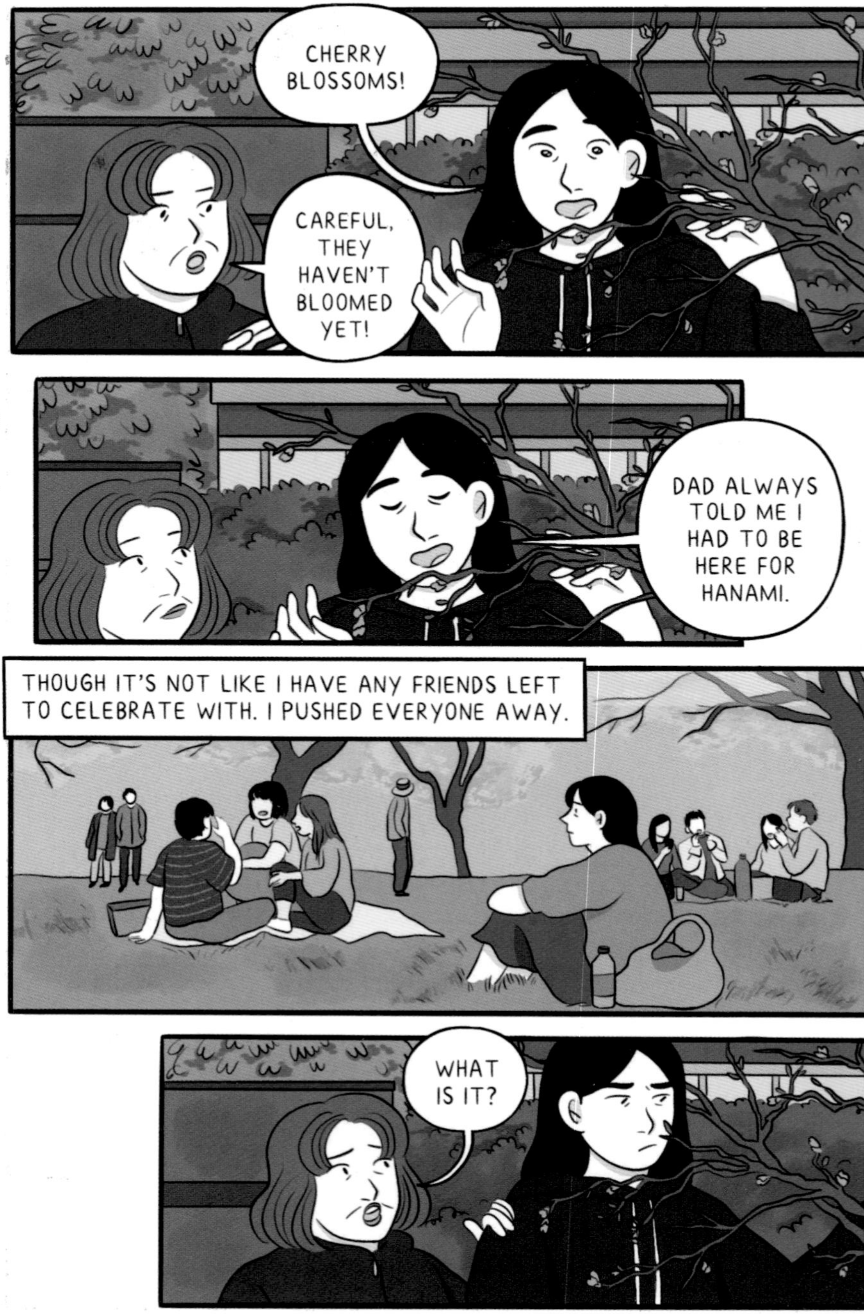
CHERRY BLOSSOMS!
CAREFUL, THEY HAVEN'T BLOOMED YET!
DAD ALWAYS TOLD ME I HAD TO BE HERE FOR HANAMI.
THOUGH IT'S NOT LIKE I HAVE ANY FRIENDS LEFT TO CELEBRATE WITH. I PUSHED EVERYONE AWAY.
WHAT IS IT?

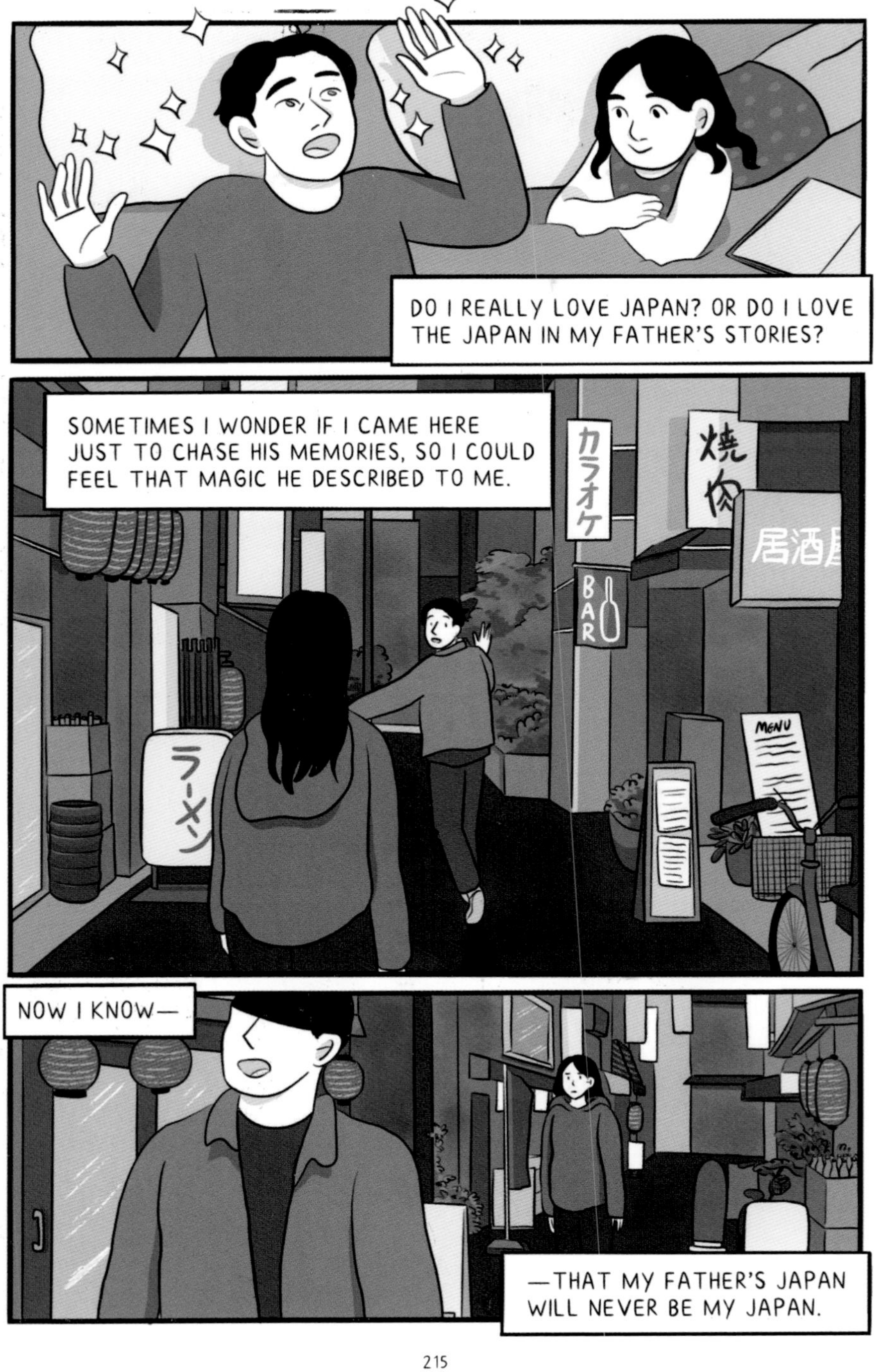
DO I REALLY LOVE JAPAN? OR DO I LOVE THE JAPAN IN MY FATHER'S STORIES?
SOMETIMES I WONDER IF I CAME HERE JUST TO CHASE HIS MEMORIES, SO I COULD FEEL THAT MAGIC HE DESCRIBED TO ME.
カラオケ
焼肉
居酒屋
BAR
MENU
ラーメン
NOW I KNOW—
—THAT MY FATHER'S JAPAN WILL NEVER BE MY JAPAN.

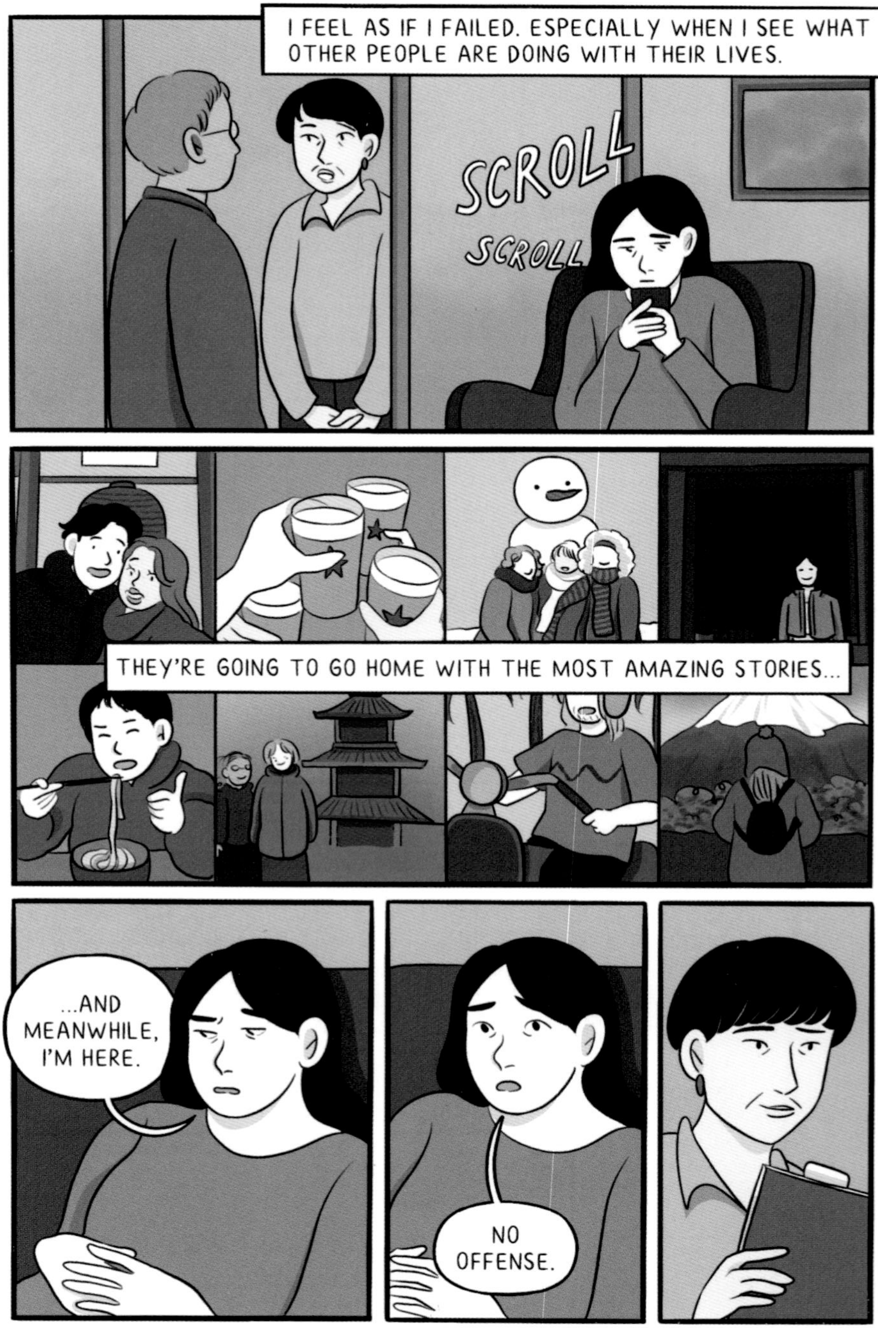
I FEEL AS IF I FAILED. ESPECIALLY WHEN I SEE WHAT OTHER PEOPLE ARE DOING WITH THEIR LIVES.
SCROLL
SCROLL
THEY'RE GOING TO GO HOME WITH THE MOST AMAZING STORIES...
...AND MEANWHILE, I'M HERE.
NO OFFENSE.

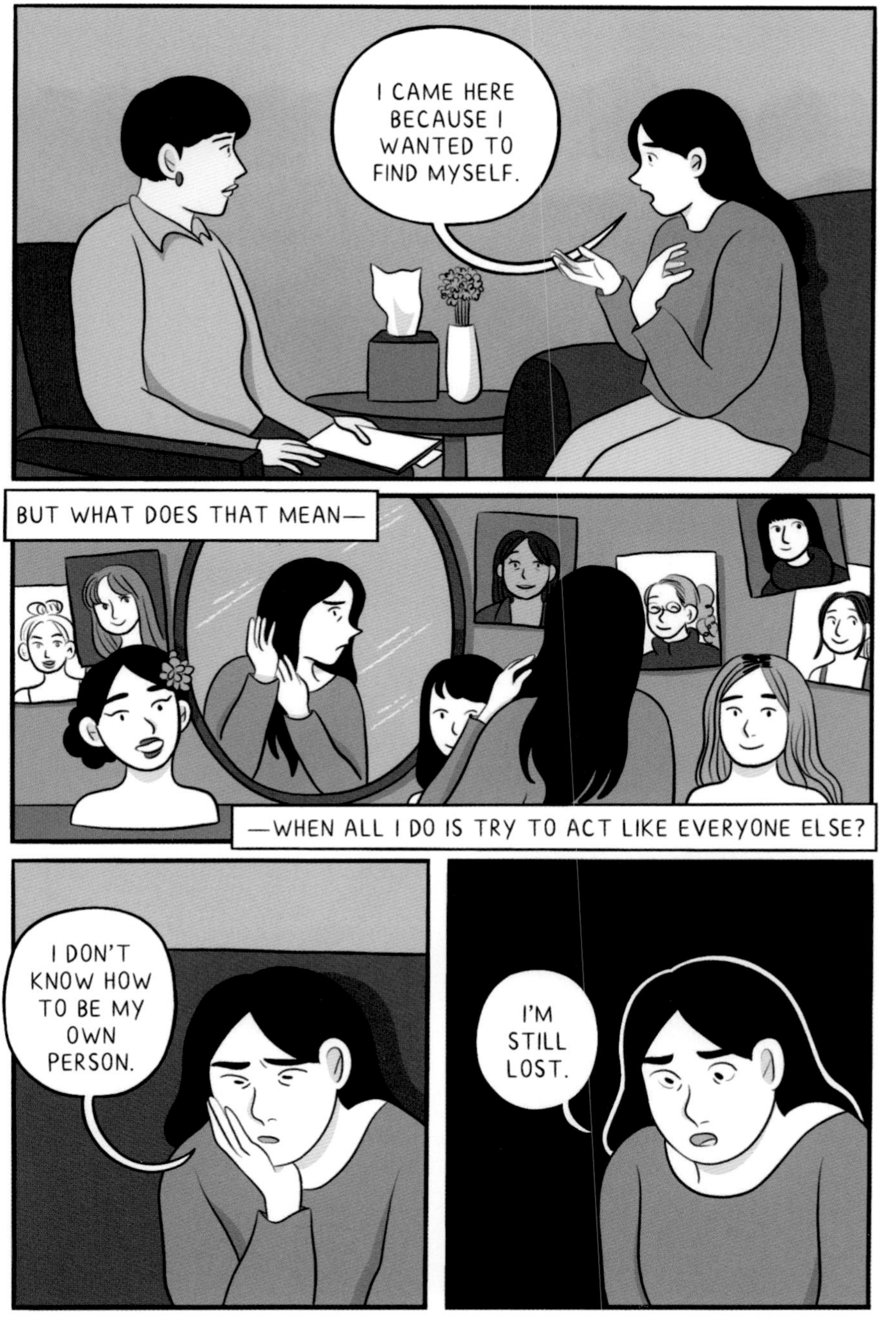
I CAME HERE BECAUSE I WANTED TO FIND MYSELF.
BUT WHAT DOES THAT MEAN—
—WHEN ALL I DO IS TRY TO ACT LIKE EVERYONE ELSE?
I DON'T KNOW HOW TO BE MY OWN PERSON.
I'M STILL LOST.

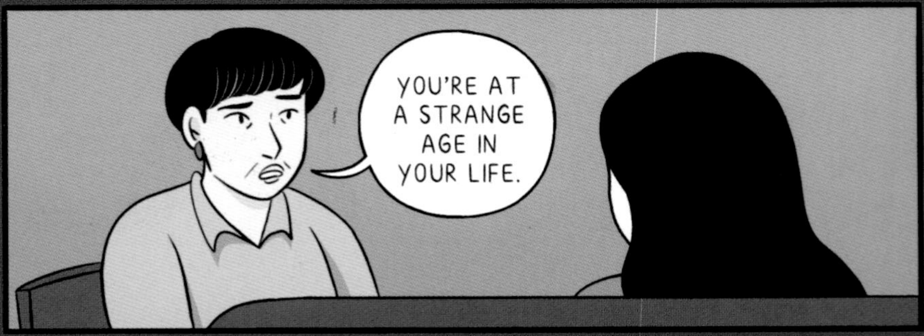
YOU'RE AT A STRANGE AGE IN YOUR LIFE.

"YOU'RE TECHNICALLY NOT A CHILD ANYMORE
BUT YOU DON'T FEEL LIKE AN ADULT, EITHER.

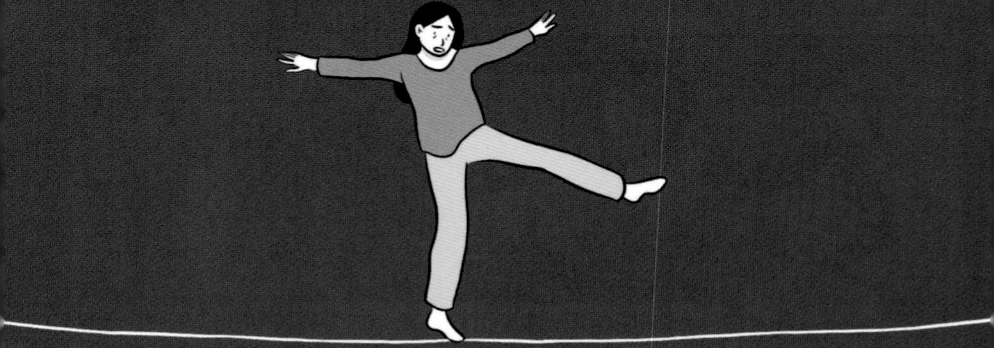

"YOU'RE SOMEWHERE CAUGHT IN BETWEEN."

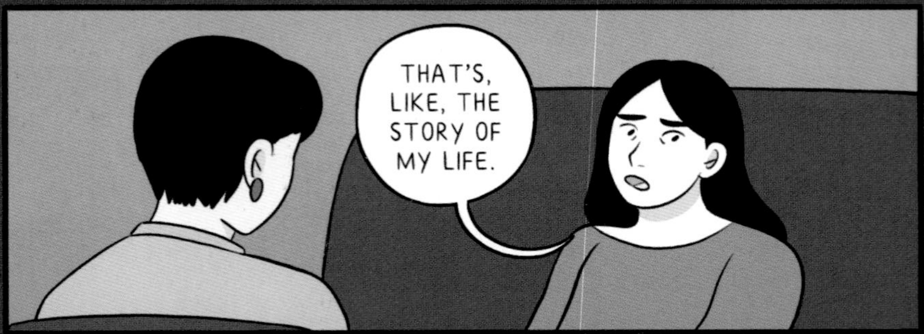
THAT'S, LIKE, THE STORY OF MY LIFE.

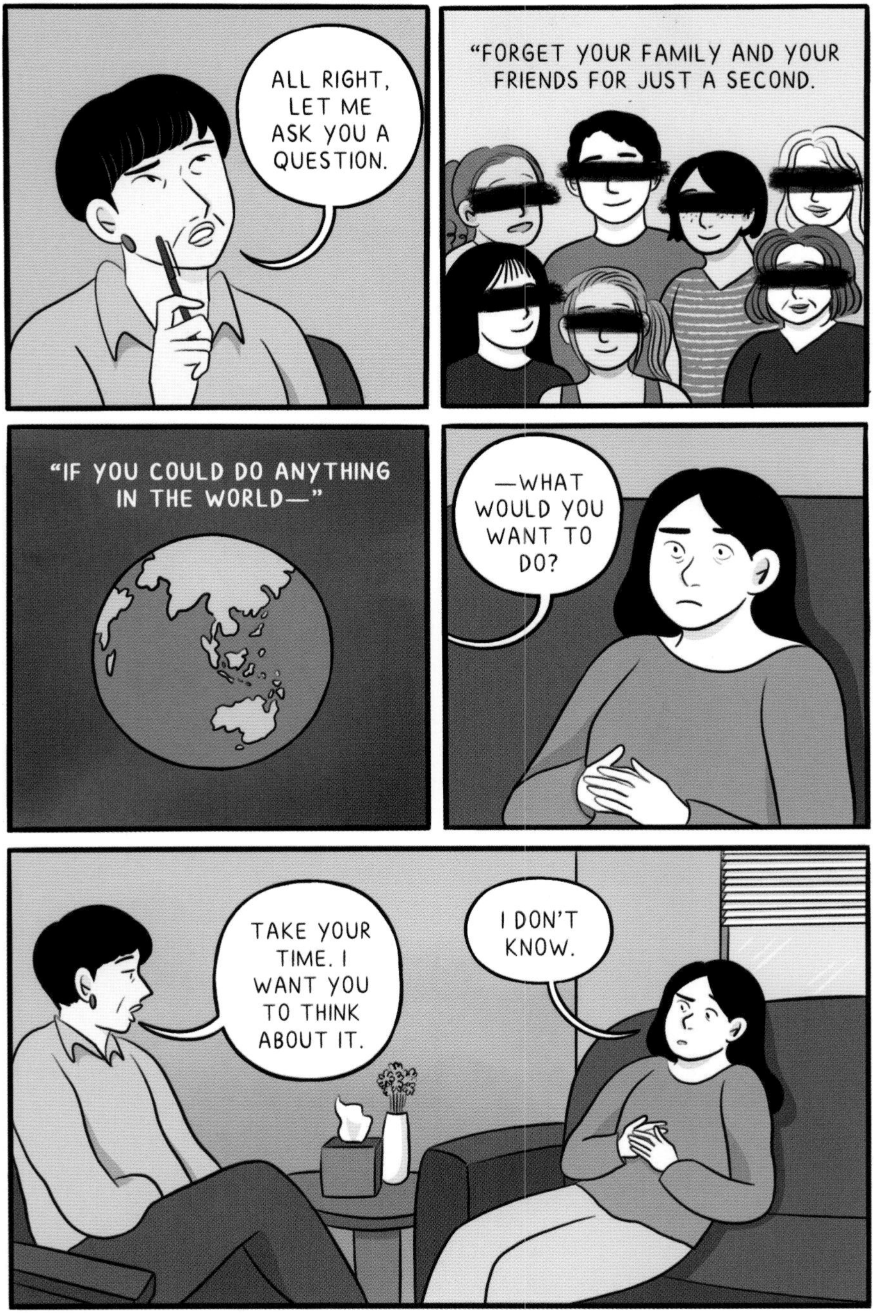
ALL RIGHT, LET ME ASK YOU A QUESTION.
"FORGET YOUR FAMILY AND YOUR FRIENDS FOR JUST A SECOND.
"IF YOU COULD DO ANYTHING IN THE WORLD—"
—WHAT WOULD YOU WANT TO DO?
TAKE YOUR TIME. I WANT YOU TO THINK ABOUT IT.
I DON'T KNOW.

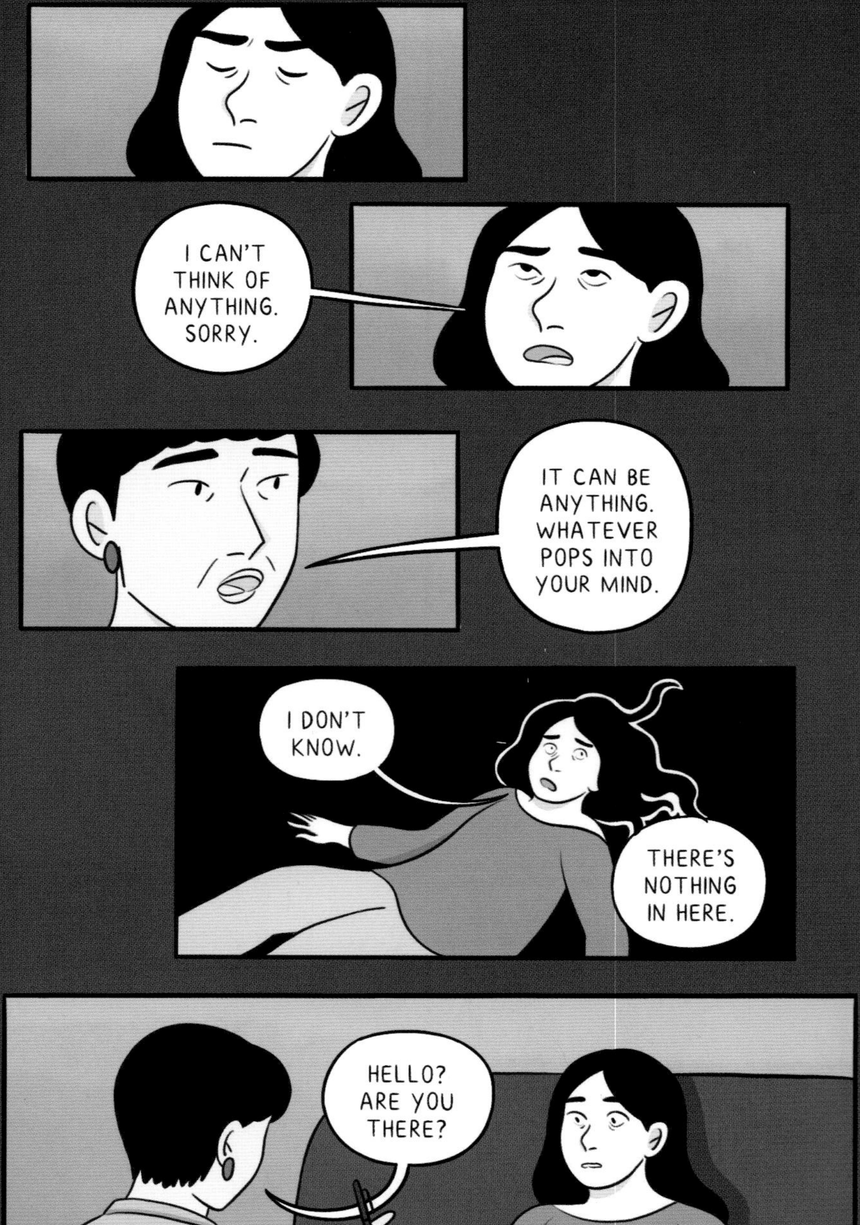

I CAN'T THINK OF ANYTHING. SORRY.
IT CAN BE ANYTHING. WHATEVER POPS INTO YOUR MIND.
I DON'T KNOW.
THERE'S NOTHING IN HERE.
HELLO? ARE YOU THERE?

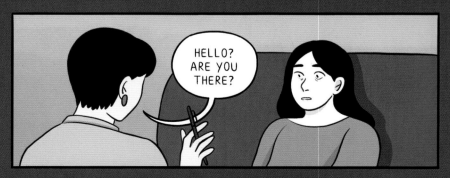

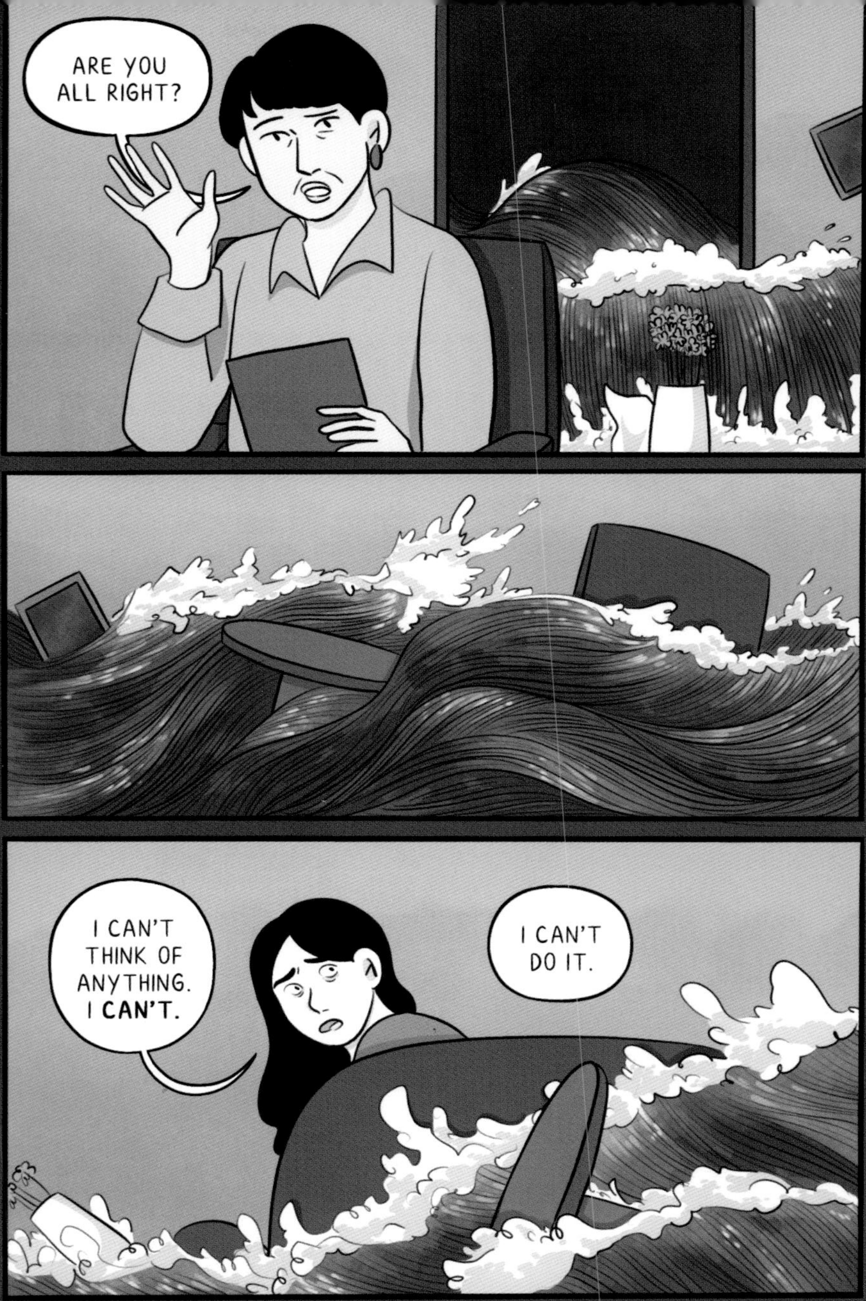
ARE YOU ALL RIGHT?
I CAN'T THINK OF ANYTHING. I **CAN'T.**
I CAN'T DO IT.

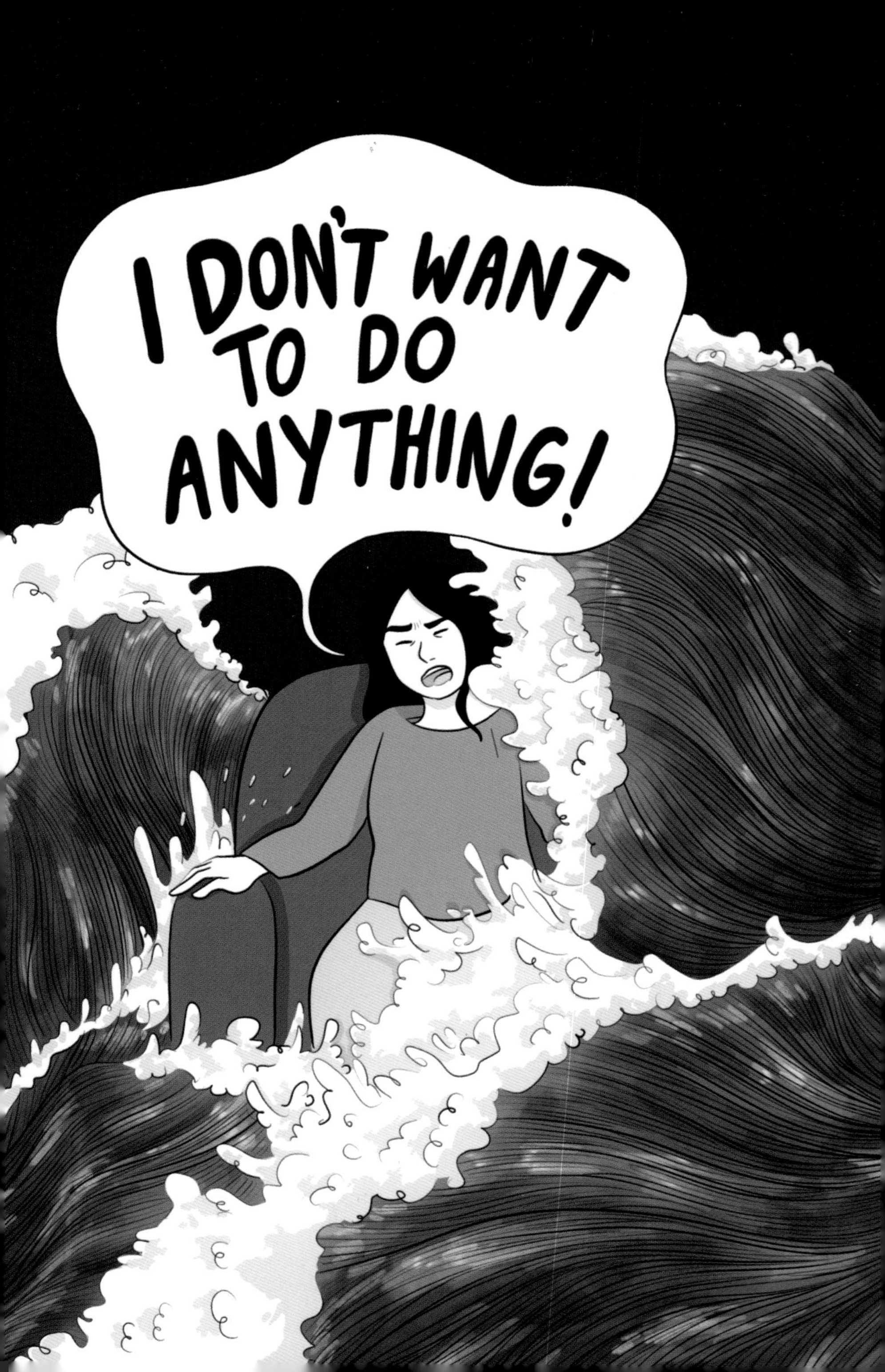
I DON'T WANT TO DO ANYTHING!

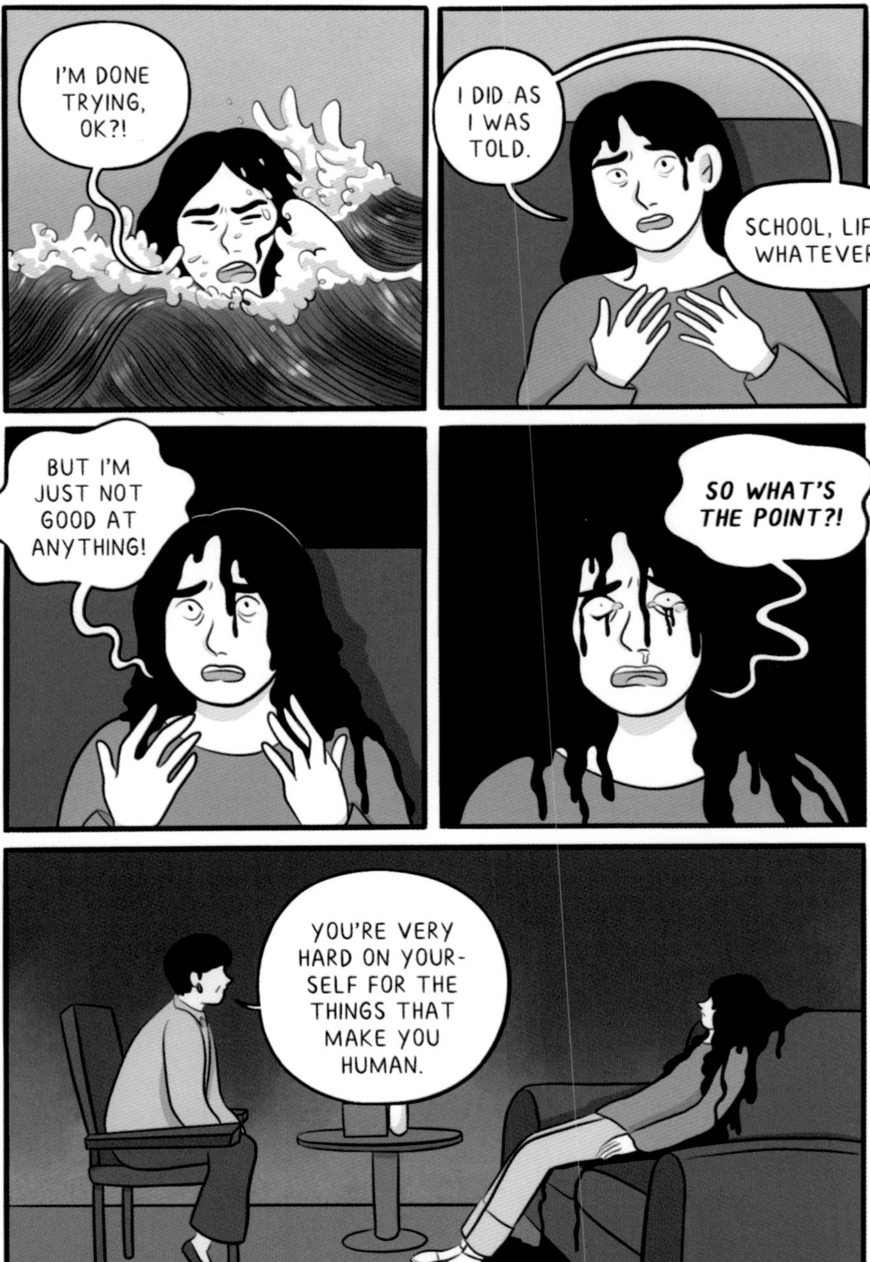
I'M DONE TRYING, OK?!
I DID AS I WAS TOLD.
SCHOOL, LIFE, WHATEVER.
BUT I'M JUST NOT GOOD AT ANYTHING!
SO WHAT'S THE POINT?!
YOU'RE VERY HARD ON YOUR-SELF FOR THE THINGS THAT MAKE YOU HUMAN.

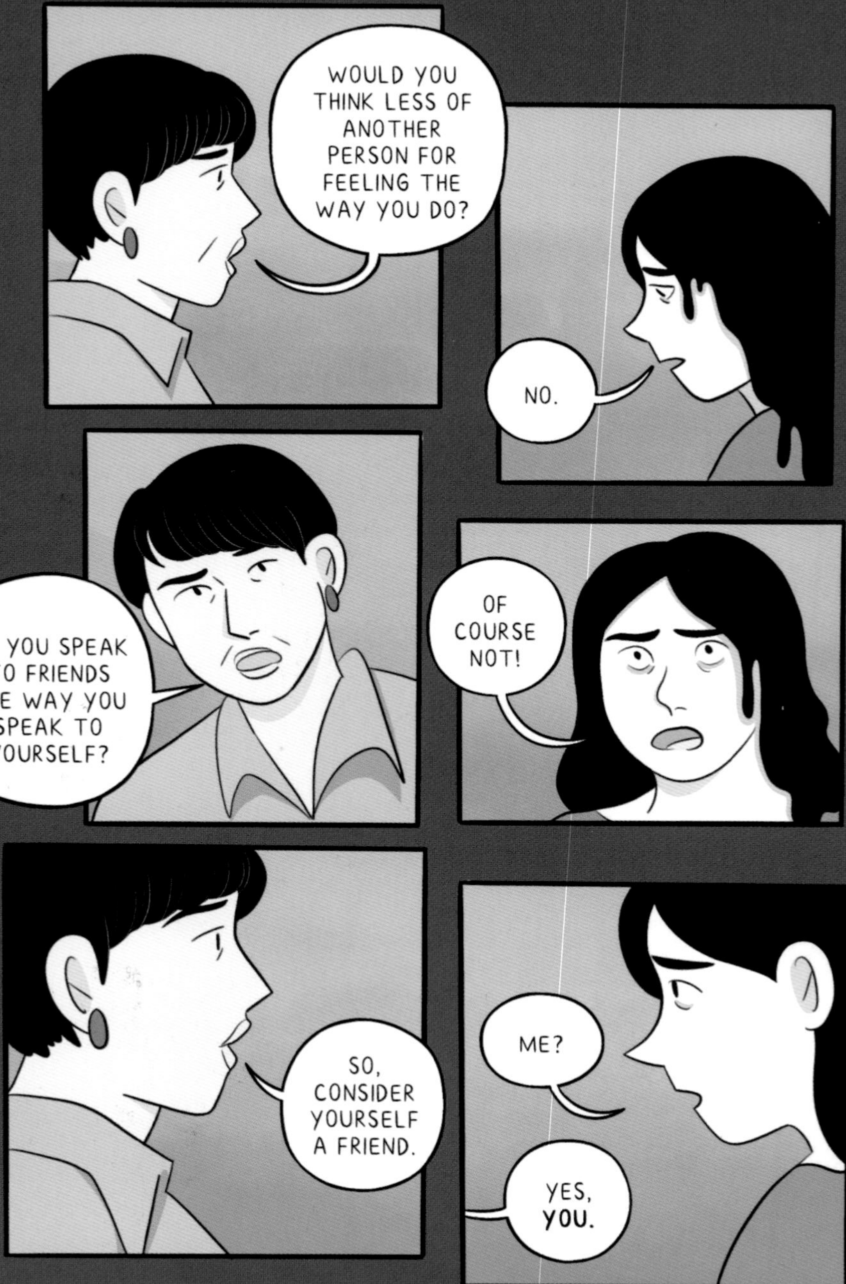
WOULD YOU THINK LESS OF ANOTHER PERSON FOR FEELING THE WAY YOU DO?
NO.
DO YOU SPEAK TO FRIENDS THE WAY YOU SPEAK TO YOURSELF?
OF COURSE NOT!
SO, CONSIDER YOURSELF A FRIEND.
ME?
YES, **YOU.**

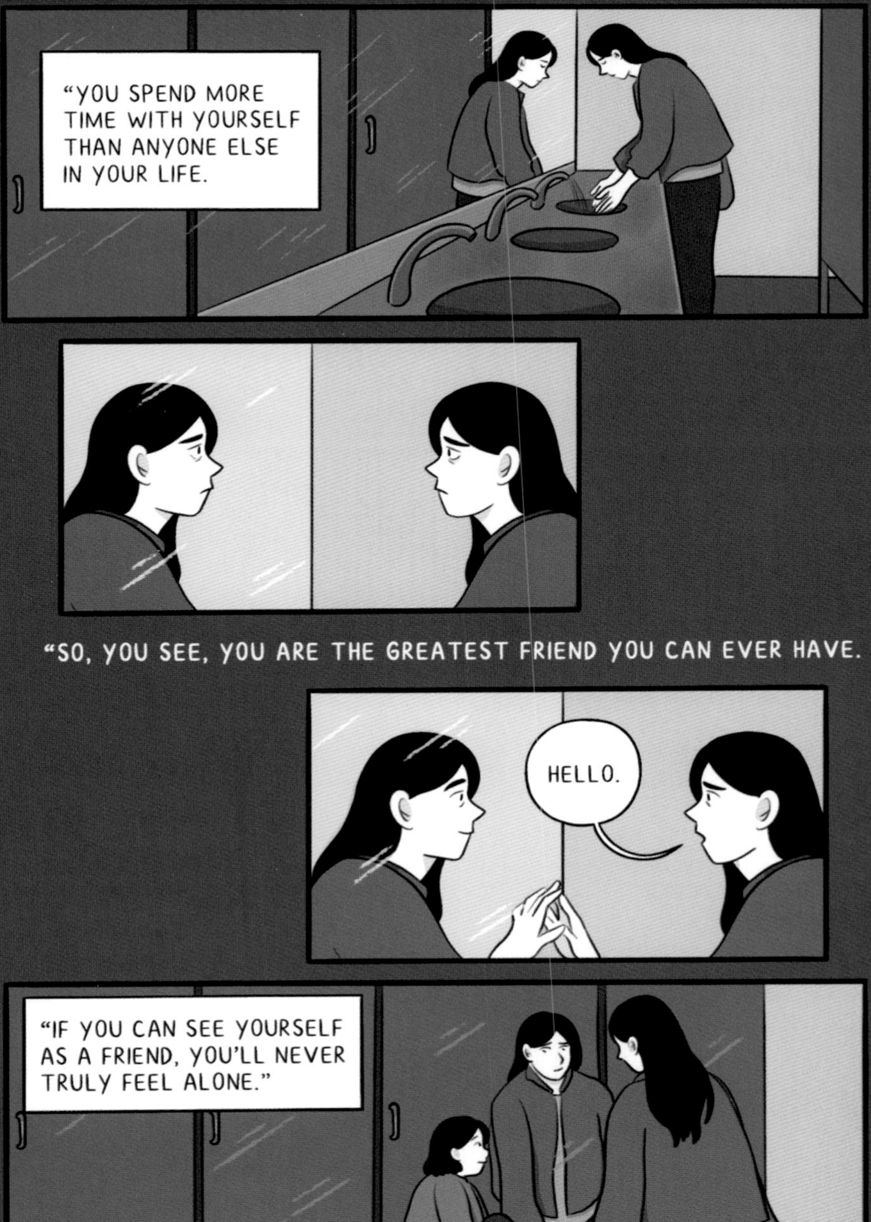
"YOU SPEND MORE TIME WITH YOURSELF THAN ANYONE ELSE IN YOUR LIFE.
"SO, YOU SEE, YOU ARE THE GREATEST FRIEND YOU CAN EVER HAVE.
HELLO.
"IF YOU CAN SEE YOURSELF AS A FRIEND, YOU'LL NEVER TRULY FEEL ALONE."

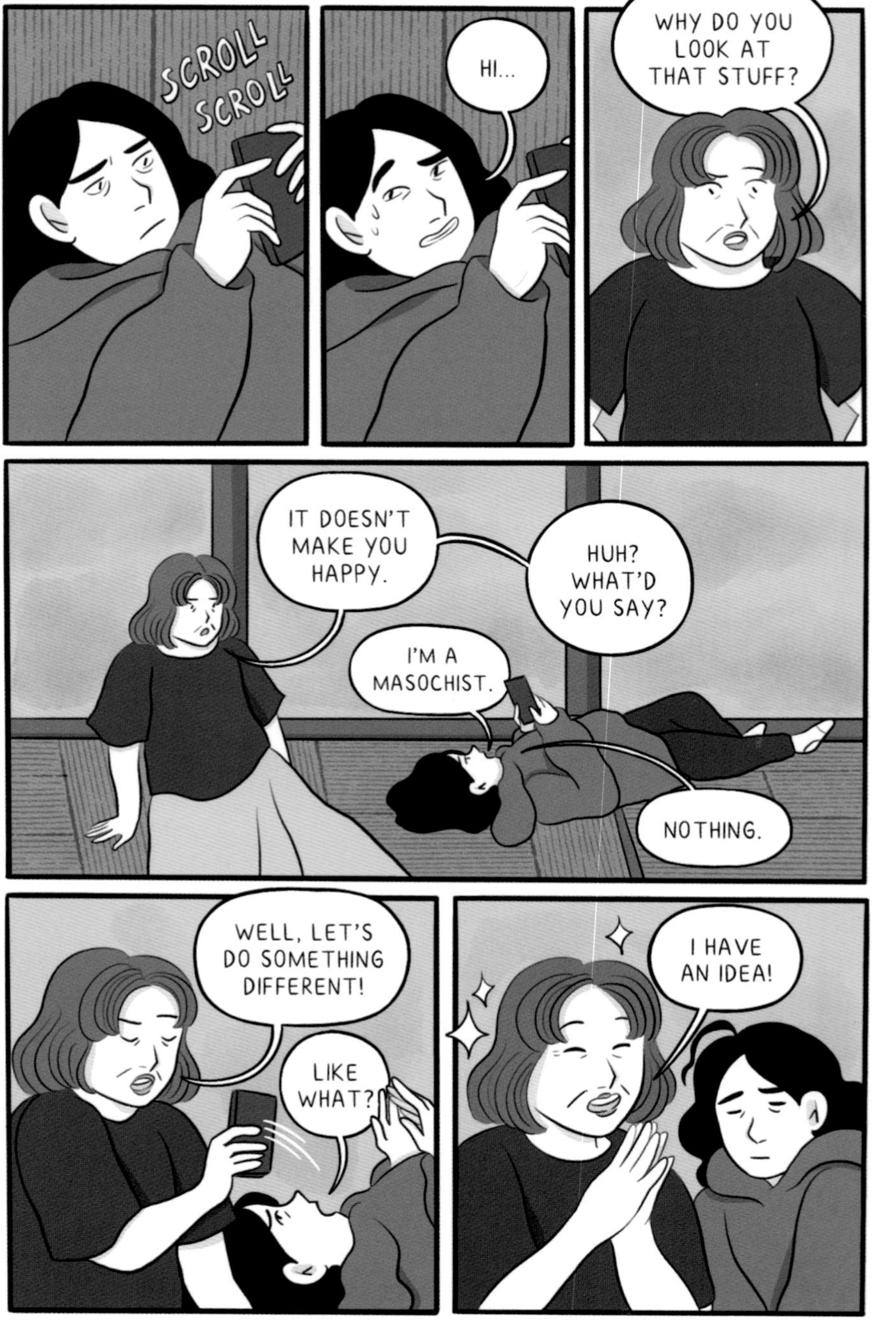
SCROLL
SCROLL
HI...
WHY DO YOU LOOK AT THAT STUFF?
IT DOESN'T MAKE YOU HAPPY.
HUH? WHAT'D YOU SAY?
I'M A MASOCHIST.
NOTHING.
WELL, LET'S DO SOMETHING DIFFERENT!
LIKE WHAT?
I HAVE AN IDEA!

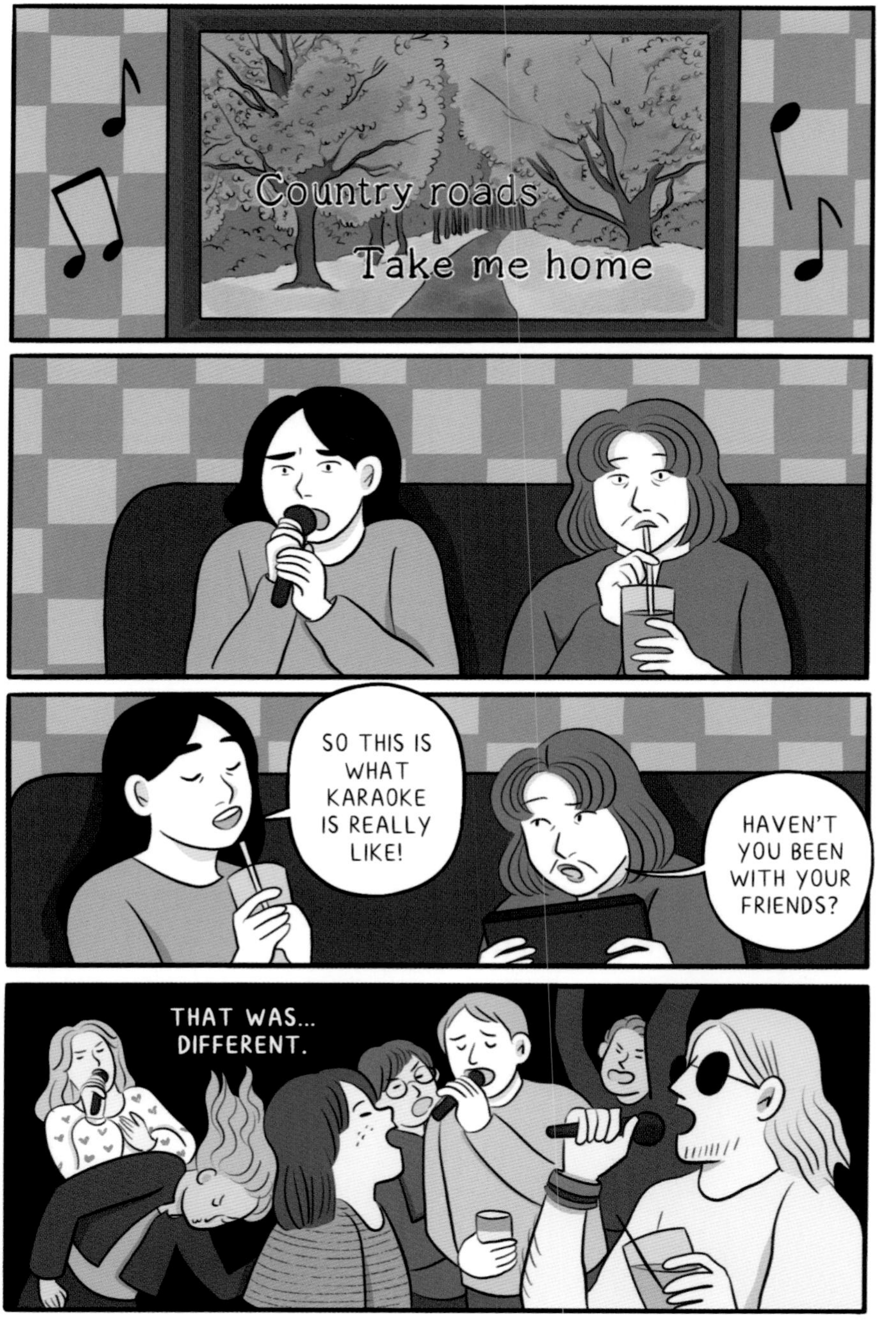
Country roads
Take me home
SO THIS IS WHAT KARAOKE IS REALLY LIKE!
HAVEN'T YOU BEEN WITH YOUR FRIENDS?
THAT WAS... DIFFERENT.

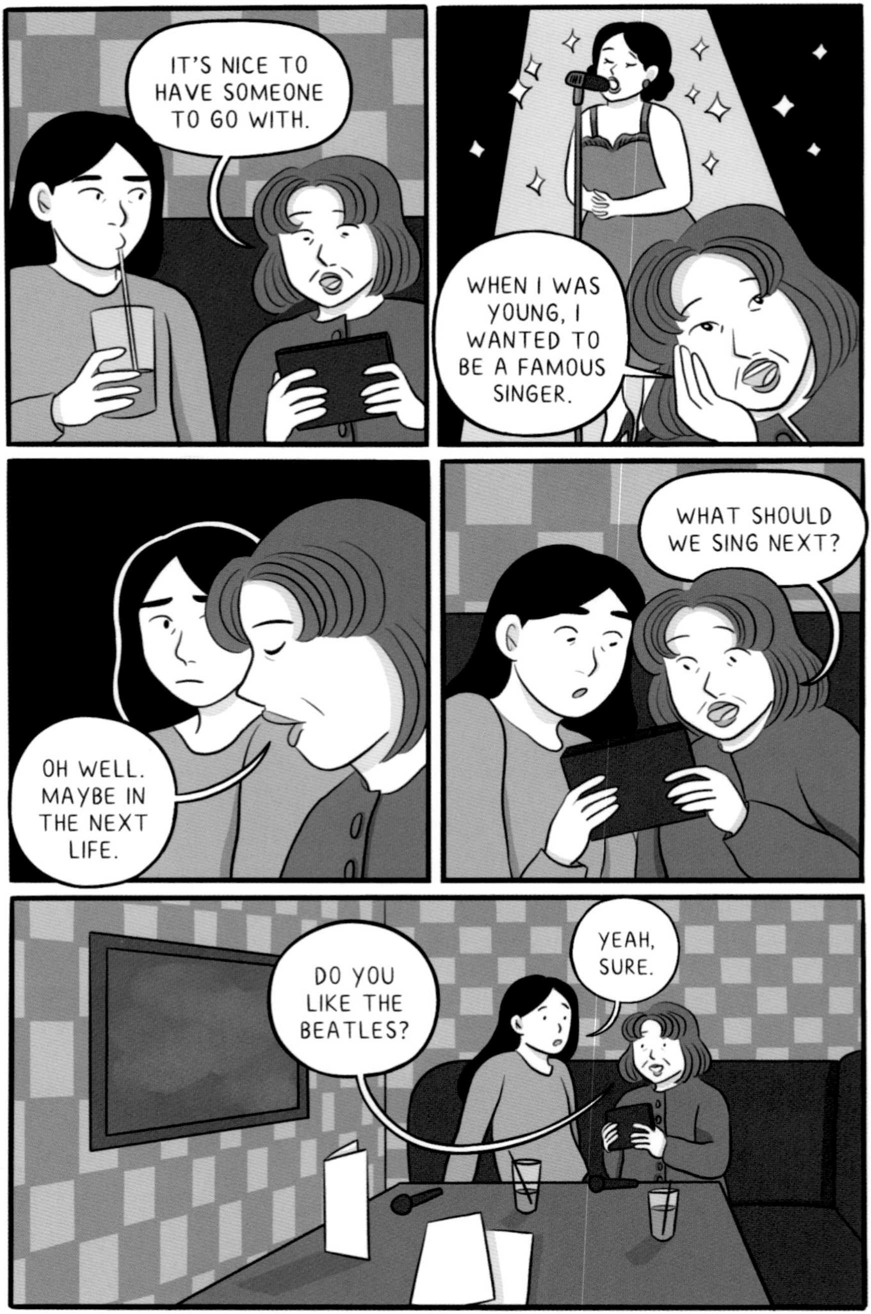
IT'S NICE TO HAVE SOMEONE TO GO WITH.
WHEN I WAS YOUNG, I WANTED TO BE A FAMOUS SINGER.
OH WELL. MAYBE IN THE NEXT LIFE.
WHAT SHOULD WE SING NEXT?
DO YOU LIKE THE BEATLES?
YEAH, SURE.

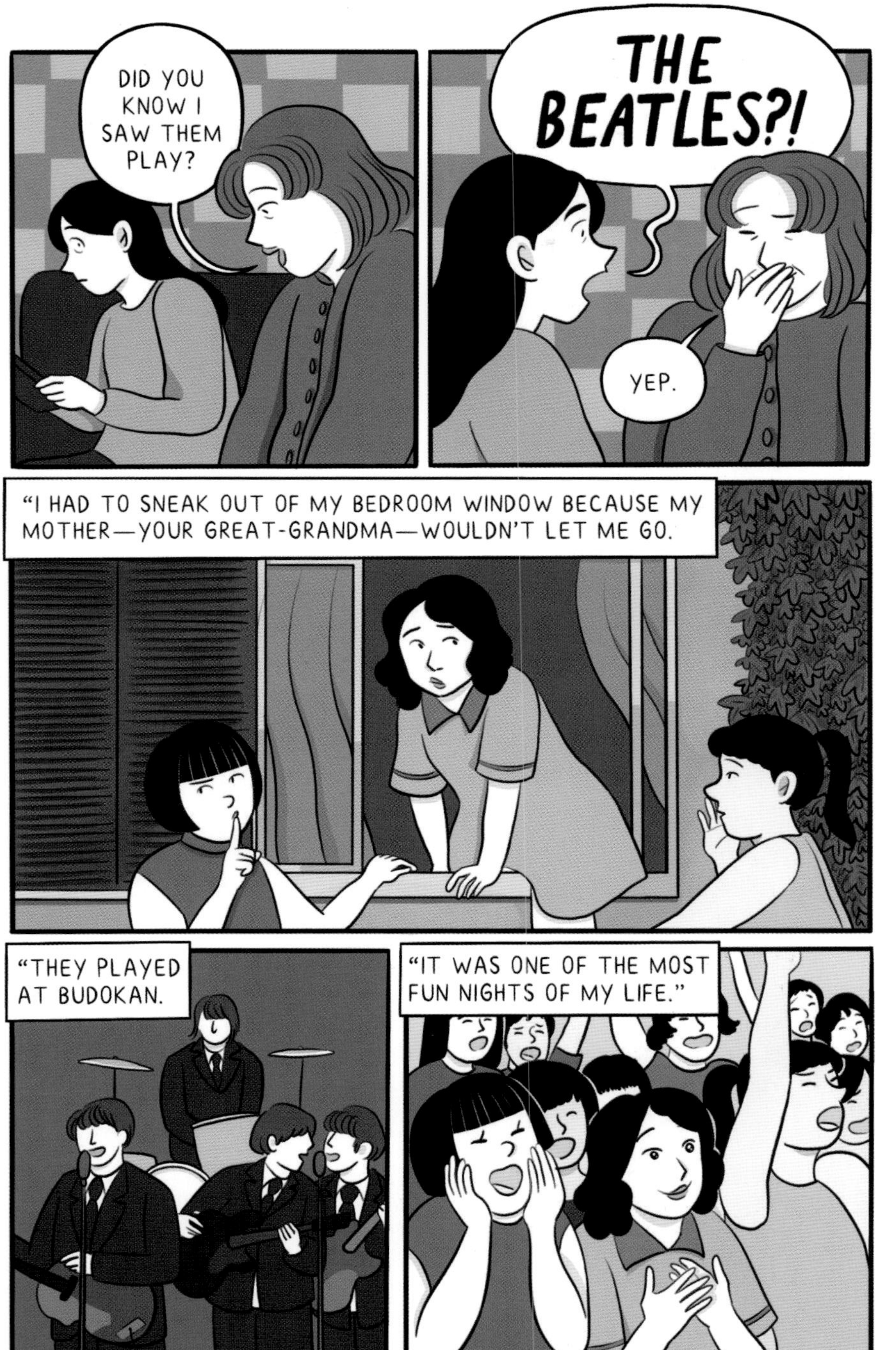
DID YOU KNOW I SAW THEM PLAY?
THE BEATLES?!
YEP.
"I HAD TO SNEAK OUT OF MY BEDROOM WINDOW BECAUSE MY MOTHER—YOUR GREAT-GRANDMA—WOULDN'T LET ME GO.
"THEY PLAYED AT BUDOKAN.
"IT WAS ONE OF THE MOST FUN NIGHTS OF MY LIFE."

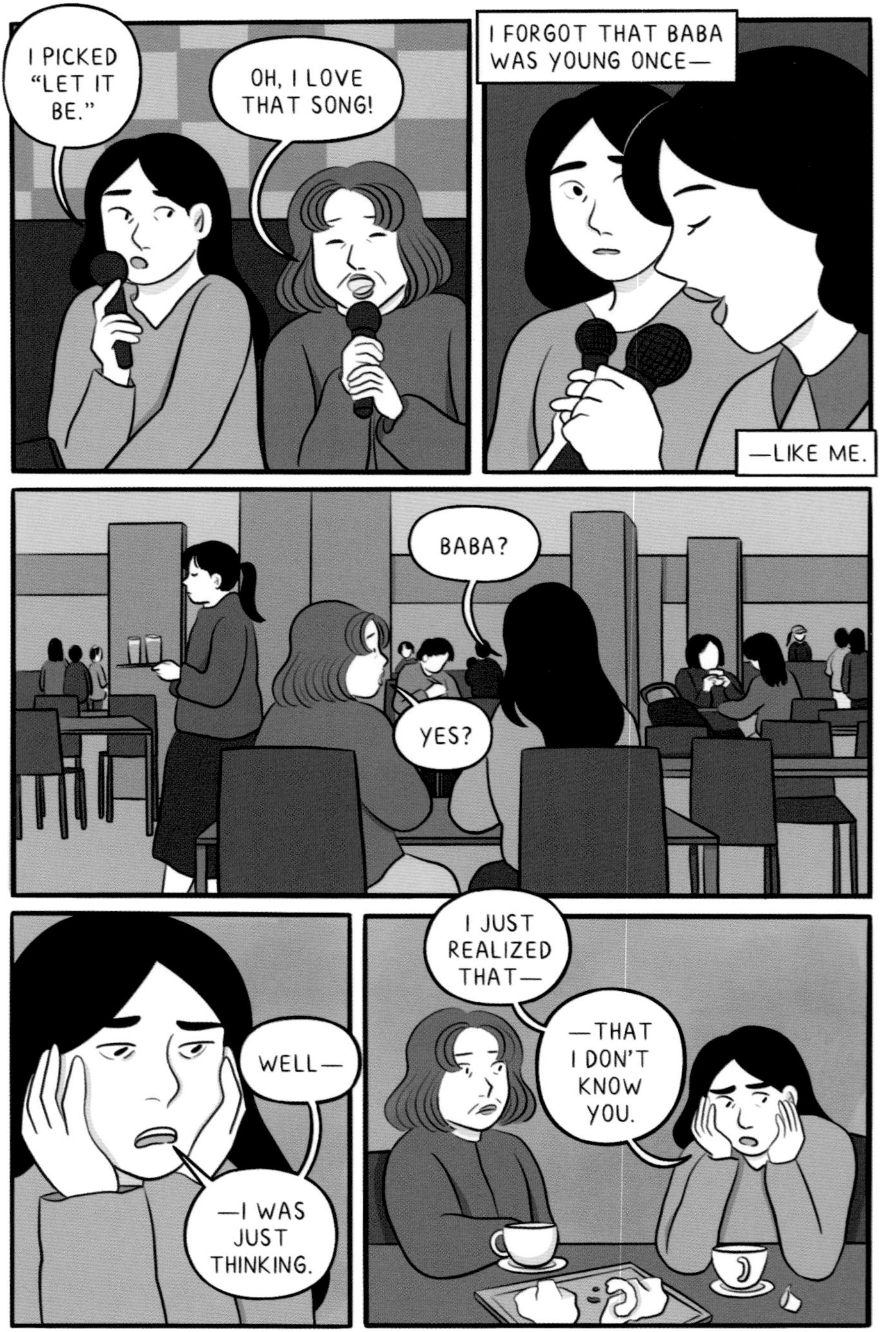
I PICKED "LET IT BE."
OH, I LOVE THAT SONG!
I FORGOT THAT BABA WAS YOUNG ONCE—
—LIKE ME.
BABA?
YES?
WELL—
—I WAS JUST THINKING.
I JUST REALIZED THAT—
—THAT I DON'T KNOW YOU.

ALL I HAVE ARE HAZY MEMORIES. OLD PICTURES WHERE WE LOOK HAPPY.

SOMETIMES YOU AND JIJI JUST FELT LIKE STRANGERS WHO LOVED ME.

IT'S AS IF I WAS NEVER REALLY HERE.

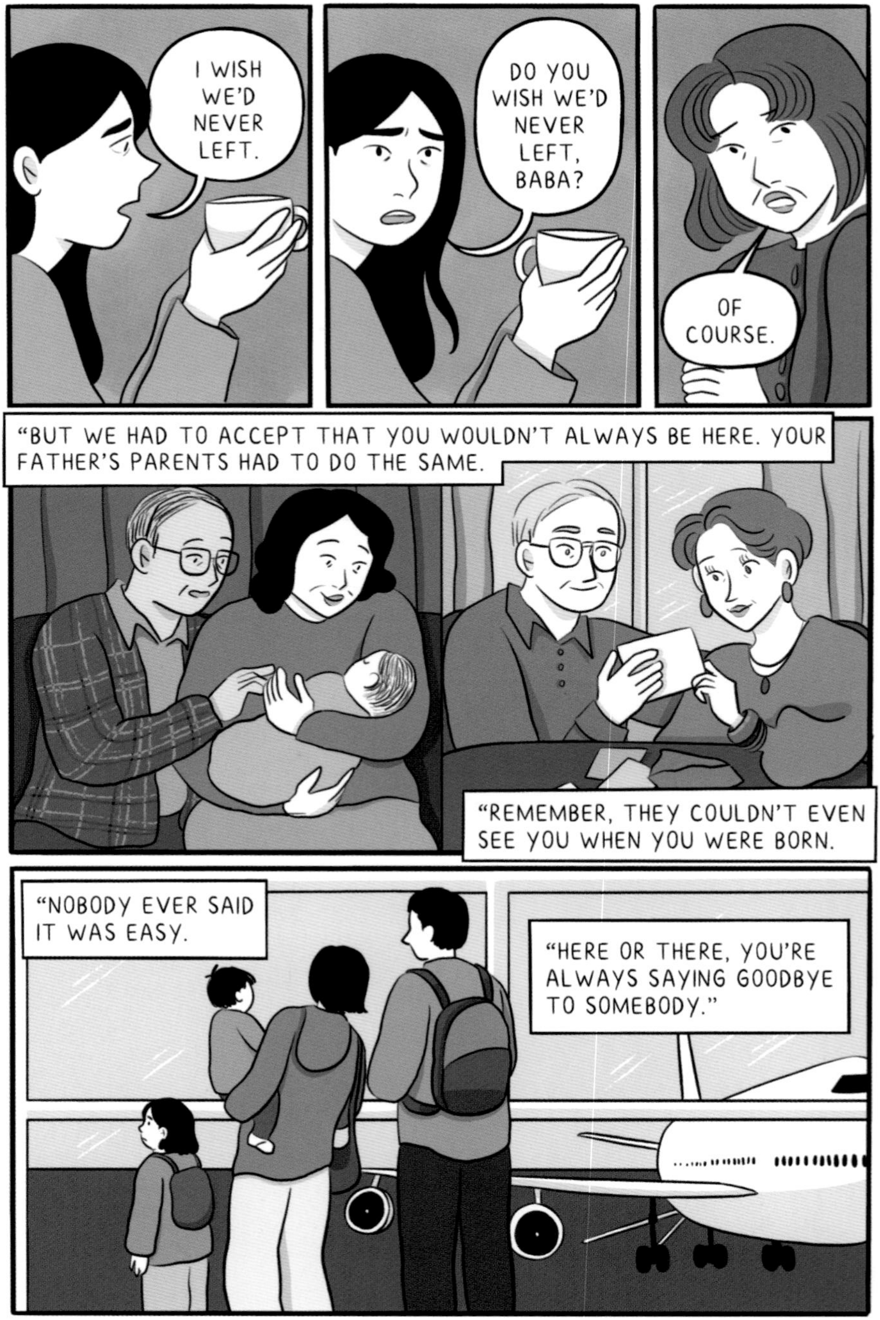
I WISH WE'D NEVER LEFT.
DO YOU WISH WE'D NEVER LEFT, BABA?
OF COURSE.
"BUT WE HAD TO ACCEPT THAT YOU WOULDN'T ALWAYS BE HERE. YOUR FATHER'S PARENTS HAD TO DO THE SAME.
"REMEMBER, THEY COULDN'T EVEN SEE YOU WHEN YOU WERE BORN.
"NOBODY EVER SAID IT WAS EASY.
"HERE OR THERE, YOU'RE ALWAYS SAYING GOODBYE TO SOMEBODY."

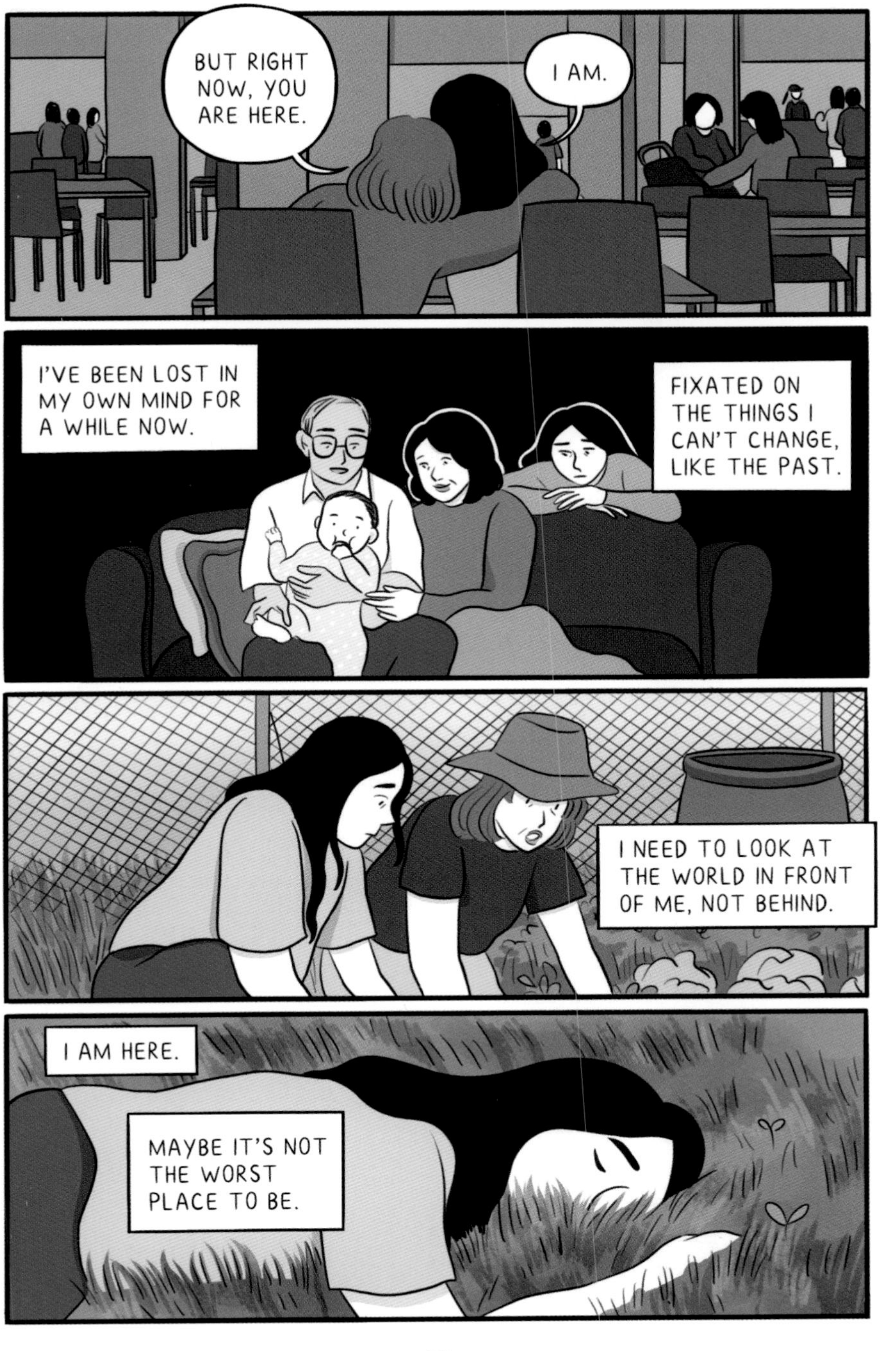
BUT RIGHT NOW, YOU ARE HERE.
I AM.
I'VE BEEN LOST IN MY OWN MIND FOR A WHILE NOW.
FIXATED ON THE THINGS I CAN'T CHANGE, LIKE THE PAST.
I NEED TO LOOK AT THE WORLD IN FRONT OF ME, NOT BEHIND.
I AM HERE.
MAYBE IT'S NOT THE WORST PLACE TO BE.

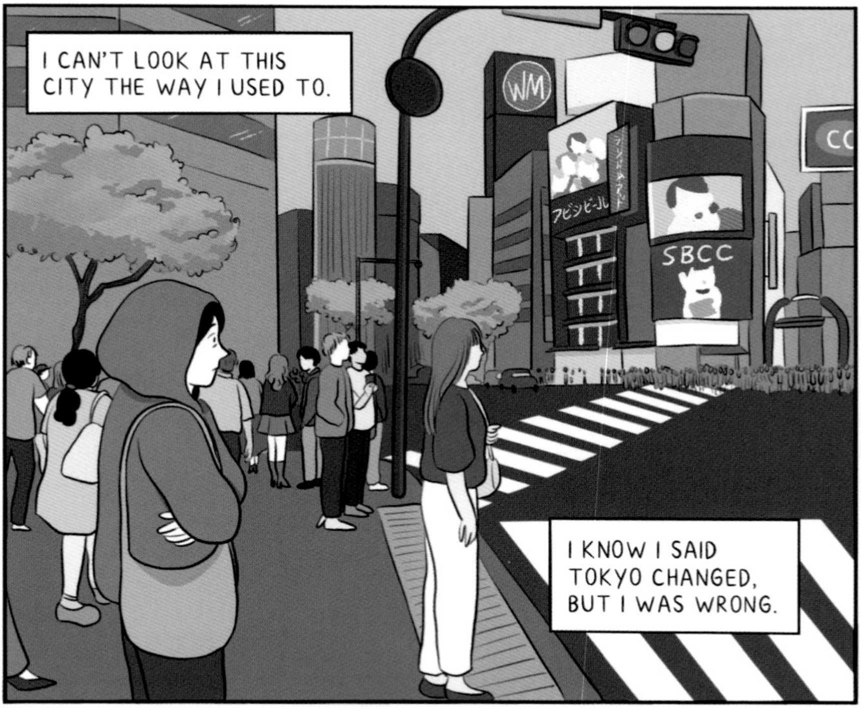
I CAN'T LOOK AT THIS CITY THE WAY I USED TO.
WM
SBCC
I KNOW I SAID TOKYO CHANGED, BUT I WAS WRONG.

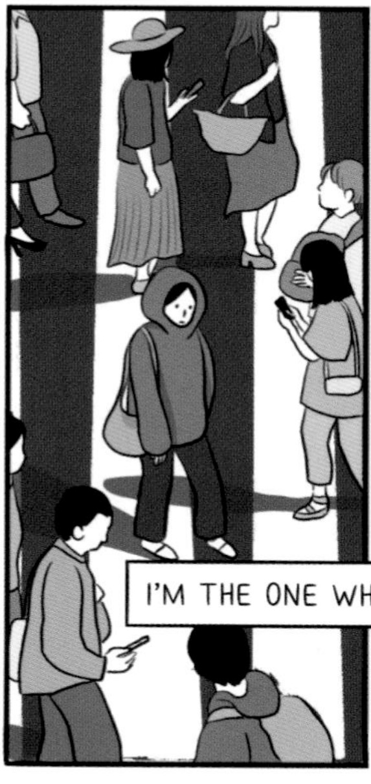
I'M THE ONE WHO CHANGED.

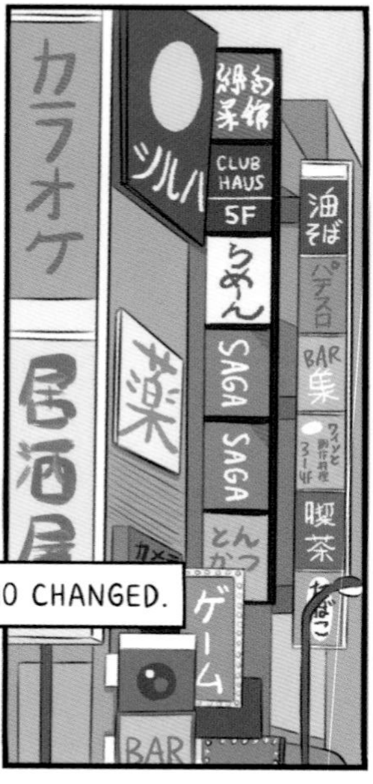
カラオケ
居酒屋
CLUB HAUS
5F
らめん
薬
SAGA
SAGA
とんかつ
油そば
BAR
集
喫茶
ゲーム
BAR

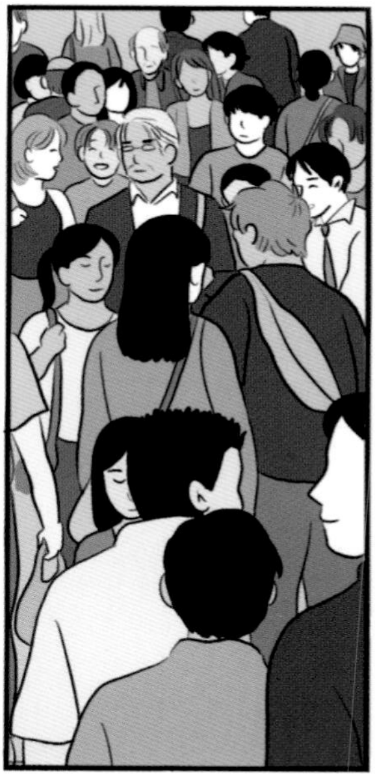

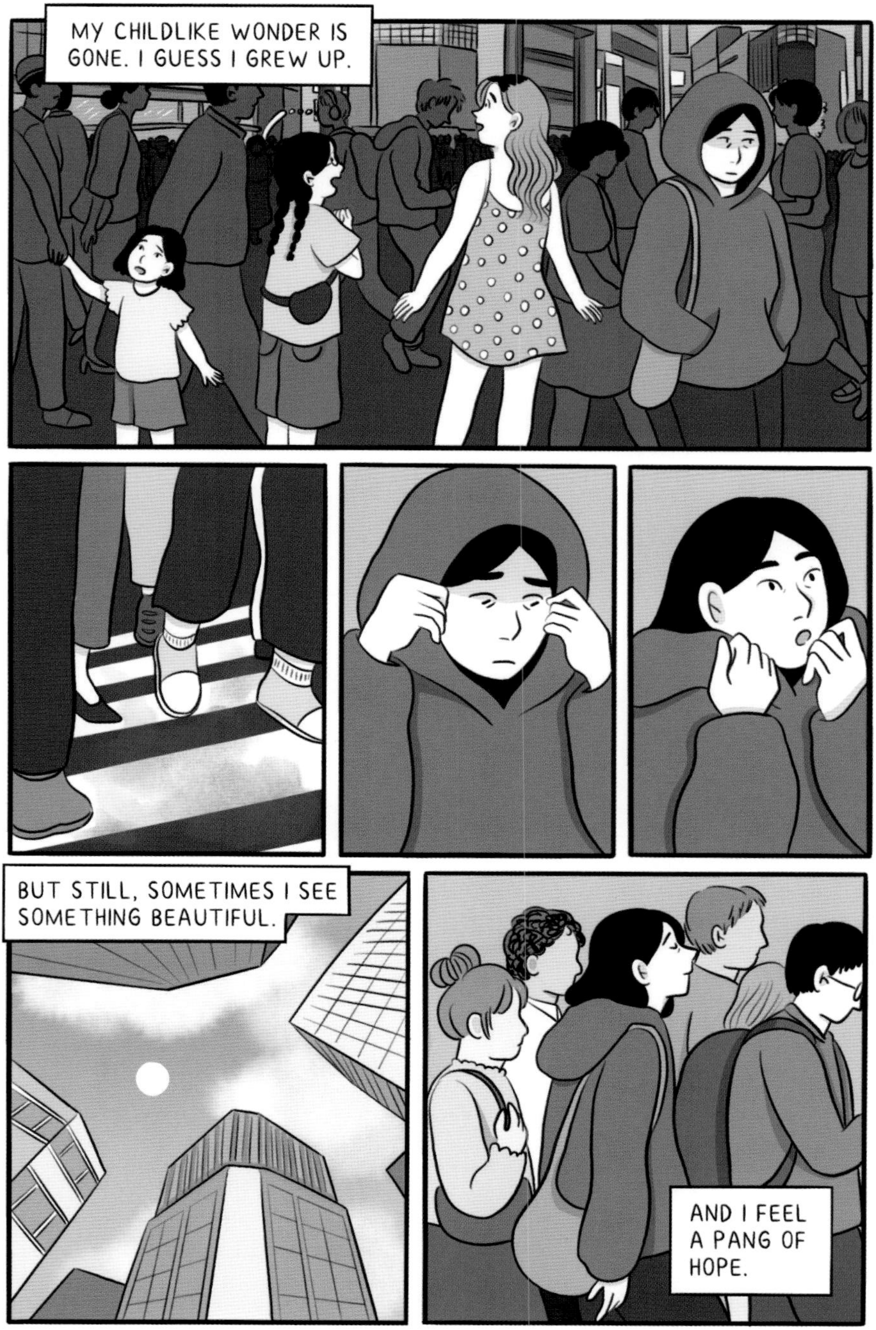
MY CHILDLIKE WONDER IS GONE. I GUESS I GREW UP.
BUT STILL, SOMETIMES I SEE SOMETHING BEAUTIFUL.
AND I FEEL A PANG OF HOPE.

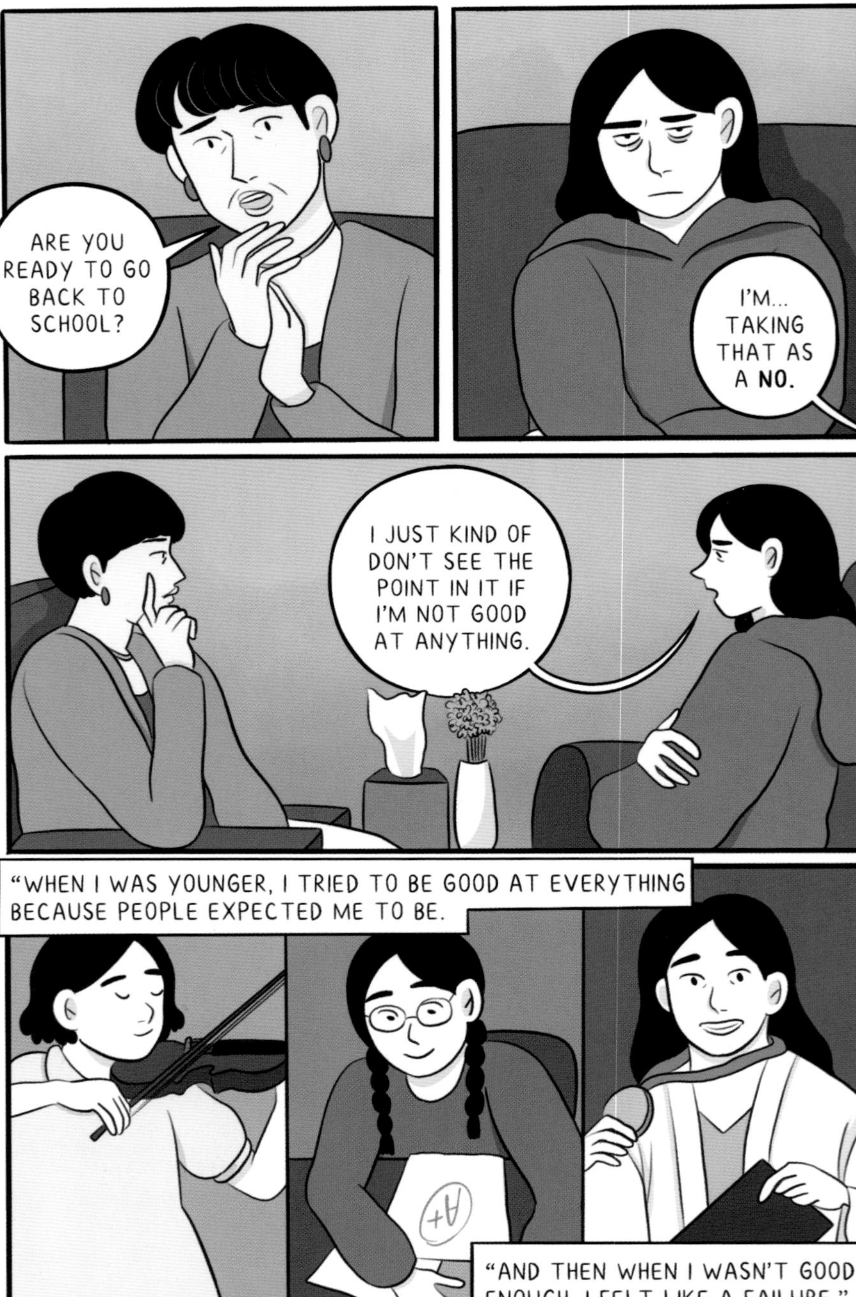
ARE YOU READY TO GO BACK TO SCHOOL?
I'M... TAKING THAT AS A **NO.**
I JUST KIND OF DON'T SEE THE POINT IN IT IF I'M NOT GOOD AT ANYTHING.
"WHEN I WAS YOUNGER, I TRIED TO BE GOOD AT EVERYTHING BECAUSE PEOPLE EXPECTED ME TO BE.
A+
"AND THEN WHEN I WASN'T GOOD ENOUGH, I FELT LIKE A FAILURE."

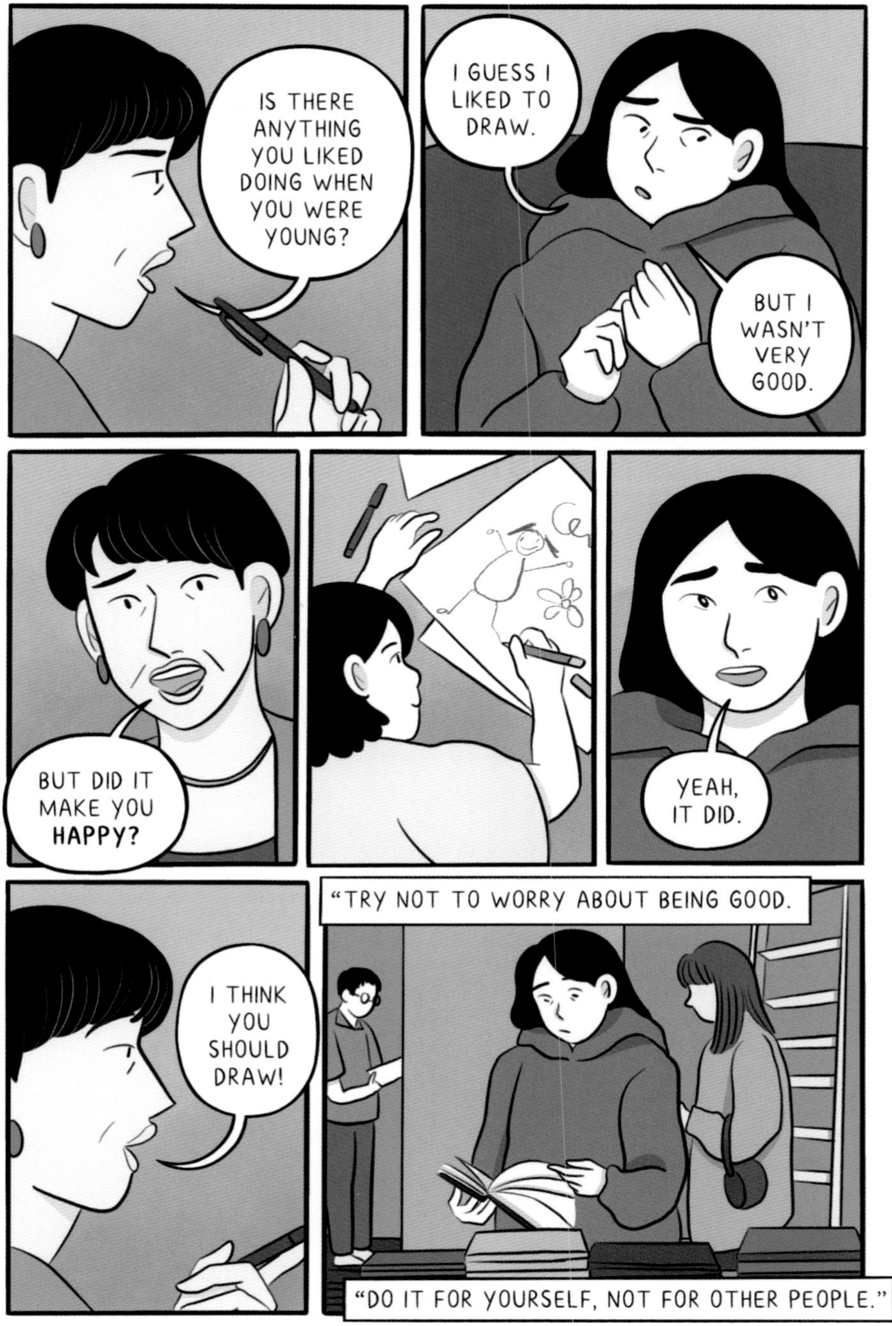
IS THERE ANYTHING YOU LIKED DOING WHEN YOU WERE YOUNG?
I GUESS I LIKED TO DRAW.
BUT I WASN'T VERY GOOD.
BUT DID IT MAKE YOU **HAPPY?**
YEAH, IT DID.
I THINK YOU SHOULD DRAW!
"TRY NOT TO WORRY ABOUT BEING GOOD.
"DO IT FOR YOURSELF, NOT FOR OTHER PEOPLE."

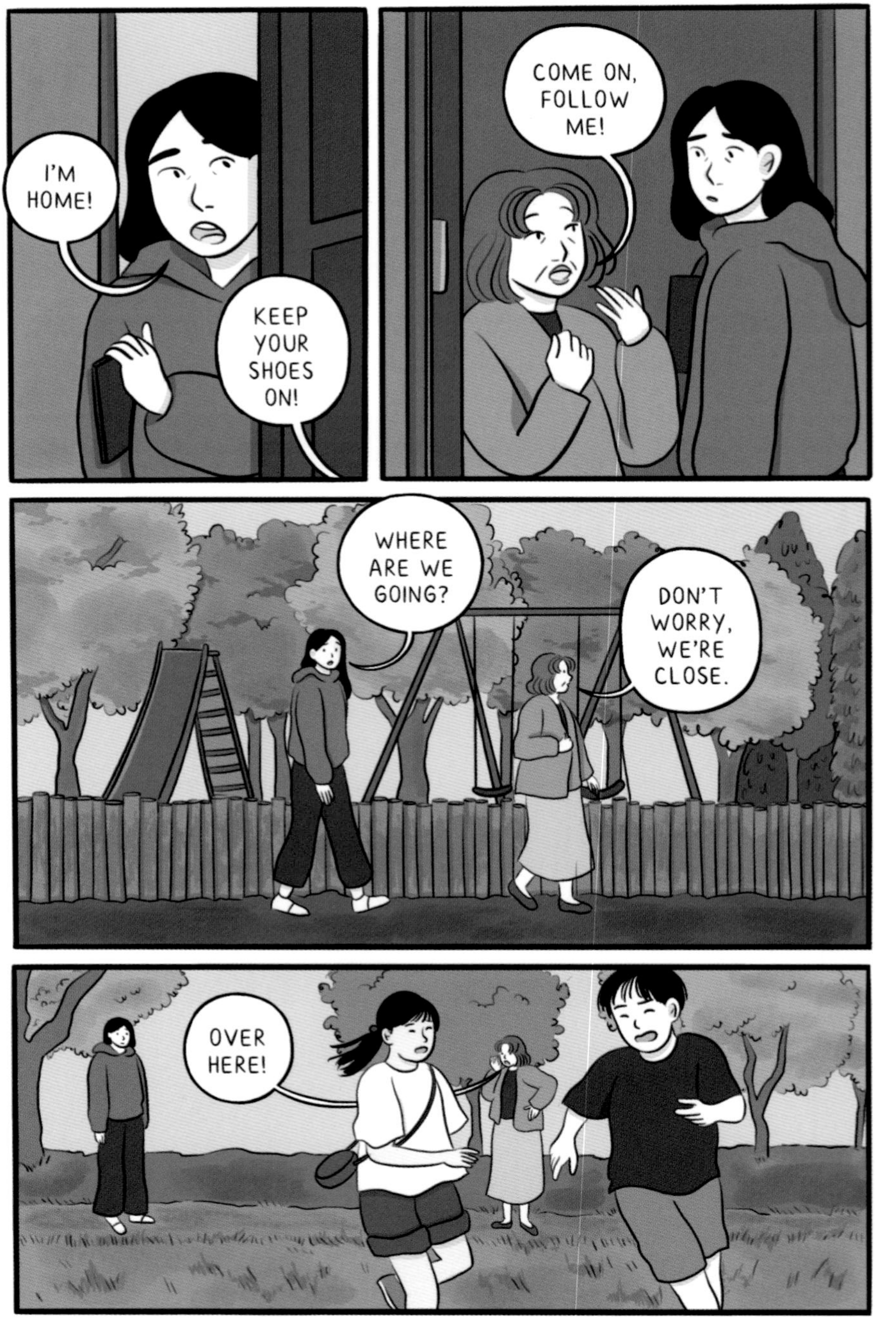
I'M HOME!
KEEP YOUR SHOES ON!
COME ON, FOLLOW ME!
WHERE ARE WE GOING?
DON'T WORRY, WE'RE CLOSE.
OVER HERE!

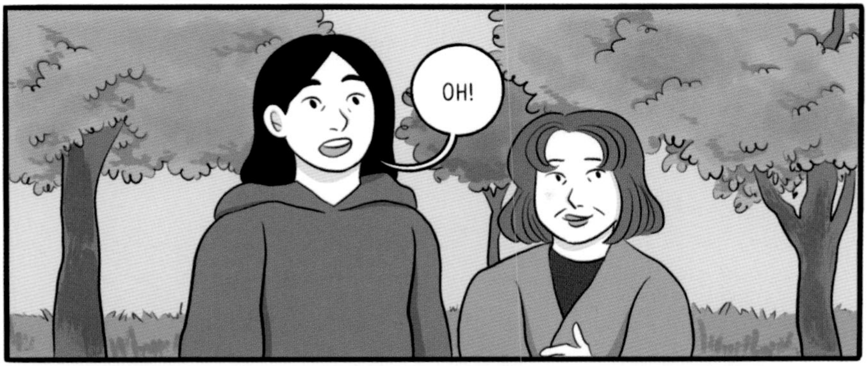
OH!

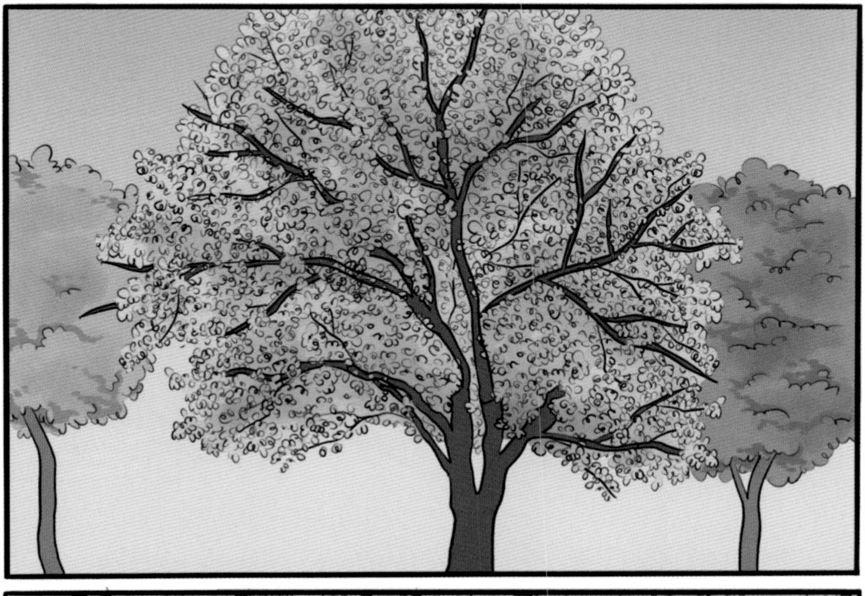

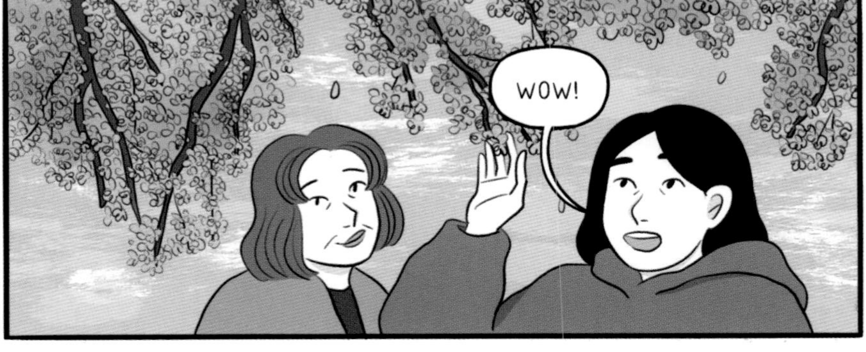
WOW!

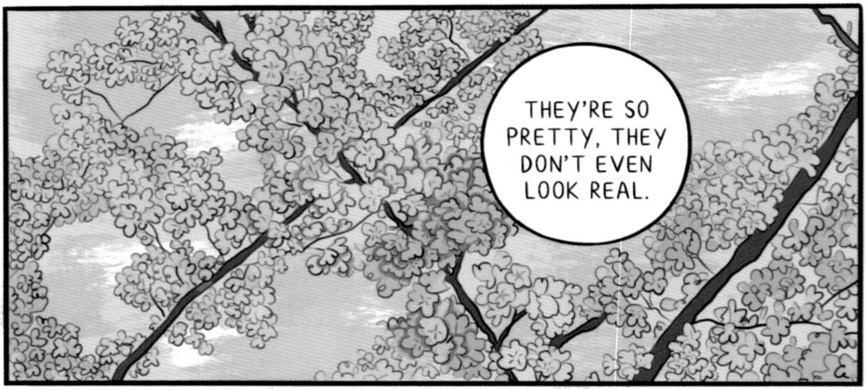
THEY'RE SO PRETTY, THEY DON'T EVEN LOOK REAL.

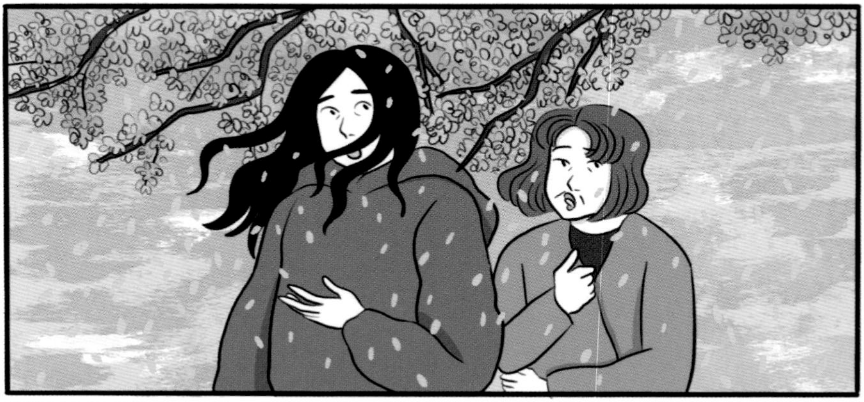

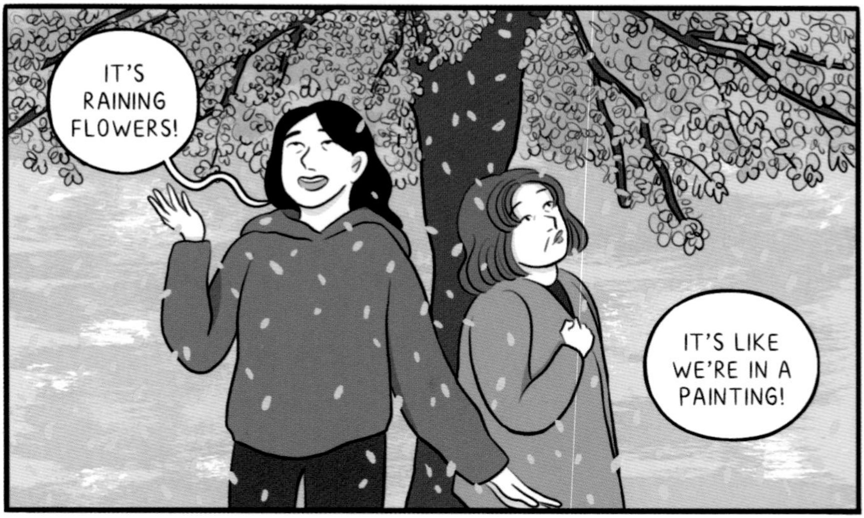
IT'S RAINING FLOWERS!
IT'S LIKE WE'RE IN A PAINTING!

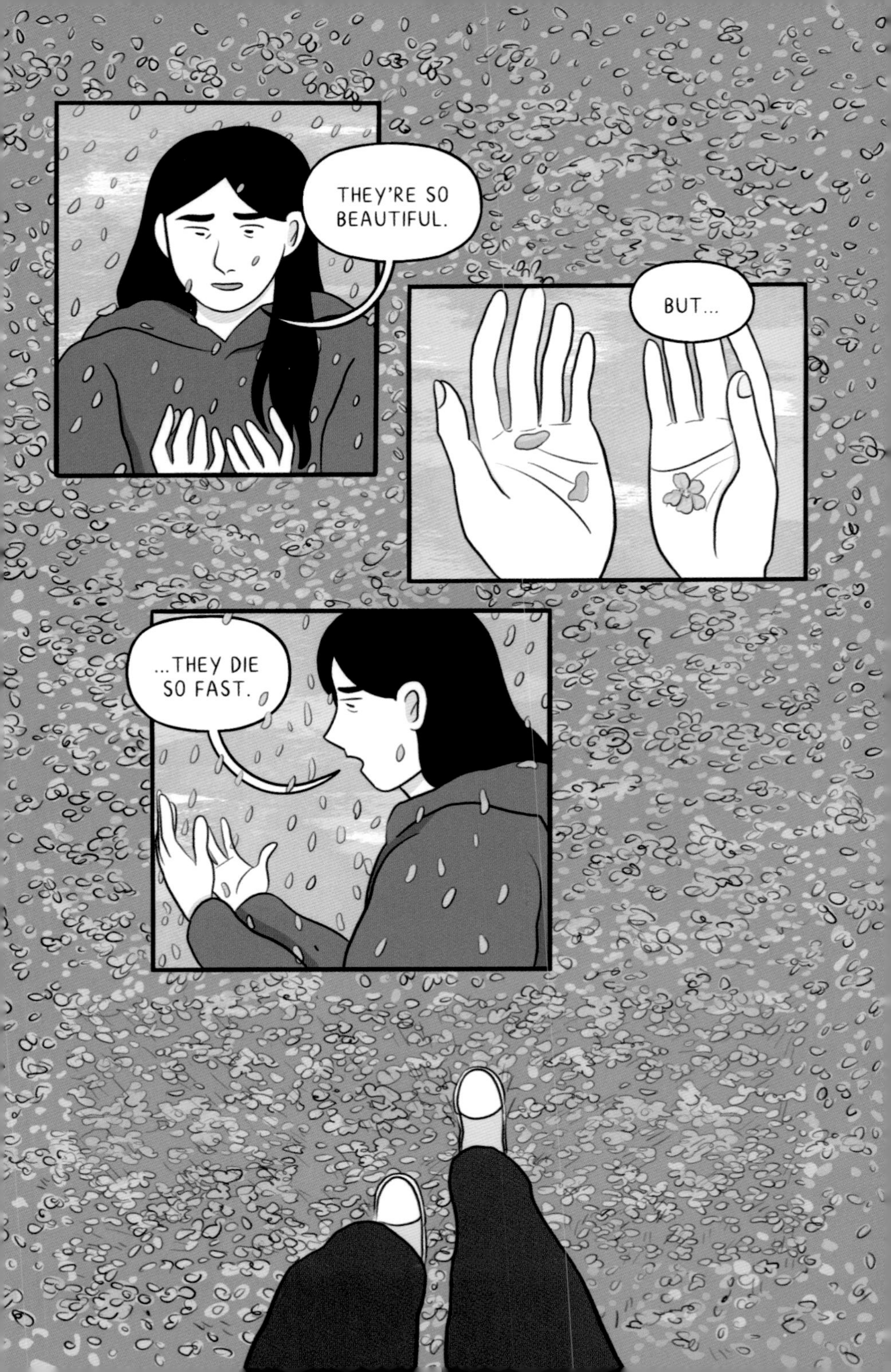
THEY'RE SO BEAUTIFUL.
BUT...
...THEY DIE SO FAST.

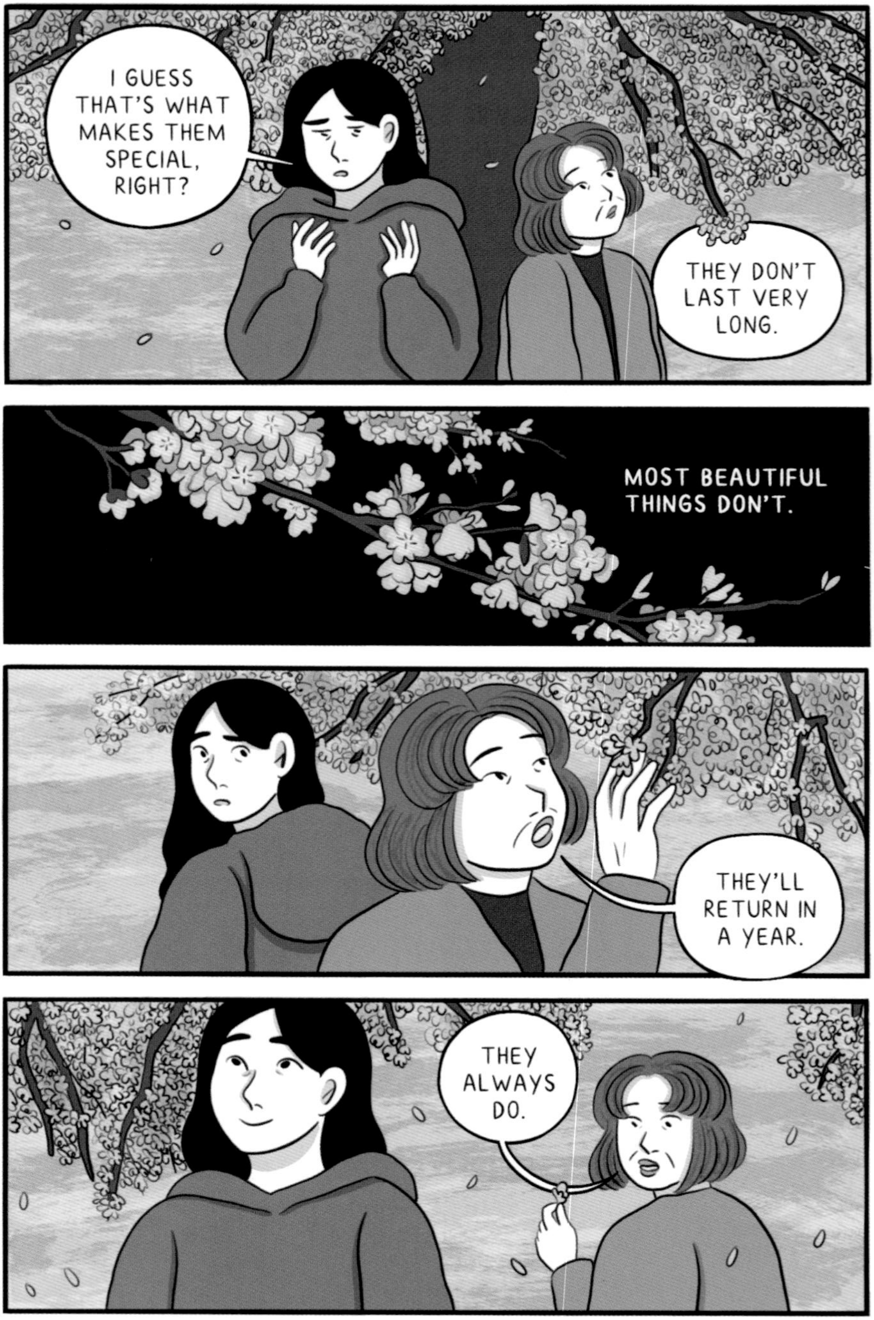
I GUESS THAT'S WHAT MAKES THEM SPECIAL, RIGHT?
THEY DON'T LAST VERY LONG.
MOST BEAUTIFUL THINGS DON'T.
THEY'LL RETURN IN A YEAR.
THEY ALWAYS DO.

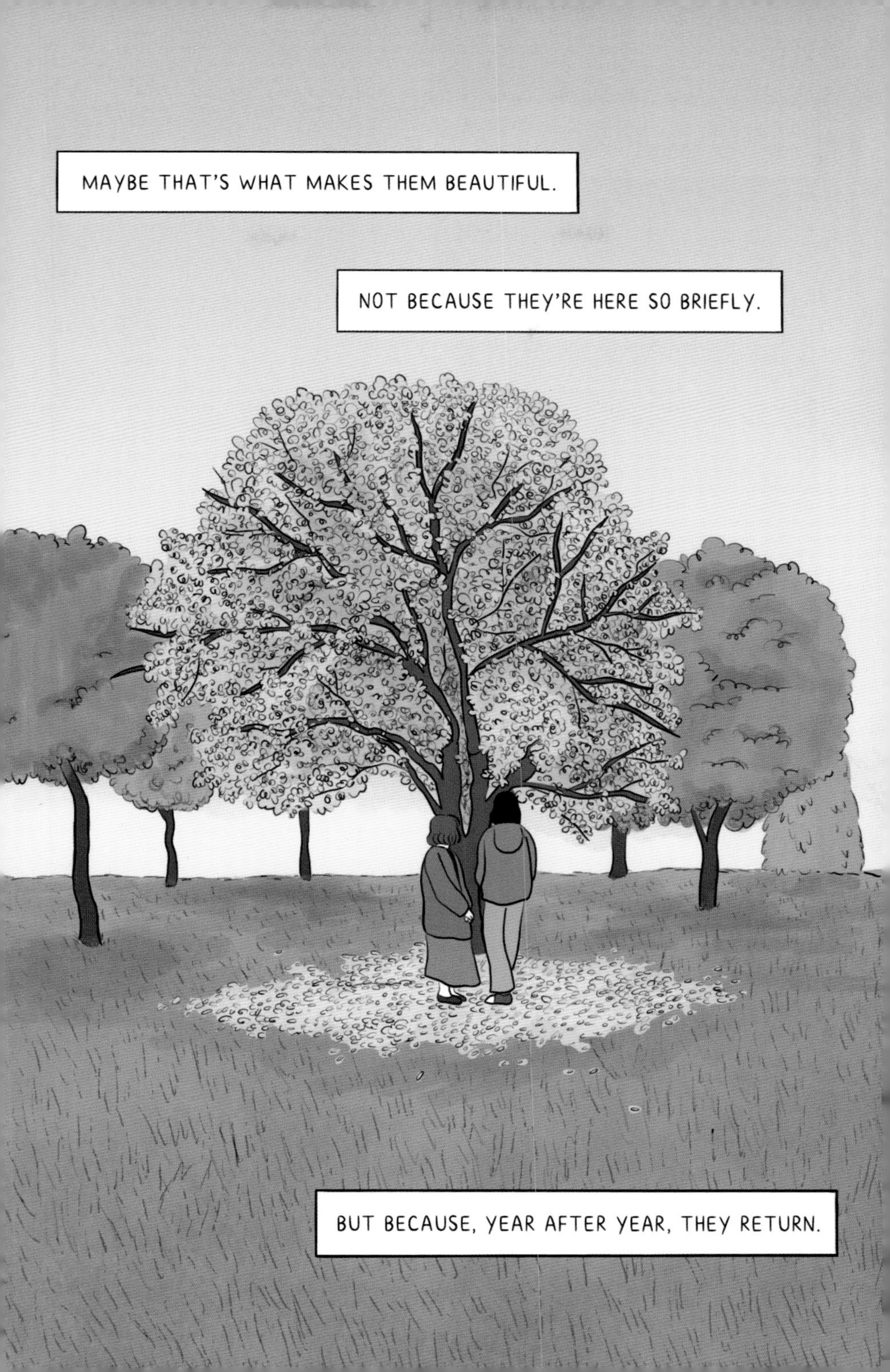
MAYBE THAT'S WHAT MAKES THEM BEAUTIFUL.
NOT BECAUSE THEY'RE HERE SO BRIEFLY.
BUT BECAUSE, YEAR AFTER YEAR, THEY RETURN.

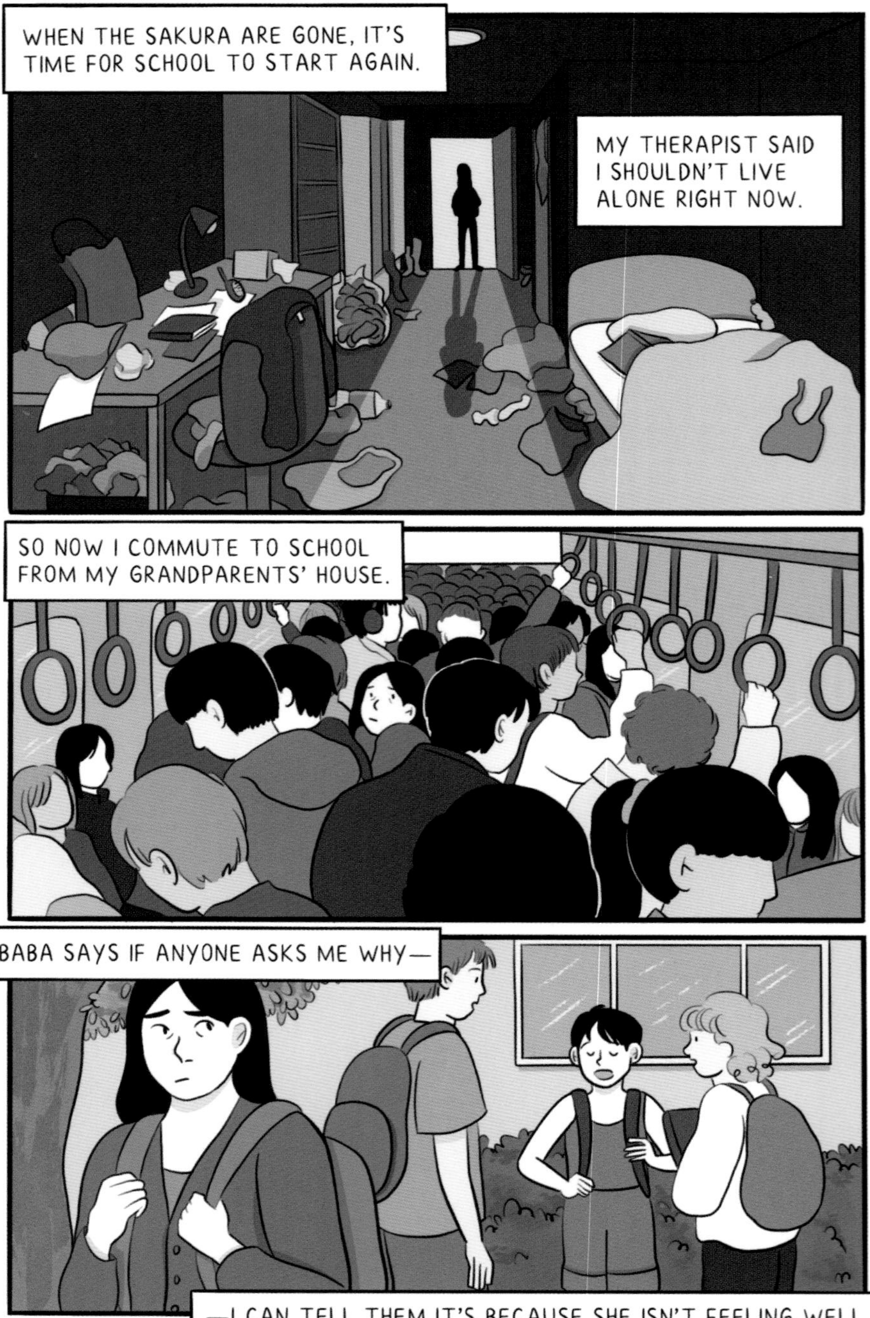
WHEN THE SAKURA ARE GONE, IT'S TIME FOR SCHOOL TO START AGAIN.
MY THERAPIST SAID I SHOULDN'T LIVE ALONE RIGHT NOW.
SO NOW I COMMUTE TO SCHOOL FROM MY GRANDPARENTS' HOUSE.
BABA SAYS IF ANYONE ASKS ME WHY—
—I CAN TELL THEM IT'S BECAUSE SHE ISN'T FEELING WELL.

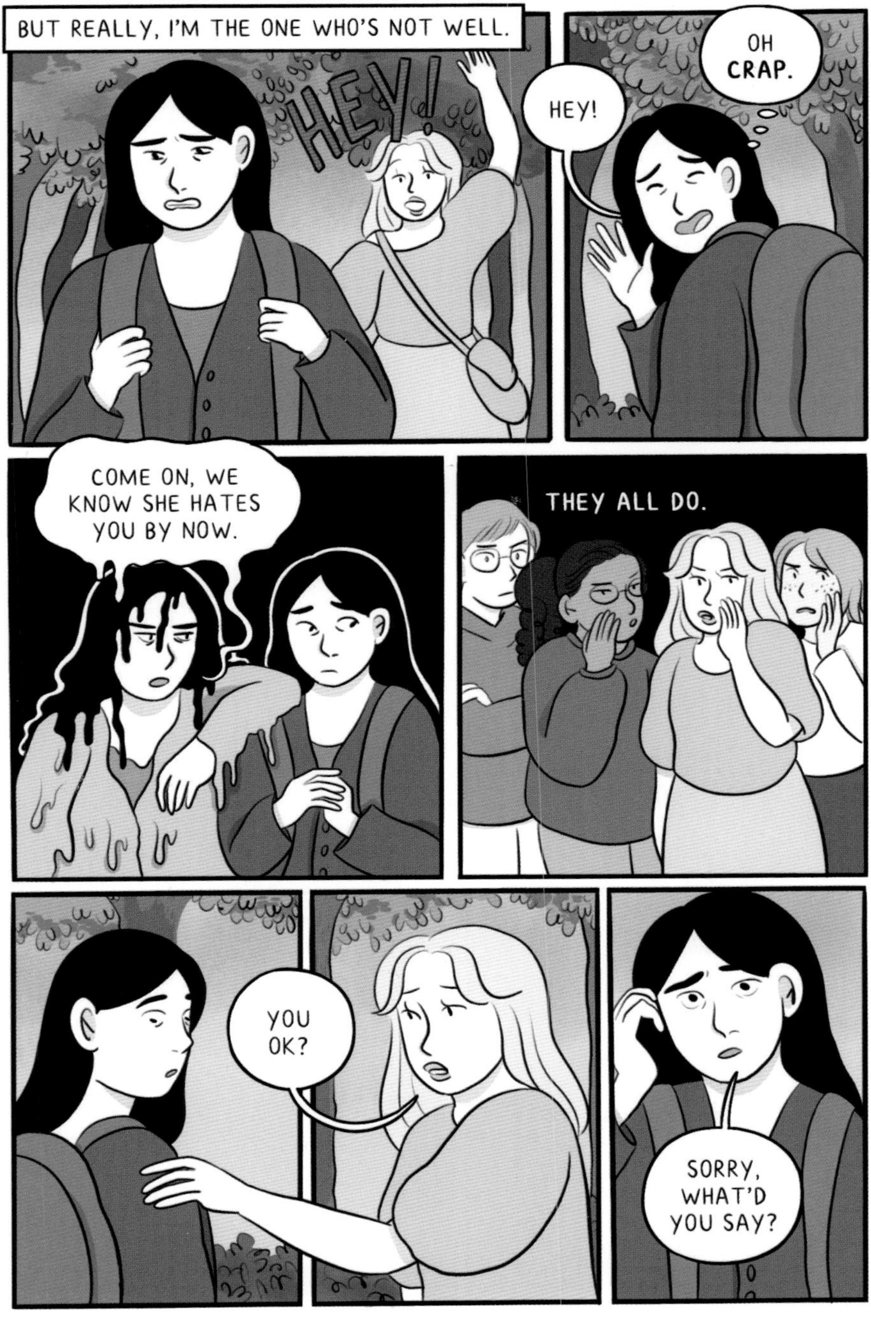
BUT REALLY, I'M THE ONE WHO'S NOT WELL.
HEY!
HEY!
OH CRAP.
COME ON, WE KNOW SHE HATES YOU BY NOW.
THEY ALL DO.
YOU OK?
SORRY, WHAT'D YOU SAY?

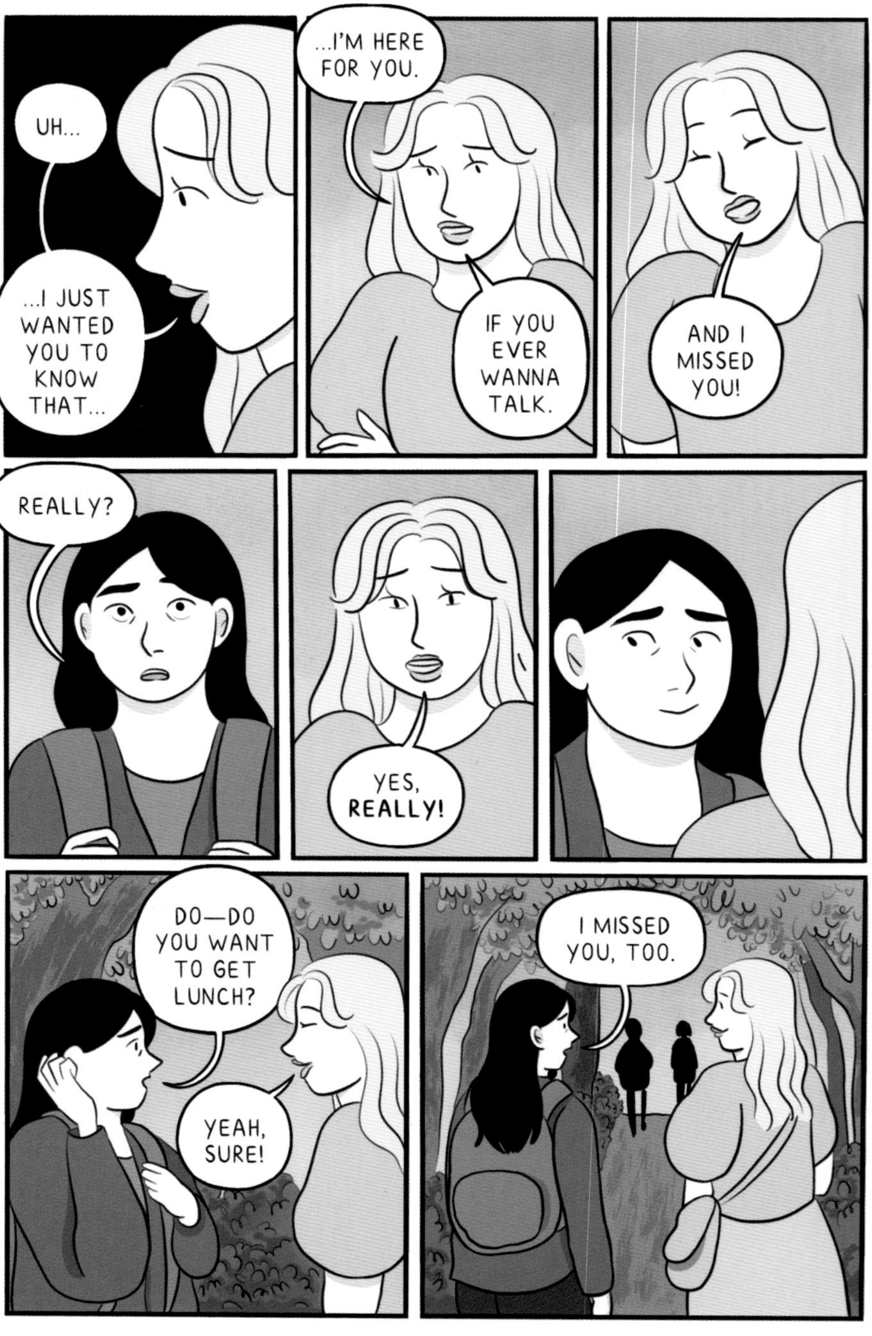
UH...
...I JUST WANTED YOU TO KNOW THAT...
...I'M HERE FOR YOU.
IF YOU EVER WANNA TALK.
AND I MISSED YOU!
REALLY?
YES, **REALLY!**
DO—DO YOU WANT TO GET LUNCH?
YEAH, SURE!
I MISSED YOU, TOO.

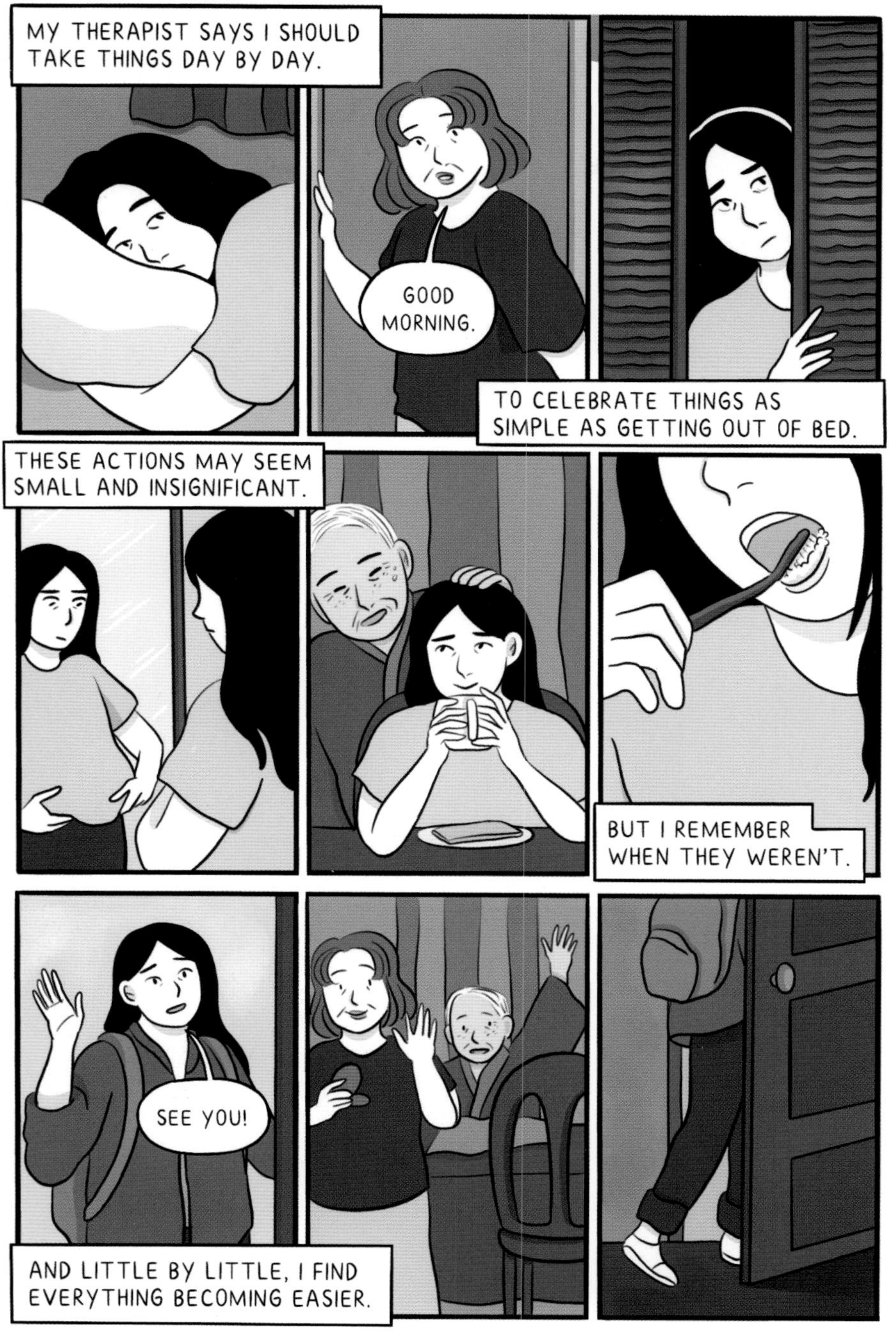

MY THERAPIST SAYS I SHOULD TAKE THINGS DAY BY DAY.
GOOD MORNING.
TO CELEBRATE THINGS AS SIMPLE AS GETTING OUT OF BED.
THESE ACTIONS MAY SEEM SMALL AND INSIGNIFICANT.
BUT I REMEMBER WHEN THEY WEREN'T.
SEE YOU!
AND LITTLE BY LITTLE, I FIND EVERYTHING BECOMING EASIER.

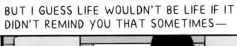

BUT I GUESS LIFE WOULDN'T BE LIFE IF IT DIDN'T REMIND YOU THAT SOMETIMES—

BUMP!

COME ON!

—IT SUCKS.

THERE ARE DAYS WHEN IT FEELS SO EASY TO FALL BACK INTO THINKING NOTHING IS EVER GONNA GET BETTER.

BUT SOMETIMES THE WORLD SURPRISES ME.

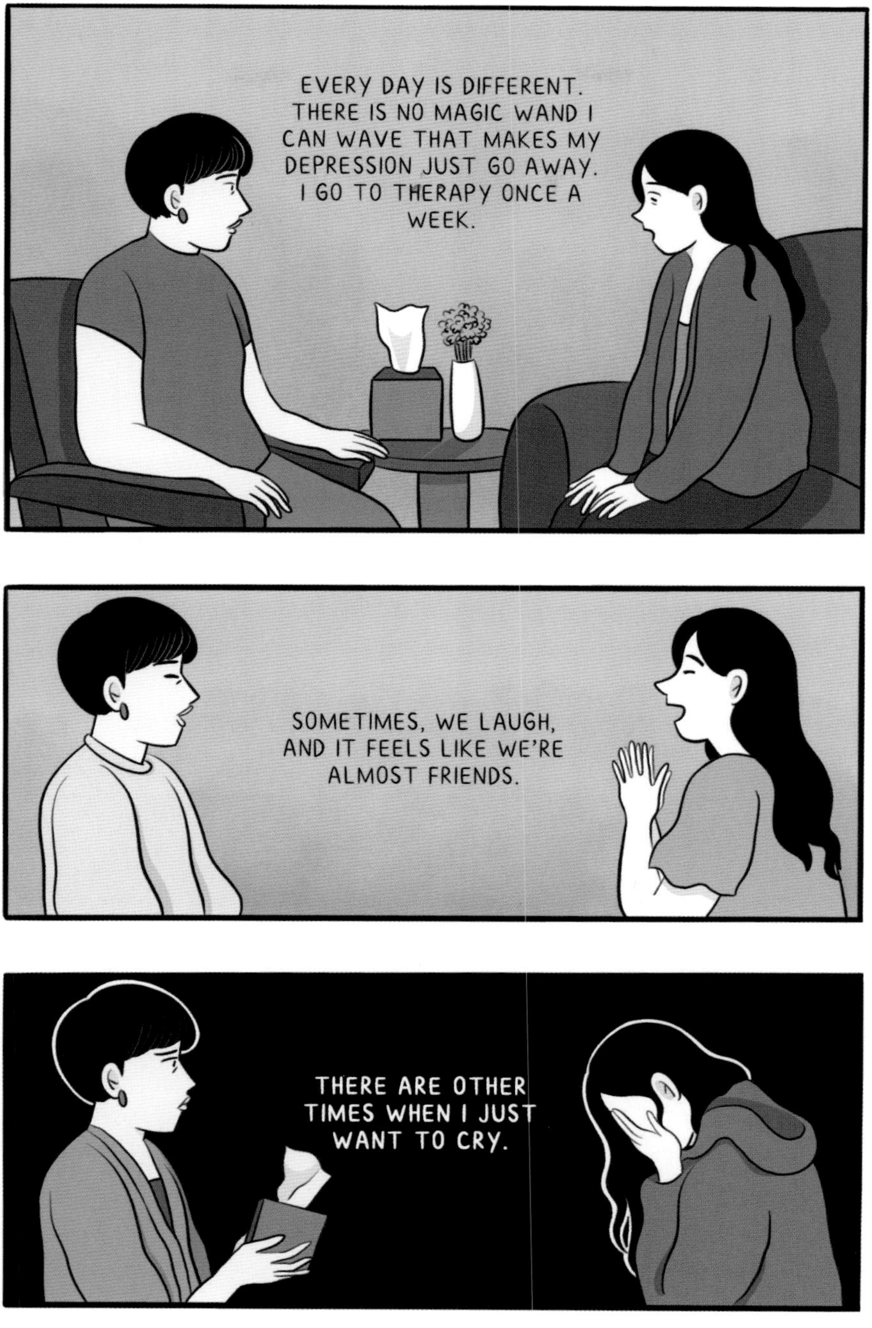
EVERY DAY IS DIFFERENT. THERE IS NO MAGIC WAND I CAN WAVE THAT MAKES MY DEPRESSION JUST GO AWAY. I GO TO THERAPY ONCE A WEEK.
SOMETIMES, WE LAUGH, AND IT FEELS LIKE WE'RE ALMOST FRIENDS.
THERE ARE OTHER TIMES WHEN I JUST WANT TO CRY.

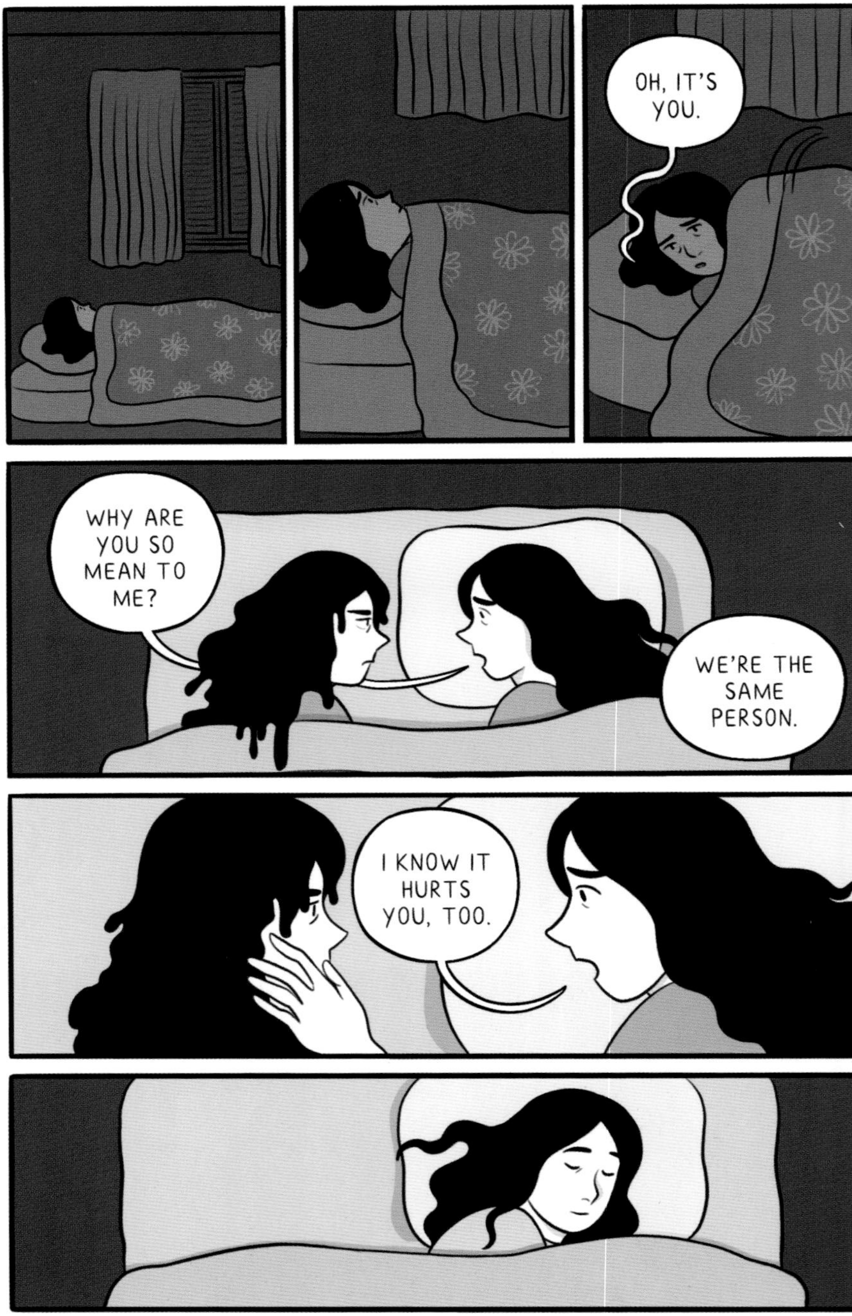
OH, IT'S YOU.
WHY ARE YOU SO MEAN TO ME?
WE'RE THE SAME PERSON.
I KNOW IT HURTS YOU, TOO.

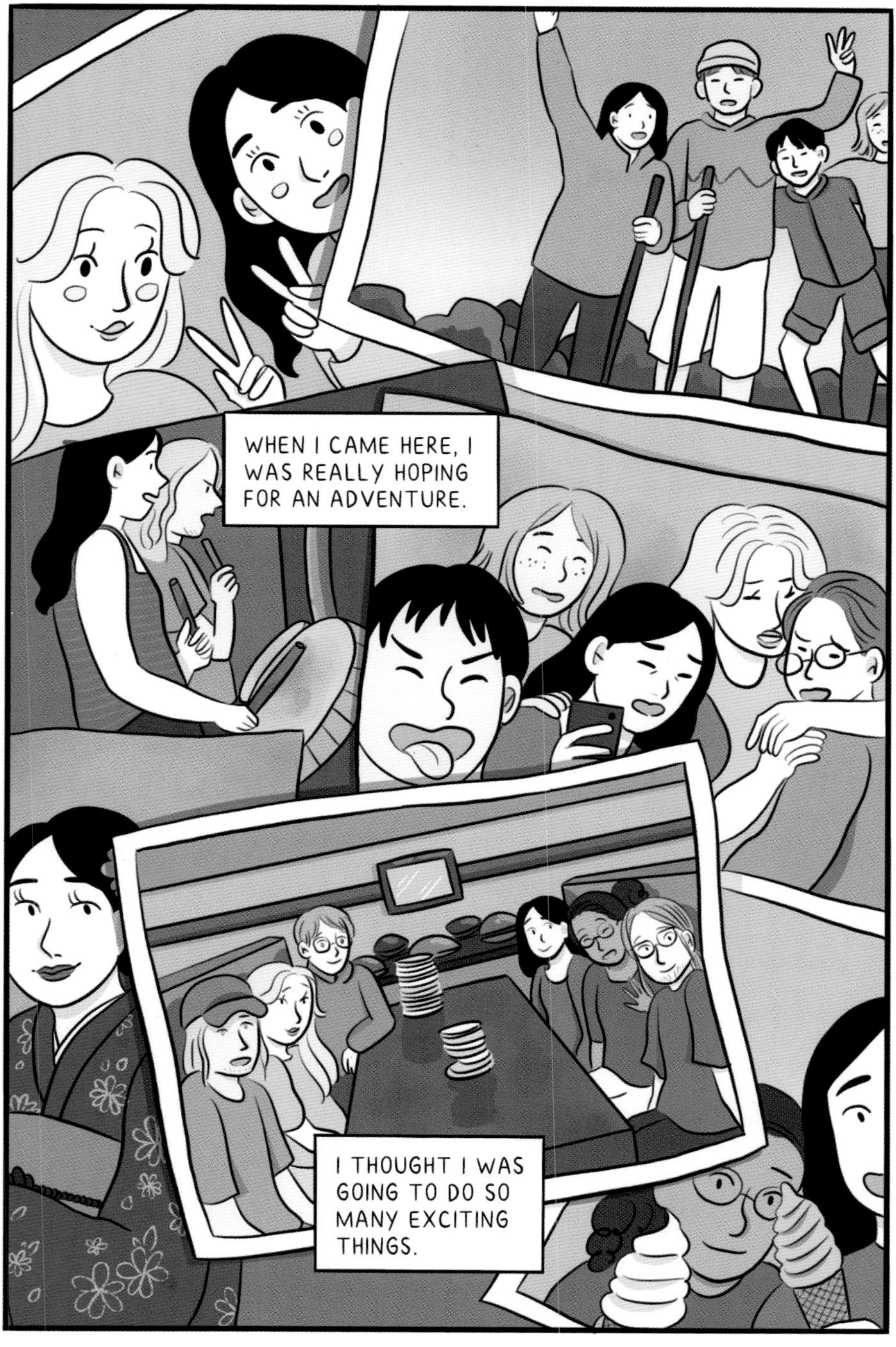
WHEN I CAME HERE, I WAS REALLY HOPING FOR AN ADVENTURE.
I THOUGHT I WAS GOING TO DO SO MANY EXCITING THINGS.

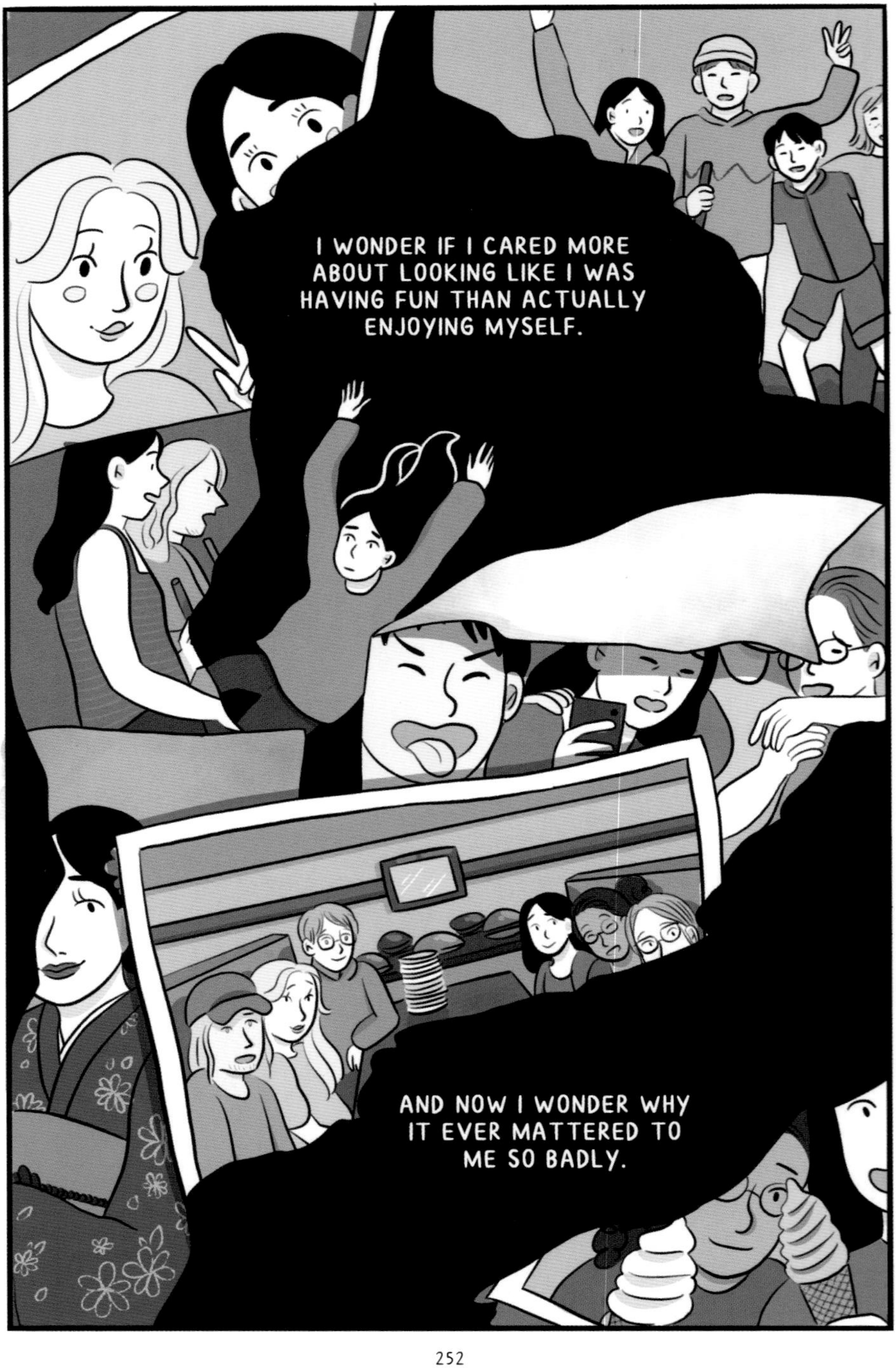
I WONDER IF I CARED MORE ABOUT LOOKING LIKE I WAS HAVING FUN THAN ACTUALLY ENJOYING MYSELF.
AND NOW I WONDER WHY IT EVER MATTERED TO ME SO BADLY.

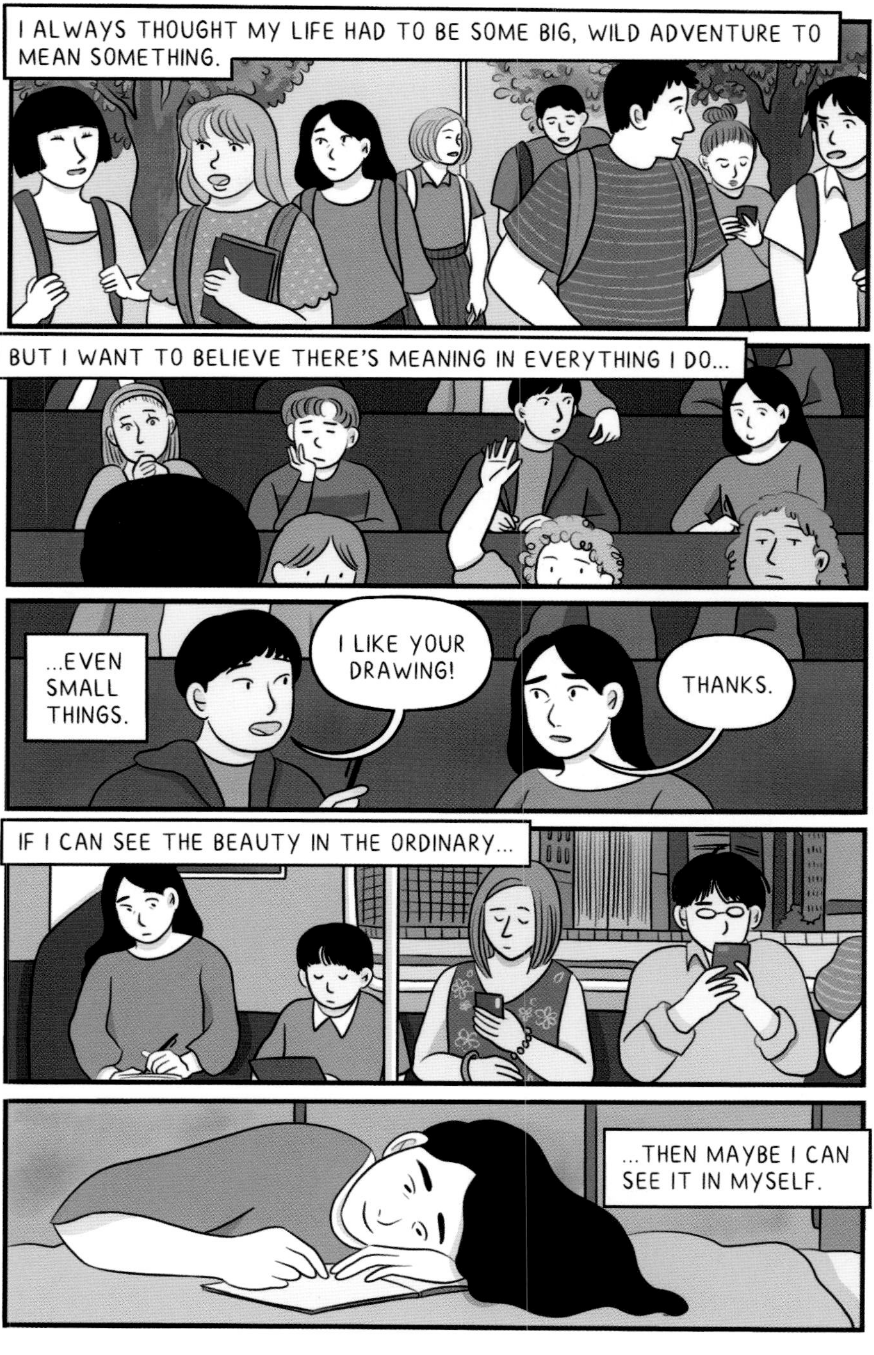
I ALWAYS THOUGHT MY LIFE HAD TO BE SOME BIG, WILD ADVENTURE TO MEAN SOMETHING.
BUT I WANT TO BELIEVE THERE'S MEANING IN EVERYTHING I DO...
...EVEN SMALL THINGS.
I LIKE YOUR DRAWING!
THANKS.
IF I CAN SEE THE BEAUTY IN THE ORDINARY...
...THEN MAYBE I CAN SEE IT IN MYSELF.

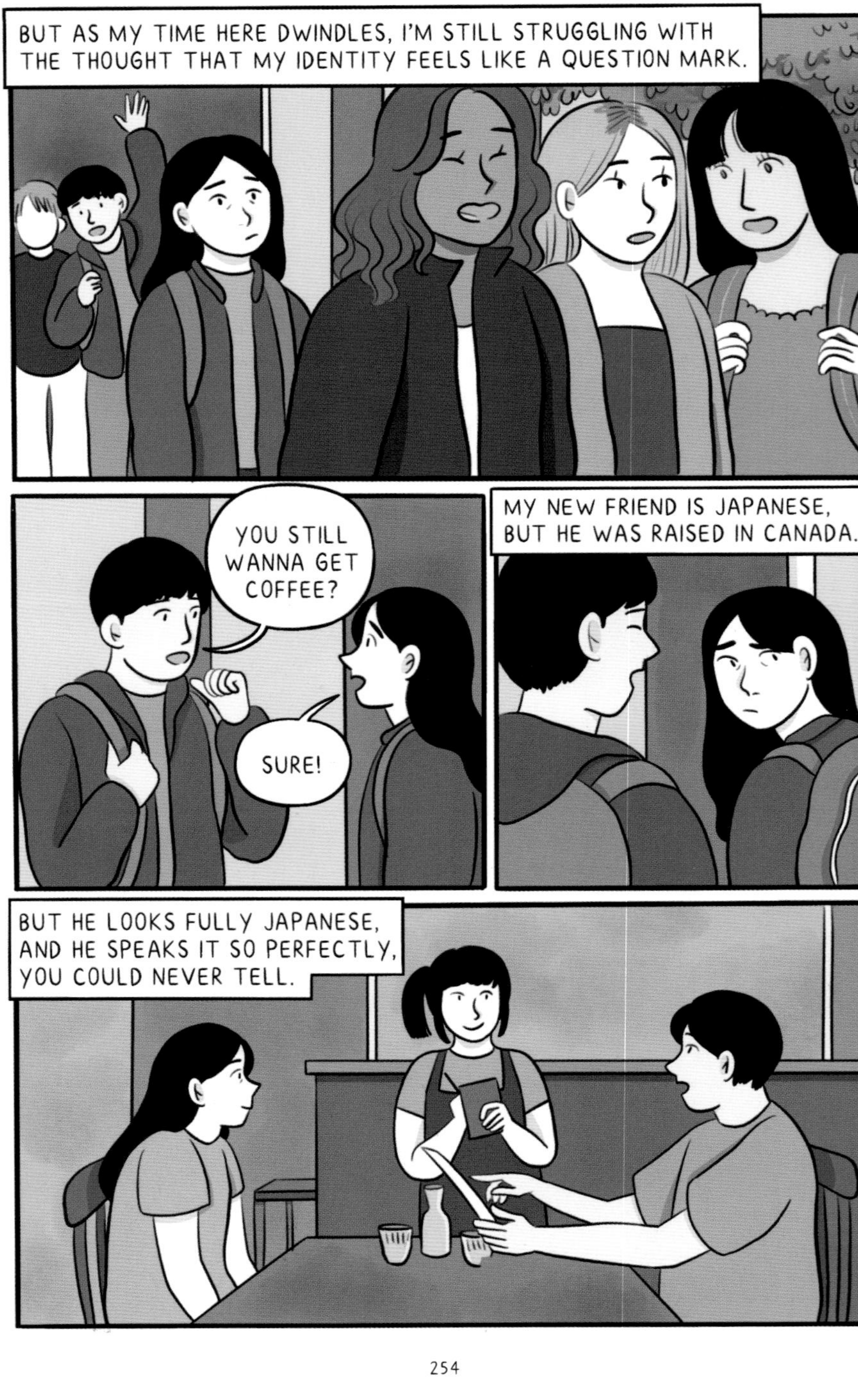
BUT AS MY TIME HERE DWINDLES, I'M STILL STRUGGLING WITH THE THOUGHT THAT MY IDENTITY FEELS LIKE A QUESTION MARK.
YOU STILL WANNA GET COFFEE?
SURE!
MY NEW FRIEND IS JAPANESE, BUT HE WAS RAISED IN CANADA.
BUT HE LOOKS FULLY JAPANESE, AND HE SPEAKS IT SO PERFECTLY, YOU COULD NEVER TELL.

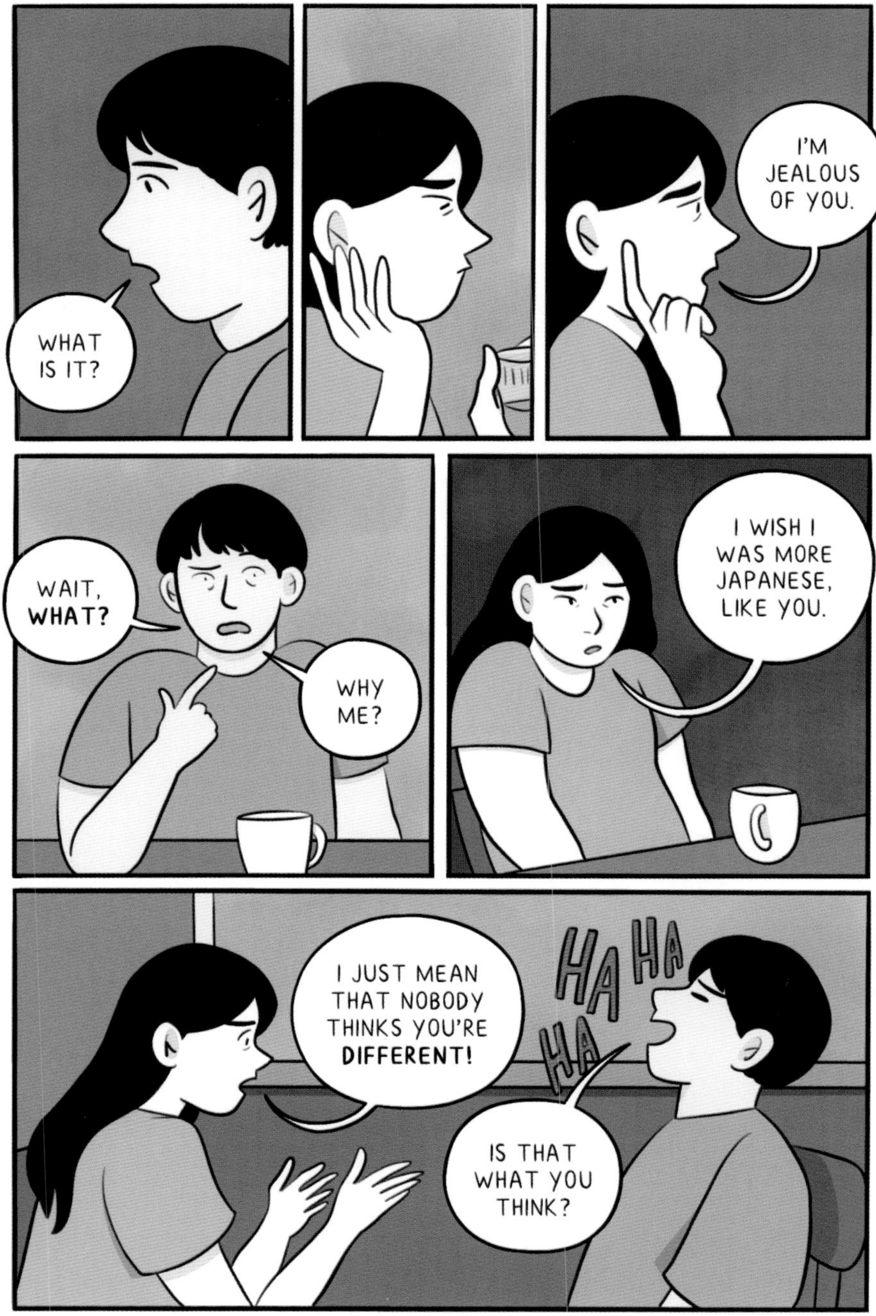
WHAT IS IT?
I'M JEALOUS OF YOU.
WAIT, **WHAT?**
WHY ME?
I WISH I WAS MORE JAPANESE, LIKE YOU.
I JUST MEAN THAT NOBODY THINKS YOU'RE **DIFFERENT!**
HA HA HA HA
IS THAT WHAT YOU THINK?

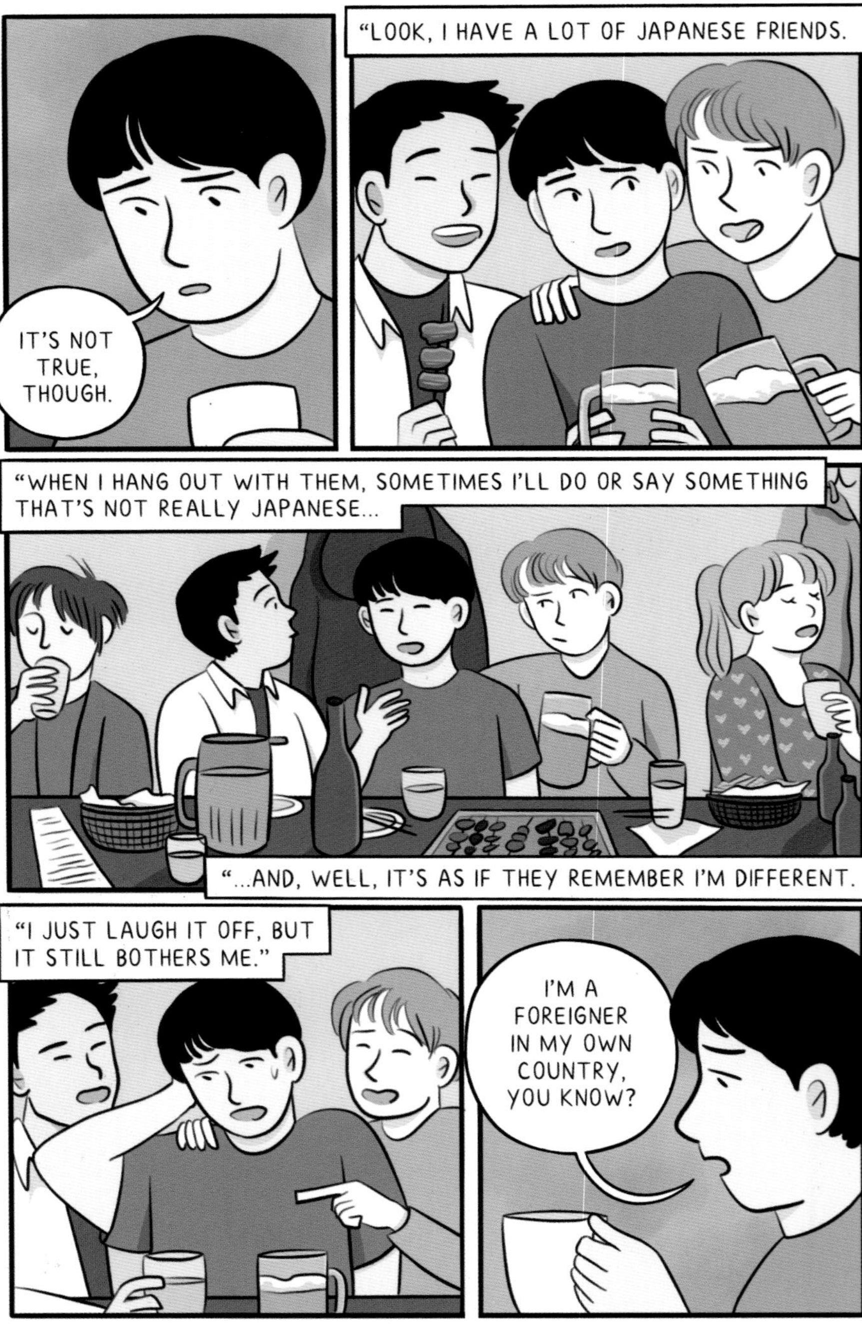
IT'S NOT TRUE, THOUGH.
"LOOK, I HAVE A LOT OF JAPANESE FRIENDS.
"WHEN I HANG OUT WITH THEM, SOMETIMES I'LL DO OR SAY SOMETHING THAT'S NOT REALLY JAPANESE...
"...AND, WELL, IT'S AS IF THEY REMEMBER I'M DIFFERENT.
"I JUST LAUGH IT OFF, BUT IT STILL BOTHERS ME."
I'M A FOREIGNER IN MY OWN COUNTRY, YOU KNOW?

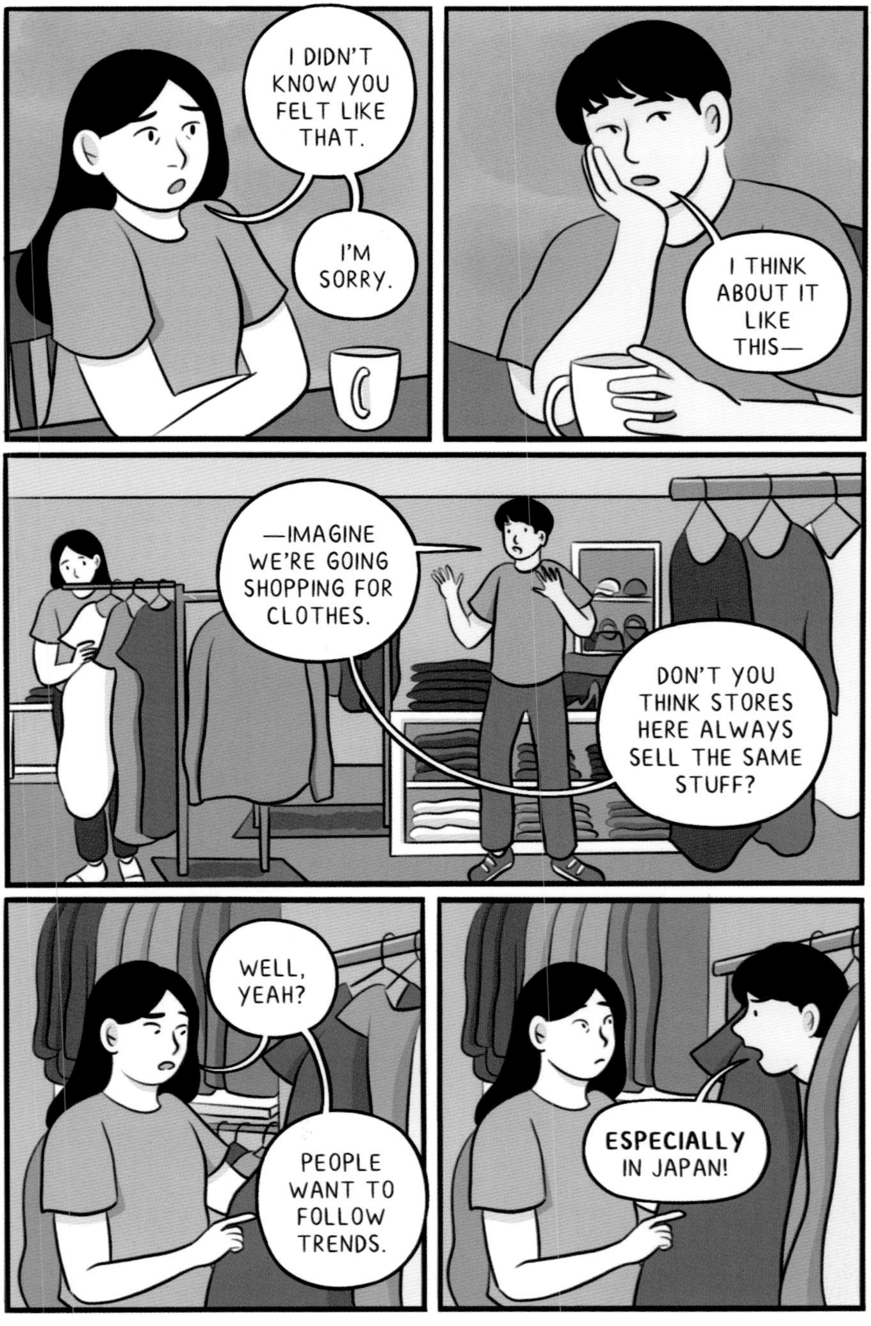
I DIDN'T KNOW YOU FELT LIKE THAT.
I'M SORRY.
I THINK ABOUT IT LIKE THIS—
—IMAGINE WE'RE GOING SHOPPING FOR CLOTHES.
DON'T YOU THINK STORES HERE ALWAYS SELL THE SAME STUFF?
WELL, YEAH?
PEOPLE WANT TO FOLLOW TRENDS.
ESPECIALLY IN JAPAN!

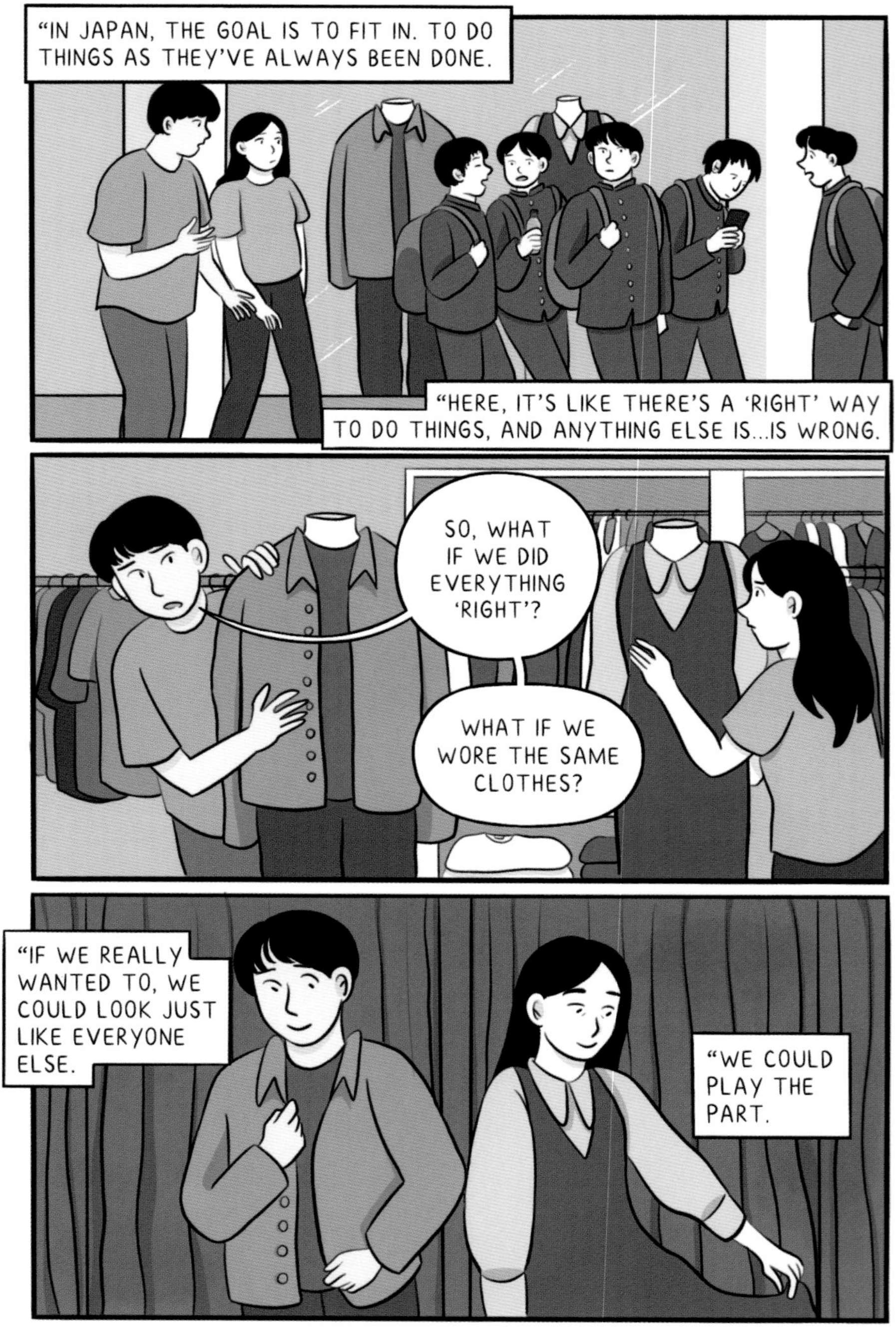
"IN JAPAN, THE GOAL IS TO FIT IN. TO DO THINGS AS THEY'VE ALWAYS BEEN DONE.
"HERE, IT'S LIKE THERE'S A 'RIGHT' WAY TO DO THINGS, AND ANYTHING ELSE IS...IS WRONG.
SO, WHAT IF WE DID EVERYTHING 'RIGHT'?
WHAT IF WE WORE THE SAME CLOTHES?
"IF WE REALLY WANTED TO, WE COULD LOOK JUST LIKE EVERYONE ELSE.
"WE COULD PLAY THE PART.

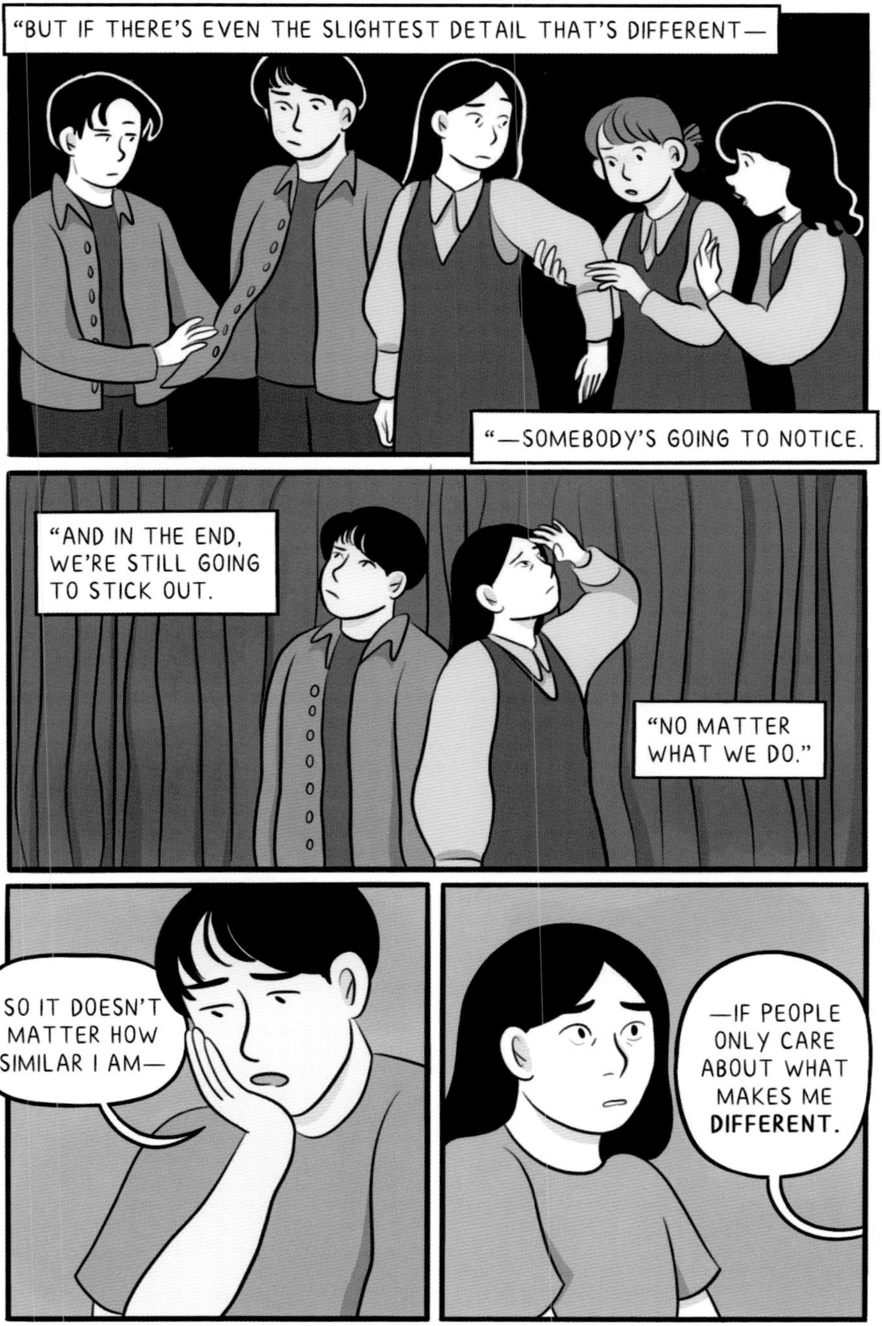
"BUT IF THERE'S EVEN THE SLIGHTEST DETAIL THAT'S DIFFERENT—
"—SOMEBODY'S GOING TO NOTICE.
"AND IN THE END, WE'RE STILL GOING TO STICK OUT.
"NO MATTER WHAT WE DO."
SO IT DOESN'T MATTER HOW SIMILAR I AM—
—IF PEOPLE ONLY CARE ABOUT WHAT MAKES ME **DIFFERENT**.

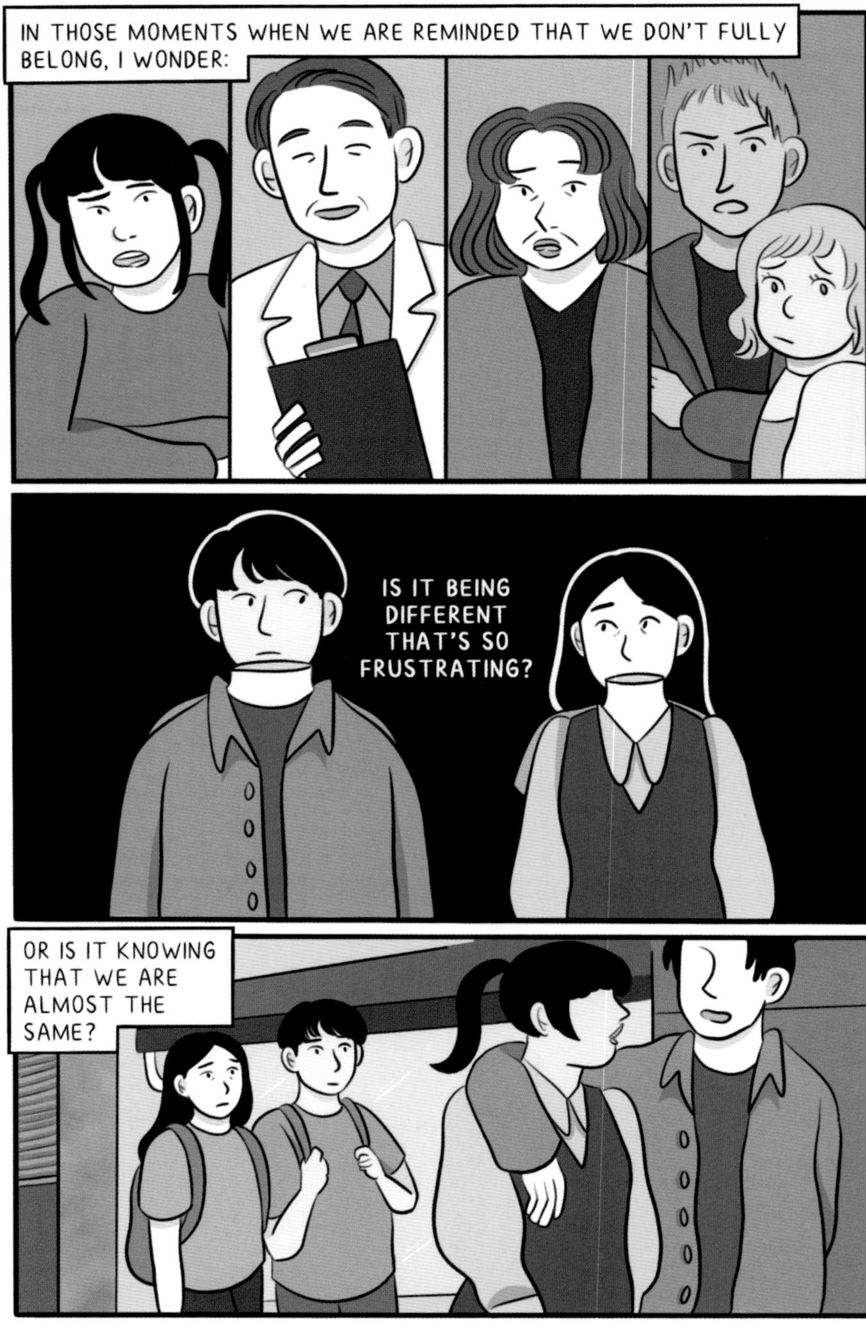
IN THOSE MOMENTS WHEN WE ARE REMINDED THAT WE DON'T FULLY BELONG, I WONDER:
IS IT BEING DIFFERENT THAT'S SO FRUSTRATING?
OR IS IT KNOWING THAT WE ARE ALMOST THE SAME?

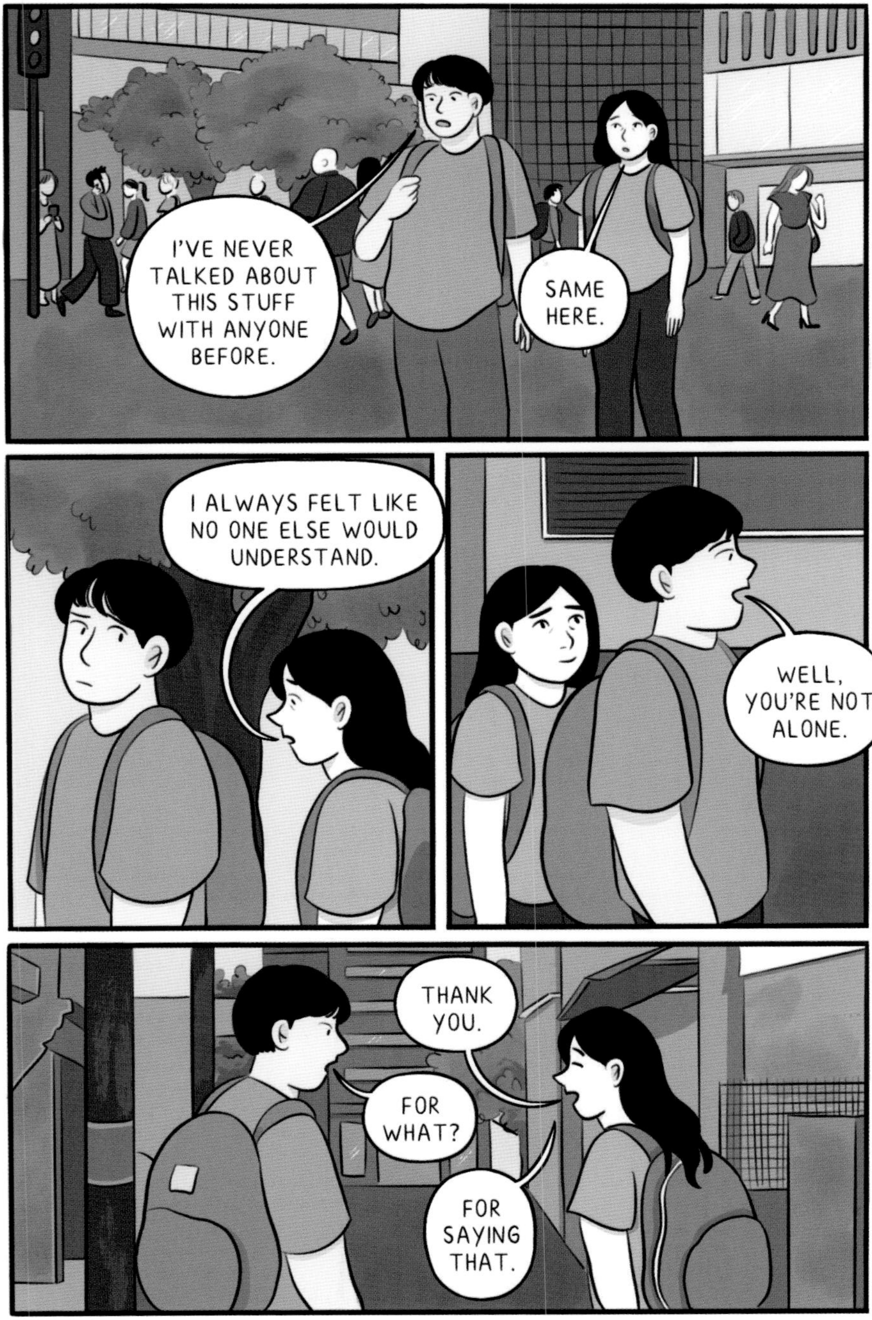
I'VE NEVER TALKED ABOUT THIS STUFF WITH ANYONE BEFORE.
SAME HERE.
I ALWAYS FELT LIKE NO ONE ELSE WOULD UNDERSTAND.
WELL, YOU'RE NOT ALONE.
THANK YOU.
FOR WHAT?
FOR SAYING THAT.

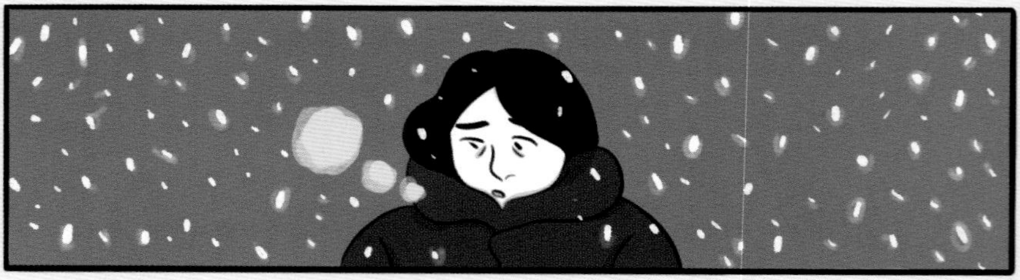

IT HAD BEEN A LONG AND COLD WINTER.

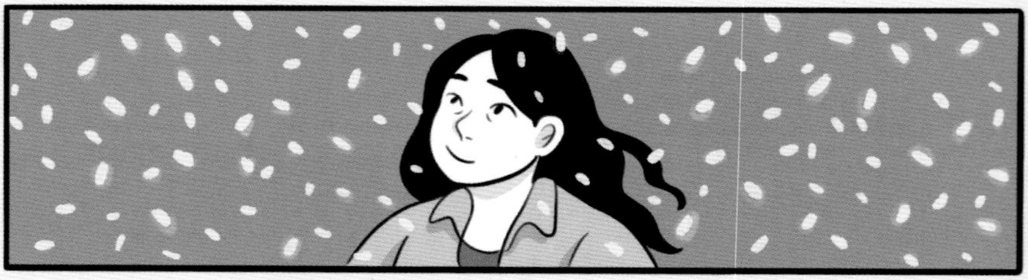

BUT SPRING BLURS INTO SUMMER IN THE BLINK OF AN EYE.

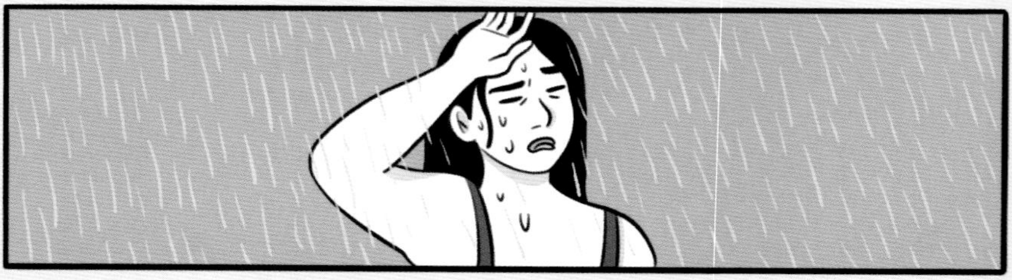

SOON, THE DAYS ARE STICKY AND HOT—

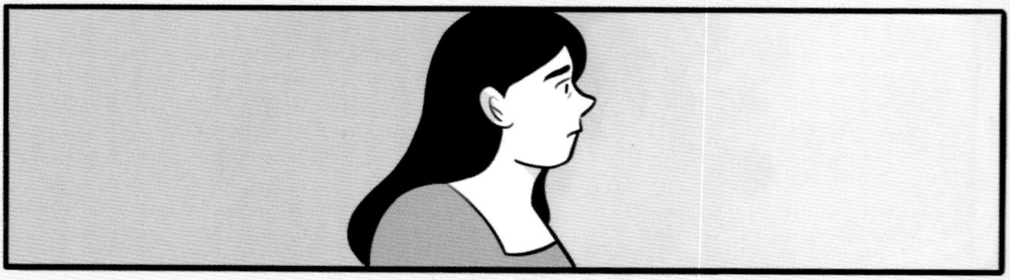

—AND I HEAR PEOPLE BEGINNING TO TALK ABOUT GOING HOME.

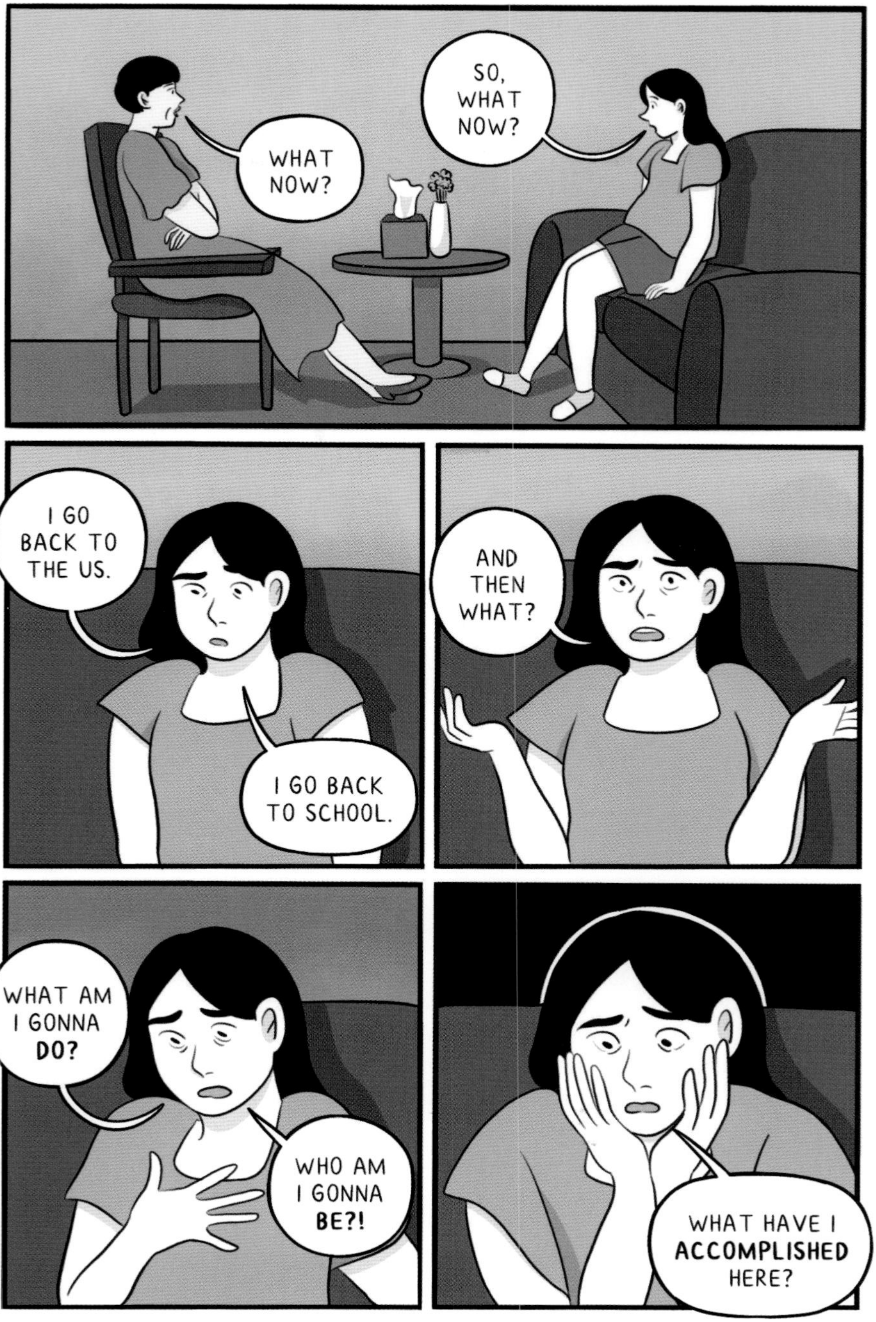
WHAT NOW?
SO, WHAT NOW?
I GO BACK TO THE US.
I GO BACK TO SCHOOL.
AND THEN WHAT?
WHAT AM I GONNA **DO?**
WHO AM I GONNA **BE?!**
WHAT HAVE I **ACCOMPLISHED** HERE?

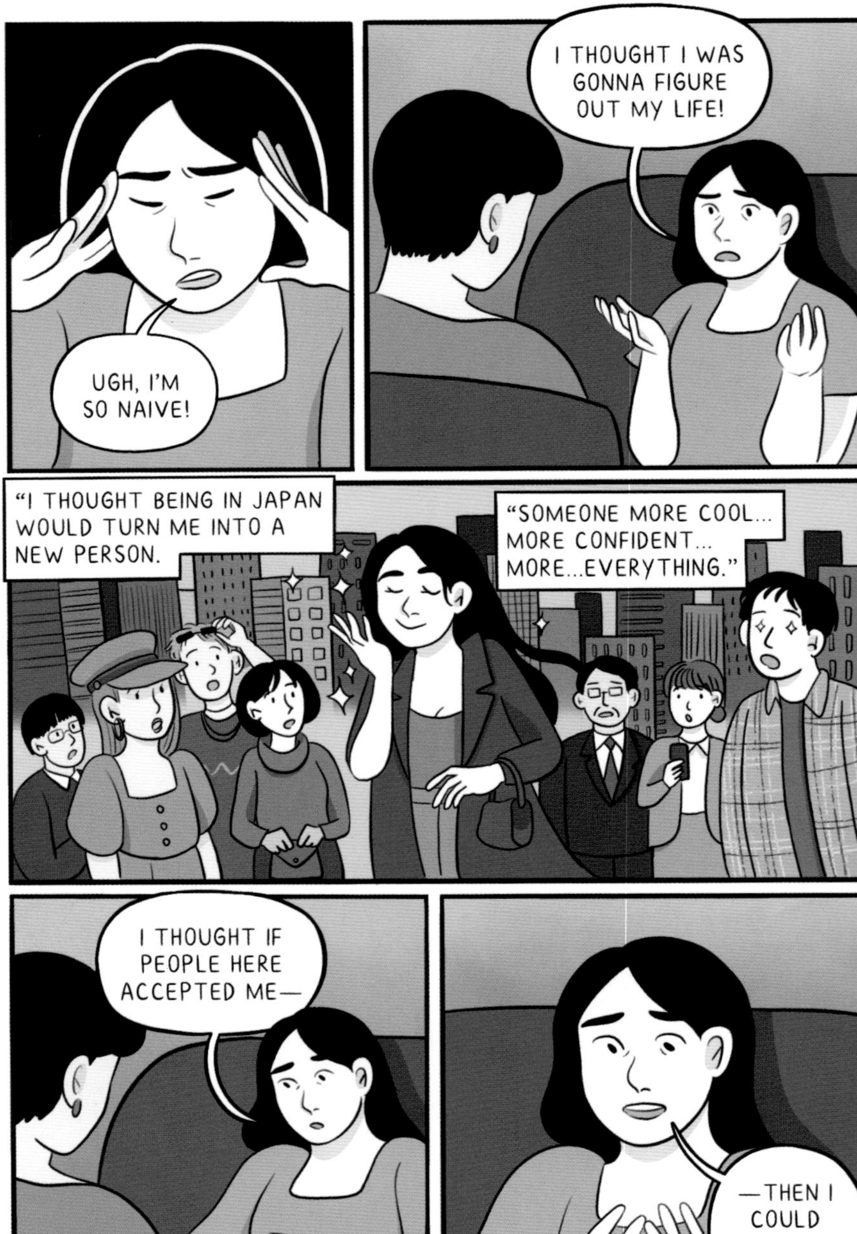
UGH, I'M SO NAIVE!
I THOUGHT I WAS GONNA FIGURE OUT MY LIFE!
"I THOUGHT BEING IN JAPAN WOULD TURN ME INTO A NEW PERSON.
"SOMEONE MORE COOL... MORE CONFIDENT... MORE...EVERYTHING."
I THOUGHT IF PEOPLE HERE ACCEPTED ME—
—THEN I COULD ACCEPT MYSELF.

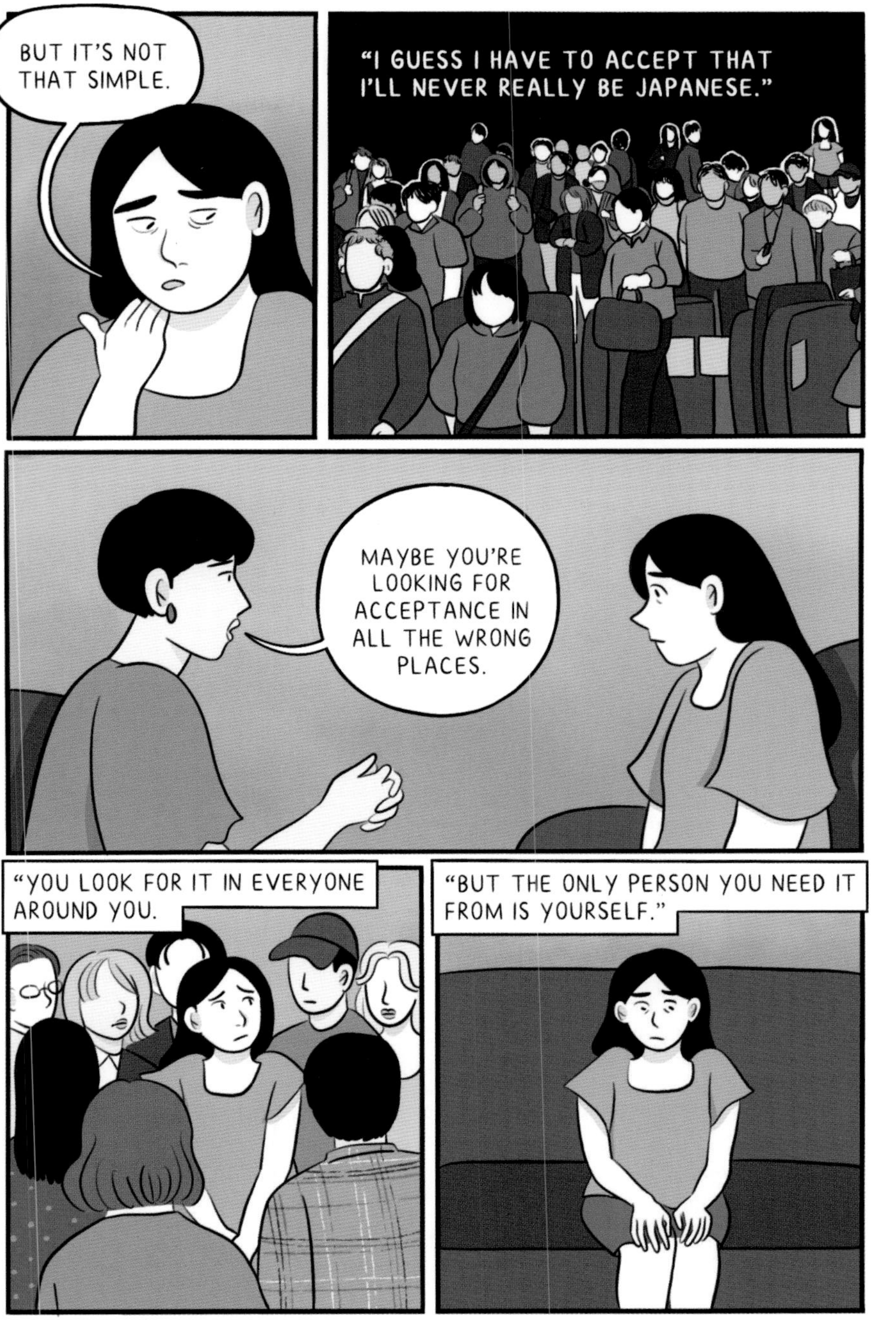
BUT IT'S NOT THAT SIMPLE.
"I GUESS I HAVE TO ACCEPT THAT I'LL NEVER REALLY BE JAPANESE."
MAYBE YOU'RE LOOKING FOR ACCEPTANCE IN ALL THE WRONG PLACES.
"YOU LOOK FOR IT IN EVERYONE AROUND YOU.
"BUT THE ONLY PERSON YOU NEED IT FROM IS YOURSELF."

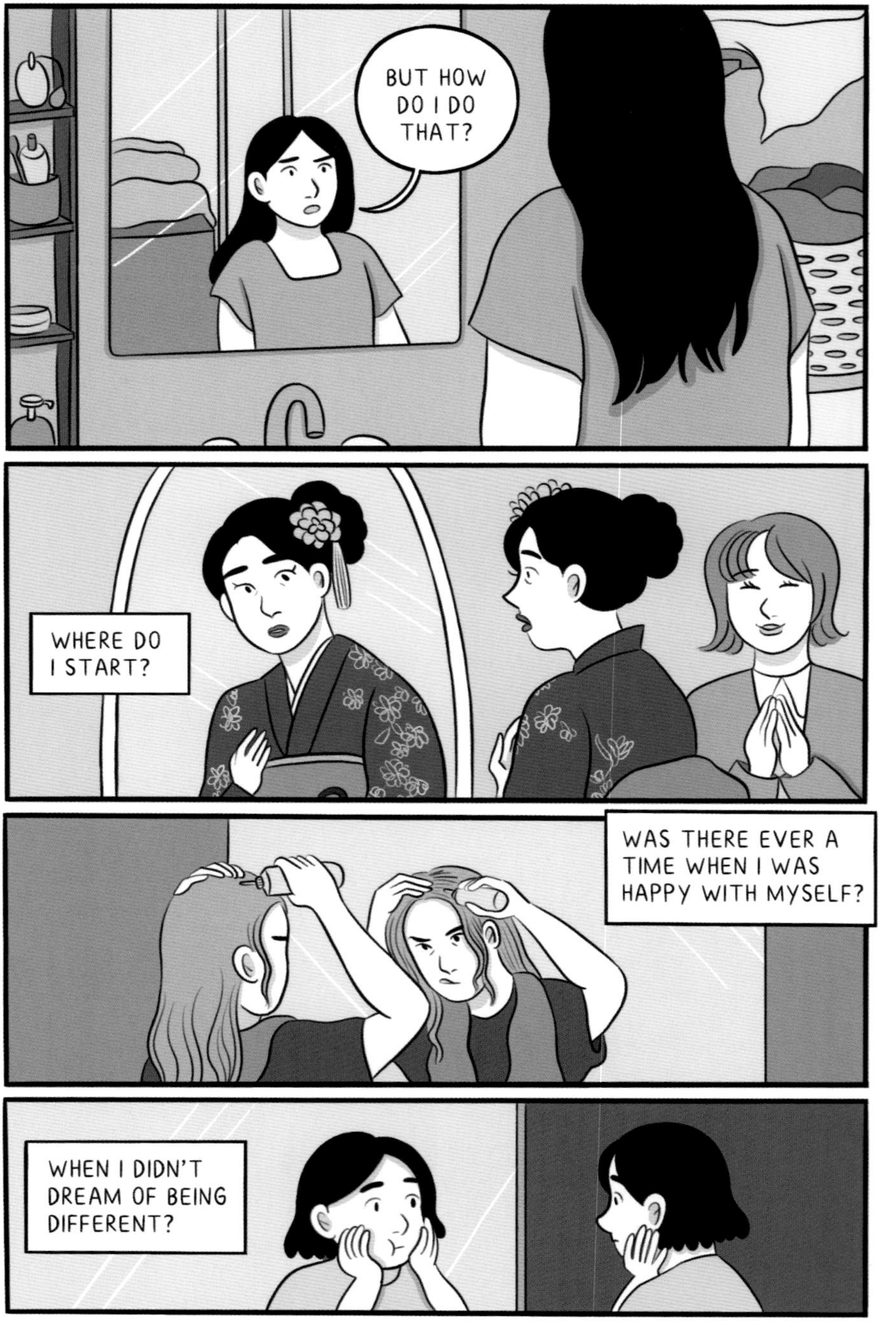
BUT HOW DO I DO THAT?
WHERE DO I START?
WAS THERE EVER A TIME WHEN I WAS HAPPY WITH MYSELF?
WHEN I DIDN'T DREAM OF BEING DIFFERENT?

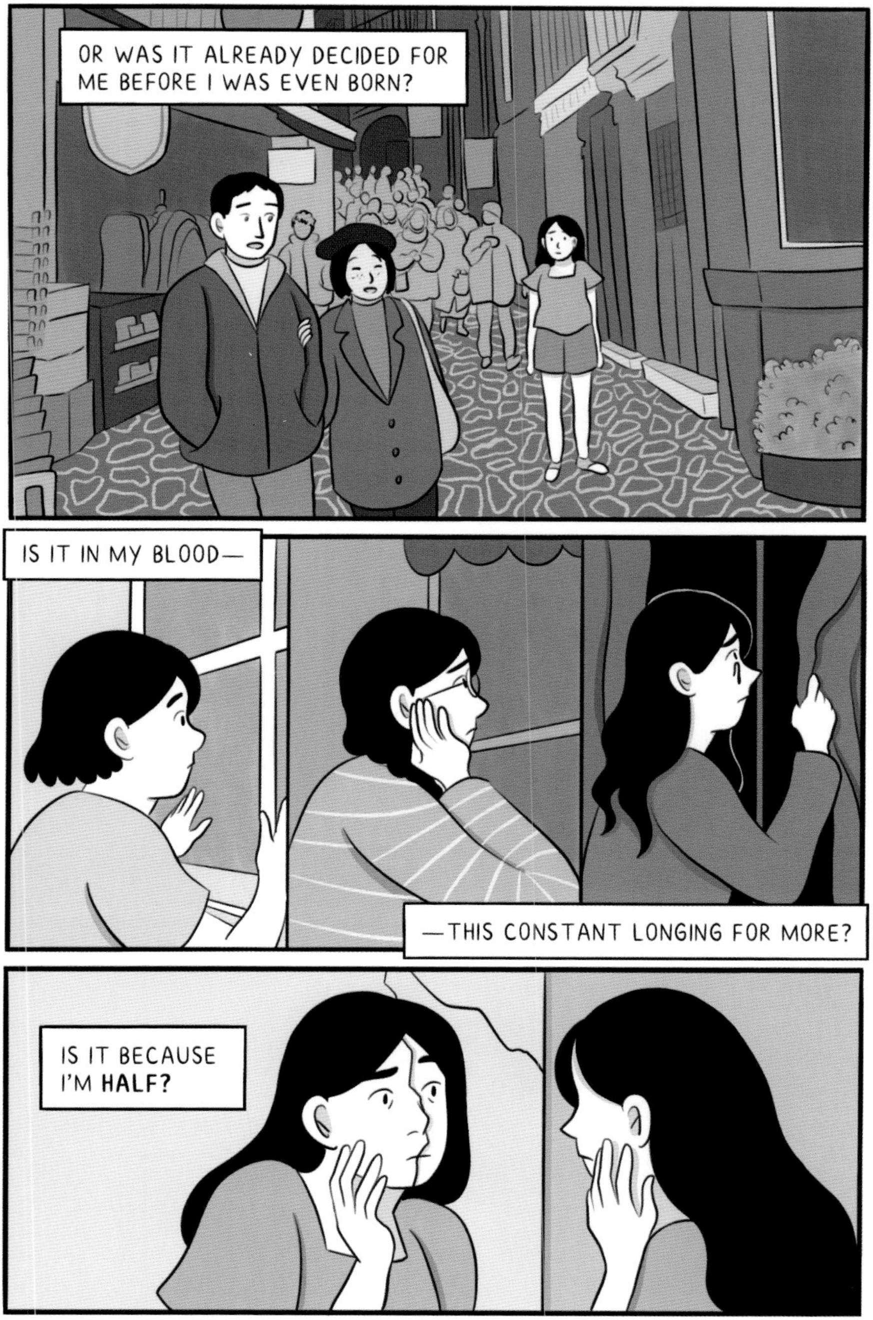
OR WAS IT ALREADY DECIDED FOR ME BEFORE I WAS EVEN BORN?
IS IT IN MY BLOOD—
—THIS CONSTANT LONGING FOR MORE?
IS IT BECAUSE I'M **HALF?**

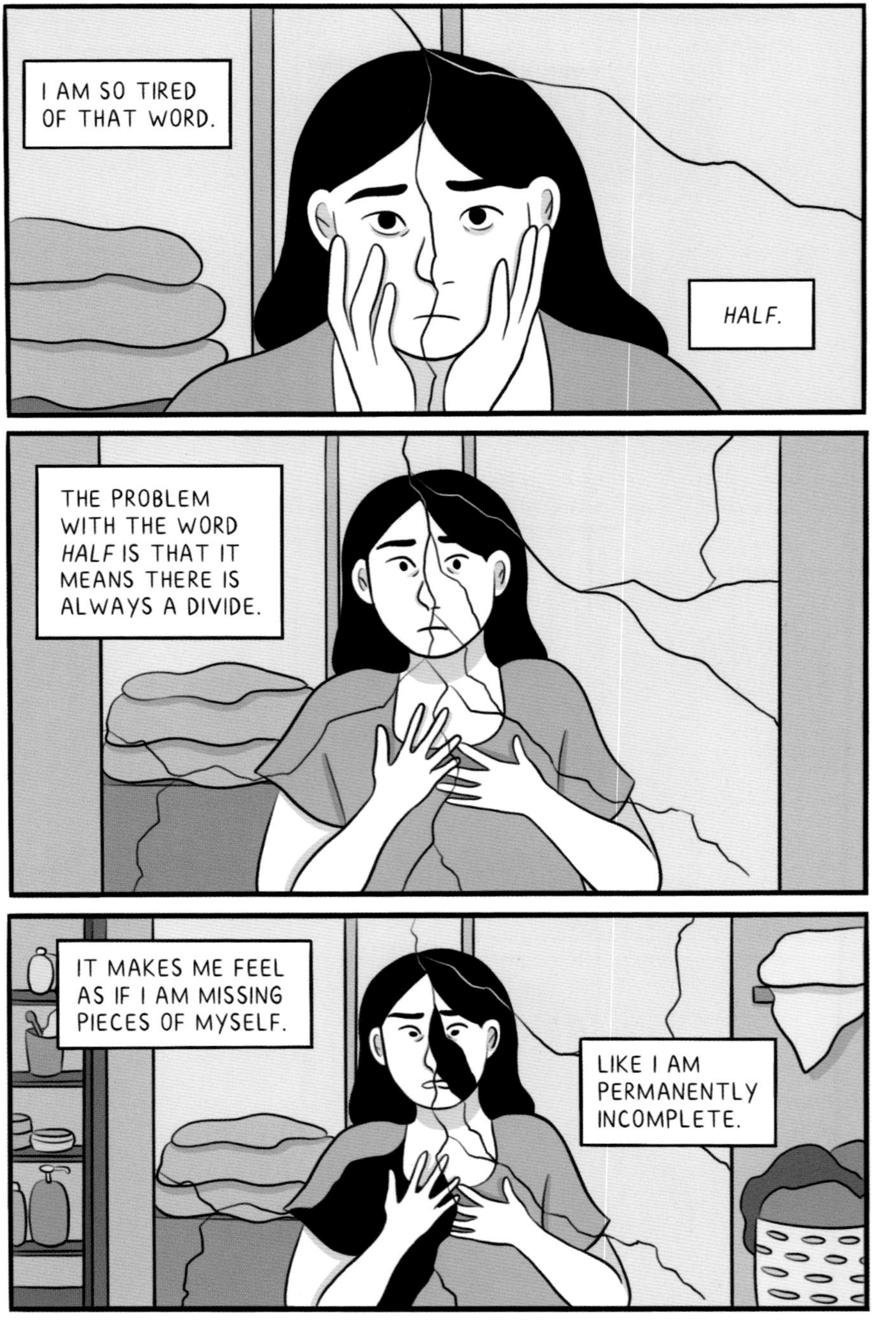
I AM SO TIRED OF THAT WORD.
HALF.
THE PROBLEM WITH THE WORD *HALF* IS THAT IT MEANS THERE IS ALWAYS A DIVIDE.
IT MAKES ME FEEL AS IF I AM MISSING PIECES OF MYSELF.
LIKE I AM PERMANENTLY INCOMPLETE.

SO I CAME TO JAPAN TO PROVE MYSELF.

TO PROVE THAT I COULD REALLY BE JAPANESE, NOT JUST HALF.

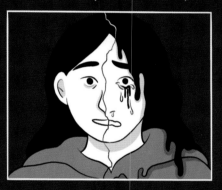

TO PROVE THAT I WAS HAPPY, EVEN WHEN I WASN'T.

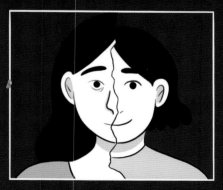

TO PROVE THAT I WAS GROWN-UP AND NO LONGER A CHILD.

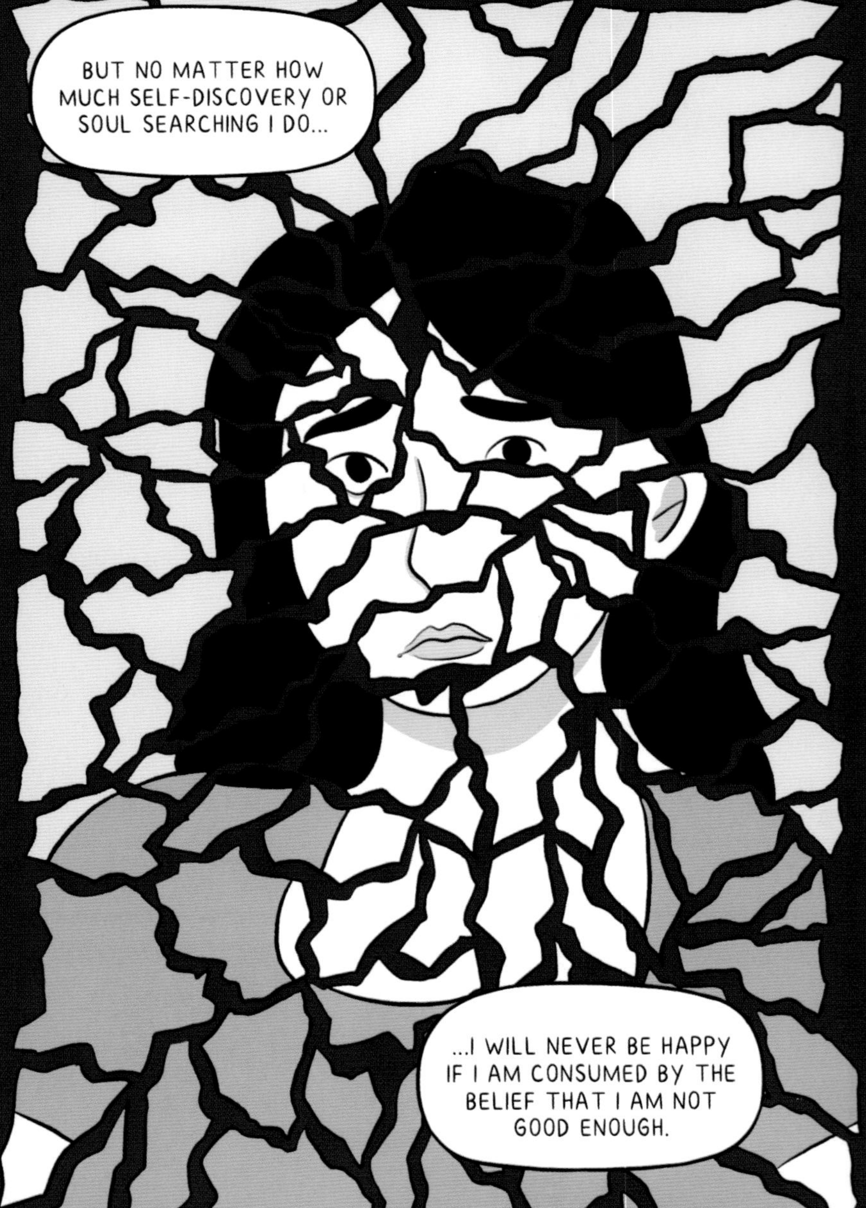
BUT NO MATTER HOW MUCH SELF-DISCOVERY OR SOUL SEARCHING I DO...
...I WILL NEVER BE HAPPY IF I AM CONSUMED BY THE BELIEF THAT I AM NOT GOOD ENOUGH.

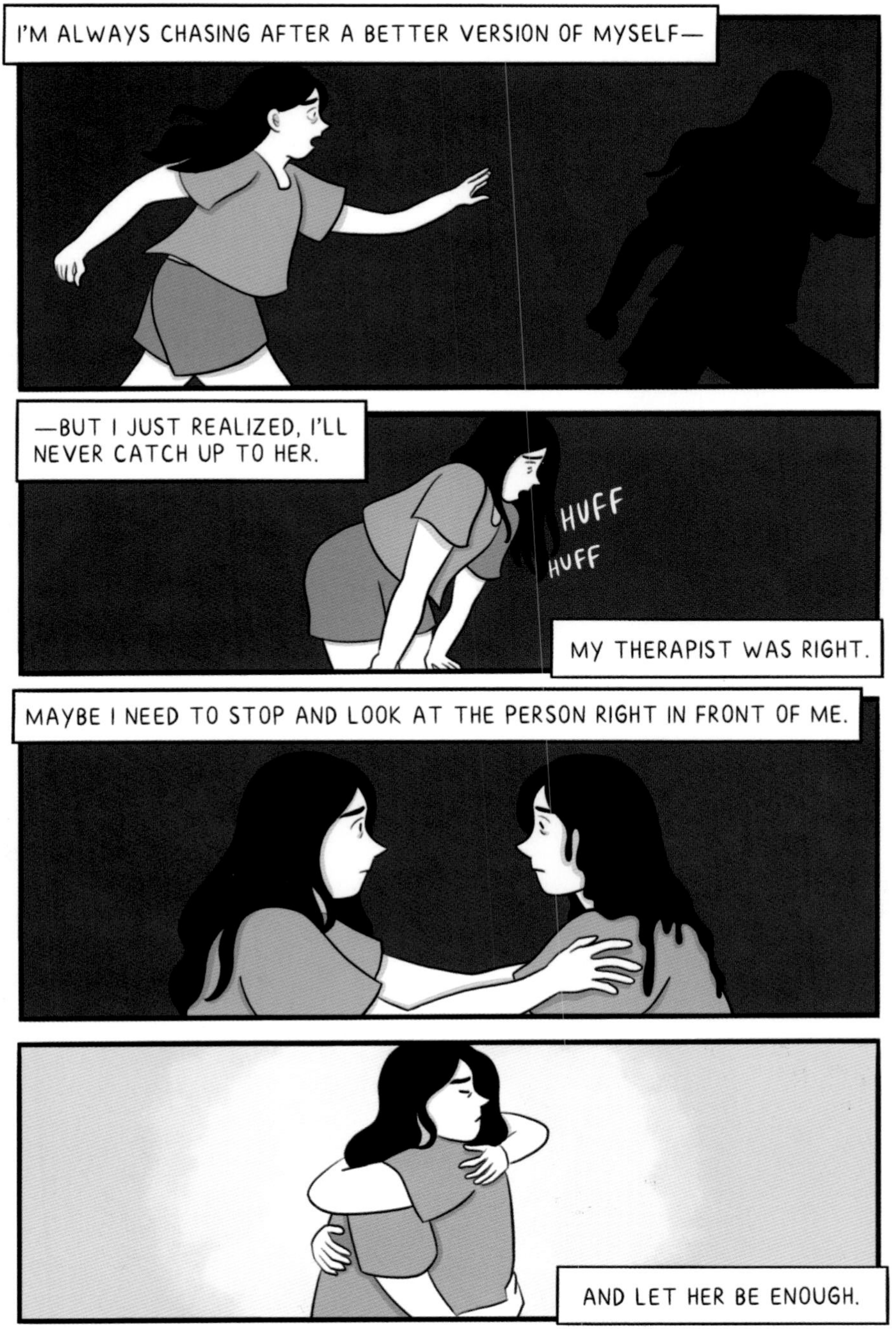
I'M ALWAYS CHASING AFTER A BETTER VERSION OF MYSELF—
—BUT I JUST REALIZED, I'LL NEVER CATCH UP TO HER.
HUFF
HUFF
MY THERAPIST WAS RIGHT.
MAYBE I NEED TO STOP AND LOOK AT THE PERSON RIGHT IN FRONT OF ME.
AND LET HER BE ENOUGH.

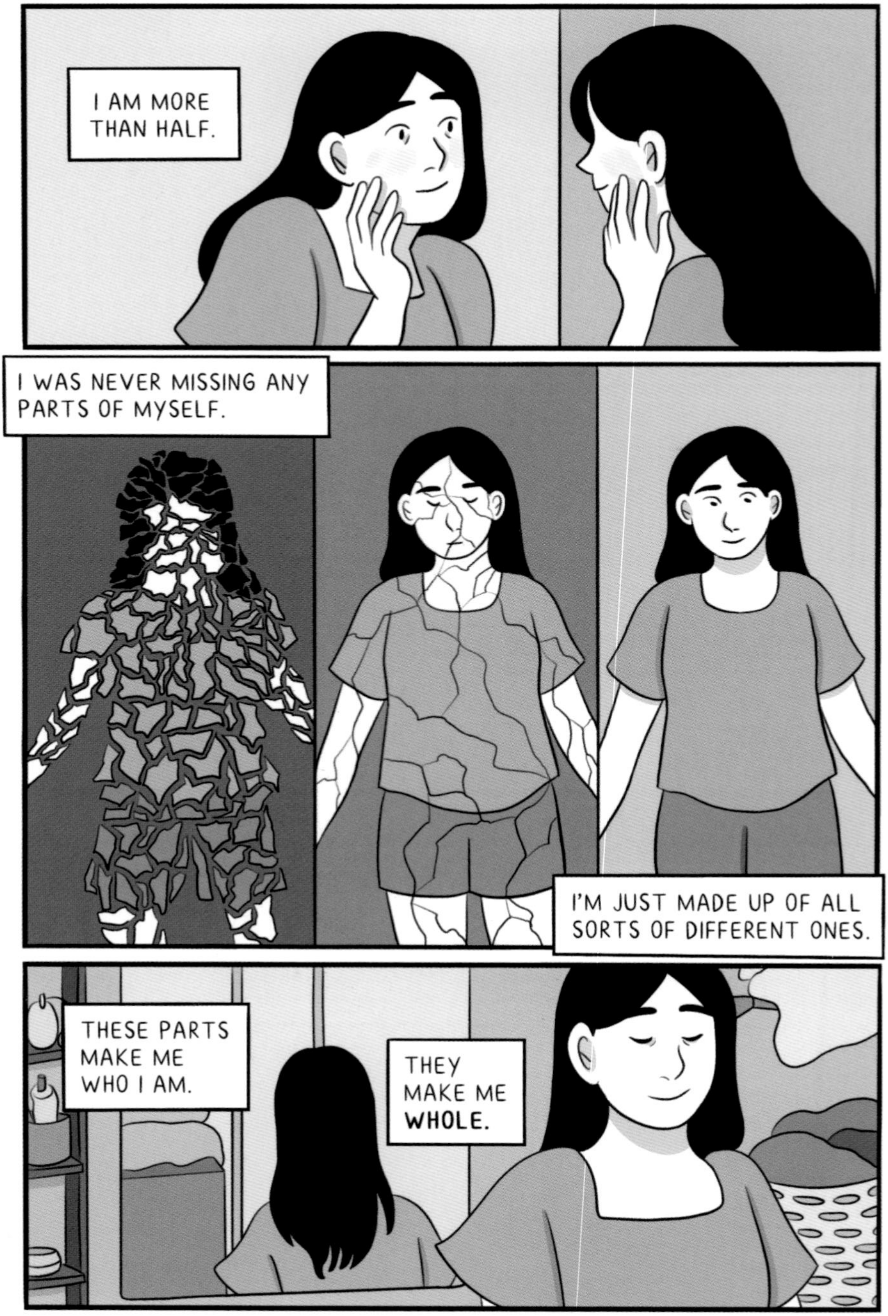
I AM MORE THAN HALF.
I WAS NEVER MISSING ANY PARTS OF MYSELF.
I'M JUST MADE UP OF ALL SORTS OF DIFFERENT ONES.
THESE PARTS MAKE ME WHO I AM.
THEY MAKE ME **WHOLE.**

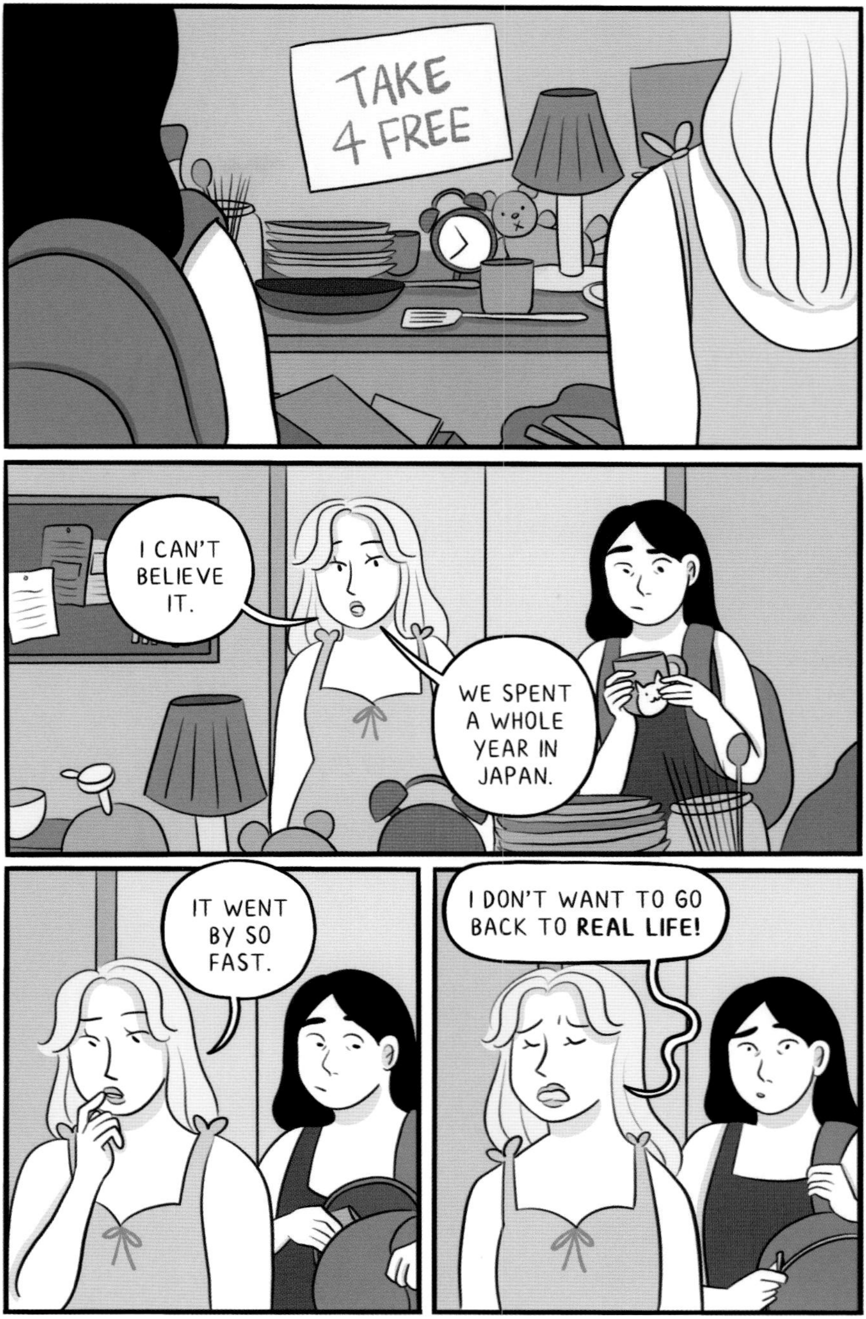
TAKE 4 FREE
I CAN'T BELIEVE IT.
WE SPENT A WHOLE YEAR IN JAPAN.
IT WENT BY SO FAST.
I DON'T WANT TO GO BACK TO **REAL LIFE!**

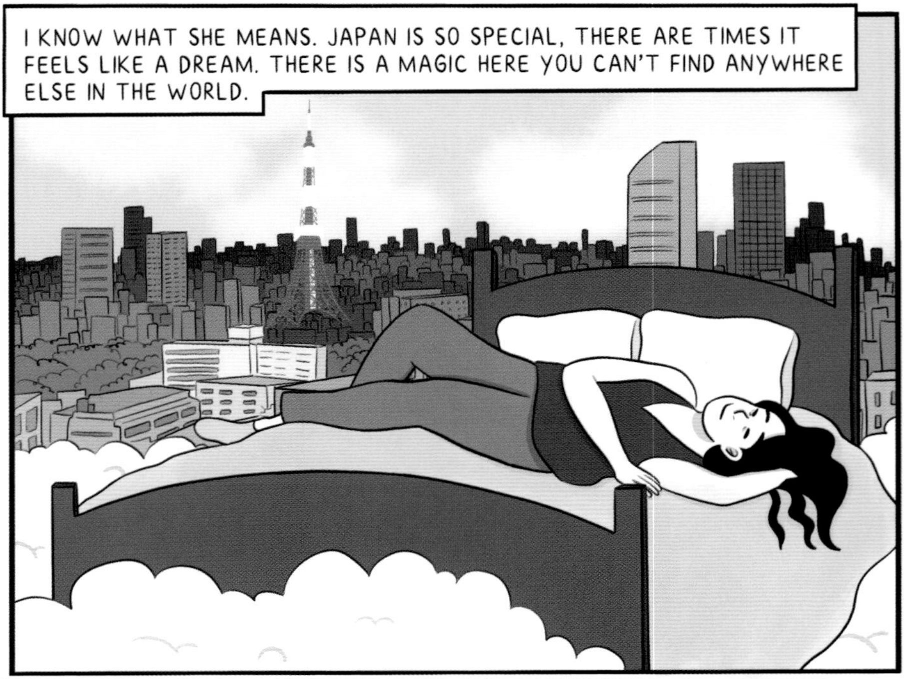
I KNOW WHAT SHE MEANS. JAPAN IS SO SPECIAL, THERE ARE TIMES IT FEELS LIKE A DREAM. THERE IS A MAGIC HERE YOU CAN'T FIND ANYWHERE ELSE IN THE WORLD.

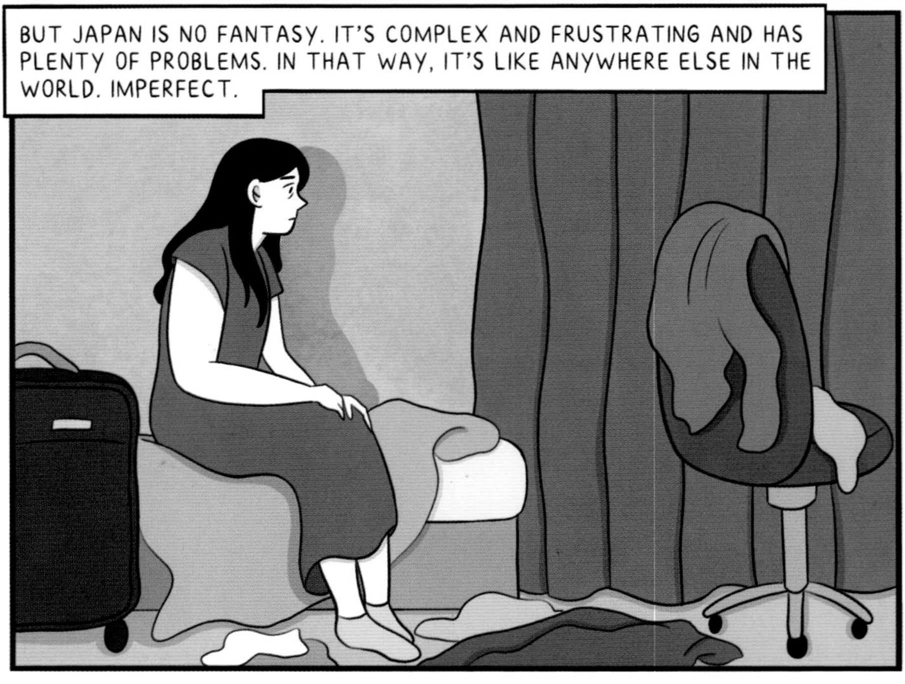
BUT JAPAN IS NO FANTASY. IT'S COMPLEX AND FRUSTRATING AND HAS PLENTY OF PROBLEMS. IN THAT WAY, IT'S LIKE ANYWHERE ELSE IN THE WORLD. IMPERFECT.

THERE IS STILL MAGIC, THOUGH. IN THE MOST ORDINARY OF THINGS.

THINGS LIKE LAUNDRY BLOWING IN THE BREEZE.

THE CHEAP BENTOS I EAT IN BETWEEN CLASSES.

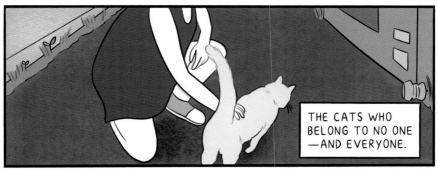

THE CATS WHO BELONG TO NO ONE —AND EVERYONE.

THE SOLITUDE OF AN EMPTY TRAIN CAR.

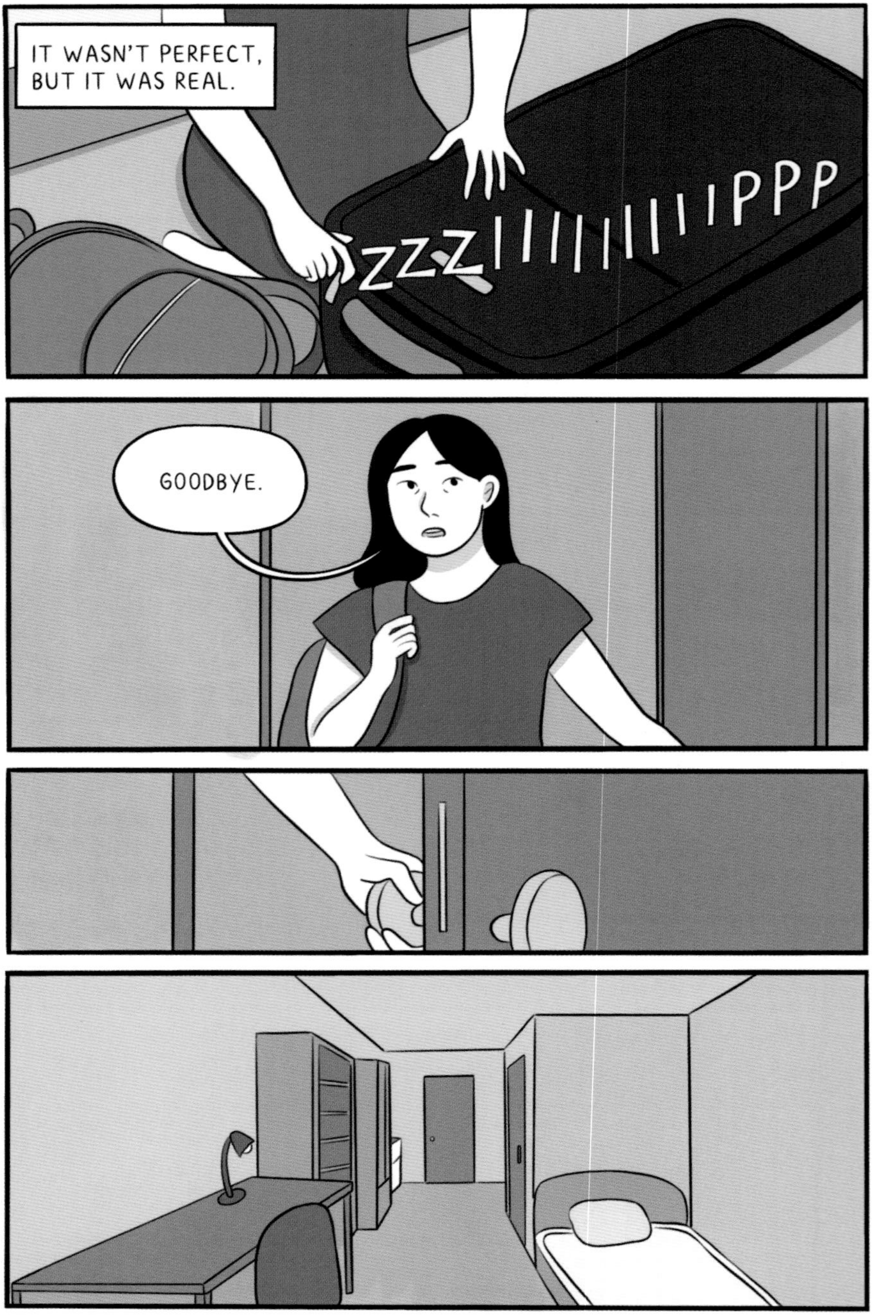
IT WASN'T PERFECT, BUT IT WAS REAL.
ZZZIIIIIIIIIIPPP
GOODBYE.

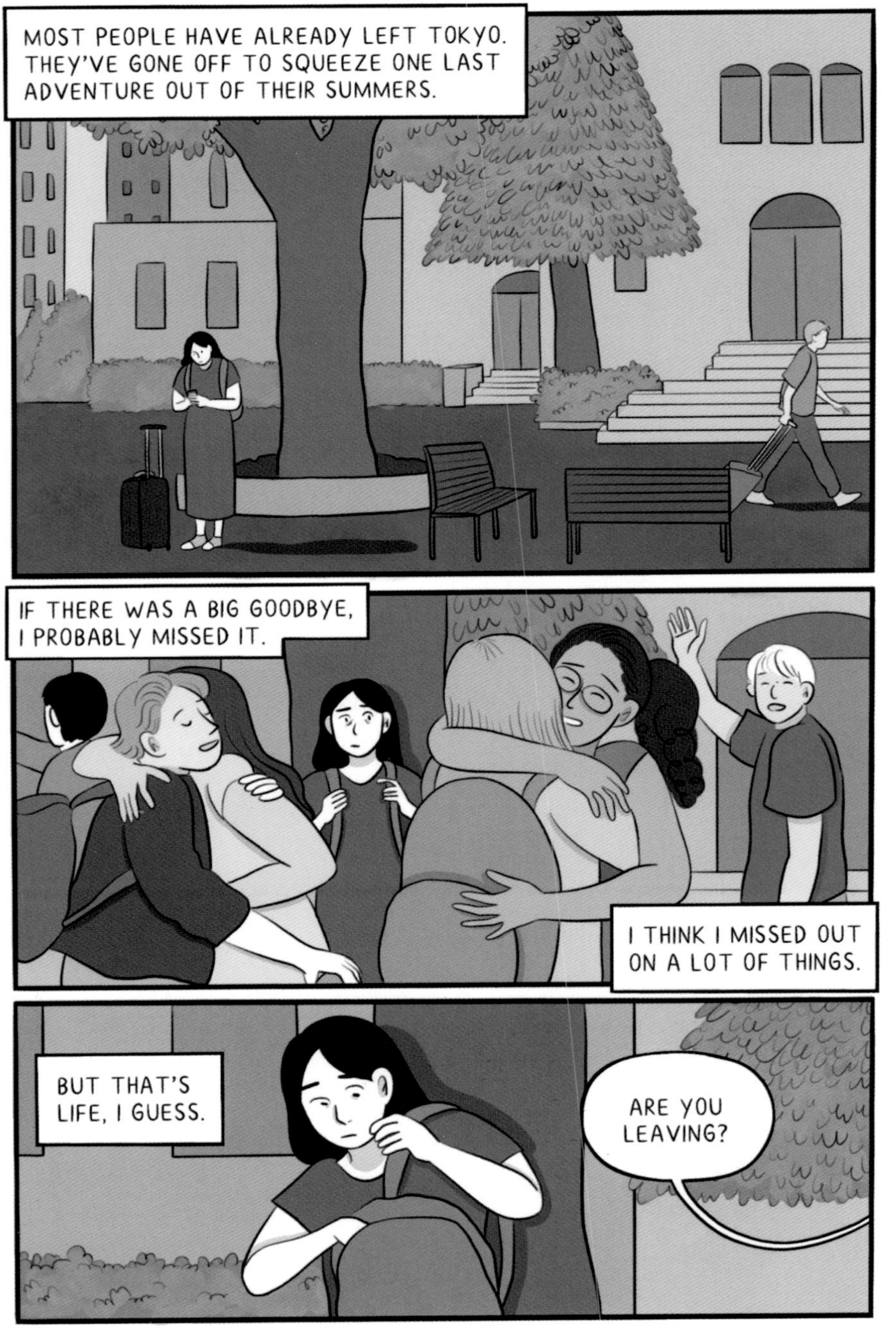
MOST PEOPLE HAVE ALREADY LEFT TOKYO. THEY'VE GONE OFF TO SQUEEZE ONE LAST ADVENTURE OUT OF THEIR SUMMERS.
IF THERE WAS A BIG GOODBYE, I PROBABLY MISSED IT.
I THINK I MISSED OUT ON A LOT OF THINGS.
BUT THAT'S LIFE, I GUESS.
ARE YOU LEAVING?

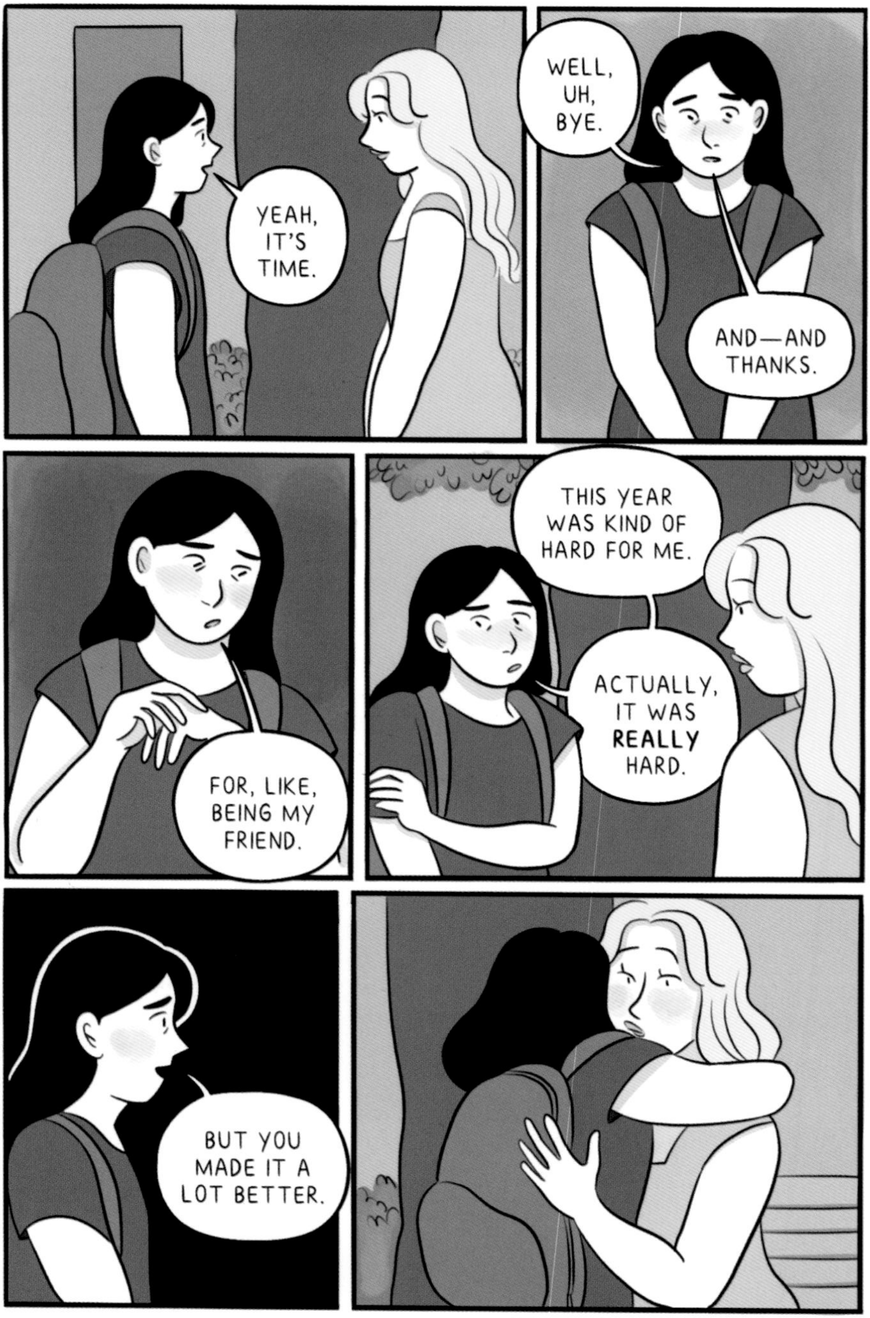
YEAH, IT'S TIME.
WELL, UH, BYE.
AND—AND THANKS.
FOR, LIKE, BEING MY FRIEND.
THIS YEAR WAS KIND OF HARD FOR ME.
ACTUALLY, IT WAS **REALLY** HARD.
BUT YOU MADE IT A LOT BETTER.

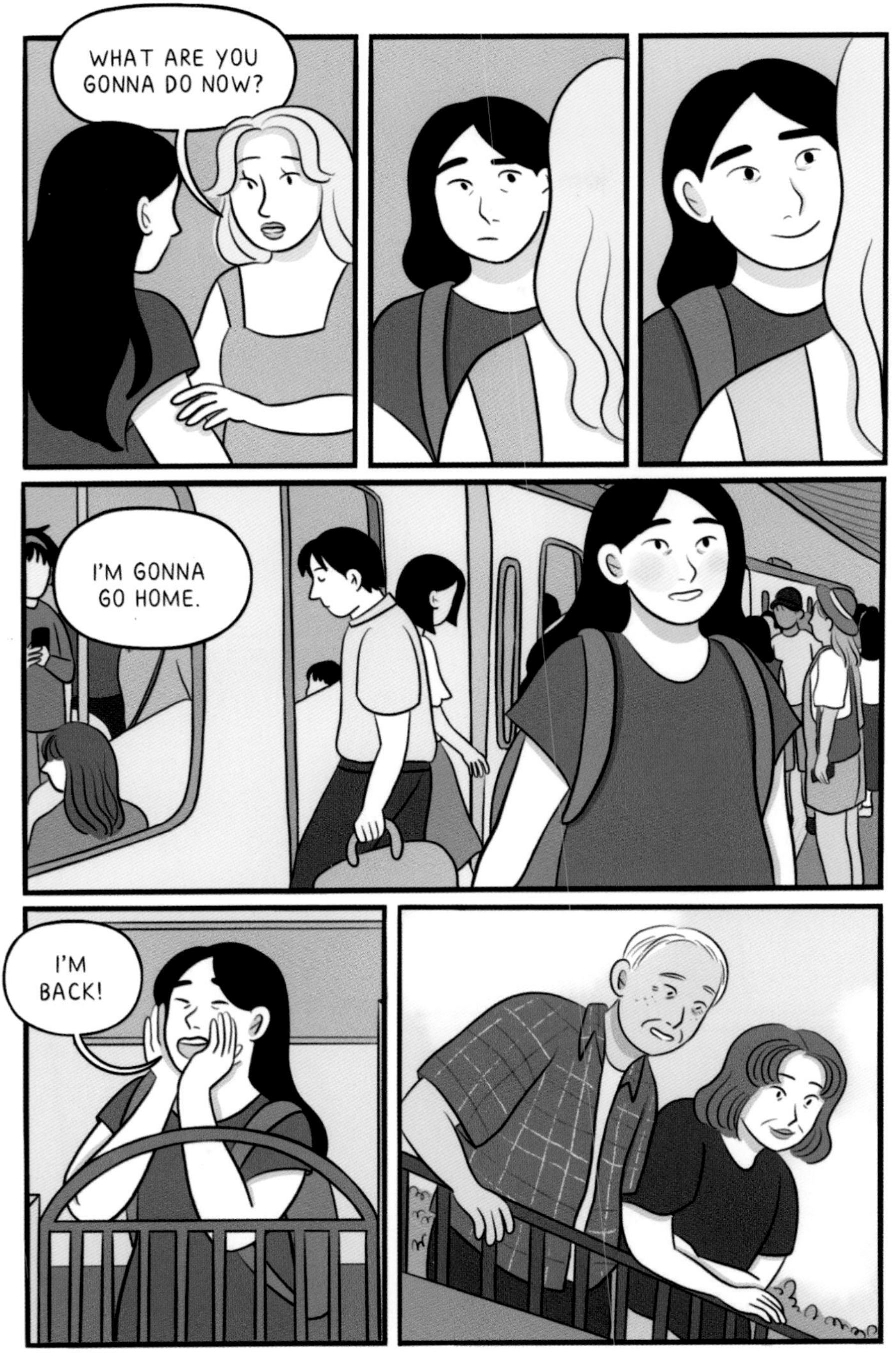
WHAT ARE YOU GONNA DO NOW?
I'M GONNA GO HOME.
I'M BACK!

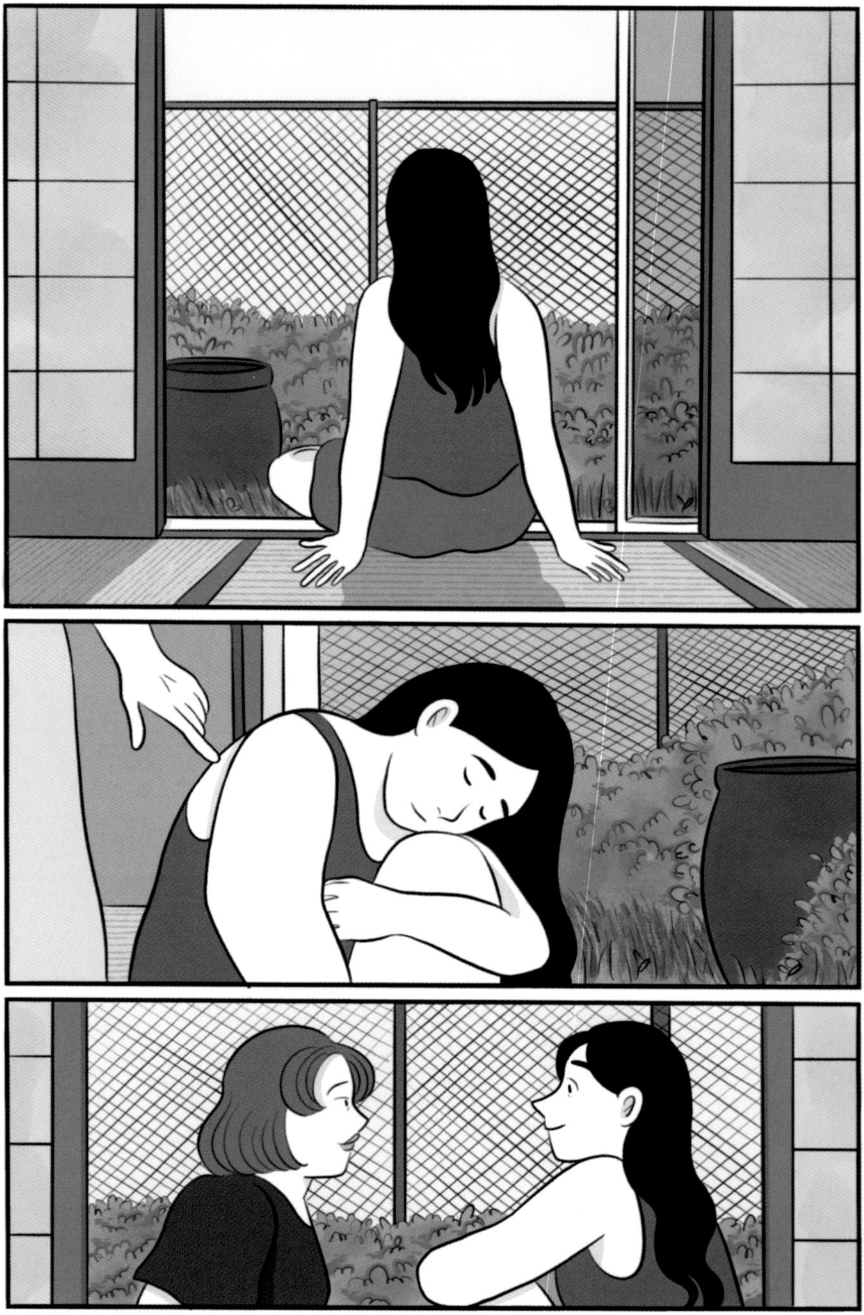

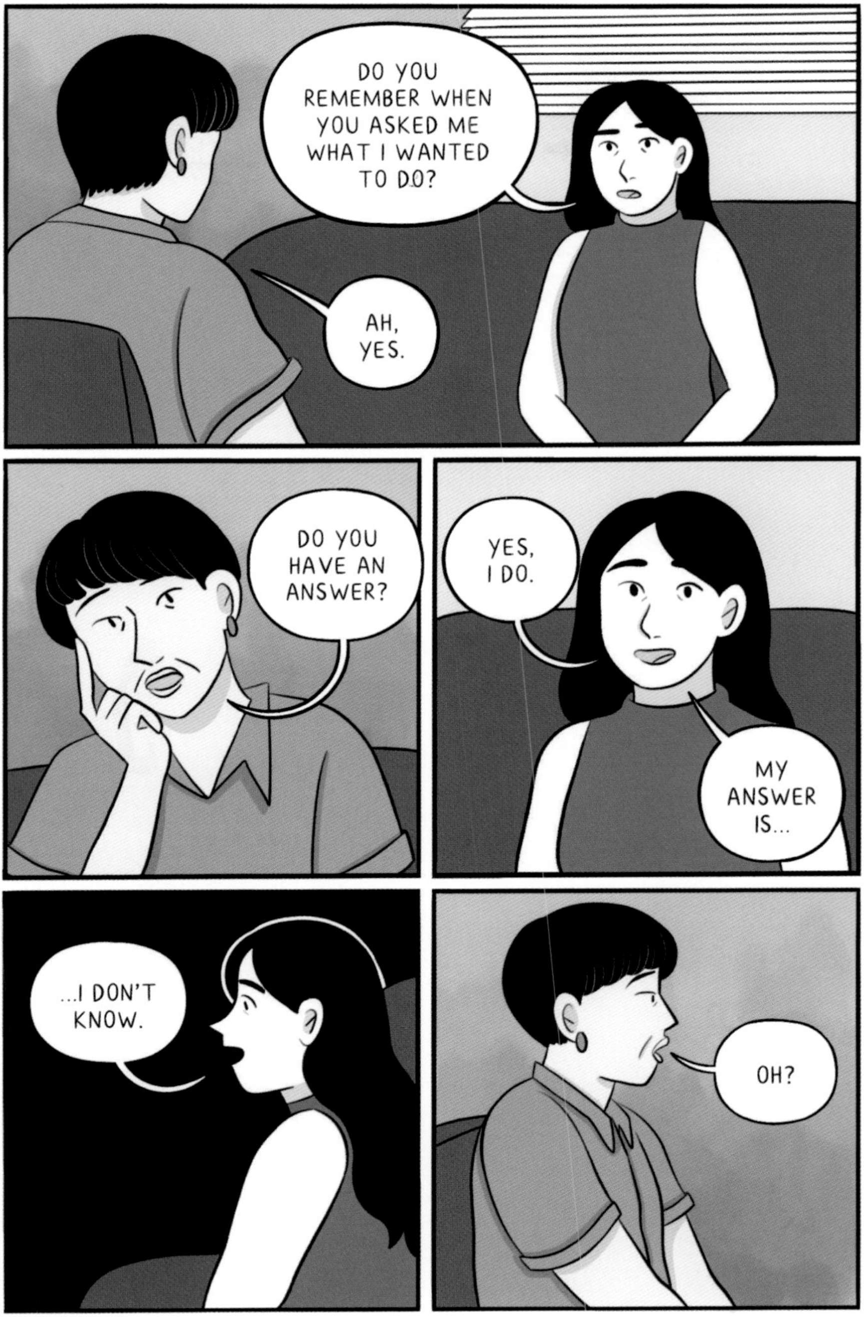
DO YOU REMEMBER WHEN YOU ASKED ME WHAT I WANTED TO DO?
AH, YES.
DO YOU HAVE AN ANSWER?
YES, I DO.
MY ANSWER IS...
...I DON'T KNOW.
OH?

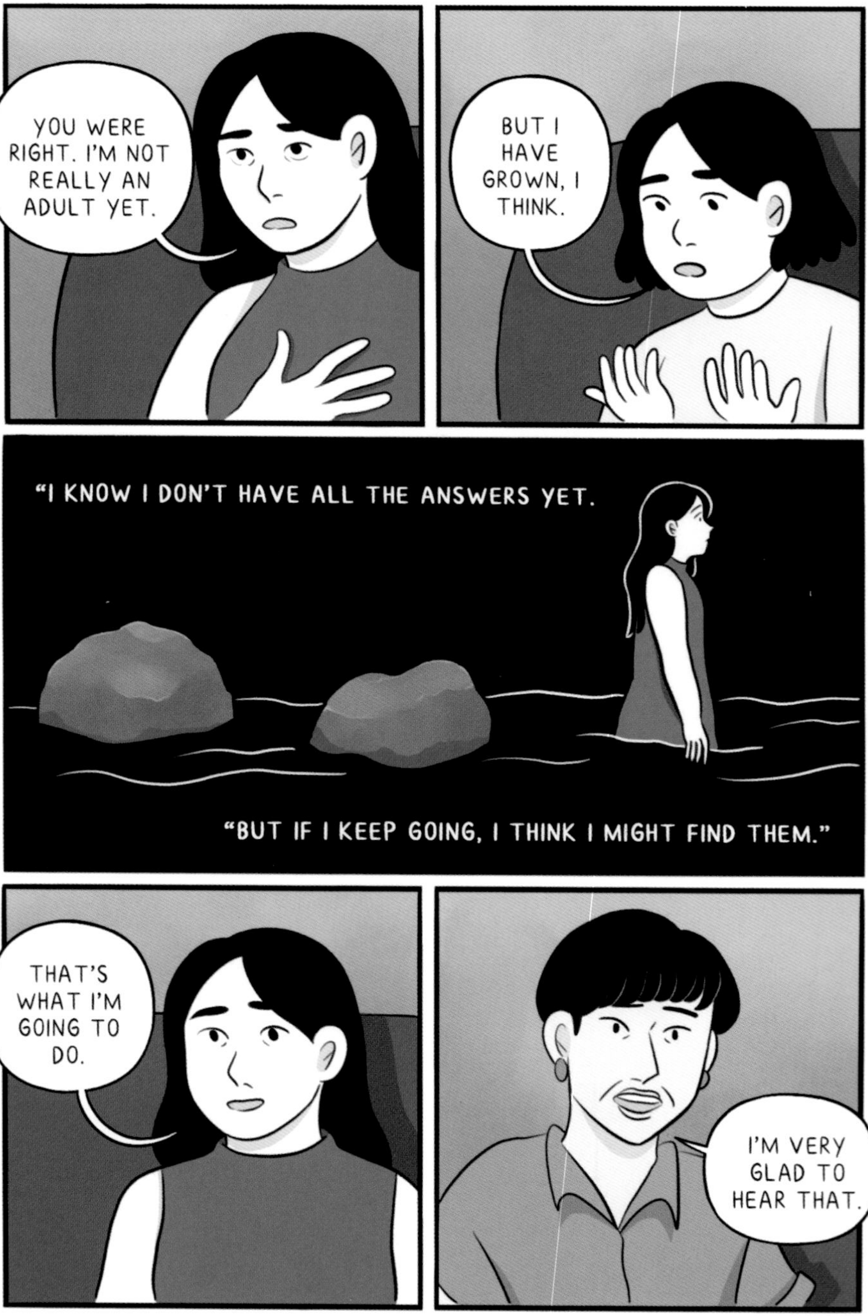
YOU WERE RIGHT. I'M NOT REALLY AN ADULT YET.
BUT I HAVE GROWN, I THINK.
"I KNOW I DON'T HAVE ALL THE ANSWERS YET.
"BUT IF I KEEP GOING, I THINK I MIGHT FIND THEM."
THAT'S WHAT I'M GOING TO DO.
I'M VERY GLAD TO HEAR THAT.

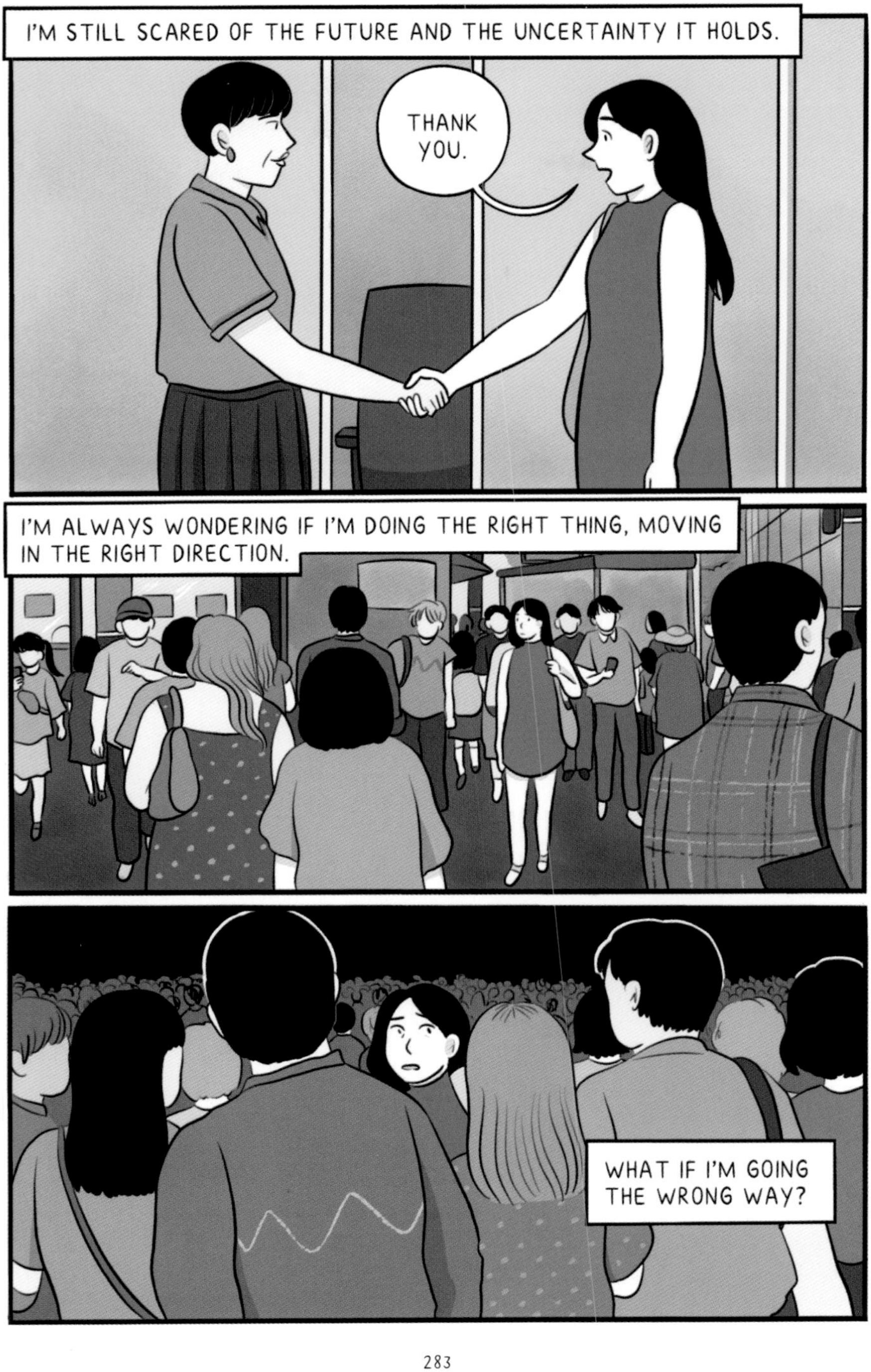
I'M STILL SCARED OF THE FUTURE AND THE UNCERTAINTY IT HOLDS.
THANK YOU.
I'M ALWAYS WONDERING IF I'M DOING THE RIGHT THING, MOVING IN THE RIGHT DIRECTION.
WHAT IF I'M GOING THE WRONG WAY?

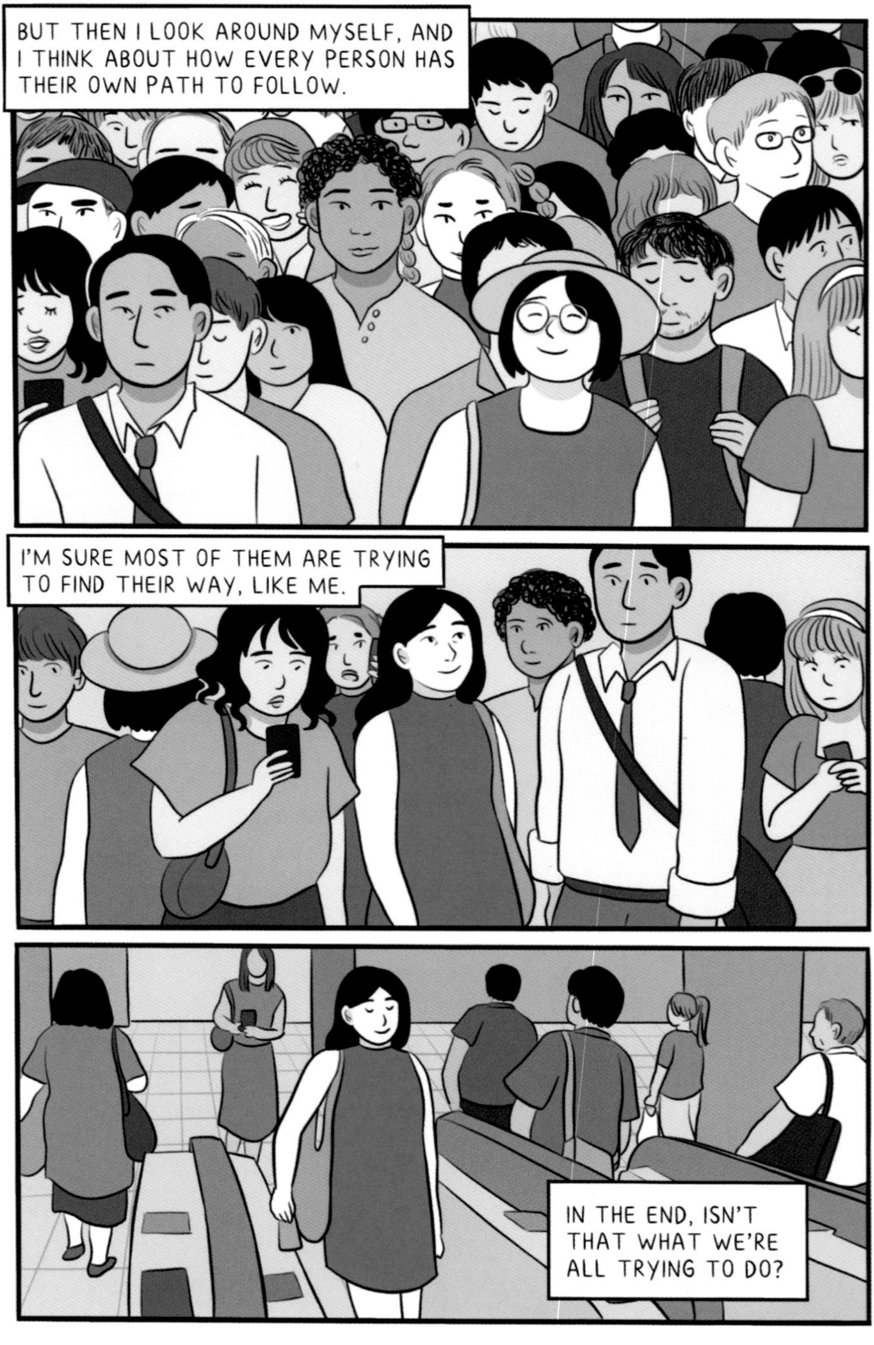
BUT THEN I LOOK AROUND MYSELF, AND I THINK ABOUT HOW EVERY PERSON HAS THEIR OWN PATH TO FOLLOW.
I'M SURE MOST OF THEM ARE TRYING TO FIND THEIR WAY, LIKE ME.
IN THE END, ISN'T THAT WHAT WE'RE ALL TRYING TO DO?

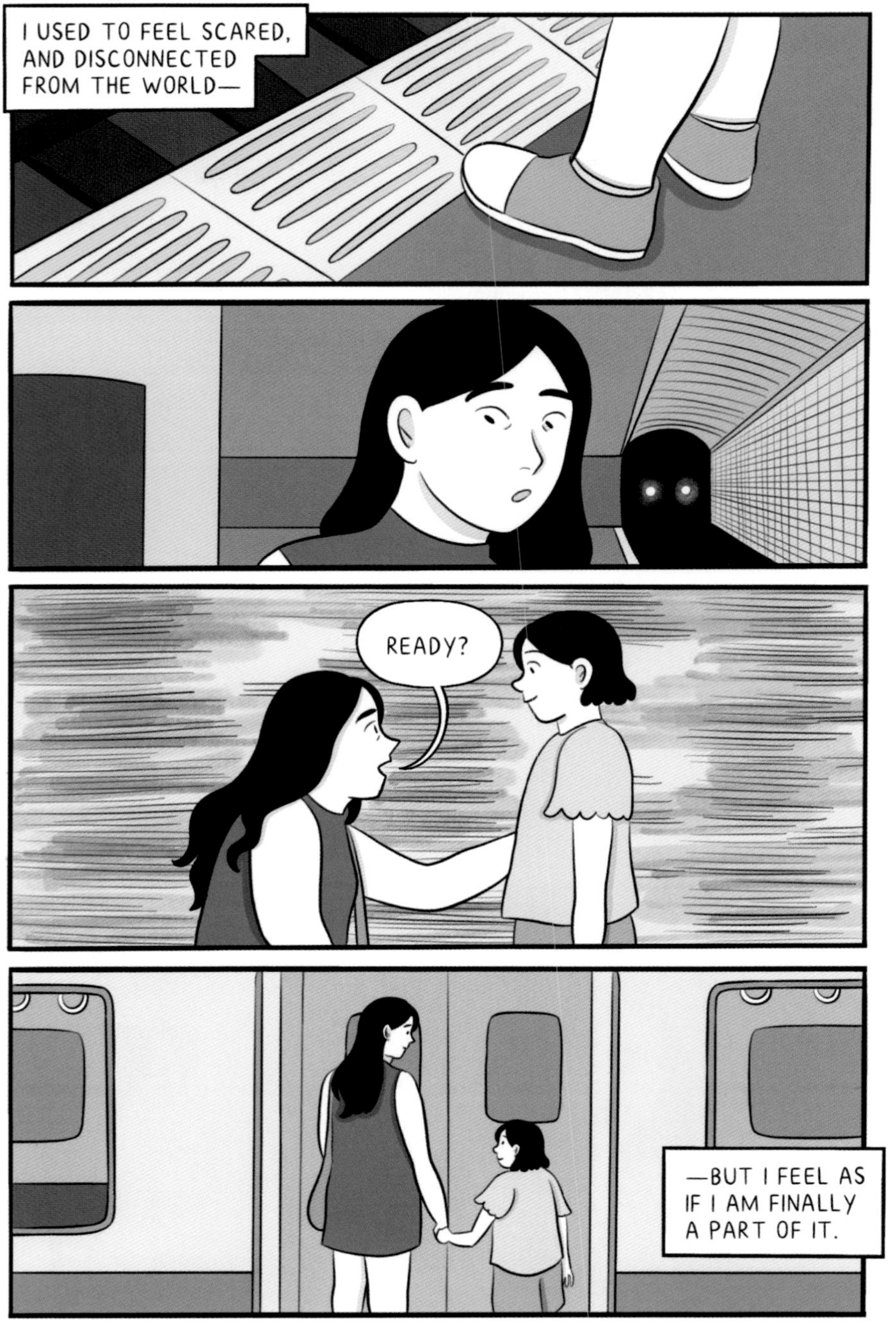
I USED TO FEEL SCARED, AND DISCONNECTED FROM THE WORLD—
READY?
—BUT I FEEL AS IF I AM FINALLY A PART OF IT.

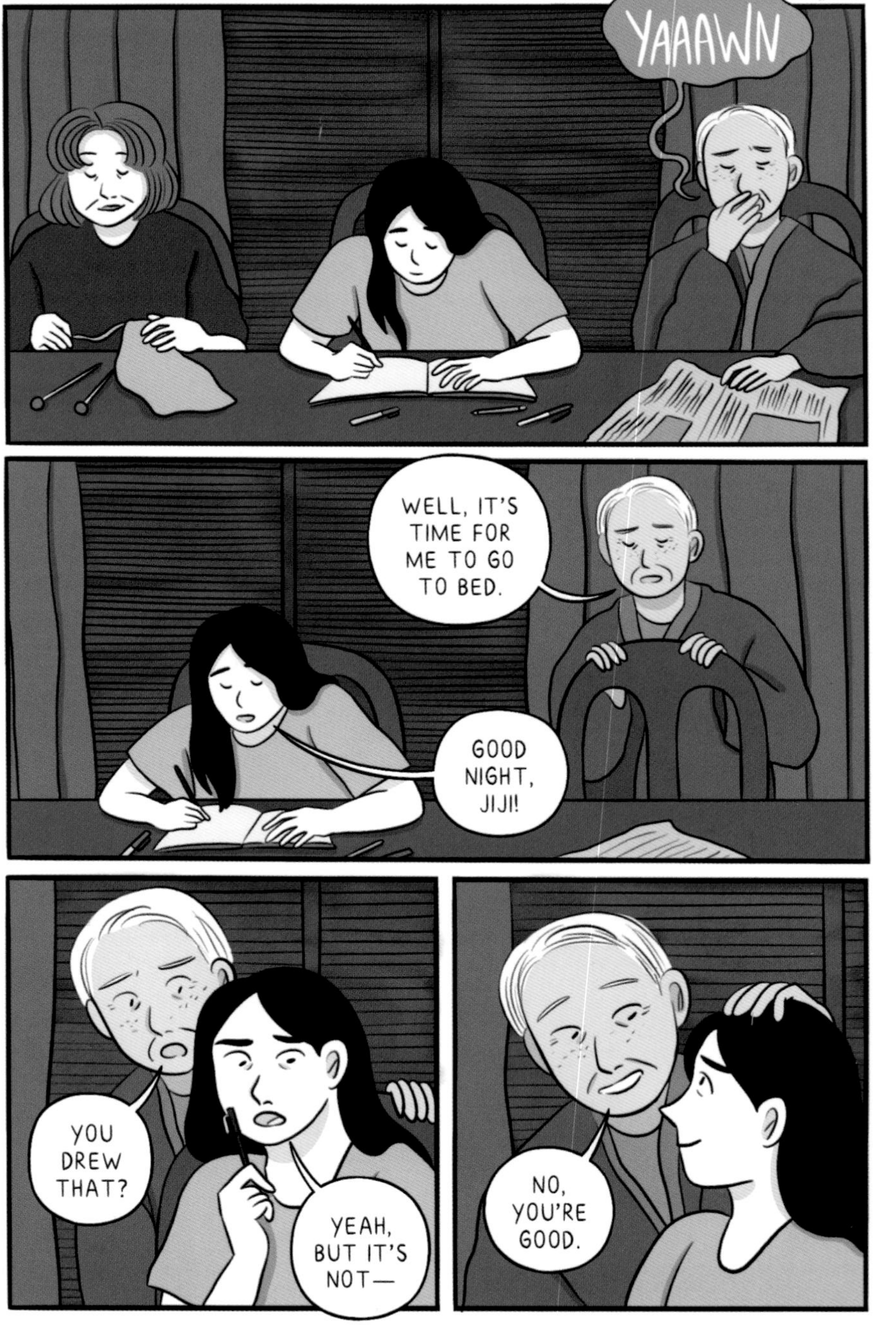
YAAAWN
WELL, IT'S TIME FOR ME TO GO TO BED.
GOOD NIGHT, JIJI!
YOU DREW THAT?
YEAH, BUT IT'S NOT—
NO, YOU'RE GOOD.

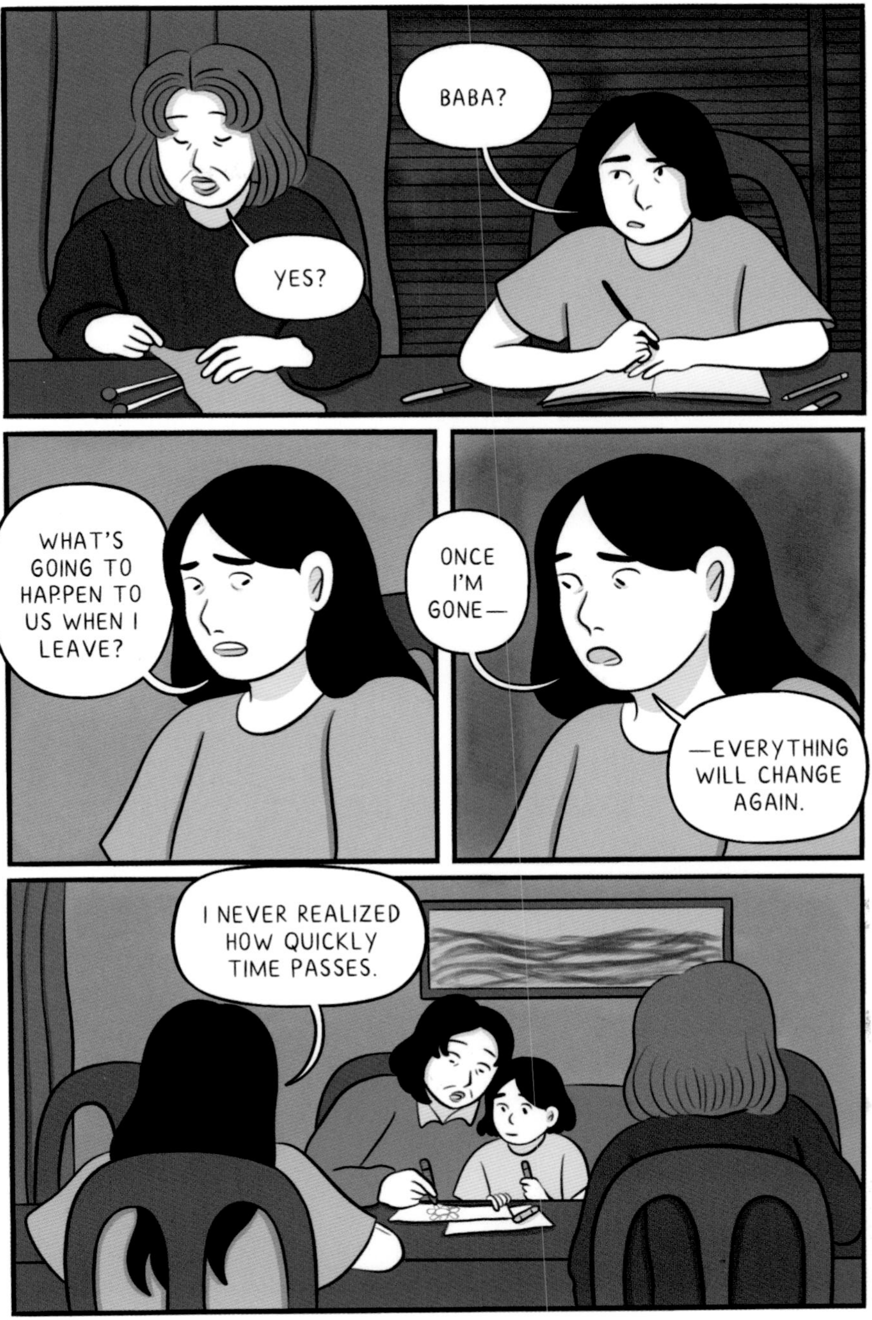
BABA?
YES?
WHAT'S GOING TO HAPPEN TO US WHEN I LEAVE?
ONCE I'M GONE—
—EVERYTHING WILL CHANGE AGAIN.
I NEVER REALIZED HOW QUICKLY TIME PASSES.

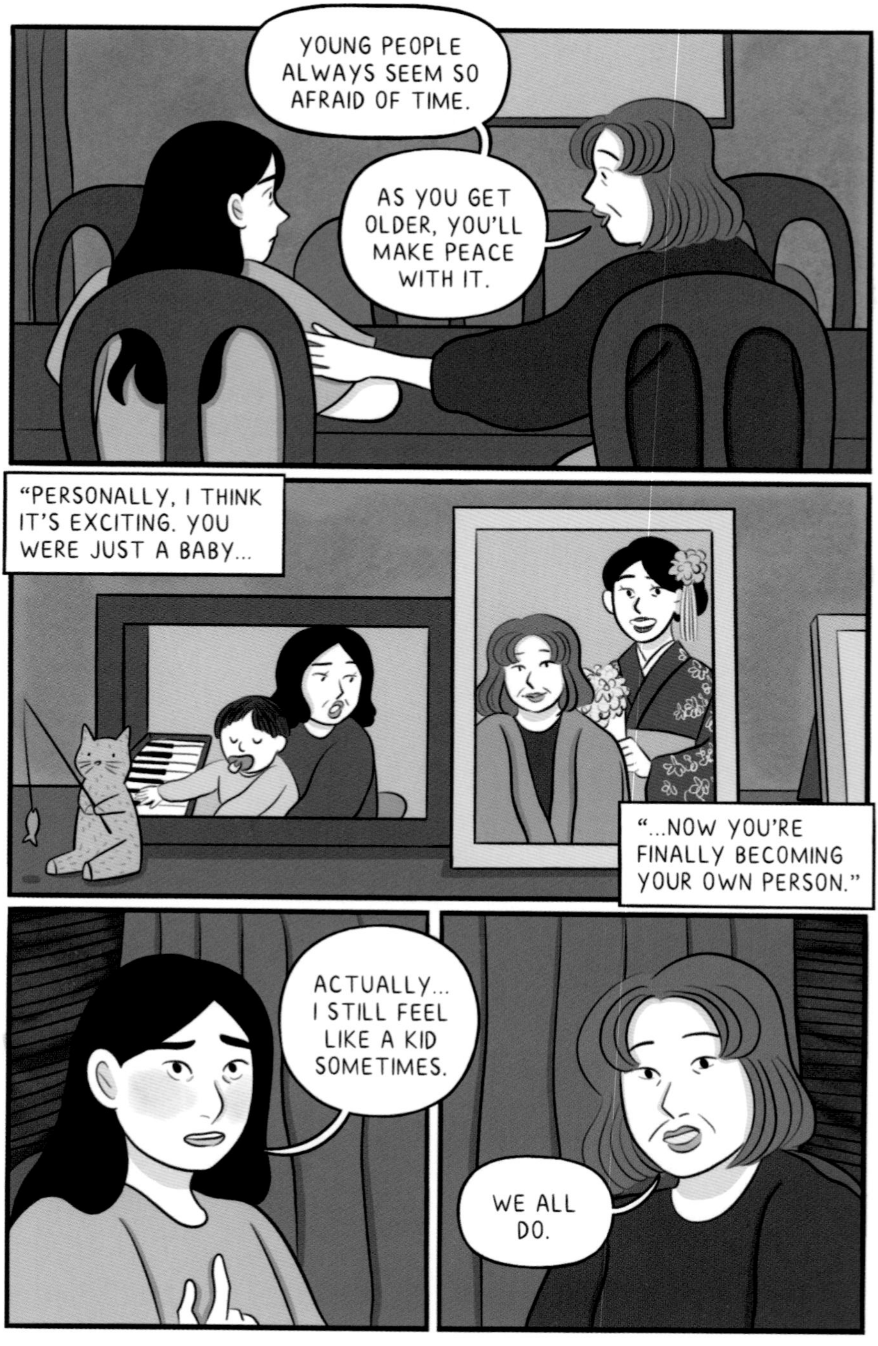
YOUNG PEOPLE ALWAYS SEEM SO AFRAID OF TIME.
AS YOU GET OLDER, YOU'LL MAKE PEACE WITH IT.
"PERSONALLY, I THINK IT'S EXCITING. YOU WERE JUST A BABY...
"...NOW YOU'RE FINALLY BECOMING YOUR OWN PERSON."
ACTUALLY... I STILL FEEL LIKE A KID SOMETIMES.
WE ALL DO.

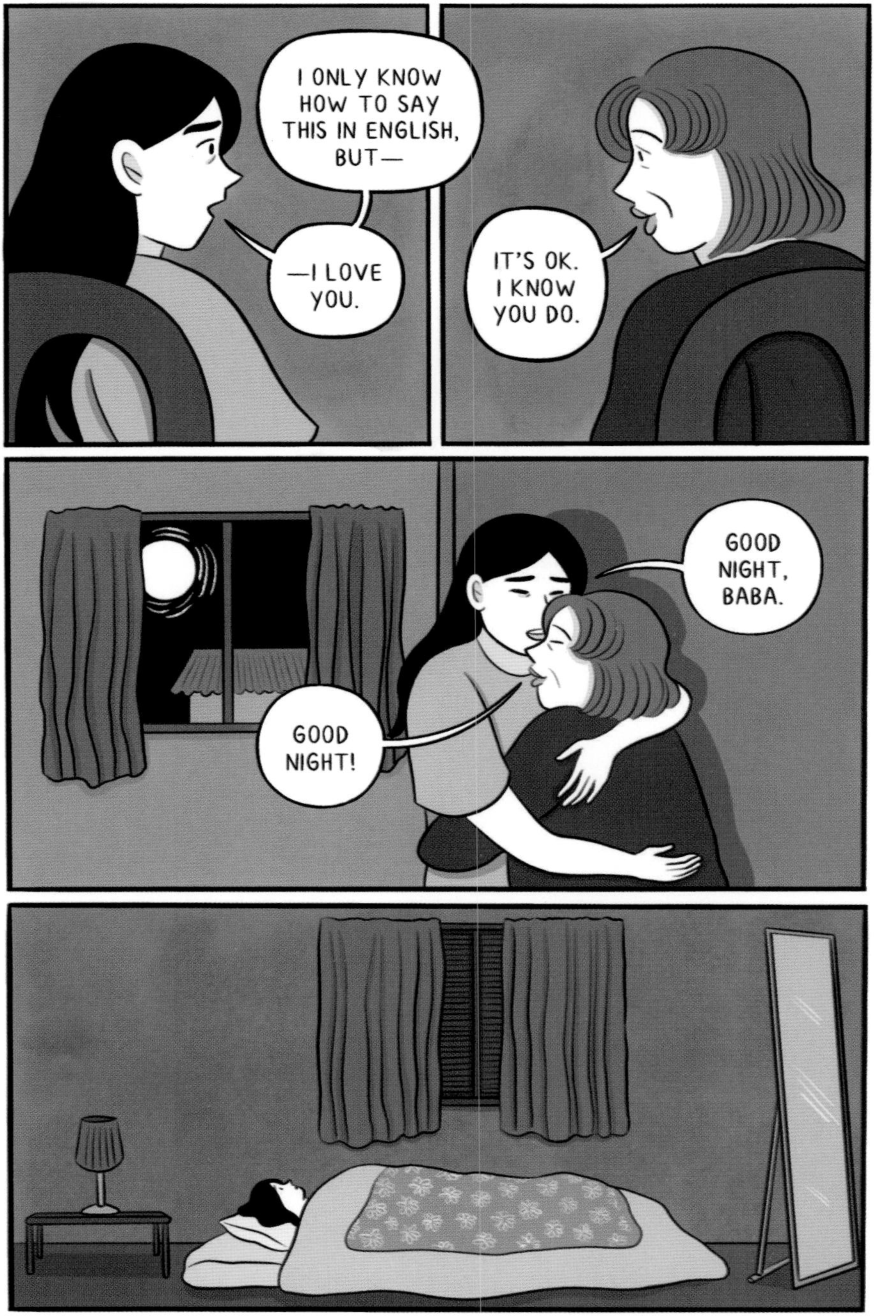
I ONLY KNOW HOW TO SAY THIS IN ENGLISH, BUT—
—I LOVE YOU.
IT'S OK. I KNOW YOU DO.
GOOD NIGHT, BABA.
GOOD NIGHT!

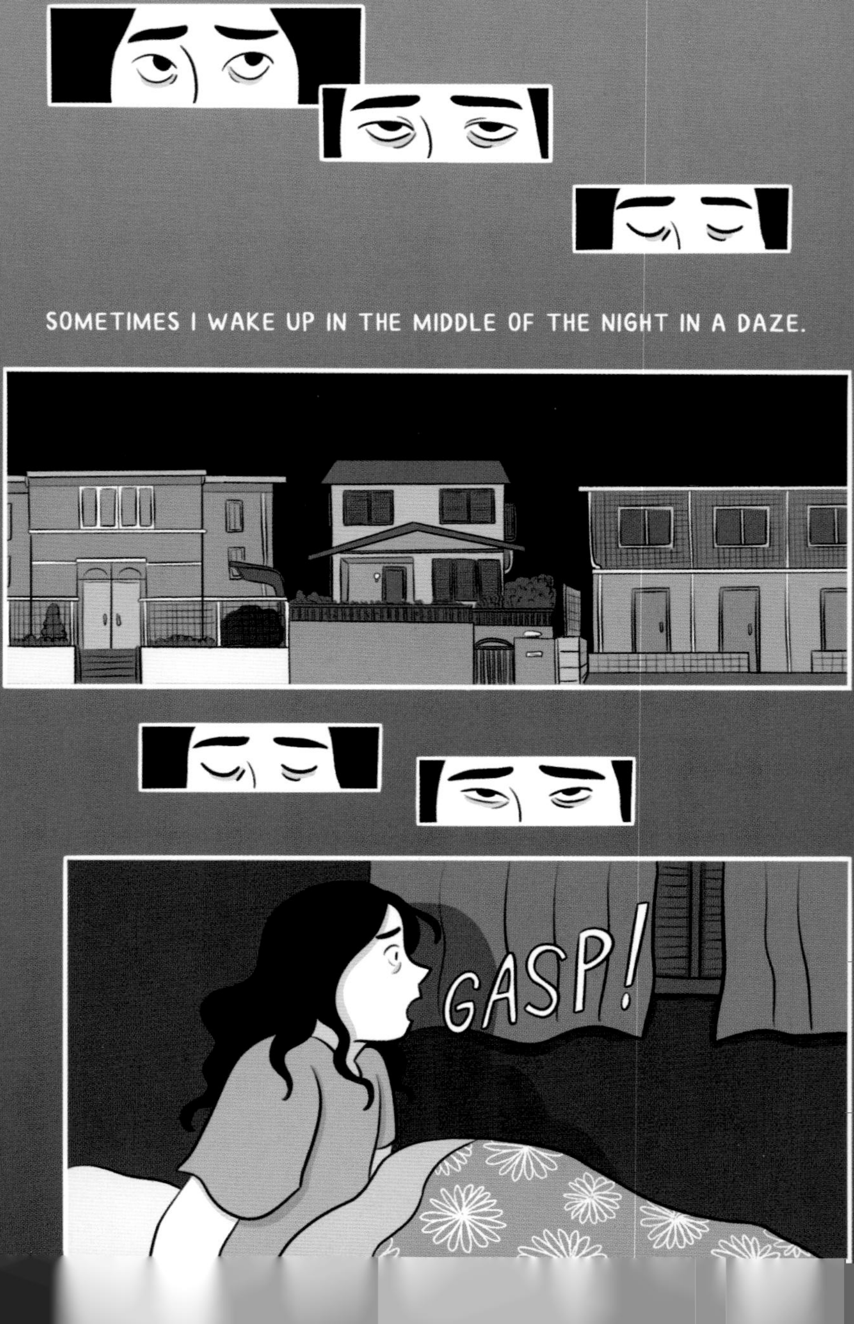
SOMETIMES I WAKE UP IN THE MIDDLE OF THE NIGHT IN A DAZE.
GASP!

—I FIND MYSELF WANDERING THROUGH THE HOUSE—

—AS QUIETLY AS I CAN—

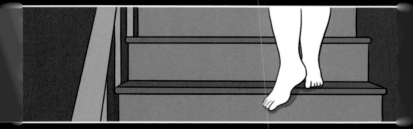

—TIPTOEING IN THE DARKNESS.

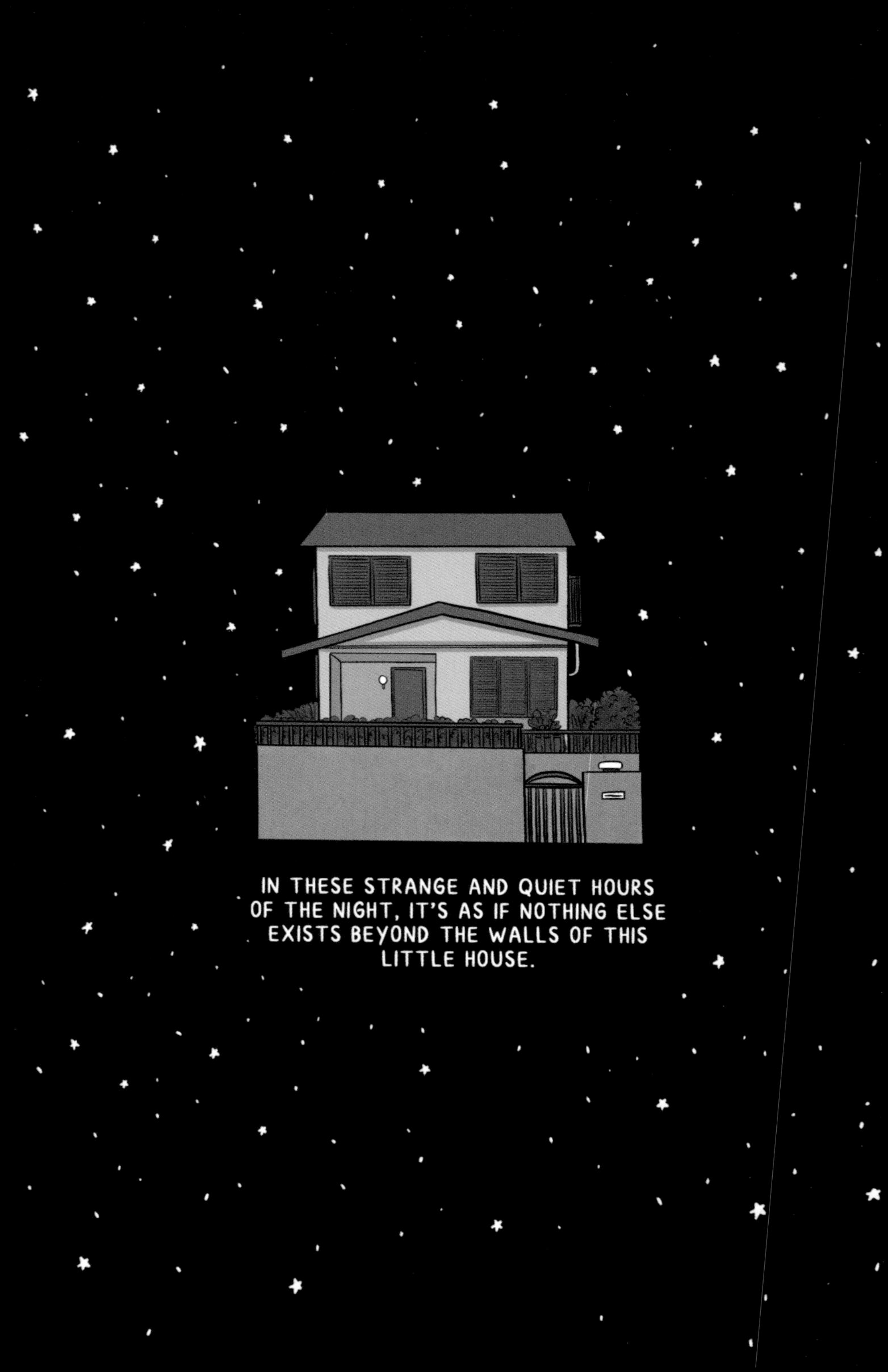
IN THESE STRANGE AND QUIET HOURS OF THE NIGHT, IT'S AS IF NOTHING ELSE EXISTS BEYOND THE WALLS OF THIS LITTLE HOUSE.

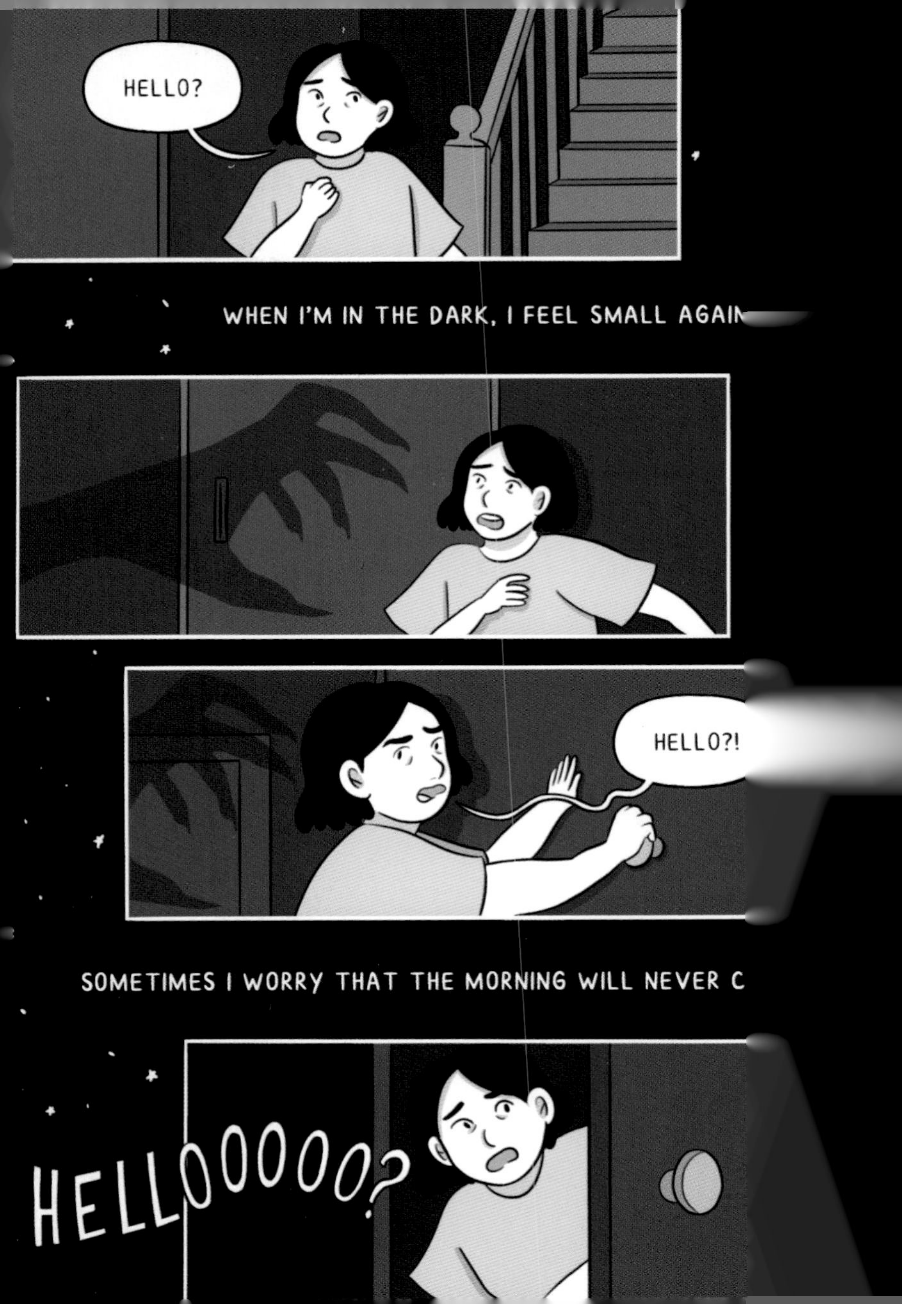
HELLO?
WHEN I'M IN THE DARK, I FEEL SMALL AGAIN
HELLO?!
SOMETIMES I WORRY THAT THE MORNING WILL NEVER C
HELLOOOOO?

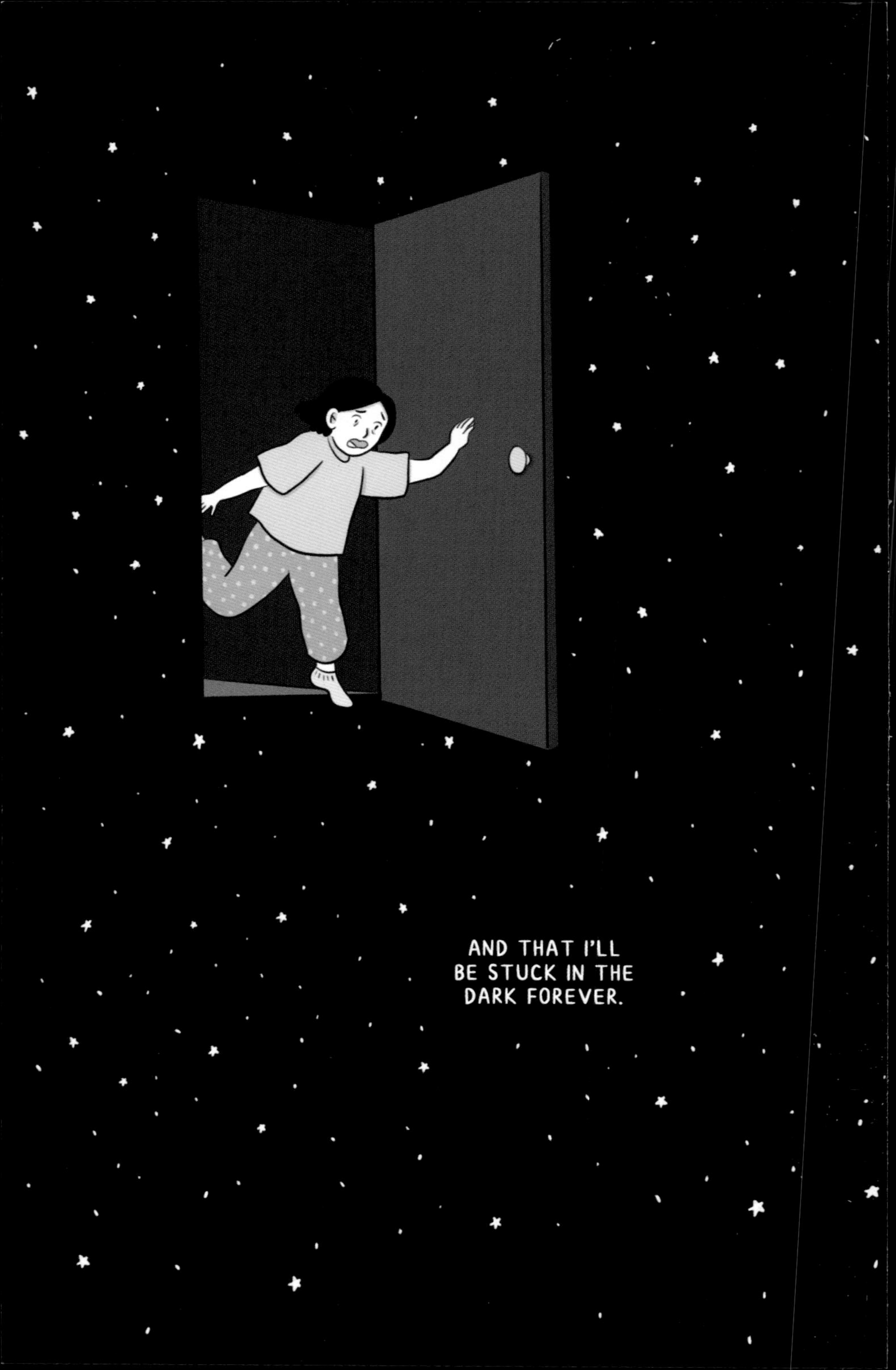
AND THAT I'LL BE STUCK IN THE DARK FOREVER.

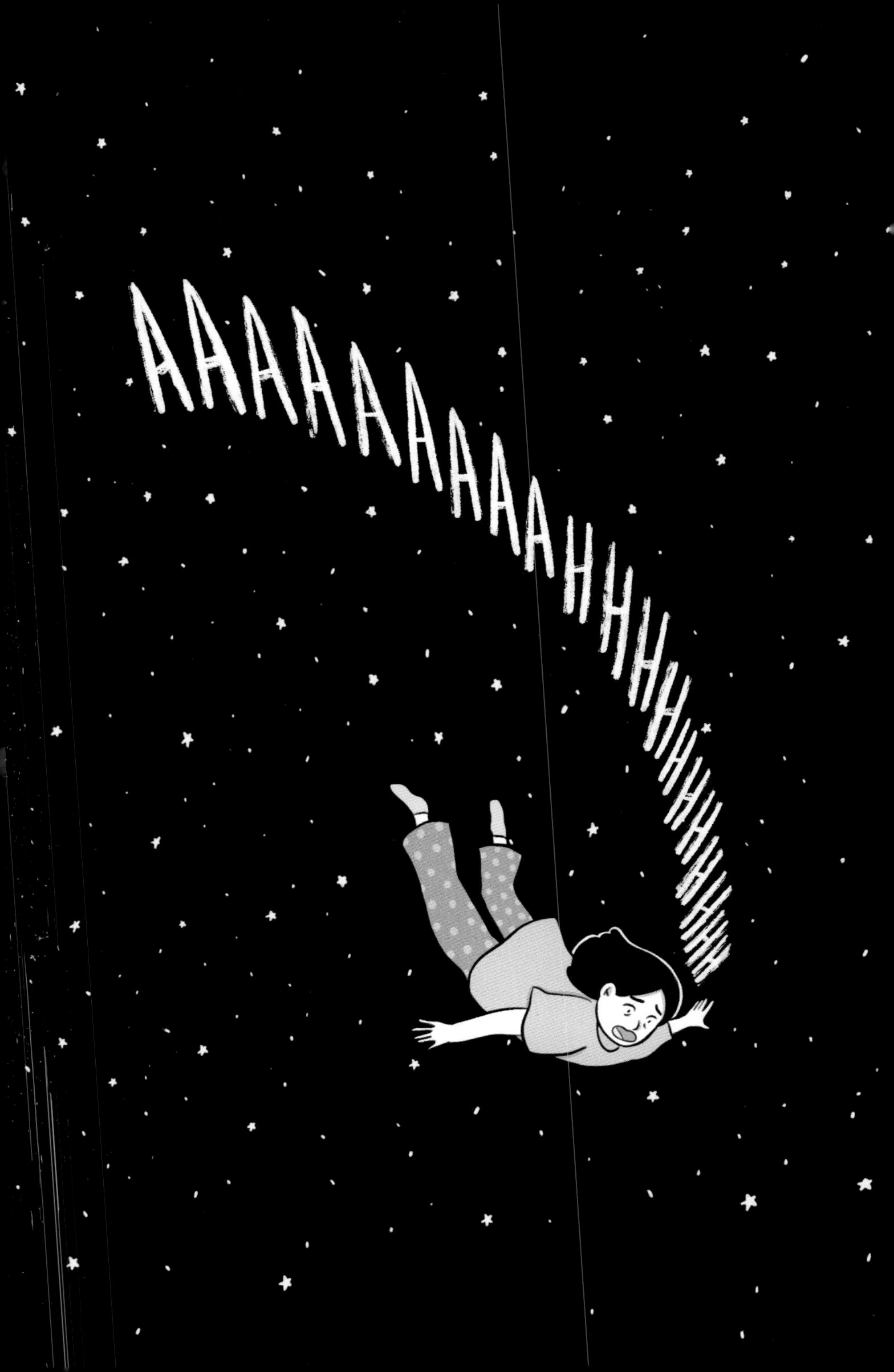
AAAAAAAAAHHHHHHHHHHHHH

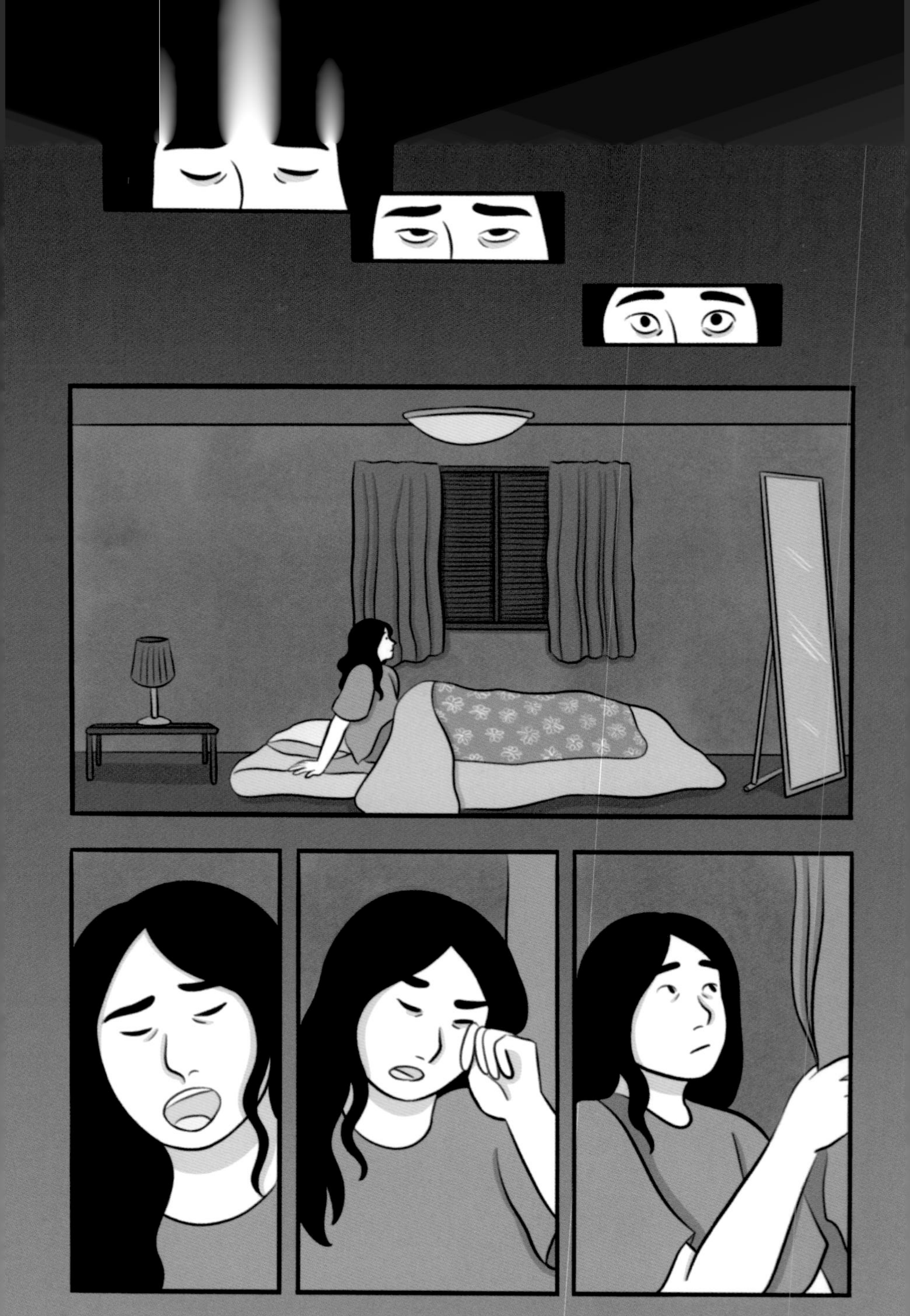

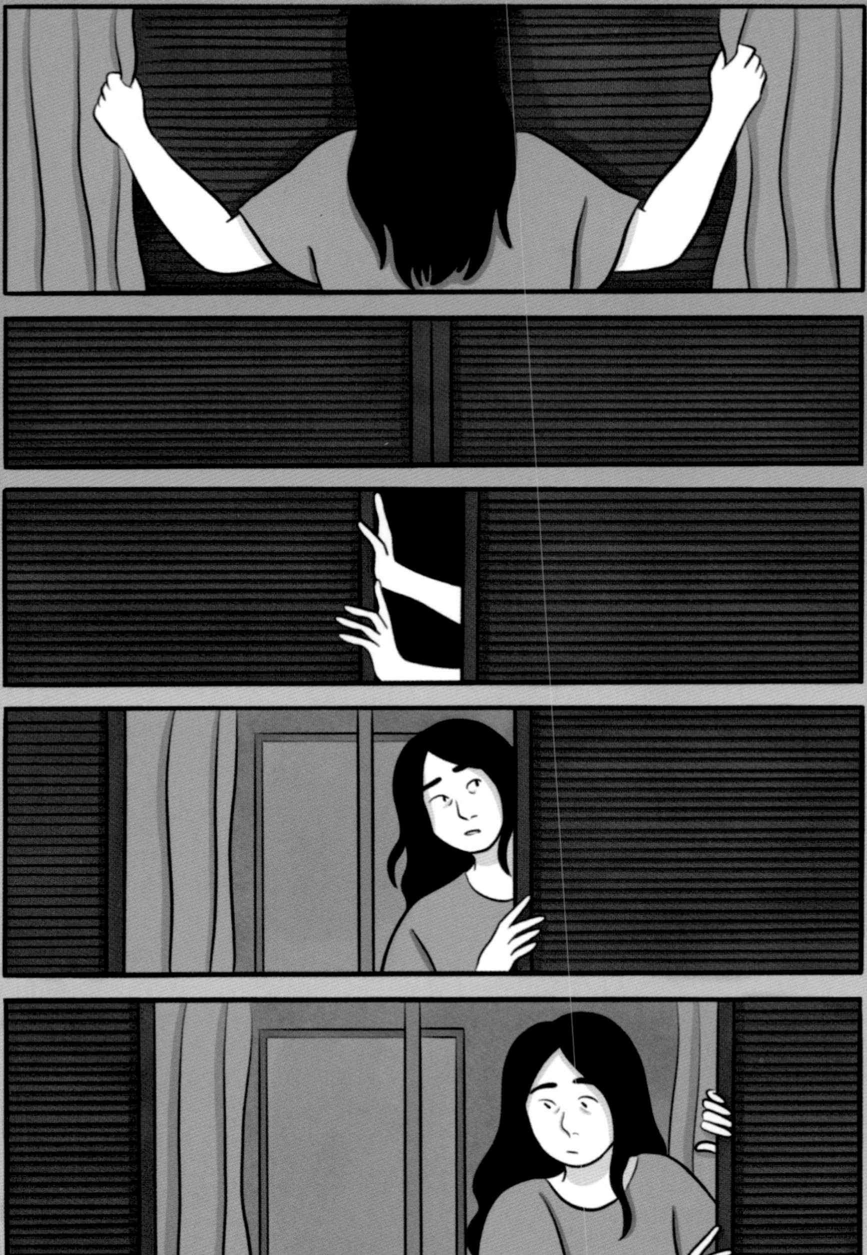

BUT NOW I KNOW THAT MORNING ALWAYS COMES...

...AND A NEW DAY IS WAITING.

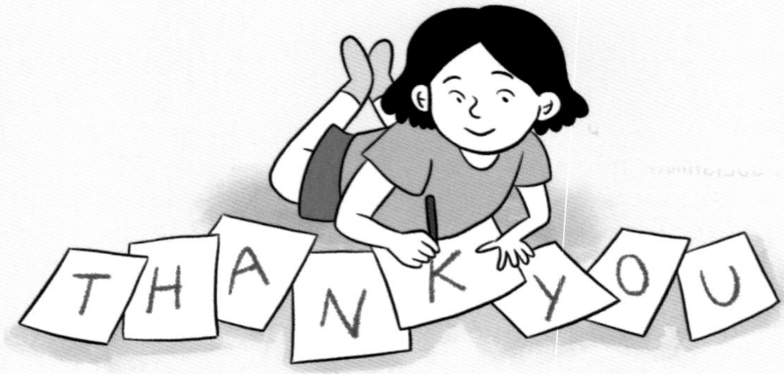
THANK YOU

ACKNOWLEDGMENTS

THIS BOOK WOULD NOT HAVE BEEN POSSIBLE WITHOUT THE WONDERFUL SUPPORT OF THE FOLLOWING PEOPLE:

TO MY AGENT, SAM HAYWOOD, THANK YOU FOR BEING A CHAMPION OF MY WORK. YOUR BELIEF IN THIS PROJECT (AND ME) IS WHAT MADE IT POSSIBLE TO BEGIN WITH.

TO MY EDITOR, ANDREA COLVIN, THANK YOU FOR BELIEVING THAT THIS STORY WAS WORTH TELLING, AND FOR GIVING ME THE OPPORTUNITY TO CREATE SOMETHING BIGGER AND MORE BEAUTIFUL FROM IT. I'M SO GRATEFUL TO HAVE WORKED WITH YOU ON THIS PROJECT.

THANK YOU TO EVERYONE ON THE LITTLE, BROWN INK TEAM FOR HELPING ME BRING THIS BOOK TO LIFE, WITH SPECIAL THANKS TO MEGAN, ANN, AND LAUREN FOR THEIR ARTISTIC DIRECTION AND EDITORIAL SUPPORT.

A BIG THANK YOU TO MARINAOMI, WHO HELPED ME COME UP WITH THE TITLE OF THIS BOOK (AND IS SUCH A GREAT ARTIST FRIEND AND INSPIRATION!). AND TO DEVON HALLIDAY, WHO HELPED GUIDE ME THROUGH SO MANY NEW EXPERIENCES ON THIS PUBLISHING JOURNEY.

TO MY PARENTS, THANK YOU FOR EVERYTHING. DAD, THANK YOU FOR BEING MY BIGGEST FAN AND FOR ALWAYS BELIEVING IN ME. MOM, THANK YOU FOR ALWAYS SUPPORTING ME EVEN WHEN YOU DON'T UNDERSTAND ME. EVERYTHING I DO IN MY LIFE IS FOR YOU AND BECAUSE OF YOU.

I WANT TO THANK MY ENTIRE FAMILY, ESPECIALLY MY SIBLINGS (HI, STEFAN AND ZOE) AND MY GRANDPARENTS IN THE US AND IN JAPAN, WHO WILL BE READING THIS BOOK ON OPPOSITE SIDES OF THE WORLD.

BABA, I'M REALLY GLAD I GOT TO SPEND THAT YEAR WITH YOU. THANK YOU FOR EVERYTHING.

I DON'T HAVE A TON OF FRIENDS, BUT I FEEL VERY LUCKY FOR THE ONES I DO HAVE, AND I WANT TO THANK THEM FOR ALWAYS BEING THERE FOR ME AND CHEERING ME ON WHILE I CRIED ABOUT HOW HARD IT IS TO MAKE A BOOK. ESPECIALLY LEYLA, HANNA, SOFIA, CAROLINE, WINNIE, AND RYO: THANK YOU FOR BEING MY CONSTANTS.

AND FINALLY, THANK YOU TO EVERYONE WHO HAS SUPPORTED MY ONLINE COMICS AND *KOKORO*, WHO HAVE GONE OUT OF THEIR WAY TO SHOW ME KINDNESS ON THIS LONG JOURNEY. I WILL NOT FORGET YOU.

Anonymous

CHRISTINE MARI

IS A COMIC ARTIST BASED IN LOS ANGELES, CALIFORNIA. WHEN
SHE WAS 15 YEARS OLD, SHE WROTE HER FIRST BOOK, *DIARY OF
A TOKYO TEEN*, AN ILLUSTRATED TRAVELOGUE DETAILING ONE
SUMMER IN JAPAN. HER ARTISTIC JOURNEY CONTINUED IN HER
ONLINE COMICS, WHICH DEAL WITH TOPICS RANGING FROM HER
MULTIRACIAL IDENTITY TO NAVIGATING ADULTHOOD AND
THE JOYS AND CHALLENGES OF DAILY EXISTENCE. SHE LOVES
RAINY DAYS AND GROCERY STORE BIRTHDAY CAKE. THIS IS HER
FIRST GRAPHIC NOVEL. CHRISTINE INVITES YOU TO VISIT
HER AT CHRISTINEMARI.COM OR FOLLOW HER ON INSTAGRAM
@CHRISTINEMARICOMICS.